Crime & Justice in America

Present Realities and Future Prospects

Second Edition

Edited by

Wilson R. Palacios
University of South Florida

Paul F. Cromwell
Wichita State University

Roger G. Dunham
University of Miami

Prentice
Hall

Upper Saddle River, New Jersey 07458

Library of Congress Cataloging-in-Publication Data

Crime & justice in America : present realities and future prospects / [edited by] Wilson
R. Palacios, Paul F. Cromwell, Rodger G. Dunham.—2nd ed.
    p. cm.
  Includes bibliographical references and index.
  ISBN 0-13-091105-4
    1. Crime—United States. 2. Criminal justice, Administration of—United States. I. Title:
Crime and justice in America. II. Palacios, Wilson R. III. Cromwell, Paul F. IV.
Dunham, Roger G.
HV6789 .C6882 2002
364.973—dc21

2001018538

Publisher: Jeff Johnson
Executive Assistant & Supervisor: Brenda Rock
Senior Acquisitions Editor: Kim Davies
Editorial Assistant: Sarah Holle
Managing Editors: Mary Carnis/Patrick Walsh
Production Management: Clarinda Publication Services
Production Editor: Rosie Jones
Interior Design: Clarinda Publication Services/ Cindy Miller
Production Liaison: Adele M. Kupchik
Director of Manufacturing and Production: Bruce Johnson
Manufacturing Buyers: Cathleen Petersen/ Ilene Sanford
Cover Design Coordinator: Miguel Ortiz

Formatting: The Clarinda Company
Electronic Art Creation: The Clarinda Company
Marketing Manager: Ramona Sherman
Marketing Assistant: Barbara Rosenberg
Marketing Coordinator: Adam Kloza
Printer/Binder: R.R. Donnelley and Sons, Inc.
Copy Editor: Clarinda Publication Services/Robyn Durand
Proofreader: Clarinda Publication Services/Carol Singer
Cover Design: Lorraine Castellano
Cover Illustration: Sandra Dionisi, SIS/Images.com
Cover Printer: Phoenix Color Corporation

Prentice-Hall International (UK) Limited, *London*
Prentice-Hall of Australia Pty. Limited, *Sydney*
Prentice-Hall Canada Inc. *Toronto*
Prentice-Hall Hispanoamericana, S.A., *Mexico*
Prentice-Hall of India Private Limited, *New Delhi*
Prentice-Hall of Japan, Inc., *Toyoko*
Prentice-Hall Singapore Pte. Ltd.
Editora Prentice-Hall do Brasil, Ltda., *Rio de Janeiro*

10   9   8   7   6   5   4   3   2   1
ISBN 0-13-091105-4

To my wife and best friend, Polly Palacios.
—**Wilson Palacios**

For my mother, Thelma Cromwell and my mother-in-law, Bernice Douglas.
You have both been an inspiration to me.
—**Paul Cromwell**

To my wife Vicki, and our children, Jenny, Jason, Joshua, Ben,
Seth and Zack.
—**Roger Dunham**

CONTENTS

PREFACE

The criminal fascinates us even as he repels us. Like Cain, he is not his brother's keeper. Like the serpent, he tempts us to guilty knowledge and disobedience. He is to men what Lucifer was to the angels, the eternal outcast and rebel, challenging all the assumptions of the moral order and risking heaven to do so. We are dismayed by his often dark and bloody deeds, and we run from him when the sun goes down, leaving the streets of our central cities dark and deserted. But even as we escape in terror, we seek him out in our imagination, as though he held locked within him some dirty secret of our own. He is, after all, a brother, acting out the primitive part in us that we struggle to keep dark. He is hated for being too much like us; he is envied for his freedom and the blessed gift of unrepentance.

Ysabel Rennie

The purpose of this Second Edition is to provide a comprehensive range of perspectives on topics and issues critical to the study of criminal justice. We have selected readings from many sources, including recent criminal justice research monographs and articles from the professional and academic literature, case studies, sociological, phychological, and criminological analyses, the popular media and literature, as well as historical and philosophical approaches to understanding the complex issues confronting criminal justice today. This interdisciplinary approach provides a broad coverage of the various topics and issues, presented in an interesting and readable format. We believe that the selections will capture the students' and teachers' imagination and help make the fascinating study of criminal justice even more appealing.

In this edition we have included 27 new chapters and have updated and revised three others. Others we have left as is. Some of those may appear by their copyright dates to be outdated. We believe, however, that some materials, regardless of their original date of publication, remain valid, vibrant and important contributions to the knowledge base of criminal justice. Lawrence Sherman's brilliant chapter entitled "Learning Police Ethics" is one of these, as is Herman Goldstein's classic paper, "The New Policing: Confronting Complexity." Likewise, Craig Uchida's chapter on the history of policing is not in need of updating. We have retained these and several others for their valuable insights which have not been made obsolete by time or new research.

The second edition is divided into four sections or topic areas: (1) Crime and Justice in America; (2) The Police in America; (3) Adjudication and Sentencing; and, (4) Jails, Prisons, and Community-Based Corrections. Each section contains selected discussions and analyses of current issues and problems, ethical consideration, and materials related to criminal justice career opportunities, including employment standards and qualifications, and strategies for pursing employment in the public or private sector of criminal justice. Each section is preceded by brief comments by the editors and is followed by questions to stimulate classroom discussion. In the first edition we included a fifth section on the future of criminal justice, "Looking Toward the 21st Century." In reorganizing, the book for this second edition we moved those "futures" chapters into the sections in which they were most relevant. Thus, each section now contains one or more chapters in which the possible future directions of the criminal justice system are analyzed and discussed. *Crime and Justice in America: Present Realities and Future Prospects, Second Edition* also contains an index to assist the reader in locating topics of interest.

This volume may readily be used as a stand-alone text for introductory criminal justice courses or as a supplement to most introductory texts. We have also sought to provide readings that create a balance between theory and practice; that promote critical thought about current criminal justice issues; and that encourage a vision for the future. As criminal justice teachers with a combined thirty years teaching and research and over two decades of experience in criminal justice practice and administration, we realize the need to present students with materials that challenge their minds yet keep their interest and make them want to read further. We believe we have accomplished that goal in this volume.

ACKNOWLEDGMENTS

Many persons helped make this second edition a reality. Primary among them are our students. We have endeavored to make this book readable, informative and to the extent possible in a textbook, exciting. They told us which of the first edition articles they liked and disliked and suggested changes. We thank them for their continuing efforts to educate us as we attempt to educate them.

Secondly, we owe a great debt to those faculty members across the country who reviewed the first edition and suggested changes and improvements to this new edition. We are particularly grateful for the efforts of Professors Clyde Cronkhite, Western Illinois University, Tere Chipman, Fayetteville Technical Community College, Barry Schmelzer, St. Ambrose University and Stacy Wyland of the University of Hawaii at Hilo.

We also owe a debt of gratitude to those authors whose work is reproduced here. This book is their work. We have simply selected the best examples of research to illustrate and illuminate the topics.

Our efforts were greatly assisted by the School of Community Affairs staff at Wichita State University. These stalwart individuals, Cathy Blackmore, Dee Pritchett and Bill Artz provided invaluable support. Finally we thank our editors at Prentice-Hall, Kim Davies and Cheryl Adam, and our project manager at Clarinda Publications Services, Rosie Jones. Their assistance and encouragement made our task easier and more efficient.

Wilson Palacios
Tampa, Florida

Paul Cromwell
Wichita, Kansas

Roger Dunham
Coral Gables, Florida

Section 1

Crime and Justice in America

INTRODUCTION

Every known society or group has rules for its members to follow and, as a result of this and simple human nature, every known society or group has rule-breakers. Once some members break the rules, it is only natural for the remaining members to respond to the rule-breakage. If the sentiment is strong concerning the importance of the rules to the group, the response will be severe. This is the bottom line of crime and justice. Crime is nothing more than the breaking of rules we consider important to our society, and justice is the official response to breaking those rules. The focus of Section I is on these more general aspects of crime and justice.

In the first selection, "The Criminal Justice Process" exposes the reader to a general procedural schematic illustrating how criminal cases are channeled through the legal system. The article covers every step of the process from the time a crime is committed to the final disposition of the case. The reader gains an appreciation of how criminal cases are actually handled by justice agencies.

The second selection, "American Criminal Justice Philosophy: What's Old—What's New?" by Curtis R. Blakely and Vic W. Bumphus, offers a unique sociohistorical perspective concerning recent community-oriented policing and restorative justice programs. In an era where many such programs are applauded for being innovative in design, Blakely and Bumphus contend that such philosophical approaches are merely contemporary versions of earlier programmatic innovations.

The third selection, "Crime and Policy: A Complex Problem," by criminologist Samuel Walker, is a direct and straightforward presentation of the facts concerning crime control policy in the United States during the last ten years. Walker examines the reasons for the reduction in crime with one question: What did work? He dispenses with the political and moralistic overtones, which surround much of the current dialogue concerning the crime problem, by presenting a factual account of the social impact such crime control initiatives as the "War on Drugs", "three strikes" law, and "selective incapacitation" have on society. Walker argues that current crime control policies are actually more harmful than anyone ever anticipated.

The fourth selection, "Fallacies About Crime," by Rutgers University criminologist Marcus Felson, is a unique and provocative analysis of crime in America, with particular reference to the misunderstandings and outright erroneous information that many

Americans use as a foundation for their concepts of crime and punishment. Felson provides a general perspective or image of crime and criminals that he sums up as temptation and control. Society provides both temptations and controls, and it is the balance of the two that dictates the amount and nature of our crime problem.

In the fifth selection, "Race, Crime, and the Administration of Justice," Christopher Stone, president and director of the Vera Institute of Justice, presents the facts concerning patterns of criminal victimization, disparities in conviction rates, and the use of stereotypes and criminal profiles as applied to individuals of color. Stone discusses what has become an enduring reality for many people of color, a very different type of criminal justice system from that experienced by white America.

The final selection in this section is entitled "Peeking Over the Rim: What Lies Ahead?" University of Nevada criminal justice professor Ken Peak reviews challenges for the future in policing, courts, and corrections. He examines several methods for determining what the future will be like and then discusses forecasted changes in police technology to cope with crime, the courts, and corrections. Computers and AIDS/HIV (AIDS) play a role in these forecasts.

FACTS ABOUT CRIME AND CRIMINALS

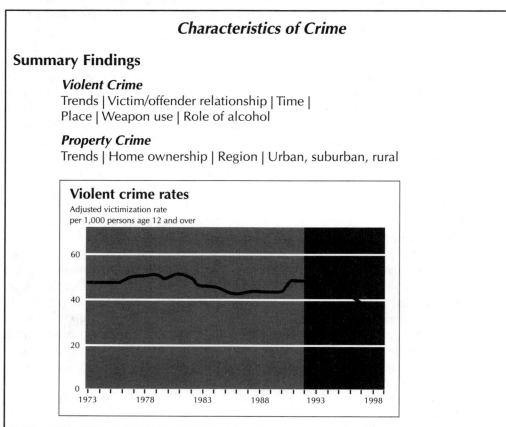

Source: http://www.ojp.usdoj.gov/bjs/cvict_c.htm

Violent Crime

Murder, Rape and sexual assault, Robbery, Assault

Trends

Violent crime rates have declined since 1994, reaching the lowest level ever recorded by the National Crime Victimization Survey in 1999.

Victim/offender relationship

Males were more likely to be victimized by a stranger, and females were more likely to be violently victimized by a friend, an acquaintance, or an intimate. During 1999—

- Almost seven in ten rape or sexual assault victims stated the offender was an intimate, other relative, a friend or an acquaintance.
- Seventy-four percent of males and 42% of females stated the individual(s) who robbed them was a stranger.

Violence against men and women by friends/acquaintances and strangers and intimate partner violence against females fell significantly between 1993 and 1998.

Family members were most likely to murder a young child—about one in five child murders was committed by a family member—while a friend or acquaintance was most likely to murder an older child age 15 to 17.

Intimates were identified by the victims of workplace violence as the perpetrator in about 1% of all workplace violent crime. About 40% of the victims of nonfatal violence in the workplace reported that they knew their offender.

For murder victims, 45% were related to or acquainted with their assailants; 15% of victims were murdered by strangers, while almost 40% of victims had an unknown relationship to their murderer.

Intimate Violence

- In 1998, women experienced an estimated 876,340 rape, sexual assault, robbery, aggravated assault and simple assault victimizations at the hands of an intimate, down from 1.1 million in 1993. In both 1993 and 1998, men were victims of about 160,000 violent crimes by an intimate partner.
- On average, from 1976–1998, the number of murders by intimates decreased by 4% per year for male victims and 1 percent per year for female victims.
- The sharpest decrease in number of intimate murders has been for black male victims. A 74% decrease in the number of black men murdered between 1976 and 1998 occurred.
- Intimate violence is primarily a crime against women—in 1998, females were the victims in 72% of intimate murders and the victims of about 85% of nonlethal intimate violence.
- Women age 16–24 experienced the highest per capita rates of intimate violence (19.6 victimizations per 1,000 women).

- Intimates (current and former spouses, boyfriends and girlfriends) were identified by the victims as the perpetrators of about 1% of all workplace violent crime.

In surveys of 12 cities in 1998, the percentage of violent crime in which the offender was a stranger to the victim ranged from 42% in Tucson to 74% in Los Angeles.

Time of Occurrence

While overall violent crimes were more likely to occur during the day than at night, some crimes exhibited different patterns.

Fifty-four percent of incidents of violent crime occurred between 6 AM and 6 PM. Approximately two-thirds of rapes/sexual assaults occurred at night—6 PM to 6 AM.

Place of Occurrence

Workplace | School | Region | Urban, suburban, rural

In 1995, about a quarter of incidents of violent crime occurred at or near the victim's home. Among common locales for violent crimes were on streets other than those near the victim's home (19%), at school (14%), or at a commercial establishment (12%).

One in four violent crimes occurred in or near the victim's home. Including these, almost half occurred within a mile from home and 73% within five miles. Only 4% of victims of violent crime reported that the crime took place more than fifty miles from their home.

Twenty-three percent of victims of violent crime reported being involved in some form of leisure activity away from home at the time of their victimization. Twenty-one percent said they were at home, and another 21% mentioned they were at work or traveling to or from work when the crime occurred.

Workplace Violence

Of selected occupations examined from 1992 to 1996, law enforcement officers were the most vulnerable to be victims of workplace violence, as well as private security guards, taxi drivers, prison guards, jail guards, and bartenders.

While they were working or on duty, U.S. residents experienced more than 2 million violent victimizations annually from 1992 to 1996, including 1.5 million simple assaults, 396,000 aggravated assaults, 51,000 rapes and sexual assaults, 84,000 robberies, and 1,000 homicides.

Annually, more than 230,000 police officers became victims of a nonfatal violent crime while they were working or on duty between 1992 and 1996.

School Violence

Students age 12 through 18 were victims of about 202,000 violent crimes at school, and about 636,000 away from school. Between 1992 and 1997 victimization rates at school and away from school declined.

- In 1993, 1995 and 1997, about 7% to 8% of students in grades 9 to 12 reported being threatened or injured with a weapon such as a gun, knife, or club on school property in the past 12 months.
- There were few racial-ethnic differences in the percentage of students being threatened or injured with a weapon on school property.
- The percent of students reporting street gang presence at school nearly doubled from 15.3% to 28.4% between 1989 and 1995.

Region

Crime rates differ across regions. In 1999 Western and Midwestern residents experienced the highest rates of violent victimization, and Western households had the highest rate of property crime in the nation.

- 37 Westerners, 36 Midwesterners, and 30 Northeasterners and Southerners per 1,000 were violent crime victims.
- Westerners and Northeasterners had higher robbery rates than Midwesterners or Southerners.

Urban, Suburban and Rural

Urban residents had the highest violent victimization rates, followed by suburban resident rates. Rural residents had the lowest rates.
In 1999—

- Nine urban residents, seven suburban residents and five rural residents per 1,000 were victims of an aggravated assault, and urban residents were robbed at almost four times the rate of rural residents.
- Urban and suburban residents were victims of simple assault at equal rates.

Surveys of 12 cities in 1998 found that black residents in urban areas experienced a higher rate of violent crime than urban whites in a majority of the cities.

Weapon Use

In one-quarter of the incidents of violent crime, offenders used or threatened to use a weapon. National Crime Victimization Survey defines assaults involving weapons as aggravated; thus almost all aggravated assaults (95%) involved a weapon. (Assaults without weapons are classified as aggravated if the victim suffers a serious injury.)

Offenders had or used a weapon in slightly less than half of all robberies, compared with 5% of all rapes/sexual assaults in 1999.

Homicides are most often committed with guns, especially handguns. In 1998, 52% of homicides were committed with handguns, 13% with other guns, 13% with knives, 5% with blunt objects, and 17% with other weapons.

In each of 12 cities surveyed in 1998, victims said that less than half of the violent crimes involved a weapon.

The Role of Alcohol in Crime Victimization

About 3 million violent crimes occur each year in which victims perceive the offender to have been drinking at the time of the offense. Among those victims who provided information about the offender's use of alcohol, about 35% of the victimizations involved an offender who had been drinking.

Two-thirds of victims who suffered violence by an intimate (a current or former spouse, boyfriend, or girlfriend) reported that alcohol had been a factor. Among spouse victims, three out of four incidents were reported to have involved an offender who had been drinking. By contrast, an estimated 31% of stranger victimizations, where the victim could determine the absence or presence of alcohol, were perceived to be alcohol-related.

For about one in five violent victimizations involving perceived alcohol use by the offender, victims also reported they believed the offender to have been using drugs as well.

Property Crime

Property crimes include burglary, theft, and motor vehicle theft.

Property crime continued a 25-year decline.

Property crime makes up about three-quarters of all crime in the United States.

Overall, about 80% of all burglaries were successful. In the remaining percentage, the offender attempted forcible entry. In four of ten of the completed burglaries, the burglar forced entry into the home; in six of ten, the burglar gained entry through an unlocked door or open window.

About 75% of all motor vehicle thefts were successful.

Of the 16 million completed thefts of property in 1999, there were 5.7 million (36%) property thefts of less than $50, 5.8 million (36%) between $50 and $249, and 3.4 million (21%) of $250 or more.

Home Ownership

Property crime occurs most often to those living in rented property.
In 1999—

- Households in rented property experienced 48% higher rates of overall property crime.
- Rented households were burglarized at rates 85% higher than owned households.
- Households living in rented property had 55% higher rates of motor vehicle theft than those in owned property.
- Households residing in rented housing experienced 40% higher rates of theft than households residing in owned dwellings.

Region

The Western portion of the nation experiences the highest rates of property crime overall in the nation.

In 1999—

- Western households had the highest rates of property crime and theft of all regions.
- Western, Southern and Midwestern households experienced similar burglary rates. Northeastern households had the lowest burglary rate in the nation.

Urban, Suburban and Rural

Urban households have historically been the most vulnerable to property crime, burglary, motor vehicle theft and theft in the United States.
In 1999—

- Suburban households were more likely to experience overall property crime, motor vehicle theft and theft than were rural households.
- Rural households were burglarized at rates significantly greater than suburban households.

Chapter 1

The Criminal Justice Process

The private sector initiates the response to crime

This first response may come from individuals, families, neighborhood associations, business, industry, agriculture, educational institutions, the news media, or any other private service to the public.

It involves crime prevention as well as participation in the criminal justice process once a crime has been committed. Private crime prevention is more than providing private security or burglar alarms or participating in neighborhood watch. It also includes a commitment to stop criminal behavior by not engaging in it or condoning it when it is committed by others.

Citizens take part directly in the criminal justice process by reporting crime to the police, by being a reliable participant (for example, a witness or a juror) in a criminal proceeding and by accepting the disposition of the system as just or reasonable. As voters and taxpayers, citizens also participate in criminal justice through the policymaking process that affects how the criminal justice process operates, the resources available to it, and its goals and objectives. At every stage of the process from the original formulation of objectives to the decision about where to locate jails and prisons to the reintegration of inmates into society, the private sector has a role to play. Without such involvement, the criminal justice process cannot serve the citizens it is intended to protect.

The response to crime and public safety involves many agencies and services

Many of the services needed to prevent crime and make neighborhoods safe are supplied by noncriminal justice agencies, including agencies with primary concern for public health, education, welfare, public works, and housing. Individual citizens as well as public and private sector organizations have joined with criminal justice agencies to prevent crime and make neighborhoods safe.

Criminal cases are brought by the government through the criminal justice system

We apprehend, try, and punish offenders by means of a loose confederation of agencies at all levels of government. Our American system of justice has evolved from the English common law into a complex series of procedures and decisions. Founded on the concept that crimes against an individual are crimes against the state, our justice system prosecutes individuals as though they victimized all of society. However, crime victims are involved throughout the process and many justice agencies have programs which focus on helping victims.

From the *Report to the Nation on Crime and Justice,* January 1998. © 1998 by the U.S. Department of Justice, Office of Justice Programs, Bureau of Justice Statistics. Reprinted by permission.

There is no single criminal justice system in this country. We have many similar systems that are individually unique. Criminal cases may be handled differently in different jurisdictions, but court decisions based on the due process guarantees of the U.S. Constitution require that specific steps be taken in the administration of criminal justice so that the individual will be protected from undue intervention from the state.

The description of the criminal and juvenile justice systems that follows portrays the most common sequence of events in response to serious criminal behavior.

ENTRY INTO THE SYSTEM

The justice system does not respond to most crime because so much crime is not discovered or reported to the police. Law enforcement agencies learn about crime from the reports of victims or other citizens, from discovery by a police officer in the field, from informants, or from investigative and intelligence work.

Once a law enforcement agency has established that a crime has been committed, a suspect must be identified and apprehended for the case to proceed through the system. Sometimes, a suspect is apprehended at the scene; however, identification of a suspect sometimes requires an extensive investigation. Often, no one is identified or apprehended. In some instances, a suspect is arrested and later the police determine that no crime was committed and the suspect is released.

PROSECUTION AND PRETRIAL SERVICES

After an arrest, law enforcement agencies present information about the case and about the accused to the prosecutor, who will decide if formal charges will be filed with the court. If no charges are filed, the accused must be released. The prosecutor can also drop charges after making efforts to prosecute *(nolle prosequi).*

A suspect charged with a crime must be taken before a judge or magistrate without unnecessary delay. At the initial appearance, the judge or magistrate informs the accused of the charges and decides whether there is probable cause to detain the accused person. If the offense is not very serious, the determination of guilt and assessment of a penalty may also occur at this stage.

Often, the defense counsel is also assigned at the initial appearance. All suspects prosecuted for serious crimes have a right to be represented by an attorney. If the court determines the suspect is indigent and cannot afford such representation, the court will assign counsel at the public's expense.

A pretrial-release decision may be made at the initial appearance, but may occur at other hearings or may be changed at another time during the process. Pretrial release and bail were traditionally intended to ensure appearance at trial. However, many jurisdictions permit pretrial detention of defendants accused of serious offenses and deemed to be dangerous to prevent them from committing crimes prior to trial.

The court often bases its pretrial decision on information about the defendant's drug use, as well as residence, employment, and family ties. The court may decide to release the accused on his/her own recognizance or into the custody of a third party after the posting of a financial bond or on the promise of satisfying certain conditions, such as taking periodic drug tests to ensure drug abstinence.

In many jurisdictions, the initial appearance may be followed by a preliminary hearing. The main function of this hearing is to discover if there is probable cause to believe that the accused committed a known crime within the jurisdiction of the court. If the judge does not find probable cause, the case is dismissed; however, if the judge or magistrate finds probable cause for such a belief, or the accused waives his or her right to a preliminary hearing, the case may be bound over to a grand jury.

A grand jury hears evidence against the accused presented by the prosecutor and decides if there is sufficient evidence to cause the accused to be brought to trial. If the grand jury finds sufficient evidence, it submits to the court an indictment, a written statement of the essential facts of the offense charged against the accused.

Where the grand jury system is used, the grand jury may also investigate criminal activity generally and issue indictments called grand jury originals that initiate criminal cases. These investigations and indictments are often used in drug and conspiracy cases that involve complex organizations. After such an indictment, law enforcement tries to apprehend and arrest the suspects named in the indictment.

Misdemeanor cases and some felony cases proceed by the issuance of an information, a formal, written accusation submitted to the court by a prosecutor. In some jurisdictions, indictments may be required in felony cases. However, the accused may choose to waive a grand jury indictment and, instead, accept service of an information for the crime.

In some jurisdictions, defendants, often those without prior criminal records, may be eligible for diversion from prosecution subject to the completion of specific conditions such as drug treatment. Successful completion of the conditions may result in the dropping of charges or the expunging of the criminal record, where the defendant is required to plead guilty prior to the diversion.

ADJUDICATION

Once an indictment or information has been filed with the trial court, the accused is scheduled for arraignment. At the arraignment, the accused is informed of the charges, advised of the rights of criminal defendants, and asked to enter a plea to the charges. Sometimes, a plea of guilty is the result of negotiations between the prosecutor and the defendant.

If the accused pleads guilty or pleads *nolo contendere* (accepts penalty without admitting guilt), the judge may accept or reject the plea. If the plea is accepted, no trial is held and the offender is sentenced at this proceeding or at a later date. The plea may be rejected and proceed to trial if, for example, the judge believes that the accused may have been coerced.

If the accused pleads not guilty or not guilty by reason of insanity, a date is set for the trial. A person accused of a serious crime is guaranteed a trial by jury. However, the accused may ask for a bench trial where the judge, rather than a jury, serves as the finder of fact. In both instances, the prosecution and defense present evidence by questioning witnesses while the judge decides on issues of law. The trial results in acquittal or conviction on the original charges or on lesser included offenses.

After the trial, a defendant may request appellate review of the conviction or sentence. In some cases, appeals of convictions are a matter of right; all states with the death penalty provide for automatic appeal of cases involving a death sentence. Appeals may be subject to the discretion of the appellate court and may be granted only on acceptance of a defendant's petition for a *writ of certiorari*. Prisoners may also appeal their sentences through civil rights petitions and writs of *habeas corpus* where they claim unlawful detention.

SENTENCING AND SANCTIONS

After a conviction, the sentence is imposed. In most cases, the judge decides on the sentence, but in some jurisdictions the sentence is decided by the jury, particularly for capital offenses.

In arriving at an appropriate sentence, a sentencing hearing may be held at which evidence of aggravating or mitigating circumstances is considered. In assessing the circumstances surrounding a convicted person's criminal behavior, courts often rely on presentence investigations by probation agencies or other designated authorities. Courts may also consider victim impact statements.

The sentencing choices that may be available to judges and juries include one or more of the following:

- the death penalty
- incarceration in a prison, jail, or other confinement facility
- probation—allowing the convicted person to remain at liberty but subject to certain conditions and restrictions, such as drug testing, or drug restrictions, such as drug testing or drug treatment
- fines—primarily applied as penalties in minor offenses
- restitution—requiring the offender to pay compensation to the victim. In some jurisdictions, offenders may be sentenced to alternatives to incarceration that are considered more severe than straight probation but less severe than a prison term. Examples of such sanctions include boot camps, intense supervision often with drug treatment and testing, house arrest and electronic monitoring, denial of federal benefits, and community service.

In many jurisdictions, the law mandates that persons convicted of certain types of offenses serve a prison term. Most jurisdictions permit the judge to set the sentence length within certain limits, but some have determinate sentencing laws that stipulate a specific sentence length that must be served and cannot be altered by a parole board.

CORRECTIONS

Offenders sentenced to incarceration usually serve time in a local jail or a state prison. Offenders sentenced to less than 1 year generally go to jail; those sentenced to more than 1 year go to prison. Persons admitted to the federal system or a state prison system may be held in prison with varying levels of custody or in a community correctional facility.

A prisoner may become eligible for parole after serving a specific part of his or her sentence. Parole is the conditional release of a prisoner before the prisoner's full sentence has been served. The decision to grant parole is made by an authority such as a parole board, which has power to grant or revoke parole or to discharge a parolee altogether. The way parole decisions are made varies widely among jurisdictions.

Offenders may also be required to serve out their full sentences prior to release (expiration of term). Those sentenced under determinate sentencing laws can be released only after they have served their full sentence (mandatory release) less any "goodtime" received while in prison. Inmates get goodtime credits against their sentences automatically or by earning them through participation in programs.

If released by a parole board decision or by mandatory release, the releasee will be under the supervision of a parole officer in the community for the balance of his or her unexpired sentence. This supervision is governed by specific conditions of release, and the releasee may be returned to prison for violations of such conditions.

Recidivism

Once the suspects, defendants, or offenders are released from the jurisdiction of a criminal justice agency, they may be processed through the criminal justice system again for a new crime. Long-term studies show that many suspects who are arrested have prior criminal histories and those with a greater number of prior arrests were more likely to be arrested again. As the courts take prior criminal history into account at sentencing, most prison inmates have a prior criminal history and many have been incarcerated before. Nationally, about half the inmates released from state prison will return to prison.

The Juvenile Justice System

Juvenile courts usually have jurisdiction over matters concerning children, including delinquency, neglect, and adoption. They also handle "status offenses," such as truancy and running away, which are not applicable to adults. State statutes define which persons are under the original jurisdiction of the juvenile court. The upper age of juvenile court jurisdiction in delinquency matters is 17 years in most states.

The processing of juvenile offenders is not entirely dissimilar to adult criminal processing, but there are crucial differences. Many juveniles are referred to juvenile courts by law enforcement officers, but many others are referred by school officials, social services agencies, neighbors, and even parents for behavior or conditions that are determined to require intervention by the formal system for social control.

At arrest, a decision is made either to send the matter further into the justice system or to divert the case out of the system, often to alternative programs. Examples of alternative programs include drug treatment, individual or group counseling, or referral to educational and recreational programs.

When juveniles are referred to the juvenile courts, the court's intake department or the prosecuting attorney determines whether sufficient grounds exist to warrant filing a petition that requests an adjudicatory hearing or a request to transfer jurisdiction to criminal court. At this point, many juveniles are released or diverted to alternative programs.

All states allow juveniles to be tried as adults in criminal court under certain circumstances. In many states, the legislature *statutorily excludes* certain (usually serious) offenses from the jurisdiction of the juvenile court, regardless of the age of the accused. In some states and at the federal level under certain circumstances, prosecutors have the *discretion* to either file criminal charges against juveniles directly in criminal courts or proceed through the juvenile justice process. The juvenile court's intake department or the prosecutor may petition the juvenile court to *waive* jurisdiction to criminal court. The juvenile court also may order *referral* to criminal court for trial as adults. In some jurisdictions, juveniles processed as adults may, upon conviction, be sentenced to either an adult or a juvenile facility.

In those cases where the juvenile court retains jurisdiction, the case may be handled formally by filing a delinquency petition or informally by diverting the juvenile to other agencies or programs in lieu of further court processing.

If a petition for an adjudicatory hearing is accepted, the juvenile may be brought before a court quite unlike the court with jurisdiction over adult offenders. Despite the considerable discretion associated with juvenile court proceedings, juveniles are afforded many of the due-process safeguards associated with adult criminal trials. Several states permit the use of juries in juvenile courts; however, in light of the U.S. Supreme Court holding that juries are not essential to juvenile hearings, most states do not make provisions for juries in juvenile courts.

In disposing of cases, juvenile courts usually have far more discretion than adult courts. In addition to such options as probation, commitment to a residential facility, restitution, or fines, state laws grant juvenile courts the power to order removal of children from their homes to foster homes or treatment facilities. Juvenile courts also may order participation in special programs aimed at shoplifting prevention, drug counseling, or driver education.

Once a juvenile is under juvenile court disposition, the court may retain jurisdiction until the juvenile legally becomes an adult (at age 21 in most states). In some jurisdictions, juvenile offenders may be classified as youthful offenders, which can lead to extended sentences.

Following release from an institution, juveniles are often ordered to a period of aftercare, which is similar to parole supervision for adult offenders. Juvenile offenders who violate the conditions of aftercare may have their aftercare revoked, resulting in being recommitted to a facility. Juveniles who are classified as youthful offenders and violate the conditions of aftercare may be subject to adult sanctions.

The governmental response to crime is founded in the intergovernmental structure of the United States

Under our form of government, each state and the federal government has its own criminal justice system. All systems must respect the rights of individuals set forth in court interpretation of the U.S. Constitution and defined in case law.

State constitutions and laws define the criminal justice system within each state and delegate the authority and responsibility for criminal justice to various jurisdictions, officials, and institutions. State laws also define criminal behavior and groups of children or acts under jurisdiction of the juvenile courts.

Municipalities and counties further define their criminal justice systems through local ordinances that prescribe the local agencies responsible for criminal justice processing that were not established by the state.

Congress has also established a criminal justice system at the federal level to respond to federal crimes such as bank robbery, kidnapping, and transporting stolen goods across state lines.

Discretion Is Exercised Throughout the Criminal Justice System

Discretion is "an authority conferred by law to act in certain conditions or situations in accordance with an official's or an official agency's own considered judgment and conscience."[1] Discretion is exercised throughout the government. It is a part of decisionmaking in all government systems from mental health to education, as well as criminal justice. The limits of discretion vary from jurisdiction to jurisdiction.

Concerning crime and justice, legislative bodies have recognized that they cannot anticipate the range of circumstances surrounding each crime, anticipate local mores, and enact laws that clearly encompass all conduct that is criminal and all that is not.[2]

Therefore, persons charged with the day-to-day response to crime are expected to exercise their own judgment within limits set by law. Basically, they must decide—

- whether to take action
- where the situation fits in the scheme of law, rules, and precedent
- which official response is appropriate.[3]

To ensure that discretion is exercised responsibly, government authority is often delegated to professionals. Professionalism requires a minimum level of training and orientation, which guide officials in making decisions. The professionalism of policing is due largely to the desire to ensure the proper exercise of police discretion.

The limits of discretion vary from state to state and locality to locality. For example, some state judges have wide discretion in the type of sentence they may impose. In recent years, other states have sought to limit the judge's discretion in sentencing by passing mandatory sentencing laws that require prison sentences for certain offenses.

Notes

[1] Roscoe Pound, "Discretion, dispensation and mitigation: The problem of the individual special case," *New York University Law Review* (1960) 35:925, 926.

[2] Wayne R. LaFave, *Arrest: The decision to take a suspect into custody* (Boston: Little, Brown & Co., 1964), p. 63–184.

[3] Memorandum of June 21, 1977, from mark Moore to James Vorenberg, "Some abstract notes on the issue of discretion."

Who Exercises Discretion?

These criminal justice officials . . .	must often decide whether or not or how to—
Police	Enforce specific laws
	Investigate specific crimes; search people
Prosecutors	File charges or petitions for adjudication
	Seek indictments
	Drop cases
	Reduce charges
Judges or magistrates	Set bail or conditions for release
	Accept pleas
	Determine delinquency
	Dismiss charges
	Impose sentences
	Revoke probation
Correctional officials	Assign to type of correctional facility
	Award privileges
	Punish for disciplinary infractions

Bureau of Justice Statistics *(www.ojp.us-doj.gov/bjs/)*. January 1998. NCJ 167894.

The response to crime is mainly a state and local function

Very few crimes are under exclusive federal jurisdiction. The responsibility to respond to most crime rests with state and local governments. Police protection is primarily a function of cities and towns. Corrections is primarily a function of state governments. Most justice personnel are employed at the local level.

Chapter 2

American Criminal Justice Philosophy

What's Old—What's New?

by Curtis R. Blakely and Vic W. Bumphus

INTRODUCTION

Contemporary movements in criminal justice, such as community-oriented policing and certain community corrections strategies, have been portrayed as new innovations, having little historical precedent. While specific programs are genuinely original, criminologists have advocated the importance of proactive and preventive programming for decades. Toward that end, the criminal justice system is currently integrating its adversarial approach to the identification, apprehension, and correction of offenders with an increased service orientation by emphasizing community involvement. As such, criminal justice scholars and activists are encouraging officials to cultivate community partnerships to solicit citizen input.

The following review of literature explores the idea that the underlying objectives of the early American criminal justice system remain largely unaltered. What has changed is public attitudes about crime, police organization, police and public perceptions about each other, and the complex relationship between politics and justice initiatives. Community policing and restorative justice paradigms are briefly discussed. The specifics are less important than the guiding philosophy behind their growing popularity. While the political rhetoric surrounding these "new" programs envisions them as novel approaches, a review of the extant literature suggests that they are nothing more than modern adaptations to earlier innovations. The authors do not intend an exhaustive historical account of either policing or corrections. Instead, they hope to provoke more comprehensive thought by briefly examining criminal justice change from a socio-historical perspective.

POLICE: A HISTORICAL REVIEW

The impact of European ideals upon early American policing is evident (Uchida, 1993; Walker, 1980; Carter & Radelet, 1999); however, unlike English protocol, original attempts at policing within America were characterized by direct citizen participation. This may be due to philosophical beliefs regarding governmental intervention and the slow,

From *Federal Probation*, June 1999.

often hesitant, establishment of colonial law enforcement agencies. Colonists were attempting to escape a strong, often tyrannical government; therefore, they naturally valued individual freedom, discretion, and participation. Due to this vacuum in official authority, individuals participated directly in criminal justice activities (Walker, 1980). Uchida (1993: 20) notes that an organized police force was viewed with suspicion due to its potential for "despotic control over citizens and subjects." However, as the colonies became more permanent and socially complex, the need for a more organized style of policing developed.

An early forerunner of contemporary policing was the night watch system, and as the name suggests, it was nothing more than night-time patrol. New York began experimenting with a night watch as early as 1684 (Walker, 1980; Uchida, 1993; Carter & Radelet, 1999; Lyman, 1999). These sentry men were primarily charged with patrolling the city for fires, suspicious individuals, riots, or other incidents requiring immediate intervention. This system was eventually modified to include a day watch component. Thus, the first forerunner of the modern police force emerged. Walker (1980: 59) credits these early attempts with engaging in "preventive patrol,"—arguably, the first attempt at proactive policing within America. Another example of early policing can be found in the use of "frank pledges" which compelled all males twelve years of age and older to serve in a quasi-police role. These were small groups of citizens that vowed to deliver to court any group member committing an unlawful act. According to Uchida (1993: 17), this style of community policing became increasingly popular in England after 1066.

While these two approaches were primarily designed to prevent and control crime, they also served to reinforce the value of community involvement in law enforcement activities. Likewise, when reviewing the early epoch of American policing, it can be seen that police were involved in a wide variety of social service tasks, including providing food to the hungry and shelter to the homeless (Uchida, 1993: 22; Kelling & Moore, 1995: 7).

It was during the reform era (beginning in the 1930s), under the direct tutelage of the Federal Bureau of Investigation, that professionalism and technology began to become paramount. The Wickersham Commission, under President Hoover, also advocated changes in policing envisioned as efforts to professionalize law enforcement (Carter & Radelet, 1999; Lyman, 1999). Departments nationwide followed suit and began to adopt a "professional" style of policing. This movement was characterized by a reduction of the social service role and an official emphasis upon crime control and offender apprehension. Therefore, police began to rely upon arrests and percentages of crimes cleared to measure effectiveness (Walker, 1980: 191; Kelling & Moore, 1995: 14). This shifted the human approach to a much lesser profile in formalized policing (Kelling & Moore, 1995: 12). Walker (1980: 135) states that this model remained dominant and unchallenged until the 1970s. However, he has also noted (1980: 189), that "while the police role was redefined toward crime fighting, day to day police work increasingly involved miscellaneous services to the public." Reiss (1971) and Walker (1980) both conclude that during the 1960s, as much as 80 percent of police work was consumed by noncriminal matters. This suggests that even during an era characterized by growing police professionalism and isolation, delivery of informal policing tasks remained the norm.

CONTEMPORARY POLICING ISSUES

Those familiar with the history of American policing are aware of the many challenges inhibiting the effective application of law enforcement. These include organizational (fiscal restraints, staffing problems, and large patrol districts), ethical, and socio-legal problems. Increasingly, police have been placed under closer scrutiny due to high-profile incidents such as the Rodney King beating, the Los Angeles riots and, more recently, the flurry of misconduct complaints landing on the New York City Police Department. Substantial criticism has involved the treatment of the young, poor, and those of minority status. These various problems have subjected nearly all police agencies to critical examination in areas of public relations and citizen contact. Likewise, police administrators across America are currently concerned with managing public relations, often accompanied by some degree of community-oriented policing.

The 1970s marked a time in which the public, somewhat dissatisfied with police services, increasingly demanded that the police take a proactive and personal approach toward community issues. This desire is summarized by Meese (1993), who proposes that the police should be more than merely reactive, responding to crimes already committed. It is important that law enforcement develop a proactive posture toward community disorder, social problems, and quality of life issues.

In response, police establishments began to abandon a strict "law enforcement" approach, replacing it with a greater "peace and service" orientation. The latter, of course, embraces a more social service and holistic approach to policing. This shift away from a strict crime control approach to one that encourages citizen involvement in police operations, and police involvement in community activities, has been referred to as strategic, problem solving, and neighborhood oriented policing (Meese, 1993). Kelling and Moore (1995) have noted that this movement signifies a new era, distinguishable from the political and reform eras.

Central to community policing is a belief that the police can more effectively achieve their basic goals of crime prevention and control through the assistance and support of the community (Meese, 1993). By establishing partnerships with other institutions like families, schools, churches, and neighborhood associations, police potentially widen their ability to identify and solve community problems. This approach envisions the importance of peace-keeping and social service tasks as equal to enforcement activities.

CORRECTIONS: A HISTORICAL REVIEW

Many of the major shifts in correctional ideology parallel changes in approaches to law enforcement. Beginning in the 16th century, "workhouses, or houses of correction," spread widely over northwestern Europe (Shichor, 1995: 23). While little is known about these early institutions and their practices, anecdotal accounts present them as an attempt to systematically address and rectify increasing crime and disorder problems. Walker (1980: 16) adds that these institutions resembled modern prisons in their attempts to rehabilitate the offender and make him or her a productive member of society. Then in 1576, the English Parliament passed an act providing for the establishment of the "bride well" (Shichor, 1995). These institutions were places where vagrants, prostitutes, and offenders were instilled with rehabilitative rationale and provided rudimentary skills training (Welch, 1996: 44). Shichor (1995: 24) identifies these institutions as early forerunners to reformatories and prisons. Likewise, Welch (1996: 44) recounts that these institutions formed the basis for rehabilitative rationale and the work ethic. Philosophical statements like, "It is of little advantage to restrain the bad by punishment, unless you render them good by discipline," reverberated this sentiment (Walker, 1980: 42). According to Walker (1980: 66), incarceration was meant to rehabilitate the offender through "creating a better environment, separating the individual from harmful influences and subjecting him to a corrective prison discipline of solitude, hard work, and religious study." Morris (1998: 32) concludes that the penitentiary was intended to reform criminals by "isolating them from each other and other infectious diseases." Thomas (1987: 60) states that this rehabilitative ideal began to take root in Europe long before the 17th century and the colonization of America. Likewise, he states that an "argument can be made that enthusiasm for rehabilitation as a major objective of penal sanctions dates back to the time of Plato or before" (Thomas, 1987: 91).

Colonial America adopted many of the same European philosophies and practices. However, Walker (1980: 12) notes that colonial criminal codes were often more lenient in their punishments than were their English counterparts. This comparative leniency may indicate an early philosophical difference existing between the colonists and England: a perception that English sanctions were more punitive than corrective. Thomas (1987: 66) recognizes this and states that well before the Civil War, sanctions were being applied within America's prisons with the conviction that they could serve the goal of crime prevention. Toward the end of the 18th century, the penitentiary arose (Shichor, 1995: 26). As the name implies, the penitentiary had as its main objectives repentance, penitence, and rehabilitation (Shichor, 1995: 26; Walker, 1980: 65).

Much like the blind men of Hindustan who gave despairingly divergent descriptions of an elephant, penologists also maintain individualistic ideals regarding correctional objectives. Most researchers, however, have consistently identified four goals. For example, Barak (1998: 75) lists these goals as revenge/retribution, deterrence, incapacitation, and rehabilitation. Shichor (1995: 65) identifies these same four goals but substitutes retribution for revenge. Wilkinson (1997) identifies the same four, but substitutes vengeance for retribution. Thomas (1987: 51) reduces the number of correctional goals to three, including retribution, crime prevention, and rehabilitation. The designation of correctional objectives suggests only a slight difference in semantics, not in overall philosophy. Morris (1998) notes that whether prisons are considered tools of retribution or rehabilitation, most people believe that they fail to achieve either goal. He states:

> Instead, the institution has unintentionally spawned a subculture that is antithetical to both goals—and it has become clear that the beliefs and behavior of inmates are far more likely to be shaped by this subculture than by prison and its programs (Morris, 1998: 8).

Thomas (1987: 85) notes that the life and death struggle of rehabilitative efforts may be the single most pervasive issue that has occurred in corrections over the past decade.

As already observed, one objective of the American correctional system has traditionally been rehabilitation. Historically, a belief in the innate goodness of humanity and one's ability to change have been valued in American correctional policies. This can be seen in the implementation of indeterminate sentencing, probation, and parole (Thomas, 1987: 93). Rehabilitation was strongly emphasized until the early 1970s when the United States began to experience unparalleled increases in crime rates and prison commitments (Shichor, 1995: 9; Blakely, 1997). Morris (1998: 8) observes that, due to overcrowding, correctional facilities are increasingly de-emphasizing their original mandate of offender rehabilitation, focusing instead on maintaining facility control. To manage the ever-increasing inmate population, rehabilitative efforts—which provide ample opportunity for inmate conflict, divert fiscal and personnel resources, and are labor intensive—increasingly become secondary to the orderly operation of the facility (Cullen, Latessa, Burton, & Lombardo, 1993; Thomas, 1995). Conditions associated with overcrowding and the violence that it spawns (Montgomery & Crews, 1998), are increasingly convincing prison officials that a strict model of incapacitation might be necessary. Contemporary correctional efforts appear less concerned with initiating inmate change and more interested in maintaining facility control by limiting opportunities for inmate misconduct. However, amidst the emergence of punitive, crime-control ideology, inmate enhancement and life skills programming remain central to correctional practices.

In the recent past, it appears that, much like the police, corrections has been guided by a strict crime control mandate. This is reflected in that large segment of society that values incarceration of offenders over the remaining three goals (Blakely, 1997; Briscoe, 1997; Wittenberg, 1997). The current "get tough" response to crime is resulting in a growing reliance upon confinement strictly as a punitive measure (Cullen, Latessa, Burton, & Lombardo, 1993; Blakely, 1997; Briscoe, 1997; Wittenberg, 1997; Montgomery & Crews, 1998). The Congress' "Safe Streets" and "3-Strikes You're Out" bills as well as the president's "War on Crime" and "Get Tough" campaigns clearly indicate a more punitive ideology (Blakely, 1998; Montgomery & Crews, 1998). Additionally, the popularity of "Truth in Sentencing" laws requires offenders to serve increasingly longer terms of confinement (Cowley, 1998; Montgomery & Crews, 1998). In a recent study conducted by Cullen, Latessa, Burton, and Lombardo (1993), rehabilitation was ranked as a secondary goal by a large percentage of prison administrators. Wittenberg (1996: 46) reports that a substantial number of Americans currently prefer punishment to rehabilitation. Thomas (1987: 99) notes that this "get tough" response is culminating in an organized "anti-rehabilitation" trend, emphasizing the protection of society through incapacitation (Shichor, 1995: 10; Montgomery & Crews, 1998).

This apparent shift in goals has prompted Albanese (1996: 558) to state, "We just can't seem to punish enough." Wilkinson (1997: 100) observes that this approach has often been at the expense of both the offender and community. These scholars concur that the current punitive approach within corrections lacks any identifiable objective, other than punishment itself.

CONTEMPORARY CORRECTIONAL ISSUES

A new paradigm in criminal justice has recently emerged. The restorative justice paradigm envisions a more proactive criminal justice system emphasizing preventing crime in the early stages, protecting society, and relying on incarceration as a last resort (Hahn, 1998; Bazemore & Umbreit, 1997). This philosophy advocates a more integrated approach to justice, encouraging community, victim, and offender participation. Restorative justice involves long-term commitment to systemic changes (Umbreit, 1995) and builds on existing programs like victim-offender mediation, restitution, community service, and police-community partnerships (Bazemore & Umbreit, 1997; Hahn, 1998).

To pursue rehabilitation again, corrections is currently experimenting with a number of restorative justice programs. At the nucleus of this movement is a belief in an offender's ability to change, and an expectation that offenders will accept responsibility for their actions. In a recent study conducted in Vermont, Gorczyk and Perry (1997: 79) report that 93 percent of that state's population wanted violent offenders to serve their entire sentences with no opportunity for early release. But these same researchers also found that Vermonters expect the system to operate with specific concern for future behavior. While these findings cannot be generalized nationwide, they may indicate a desire by many for proactive and rehabilitative measures. Maryland, too, has implemented a restorative justice approach to its juvenile justice system. This program has the expressed objectives of increasing "public safety," and offender "accountability," while initiating "rehabilitative" measures (Simms, 1997).

A COMPARISON OF PROACTIVE POLICING AND PROACTIVE CORRECTIONS

After reviewing the historical objectives of policing and corrections, and current attempts to implement community policing and restorative justice programs, the question persists whether these philosophical approaches are new, or an attempt to return to earlier criminal justice pursuits. While it may initially appear unnecessary to make this determination, there are two compelling reasons to do so. First, a strong grounding in historical precedent is essential for the application of criminal justice and permits contemporary practitioners to make intelligent and informed decisions about crime control strategies and tactics. Secondly, this determination permits contemporary practitioners to further refine their approach to the ever-changing nature of criminal justice. This, in turn, allows for a more informed perspective on the evolution of correctional ideologies.

It appears that the early criminal justice system was originally more forward-looking than its contemporary counterpart. This is evidenced in the early establishment of peacekeeping and rehabilitative goals. While we are less interested in the methods of early justice than in the philosophical basis for their implementation, evidence indicates that early practitioners wished to cultivate a strong interpersonal relationship with society.

Likewise, with the advent of community policing, it appears that American policing is attempting to return to its original functions of public service and crime control. Faced with increasing crime rates during the reform era, police were largely unprepared to address social problems effectively. Therefore, police agencies adopted a defensive position of quick response times and the ready application of force. Rising crime rates also began to drive a wedge between the police and community. Increasingly, the police were being relegated to responding to incidents rather than intervening proactively. This encouraged society to view police efforts as unproductive and uncaring, and police to view communities as uncaring and nonsupportive.

Increasing crime rates and a defensive orientation readily lent itself to an adoption of military-style structuring. As can be expected, this further weakened the peacekeeping mandate of police agencies. Meese (1993) and Walker (1980) have noted the general negative impact of the military structure upon police agencies. Further, the inherent nature of military structuring stifled individual discretion and creative problem-solving techniques. Police departments began to departmentalize and internalize operations. Society also began to view government apprehensively. With growing discontent with government and police services, anti-government public sentiment emerged. This was compounded by the unpopularity of the Vietnam War and skyrocketing claims of police brutality.

The increased reliance by police agencies on the automobile also took its toll. Walker (1980) credits the introduction of the automobile with isolating the police officer from the community and ultimately increasing the officer's adversarial relationship with new segments of society. While the car allowed a rapid response to calls for service, it ultimately removed officers from the neighborhood, relegating them to the confines of the cruiser. Motorized patrol demanded that an officer be reactive rather than proactive. Along with the automobile came new forms of communication, which inhibited personalized contact with the public, and instead, encouraged a reliance on other police personnel such as the dispatcher. The dispatcher became the source of information for police personnel and effectively replaced face-to-face contact with citizenry.

Likewise, corrections, which was largely a victim in this crime control approach, increasingly emphasized incapacitation. With increases in arrests, convictions, and imprisonments, they too were unprepared to continue emphasizing service through treatment programs. Morris (1998: 8) observes, "Instead of concerning themselves with the original purpose of the institution, prison officials are forced to focus almost exclusively on simply keeping control over their wards." Between 1970 and 1995, the number of inmates being housed in state and federal prison more than quintupled (Morris, 1998: 7). This "explosion" led Morris to state: "America's prison populations have been growing at such a rate that prison authorities may soon be forced to post 'no vacancy' signs outside their gates." In an attempt to "tread water," efforts to impart skills and increase education became secondary to the safe management of large inmate populations (Morris, 1998: 8). Because of overcrowding and increases in prison violence, correctional officials increasingly limited or eliminated activities not seen as absolutely necessary. The 1970s and early 1980s became known for prison riots like those that ravaged Attica and the Penitentiary of New Mexico. These and similar events convinced prison officials that a strict model of incapacitation might best suit criminal justice policy. And yet, through all these changes, America's penal system did not totally abandon its original intent, and increasingly began to use terms like "correctional officer," "correctional center," and "departments of corrections." While many argue, like Thomas (1987: 96) that a change in terminology does not necessarily imply a change in practice, this change may indicate an attempt to identify with an overall objective.

CONCLUSION

The historical record does not support community policing and restorative justice as contemporary innovations, but as attempts to return to an earlier model of justice emphasizing people, discretion, and a belief in the inherent goodness of humanity. Though criminal justice perspectives have gained and lost momentum due to social change, the symbiotic relationship between the various objectives ensures a criminal justice system that places emphasis on both reactive and proactive strategies. Therefore, contemporary proactive justice is part and parcel of the larger philosophical basis of the modern criminal justice system. In sum, it is the various interpretations of historical events in criminal justice that suggests that what is *old* (proactive or reactive) will eventually become *new,* again and again.

REFERENCES

Albanese, J. (1996). Five fundamental mistakes of criminal justice. *Justice Quarterly,* 13(4): 551–565.

Barak, G. (1998). *Integrating criminologies.* Boston, MA: Allyn and Bacon.

Bazemore, G. & Umbreit, M. (1997). *Balanced and restorative justice for juveniles: a framework for juvenile justice in the 21st century.* Washington DC: Office of Juvenile Justice and Delinquency Prevention.

Blakely, C. (1998). The rehabilitative benefits of education. *The (British) Prison Service Journal* (120): 29.

Blakely, C. (1997). Offender rehabilitation: A worthy goal. *Corrections Compendium.* 22(5): 1–2.

Bloomer, K. (1997) America's newest growth industry. *In These Times* (March).

Briscoe, J. (1997). Breaking the cycle of violence: A rational approach to at-risk youth. *Federal Probation,* 51(3): 3.

Carter, D., & Radelet, L. (1999). *The police and the community* (6th edition). Upper Saddle River, NJ: Prentice Hall.

Cowley, J. (1998). Changing public opinion. *Corrections Today* (February).

Cullen, F., Latessa, E., Burton, V., & Lombardo, L. (1993). Prison wardens: Is the rehabilitative ideal supported? *Criminology,* 31(1): 69–87.

Gorczyk, J., & Perry, J. (1997). What the public wants. *Corrections Today* (December).

Hahn, P. (1998). *Emerging criminal justice: three pillars for proactive justice system.* Thousand Oaks, CA: Sage Publications.

Johnson, B. R., & Ross, P. P. (1990). The privatization of correctional management: A review. *Journal of Criminal Justice,* 18: 351–355.

Kelling, G. and Moore, M. (1995). The evolving strategy of policing. In Kappeler's *The police and society: Touchstone Readings.* Prospect Heights, IL: Waveland Press, Inc.

Lyman, M. (1999). *The police: an introduction.* Upper Saddle River, NJ: Prentice Hall.

Meese III, E. (1993). *Community policing and the police officer.* Washington DC: U.S. Dept. of Justice.

Montgomery Jr., Reid, & Crews, G. (1998). *A history of correctional violence: An examination of reported causes of riots and disturbance.* Lanham, MD: American Correctional Association.

Morris, J. (1998). *Jailhouse journalism: The fourth estate behind bars.* Jefferson, NC: McFarland and Company, Inc.

Reiss, A. (1971). *The police and the public.* New Haven: Yale University Press.

Rothman, D. (1971). *The discovery of the asylum.* Boston: Little, Brown.

Shichor, D. (1995). *Punishment for profit.* Thousand Oaks, CA: Sage Publications.

Simms, S. (1997). Restorative juvenile justice. *Corrections Today* (December).

Thomas, J. (1995). The ironies of prison education. In Davidson's *Schooling in a Total Institution.* Westport, CT: Bergin and Garvey.

Thomas, C. (1987). *Corrections in America—Problems of the past and the present.* Thousand Oaks, CA: Sage Publications.

Uchida, C. (1993). The development of two American police: An historical overview. In Dunham and Alpert's *Critical issues in policing.* Prospect Heights, IL. Waveland Press, Inc.

UC Research (1993/94). *Punishment vs. rehabilitation.* Cincinnati: University of Cincinnati.

Umbreit, M. (1995). Holding juvenile offenders accountable: a restorative justice perspective. *Juvenile and Family Court Journal,* 42(2): 31–42.

Walker, S. (1980). *Popular justice: A history of American criminal justice.* New York: Oxford University Press.

Welch, M. (1996). *Corrections: a critical approach.* New York: McGraw-Hill.

Wilkinson, R. (1997). Community justice in Ohio. *Corrections Today* (December).

Wittenberg, P. (1997). Leadership and the management of agency image. *Federal Probation,* 61(3): 46.

Wittenberg, P. (1996). Power, influence and the development of correctional policy. *Federal Probation,* 60(2): 43.

Chapter 3

Crime and Policy

A Complex Problem

THE MIRACLE OF FALLING CRIME RATES

Crime in America is down. For almost seven years now, beginning in the early 1990s, serious crime has been dropping dramatically. The FBI reports that the crime rate dropped 22 percent between 1991 and 1998 (and dropped another 10 percent in the first six months of 1999). The National Criminal Victimization Survey (NCVS), meanwhile, reports that "every major type of crime . . . decreased significantly between 1993 and 1998." Violent crime was down 27 percent and property crimes down 34 percent.[1]

The reduction has been particularly dramatic in certain cities. Both the murder and robbery rates in San Diego in 1999 were one-third the levels in 1991. A similar decline has occurred in New York City, where the number of murders in 1998 fell to levels not seen since the mid-1960s. In Boston, the number of homicides dropped from 152 in 1990 to 43 in 1997; among persons age 24 and under, they fell from 62 to 15, while firearms homicides among juveniles age 16 and under fell from 10 to none in 1996 (with one in 1997).[2]

Coming after three decades of high crime rates, the drop in serious crime seems like a miracle to many Americans. For the first time in a generation, there is good news. Something seems to be working. Since crime rates began to soar around 1962 and 1963, crime has ripped the social fabric of American society. In addition to the very real harm of particular crimes—the terrible human suffering of murder and rape, and the financial losses of burglary and theft—crime has generated massive fear in ordinary Americans and damaged the quality of life in our neighborhoods. Moreover, as a political issue, "crime" has been intertwined with the race issue and has contributed to the racial polarization of American society.

The current decline in serious crime is particularly surprising because only a few years ago some criminologists were predicting just the opposite. In 1996, for example, James Alan Fox warned of a "ticking time bomb" of violent crime in the near future because of the projected increase in the number of teenagers. But in fact, the homicide trends moved in exactly the opposite direction.[3]

Is it for Real?

Many skeptics ask whether the current decline in crime is real. Is it genuine or the result of a statistical artifact, or manipulated crime data, or simply a temporary drop? All of the evidence indicates that it is genuine. First, both of the two sets of government crime data, the Uniform Crime Reports (UCR) and the National Crime Victimization Survey (NCVS),

From *Sense and Nonsense About Crime and Drugs: A Policy Guide, 3rd edition,* by S. Walker © 1998. Reprinted with permission of Wadsworth, an imprint of the Wadsworth Group, a division of Thomson Learning.

confirm the trend. In the past, they have often reported different trends. Now, however, these two reports take the nation's temperature with different thermometers and get the same readings. It might be possible for one city to manipulate its crime data to make itself look good, but it is not possible that both the UCR and NCVS could be manipulated to this extent. Second, the decline in crime has continued now for about seven years and does not appear to be a temporary blip. One of the reasons for this conclusion is that so many other social indicators—unemployment, births to teenage girls, and others— are moving in a positive direction and began moving at about the same time. We will have more to say about the trends in other social indicators shortly.

The Great American Paternity Fight

There is an old adage that failure is an orphan but success has many parents. So it is with the reduction in crime; everyone wants to claim responsibility for it. New York City officials claim that it is the result of the NYPD's "zero-tolerance" policy.[4] The White House claims it is the result of the 100,000 new police officers funded by the 1994 Violent Crime Control Act. Other policy makers believe it is the result of tough new sentencing laws that have incapacitated a large number of serious offenders. Some criminologists believe that the reduction is associated with a decline in the use of crack cocaine. Still others believe that it is one of several positive consequences of an extremely healthy economy.[5]

Where does the truth lie? Most leading criminologists are still reluctant to provide any definitive answers. Criminologist Lawrence W. Sherman says that "it is very hard to say with any certainty" what caused this change. Michael Smith of the Vera Institute believes that it is may be a broader "cultural trend which is difficult to define."[6]

This section attempts to answer these questions. It is . . . about crime policy, a search for sensible answers to the basic question: *What works?* What policies are effective in reducing serious crime? Our agenda here is to review some of the major crime control proposals and evaluate their effectiveness in light of what we know about crime and justice. [We have previously sought to determine what might work.] Now, in the face of steadily falling crime rates, we have to turn the question around: What *did* work? Did certain crime policies contribute to this phenomenon? If so, which ones? What is the evidence? For all practical purposes, the analysis . . . is the same. We want to determine the impact of particular policies, if any, on serious crime.

One of the major obstacles to finding sensible crime policies is that there are so many *bad* ideas. In the face of high crime rates, people have grasped desperately at any idea that seemed to offer a quick solution. Politicians readily obliged them, offering simplistic solutions that promised quick and dramatic results. One of the most recent examples is the so-called "three strikes" law, providing mandatory life prison sentences to persons convicted of a third felony, enacted by 15 states between 1993 and 1994 alone.[7]

We will frame our discussion in terms of a series of propositions. Our first proposition is this:

PROPOSITION 1
Most current crime control proposals are nonsense.

UNDERSTANDING THE CRIME PROBLEM

Crime in the United States is surrounded by myths. Public fear and concern about crime has been high for over 30 years. Gallup polls in 1994, 1995, and 1996 consistently found that despite falling crime rates, people regarded crime as "the most important problem facing the country."[8]

America's Two Crime Problems

Your risk of being a crime victim depends a lot on who you are. The victimization rate for robbery in 1994 was 4.8 per 1,000 for white Americans and 14.0 for African Americans. The burglary rate was 78.6 per 1,000 for the poorest Americans (annual income of less than $7,500), compared with 40.9 for the wealthiest (income of $75,000 or more).[9] Data on homicides provide especially dramatic evidence of the racial disparity in victimization. The number of murders reached an all-time high of 26,250 in 1992. While the overall murder rate that year was 10 per 100,000, it was 9.1 for white males and 67.5 for African-American males. For white females it was only 2.8 but 13.1 for African-American women.[10]

In short, many analysts believe that the United States has *two* crime problems: one that affects most white, middle-class Americans and another that affects people of color, the poor, and young people of color in particular.

Very poor neighborhoods have been overwhelmed by crime and drugs. For their residents, whom some analysts call the *underclass*, the quality of daily life worsened significantly in the 1980s.[11] In many neighborhoods, the drug trade almost completely took over the streets, with open drug use and selling. One block in Brooklyn was described as an open "drug bazaar," where drugs occupied "the entire life of [the] neighborhood." Despite a steady stream of arrests, one police officer conceded that "the whole neighborhood is into it."[12]

Elliott Currie, meanwhile, citing the evidence from two different surveys of drug use, argues that we have two drug problems: one involving the majority of the population and the other concentrated in the inner cities.[13] The National Household Survey (NHS) indicates that despite public hysteria about drugs, use of illicit drugs dropped substantially between 1979 and 1996. The number of current users of cocaine in 1996 was one-third the level reached in 1985. Current marijuana use is less than half the 1979 to 1982 levels.[14] The methodology of the NHS, however, probably undercounts many people who are most at risk for serious drug abuse: low-income adults who do not have stable employment or residence. The Drug Abuse Warning Network (DAWN) surveys hospital emergency room admissions in urban areas (489 hospitals in 1995). "Drug-related episodes" rose by 65 percent between 1978 and 1995. Cocaine-related episodes quadrupled between 1985 and 1989, declined for one year, then increased significantly from 1991 to 1995. Heroin-related episodes have also increased.[15] These data suggest a worsening drug problem for one segment of the population at the same time that the NHS data indicate a significant decline in drug use for the general population.

The American crime problem is actually a problem of *violent* crime—murder and robbery, in particular. In a careful review of comparative crime rates, James Lynch points out that property crime rates in other industrialized countries are similar to, and in some cases higher than, those in the United States. The types of robbery also differ. Far more American robberies involve the use of a firearm than in other countries. In this respect, they instill more fear in their victims.[16]

As we search for sensible crime policies, we need to keep in mind which crime problem and which drug problem we are talking about. Many proposed policies are unrelated to the most serious parts of the crime problem. Some policies are justified in the name of serious crime but in practice affect less serious crimes. The National Criminal Justice Commission, a private group that includes many leading criminologists, argues that the war on crime has been a case of "bait and switch."[17] (The term comes from the area of consumer fraud, where a retailer advertises a low-priced item and then claims that it is sold out and tries to sell a higher-priced item). According to the commission, the war on crime has promised to attack *violent* crime but has mainly resulted in the imprisonment of more *nonviolent* offenders. In California, for example, 73 percent of the increase in the prison population between 1980 and 1993 involved persons convicted of nonviolent crimes. As we examine different crime policies in the chapters ahead, we want to make sure that they have an impact on their intended target.

WAGING WAR ON CRIME

For over thirty years, we have waged a "war on crime." President Lyndon Johnson first declared war on crime in 1965. President Richard Nixon then announced his own war in 1969, and President George Bush declared war on drugs on September 5, 1989.[18] Other politicians and policy makers have followed their lead and used the rhetoric of "war" to characterize our crime policy.

The consequences of the war on crime and drugs have been enormous. The number of prisoners increased six-fold from 196,429 in 1970 to 1.9 million by the end of 1998. The United States has been on an imprisonment orgy, and the last twenty-five years represent a radical break with the past. The incarceration rate rose from 96 per 100,000 in 1970 to 452 per 100,000 in 1998 (state and federal prisoners). This compares with incarceration rates of 111 per 100,000 in Canada, 79 in Australia, and 42 in Japan.[19]

The prisons are only part of the story. The national jail population more than doubled between 1979 and 1998, rising from 153,394 to 592,462 inmates. The number of people on probation grew from 1,079,258 adults in 1976 to 3,417,613 by the end of 1998, and the number of adults on parole soared from 156,194 to 704,904 in the same period. Thus, the total number of people "under correctional supervision" by the late 1990s was about 5 million!

The imprisonment boom is the product of several forces. Public attitudes about crime and criminals became increasingly punitive, particularly with respect to drugs. These attitudes have been translated into laws producing more and longer prison sentences, particularly for drug offenses. The Clark Foundation report *Americans Behind Bars* concludes that "much of the growth in prison population has resulted from a doubling of the number of arrests for drug law violations and a tripling of the rate of incarceration for arrested drug offenders."[20]

The impact of the war on crime is one of the main themes of this section. Is it responsible for the recent decline in crime? Has it contributed to the recent reduction in crime rates? Or has it made things worse, increasing the alienation of African-American young men in particular?

Conservatives such as John J. Dilulio and the Council on Crime in America argue that a punitive policy is necessary, morally justified, and if used properly, effective. As the council puts it, prison is "socially beneficial and cost-effective." They believe that the recent decline in the crime rate is proof that punishment works.[21]

Race and the War on Crime

Elliott Currie, Jerome Miller, the Sentencing Project, the Clark Foundation, and the National Criminal Justice Commission believe that the war on crime has made things worse: that it has not deterred crime, that it is racially biased, and that it has contributed to the destruction of inner-city communities, and as a consequence it has increased the likelihood of juvenile violence.

Currie and others argue that the war on drugs has been waged primarily against young black men. The Sentencing Project found that African Americans represent 13 percent of the population, 15 percent of all illicit drug users (according to the National Household survey), but 35 percent of all people arrested for drug offenses, 55 percent of those convicted, and 74 percent of those sentenced to prison for drug offenses.[22]

Jerome Miller characterizes the war on crime as a case of "search and destroy" directed at young African-American men.[23] The National Center on Institutions and Alternatives estimates that on any given day, 42 percent of the young black men (ages 18 to 35) in Washington, D.C., are under the control of the justice system: either in prison or jail or on probation or parole. The figure for Baltimore was 56 percent. About 75 percent of the Washington black men were likely to be arrested before they reach age 35.[24] A study by the California legislature painted a similar picture: one-sixth of the African-American men over the age of 16 are arrested every year. Many of these arrests are for drug offenses. Yet the same study found that 92 percent of African-American men arrested for drugs were subsequently released for lack of evidence.[25] In short, a huge number of African-American men are acquiring arrest records as a result of the war on drugs. By 1990, more black men were in prison than in college.

The disparate impact of the war on crime has had a profound impact on attitudes toward the justice system. One survey found that 80 percent of whites believed that O. J. Simpson was guilty of murdering his ex-wife Nicole Brown Simpson and her friend Ronald Goldman. But 80 percent of African Americans thought he was innocent.[26] The war on crime has contributed to deep distrust of the justice system among minorities.

Discrimination and the *sense* of unfairness contributes to the crime problem. Social psychologists in the field of procedural justice argue that people are more inclined to obey the law if they feel that the law and legal institutions are fair and treat them with respect. The sense of unfairness and alienation from the justice system, meanwhile, leads to disrespect for the law and a greater likelihood of law breaking.[27]

The War on Crime and the Criminal Justice System

The war on crime has also overloaded the criminal justice system so that in some instances it cannot perform some of its basic functions. In Philadelphia, the police commissioner described the criminal courts as being "on the verge of collapse" in 1990. The massive increase in arrests created a backlog of 12,129 cases, with the result that many more defendants failed to make their scheduled court dates. The number of defendants who did not appear soared from 13,807 in January 1987 to a whopping 32,880 by July 1990. The system was incapable of tracking them down and bringing them into court. Law professor Gerald Caplan described it as "a kind of amnesty for some criminals."[28]

"Getting tough" has actually backfired in many states. As prisons become over-crowded, correctional officials are forced to release many offenders earlier than they normally would just to make room for the new arrivals. The percentage of sentences served in Texas dropped from about 30 to 35 percent during 1977–1980 to approximately 20 percent in 1990.[29] This process undermines the original intent of the tough sentencing law—to reduce crime through deterrence and incapacitation.

A very basic lesson is apparent here: The justice system can only handle so much business. It does not "collapse" like a building. It keeps on going, but only through adjustments that are often undesirable. . . .

Finally, the enormous cost of the war on crime has drained tax dollars from other social needs, such as education, public health, and the economic infrastructure of roads and bridges. In California, for example, state expenditures for corrections were only half the amount spent on higher education in the early 1980s; by 1994, they were equal, at $3.8 billion. Prison budgets had risen dramatically, whereas the state colleges and universities had suffered drastic cuts.[30] If education has historically been an investment in the future of society, then the cuts in education to finance prison represent a *dis*investment in the future.

The Futility of Waging "War" on Crime

"War" is the wrong metaphor to use for reducing crime for several reasons. It raises unrealistic expectations, promising a "victory." The effective control of crime, however, will not come quickly or easily. A final victory in the military sense will never be achieved; there will always be some crime. A sensible goal is to get it down to some tolerable level.[31]

The war metaphor is also wrong because it suggests that we are fighting a foreign enemy. The "us versus them" attitude encourages police officers to think that suspects do not have the rights of American citizens. Community policing, which emphasizes close working relations between police and citizens, is a far more appropriate approach for a democratic society. Finally, as we have already seen, the current war on crime has had a terrible effect on American society, particularly on racial and ethnic minority communities.

These facts lead us to the following proposition:

PROPOSITION 2
Waging "war" is the wrong way to fight crime.

The truth is, we do not face a foreign enemy. We are up against ourselves. We need to deal with our own social institutions, our own values, our own habits, and our own crime control policies. The weight loss problem offers a more useful comparison. The solution does not lie in a miracle cure; instead, it involves difficult long-term changes in one's own behavior: eating less, eating less-fattening food, and exercising more. By the same token, we will reduce crime when we make basic changes in all of our social policies that affect families, employment, and neighborhoods. There is no quick easy "miracle" cure for crime.

Crime Policy: A Plague of Nonsense

Americans have trouble thinking clearly about crime. The result is a lot of crime control proposals that are nonsense. Why?

The main reason is that we have been overwhelmed by violent crime. Despite the substantial decline in recent years, we still have far more violent crime than any other industrialized country. We murder each other eight to twelve times as often as do people in Europe or Japan. In 1990, the American murder rate was 9.4 per 100,000, compared with only 1.3 for England and Wales. The American robbery rate was 257 per 100,000 but only 55 in West Germany and 47 in Ireland.[32]

Fear of crime still pervades our daily lives like a plague, affecting the way we think, the way we act, the way we respond to one another. It has a corrosive effect on interpersonal relations, making us wary of small acts of friendliness toward strangers. It also distorts the political process, with politicians offering quick-fix solutions that offer no realistic hope of reducing crime. Fear and frustration about crime produce irrational thinking. Almost every year some new proposal promises to reduce crime by 30 percent or 50 percent.

Even some of the most informed experts on criminal justice are overwhelmed by the problem. When Jerome Miller first sent the manuscript of his book *Search and Destroy* to the publisher, his editor wrote back that it was "too pessimistic," with no optimistic recommendations on how to solve the crime problem. Miller admitted that his editor was right; he did not "have many suggestions—and those I do have, aren't likely to be taken."[33] Many other people have had the same problem: an inability to formulate sensible, realistic proposals for reducing crime.

Our response to the crime problem also resembles the way many people deal with being overweight—by "binging." Just as people go on crash diets, lose weight, put it all back on, and then take up another diet fad a year later, so we tend to "binge" on crime control fads. Yesterday it was "selective incapacitation." Today it is "three strikes." And so it goes. Typically, everyone forgets yesterday's fad without examining whether it really worked.

We need to make an important distinction regarding the goals of different reform proposals. Many sensible proposals involve reducing the *harm* done by the criminal justice system. The Sentencing Project, the Edna McConnell Clark Foundation, and the National Criminal Justice Commission have all made proposals for reducing the harm done by our current sentencing practices. In *Malign Neglect*, Michael Tonry offers a specific proposal for reducing racial disparities in sentencing.[34] Reducing the harm done by the criminal justice system is an important and laudable goal, but our focus here is on policies that will reduce *crime*, particularly serious crime.

THE GROUND RULES

The goal of this section is to identify sensible and effective crime policies. Let us begin by establishing the ground rules for our inquiry. First, we will focus on crime control. We are concerned with policies that will reduce the level of serious crime. We will consider questions of justice and fairness as a basic constraint on crime policy. Effectiveness—defined as reduction in crime—is not the only criterion for a sensible crime control policy. We have limits to what we can do. A democratic society respects the rule of law and standards of justice and fairness, unlike totalitarian societies that are based on the principle of unlimited government power. It might reduce crime if we just shot all robbers and drug dealers on sight. When an Islamic rebel group took power in Kabul, the capital of Afghanistan, in 1996, the group restored punishments such as stoning to death people guilty of adultery and cutting off the hands of thieves. One criminal was driven through the streets on a truck with an amputated hand and heavy weights holding his jaw open. Such practices, however, violate our standards of decency and due process.

Second, we will focus primarily on the crimes of robbery and burglary. This limited focus helps impose discipline on our thinking. Too many people evade the hard questions about crime by changing the subject. Liberals often find it difficult to talk about robbery and burglary, changing the subject to victimless crimes such as gambling, marijuana use, and unconventional sexual behavior. Conservatives focus on celebrated cases (particularly mass murders or extremely vicious crimes) that have little to do with the routine felonies of robbery and burglary. . . .

Thinking Clearly About Crime Prevention

As the 1997 University of Maryland report on *Preventing Crime* argues, many people are confused about the term *crime prevention*. The report points out that "the national debate over crime often treats "prevention" and "punishment" as mutually exclusive concepts, polar opposites on a continuum of 'soft' versus 'tough' responses to crime. . . ."[35] As we explain shortly, this dichotomy generally defines conservatives as the advocates of "tough" policies and liberals as the advocates of "soft" policies.

The Maryland report persuasively argues that this is a false dichotomy. Regardless of their label, all crime policies are designed to prevent crime. Particular polices are simply different means to that end. An allegedly "soft" treatment program (e.g., out-patient drug abuse counseling) is intended to prevent crime no less than is an allegedly "tough" sentencing policy (e.g., a "three strikes" law). From the standpoint of effective crime prevention, the real issue is not one of intentions or methods but consequences. Which policies reduce crime?

The question of reasonable goals.   Our search for sensible and effective crime policies raises a difficult question of criteria. What do we mean by *effective*? Let us say we find a policy that would reduce crime by 5 percent without doing any serious harm. Is that a goal worth pursuing? A 5 percent reduction is not much, given the size of our crime problem. We would still be swamped by murder, robbery, rape, and drug abuse. It would be easy to dismiss that policy as hardly worth the effort.

The issue here is one of reasonable goals. In his discussion of gun crimes, Gary Kleck makes a persuasive case in favor of modest goals. We should not expect quick and dramatic changes. Unreasonable expectations lead to disappointment and frustration. Kleck advises thinking in terms of modest goals that can be achieved.[36] In the long run, a sensible approach to crime will probably include a series of different policies, each one focusing on a different aspect of the larger problem and each one producing a modest reduction in crime.

Reducing Crime: The New Community Focus

The most comprehensive survey of the effectiveness of crime policies is the 1997 University of Maryland report *Preventing Crime*. One of the report's most important conclusions involves the *interdependency* of different policies and the context in which policies operate. "Crime prevention policies are not delivered in a vacuum."[37] A particular program may be effective in an economically healthy community but ineffective in one with a very high unemployment rate. One potentially effective program may need to be supported by other programs in order to fulfill its potential. The report suggests that "it may be necessary to mount programs in several institutional settings simultaneously—such as labor markets, families, and police—in order to find programs in any one institution to be effective."

The interrelatedness of crime policies, other policies, and the external environment may seem self-evident. Unfortunately, it has not been self-evident to most criminal justice researchers. Most evaluations of programs focus very narrowly on the programs themselves. To a certain extent, this limited scope is dictated by the canons of social science research, which call for controlling for the relevant variables. Thus, for example, an evaluation of a new sentencing law will control for variables related to sentenced offenders, judges, and, if it is a cross-jurisdictional study, different court systems. Such evaluations do not, however, control for the community environments into which offenders eventually return, either through probation or parole. A study of a police "crackdown" on crime typically does not control for changes in the local labor market or the nature of and changes in sentencing or correctional programs that affect the area being policed. This narrow focus is also the result of practical considerations: Given the limits of time and money, it is simply not possible to investigate all of these other factors.

The Maryland report represents a major conceptual breakthrough in thinking about effective crime reduction. The report identifies seven "institutional settings" in which crime policies are delivered: communities, families, schools, labor markets, "places" (e.g., crime hot spots), policing, and other criminal justice system institutions. One of the important aspects of this framework is that it reduces the criminal justice system—the major focus of most analyses of crime policy—to the humble status of merely one of seven institutional settings (although policing is designated as a separate institution, perhaps because that is the speciality of the report's principal author, Lawrence W. Sherman). The report suggests, again persuasively, that "the effectiveness of crime prevention in each of the seven institutional settings depends heavily on local conditions in the other settings" [boldface in the original].[38]

The Larger Context: Recent Social Trends

The importance of the larger social and economic context of crime is highlighted by recent trends in a number of social indicators. Not only is crime down, but a number of other indicators of the well-being of American society have also been moving in a positive direction. Unemployment in the late 1990s was the lowest since the 1960s. Welfare caseloads dropped significantly in the 1990s, and had begun dropping even before enactment of the 1994 Welfare Reform Law. New AIDS cases were also down. Births to teenage women declined sharply between 1992 and 1998.[39]

What is particularly striking is that all of these social trends closely parallel the trends in the crime rate. Not only are they moving in the same direction, but in several cases they turned in a positive direction at *almost exactly the same time*—in the early 1990s. This points in the direction of an important hypothesis: Crime is down because of the general social and economic health of the country, not because of any particular crime policy or policies.

GUILTY: LIBERALS AND CONSERVATIVES

Nonsense about crime is politically nonpartisan. Over the years, both liberals and conservatives have been guilty of making extravagant promises about crime reduction. In 1967, the President's Crime Commission, representing a liberal perspective, promised "a significant reduction in crime" if its recommendations were "vigorously pursued."[40] In 1975, the conservative James Q. Wilson offered a program that he claimed would reduce serious crime by 30 percent.[41] Neither of these promises, or many others like them, were realistic. Consequently, our third proposition is as follows:

PROPOSITION 3
Both liberals and conservatives are guilty of peddling nonsense about crime.

Crime policies are guided by certain underlying assumptions. Liberals and conservatives begin with different assumptions about crime, the administration of justice, and human nature. To make sense of different crime control proposals, it is helpful to analyze the underlying assumptions of each side.

CRIME CONTROL THEOLOGY

A serious problem with the debate over crime policy is that faith usually triumphs over facts. Both liberals and conservatives begin with certain assumptions that are almost like religious beliefs. Too often, these assumptions are not supported by empirical evidence. We call this phenomenon *crime control theology*.[42]

Most conservatives, for example, believe that the death penalty deters crime. This view persists despite the fact that no evidence conclusively supports it. Most liberals, meanwhile, believe that "treatment" works as a cure for crime and drug abuse, despite considerable evidence on the limited effectiveness of treatment programs.

In *Point Blank*, Gary Kleck points out how people switch sides on the deterrence question to suit their beliefs. Conservatives believe that the death penalty deters crime but then argue that the exclusionary rule will not deter police misconduct. Liberals switch sides in the opposite direction, arguing that the death penalty does not deter crime but that the exclusionary rule does work.[43] This leads us to the following proposition.

PROPOSITION 4
Most crime control ideas rest on faith rather than facts.

Conservative Theology

Crime control theologies represent idealized worlds that express people's highest hopes and deepest fears. Conservative crime control theology envisions a world of discipline and self-control in which people exercise self-restraint and subordinate their personal passions to the common good. It is a world of limits and clear rules about human behavior.

The problem, according to conservatives, is that criminals lack self-control. They succumb to their passions and break the rules. They kill because they cannot control their anger. They steal because they want something now and are unable to defer gratification. For conservatives, poverty is no excuse for crime. People remain poor because they lack the self-discipline to get an education, find a job, and steadily try to improve themselves.

Free will, rational choice, and moral responsibility reign supreme in conservative crime control theology. People are responsible for their own fate; they *choose* to commit crime. James Q. Wilson and Richard J. Herrnstein argue: "At any given moment, a person can choose between committing a crime and not committing it."[44] A good example of a policy based on rational choice theory is the "Just say no!" antidrug campaign. It assumes that all we have to do is persuade people to make the decision not to use drugs.

Rational choice theory holds that people weigh the relative risks and rewards of committing crime. If the risk of punishment is low or the punishments are relatively light, more people will tend to commit crime. If the chance of being caught and punished is high and the punishments are relatively severe, fewer people will choose to commit crime. Thus, the certainty and severity of punishment directly affects the crime rate.[45]

In conservative crime control theology, punishment has both a moral and a practical element. Because criminals choose to offend, they deserve punishment. They are morally responsible for their actions. Rules are the basis of a civil society, and rule breaking should be punished. This is called *retribution* or *desert*. James Q. Wilson summed it up in a frequently quoted statement: "Wicked people exist. Nothing avails except to set them apart from innocent people."[46] Conservatives also believe that punishment shapes future behavior through the process of *deterrence*. Specific deterrence is directed at the individual offender, teaching him or her that bad actions have unpleasant consequences. General deterrence is directed at the general population, teaching by example.

Conservatives are deeply ambivalent about the role of government in controlling crime. William J. Bennett, John J. Dilulio, Jr., and John P. Walters argue that the "root cause" of crime is "moral poverty" (as opposed to material poverty). Too many children grow up not learning right from wrong. Moral health, they argue, is nurtured primarily by strong, two-parent families, religious training, and social institutions that reinforce the right values. "Can government supply manner and morals?" they ask. "Of course it cannot," they answer. People are socialized into law-abiding behavior primarily by private institutions, beginning with the family. But, these conservatives argue, government does have an important role to play in providing effective examples of holding people responsible for their behavior. Thus, the swift, certain punishment of offenders helps breed moral health. Moral poverty is fostered by the failure of the criminal justice system to punish criminals. Thus, while government cannot do everything, it can do something.[47]

Underlying conservative crime control theology is an idealized image of the patriarchal family. Punishment resembles parental discipline. Minor misbehavior is greeted with a gentle warning, a second misstep earns a sterner reprimand, and serious wrongdoing receives a severe punishment. The point is to teach the wisdom of correct behavior by handing out progressively harsher sanctions and threatening even more unpleasant punishment if the behavior continues.

The real world of crime and justice, unfortunately, does not work like the family. It is filled with some very incorrigible children. Some are so deeply alienated from society that they do not respect the overall structure of authority. Punishment, in fact, may only distance them further. Some observers believe, for example, that arrest and imprisonment are such common experiences in some poor minority neighborhoods that they have lost whatever deterrent threat they might have once had.[48]

John Braithwaite's provocative book *Crime, Shame, and Reintegration* offers a useful perspective on this problem. Braithwaite describes the process of "reintegrative shaming" as being very much like the way a family handles someone who breaks the rules. But his theory also clearly indicates that informal sanctions work when close social bonds link the sanctioner and the sanctioned, and where no great differences in values exist in the community—that is, when the relationship more closely resembles a family.[49]

This is the heart of the problem. The family analogy breaks down in the real world because we have a highly fragmented society, characterized by great differences in wealth, race, religion, and lifestyles. Our society is anything but a tight-knit community with shared values. Braithwaite's theory, in fact, is a good explanation of why informal, family-style sanctions do not work in our society. His description of the conditions under which a system of reintegrative shaming can work is actually a very accurate description of a seventeenth-century New England village, where that approach to crime control was used very effectively.[50]

The limits of reintegrative shaming lend further support to the importance of a community orientation and the interdependency of institutions and policies emphasized by the Maryland *Preventing Crime* report. Effective reintegration requires a reasonably healthy community. Achieving a healthy community, in turn, probably requires a series of crime prevention programs directed toward a number of different institutions: families, schools, the local labor market, and so on.

Conservatives explain the failure of punishment to work by focusing on problems in the criminal justice system. Punishment, they say, is not certain or severe enough. Too many loopholes allow criminals to beat the system: the exclusionary rule, the Miranda warning, the insanity defense, plea bargaining, and so on. The idea that many criminals "beat the system" and "get off easy" is an article of faith in conservative crime control theology. Close these loopholes, ensure certainty of punishment, and we can reduce crime. Longer prison terms and the death penalty, meanwhile, will increase the deterrent effect and reduce crime. . . .

Liberal Theology

Liberal crime control theology views crime in a social context. According to liberals, criminal behavior is largely the result of social influences such as the family, the peer group, the neighborhood, economic opportunities, and discrimination.

Liberal crime policy seeks to alter these influences. Rehabilitation programs, for example, are designed to provide a structured set of influences that will shape the offender's behavior in a positive direction. Liberals favor community-based alternatives to imprisonment because they represent a healthier environment than prison. Supervised probation and parole are designed to provide positive external influences. Basic education and vocational training programs, meanwhile, are designed to equip the offender for success in life.

Liberals are as guilty of wishful thinking as are conservatives. A fundamental article of faith in liberal crime control theology is the belief that people's behavior can be reshaped through some kind of formal treatment program. The history of prison and correctional reform is the story of a continuing search for the Holy Grail of rehabilitation: a program that will truly reform offenders. The people who invented the prison in the nineteenth century thought that institution would do the job.[51] When it had obviously failed, reformers invented parole and the indeterminate sentence, advertising them as the magic keys to rehabilitation. When these measures did not solve the problem of crime, reformers came up with new variations (group counseling, intensive supervision, and so forth). None of these programs has demonstrated consistent effectiveness.

If conservatives refuse to face the facts about the failure of punishment, liberals refuse to look at the sad history of the failure of rehabilitation. Faith continues to survive in the face of repeated failure.

It is also an article of faith among liberals that the United States is the most punitive country in the world. We do, in fact, lock up more people than any other country. Our current incarceration rate of 452 per 100,000 leads the world. James Lynch's research offers a valuable comparative perspective on this figure. Using arrests as a baseline, he notes that the probabilities of an offender's going to prison are only slightly different in the United States, Canada, England, and the former West Germany. In this regard, we are no more punitive than most other countries. We do, however, give much longer prison sentences. Our incarceration rate is greater primarily because we have more serious crime than these other countries.[52]

If conservatives believe that most of our problems are the result of loopholes that let too many people off easy, liberals are guilty of blaming everything on overly harsh punishments.

Liberals are ambivalent on the question of individual responsibility. Although they emphasize the importance of social conditions in causing crime and reject the conservative preoccupation with individual responsibility, they cannot completely ignore the role of individual choice. Rehabilitation programs, in fact, are designed to influence individuals to make different (and better) choices. In the realm of the public policy debate, however, liberals tend to downplay the element of individual responsibility.

A Word About Rules

One way to distinguish between conservatives and liberals with respect to crime policy is their attitude toward *rules*. Everyone believes in rules and their application in a consistent fashion. This is what people mean when they refer to the "rule of law."

Conservatives and liberals mainly disagree over which set of rules to emphasize. In criminal justice, we have two basic sets: criminal law and criminal procedure. The substantive *criminal law* is a set of rules governing everyone's behavior. It defines certain behavior as criminal and specifies the penalty for breaking the rules. *Criminal procedure*, on the other hand, is a set of rules governing criminal justice officials. It tells them what they may not do (conduct unreasonable searches and seizures) and what they must do (bring the suspect before a magistrate without unnecessary delay).[53]

Conservatives emphasize the rules of the criminal law. Harming a person or taking someone else's property violates the basic standards of a decent society. Anyone who violates these rules should be punished. Liberals tend to emphasize the rules of criminal procedure. A free society is one that strictly limits the potentially awesome power of government officials.

One way to understand the difference between liberal and conservative attitudes toward rules is to recognize what each side sees as its worst nightmare. For conservatives, unchecked criminality leads to anarchy and the death of freedom. For liberals, unchecked government power leads to tyranny and the death of freedom. The difference is really a question of what represents the greatest threat to freedom.

Both sides are ambivalent about rule breaking. Conservatives tend to be willing to excuse violations of the rules of procedure to control crime. They will overlook the unreasonable search if it helps convict a criminal. Liberals, on the other hand, are more concerned about official rule breaking. They are willing to see a criminal suspect go free if a police officer or some other official has made a serious mistake. These differences are not absolute, of course. They are really matters of emphasis. Conservatives do not endorse gross abuses by the police, and liberals do not endorse crime.

The classic statement of the difference between conservatives and liberals on this issue is Herbert Packer's essay on the "two models of the criminal process."[54] Conservatives embrace the *crime control model*, which puts a high priority on the effective control of crime. To this end, they are willing to grant officials considerable leeway, not restricting them with a lot of rules. Liberals prefer the *due process model*, in which the highest priorities are fair treatment and the presumption of innocence. Formal rules (due process guarantees) are designed to achieve these goals.

Ideological Confusion: Switching Sides

The conservative/liberal dichotomy is a useful way to think about crime policy. It helps identify the basic assumptions that underlie different policies. In the last few years, however, this dichotomy is not quite as sharp as it was a few years ago. Strange things have been happening. Some conservatives have adopted traditional liberal policies, and many liberals have embraced traditional conservative ideas. Understanding the crime debate today requires sorting our way through this ideological confusion.

One major change involves the issue of legalizing drugs. Decriminalization has traditionally been a liberal proposal. They have argued that we should not criminalize behavior that does not harm others. Moreover, criminalizing a lot of behavior often tends to make things worse, by overloading the criminal justice system, encouraging corruption, and failing to respond effectively to what are really social and medical problems.

Surprisingly, many prominent conservatives endorse legalizing drugs. The most prominent is the writer and television talk show host William F. Buckley. . . . For the moment, it is important to note that some conservatives have switched sides and adopted a traditional liberal position.

Meanwhile, many liberals have adopted some conservative crime control proposals. The best example is President Bill Clinton. The 1994 Violent Crime Control Act, which he supported, calls for more police and longer prison sentences. In the 1996 presidential election campaign, political observers said that Clinton had moved to the right and embraced the traditional Republican position on crime.

In short, the ideological lineup on crime control policies has become very muddled. Nonetheless, it is still possible to identify a set of crime policies that, because of their underlying assumptions, can be classified as conservative and another set that can be classified as liberal. These categories will help us analyze the different policies we will consider in this book.

CONCLUSION

Crime is a serious problem in the United States. The recent dramatic reductions in the crime rate still leave a problem of violent crime that is far higher than other industrialized countries. Unfortunately, we do not have many good ideas about how to solve the crime problem.

NOTES

1. Bureau of Justice Statistics, *Criminal Victimization 1998: Changes 1997–98 with Trends 1993–98* (Washington DC: Government Printing Office, 1999). Federal Bureau of Investigation, *1999 Preliminary Estimate* (11 November 1999).

2. Boston Police Department and Partners, *The Boston Strategy to Prevent Youth Violence* (Boston: Boston Police Department, 1998).

3. James Alan Fox, *Trends in Juvenile Violence* (Washington, DC: Government Printing Office, 1996). Philip J. Cook and John H. Laub, "The Unprecedented Epidemic in Youth Violence," in Michael Tonry and Mark H. Moore, eds., *Youth Violence* (Chicago: University of Chicago Press, 1998), pp. 27–64.

4. William Bratton and Peter Knoblach, *Turnaround* (New York: Random House, 1998).

5. A variety of explanations by prominent criminologists are offered in the symposium, "Crime's Decline—Why," *National Institute of Justice Journal* (October 1998), pp. 7–20.

6. Quotes from Clifford Krauss, "Murder Rate Plunges in New York City," *New York Times*, 8 July 1995: 1, 16.

7. Michael G. Turner, Jody L. Sundt, Brandon K. Applegate, and Francis T. Cullen, "'Three Strikes and You're Out' Legislation: A National Assessment," *Federal Probation 59* (September 1995): 16–35.

8. Bureau of Justice Statistics, *Sourcebook of Criminal Justice Statistics—1995* (Washington, DC: Government Printing Office, 1996), p. 128.

9. Bureau of Justice Statistics, *Criminal Victimization 1994* (Washington, DC: Government Printing Office, 1996).

10. Bureau of the Census, *Statistical Abstract of the United States, 1995* (Washington, DC: Government Printing Office, 1995), p. 202.

11. Elliott Currie, *Reckoning: Drugs, The Cities, and the American Future* (New York: Hill & Wang, 1992).

12. Mary B. Tabor, "The World of a Drug Bazaar," *New York Times*, 1 October 1992: 1, 20; Mary B. Tabor, "Neighborhood Ruled by Drug Culture," *New York Times*, 2 October 1992: 18.

13. Currie, *Reckoning*.

14. The data are summarized in Office of National Drug Control Policy, *Data Snapshot: Drug Abuse in America, 1998* (Washington, DC: Government Printing Office, 1998). Department of Health and Human Services, *Preliminary Estimates From the 1995 National Household Survey on Drug Abuse*, Advance Report 18 (Washington, DC: Government Printing Office, 1996).

15. Office of National Drug Control Policy, *Data Snapshot: Drug Abuse in America, 1998*, plate 76.

16. James Lynch, "Crime In International Perspective," in James Q. Wilson and Joan Petersilia, eds. *Crime* (San Francisco: ICS Press, 1995), pp. 11–38.

17. Steven R. Donziger, ed., *The Real War on Crime: The Report of The National Criminal Justice Commission* (New York: HarperCollins, 1996), pp. 18–19.

18. On the history of "wars" on crime, see Samuel Walker, *Popular Justice: A History of American Criminal Justice*, 2nd ed. (New York: Oxford University Press, 1998).

19. Marc Mauer, *Americans Behind Bars: One Year Later* (Washington, DC: The Sentencing Project, 1992).

20. Edna McConnell Clark Foundation, *Americans Behind Bars* (New York: Edna McConnell Clark Foundation, 1994), p. 8.
21. Council on Crime in America, *The State of Violent Crime in America* (Washington, DC: Council on Crime in America, 1996). William J. Bennett, John J. Dilulio, Jr., and John P. Walters, *Body Count* (New York: Simon & Schuster, 1996).
22. Mauer, *Americans Behind Bars: One Year Later*.
23. Jerome G. Miller, *Search and Destroy: African American Males in the Criminal Justice System* (New York: Cambridge University Press, 1996).
24. National Center on Institutions and Alternatives, *Hobbling a Generation: African American Males in the District of Columbia's Criminal Justice System* (Alexandria, VA: National Center on Institutions and Alternatives, 1992); Miller, *Search and Destroy*, p. 7.
25. Miller, *Search and Destroy*, p. 8.
26. Donziger, ed., *The Real War on Crime*, pp. 169–70.
27. Tom R. Tyler, *Why People Obey the Law* (New Haven: Yale University Press, 1990).
28. Michael de Courcy Hinds, "Philadelphia Justice System Overwhelmed," *New York Times*, 15 August 1990: 1, 13.
29. Sheldon Ekland-Olson, "Crime and Incarceration: Some Comparative Findings From the 1980s," *Crime and Delinquency* 38 (July 1992): 392–16.
30. Edna McConnell Clark Foundation, *Americans Behind Bars*.
31. Egon Bittner, "The Police and the 'War on Crime,'" in *The Functions of the Police in Modern Society* (Washington, DC: Government Printing Office, 1970), pp. 48–51.
32. Ineke Haen Marshall, "How Exceptional Is the United States? Crime Trends in Europe and the US," *European Journal on Criminal Policy and Research* 4(2): 7–35.
33. Miller, *Search and Destroy*, p. 235
34. Michael Tonry, *Malign Neglect* (New York: Oxford University Press, 1995).
35. University of Maryland, *Preventing Crime: What Works, What Doesn't, What's Promising* (Washington, DC: Government Printing Office, 1997), pp. 2–2.
36. Gary Kleck, *Point Blank: Guns and Violence in America* (New York: Aldine de Gruyter, 1991). pp. 432–33.
37. University of Maryland, *Preventing Crime*, pp. 2–4.
38. *Ibid.*, pp. 2–5.
39. A particularly valuable source is Marc Miningoff and Marque-Luisa Miningoff, *The Social Health of the Nation* (New York: Oxford University Press, 1999).
40. President's Commission on Law Enforcement and Administration of Justice, *The Challenge of Crime in a Free Society* (Washington, DC: Government Printing Office, 1967) p. vi.
41. James Q. Wilson, *Thinking About Crime* (New York: Basic Books, 1975).
42. George C. Thomas and David Edelman, "An Evaluation of Conservative Crime Control Theology," *Notre Dame Law Review* 63(2) (1988): 123–60.
43. Kleck, *Point Blank*, pp. 7, 13.
44. James Q. Wilson and Richard J. Herrnstein, *Crime and Human Nature: The Definitive Study of the Causes of Crime* (New York: Simon & Schuster, 1985), p. 44.
45. But everyone should read the article Wilson coauthored: James Q. Wilson and Allen Abrahamse, "Does Crime Pay?" *Justice Quarterly* 9 (September 1992): 359–77.
46. Wilson, *Thinking About Crime* [1975 ed.], p. 209.

47. William J. Bennett, John J. Dilulio, Jr., and John P. Walters, *Body Count* (New York: Simon & Schuster, 1996), p. 205.

48. See the discussion of this point in Daniel S. Nagin, "Criminal Deterrence Research at the Outset of the Twenty-First Century," in Michael Tonry, ed., *Crime and Justice: A Review of Research*, vol. 23 (Chicago: University of Chicago Press, 1998), pp. 4–5.

49. John Braithwaite, *Crime, Shame, and Reintegration* (New York: Cambridge University Press, 1989). John Braithwaite, "Restorative Justice: Assessing Optimistic and Pessimistic Accounts," in Michael Tonry, ed., *Crime and Justice: A Review of Research*, vol. 25 (Chicago: University of Chicago Press, 1999), pp. 1–127.

50. Lawrence M. Friedman, *Crime and Punishment in American History* (New York: Basic Books, 1993); Walker, *Popular Justice*, chap. 1.

51. David Rothman, *The Discovery of the Asylum* (Boston: Little, Brown, 1971).

52. Lynch, "Crime in International Perspective."

53. On the subject of rules and discretion, see Samuel Walker, *Taming the System: The Control of Discretion in American Criminal Justice, 1950–1990* (New York: Oxford University Press, 1993).

54. Herbert L. Packer, "Two Models of the Criminal Process," in *The Limits of the Criminal Sanction* (Stanford, CA: Stanford University Press, 1968), chap. 8.

Chapter 4

Fallacies About Crime

by Marcus Felson

For years, Roberto Alomar had been the model major league baseball player—polite, professional, and competent. No one had an ill word to say about him. Then one day he lost his temper and spit in the face of an umpire. Worse still, he did this on national television, and his act was replayed over and over for millions of people who were not even interested in baseball. He was punished, as he deserved, but his overall reputation was ruined by one incident. Even though the facts were reported accurately, they gave an unfair overall impression of the man, who also deserved credit for his good acts.

Similarly, the more severe fallacies about crime arise from a poor selection of facts. This chapter tries to help the student of crime acquire a better focus by taking a number of these fallacies and filling in some facts.

SOURCES OF INFORMATION ABOUT CRIME

Many people rely on nonprofessional sources of information about crime, including the news media, personal experience, and friends, family, and associates. There is nothing wrong with using this information as part of the recipe, but some ingredients should be added from professional sources. There are at least seven systematic sources of crime information:

- Reports to police
- Reports by victims
- Self-reported offending
- Business data
- Medical reports
- Mortality statistics
- Systematic observations

The first three of these types provide the broadest coverage. The most famous American police data are the *Uniform Crime Reports* (UCR), compiled by the Federal Bureau of Investigation (FBI) from local police agencies (see FBI, 1995; U.S. Department of Justice, Bureau of Justice Statistics, 1995b).[1]

People do not report all crime to the police. To get beyond that shortcoming, surveys ask the general public about crime victimizations. The most widely known victim reports are in the National Crime Victim Survey (NCVS), which interviews a large sam-

Marcus Felson, *Crime in Everyday Life*, Thousand Oaks, Ca.: Forge Press, pp. 1-22.

ple of citizens about whether they were victimized personally or as a household (U.S. Department of Justice, 1995a, 1995b). These surveys turn up about twice as many crime victimizations as show up in the UCR, adding millions of offenses never reported to the police. Many offenses, however, do not have a clear and immediate victim. To cast a still wider net, it makes sense to interview people about their personal criminal behavior. The most widely known self-report survey is Monitoring the Future, consisting of interviews with high school seniors (see U.S. Department of Justice, 1995b). This annual survey asks questions about underage drinking, using marijuana and more serious drugs, minor shoplifting, and other offenses. Some of the questions ask about delinquency in the prior month, thus giving some currency to the indicators without creating so much threat that respondents will not answer.

More specialized sources also turn up important information about crime. To learn about stealing by customers and employees, businesses have used not only surveys but also accounting studies of merchandise that should be there but isn't— "shrinkage." Businesses often keep their records confidential, but the National Retail Security Survey (Hollinger, 1993, 1997) and other business studies (see Beck & Willis, 1995; DiLonardo, 1997) have compiled some of their information.

Medical reports include compilation of emergency room episodes by the Drug Use Warning Network and the National Institute of Justice's Drug Use Forecasting Program, which is based on testing already arrested adults for the presence of drugs in their bodies (U.S. Department of Justice, 1995b). Given that homicide victims do not report their own demise on self-report surveys, vital statistics compiled from morgues have provided an important supplement to the UCR homicide data (Department of Health and Human Services, 1995).

Last, one can observe criminal behavior systematically. It usually is inefficient to wait around for crimes to happen, but it is not so difficult to count prostitutes on the street (McNamara, 1994), drunks hanging out, graffiti scrawled on walls, vandalized public telephones (Challinger, 1992), or pieces of litter or piles of dog droppings (Coleman, 1985). You can see that there is no shortage of facts linked to crime. The problem is how to put these facts together.

This is the only negative chapter in an otherwise positive book. In this chapter, I point out several fallacies about crime, but I could not resist slipping in some positive ideas in presenting these fallacies.

TEN FALLACIES ABOUT CRIME

No human mind is completely consistent. Inside our minds, each of us holds some of the fallacies listed here, but also some ideas contrary to the fallacies. As you read on, you will recognize these as fallacies. But can you resist them? Even though I am the author, I often fall back on these simple fallacies, to my own surprise. Perhaps naming and explaining the fallacies will help all of us to resist them.

The Dramatic Fallacy

Watching television leads us astray in studying crime (see Kappeler, Blumberg, & Potter, 1993). The "cop shows" and news shows have the same problem: They need to keep people watching. Television and other media seek strange and violent incidents to keep their ratings high; thus, they are interested in such events as romantic murders by jealous lovers, shoot-outs between felons and police officers, and fiendishly clever types of murder. These portrayals give a highly inaccurate general picture of crime, or even of murder. I call this the *dramatic fallacy*.

In the UCR, the FBI lists just under 2.9 million offenses in 1994 for the eight categories of major crime: murder,[2] forcible rape, aggravated assault, robbery, burglary, motor vehicle theft, larceny-theft, and arson. Almost 9 out of 10 of these crimes are property crimes: burglaries, motor vehicle thefts, and larceny-thefts. Murder and rape, which get the most attention in the media, are greatly outnumbered by the other violent offenses. Indeed, murders are less than 1% of the major crime total, and we have not yet begun to consider all the minor criminal offenses reported or all the offenses not reported.

Sherlock Holmes would have no interest whatever in most of the 22,076 murders reported in the United States for 1994. Only 20 involved poison or explosives. Only 22 were by narcotics overdose. Some 78 murders were classified as involving rape. Just 15 involved prostitution and commercialized vice. Sniper attacks make good television, but only two such homicides occurred in the entire United States in 1994. About 1.7% of the murders involved romantic triangles (U.S. Department of Justice, 1995b, Tables 3.110, 3.127, 3.124, and 3.126). Although 1,157 of the murders were coded as juvenile gang killings, the world's leading expert in juvenile gangs, Malcolm W. Klein (1995), has warned that police often overdo their coding of gang involvement. Thus, if a store owner gets shot in a robbery and the offender seemed to be a gang member, many departments count that incident as a gang murder rather than something more plain. Gang members may be highly criminal, but that does not mean that most of the crimes they commit are of, by, or for the gang itself. Members do most crime for themselves, as explained in a later section.

Michael Maxfield reminds us that we often do best to regard murder not as a crime but as an outcome (Maxfield, 1989; Block & Block, 1992). A murder is not much different from an ordinary fight, except that someone happened to die. Murder is in general the tragic result of a stupid little quarrel.[3] Indeed, murder has two central features: a lethal weapon too near and a hospital too far. Indeed, Tedeschi and Felson (1994) find many parallels between murder and simple fights. Some murderers, though, intend to kill from the outset (see Felson & Messner, 1996). Even so, murders usually are carried out for mundane reasons. In any case, they are swamped by the vast numbers of minor offenses.

The 1994 total of arrests for all reasons is 14.6 million. This number includes 1.2 million arrests for minor assaults, which outnumbered murders 55 to 1 (1995b, Table 4.1). Most of these arrests were for drunkenness, disorderly conduct, liquor violations, teens running away from home, and the like. Some were for drug violations, which are not included in the major crime index because police have great discretion in arrest decisions when they encounter drug use or sales, and in searching for these offenses. For each homicide reported in the major crime index, police arrest about 700 people for other offenses.

Victim surveys also make everyday crime look more ordinary and less ornery. The 1994 NCVS estimates about 40 million victimizations nationally [see U.S. Department of Justice, 1995b, Table 3.1]. This dragon diagram shows that rapes and sexual assaults are greatly outnumbered by the more ordinary crimes. Thefts outnumber robberies about 19 to 1. Simple assaults outnumber aggravated assaults. Nine out of 10 aggravated assaults do not involve a firearm. Nor do victims usually act dramatically: Only 6 in 1,000 attacked the offender using a weapon, and only 1.5% threatened the offender with a weapon (U.S. Department of Justice, 1995b, Table 3.17).

Self-report crime surveys also tell us that crime is not very dramatic. These surveys pick up a lot of illegal consumption and minor offenses, but little major crime. About 4 out of 5 high school seniors admit to underage alcohol consumption. About half of them admit drinking alcohol in the 30 days prior to the interview. Self-report data indicate that it is also common for adolescents to engage sometimes in shoplifting, theft, small consumption of marijuana, and other minor delinquency (U.S. Department of Justice, 1995b, Table 3.41). The more extreme behaviors are less common. About 6% admit ever having tried cocaine. Some 2% say they used cocaine in the past 30 days (U.S. Department of Justice, 1995b, Table 3.60).

Even police work is by and large mundane. Ordinary police activity includes these sorts of activities:

- Driving around a lot
- Asking people to quiet down
- Hearing complaints about barking dogs
- Filling out paperwork
- Meeting with other police officers
- Waiting to be called up in court

To quote the standard line, "Police work consists of hour upon hour of boredom, interrupted by moments of sheer terror." Some police have to wait years for these moments. Most seldom or never take their revolver out of its holster. Most are never shot at and never shoot at anybody else. In 1994, some 76 officers were killed. Of these incidents, 6 occurred in ambush situations and 16 during robberies in progress. Few of these incidents involved federal officers (U.S. Department of Justice, 1995b, Tables 3.158 and 3.159; FBI, 1995). This is not to deny that police have legitimate concerns about such incidents. They do not like a persistent threat, and close calls are no fun. They are justifiably upset to have a friend shot, or even an officer they do not know by name. Overall, however, their mortality rates are not high. Their more common problems are rude encounters with people who cannot keep their mouths shut.

We can see, then, that most offenses are not dramatic. Property crime swamps violent crime. Even violent crime is largely minor and leaves no lasting physical harm. Even when there is harm, it is usually self-containing and not classified as aggravated assault, much less homicide.

Meanwhile, the "cop shows" prefer dramatic plots, interesting offenses, stunning conflicts, thrilling car chases, and struggles to the death—anything but ordinary criminal acts. The TV screen is smaller than life. Something must jump out from it, or people will turn it off or go in the other room. My brother Stephen Felson, an appeals lawyer and playwright, explains the three principles that screenwriters consider:

- Find a cohesive story.
- Present a single character's inner conflict.
- Show a time or place unlike all others.

Because television has to fight so hard for the attention of the audience in their own homes, this medium has to keep its story clear and dramatic. To achieve that, a screenwriter has no choice but to rearrange reality. The "real crime" story is usually not much of a story: Someone drinks too much and gets in a fight. There is little inner conflict: He saw, he took, he left. Not much is resolved: He won't give it back.

Newspapers offer more space than does television for covering ordinary criminal events. Historically, newspapers were able to go into greater detail and to present information that was less dramatic and more deep. Newspapers today, however, have to compete with the other media. An ordinary break-in, theft, or minor assault might make a small-town, community, or college paper, but the big-city papers are not interested. They gravitate instead to such stories as the Oklahoma City bombing, which killed and maimed hundreds, the killing of TV star Bill Cosby's son, the O.J. Simpson case, or hate crimes (see Jacobs & Potter, 1997). A lot of media attention surrounded the gang rape in Glen Ridge, New Jersey, a town I drive through daily to get to my office. It seems quite peaceful to me. By the time this book is in your hands, there will be other dramatic crimes to distract you from thinking clearly about crime.

I am reminded of my late dog, Lucia, a gentle border collie that kids would pet and smile at. Even people afraid of dogs usually were not afraid of Lucia. One month, the television news got hold of some stories of pit bull attacks on people, including the death of a child and serious injuries to some adults. Lucia was transformed immediately from neighborhood sweetheart into a terrifying criminal. People started screeching at me, "Is that a pit bull?" even though a border collie–spaniel mix looks nothing like a pit bull. This is a reminder of the sheer power of the press and the images it presents. That power challenges every student of crime to resist media images and stick to the facts.

The Cops-And-Courts Fallacy

It is easy to exaggerate the importance of the police, courts, and prisons as the key actors in crime production and prevention. I cannot deny the importance of the criminal justice system, which goes beyond the individuals processed by it (Gorecki, 1979). We must not forget, however, that crime itself happens first. The criminal justice system merely responds. The *cops-and-courts fallacy* warns us against overrating the importance of the criminal justice system.

The short arm of the law is best explained by one fact: Most crimes are never reported to the police in the first place. Two thirds of the respondents to the 1994 NCVS who stated they were victimized did not report the crime to the police. For plain theft, three-quarters of the incidents were not reported. For robbery, 45% were not reported. Self-report data turn up even greater numbers of illegal acts that never gain the attention of the police, notably in the area of marijuana consumption, underage use of alcohol, and shoplifting. With so much crime never coming to the attention of the police, we have to begin putting the criminal justice system into a smaller perspective.

The arithmetic is quite telling. Of those crimes that occur in society, most are not known to the police. Of those the police know about, the vast majority result in no arrest. Most arrests do not lead to trial or a guilty plea. Of cases that get to trial, most do not result in incarceration. For example, some 5.5 million burglaries were estimated [to have occurred] in the United States in 1994 (NCVS). . . .

In addition, some burglars are convicted of a lesser offense after a plea bargain, and multiple burglaries may be statistically "cleared" by arrest, even if only one offense leads to conviction. It also should be noted that the past few years have seen an increase in the number of convictions and incarcerations per 1,000 burglaries. The law, however, still has serious limits.

These limits are even more evident for some other crimes. For example, for every thousand larcenies, only about three offenders are sentenced to jail or prison. Equivalent estimates for the millions of instances of drug abuse are difficult to make, but the chance of being punished has to be much smaller still.

Even when the criminal justice system delivers punishment, it does so after long delays. For example, in state courts the median time elapsing between arrest and conviction for burglary was estimated as 6 months for cases involving trials and 5 months for those involving guilty pleas (by far the busiest road toward conviction). For violent crimes, jury trial convictions take almost 10 months, bench trials 7 months, and guilty pleas 6 months (U.S. Department of Justice, 1995b, Table 5.62).

To put the U.S. system of punishment into perspective, consider what happens when you touch a hot stove: You receive quick and certain, but minor, pain. After being burned once, you will not touch a hot stove again. Now think of an imaginary hot stove that burns you only once every 500 times you touch it, with the burn not hurting until 5 months later. Psychological research and common sense alike tell us that this imaginary stove will not be as effective in deterring behavior as the real stove. Psychologists have long studied rewards and punishments, finding that it is easiest to get someone to do what you want if you reward more than you punish, doing so quickly, often, and mildly. We can see that the U.S. criminal justice system does everything wrong: It punishes bad rather than rewarding good, and it relies on rare and delayed, but extreme, penalties. Meanwhile, crime gives sure and quick rewards to offenders. It should come as no surprise that many people continue to commit crimes.

Even without punishment, police theoretically can reduce crime by patrolling, inhibiting wrongdoing by their sheer presence on the streets. The Kansas City Patrol Experiment investigated this point. The experiment discovered that intensified police patrols are scarcely noticed by offenders or citizens and have no impact on crime rates (Kelling, Pate, Dieckman, & Brown, 1974). More recent work finds that police patrols *can* reduce crime, but only if they concentrate police efforts very intelligently (McGarrell & Weiss, 1996; Sherman & Weisburd, 1995). . . . We cannot expect results from the police if we give them an impossible task. They cannot protect one-quarter of 1 billion people and billions of pieces of property all the time, least of all when these potential crime targets are dispersed over vast amounts of space. Like all of us, the police have to focus their efforts.

Can a police officer look after your home or business for you? Let's take the case of Los Angeles County. The protection task is awesome, with 4,070 square miles to cover. Some 8.8 million people, 4 million households (U.S. Bureau of the Census, 1990), and perhaps a million businesses, schools, government buildings, and other locations need protecting. Each week has 168 hours. Each day has 1,440 minutes (86,400 seconds) to cover.

To accomplish this, Los Angeles County has some 15,000 sworn police officers (U.S. Department of Justice, 1995b, Table 1.35). If a third of these officers have special assignments or full-time desk duties, that leaves 10,000 for patrol duties. Each officer needs time for roll call, paperwork, court appearances, instruction, consultation, and breaks. Even with overtime, we cannot assume that an officer patrols more than 30 hours per week, on the average. Dividing 168 hours per week by 30 hours per officer (driving alone), we can estimate that it takes 5.6 officers to cover one beat fully (24 hours a day,

7 days a week). Dividing the 10,000 patrol officers by 5.6 beats, we learn that only 1,786 beats can be covered fully for all of Los Angeles County.

Next, divide the protection tasks mentioned above by the 1,786 beats. Each beat must cover 2.28 square miles, protecting 4,927 people, 2,240 households, and perhaps 560 other locations (for a total of 2,800 locations per beat). Although officers have to cover 86,400 seconds per day, they probably lose at least half that time driving between places or just looking ahead to avoid smashing up the police car. This leaves no more than 43,200 seconds per day to protect 2,800 locations. That leaves only about 15 seconds per day to watch each place. You can expect that your house will lack on-the-spot police protection 99.98% of the time.

There is also precious little time for an officer to learn, for example, who has a right to be leaving your home with a CD player. Given that officers are quite often shifted from one beat to another, they have no chance to learn the "names and numbers" of all the players. It is not surprising that less than 1% of offenses end with the offender "caught in the act" by police on patrol. Doubling the number of police in a U.S. metropolis is like putting two drops in a bucket instead of one.

My point is not to blame the people in the criminal justice system. They are subject to the practical limits of our society as we know it. Nor do I wish to live in a society that abolishes its criminal justice system. These data suggest, however, that the criminal justice system is actually quite marginal in its direct effect on everyday crime, at least when incidents are taken one by one. Let's not place unreasonable demands on that system and the people who work in it.

On the other hand, very active offenders do get into a lot of trouble in their lives. The paradoxical conclusion is that the average crime pays in the short run, but a life of crime does not pay at all. For example, getting drunk makes you feel good for a while, but the hangover comes tomorrow and the deterioration of the liver well after that. Stealing one item is profitable today, but stealing a thousand things puts you on a slippery slope toward substance abuse, counterattacks by others, unemployment, jail, and prison. The arithmetic of Wilson and Abrahamse (1992) confirms that crime does not pay over time, even if it lures people in at the moment. Unfortunately, offenders may put their pains out of mind while remembering gains, calculating more success than they really have. Their short-term orientation leads them away from the long-term cost-benefit analysis.

The research of Marianne Junger and colleagues (Junger & Marshall, 1997; Junger, Terlouw, & van der Heijden, 1995) helps us to understand another peculiar fact about living a life of crime: Offenders almost certainly suffer more from the consequences of their own lifestyles than from the actions of public officials. If they took a close look at substance abuse and what it does to their bodies over time, that really ought to be enough motivation to go clean.

The Not-Me Fallacy

The false image of crime and criminals leads to something worse: a false image of oneself. Most individuals would like to think that they are *fundamentally* different from serious offenders. The *not-me fallacy* is the illusion that *I* could never do a crime. It includes the acquired ability to forget every illegal act I ever commit. It also includes that special talent for breaking the law while declaring, as did Richard Nixon, that "I am not a crook."

Part of the not-me fallacy is to take note of any crimes I did *not* commit and to interpret them as proof of my goodness. Why haven't I stolen anything lately? Perhaps

- I could never do anything wrong.
- Nobody tempted me.
- I was afraid to do it.

It is far more pleasant to believe the first of the above. The other interpretations take me down a peg. They make me admit my imperfections.

Consider, however, how everyday life often keeps temptations limited, denies chances to respond to these temptations, or makes people afraid to act on them. This requires each of us to admit imperfections. Sir Winston Churchill supposedly asked Lady Astor whether she would sleep with him for 5 million pounds. She said she supposed she would. Then he asked whether she would sleep with him for only 5 pounds. She answered, "What do you think I am?" His response was, "We've already established that; we're merely haggling over price." Ask yourself the tough questions about whether you can be tempted or whether you behave well for the wrong reasons.

The reality is that ordinary people [—young and old alike—] can do ordinary crime. Everybody could do at least some crime at some time (Gabor, 1994). This is not a claim that crime involvement is uniform; however, more active offenders are more easily understood when we recognize their similarity to others and get back to the notion that crime is very human.

People apply the denial principle not only to themselves but also to their children. When my father heard of any rule breaking when we were growing up, his response was, "Not *my* kid." In his case, he did not deny the facts, but he used them to raise our standards as best he could. Facing facts is hard for many parents. It is easier to tell yourself that your own children could do no wrong, or at least no major wrong. Just as it is not necessary to be bad to do bad, one need not be a bad parent to have a child who does bad things, even often.

Because our society so often associates bad behavior with bad parenting, parents have a strong incentive to hear and see no evil done by their own children. This encourages them not to dig too deeply to find bad facts, not to believe those that come to their attention, and to find excuses for those they cannot deny. Youths help parents persist in this denial by neglecting to inform them of all the bad things they do or by finding scapegoats outside the home when they are caught.

Some parents get angry at anyone, including police or neighbors, who informs them that their children have done wrong. This problem is all the more severe when those providing such information are strangers. Accusations by strangers are threatening to parents, and strangers themselves may feel that it makes more sense to look the other way than to inform parents and create resentment and distrust. Sometimes parents are the last to know the facts about their own children.

The Innocent Youth Fallacy

My brother Ed is a criminal lawyer who often handles juvenile cases. He once told me, "I look at some of my young clients and tell myself, 'That's a kid.' Then I say to myself, 'That's also a criminal.'" Perhaps none of us can easily resolve this conflict in our own minds.

The television version of crime usually portrays middle-aged offenders or victims. When the young are there, they are portrayed as innocents corrupted by those older. This is the *innocent youth fallacy*.

Are young people really so innocent? I have heard many people say, "Let's keep the young offenders separate from the hard-bitten older offenders, who will be a bad influence on them." If you ask the prison officials, they tell you something different. The young offenders give them most of the trouble. The reason to keep the ages separate is to protect the older prisoners from the young thugs.

Several types of data show repeatedly that young people have a very strong presence in various aspects of crime (Gottfredson & Hirschi, 1990, Chapter 6). Victim surveys repeatedly show risk of victimization for ordinary crimes to be highest among teenagers and those in their early 20s. This risk declines noticeably in the late 20s, continuing to later ages. Except for purse snatching, the victimization risk is relatively low among senior citizens.

The youth of offenders is also reported in victim surveys. . . . According to victims [responding to the 1994 NCVS], multiple offenders have a much younger pattern. Lone offenders are reported as somewhat older, but still mostly under 30. This finding is consistent with other work showing young offenders to be more group oriented (Erickson & Jensen, 1977).

Official police data for 1994 support the argument that offenders are very young. For example, burglary arrests peak at age 16 and decline after that. . . . Furthermore, the number of arrests is halved for those in the 35- to 49-year age group as compared with those in their early 20s, and the number of arrests is even lower for older groups. This general pattern has some complexities. For instance, the general tendency for crime to occur at young ages is somewhat offset by the addiction pattern. As people addicted to drugs or alcohol get older, they get deeper into trouble, at least until they fall apart. That is why drunk driving arrests do not drop off as fast with age as does burglary. Youths of driving age, however, are still very well represented in drunk driving arrest statistics. The young are probably even more involved as offenders than these statistics indicate, for these reasons:

- Juvenile offenses often are handled internally by schools or noncriminally by other authorities.
- Juveniles have less access to some crime targets. For example, few 17-year-olds have full-time jobs, so they have less chance to commit employee theft (Gottfredson & Hirschi, 1990).
- Juvenile offenses, such as substance abuse, are difficult to discover.
- Active young offenders still look young and innocent. Their bodies do not yet show the deterioration that comes from living a fast life.

In general, the age curve is as follows: People get in trouble as offenders (and as victims) as they reach adolescence. After adolescence, crime involvement continues at somewhat lower levels in the early 20s and continues declining, getting much lower into later middle-age and senior years. Victimization risk declines more slowly with age than does offending. After age 30, the declines in crime involvement are especially marked, but alcohol violations hold on to some extent.

The Ingenuity Fallacy

The false image of "the criminal" derived from the media makes this self-deception easy. To be good foils for the hero, criminals must be almost as crafty and tough. Consider Professor Moriarty as the evil and brilliant criminal in epic struggle with Sherlock Holmes. Nobody but Holmes could outsmart him. It would not have been fair to have the brilliant Sherlock Holmes chasing a drunken fool.

Our ideas about classic criminals include the skilled cat burglar who can slip into a third-story room while victims sleep, quietly pocketing valuables and then slipping down the drainpipe without a sound. A book more than six decades old, *The Professional Thief, by a Professional Thief*, resulted from Edwin Sutherland's interviews with "Chick Conwell" (Sutherland, 1933/1956). The book described what a professional thief of the 1930s did and how he learned such tactics as switching fake jewels for real ones right in front of a jeweler, pickpocketing and safecracking, and tricking people out of money.

Advanced skills do not apply widely today to crime as we know it. Maurice Cusson (1993) of the University of Montreal writes about the "de-skilling" of crime in recent decades. As technology makes safes difficult to crack, it also puts lots of cars on the streets with windows that are easy to smash. As crowds suitable for old-fashioned pocket picking decline, offenders find they can grab someone's wallet or purse near the bank or ATM, or when the victim is paying for a hot dog. Walsh (1994) has generalized this issue in what he calls the "obsolescence of crime forms." Walsh lists 24 offenses that have become largely obsolete, including bribery of voters, eavesdropping, and illegal abortion. Following on the work of Cohen and Felson (1979) on how changing technology brings new crime, Walsh demonstrates that changes in technology also can cause some crimes to fall by the wayside.

The de-skilling of crime is illustrated by modern robberies. The lack of planning in robbery is often surprising. For example, most bank robbers had never been in the bank they robbed and made no particular plans. Feeney's (1986) interviews with California robbers found some other surprises. Only 60% of the robbers wanted money at the outset. One in four were after something else, and one in five got into "accidental robberies" that resulted from burglaries, fights, or something else not originally intended as a robbery. . . . Only 3 of 112 robbers reported doing a lot of planning. Feeney gives examples of offenders driving along with passengers "totally unaware of what was about to happen." Many a robber even surprises himself. This does not mean, however, that robbers do not make any decisions. It merely indicates that they do not act with great care or necessarily have to. This view of robbery is confirmed by other studies (Bellot, 1983; Gabor et al, 1987; Indermaur, 1995; Morrison & O'Donnell, 1996).

The *ingenuity fallacy* exaggerates the offender's cleverness. Chick Conwell aside, most criminals take a very casual approach. For them, the point of crime is to get things without having to work hard and without much dedication; thus, most crime is quick and easy, and most offenders are unskilled. That does not mean they are stupid, merely that they do not usually put forth a lot of effort or show a lot of daring.

Victims often have trouble admitting how foolish they were in making crime easy, so they tell themselves, the police, and anyone else who asks, "A professional criminal broke into my house." People who hide the jewels in the cookie jar or the money in the bathroom think that nobody else ever thought of those hiding places. If you were looking for someone else's valuables, where would you look?

Offenders themselves have admitted that much of what they do is casual and unplanned, yet they still do some thinking, however simple and quick the crime may be. The Latin words *modus operandi* mean "method of doing something." Cromwell, Olson, and Avary (1991, 1993) learned a great deal about the modus operandi for burglary. They simply drove around with local burglars, peppering them with questions on the spot. This gave the offenders less time to make things up.[4] They asked:

- Why do you pick this street?
- Would you break into that house?
- Why would you skip that other house?
- If you won't break in now, will you go back?

Almost all these burglars said they wanted easy and low-risk homes. They start by looking to see if anybody is in the house and the ones next to it. Three clearly empty houses in a row put the middle house at greater risk, because the neighbors are not there to prevent the crime. Burglars first look for activity, then they might probe by ringing doorbells or knocking on the door to see if anybody is there. They drive around a little to find the easy pickings. The idea is to look and act quickly.

Most crimes take very little time, much less than the general public realizes. A burglary takes a minute or two, sometimes as much as five. Burglars act quickly, before anyone can discover them. That also explains why they make such a mess rummaging through a victim's belongings. Indeed, burglary as a routine phenomenon carried out in the easiest and fastest way is confirmed in several studies (Bennett & Wright, 1984; Rengert & Wasilchick, 1985; Tunnell, 1992; Walsh, 1980; Wright & Decker, 1994; see the overall review by Shover, 1991).

Robbery also is a quick crime. If someone points a gun at you and asks, "Your money or your life?" how long does it take you to reply?

The Organized Crime Fallacy

Many a dollar has been made on Mafia movies. Genius, organization, drama, crime families—these are the images of organized crime. Many a headline also has been devoted to big-time "white-collar criminals" who carry out massive thefts through clever manipulations of stocks or finances. These images are exaggerated with respect to crime in the United States (see Kappeler et al, 1993, pp. 11–14). In their book *Crimes of the Middle Classes*, Weisburd, Wheeler, Waring, and Bode (1991) find that most such crime is extremely mundane. For example, owners of two or three local laundries can agree to fix the prices they charge the local hospital, which is blatantly illegal and not very nice. This crime takes only one short meeting or a quick chat over beer. The owners make money from this crime, but you cannot make much of a movie out of it.

If anything, these researchers underestimated the ordinariness of white-collar crime by using court data. I do not deny that simple local finagling adds up and hurts society, but we cannot prevent the crimes without dropping our fantasies about them.

Criminologists have long advanced a network model of organized crime. This approach finds that such offenders are not very likely to meet in a single room to plan everything carefully. Let's say that Joe grows marijuana and sells a larger amount to Mary, who distributes smaller packages among five others. These folks take their packages and further break them up among a few people, who do the same. Like a chain letter, the marijuana gets to user step by step. The illegal network involves many people, but most of them do not know the others. Some offenders may get together briefly here and there, but if they are together for very long, it probably is to get high. Peter Reuter, a leading economist of organized crime and drugs, finds similar simplicity in illegal gambling (Reuter, 1984).

The fancy image inherent in the *organized crime fallacy* does not really fit the tasks such criminals carry out. Does it really take much time, skill, or organization to hand someone a package of drugs and take the money, or to take a bet, or to sell quick sex? Does it require skill or organization to kill someone in an age of firearms? Or for Fred to pay George to threaten Bill? Ongoing and as-yet-unpublished research by Mangai Natarajan, who is examining thousands of hours of wiretaps of high- and middle-level drug dealers, indicates that they are not very businesslike. One of them might ask, "Where's the pickup? What time? Where's the party tonight?" They spend more time talking about the party than the work. Indeed, the purpose of crime is to work less. The purpose of organized crime is to make even more money even more easily. That means avoiding long meetings.

The Juvenile Gang Fallacy

Not only the media but even law enforcement has played a role in nurturing the image of juvenile gangs as cohesive, ruthless groups of alienated youths who

- Dominate local crime
- Do the nation's drug trafficking
- Fit the organized crime pattern
- Provide a surrogate family
- Kill anybody who quits

This *juvenile gang fallacy* has led to public misplacement of crime concerns. The leading expert on juvenile gangs, Professor Malcolm W. Klein, started by studying gangs face to face (Klein, 1971). He expected to find coherent groups of boys involved in exciting things. Instead, he found weak-structured groups that break up often and have members constantly entering and leaving. They were extremely boring, and members hung out doing mostly nothing. Klein described the street gang as an onion, with each part peeling off to reveal another part, then another, until you got to the core. A few core members were more active than the others (that is, they hung out regularly, doing nothing), but most members were peripheral, there one day and not the next. Klein's landmark book, *The American Street Gang: Its Nature, Prevalence, and Control* (1995), punctures many preconceptions (see also Klein, Maxson, & Cunningham, 1991). How can a gang be compared to a family, when families last for years or lifetimes rather than for weeks or months? If you want to quit a street gang, all you have to do is come around less often, or hang out with peripheral rather than core members. Paradoxically, juvenile gangs are still harmful, mainly because their members are criminally active, not because they are coherent. Even if they put on something of a show, however, that does not mean you have to believe all of it.

Let me describe a typical street gang. For the sake of convenience, I shall name the gang the Undependables. They are involved in substantial amounts of crime, and it is a part of their identity. Most of their crime is petty and very local, but some of them get into serious trouble. The Undependables have an extra presence in local crime, but a majority of such crime is done by youths who are not members of the Undependables. When a small group of Undependables steals something, they do not share it with the group but keep it for themselves. Nor can they be depended on to keep crime to themselves. For example, two Undependables may well get together with two not in the gang to break into a house. Although some members of the Undependables may play a role in selling illegal drugs, the gang as a whole is not organized to sell drugs, despite its reputation for doing that.

Even the membership of the Undependables is unclear, changing by the month. Core members are not necessarily there for a very long term, and most members are very volatile, at the fringes. The group is loosely linked in the immediate vicinity, and its connection with others who use the same gang name is looser: There may be the Bay Street Undependables and the James Park Undependables, who seldom talk to each other and may even fight each other. There may also be Wannabe Undependables, boys who imitate the Undependables or even join the Junior Undependables. The looseness of the Undependables does not deny that they create a lot of trouble for others, and even for themselves, but they do not have the kind of hierarchy described in Weber's (1991/1920–1921) classic essay on bureaucracy.

Klein's early experience revealed that the group social workers who were supposed to help boys get away from gangs were actually helping to keep the gangs cohesive: The other gangs fell apart without social workers to help them stick together.

So much for the gang as a machine of cohesive evil. Indeed, one of the fascinating features of crime is that a lot of evil can be done with very little ingenuity, planning, or cohesiveness. We nevertheless keep hearing about the juvenile gang of a different sort. I wonder whether it is too hard for the public to accept the notion that young people acting in small numbers can do a lot of bad things, because young people are supposed to be innocent. It is much easier to conceive of evil gangs than evil kids. Evil gangs also make a much better story for the media.

The Pestilence Fallacy

We now turn to misconceptions about how crime relates to other phenomena in society at large. For individuals, we know that bad things often are related. If you get drunk too often, you have accidents and get sick. If two lovers split up, they also become depressed and unattractive to potential new lovers. Later, we take up the question of how some individuals mess up many things and how that tendency relates to crime. We also consider how bad things are related within localities.

Beyond individuals and localities, however, it is not quite the same. Social bads do not necessarily go together. I call this the *pestilence fallacy*, for it treats crime as one of many evils that comes from other evils in society. For example, some people assume that crime comes from such ills as unemployment, poverty, cruelty, and the like.

The pestilence fallacy also would tell us that prosperity ought to bring lower crime rates. Why, then, do the most prosperous nations of the world, including the United States, have high property crime rates? Why do the poor nations of the world so often have lower property crime rates? (See Brantingham & Brantingham, 1984; Van Dijk, Mayhew, & Killias, 1990.) Why does the United States, despite its prosperity, have such high violent crime rates? Why does The Netherlands, despite its high level of social welfare spending and emphasis on social equality, also have high violent crime rates? Why was the major period of crime rate increase in the United States, 1963 to 1975, also a period of healthy economic growth and relatively low unemployment? (see Cohen & Felson, 1979; Felson & Cohen, 1981.) Why was the Great Depression devoid of a general crime rate increase?

Why did Sweden's crime rates increase greatly, despite the fact that its Social Democratic government brought more and more programs to enhance equality and protect the poor (Smith, 1995)? For example, Sweden had some 8,000 violent crimes in 1950, which increased to nearly 40,000 in 1988. During the same period, burglaries grew to seven times their former number, and robberies increased to 20 times their former level (Dolmen, 1990; Wikstrom, 1985). This is not to argue that Sweden's welfare state contributed to its crime rate (nonwelfare states also had proliferating crime), but to show that crime seems to march to its own drummer, largely ignoring social justice, inequality, government social policy, welfare systems, poverty, unemployment, and the like. To the extent that crime rates respond at all to these phenomena, they may actually rise somewhat with prosperity. In any case, crime does not simply flow from other ills.

This is not an argument against fighting poverty, discrimination, or unemployment. Rather, it is an attempt to detach criminology from a knee-jerk link to other social problems.

The Agenda Fallacy

All too many observers tend to link crime to their larger political or religious agenda (Walker, 1989). For example, a "liberal" agenda promises to reduce crime by enacting poverty programs and increasing social or economic justice. A "conservative" agenda offers to reduce crime by decreasing welfare support or by using capital punishment (even though it does not apply to most crimes). Some religious groups claim that conversion to their faith or values will prevent crime. In each case, crime is treated not for its own sake but instead for how it can be added to a larger agenda.

A wide array of political and social agendas have been linked with crime prevention. If you are in favor of a minimum wage as part of your agenda, then why not argue that it will prevent crime? If you are concerned about sexual morality, tell people that sexual misbehavior leads to crime. If you are a feminist, proclaim that rape is produced by anti-feminism. If you dislike pornography, link it to sexual or other crimes. If the entertainment media offend your sensibilities, blame them for crime and demand censorship as a crime prevention method. Right-wing, left-wing, or whatever your agenda, if there is something you oppose, blame that for crime; if there is something you favor, link that to crime prevention. If there is some group you despise, blame them and protect others (R. Felson, 1991; Felson & Felson, 1993). These are political tactics, not the way to gain more knowledge about crime. Indeed, they may eventually harm the agenda if promises are not fulfilled.

Those who really want to learn about crime should observe the following advice:

- Learn everything you can about crime for its own sake rather than to satisfy ulterior motives, such as gaining political power or religious converts.

- Set your agenda aside while learning about crime. If your political and religious ideas are worthwhile, they should stand on their own merits.

The Morality Fallacy

A special case of the pestilence fallacy is the *morality fallacy*. This is the belief that crime is produced by declining morality. The fallacy follows from this line of thinking:

1. Crime is immoral.
2. Crime is widespread.
3. Therefore, wider teaching of moral values will reduce crime.

The above reasoning forgets about hypocrisy. People can easily talk about good without doing good. They can even believe in good without putting their beliefs in action all the time (Hirschi & Stark, 1969). Moral training does not guarantee moral behavior (Wrong, 1961). Nor does a lack of moral behavior prove the absence of moral training. For example, the high murder rate in the United States does not prove that Americans believe in murder or that they are trained to commit murder. If that were the case, why do U.S. laws set such high levels of punishment for murder? Why would U.S. public opinion show such outrage at murderers and other serious criminals?

Consider a parallel question: Why do people become overweight? This set of statements is analogous to the earlier triplet of crime statements:

1. Being overweight is bad.
2. Being overweight is widespread.
3. Therefore, a lot of people must want to be fat, and we have to teach them that being fat is bad.

If the conclusion is correct, then why do so many overweight people want to lose weight? Many people already know that it is better to be thinner but find it difficult to accomplish that goal, given America's cornucopia of rich food at low prices. When I lived in Sweden, I noticed that visiting American scholars lost weight, inspired by food prices triple those back home.

CONCLUSION

The many fallacies in our perceptions of crime fit a pattern. All of them point toward a moral struggle between evil offenders and the criminal justice system, which acts on behalf of society's good people. Even criminologists are often tempted to describe a world of criminals distinct from the world of general citizens. We must resist that temptation. In the old cowboy movies, good guys wore white hats and were kind to their white horses, and bad guys wore black hats and mistreated their black horses and everyone else. Real human life is not so clear-cut.

It is true that some people commit far more than their share of offenses, but Fattah (1991) documents that both offenders and victims tend to be in the same groups: young, male, and unmarried. Several scholars have found that offenders themselves have higher rates of crime victimization than the rest of the population (Fattah, 1991; Gottfredson, 1984). To quote Susan Smith, "Empirical research is increasingly gnawing away at the concept of mutually exclusive offender and victim populations, showing it to be a figment of political imagination and a sop to social conscience" (1986, p. 98).

We have to face the fact that most crime and most delinquency is ordinary and non-dramatic, involving little ingenuity. The mostly young participants act outside the reach of the criminal justice system and the various popular agendas. In short, crime must be studied in its own terms.

ENDNOTES

1. For the reader's convenience, I have taken as many crime statistics as possible from the *Sourcebook of Criminal Justice Statistics*. This is put out by the U.S. Department of Justice, Bureau of Justice Statistics. Look in the references under that agency. Most data refer to 1994, for which counts were more complete at the time of publication. Students can get the latest data on the Internet as follows. The *Sourcebook* is available via http://www.ojp.usdoj.gov/bjs. The *Uniform Crime Reports* is available via http://www.fbi.gov. The reader has a choice between recent but preliminary data or data that are a few years old but finalized. For most purposes in this chapter, the final data suffice.
2. I have used murder and homicide interchangeably, but this is not strictly correct. Homicide is the larger category, including justifiable killings not classified as murder. For exact definitions of these and other crime terms, see the *Sourcebook*'s appendices or original sources cited.
3. Quarrels are enumerated in homicide analysis as part of the UCR each year.
4. Offenders often distort things, telling you what they think you want to hear, what will make them look tough or important, or what they think will help them get out of jail. So how can we get a straight answer about what happens in a crime? One does best to ask specifically how a crime is committed. The same offenders who say nothing or pour out nonsense in response to some questions suddenly get down to earth when asked more basic questions, such as exactly how to break into a car, how to get shirts past a store's cashier, or where to go to grab a victim.

REFERENCES

Beck, A., & Willis, A. (1995). *Crime and security: Managing the risk to safe shopping*. Leicester, UK: Perpetuity Press.

Bellot, S. (1983). Portrait du voleur à main armée occasional [A portrait of the casual armed robber] (Technical Report No. 7). Montreal: International Center of Comparative Criminology, University of Montreal.

Bennett, T., & Wright, R. (1984). *Burglars on burglary: Prevention and the offender*. London: Gower.

Block, R. L., & Block, C. R. (1992). Homicide syndromes and vulnerability: Violence in Chicago's community areas over 25 years. *Studies on Crime and Crime Prevention*, 1, 61–65.

Brantingham, P. J. & Brantingham, P. L. (1984). *Patterns in Crime*, New York: MacMillan.

Challinger, D. (1992). Less telephone vandalism: How did it happen? In R. V. Clarke (Ed.), *Situational crime prevention: Successful case studies*. New York: Harrow & Heston.

Cohen, L. E., & Felson, M. (1979). Social change and crime rate trends: A routine activity approach. *American Sociological Review*, 44, 588–608.

Coleman, A. (1985). *Utopia on trial: Vision and reality in planned housing*, London: Hilary Shipman.

Cromwell, P. F., Olson, J. N., & Avary, D. W. (1991). *Breaking and entering: An ethnographic analysis of burglary*. Newbury Park, CA: Sage.

Cromwell, P. F., Olson, J. N., & Avary, D. W. (1993). Who buys stolen property: A new look at criminal receiving. *Journal of Crime and Justice*, 56, 75–95.

Cusson, M. (1993). A strategic analysis of crime: Criminal tactics as responses to precriminal situations. In R. V. Clarke & M. Felson (Eds.), *Routing activity and rational choice: Advances in criminological theory*, 5. New Brunswick, NJ: Transaction Books.

Department of Health and Human Services. (1995). *Morbidity and mortality*. Washington, DC: Government Printing Office. (Published annually)

DiLonardo, R. L. (1997). The economic benefit of electronic article surveillance. In R. V. Clarke (Ed.), *Situational crime prevention: Successful case studies* (2nd ed.). New York: Harrow & Heston.

Dolmen, L. (Ed.). (1990). *Crime trends in Sweden, 1988*. Stockholm: National Council for Crime Prevention.

Erickson, M., & Jensen, G. F. (1977). Delinquency is still group behavior! Toward revitalizing the group premise in the sociology of deviance. *Journal of Criminal Law and Criminology*, 68, 262–273.

Fattah, E. A. (1991). *Understanding criminal victimization: An introduction to theoretical victimology*. Scarborough: Prentice Hall Canada.

Federal Bureau of Investigation, Department of Justice. (1995). *Uniform Crime Reports: Crime in the United States*. Washington, DC: Government Printing Office. (Published annually)

Feeney, F. (1986). Robbers as decision makers. In D. Cornish & R. V. Clarke (Eds.), *The reasoning criminal*. New York: Springer-Verlag.

Felson, M., & Cohen, L. E. (1981). Modeling crime rate trends—A criminal opportunity perspective. *Journal of Research in Crime and Delinquency*, 18, 138–164 (as corrected, 1982, 19, 1).

Felson, R. B. (1991). Blame analysis: Accounting for the behavior of protected groups. *American Sociologist*, 22, 5–23.

Felson, R. B., & Felson, S. (1993, September/October). Predicaments of men and women. *Society*, pp. 16–20.

Felson, R. B., & Messner, S. F. (1996). To kill or not to kill? Lethal outcomes in injurious attacks. *Criminology*, 34, 519–546.

Gabor, T. (1994). *Everybody does it! Crime by the public*. Toronto: University of Toronto Press.

Gabor, T., Baril, M., Cusson, M., et al. (1987). *Armed robbery: Cops, robbers and victims*. Springfield, IL: Charles C. Thomas.

Gorecki, J. (1979). *A theory of criminal justice*. New York: Columbia University Press.

Gottfredson, M. (1984). *Victims of crime: The dimensions of risk* (Home Office Research and Planning Unity Report No. 81).

Gottfredson, M. & Hirschi, T. (1990). *A general theory of crime*. Stanford, CA: Stanford University Press.

Hirschi, T., & Stark, R. (1969). Hellfire and delinquency. *Social Problems*, 17, 202–212.

Hollinger, R. C. (1993). *National Retail Security Survey*. Gainesville: University of Florida, Department of Sociology.

Hollinger, R. C. (1997). Measuring crime and its impact in the business environment. In M. Felson & R. V. Clarke (Eds.), *Business and crime prevention*, Monsey, NY: Criminal Justice Press.

Indermaur, D. (1995). *Violent property crime*. Sydney: Federation Press.

Jacobs, J. B., & Potter, K. A. (1997). Hate crimes: A critical perspective. In M. Tonry (Ed.), *Crime and justice: A review of research* (Vol. 22). Chicago: University of Chicago Press.

Junger, M., & Marshall, I. H. (1997). The interethnic generalizability of social control theory: An empirical test. *Journal of Research in Crime and Delinquency*, 34, 79–112.

Junger, M., Terlouw, G-J., & van der Heijden, P. G. (1995). Crime, accidents and social control. *Criminal Behaviour and Mental Health*, 5, 386–410.

Kappeler, V. E., Blumberg, M., & Potter, G. W. (1993). *The mythology of crime and criminal justice*, Prospect Heights, IL: Waveland.

Kelling, G. L., Pate, T., Dieckman, D., & Brown, C. (1974). *The Kansas City preventive patrol experiment: A summary report*. Washington, DC: Police Foundation.

Klein, M. W. (1971). *Street gangs and street workers*. Englewood Cliffs, NJ: Prentice Hall.

Klein, M. W. (1995). *The American street gang: Its nature, prevalence, and control*. New York: Oxford University Press.

Klein, M. W., Maxson, C. L., & Cunningham, L. C. (1991). "Crack," street gangs, and violence. *Criminology*, 29, 623–650.

Light, R., Nee, C., & Ingham, H. (1993). *Car theft: The offender's perspective* (Home Office Research Study #130). London: Her Majesty's Stationery Office.

Maxfield, M. G. (1989). *Circumstances in supplementary homicide reports: Variety and validity*.

McGarrell, E. F., & Weiss, A. (1996, November). *The impact of increased traffic enforcement on crime*. Paper presented at the Annual Meetings of the American Society of Criminology, Bloomington, IN.

McNamara, R. P. (1994). *The Times Square hustler: Male prostitution in New York City*, Westport, CT: Praeger.

Morrison, S., & O'Donnell, I. (1996). An analysis of the decision making processed of armed robbers. In R. Homel (Ed.), *Crime prevention studies: Vol. 5. The politics and practice of situational crime prevention*. Monsey, NY: Criminal Justice Press.

Rengert, G. F. & Wasilchick, J. (1985). *Suburban burglary*. Springfield, IL: Charles C. Thomas.

Reuter, P. (1984). *Disorganized crime: Illegal markets and the Mafia*. Cambridge: MIT Press.

Sherman, L., & Weisburd, D. (1995). General deterrent effects of police patrol in crime "hot spots": A randomized controlled trial. *Justice Quarterly*, 12, 625–648.

Shover, N. (1991). Burglary. In M. Tonry (Ed.), *Crime and justice: A review of research* (Vol 14). Chicago: University of Chicago Press.

Smith, D. J. (1995). Youth crime and conduct disorders: Trends, patterns and causal explanations. In M. Rutter & D. J. Smith (Eds.), *Psychosocial disorders in youth populations: Time trends and their causes*. Chichester, UK: Wiley.

Smith, S. J. (1986). *Crime, space and society*. Cambridge, UK: Cambridge University Press.

Sutherland, E. H. (1956). *The professional thief, by a professional thief*. Chicago: University of Chicago Press. (Original work published 1933.)

Tedeschi, J., & Felson, R. B. (1993). Predatory and dispute-related violence: A social-interactionist approach. In R. V. Clarke & M. Felson (Eds.), *Routine activity and rational choice: Advances in criminological theory*, 5 New Brunswick, NJ: Transaction Books.

Tunnell, K. D. (1992). *Choosing crime: The criminal calculus of property offenders*. Chicago: Nelson-Hall.

U.S. Bureau of the Census. (1990). *U.S. census of population*. Washington, DC: Government Printing Office.

U.S. Department of Justice, Bureau of Justice Statistics. (1995a). *Criminal victimization in the United States*. Washington, DC: Government Printing Office. (Published annually).

U.S. Department of Justice, Bureau of Justice Statistics. (1995b). *Sourcebook of criminal justice statistics*. Washington, DC: Government Printing Office. (Published annually).

Van Dijk, J. J., Mayhew, P., & Killias, M. (1990). *Experiences of crime across the world—Key findings of the 1989 International Crime Survey*. Deventer, The Netherlands: Kluwer Law and Taxation Publishers.

Walker, S. (1989). *Sense and nonsense about crime: A policy guide* (2nd ed.). Belmont, CA: Brooks-Cole.

Walsh, D. P. (1980). *Break-ins: Burglary from private houses*. London: Constable.

Walsh, D. P. (1994). The obsolescence of crime forms. In R. V. Clarke (Ed.), *Crime prevention studies* (Vol. 2). Monsey, NY: Criminal Justice Press.

Weber, M. (1991). *From Max Weber: Essays in sociology; Bureaucracy*. London: Routledge. (Original work published 1920, 1921.)

Weisburd, D., Wheeler, S., Waring, E., & Bode, N. (1991). *Crimes of the middle classes*. New Haven, CT: Yale University Press.

Wikstrom, P.O. (1985). *Everyday violence in contemporary Sweden: Situational and ecological aspects* (Report No. 15). Stockholm: National Council for Crime Prevention.

Wilson, J. Q. & Abrahamse, A. (1992). Does crime pay? *Justice Quarterly*, 9, 359–377.

Wright, R. T. & Decker, S. H. (1994). *Burglars on the job*. Boston: Northeastern University Press.

Wrong, D. H. (1961). The oversocialized conception of man in modern sociology. *American Sociological Review*, 26, 183–193.

Chapter 5

Race, Crime, and the Administration of Justice

A Summary of the Available Facts

by Christopher Stone

We each know about race, crime, and the administration of justice in many ways: from our own experience, through stories we hear, and from our various understandings of history. We may also retain a current statistic or two, especially if we have stumbled on one that reinforces what we already believe. But what does the subject of race, crime, and justice look like if approached empirically, and with reference to all of what we refer to today as racial groups?

At the most general level, we know that many people of color—Native Americans, Asian Americans, Hispanic Americans, black Americans—do not trust the justice system. For example, a study of Hispanic Texans in the mid-1980s found that fewer than 30 percent rated the job performance of their local police as good.[1] In a 1995 Gallup poll, more than half of black Americans said the justice system was biased against them. Moreover, two-thirds of black Americans in that same Gallup poll said that police racism against blacks is common across the country, and a majority of white Americans (52 percent) agreed.[2]

Social scientists usually explain this broad distrust in two ways: historical experience and present-day practice. The historical experience with the justice system among Native Americans, Asian immigrants, black Americans, and Hispanic Americans is more than enough to provoke distrust, but is it being reinforced by current practice? How does the pattern of crime and victimization keep us from living as one America? How do stereotypes work to cause people of some races and ethnic groups to be unfairly suspected of crime? How and when does the justice system itself treat defendants and offenders differently on the basis of race or ethnicity? Does a lack of diversity in the justice system add to the distrust?

Social science research has shed some light on each of these concerns, but our empirical knowledge is uneven. We know a lot about some of these issues, but there are great gaps in what we know through research. We know much less about discrimination in judicial decisions regarding Asian-American defendants, for example, than we do about "black and white" discrimination. And we know much more about reported index crimes (homicide, robbery, rape, burglary, aggravated assault, larceny, auto theft, and arson) than we do about other criminal conduct. The lack of data and good research on the experience of Asian Americans and Native Americans in particular is a problem.

Christopher Stone, *National Institute of Justice Journal*, April 1999.

PATTERNS OF CRIME VICTIMIZATION

Consider first the pattern of crime victimization. In general, whites have the lowest victimization rates, followed by Asians, followed by Native Americans, then Hispanics, then blacks. But the differences are dramatic. In 1995, for example, there were 5.1 homicide victims per 100,000 non-Hispanic white males. The rate for Asian-American males was more than one-and-a-half times higher, at 8.3 per 100,000. But the rate for Native American males was 18 per 100,000, more than three times the white rate, and the rate for Hispanics was 25.1 per 100,000, almost five times the white rate. And the rate for blacks was 57.6 per 100,000, more than 10 times the white rate.[3]

This pattern changes somewhat for different crimes. For more common violent crimes, such as robbery, the relative position of the groups is the same, but the differences are not as great. For household crimes, such as burglary, Hispanics report the highest rates of victimization in the annual victimization surveys conducted by the Census Bureau for the Justice Department.[4]

Why the differences? The crudest analyses focus on the offenders, telling us that most crime is intraracial. More than 80 percent of homicides where we know the race of the killer are either white-on-white or black-on-black. Research among Vietnamese and Chinese in California has also shown that most crime there is intraracial.[5]

Does this mean that groups with high victimization rates also have high offending rates? Yes, but with three crucial caveats. First, it is essential to remember that most crime is committed by whites. Their offending rates may be low, but there are so many of them that they still manage to commit most of the crime.

Second, the chances that a young adult has ever committed a violent offense is roughly equal across races. This is what social scientists call the "ever prevalence rate," and it is the percentage of people who, by a certain age, have at least once in his or her lifetime committed a certain act. The ever prevalence rate for committing a violent crime is roughly the same for black and white people. The difference in violent crime rates among these two groups is a function of the greater number of offenses committed each year by those in certain groups and of their persistence in such behavior over time.[6]

Third, community conditions seem to be the reason that crime falls so heavily on some groups. The more sophisticated analyses today focus on neighborhoods, and they show us that the differences in victimization and offending rates between groups may have more to do with neighborhood and community conditions than with race itself. Where people live in neighborhoods of concentrated disadvantage, victimization and offending rates are high. When researchers compare similar neighborhoods of different races, the racial differences seem to disappear.[7] The problem is that researchers cannot find white communities to compare to the most disadvantaged urban communities.

STEREOTYPES AND CRIMINAL PROFILES

Most people of all races and ethnic groups are never convicted of a crime, but stereotypes can work to brand all members of some groups with suspicion. These stereotypes may have their roots in past biases, but they also can be reinforced through broadcast news and newspaper reports. One social scientist, for example, finds that Asians are overidentified with Asian gangs.[8] A team of researchers at the University of California at Los Angeles has found that blacks and Hispanics are overrepresented in TV news depictions of violent crime, while whites are overrepresented in stories involving nonviolent crime.[9]

These stereotypes are bad enough in the culture at large, but they also work their way into law enforcement through the use of criminal profiles, putting an undue burden on innocent members of these groups. A particularly clear example of this phenomenon is found in a study of Maryland state troopers and the searches they made of motorists on Interstate Highway 95 in 1995. On this particular stretch of highway, motorists were found to be speeding equally across races. Black motorists, for example, constituted 17 percent of the motorists and 17.5 percent of the speeders. But black motorists were the subject of 409 of the 533 searches made by the police looking for contraband.[10]

Why were black motorists searched so often? The police might justify such practices on the ground that blacks are more likely to be carrying contraband. And the statistics show this to be true: the police found contraband in 33 percent of the searches of black motorists, and in 22 percent of the searches of white motorists. But the mischief in this practice is quickly exposed. Blacks had a 50 percent higher chance of being found with contraband, but were searched more than 400 percent more often. The result is that 274 innocent black motorists were searched, while only 76 innocent white motorists were searched. The profiles apparently used by the Maryland state troopers make 17 percent of the motorists pay 76 percent of the price of law enforcement strategy, solely because of their race.

DISPARITIES IN CONVICTION RATES

The combination of higher rates of crime and higher levels of police attention produce disproportionate numbers of arrests among some groups. Arrest rates for violent crimes among Asian Americans are about half of that among white Americans. Rates for Native Americans are about one-and-a-half times that for whites, and rates for blacks are about five times that for whites. Again, as with crime, the arrest rate for whites may be low, but there are so many whites that they account for 55 percent of all arrests for violent crime.[11]

But then what happens? Here is the problem that has attracted more research than any other area under discussion today. Black Americans account for fewer than half of the arrests for violent crimes, but they account for just over half of the convictions and approximately 60 percent of the prison admissions.[12] At the beginning of this decade, the chance that a black male born in the United States would go to prison in his lifetime—not reform school, not a few days or weeks in jail, but state or federal prison following conviction for a felony and a sentence of more than a year—was more than 28.5 percent. The corresponding chance for an Hispanic male was 16 percent, and for a white male, 4.4 percent.[13]

A similar pattern of disproportionate representation of black and Hispanic Americans appears in juvenile detention facilities, where in 1994, 43 percent of juveniles were black, 19 percent were Hispanic, and 35 percent were white.[14]

These are national figures, but the reality in many individual juvenile and adult institutions is even more stark as geography and classification systems increase the segregation and concentration of minority inmates. How has this happened? Is this simply the result of fair-minded prosecutors and courts applying the law to disproportionate arrests, or is there bias at work at these later stages of the justice process?

Researchers have looked carefully for evidence of bias, reaching different conclusions. Some of the disparity we see when we visit these institutions is clearly explained by differences in arrest charges, and much more is explained by differences in the prior records of those convicted. There is no evidence of disparity that stretches across the justice system as a whole when we consider index crimes. But studies of individual jurisdictions and specific parts of the court process do find some evidence of race bias in a significant number of cases.

The most we can say is that when crime type and prior record are taken into account, black defendants in some jurisdictions are more likely to receive prison sentences than are white defendants. In addition, there is some evidence that race influences detention and placement decisions in juvenile justice processing.[15] The problems we encounter in this research are illustrated in a recent study of sentencing disparity of Native Americans in Arizona. After accounting for prior felony records and other factors, American Indians were found to receive longer sentences than whites only for robbery and burglary, while whites received significantly longer sentences for homicide than did American Indians.[16]

Of course, both of these findings could be evidence of bias. The longer sentences could be evidence of harsher treatment of Native American offenders for crimes against strangers, while the lower sentences for homicide could be evidence that the courts do not treat seriously offenses among acquaintances within this population. Across race and ethnic groups, concerns about both of these kinds of bias are regularly reported: under-enforcement of laws within a minority community and overpunishment when that community is seen as a threat to the majority. These two kinds of bias can balance each other in simple studies. Their interaction is captured most famously in the research on the death penalty, showing that black offenders found guilty of murdering white victims are at the highest risk for the death penalty, while offenders of any race found guilty of murdering black victims are least likely to receive the death penalty.[17]

Finally, in considering the work of the justice system itself, the special case of drug offenses needs to be considered separately. Asian-American youth report very low drug use compared with other groups. Black youth consistently report lower rates of use than whites; Hispanic youth report more use than black youth, but less than white youth.[18] Yet police activity, new criminal legislation, special courts, and longer sentences were all brought to bear in the late 1980s against the use and sale of drugs, particularly crack cocaine. Whatever one believes about the rationality of the decision to create special, harsher penalties for crack cocaine, the concentration of these sentences on black defendants is striking. For example, of the drug defendants sentenced for powdered cocaine in the United States District Courts during the 1995 Federal fiscal year, 35 percent were black, 37 percent were Hispanic, and 21 percent were white. In contrast, of those sentenced for crack cocaine, 86 percent were black, 9 percent were Hispanic, and fewer than 5 percent were white.[19]

As striking as these statistics can be, the most powerful reminder of bias in these stages of the justice system sometimes comes from qualitative research. That is because bias in the system is most often found in local practices rather than aggregate statistics. For example, in a study in Washington state in the late 1980s, researchers found that nonwhites were sentenced to prison at higher rates in counties with large minority populations. In follow-up interviews, justice officials and community leaders told the researchers directly that citizens in their countries were concerned about the "danger-ousness" of minorities and admitted using race as a code for a culture that to them sig-nified criminality.[20]

STRENGTHENING DIVERSITY WITHIN THE CRIMINAL JUSTICE SYSTEM

If these biases were eliminated from the justice system, would we still have a problem? If the police abandoned the use of offensive stereotypes, if the remnants of institutional bias were driven from the courts, would the justice system deserve and win respect across lines of race and ethnicity? Or is the sheer volume of black and Hispanic prisoners in America a problem in its own right?

There is little empirical evidence on this, but it is a question worth considering. Re-spect for the justice system can be won or lost not just in its decisions, but in who is making them.

Slow but real progress has been made in strengthening the diversity of law enforce-ment throughout the United States, but some signs indicate that this effort is losing mo-mentum. A recent study commissioned by NIJ focusing on the hiring of police executives in Florida, for example, concluded that the number of minority law enforcement execu-tives has declined in recent years, after earlier gains. A large percentage of minority of-ficers remain in entry-level positions throughout their careers and the outlook for any change, the researchers concluded, is bleak.[21]

DECLINING CRIME RATES: A REASON FOR OPTIMISM

If there is a strong reason for optimism among all these data, it is in the steady decline in crime over the last several years in most large U.S. cities. Let me focus here on the often neglected yet dramatic decline in domestic homicide, where we again find a stark dif-ference between blacks and whites. Twenty years ago, white men were rarely victims of domestic homicide—approximately 1 victim per 100,000 males ages 20 to 44. White women were victims at about twice that rate. Both rates have declined modestly over these two decades. Rates for black victims of domestic homicide were roughly 7 times higher 20 years ago, and they have plummeted since. The rate for black male victims has dropped from more than 16 to fewer than 3 homicides per 100,000; and for black women the rate has fallen from more than 12 to fewer than 5.[22]

These declines leave us with two important lessons. First, they remind us of the power of neighborhood disadvantage, for as stark as the black/white differences are, they disappear when researchers control for housing conditions.[23] Second, they remind us of the power these communities have to help themselves. There are some aspects of the drop in crime for which police can claim the credit, and there is plenty of crime reduc-tion for everybody to claim some, but this drop, occurring over 20 years, exceeds the reach of any single program or administration. It is an example of cultural change and communities working to heal themselves.

In sum, these declines hold out the promise of a day when race will no longer be a proxy for suspicion, and crime no longer a proxy for concentrated community disadvantage.

NOTES

1. Carter, David L., "Hispanic Perception of Police Performance: An Empirical Assessment," *Journal of Criminal Justice* 13:487–500 (1985).
2. *Gallup Poll Monthly*, October 1995.
3. Unpublished analysis of various data provided to the author by the U.S. Department of Justice, Bureau of Justice Statistics.
4. Bureau of Justice Statistics, *Criminal Victimization Rates in the United States, 1994*, Washington, D.C.: U.S. Department of Justice, Bureau of Justice Statistics, May 1997.
5. Song, J. H-L., "Attitudes of Chinese Immigrants and Vietnamese Refugees Toward Law Enforcement in the United States," *Justice Quarterly* 9(4):703–19 (1992) (NCJ 143561).
6. Elliott, Delbert S., "Serious Violent Offenders: Onset, Developmental Course, and Termination—The American Society of Criminology 1993 Presidential Address," *Criminology* 32(1):8 (1994).
7. Sampson, Robert J., Stephen W. Raudenbush, and Felton Earls, "Neighborhoods and Violent Crime: A Multilevel Study of Collective Efficacy," *Science* 277:2–25 (August 15, 1997) (NCJ 173119).
8. "Asians Are Automatically Labeled Gang Members," *Los Angeles Times*, December 12, 1994, B-5.
9. Gilliam Jr., Frank D., Shanto Iyengar, Adam Simon, and Oliver Wright, "Crime in Black and White: The Violent Scary World of Local News," *Press/Politics* 1(3):6–23 (1996).
10. This discussion of stops by Maryland state troopers is based on statistics published in Katheryn K. Russell, *The Color of Crime* (New York: New York University Press, 1998), 41–2. Since the presentation of this paper, additional data from this study have been presented showing that black motorists were no more likely to be found with contraband than white motorists. In either case, the burden of this enforcement practice falls disproportionately on innocent black motorists.
11. Federal Bureau of Investigation, *Uniform Crime Reports*, Washington, D.C.: U.S. Department of Justice, Federal Bureau of Investigation, 1996.
12. Unpublished analysis of various data provided to the author by the U.S. Department of Justice, Bureau of Justice Statistics.
13. Bonczar, Thomas P., and Allen J. Beck, *Lifetime Likelihood of Going to State or Federal Prison*, Washington, D.C.: U.S. Department of Justice, Office of Justice Programs, March 1997 (NCJ 160092).
14. Roscoe, Mark, and Reggie Morton, *Disproportionate Minority Confinement*, Washington, D.C.: U.S. Department of Justice, Office of Juvenile Justice and Delinquency Prevention, April 1994.
15. Sampson, Robert J., and Janet L. Lauritsen, "Racial and Ethnic Disparities in Crime and Criminal Justice in the United States," in Michael Tonry, (ed.) *Ethnicity, Crime, and Immigration: Comparative and Cross-National Perspectives*, Chicago, IL: The University of Chicago Press, 1997, 355 (NCJ 165176).
16. Alvarez, A, and R. D. Bachman, "American Indians and Sentencing Disparity, An Arizona Test," *Journal of Criminal Justice* 24:549–61 (1996).
17. Sampson and Lauritsen, pp. 354–5.

18. National Institute on Drug Abuse, "Drug Use Among Racial/Ethnic Minorities," Washington, D.C.: U.S. Department of Health and Human Services, National Institute on Drug Abuse, 1995 (Pub. No. 95-30008).

19. U.S. Sentencing Commission, 1996 datafile, MONFY96.

20. Sampson and Lauritsen, p. 357.

21. National Institute of Justice, *The Future of Minority Law Enforcement Executives in the State of Florida*, Washington, D.C.: U.S. Department of Justice, National Institute of Justice, 1994 (NCJ 153059).

22. Greenfeld, Lawrence A., et al, "Violence by Intimates: Analysis of Data on Crimes by Current or Former Spouses, Boyfriends, and Girlfriends," Washington, D.C.: U.S. Department of Justice, Bureau of Justice Statistics, March 1998 (NCJ 167237).

23. Short, Jr., James F., "Measuring Violent Crime: Trends and Social Distributions" in John Hagan (ed.) *Poverty, Ethnicity, and Violent Crime*, Boulder, CO: Westview Press, 1997, 24 (NCJ 169786).

Chapter 6

Peeking Over the Rim

What Lies Ahead

by Kenneth J. Peak

I like the dreams of the future better than the history of the past.
—Patrick Henry

The trouble with our times is that the future is not what it used to be.

—Paul Valery

INTRODUCTION

What will the future bring? In attempting to answer that impossible question, we all have probably wished at some time that we could gaze into a crystal ball and have what former President George Bush referred to as "the vision thing." It is important that today's criminal justice students listen to what the prognosticators tell us about the future and understand their methods; they could well be the administrators of justice in a mere decade. They, like current justice administrators, must take the time today to "peek over the rim" to anticipate and plan for the future.

This chapter opens by examining several methods by which futurists attempt to determine what the future holds—in short, tools for prediction. Using those best-guess methods, we then look at what appears imminent with respect to demographics and crime in the United States. We then view what the experts portend in terms of police technology to cope with crime, as well as forecasted changes in both courts (including possibilities for reform) and corrections (population growth and the need to build more prisons). We close with discussions of how computers have changed (and will continue to change) justice administration, and how AIDS has affected personnel, policy, and litigation, and clients of the justice system.

HOW TO PREDICT THE FUTURE

Many variables can affect predictions and trends, one of the most important being money. If you have unlimited funds, you do not need to be concerned with futures. Over the next 14 to 20 years, the driving force for major changes in law enforcement agencies will be

Kenneth J. Peak, *Justice Administration: Police, Courts, and Corrections Management*, (c) 1995, pp. 436–455.
Reprinted by permission of Prentice-Hall, Inc., Englewood Cliffs, N.J.

the economy. In a phrase, "there is a lot of crime prevention in a T-bone steak." Unfortunately, with the volatile nature of the world's oil supplies, the value of the dollar, and many other related matters, our economy is in a delicate balance and our future is uncertain.

Contemporary futures research has two major aspects: environmental scanning and scenario writing. Environmental scanning is an effort to put a social problem under a microscope, with an eye toward the future. We may consult experts on their opinions, such as demographers, social scientists, technologists, and economists. A Delphi process may also assist, gathering experts, looking at all possible factors, and getting an idea of what will happen in the future. Thus environmental scanning permits us to identify, track, and assess changes in the environment.

Through scanning, we can examine the factors that seem likely to "drive" the environment. "Drivers" are factors or variables—economic conditions, demographic shifts, governmental policies, social attitudes, technological advances, and so on—that will have a bearing on future conditions. Three categories of drivers will serve to identify possible trends and impacts on the American criminal justice system by and beyond the year 2000: (1) social and economic conditions (e.g., size and age of the population, immigration patterns, nature of employment, and lifestyle characteristics); (2) shifts in the amounts and types of crimes (including the potential for new types of criminality and for technological advances that might be used for illegal behavior); and (3) possible developments in the criminal justice system itself (e.g., changes in the way the police, courts and corrections subsystems operate; important innovations).

Scenario writing is simply the application of drivers to three primary situations or elements: public tolerance for crime, amount of crime, and the capacity of the criminal justice system to deal with crime. An important consideration is whether each will occur in high or low degrees. For example, drivers may be analyzed in a scenario of *low* public tolerance for crime, a *high* amount of crime, and a *high* capacity of the criminal justice system to deal with crime. Conversely, a scenario may include a view of the future where there is a *high* tolerance for crime, a *low* amount of crime, and a *low* capacity for the system to cope with crime; and so on.

THE CHANGING FACE OF AMERICA

In 1996 the first wave of "baby boomers" will turn 50; by 2010 one in every four Americans will be 55 or older. By the year 2000, an estimated 34.9 million elderly people will constitute 13 percent of the population. The minority population is increasing rapidly; by the year 2000 an estimated 34 percent of American children will be Hispanic, black, or Asian. More than 25 million women headed their own households in 1990, 28 percent of the nation's 91 million households. Two-thirds of black and Hispanic households are headed by women. And if present trends continue, one-half of all marriages occurring today will end in divorce within a decade.

In our "postindustrial" society, there are fewer blue-collar jobs and more white-collar jobs. Jobs that are declining in number are those that could be filled by those with fewer skills. The fastest-growing jobs are those requiring more language, math, and reasoning skills. For the next decade, 90 percent of all new jobs will be in the service sector—fields that often require high levels of education and skill. Ten years ago, 77 percent of all jobs required some type of generating, processing, retrieving, or distribution of information; by the year 2000, heavily computerized information processing will be involved in 95 percent of all jobs. Statistics indicate that America is becoming a bifurcated society with more wealth, poverty, and a shrinking middle class. The gap between the "haves" and "have nots" is widening. An underclass of people—those who are chronically poor and live outside of society's rules—is growing. Between 1970 and 1980 the underclass tripled.

The influence of immigration to America, and the growth of minority-group populations in general, cannot be overstated. America now accepts nearly a million newcomers per year, which equates to about 10 million new residents each decade (excluding their offspring) even if immigration rates do not rise. Shortly after the turn of the twenty-first century, Asians are expected to reach 10 million; today's 18 million legal and illegal Hispanics may well double by then. In less than 100 years we can expect white dominance of the United States to end, as the growing number of blacks, Hispanics, and Asians together become the new majority. History has shown that where newcomers cluster together in poor neighborhoods with high crime rates, the police are soon involved. And when these various minority groups are forced to compete for increasingly scarce, low-paying service jobs, intergroup relations sour and can even become combative, as has occurred recently in Los Angeles, Miami, and other cities.

In sum, today's economy is based on knowledge. Whereas employers in the past mostly wanted muscle, today more and more jobs presuppose skills, training, and education. Fewer jobs remain for those on the bottom rung; the results are clear in our inner cities.

A CHANGING NATURE OF CRIME

Three important drivers contribute to the changing nature of crime in the West: (1) the advent of high technology in our society; (2) the distribution and use of narcotics; and (3) a declining population in the 15 to 24 [years] age bracket.

The nature of crime is rapidly changing. The new crimes of data manipulation, software piracy, industrial espionage, bank card counterfeiting, and embezzlement by computer are here to stay. What will probably tend to decrease will be the traditionally illegal means of obtaining funds: robbery and burglary. These new crimes will require the development of new investigative techniques, specialized training for law enforcement investigators, and the employment of people with specialized, highly technological backgrounds.

The abuse of narcotics is spreading in numbers and throughout various social classes, continuing to demand an ever-increasing amount of law enforcement time and resources. The real solution to the drug problem is for people to stop demanding a supply. However, that is probably an impossible goal at this time.

The decline in the size of the 15 to 24 cohort, the crime-prone youth of our society, has significantly affected crime rates. We are witnessing a decline in several types of crime, although crimes of violence are increasing. As we see the increase in the "graying of America," however, the young criminals will increasingly prey on the elderly and flourish. The growing numbers of crime-prone youths in our metropolitan areas virtually ensures that high crime rates will continue in the inner city.

Future criminal justice recruiting efforts are implicated by the nation's shift in demographic makeup. A change toward older workers, fewer entry-level workers, and more women, minorities, and immigrants in the population will force criminal justice and private industry to become more flexible to compete for qualified applicants. With the aging of America, justice agencies that recruit only recent high school graduates will probably face a shortage of qualified workers. Agencies must devise new strategies to attract

21- to 35-year-olds. This age group will be at a premium over the next 10 years, and the trend will continue well into the middle of the next century. Criminal justice will also need to offer better wage and benefits packages to compete with private businesses, such as day care, flexible hours, and paid maternity leave.

[In] the year 2000, an estimated 75 percent of the labor force will need retraining; justice agencies will have to train existing personnel, both professional and clerical, and a major thrust will be toward communication with non–English-speaking communities.

POLICING AND TECHNOLOGY IN THE FUTURE

The high-speed technological revolution, which has barely begun, will introduce new weapons for criminals and the police alike. Some futurists feel that the old methods and equipment for doing police work will soon fall by the wayside, replaced, for example, by electric and methane-fueled scooters and bubble-topped tricycles for densely populated areas; steamwagons and diesel superchargers for police in the rural and suburban areas; and methane-filled helium dirigibles, equipped with infrared night goggles and sophisticated communications and lighting devices, for patrol and assistance in planning barricades to trap high-speed drivers and search and rescue operations.

Patrol officers in this scenario will be able to type in an analysis of how a crime was committed and receive a list of suspects. With a bit more analysis and data, the computer will also give a probability of various suspects committing that particular crime at that particular place. All homes and businesses will be linked to a central dispatch system in a police-approved, computer-based remote linkage system that will combine burglar and fire alarms. Community policing teams will be assigned by zone, the officers wearing blazers instead of paramilitary uniforms. Basic police training will last a minimum of 10 months and will be geared so that the lower one-third of the class will flunk out.

Others see the future of policing differently. The twenty-first-century cop may patrol by means of jet backpack flight equipment, and officers will be able to tie in to "language banks" of translators via their wrist radios. Holographic, or three-dimensional photography may be used for mug photos, and satellite photography will probably be used to assist in criminal investigations. Police vehicles will have all electronic equipment built in, and private vehicles will have a factory-installed "kill switch" that can be activated by depressing a button in a nearby patrol vehicle, thus preventing high-speed pursuits. Police officers may spend no time in court, instead transmitting their testimony by home computer/video systems.

Obviously, law enforcement needs to assign some of its best thinkers to the task of probing the future. What should be the agency's budget? How should police personnel be trained? What skills will be needed? What new technologies will the police face? How should forces be deployed?

An area of concern among futurists is law enforcement's organizational structure. Increasing numbers of law enforcement executives are beginning to question whether or not the "pyramid"-shaped police bureaucracy will be effective in the future. Communications within the pyramid structure are often broken down and frustrated by the levels of bureaucracy; perhaps the organizational structure, the argument goes, could be changed to a more horizontal design to facilitate the flow of information and ideas.

Personnel and labor/management problems will continue to loom large in the future. Opportunities for graft and corruption will not decline, so police administrators must be sure to develop personnel policies that will protect the integrity of the profession. Debate is currently underway regarding mandatory drug testing and the use of the polygraph to safeguard the organizations. Traditional police personnel problems are not anticipated to decline either. Such matters as age discrimination, employment misconduct, sexism, new employee attitudes, and poor work habits will not be resolved in the near future.

FUTURE ADAPTATIONS BY THE COURTS

Major Modification on the Horizon

Many people believe that the inability to think systematically about the future is particularly apparent in the court community. In 1990 the chairman of the board of directors of the State Justice Institute and former Chief Justice of the Supreme Court of Alabama noted with regret that "The common picture of an American court is that of an institution rooted in the past, resistant to change, and resigned to inefficiency." And in the early 1980s, a futurist working with the Hawaii judiciary asked what were the most important long-term issues facing the courts; one reply was "how the parking spaces are allocated." The reasons for this short-term focus in the courts are several: the urgent pressure to attend to the present; judicial priorities set in annual or biannual legislative sessions; legal personnel being trained to apply the past (precedent-guiding decisions made in the present), the common law assumes the future will take care of itself; and judges, in particular, having an inherent preference for sensing the facts before them, not intuiting probable or possible future possibilities.

Looking at current trends, however, futurist Clement Bezold offered some court-related speculation for the early twenty-first century:

1. Rise of courts as a business: Efficiency and cost/benefit focuses will become more important. Private judging, arbitration, and mediation will increasingly compete with public-run courts for faster and fairer dispute resolution.
2. Death of the adversary system: The adversary system is slow, costly, and fraught with "unfairness." New, less confrontational, more humanistic ways to resolve disputes will arise, buttressed by the increase in technology.
3. The vast majority of judicial decision making (in such grass-roots areas as small claims, traffic, and status offenses) will be by nonlawyer, citizen pro-tempore judges. The need for quick decisions will lead more and more to this system for cases requiring little legal knowledge or training.
4. Courts will be depoliticized. Appointed professional managers will become the norm, and merit selection of judges will become more commonplace.
5. Technology will allow quick, easy synthesis of information and data for judicial decision making. This will provide a "quicker path to decision" and greater efficiency.
6. Courts will increasingly be called upon to resolve social problems involving drugs, poverty, and domestic violence—with little success.
7. Court programs will become increasingly decentralized. As courts become more service oriented, court programs will move closer to client groups.
8. Court organization structures will become more informal, with less reliance on hierarchical, bureaucratic structures, and shared leadership.

Suggestions for Reform

Suggestions for reform in the federal courts include adding additional judges to handle increasing federal calendars, geographic alignment to balance the court caseloads, delegating court management to professional managers, and diverting certain cases for arbitration. However, a major problem that permeates all of these reforms is the decentralized nature of the federal judiciary.

At the state court level, three major administrative reforms have been recommended by such groups as the American Bar Association and the American Judicature Society, all of which come under the heading of "court unification": structural unification, administrative centralization, and unified budgeting. *Structural unification* involves consolidating and simplifying existing trial courts and forming a single superior court on a county-wide basis; lower courts cease to exist. *Administrative centralization* would place statewide authority for court policy and administration in the supreme court or judicial council, with overall governance placed with the chief justice of the highest court or a chief administrative judge. Such an organization "provides the state's highest court with the power to make rules, appoint managerial personnel, assign judges' nonjudicial staff, and prepare and execute a centralized, state-financed yearly budget." Under this system, a high degree of uniformity is achieved; judges can also be moved across counties on temporary assignments to reduce case backlogs.

Opponents of unification and centralization argue that such changes would lead to a large central bureaucracy which would be insensitive to local concerns; rigidity would be substituted for individual justice. *Unified budgeting* "means that the budget for the court system is prepared at the state level, regardless of the source of funds, and that the executive branch does not have the authority to modify the budget request," since this would encroach upon the separation of powers.

How to Approach Reform

In an excellent book entitled *Court Reform on Trial*, in which he examined reform with bail, pretrial diversion, sentence reform, and speedy trial rules, Malcolm Feeley provided several stages in the planned-change process for the courts; succinctly, they are: (1) diagnosis or conception (identifying problems and solutions); (2) initiation (new functions added or practices significantly altered); (3) implementation (staffing, clarifying goals, adapting to a new environment); (4) routinization (commitment to supply funding and a physical base of operations); and (5) evaluation (assessment should take place during the first three stages).

The courts, Feeley wrote, while staffed with trained professionals, are also enmeshed in a web of rules that can often be inimical to change. Because of rigid segmentation, broad perspectives and systemwide thinking are discouraged and innovation is stifled. Segmentation in the adversary process inhibits communication, feeds distrust, and breeds antagonism. Finally, because of the large numbers of cases that courts must handle, courts are forced to emphasize efficiency; the greater this emphasis, the more likely that program change will be discouraged. When change *is* initiated, it often cannot be implemented. Because attempts to change encounter at least some of these problems, the successes are few and far between. Feeley concluded that "The courts do face real problems—and problems that have not been taken seriously enough. The question is: Can proponents of planned change adequately identify these problems, diagnose them accurately, and make improvements?"

THE FUTURE AND CORRECTIONS

Continuing the "Boom Industry"

Probably nowhere in the justice system is forecasting for the future more difficult and dismal than in corrections. The most ominous problems for the future of corrections will continue to be those we have concentrated upon already and which are the most difficult to predict—crowding and its related costs.

Attempts were made in the mid-1980s to estimate future state prison populations, using a mathematical model that extrapolated crime, incarceration, and demographic patterns to the year 2020. The conclusion was that prison populations would continue to rise into the early 1990s, and then that the "birth dearth" that followed World War II would begin to affect prison admissions, and the number of persons behind bars would decline slightly for about a decade. Around the turn of the century, levels were predicted to rise again and continue upward through 2020.

However, reality has a way of outstripping forecasts and mathematical models, especially in corrections. One estimate was that by 2020, prison populations would grow between 20 and 25 percent over 1983 levels. But between 1983 and 1986 alone, those populations grew 30 percent. The projections fell short partly because the forecasters could not anticipate changes in sentencing policy and partly because they did not capture adequately the subtle and possibly changing interactions among age, race, crime, and criminal justice processing. For example, the baby boom never really stopped in the black and Hispanic communities, and these groups will constitute an increasingly large proportion of the young male cohort in the coming decades. Because young black and Hispanic men have higher arrest and incarceration rates than whites, and because there is some evidence that those rates are increasing, the slowdown in prison populations that has been forecast may not come to pass.

Even more ominous is the prediction by corrections author and futurist Douglas McDonald that the U.S. prison population might double again in the next 10 years. The current rates of growth are pointing in that direction. If the prison population doubles, governments will rapidly have to construct as many cells as now exist to handle the demand, as well as replacing currently substandard facilities. The cost of this construction, based on a projected average of $51,000 per bed, will be approximately $26 billion in constant 1986 dollars. Jail populations have also been rising quickly and could also double in the next 10 years if past trends continue. Assuming an average construction cost of nearly $49,000 per bed, doubling the size of America's jail capacity would cost approximately $12 billion.

Pains will be more severe in those states having high incarceration rates, few alternative-to-incarceration programming planned, and higher levels of poverty (with, by extension, weaker tax bases). Most states in the south are so characterized. Local governments maintaining jails will fare even worse than state governments, because their revenue bases are narrower.

Another concern today is with correctional administrators being able to "find their way." As one corrections worker observed, "Correctional administrators" . . . tend to face inward toward their organizations . . . and are little in touch with the outside world . . . and seem to be isolated from organized efforts to advance and refine general understanding of administration, especially public administration." And as Alvin Cohn noted:

> Unfortunately, many correctional managers have learned that [their bosses have] as a motto, "Let sleeping dogs lie." More unfortunately, they have learned that "barking" or "attacking" dogs generally will not survive. This is not to argue that there cannot be change; we know that change is inevitable. The question is whether an executive chooses to be reactive or proactive . . . will simply ride the currents of change . . . or deliberately attempt to harness and control change. The former is crisis management, the latter is the kind of manager we should be training to assume mantles of leadership.

Prisons: To Reform or Not to Reform

Given the extent of corrections' responsibility and problems throughout its history, it is not surprising that many people have called for its reform. The story of penal reform in the United States is an old and discouraging one. From the development of the penitentiary in the late eighteenth and early nineteenth centuries, to the determinate sentencing movement of the last two decades, penal "reforms" in this country have led to few real improvements in the practice of punishment. Even if the reforms alleviated old problems, in so doing they often created new ones, requiring new reforms, which led to further problems, and so on. However, now that we are ending the current reform cycle, that of determinate sentencing, it is timely and perhaps even necessary to consider why reforms fail, and whether or not anything will work. According to Samuel Pillsbury, "Reform begins with the proposal of a scheme for penal improvement. In most instances it is suggested by an idealist who links the proposed penal reform to a view of the ideal society prominent at the time. The idealist promotes a penal ideology which emphasizes the rightness or goodness of the proposed change in terms of society's relation to the offender."

George Bernard Shaw warned against penal reform more than a half century ago. He urged the following upon persons interested in pursuing penal reform for benevolent purposes: "To put it down and go about some other business. It is just such reformers who have in the past made the neglect, oppression, corruption, and physical torture of the common goal the pretext for transforming it into that diabolical den of torment, mischief, and damnation, the modern prison."

There are many who have sought, both from within the system as well as from without, to make prisons better places. Internally initiated reform has from time to time involved inmate rioting; although this method is not the most effective tool for the expression of inmate grievances, it has focused attention on prison problems and helped pave the way for inmate councils, grievance procedures, conflict resolution, and the position of ombudsman. Changing the internal administration is another means of attempting internal reform. An example was Arkansas Governor Winthrop Rockefeller's hiring in the 1960s of Tom Murton to administer a prison system that had become corrupted and even lethal (Murton unearthed a number of scandals and even human skeletons at the prison). This attempt at reform was made famous by the 1980 movie *Brubaker*, starring Robert Redford.

Murton was quite critical during his tenure, referring to the "facade of reform" and saying that the "reform of penal practices has often appeared to follow the motto, 'Do something, even if it proves to be wrong.'" He added that "the reformer long ago came to realize that chief executives, prison boards, prison staffs, and most inmates are not willing to risk the consequences of seeking real reform."

Normally, internally initiated reform by the staff is short-lived; either the old routine returns or the reforms settle into a new but equally sterile routine. Unless real reform occurs at all levels, there is little incentive for initiating new programs. The most lasting reforms appear to be those that have been initiated by external sources or with the knowledge and support of the outside community and public leaders.

At the state level, externally induced reform is usually brought by legislative or executive action. A state's criminal code may be revised, allowing such benefits as educational and home furloughs. The executive branch of government can enact executive orders. At the federal level, the most active reformer has been the U.S. Supreme Court. A number of major court decisions have affected prisoners' rights. External pressure is also brought to bear by private organizations, such as the John Howard Association, the American Correctional Association, and the National Council on Crime and Delinquency. All seek reform through prison certification visits and suggestions to correctional administrators. Organizations of ex-offenders who work with prisoners, such as the Seventh Step Foundation, Man-to-Man, and the Fortune Society, also seek correctional reform.

An official of the California school system provided some food for thought for simple prison reform, saying:

> You want to know where prison reform starts? I'll tell you. It's the third grade. We know the high risk groups who will drop out of school. We know individuals from these groups make up a disproportionate share of prison inmates. Give me part of the $20,000 a year we now spend on these kids as adults [in prison], give it to me now, and we can make sure they won't wind up in prison, costing the state money not only to lock them up, but for the crimes they've committed, and for the welfare payments if they have a family.

According to prison expert John Dilulio, Jr., three steps could be taken by prison officials to help create better prisons in the short and long terms:

1. Provide continuity in the commissioner's office (and, it should be added, in the warden's office; both have an average tenure that is often less than five years). The current situation of high turnover for the past 15 years fosters a power vacuum at many levels of management.
2. Adopt the practice of unit management as a means of reducing prison violence. In addition to its potential for calming the institution and its residents, there are fewer staff rotations, allowing management to measure performance better. Officers are given more authority, act more as professionals, and morale is boosted.
3. Allow products manufactured by inmates in state prisons to be sold to the federal government. This would eliminate the presently endless hours of idleness for inmates. The federal system has a large and ready market for its products.

Building More Prisons: Large, Small, or None at All?

No issue has brought criminal justice more to the forefront of public policy—and into the living rooms of America—than that of corrections cost. In fact, state spending for corrections throughout the nation grew by more than 50 percent during the 1980s—the greatest increase of any state-funded service. Furthermore, from 1975 to 1985, the cost of operating corrections in the country rose by nearly 240 percent. Americans now spend $13 billion each year to confine adult offenders.

Legal reforms have expanded the use of determinate and mandatory sentences and thus enlarged the correctional population. With the current annual cost of incarceration running as high as $50,000 per inmate, there is increasing concern over the cost of incarcerating such large numbers of offenders and crowding in general. As a result, a variety of proposals have surfaced to cope with the problem of population and save money. One purported cost-saving mechanism is privatization. . . . Others include marginally credible ideas ranging from that of a New York City mayor, to make use of old tugboats to hold prisoners, to politically volatile solutions such as early-release programs, to electronic surveillance home-detention programs.

Although it is clear that the concern among legislators, correctional administrators, and the public over the cost of corrections is justified, the public is sending mixed messages. For example, legislative changes to penal codes in the late 1980s, in the form of mandatory prison terms for drunk drivers and for those who commit gun crimes, as well as calls for the abolition of parole boards, seemed to indicate a popular sentiment for more prison space. More recently, however, the public seems to be gradually reversing itself, balking at the prospect of spending $30 million to $50 million every few years to construct a new prison for housing offenders (especially when schools, highways, health care, and social services are suffering). Thus, we now see a movement beginning toward early release and other types of programs designed to reduce the overload and divert offenders away from incarceration.

Douglas McDonald determined that larger prisons were less expensive on a per-prisoner basis than smaller ones. In addition, the average per-capita cost of operating maximum-security prisons was lower than the cost of minimum-security camps, which in turn were less expensive than medium-security facilities. These cost differences resulted largely from variations in the way each type of facility was staffed. Maximum-security prisons were larger, on average, and had fewer staff persons per inmate than other facilities. "*As the staff/inmate ratio increased, so did cost.*" [emphasis his].

All is not gloom and doom in the area of corrections costs, however. Construction and financing costs can make building prisons seem overwhelmingly expensive. However, according to the National Institute of Justice (NIJ), when these charges are amortized over the useful life of a facility, they become quite modest. But the NIJ also noted that there are other unintended costs of imprisonment for a community. Imprisonment of breadwinners may force their families into welfare dependency. There are other variables as well. For example, if an inmate was unemployed at the time of imprisonment, the state would actually gain by paying less unemployment compensation.

One estimate is that society lost an average of $408 in taxes and $84 in welfare payments per year of imprisonment. Assuming a total social loss of $5000 per year, the NIJ concluded that a year in prison implies confinement costs of roughly $20,000, for a total social cost of about $25,000. Carrying this analysis a bit further and adding new twist, by combining crime costs and offense rates, NIJ found that a typical inmate (found in a survey to commit 187 crimes per year) is responsible for $430,000 in crime costs. Sentencing 1000 more offenders to prison would obligate correctional systems to an additional $25 million per year, but about 187,000 felonies would be averted in the process of incapacitation. *These crimes represent about $430 million in social costs.* [emphasis theirs].

In addition to being sensitive to the high cost of imprisonment and the political sensitivity of this issue, correctional administrators must be adept at determining the best approach to keeping abreast with the structural needs of their criminal population. Timing can be a hidden, yet important variable, as the public is not always amenable to new, normally expensive construction proposals. Also, legislative enactments (such as those concerning mandatory sentencing or early-release proposals) also weigh into the prison construction decision. Alternatives to imprisonment must also be considered.

CAN ADMINISTRATORS "REINVENT" CRIMINAL JUSTICE?

Casting Off Old Ways

Reinventing Government, the book that recently swept the country and was on the bookshelves of many governors, city managers, and criminal justice administrators, provided ideas about how government can and should work as efficiently and productively as the best-run private businesses. It uses myriad examples of government agencies that have slashed red tape, begun focusing on the "customer," cut costs tremendously, revamped the budget-expenditure process to provide incentives for saving money, abandoned archaic civil-service systems, decentralized authority, and empowered their employees. It showed how these agencies can become more entrepreneurial and "steer" rather than "row," be driven by missions rather than by rules, encourage competition over monopoly, and invest in prevention rather than cure. Generally—and the reason for the book's widespread popularity—it demonstrated what can be accomplished when government leaders decided to "break the mold" and try new methods.

The authors of *Reinventing Government*, David Osborne and Ted Gaebler, went beyond the five principles of total quality management, espoused by W. Edwards Deming in 1950, which focused on results, customers, decentralization, prevention, and a market (or systems) approach. Osborne and Gaebler found that most entrepreneurial governments focused on promoting *competition* between service providers; they *empower* citizens by pushing control out of the bureaucracy and into the community; and they measure the performance of their agencies, focusing not on inputs but on *outcomes*. They are driven by their goals—their *missions*—rather than by rules and regulations. They redefine their clients as *customers* and offer them choices—between levels of involvement, training programs, and so on. They prevent problems before they emerge, rather than simply offering services afterward. They *decentralize* authority, embracing participatory management. They prefer *market* mechanisms to bureaucratic mechanisms. And they focus not simply on providing public services, but on *catalyzing* all sectors—public, private, and voluntary—into action to solve their community's problems.

Some Success Stories

Can some or all of these principles be applied in criminal justice agencies? Indeed, several principles are at the very heart of community-oriented policing problem solving. Perhaps a closer look at some justice-related examples will demonstrate how many of the Osborne and Gaebler principles can be implemented when administrators become determined to "reinvent" their organizations.

- The Visalia, California, Police Department pioneered a lease-purchase program for squad cars which allowed the city to cut its energy consumption by 30 percent. In a few years, the department had saved $20 million in cash, almost its entire operating budget.
- In Tulsa, Oklahoma, police studied arrest trends, school dropout statistics, drug treatment data, and the problems of the city's public housing developments. They concluded that teenagers from one section of town were creating most of the city's drug problems, so they began working with the community to attack the problem. They organized residents and together prosecuted and evicted residents who were dealing, they created an antidrug education program in the projects and established job placement and mentoring programs, they set up a youth camp for teenagers, and they worked with the schools to develop an antitruancy program.
- Sunnyvale, California, developed performance measures for all municipal departments, defining the results it wanted. In each program area, the city articulated a set of "goals," a set of "community condition indicators," a set of "objectives," and a set of "performance indicators." Objectives set the specific targets for each unit of city government. For example, in public safety, one objective was to keep the city "within the lowest 25 percent of Part I crimes for cities of comparable size, at a cost of $74.37 per capita."
- Many police agencies now survey their communities—victims, witnesses, even offenders—regarding agency performance and ways to generate revenue. The Madison, Wisconsin, Police Department mailed surveys to every thirty-fifth person it encountered. It asked citizens to rate the police on seven factors: concern, helpfulness, fairness, knowledge, quality of service, professional conduct, how well they solved the problem, and whether they put the person at ease.
- The St. Louis County (Missouri) Police Department developed a system that allows officers to call in their reports; the department licensed the software to a private company and earns $25,000 each time the package is sold to another department.
- Paulding County, Georgia, built a 244-bed jail when it needed only 60 extra beds, so that it could charge other jurisdictions $35 a night to handle their overflow. In the first year of business, the jail brought in $1.4 million, $200,000 more than its operating costs.
- Some enterprising police departments in California are earning money renting out motel rooms as weekend jails. They reserve blocks of rooms at cheap motels, pay someone to sit outside to ensure that inmates stay in their rooms, and rent the rooms to convicted drunk drivers at $75 a night.

A Shift in Governance

These examples clearly demonstrate what can happen when administrators begin thinking like entrepreneurs rather than strict bureaucrats. Unfortunately, the great majority of our federal, state, and local government agencies do not so operate. They reward failure and enhance bureaucracies rather than creating incentives to save money or serve customers. When the crime rates increase, justice agencies are given more money; if they continue to fail, they are given even more. As police departments professionalized, they began focusing on chasing crooks, not on solving community problems. This approach encourages agencies to ignore the root causes of crime, simply continue chasing criminals, and not consider possible solutions to problems.

What Osborne and Gaebler call for is nothing less than a shift in the basic model of governance used in America—a shift that is already under way, doubtless largely because of the [past] recession and demands on government agencies to "do more with less." It is now essential that justice administrators engage in strategic planning, looking beyond tomorrow and anticipating the future. Some police administrators began coping with recent revenue shortfalls in some new and unique—if not always popular—ways: charging fees for traditionally free public services, such as accident investigations, unlocking vehicles, and response to false alarms.

It will become increasingly important for justice administrators to think of such revenue-enhancing possibilities and ways to save money. They must also listen more to one of their greatest resources—the rank and file—although a revamped or "inverted" pyramidal organization structure may be necessary for accomplishing this goal. Greater collaboration with the public is also needed: the police must insist that private citizens, institutions, and organizations within their communities shoulder greater responsibility for assisting in crime control. Some examples of excellent collaborative efforts are D.A.R.E., M.A.D.D., Neighborhood Watch, and Court Watch.

In sum, justice administrators and society must rethink its approach to crime. They must play a catalytic role, not just reduce services or, as in the past, throw more money and personnel at ongoing problems. They must steer rather than row, with a clear map in hand. In short, they need a new vision of government.

COMPUTER APPLICATIONS IN CRIMINAL JUSTICE

An Information Technology Revolution

Advances in computer technology have revolutionized many concepts of organizational management, altered the value of information, and affected the flow of information within organizations. Computer technology has changed our society, the processes of government, and the disposition of justice itself. We are witnessing an "information technology revolution."

When a police officer investigates a crime, a probation officer prepares a presentence report, a court schedules a case for trial, a victim calls the district attorney's office to learn the status of his case, or a parole board tracks an inmate's parole eligibility date, information is collected, analyzed, and stored for future use. Criminal justice agencies use many different types of files, including those of criminal information, case investigation, budgets, and personnel.

Computers also allow justice administrators to engage *planning* at a level never before possible. As shown earlier in this chapter, strategic planning and forecasting are essential for developing and implementing policy within the limitations of present knowledge and decision making within political and economic realities. Data bases that contain information specifically used by management in decision making (planning, budgeting, fiscal, personnel management, or inventory control information) are called *management information systems* (MISs). Data bases that are used in agency operations (investigations, crime trend analysis, social history information, and arrest information) are called *operations data bases* (ODB).

Mainframe computer systems are designed to store, retrieve, manipulate, and analyze massive amounts of information. There are three mainframe data bases in criminal justice: (1) the National Criminal Justice Information Center (NCIC), which contains detailed arrest and intelligence information on known and wanted offenders; (2) the *Uniform Crime Reports* (UCR), published annually by the FBI, which compiles, summarizes, and reports national crime data on a quarterly and annual basis; and (3) the *Sourcebook of Criminal Justice Statistics*, published by the federal Bureau of Justice Statistics, U.S. Department of Justice, which publishes a comprehensive summary of justice activities across the country. Mainframe data-based management systems are also used extensively in criminal justice at all levels of government in functions ranging from psychological profiles of terrorists and kidnappers to automobile registration and construct descriptions and sketches of criminal subjects. Computers are also used as investigative tools in crime laboratories across the country.

Harnessing Computers in Justice Agencies

Courts use computers not only to schedule cases but also to monitor jail populations and ensure that prisoners scheduled for court appearances are brought to court on time. In San Diego, police use computers as memory banks for storing nicknames, scars and marks, and field investigations. In Dallas, the court uses a mainframe computer to issue subpoenas and summonses. Patrol cars in many jurisdictions come equipped with computers, linking officers with NCIC and other crime bases and allowing them to do reports in the field. Corrections agencies are able to use computers to manage inmate records, conduct presentence investigation, supervise offenders in the community, provide instruction to inmates, and train correctional personnel. Jail administrators, with computer assistance, receive daily reports on court schedules, inmate rosters, time served, statistical reports, maintenance costs, and other data.

The fiscal savings and overall accomplishments provided by microcomputers and mainframes is considerable. The St. Louis, Missouri, Police Department experienced a 53 percent reduction in time spent by investigators in writing and typing reports. San Diego's computerized investigations systems resulted in over 3000 arrests. In St. Petersburg, all emergency dispatching is computerized. In Chicago, computers coordinate field command communications. In Baton Rouge, drug investigators search out abusers and unethical doctors from among mountains of pharmaceutical prescriptions. Many police agencies use computer-aided instruction to train police officers. In Dallas, courts use computers to transmit subpoenas via electronic mail.

Clearly, criminal justice students as well as in-service practitioners need to become knowledgeable in basic computer operation. As strongly indicated earlier in this chapter, the future holds far greater growth and development in our information-processing society. Several questions and issues attend this development, however. Will justice agencies become overly dependent on computers? Will personnel forget how to write reports? Does efficiency and productivity mean a fairer justice system? Does computerization actually save time and eliminate unnecessary paperwork?

Administrators must be certain that the advent of high technology does not become a bane to their mission. Nonetheless, it is certain that "the future is now" in this regard.

QUESTIONS FOR THOUGHT AND DISCUSSION

Chapter 1: "The Criminal Justice Process"

1. What role does pretrial services play in the criminal justice system?
2. How does the juvenile justice system differ from its adult counterpart?
3. What role does the private sector play in the criminal justice system?

Chapter 2: "American Criminal Justice Philosophy: What's Old—What's New?" by Curtis Blakely and Vic W. Bumphus

1. What was the impetus for community-oriented policing programs?
2. What is the philosophical framework of community-oriented policing?
3. How are restorative justice programs and community-oriented policing related? How are they different?

Chapter 3: "Crime and Policy: A Complex Problem," by Samuel Walker

1. Why does the author indicate "most current crime control proposals are nonsense"?
2. Based on your understanding of Walker's thesis, is the criminal justice system racist?
3. What have been some unintended consequences of the "war on crime"?
4. What is the correct way of fighting crime?

Chapter 4: "Fallacies About Crime," by Marcus Felson

1. What are the most serious misunderstandings we have about crime and criminals?
2. Does the author's argument imply a complete change in the relationship between criminology and morality? Is this a proposal for a new criminology that is entirely amoral?
3. What does this reading imply about the role of police and the rest of the criminal justice system?

Chapter 5: "Race, Crime, and the Administration of Justice," by Christopher Stone

1. What accounts for noted disparities in conviction rates among certain racial and ethnic groups in this country?
2. What solutions can you offer to ameliorate racist attitudes and discriminatory behavior by agents of the criminal justice system?

Chapter 6: "Peeking Over the Rim: What Lies Ahead?" by Ken Peak

1. What are three important factors that will change the nature of crime in Western nations? How will each change the nature of crime?
2. What changes in policing technology are forecast to cope with the crime of the future? What possible problems could these changes cause?
3. How will the courts adapt to the changes in crime?
4. What are the major changes forecast for corrections?

Section 2

The Police in America

INTRODUCTION

The police are on the front line in the fight against crime. They are by far the most likely of any officials in the criminal justice system to come into contact with citizens. In actual practice, they exercise rather broad discretionary power in this role. It is the individual officer who decides what law to enforce, how much to enforce it, against whom it should be enforced, and under which circumstances. This fact alone places the police in a central position for determining how our justice system is viewed by the public, how effective it is in controlling various types of crime, how fairly it dispenses justice, and how our laws are translated into practice.

Most citizens do not realize the breadth of the skills needed to be an effective police officer. Most citizens are well aware of the crime-fighting activities of the police and the difficulty in performing these duties. However, many fail to realize that the majority of police work is best described as peacekeeping or order maintenance, and that these activities require a completely different type of personal demeanor and skills than crime fighting. It is the vacillation between these divergent demands on the police officer that makes the police role so complex and difficult to fulfill. Section 2 focuses on the police, trends in policing, and some current issues.

At the beginning of this section is a brief note, "Facts About Police," which provides some basic facts about police in the United States.

In Chapter 7, "The Development of American Police: An Historical Overview," Craig D. Uchida examines the development of the police since A.D. 900 and then focuses on how the role of the police has changed in American society from colonial times to the present. This review of history illustrates how many present-day issues concerning the police have their roots in different epochs of American history. This selection then gives contextual meaning to many of the current problems and issues discussed in other selections.

In Chapter 8, "The New Policing: Confronting Complexity," by law professor Herman Goldstein, outlines the importance of the relationship between the police and the public as well as importance of engaging the citizenry in the overall task of policing. He examines the complexities involved in instituting community-based policing and outlines the extraordinary accomplishments being made.

In Chapter 9, "Contemporary Policing in a Community Era," Professor Quint C. Thurman provides a theoretical and practical overview of community policing. This article offers a balanced approach by delineating both what community policing can and cannot effectively do. This piece should prove timeless because community policing will be the new benchmark used in evaluating future policing initiatives.

Chapter 10, "Police Shootings: Myths and Realities," was written especially for this volume by Roger G. Dunham and Geoffrey P. Alpert. The authors discuss what happens when police officers find it necessary to use their weapons to enforce the law. Drawing upon a ten-year study of the Metro-Dade County, Florida, police as well as other studies, the authors uncover various patterns and trends concerning this most deadly use of force. Although this issue is among the most controversial topics in policing, the image most citizens obtain from the media greatly overemphasizes the amount of police violence involved in typical police work, especially regarding the use of firearms.

In Chapter 11, "What We Know About Police Use of Force," Kenneth Adams separates fact from fiction concerning police use of force. Although an emotional topic and one usually replete with anecdotal evidence, Professor Adams reviews the extant literature and statistical evidence concerning such responsive behavior. He also offers possible areas for future scientific research.

Chapter 12, entitled "Learning Police Ethics," is becoming a classic. Author Lawrence Sherman argues that ethics codes formally laid down by police departments are bound to fail. He demonstrates that the real "code" is acquired through socialization "on the job," which creates some problems. Sherman feels it is better to learn police ethics in a setting removed from the heat of the battle and the pressures of co-workers and supervisors. He concludes that ethically sound decision-making by police requires a special effort to counteract this informal socialization of recruits to the "old" way.

Chapter 13, "Sexual Misconduct by Police Officers" was written especially for this book by Allen D. Sapp. This author discusses an often hidden form of police misconduct: sexually motivated actions and behavior by police officers. He quotes from many lengthy interviews with police officers and supervisors in numerous large metropolitan police departments, as well as with many municipal and state officers. Seven categories of sexually motivated misconduct are outlined and discussed, followed by prescriptions for controlling sexual harassment.

Chapter 14, "Public Attitudes Toward Police Pursuit Driving," by John M. MacDonald and Geoffrey P. Alpert, offers results of a multijurisdictional survey concerning the public perception of pursue/don't pursue decisions in law enforcement. The importance of understanding the public sentiment of such policing behavior is situated in an organizational and theoretical framework. The authors also discuss possible new areas of scientific inquiry.

In Chapter 15, "Race-Based Policing: Alternatives to Assessing the Problem, "Brian L. Withrow and Henry Jackson analyze the problem of racial profiling. They argue that while research shows that race plays a relatively unimportant role in a police officer's decision to issue a traffic citation, it does play a substantial role in the decision to stop or search a vehicle. Withrow and Jackson offer alternative strategies to overcome the flaws in research into this issue.

In Chapter 16, "The Future of Policing in a Community Era," Professor Jihong Zhao offers a historical account of policing. The advantages and disadvantages of a public-service ethic in policing are discussed in an organizational context. As such, he outlines the inherent differences between programmatic and institutional change, and what impact, if any, such differences may have on the future of service-oriented policing.

FACTS ABOUT POLICE

Summary findings

- Personnel
- Education and Training Requirements
- Operating Expenditures
- 9-1-1 Participation
- Drug Asset Forfeiture
- Community Policing
- Police Public Contact

Personnel

- As of June 1997, local police departments had an estimated 531,496 full-time employees, including about 420,000 sworn personnel. Sheriffs' departments had 263,427 full-time employees, including about 175,000 sworn personnel.
- From 1993 to 1997, total employment by local police departments was up by an average of 3% per year, compared with 1% per year from 1987 to 1993. Sheriffs' departments increased their number of employees by 4.4% per year from 1993 to 1997, compared with 3.1% per year from 1987 to 1993.
- From 1987 to 1997, minority representation among local police officers increased from 14.5% to 21.5%. In sheriffs' departments, minorities accounted for 19% of sworn personnel in 1997, compared with 13.4% ten years earlier.

Education and Training Requirements

- In 1997, 14% of local police departments and 11% of sheriffs' departments had some type of college education requirement for new officers. One percent of departments required a 4-year degree.
- The typical new officer recruit was required to complete 1,100 hours of training in local police departments and 900 hours in sheriffs' departments during 1997.

Operating Expenditures

- Local police departments cost about $67,000 per sworn officer and $150 per resident to operate annually. Sheriffs' departments cost about $73,000 per officer and $49 per resident annually.

9-1-1 Participation

- In 1997, 85% of all local police departments, employing 97% of all officers, were participants in an emergency 9-1-1 system. The comparative percentages for sheriffs' departments were 84% and 88%, respectively.

Drug Asset Forfeiture

- Collectively, local police departments received $490 million in cash, goods, and property from drug asset forfeiture programs during fiscal 1997. Sheriffs' departments had total receipts of $158 million.

Source: http://www.ojp.udoj.gov/bjs/lawenf.htm

Community Policing

- A majority of local police departments serving a population of 50,000 or more had a full-time community policing unit, and a majority of the departments serving a population of 10,000 or more had personnel assigned to community policing activities. A majority of sheriffs' departments serving 250,000 or more residents had personnel so assigned.

Among municipal police departments employing 100 or more officers:

As of June 30, 1997—

- 61% had a formally written community policing plan
- 71% had a community policing unit with sworn personnel assigned full-time
- 74% operated one or more community substations
- 79% had full-time school resource officers

During the 3-year period ending June 30, 1997—

- 91% trained at least some of their in-service officers in community policing.
- 80% trained all their new officer recruits in community policing.

During the 12-month period ending June 30, 1997—

- 69% offered community policing training to citizens.
- 68% formed problem-solving partnerships with local groups or agencies.

Police Public Contact

In surveys conducted in 12 cities in 1998—

- About 30% or more of the residents in each city said they had some level of contact with the police in the past 12 months.
- A majority (nearly 80%) or more of the residents in each city were satisfied with the police in their neighborhood.
- Residents who were fearful of neighborhood crime were generally less likely to be satisfied with their local police than those who were not fearful of crime in their neighborhood.

Chapter 7

The Development of the American Police

An Historical Overview

by Craig D. Uchida

INTRODUCTION

During the past 20 years, scholars have become fascinated with the history of police. A plethora of studies has emerged as a result. Early writings were concerned primarily with descriptions of particular police agencies. Roger Lane (1967) and James F. Richardson (1970) broke new ground in describing the origins of policing in Boston and New York, respectively. Since that time, others have followed suit with narratives of police organizations in St. Louis (Maniha, 1970; Reichard, 1975), Denver (Rider, 1971), Washington, D.C. (Alfers, 1975), Richmond (Cei, 1975), and Detroit (Schneider, 1980).

Other authors have focused on issues in policing. Wilbur R. Miller (1977) examined the legitimation of the police in London and New York. Samuel Walker (1977) and Robert Fogelson (1977) concentrated on professionalism and reform of errant police in the 19th and 20th centuries. Eric H. Monkkonen (1981) took an entirely different approach by using quantitative methods to explain the development of policing in 23 cities from 1860 to 1920.[1]

Overall these histories illustrate the way in which police have developed over time. They point out the origins of concepts like crime prevention, authority, professionalism, and discretion. In addition, these historical analyses show the roots of problems in policing, such as corruption, brutality, and inefficiency.

The major purpose of this selection is to examine the development of the police since A.D. 900 and, more specifically, to determine whether the role of the police has changed in American society over a period of about 300 years. This is not an easy task. The debate over the "true" or "proper" police function is an ongoing one and cannot itself be resolved in a selection such as this.[2] However, by describing the various roles, activities, and functions of law enforcement over time, we can at least acquire a glimpse of what the police do and how their activities have varied over time. To do so, we rely on a number of important contributions to the study of the history of police.

The selection is divided into seven parts and basically covers the history of law enforcement and the role of the police from colonial America to the present. Part I examines the English heritage of law enforcement and its effect on colonial America. The colonists relied heavily on the mother country for their ideas regarding community involvement in law enforcement.

Part II examines the problems of urban centers in the 18th and 19th centuries and turns to the development of the full-time uniformed police in England and America. The preventive approach to law enforcement became central to the police role in both London and American cities. Part III is concerned with police activity in 19th century American cities. Patrol work and officer involvement in corruption are discussed.

In Part IV the reform movement of the Progressive Era is examined. From 1890 to 1920 reformers attempted to implement social, economic, and political change in the cities. As part of city government, police departments were targets of change as well.

In Part V we study a second reform era. From 1910 to 1960 chiefs became involved in a movement to professionalize the police. Part VI covers the riots and disorders of the 1960s and their immediate effect on policing across the country. Finally, in Part VII, we discuss the long-term legacy of the 1960s. That is, we examine the developments of the police since 1969 in terms of research and public policy.

COMMUNITIES, CONSTABLES, AND COLONISTS

Like much of America's common-law tradition, the origins of modern policing can be linked directly to its English heritage. Ideas concerning community policing, crime prevention, the posse, constables, and sheriffs developed from English law enforcement. Beginning at about A.D. 900, the role of law enforcement was placed in the hands of common, everyday citizens. Each citizen was held responsible for aiding neighbors who might be victims of outlaws and thieves. Because no police officers existed, individuals used state-sanctioned force to maintain social control. Charles Reith, a noted English historian, refers to this model of law enforcement as "kin police" (Reith, 1956). Individuals were considered responsible for their "kin" (relatives) and followed the adage, "I am my brother's keeper." Slowly this model developed into a more formalized "communitarian," or community-based police system.

After the Norman Conquest of 1066, a community model was established, which was called frankpledge. The frankpledge police system required that every male above the age of twelve form a group with nine of his neighbors called a tything. Each tything was sworn to apprehend and deliver to court any of its members who committed a crime. Each person was pledged to help protect fellow citizens and, in turn, would be protected. This system was "obligatory" in nature, in that tythingmen were not paid salaries for their work, but were required by law to carry out certain duties (Klockars, 1985:21). Tythingmen were required to hold suspects in custody while they were awaiting trial and to make regular appearances in court to present information on wrong-doing by members of their own or other tythings. If any member of the tything failed to perform his required duties, all members of the group would be levied severe fines.

Ten tythings were grouped into a hundred, directed by a constable (appointed by the local nobleman) who, in effect, became the first policeman. That is, the constable was the first official with law enforcement responsibility greater than simply helping one's neighbor. Just as the tythings were grouped into hundreds, the hundreds were grouped into shires, which are similar to counties today. The supervisor of each shire was the shire reeve (or sheriff), who was appointed by the king.

Frankpledge began to disintegrate by the 13th century. Inadequate supervision by the king and his appointees led to its downfall. As frankpledge slowly declined, the parish constable system emerged to take its place. The Statute of Winchester of 1285 placed more authority in the hands of the constable for law enforcement. One man from each parish served a one-year term as constable on a rotating basis. Though not paid for his work, the constable was responsible for organizing a group of watchmen who would guard the gates of the town at night. These watchmen were also unpaid and selected from the parish population. If a serious disturbance took place, the parish constable had the authority to raise the "hue and cry." This call to arms meant that all males in the parish were to drop what they were doing and come to the aid of the constable.

In the mid-1300s the office of justice of the peace was created to assist the shire reeve in controlling his territory. The local constable and the shire reeve became assistants to the justice of the peace and supervised the night watchmen, served warrants, and took prisoners into custody for appearance before justice of the peace courts.

The English system continued with relative success well into the 1700s. By the end of the 18th century, however, the growth of large cities, civil disorders and increased criminal activity led to changes in the system.

LAW ENFORCEMENT IN COLONIAL AMERICA

In colonial America (17th and 18th centuries), policing followed the English systems. The sheriff, constable, and watch were easily adapted to the colonies. The county sheriff, appointed by the governor, became the most important law enforcement agent particularly when the colonies remained small and primarily rural. The sheriff's duties included apprehending criminals, serving subpoenae, appearing in court, and collecting taxes. The sheriff was paid a fixed amount for each task he performed. Since sheriffs received higher fees based on the taxes they collected, apprehending criminals was not a primary concern. In fact, law enforcement was a low priority.

In the larger cities and towns, such as New York, Boston, and Philadelphia, constables and the night watch performed a wide variety of tasks. The night watch reported fires, raised the hue and cry, maintained street lamps, arrested or detained suspicious persons, and walked the rounds. Constables engaged in similarly broad tasks, such as taking suspects to court, eliminating health hazards, bringing witnesses to court, and so on.

For the most part, the activities of the constables and the night watch were "reactive" in nature. That is, these men responded to criminal behavior only when requested by victims or witnesses (Monkkonen, 1981). Rather than preventing crime, discovering criminal behavior, or acting in a "proactive" fashion, these individuals relied on others to define their work. Public health violations were the only types of activity that required the officers to exercise initiative.

PREVENTIVE POLICE: COPS AND BOBBIES

The development of a "new" police system has been carefully documented by a number of American and English historians. Sir Leon Radzinowicz (1948–1968), Charles Reith (1956), and T.A. Critchley (1967) are among the more notable English writers. Roger Lane (1967), James F. Richardson (1970), Wilbur R. Miller (1977), Samuel Walker (1977), and Eric H. Monkkonen (1981) represent a rather diverse group of American historians who describe and analyze a number of early police departments. Taken together these works present the key elements of the activities of the first English and American police systems that used the preventive model.

During the mid- to late 1700s the growth of industry in England and in Europe led to rapid development in the cities. London, in particular, expanded at an unprecedented rate. From 1750 to 1820 the population nearly doubled (Miller, 1977) and the urban economy became more complex and specialized. The Industrial Revolution led to an increase in the number of factories, tenements, vehicles, and marketplaces. With industrial growth came a breakdown in social control, as crime, riots, disorder, and public health problems disrupted the city. Food riots, wage protests, poor sewage control, pickpockets, burglars, and vandals created difficulties for city dwellers. The upper and middle classes, concerned about these issues sought more protection and preventive measures. The constable–watch system of law enforcement could no longer deal successfully with the problems of the day, and alternative solutions were devised.

Some of the alternatives included using the militia; calling out the "yeomanry" or cavalry volunteers for assistance; swearing in more law-abiding citizens as constables; or employing the army to quell riot situations (Richardson, 1974:10). However, these were short-term solutions to a long-term problem.

Another proposal was to replace the constable–watch system with a stronger, more centralized police force. Henry and John Fielding (magistrates in the 1750s), Patrick Colquhoun (a magistrate from 1792 to 1818), and philosopher Jeremy Bentham and his followers advocated the creation of a police force whose principal object was the prevention of crime. A preventive police force would act as a deterrent to criminals and would be in the best interests of society. But the idea of a uniformed police officer was opposed by many citizens and politicians in England. An organized police too closely resembled a standing army, which gave government potentially despotic control over citizens and subjects. The proponents of a police force eventually won out, based primarily on the disorder and fear of crime experienced by London residents. After much debate in the early 1800s, the London Metropolitan Police Act was finally approved by Parliament in 1829 (see Critchley, 1967; and Reith, 1956).

The London Metropolitan Police Act established a full-time, uniformed police force with the primary purpose of patrolling the city. Sir Robert Peel, Britain's Home Secretary, is credited with the formation of the police. Peel synthesized the ideas of the Fieldings, Colquhoun, and Bentham into law, convinced Parliament of the need for the police, and guided the early development of the force.

Through Peel and his two police commissioners, Charles Rowan and Richard Mayne, the role of the London Police was formulated. Crime prevention was the primary function, but to enforce the laws and to exert its authority, the police had to first gain legitimacy in the eyes of the public. According to Wilbur R. Miller (1977), the legitimation of the London police was carefully orchestrated by Peel and his associates. These men recognized that in order to gain authority police officers had to act in a certain manner or the public would reject them. To gain acceptance in the eyes of the citizen, Peel and his associates selected men who were even-tempered and reserved; chose a uniform that was unassuming (navy blue rather than military red); insisted that officers be restrained and polite; meted out appropriate discipline; and did not allow officers to carry guns. Overall, the London police emphasized their legitimacy as based on *institutional* authority— that their power was grounded in the English Constitution and that their behavior was determined by rules of law. In essence, this meant that the power of the London "bobby" or "Peeler" was based on the institution of government.

American cities and towns encountered problems similar to those in England. Cities grew at phenomenal rates; civil disorders swept the nation, and crime was perceived to be increasing. New York, for example, sprouted from a population of 33,000 in 1790 to 150,000 in 1830. Foreign immigrants, particularly Irish and Germans, accounted for a large portion of the increase. Traveling to America in search of employment and better lifestyles, the immigrants competed with native-born Americans for skilled and unskilled positions. As a result, the American worker saw the Irishman and [the] German as social and economic threats.

Other tensions existed in the city as well. The race question was an important one in the Northern cities as well as on the Southern plantations. In fact, historians have shown that hostility to blacks was just as high in the North as in the South (Litwack, 1961). Those opposed to slavery (the abolitionists) were often met by violence when they attempted to speak out against it.

Between the 1830s and 1870s, numerous conflicts occurred because of ethnic and racial differences, economic failures, moral questions, and during elections of public officials. In New York, 1834 was designated the "Year of the Riots" (Miller, 1977). The mayoral election and anti-abolitionist sentiment were the two main reasons for the disorders. Other cities faced similar problems. In Philadelphia, the Broad Street Riot of 1837 involved almost 15,000 residents. The incident occurred because native-born volunteer firemen returning from a fire could not get by an Irish funeral procession. In St. Louis in 1850, a mob destroyed the brothels in the city in an attempt to enforce standards of public decency. To quell most of these disturbances, the local militia was called in to suppress the violence, as the constables and the night watch were ineffectual.

At the same time that the riots occurred, citizens perceived that crime was increasing. Homicides, robberies, and thefts were thought to be on the rise. In addition, vagrancy, prostitution, gambling, and other vices were more observable on the streets. These types of criminal activities and the general deterioration of the city led to a sense of a loss of social control. But in spite of the apparent immediacy of these problems, replacements for the constable–watch police system did not appear overnight.

The political forces in the large industrial cities like New York, Philadelphia, Boston, and others precluded the immediate acceptance of a London-style police department. City councils, mayors, state legislatures, and governors debated and wrangled over a number of questions and could not come to an immediate agreement over the type of police they wanted. In New York City, for example, although problems emerged in 1834, the movement to form a preventive police department did not begin until 1841; it was officially created in 1845, but officers did not begin wearing uniforms until 1853.

While the first American police departments modeled themselves after the London Metropolitan Police, they borrowed selectively rather than exactly. The most notable carryover was the adoption of the preventive patrol idea. A police presence would alter the behavior of individuals and would be available to maintain order in an efficient manner. Differences, however, between the London and American police abounded. Miller (1977), in his comparative study of New York and London police, shows the drastic differences between the two agencies.

The London Metropolitan Police was a highly centralized agency. An extension of the national government, the police department was purposely removed from the direct political influence of the people. Furthermore, as noted above, Sir Robert Peel recruited individuals who fit a certain mold. Peel insisted that a polite, aloof officer who was trained and disciplined according to strict guidelines would be best suited for the function of crime prevention. In addition, the bobbies were encouraged to look upon police work as a career in professional civil service.

Unlike the London police, American police systems followed the style of local and municipal governments. City governments, created in the era of the "common man" and democratic participation, were highly decentralized. Mayors were largely figureheads; real power lay in the wards and neighborhoods. City councilmen or aldermen ran the government and used political patronage freely. The police departments shared this style of participation and decentralization. The police were an extension of different political factions, rather than an extension of city government. Police officers were recruited and selected by political leaders in a particular ward or precinct.

As a result of the democratic nature of government, legal intervention by the police was limited. Unlike the London police, which relied on formal institutional power, the American police relied on informal control or individual authority. That is, instead of drawing on institutional legitimacy (i.e., parliamentary laws), each police officer had to establish his own authority among the citizens he patrolled. The personal, informal police officer could win the respect of the citizenry by knowing local standards and expectations. This meant that different police behavior would occur in different neighborhoods. In New York, for example, the cop was free to act as he chose within the context of broad public expectations. He was less limited by institutional and legal restraints than was his London counterpart, entrusted with less formal power, but given broader personal discretion.

POLICE ACTIVITY IN THE 19TH CENTURY

American police systems began to appear almost overnight from 1860 to 1890 (Monkkonen, 1981). Once large cities like New York, Philadelphia, Boston, and Cincinnati had adopted the English model, the new version of policing spread from larger to smaller cities rather quickly. Where New York had debated for almost ten years before formally adopting the London style, Cleveland, Buffalo, Detroit, and other cities readily accepted the innovation. Monkkonen explains that the police were a part of a growing range of services provided by urban administrations. Sanitation, fire, and health services were also adopted during this period, and the police were simply a part of that natural growth.

Across these departments, however, differences flourished. Police activity varied depending upon the local government and political factions in power. Standards for officer selection (if any), training procedures, rules and regulations, levels of enforcement of laws, and police-citizen relationships differed across the United States. At the same time, however, there were some striking similarities.

Patrol Officers

The 19th century patrolman was basically a political operative rather than a London-style professional committed to public service (Walker, 1977). Primarily selected for his political service, the police officer owed his allegiance to the ward boss and police captain that chose him.

Police officers were paid well but had poor job security. Police salaries compared favorably with other occupations. On average in 1880, most major cities paid policemen in the neighborhood of $900 a year. Walker (1977) reports that a skilled tradesman in the building industry earned about $770 a year, while those in manufacturing could expect about $450 a year. A major drawback, however, was that job security was poor, as their employment relied on election day events. In Cincinnati, for example, in 1880, 219 of the 295 members of the force were dismissed, while another 20 resigned because of a political change in the municipal government. Other departments had similar turnover rates.

New officers were sent out on patrol with no training and few instructions beyond their rule books. Proper arrest procedures, rules of law, and so on were unknown to the officers. Left to themselves, they developed their own strategies for coping with life on the streets.

Police Work

Police officers walked a beat in all types of weather for two to six hours of a 12-hour day. The remaining time was spent at the station house on reserve. During actual patrol duty, police officers were required to maintain order and make arrests, but they often circumvented their responsibilities. Supervision was extremely limited once an officer was beyond the station house. Sergeants and captains had no way of contacting their men while they were on the beat, as communications technology was limited. Telegraph lines linked district stations to headquarters in the 1850s, but call boxes on the beat were not introduced until late in the 19th century, and radio and motorized communications did not appear until the 1900s (Lane, 1980). Police officers, then, acted alone and used their own initiative.

Unfortunately, little is known about ordinary patrol work or routine interactions with the public. However, historians have pieced together trends in police work based on arrest statistics. While these data have their limitations, they nonetheless provide a view of police activity.

Monkkonen's work (1981) found that from 1860 to 1920 arrests declined in 23 of the largest cities in the United States. In particular, crimes without victims, such as vice, disturbances, drunkenness, and other public order offenses, fell dramatically. Overall, Monkkonen estimated that arrests declined by more than 33% during the 60-year period. This trend runs contrary to "common sense notions about crime and the growth of industrial cities, immigration and social conflict" (p. 75). Further analysis showed that the decline occurred because the police role shifted from one of controlling the "dangerous class" to one of controlling criminal behavior only. From 1860 to 1890, Monkkonen argues, the police were involved in assisting the poor, taking in overnight lodgers, and returning lost children to their parents or orphanages. In the period of 1890 to 1920, however, the police changed their role, structure, and behavior because of external demands upon them. As a result, victimless arrests declined, while assaults, thefts, and homicide arrests increased slightly. Overall, however, the crime trend showed a decrease.

Police Corruption and Lawlessness

One of the major themes in the study of 19th century policing is the large-scale corruption that occurred in numerous departments across the country. The lawlessness of the police—their systematic corruption and nonenforcement of the laws—was one of the paramount issues in municipal politics during the late 1800s.

Police corruption was part of a broader social and political problem. During this period, political machines ran municipal governments. That is, political parties (Democrats and Republicans) controlled the mayor's office, the city councils, and local wards. Municipal agencies (fire departments, sanitation services, school districts, the courts, etc.) were also under the aegis of political parties. As part of this system, political patronage was rampant. Employment in exchange for votes or money was a common procedure. Police departments in New York, Chicago, Philadelphia, Kansas City, San Francisco, and Los Angeles were filled with political appointees as police officers. To insure their employment, officers followed the norms of the political party, often protecting illicit activities conducted by party favorites.

Corrupt practices extended from the chief's office down to the patrol officer. In New York City, for example, Chief William Devery (1898–1901) protected gambling dens and illegal prize fighting because his friend, Tim Sullivan (a major political figure on the Lower East Side) had interests in those areas. Police captains like Alexander "Clubber" Williams and Timothy Creeden acquired extensive wealth from protecting prostitutes, saloonkeepers, and gamblers. Williams, a brutal officer (hence, the nickname Clubber), was said to have a 53-foot yacht and residences in New York and the Connecticut suburbs. Since a captain's salary was about $3,000 a year in the 1890s, Williams had to collect from illegal enterprises in order to maintain his investments.

Because police officers worked alone or in small groups, there were ample opportunities to shake down peddlers and small businesses. Detectives allowed con men, pickpockets, and thieves to go about their business in return for a share of the proceeds. Captains often established regular payment schedules for houses of prostitution depending upon the number of girls in the house and the rates charged by them. The monthly total for police protection ranged between $25 and $75 per house, plus $500 to open or re-open after being raided (Richardson, 1970).

Officers who did not go along with the nonenforcement of laws or did not approve of the graft and corruption of others found themselves transferred to less-than-desirable areas. Promotions were also denied; they were reserved for the politically astute and wealthy officer (promotions could cost $10,000 to $15,000).

These types of problems were endemic to most urban police agencies throughout the country. They led to inefficiency and inequality of police services.

REFORM, REJECTION, AND REVISION

A broad reform effort began to emerge toward the end of the 19th century. Stimulated mainly by a group known as the Progressives, attempts were made to create a truly professional police force. The Progressives were upper-middle class, educated Protestants who opposed the political machines, sought improvements in government, and desired a change in American morality. They believed that by eliminating machine politics from government, all facets of social services, including the police, would improve.

These reformers found that the police were without discipline, strong leadership, and qualified personnel. To improve conditions, the progressives recommended three changes: (1) the departments should be centralized; (2) personnel should be upgraded; and (3) the police function should be narrowed (Fogelson, 1977). Centralization of the police meant that more power and authority should be placed in the hands of the chief. Autonomy from politicians was crucial to centralization. Upgrading the rank-and-file meant better training, discipline, and selection. Finally, the reformers urged that police give up all activities unrelated to crime. Police had run the ambulances, handled licensing of businesses, and sheltered the poor. By concentrating on fighting crime, the police would be removed from their service orientation and their ties to political parties would be severed.

From 1890 to 1920, the Progressive reformers struggled to implement their reform ideology in cities across the country. Some inroads were made during this period, including the establishment of police commissions, the use of civil service exams, and legislative reforms.

The immediate responses to charges of corruption were to create police administrative boards. The reformers attempted to take law enforcement appointments out of the hands of mayors and city councilmen and place control in the hands of oversight committees. The Progressives believed that politics would be eliminated from policing by using this maneuver. In New York, for example, the Lexow Committee, which investigated the corrupt practices of the department, recommended the formation of a bipartisan Board of Police Commissioners in 1895. Theodore Roosevelt became a member of this board, but to his dismay found that the commissioners were powerless to improve the state of policing. The bipartisan nature of the board (two Democrats and two Republicans) meant that consensus could not be reached on important issues. As a result, by 1900 the New York City police were again under the influence of party politics. In the following year, the board of commissioners was abolished and the department was placed under the responsibility of a single commissioner (Walker, 1977). Other cities had similar experiences with the police commission approach. Cincinnati, Kansas City, St. Louis, and Baltimore were among those that adopted the commission, but found it to be short-lived. The major problem was still political—the police were viewed as an instrument of the political machine at the neighborhood level and reformers could not counter the effects of the Democratic or Republican parties.

Civil service was one answer to upgrading personnel. Officers would be selected and promoted based on merit, as measured by a competitive exam. Moreover, the officer would be subject to review by his superiors and removal from the force could take place if there was sufficient cause. Civil service met with some resistance by officers and reformers alike. The problem was that in guarding against the effects of patronage and favoritism, civil service became a rigid, almost inflexible procedure. Because it measured abstract knowledge rather than the qualities required for day-to-day work, civil service procedures were viewed as problematic. Eventually, the program did help to eliminate the more blatant forms of political patronage in almost all of the large police departments (Walker, 1977).

During this 30-year period, the efforts of the Progressive reformers did not change urban departments drastically. The reform movement resulted, in part, in the elimination of the widespread graft and corruption of the 1890s, but substantive changes in policing did not take place. Chiefs continued to lack power and authority, many officers had little or no education, training was limited, and the police role continued to include a wide variety of tasks.

Robert Fogelson (1977) suggests several reasons for the failure of reform. First, political machines were too difficult to break. Despite the efforts by the Progressives, politicians could still count on individual supporters to undermine the reforms. Second, police officers themselves resented the Progressives' interventions. Reformers were viewed by the police as individuals who knew little about police work and officers saw their proposals for change as ill-conceived. Finally, the reforms failed because the idea of policing could not be divorced from politics. That is, the character of the big-city police was interconnected with policymaking agencies that helped to decide which laws were enforced, which public was served, and whose peace was kept (Fogelson, 1977). Separating the police completely from politics could not take place.

THE EMERGENCE OF POLICE PROFESSIONALISM

A second reform effort emerged in the wake of the failure of the Progressives. Within police circles, a small cadre of chiefs sought and implemented a variety of innovations that would improve policing generally. From about 1910 to 1960, police chiefs carried on another reform movement, advocating that police adopt the professional model.

The professional department embodied a number of characteristics. First, the officers were experts; they applied knowledge to their tasks and were the only ones qualified to do the job. Second, the department was autonomous from external influences, such as political parties. This also meant that the department made its own rules and regulated its personnel. Finally, the department was administratively efficient, in that it carried out its mandate to enforce the law through modern technology and businesslike practices. These reforms were similar to those of the Progressives, but because they came from within police organizations themselves, they met with more success.

Leadership and technology assisted the movement to professionalize the police. Chiefs like Richard Sylvester, August Vollmer, and O.W. Wilson emphasized the use of innovative methods in police work. Samuel Walker (1977) notes that Sylvester, the chief of the Washington, D.C., police, helped to establish the idea of professionalism among police chiefs. As president of the International Association of Chiefs of Police (IACP), Sylvester inculcated the spirit of reform into the organization. He stressed acceptance of technological innovations, raised the level of discussion among chiefs to include crime control ideas, and promoted professionalism generally.

The major innovator among the chiefs was August Vollmer, chief of the Berkeley, California, police. Vollmer was known for his pioneering work in developing college-level police education programs, bicycle and automobile patrols, and scientific crime detection aids. His department was the first to use forensic science in solving crimes.

Vollmer's emphasis on the quality of police personnel was tied closely to the idea of the professional officer. Becoming an expert in policing meant having the requisite credentials. Vollmer initiated intelligence, psychiatric, and neurological tests by which to select applicants. He was the first police chief to actively recruit college students. In addition, he was instrumental in linking the police department with the University of California at Berkeley. Another concern of Vollmer's dealt with the efficient delivery of police services. His department became the first in the nation to use automobiles and the first to hire a full-time forensic scientist to help solve crimes (Douthit, 1975).

O.W. Wilson, Vollmer's student, followed in his mentor's footsteps by advocating efficiency within the police bureaucracy through scientific techniques. As chief in Wichita, Kansas, Wilson conducted the first systematic study of one-officer squad cars. He argued that one-officer cars were efficient, effective, and economical. Despite arguments from patrol officers that their safety was at risk, Wilson claimed that the public received better service with single-officer cars.

Wilson's other contributions include his classic textbook, *Police Administration*, which lays out specific ideas regarding the use of one-man patrol cars, deployment of personnel on the streets, disciplinary measures, and organizational structure. Later in his career, Wilson accepted a professorship at the University of California at Berkeley where he taught and trained law enforcement officers. In 1947, he founded the first professional school of criminology.

Other chiefs contributed to the professional movement as well. William Parker changed the Los Angeles Police Department (LAPD) from a corrupt, traditional agency to an innovative, professional organization. From 1950 to his death in 1966, Parker served as chief. He was known for his careful planning, emphasis on efficiency, and his rigorous personnel selection and training procedures. His public relations campaigns and adept political maneuvers enabled him to gain the respect of the media and community. As a result, the LAPD became a model for reform across the country.

Technological changes also enabled the police to move toward professionalism. The patrol car, two-way radio, and telephone altered the way in which the police operated and the manner in which citizens made use of the police. Motorized patrol meant more efficient coverage of the city and quicker response to calls for service. The two-way radio dramatically increased the supervisory capacity of the police; continuous contact between sergeant and patrol officer could be maintained. Finally, the telephone provided the link between the public and the police. Though not a new invention, its use in conjunction with the car and two-way radio meant that efficient response to calls for service could be realized.

Overall, the second reform movement met with more success than the Progressive attempt, though it did not achieve its goal of professionalism. Walker (1977) and Fogelson (1977) agree that the quality of police officers greatly improved during this period. Police departments turned away the ill-educated individual, but at the same time failed to draw college graduates to their ranks. In terms of autonomy, police reformers and others were able to reduce the influence of political parties in departmental affairs. Chiefs obtained more power and authority in their management abilities, but continued to receive input from political leaders. In fact, most chiefs remained political appointees. In terms of efficiency, the police moved forward in serving the public more quickly and competently. Technological innovations clearly assisted the police in this area, as did streamlining the organizations themselves. However, the innovations also created problems. Citizens came to expect more from the police—faster response times, more arrests, and less overall crime. These expectations, as well as other difficulties, led to trying times for the police in the 1960s.

RIOTS AND RENEWAL

Policing in America encountered its most serious crisis in the 1960s. The rise in crime, the civil rights movement, anti-war sentiment, and riots in the cities brought the police into the center of a maelstrom.

During the decade of the 1960s, crime increased at a phenomenal rate. Between 1960 and 1970 the crime rate per 100,000 persons doubled. Most troubling was the increase in violent crime—the robbery rate almost tripled during these ten years. As crime increased, so did the demands for its reduction. The police, in emphasizing its crime-fighting ability, had given the public a false expectation that crime and violence could be reduced. But with the added responsibility of more crime, the police were unable to live up to the expectation they had created. As a result, the public image of the police was tarnished.

The civil rights movement created additional demands for the police. The movement, which began in the 1950s, sought equality for black Americans in all facets of life. Sit-ins at segregated lunch counters, boycotts of bus services, attempts at integrating schools, and demonstrations in the streets led to direct confrontations with law enforcement officers. The police became the symbol of a society that denied blacks equal justice under the law.

Eventually, the frustrations of black Americans erupted into violence in northern and southern cities. Riots engulfed almost every major city between 1964 and 1968. Most of the disorders were initiated by a routine incident involving the police. The spark that ignited the riots occurred on July 16, 1964, when a white New York City police officer shot and killed a black teenager. Black leaders in the Harlem ghetto organized protests demanding disciplinary action against the officer. Two days later, the demonstrators marched on precinct headquarters, where rock-throwing began. Eventually, looting and burning erupted during the night and lasted for two full days. When the riot was brought under control, one person was dead, more than 100 injured, almost 500 arrested, and millions of dollars worth of property destroyed. In the following year, the Watts riot in Los Angeles led to more devastation. Thirty-four persons died, a thousand were injured, and 4,000 arrested. By 1966, 43 more riots broke out across the country and in 1967, violence in Newark and Detroit exceeded the 1965 Watts riot. Disorders engulfed Newark for five days, leaving 23 dead, while the Detroit riot a week later lasted nearly seven days and resulted in 43 deaths with $40 million in property damages.

On the final day of the Detroit riot, President Lyndon Johnson appointed a special commission to investigate the problem of civil disorder. The National Advisory Commission on Civil Disorders (The Kerner Commission) identified institutional racism as the underlying cause of the rioting. Unemployment, discrimination in jobs and housing, inadequate social services, and unequal justice at the hands of the law were among the problems cited by the commission.

Police actions were also cited as contributing to the disorders. Direct police intervention had sparked the riots in Harlem, Watts, Newark, and Detroit. In Watts and Newark, the riots were set off by routine traffic stops. In Detroit, a police raid on an after-hours bar in the ghetto touched off the disorders there. The police, thus, became the focus of national attention.

The Kerner Commission and other investigations found several problems in police departments. First, police conduct included brutality, harassment, and abuse of power. Second, training and supervision were inadequate. Third, police-community relations were poor. Fourth, the employment of black officers lagged far behind the growth of the black population.

As a means of coping with these problems in policing (and other agencies of the criminal justice system), President Johnson created a crime commission and Congress authorized federal assistance to criminal justice. The President's crime commission produced a final report that emphasized the need for more research, higher qualifications of criminal justice personnel, and greater coordination of the national crime-control effort. The federal aid program to justice agencies resulted in the Office of Law Enforcement Assistance, a forerunner of the Law Enforcement Assistance Administration (LEAA).

THE LEGACY OF THE '60S

The events of the 1960s forced the police, politicians, and policymakers to reassess the state of law enforcement in the United States. For the first time, academicians rushed to study the police in an effort to explain their problems and crises. With federal funding from LEAA and private organizations, researchers began to study the police from a number of perspectives. Sociologists, political scientists, psychologists, and historians began to scrutinize different aspects of policing. Traditional methods of patrol deployment, officer selection, and training were questioned. Racial discrimination in employment practices, in arrests, and in the use of deadly force were among the issues closely examined.

In addition, the professional movement itself came into question. As Walker notes, the legacy of professionalization was "ambiguous" (Walker, 1977:167). On one hand, the police made improvements in their level of service, training, recruitment, and efficiency. On the other hand, a number of problems remained and a number of new ones emerged. Corruption scandals continued to present problems. In New York, Chicago, and Denver, systematic corruption was discovered. Political parties persisted in their links to policing.

The professional movement had two unintended consequences. The first involved the development of a police subculture. The second was the problem of police-community relations. In terms of the subculture, police officers began to feel alienated from administrators, the media, and the public, and turned inward as a result. Patrol officers began to resent the police hierarchy because of the emphasis on following orders and regulations. While this established uniformity in performance and eliminated some abuses of power, it also stifled creativity and the talents of many officers. Rather than thinking for themselves (as professionals would), patrol officers followed orders given by sergeants, lieutenants, or other ranking officers. This led to morale problems and criticism of police administrators by the rank and file.

Patrol officers saw the media and the public as foes because of the criticism and disrespect cast their way. As the crime rate increased, newspaper accounts criticized the police for their inability to curtail it. As the riots persisted, some citizens cried for more order, while others demanded less oppression by the police on the streets. The conflicting messages given to the patrol officers by these groups led to distrust, alienation, and frustration. Only by standing together did officers feel comfortable in their working environment.

The second unintended consequence of professionalism was the problems it generated for police-community relations. Modern technology, like the patrol car, removed the officer from the street and eliminated routine contact with citizens. The impersonal style of professionalism often exacerbated police-community problems. Tactics such as aggressive patrol in black neighborhoods, designed to suppress crime efficiently, created more racial tensions.

These problems called into question the need for and effectiveness of professionalism. Some police administrators suggested abandoning the movement. Others sought to continue the effort while adjusting for and solving the difficulties. For the most part, the goal of professionalization remains operative. In the 1970s and 1980s, progressive police chiefs and organizations continue to press for innovations in policing. As a result, social science research has become an important part of policymaking decisions. By linking research to issues like domestic violence, repeat offenders, use of deadly force, training techniques, and selection procedures, police executives increase their ability to make effective decisions.

CONCLUDING REMARKS

This chapter has examined the history of American police systems from the English heritage through the 20th century. Major emphasis has been placed on the police role, though important events that shaped the development of the police have also been discussed. As can be seen through this review, a number of present-day issues have their roots in different epochs of American history. For example, the idea of community policing can be traced to the colonial period and to medieval England. Preventive patrol, legitimacy, authority, and professionalism are 18th- and 19th-century concepts. Riots, disorders, and corruption are not new to American policing; similar events occurred in the 19th century. Thus, by virtue of studying history, we can give contextual meaning to current police problems, ideas, and situations. By looking at the past, present-day events can be better understood.

ENDNOTES

1. This list of police histories is by no means a comprehensive one. A vast number of journal articles, books, and dissertations have been written since the 1960s.
2. A number of scholars have examined the "police function," particularly in the last 20 or so years. Among the most well-known are Wilson (1968), Skolnick (1966), Bittner (1971), and Goldstein (1977). Each of these authors subscribes to a different view of what the police should and should not do.

REFERENCES

Alfers, Kenneth G. 1975. "The Washington Police: A History, 1800–1886." Ph.D. Dissertation. George Washington University.

Bittner, Egon. 1970. *The Functions of the Police in Modern Society*. Chevy Chase, Maryland: National Institute of Mental Health.

Cei, Louis B. 1975. "Law Enforcement in Richmond: A History of Police Community Relations, 1737–1974." Ph.D. Dissertation. Florida State University.

Critchley, T.A. 1967. *A History of Police in England and Wales*. Montclair, New Jersey: Patterson Smith.

Douthit, Nathan. 1975. "August Vollmer: Berkeley's First Chief of Police and the Emergence of Police Professionalism." *California Historical Quarterly* 54 Spring: 101–124.

Fogelson, Robert. 1977. *Big-City Police*. Cambridge: Harvard University Press.

Goldstein, Herman. 1977. *Policing a Free Society*. Cambridge: Ballinger Press.

Klockars, Carl. 1985. *The Idea of Police*. Beverly Hills: Sage Publications.

Lane, Roger. 1967. *Policing the City: Boston, 1822–1885*. Cambridge: Harvard University Press.

——— 1980. "Urban Police and Crime in Nineteenth-Century America," in Michael Tonry and Norval Morris (eds.), *Crime and Justice: An Annual Review of Research, Volume 2*. Chicago: University of Chicago Press.

Litwack, Leon. 1961. *North of Slavery*. Chicago: University of Chicago Press.

Maniha, John K. 1970. "The Mobility of Elites in a Bureaucratizing Organization: The St. Louis Police Department, 1861–1961." Ph.D. Dissertation. University of Michigan.

Miller, Wilbur R. 1977. *Cops and Bobbies: Police Authority in New York and London, 1830–1870*. Chicago: University of Chicago Press.

Monkkonen, Eric H. 1981. *Police in Urban America, 1860–1920*. Cambridge: Cambridge University Press.

Radzinowicz, Leon. 1948–1968. *History of the English Criminal Law, Volumes 1–4*. New York: MacMillan.

Reichard, Maximilian I. 1975. "The Origins of Urban Police: Freedom and Order in Antebellum St. Louis." Ph.D. Dissertation. Washington University.

Reith, Charles. 1956. *A New Study of Police History*. Edinburgh.

Richardson, James F. 1970. *The New York Police: Colonial Times to 1901*. New York: Oxford University Press.

——— 1974. *Urban Police in the United States*. Port Washington, New York: Kennikat Press.

Rider, Eugene F. 1971. "The Denver Police Department: An Administrative, Organizational, and Operational History, 1858–1905." Ph.D. Dissertation. University of Denver.

Schneider, John C. 1980. *Detroit and the Problems of Order, 1830–1880*. Lincoln: University of Nebraska Press.

Skolnick, Jerome, 1966. *Justice Without Trial: Law Enforcement in Democratic Society*. New York: John Wiley and Sons.

Walker, Samuel. 1977. *A Critical History of Police Reform: The Emergence of Professionalism*. Lexington, Massachusetts: D.C. Heath and Company.

Wilson, James Q. 1968. *Varieties of Police Behavior: The Management of Law and Order in Eight Communities*. Cambridge: Harvard University Press.

Chapter 8

The New Policing

Confronting Complexity

by Herman Goldstein

Community policing is well on its way to becoming a common term in households across the nation. That is a satisfying development for many, but causes some anxiety and discomfort for others. What accounts for the mixed reactions?

Under the rubric of community policing, progressive police administrators and interested citizens have been working hard for more than a decade to design and implement a form of policing that better meets the extraordinary demands on the police in the 1990s. Within these circles the term "community policing" has been used to embrace and intricately web together initiatives that have long been advocated for modern-day policing. These efforts have stimulated more productive thought and experimentation than has occurred at any previous time in the history of policing in this country. They have also created a new feeling of excitement and optimism in a field that has desperately needed both. It is understandable, therefore, why the current wave of popular support for community policing is so welcome in many quarters. It gives a tremendous impetus to these new initiatives.

The downside of this new-found popularity is that "community policing" is widely used without any regard for its substance. Political leaders and, unfortunately, many police leaders latch onto the label for the positive images it evokes but do not invest in the concept itself. Some police personnel resist community policing initiatives because of the belief that they constitute an effort to placate an overly demanding and critical segment of the community that is intent on exercising more control over police operations.

Indeed, the popularity of the term has resulted in its being used to encompass practically all innovations in policing, from the most ambitious to the most mundane; from the most carefully thought through to the most casual. The label is being used in ways that increase public expectations of the police and create the impression that community policing will provide an instant solution not only for the problems of crime, disorder, and racial tension, but for many of the other acute problems that plague our urban areas as well.

With such varied meanings and such broad expectations, the use of "community policing" creates enormous problems for those seriously interested in bringing about meaningful change in the American police. Carefully developed initiatives bearing the community policing label, fragile by their very nature, are endangered because superficial programs are so vulnerable to attack.

From National Institute of Justice, *Research in Brief*, Washington, D.C.: United States Department of Justice, December, 1993.

One reaction to this dilemma is to press for definition and simplification, to seek agreement on a pure model of community policing. This pressure for simplification is joined by well-intentioned practitioners who, understandably, want to know—in specific detail—what they are supposed to do. *Oversimplification*, however, can be a deadly enemy to progress in policing. The field already suffers because so much in policing is oversimplified.

Crime, violence, and disorder, for example, are simple, convenient terms, but they disguise amorphous, complex problems. Their common and indiscriminate use, especially in defining the responsibilities of the police, places a heavy burden on the police and complicates the police task. The police respond with law enforcement and patrol— equally simple terms commonly used by the public without any awareness of the methods they embrace and their value. If community policing takes its place alongside law enforcement or patrol as just another generic response to a simplistic characterization of the police function, not much will have been gained and the concept will quickly lose its credibility.

RETHINKING THE POLICE ROLE

The policing of a free, diverse, and vibrant society is an awesome and complex task. The police are called upon to deal with a wide array of quite different behavioral problems, each perplexing in its own way. The police have tremendous power—to deny freedom and to use force, even to take a life. Individual officers exercise enormous discretion in using their authority and in making decisions that affect our lives. The very quality of life in this country and the equilibrium of our cities depend on the way in which the police function is carried out.

Given the awesome and complex nature of the police function, it follows that designing the arrangements and the organization to carry it out is equally complex. We are now in a period in which more attention is being given to the police function than at any prior time, a period in which we are rethinking, in all of its multiple dimensions, the arrangement for the policing of our society. We should not, therefore, lose patience because we have not yet come up with the perfect model; we should not get stalled trying to simplify change just to give uniform meaning to a single, catchy, and politically attractive term. We need to open up explorations rather than close them down. We need to better understand the complicated rather than search for the simple.

Some of the most common changes associated with community policing are already being implemented; for example, the permanent assignment of officers to specific beats with a mandate to get to know and relate to the community. There is now growing and persuasive support for decentralization, permanent assignments, and the development of "partnerships" between the police and the community. But these changes represent only a fragment of the larger picture.

Policing in the United States is much like a large, intricate, complex apparatus with many parts. Change of any one part requires changes in many others and in the way the parts fit and work together. For example, altering the way officers are assigned and how they patrol may be easy. But to gain full value from such changes, and to sustain them, changes are also necessary in the organization and leadership of the police department— in its staffing, supervision, training, and recruitment; and in its internal working environment. Thus, a change in direction requires more than tinkering. It requires, if it is to be effective, simultaneous changes in many areas affecting the enterprise. This, in turn, requires careful planning and coordination. And perhaps most important, it requires time, patience, and learning from experience.

Moreover, to succeed in improving policing, we need to move beyond the exclusive focus on the police *agency*. There is an urgent need to alter the public's expectations of the police. And we need to revise the fundamental provisions that we as a society make for carrying out the police function. For example:

- Refine the authority granted the police (curtail it in some areas and expand it in others).
- Recognize the discretion exercised by the police and provide a means for its review and control.
- Provide the police with the resources that will enable them to get their job done.

We need, in other words, without compromising our commitment to democratic values, to bring expectations and capacity more into harmony so that a job increasingly labeled as "impossible" can be carried out.

THE NATURE OF CHANGE

To illustrate, in some detail, the complexity of change in policing, it is helpful to examine five spheres in which change is now occurring. What types of issues arise? And what is the interrelationship and interdependence among the factors involved in these changes?

Refining the Police Function and Public Expectations

The new forms of policing expand the police function from crime fighting, without any abdication of that role, to include maintaining order, dealing with quality-of-life offenses, and fixing the "broken windows"—all now recognized as being much more important than previously believed. The police have become more proactive, committed to preventing incidents rather than simply *reacting* to them. These shifts in emphasis appear to have gained widespread support.

But we need to be aware of the avalanche of business that this expansion of the police function invites lest it constitute a serious self-inflicted wound. The volume and nature of the miscellaneous tasks that accrue to the police are many. Cutbacks in other government services only add to their number. In areas that are starved for social services, the slightest improvement in police response increases the demand on the police. As water seeks its own level, the vast array of problems that surface in a large urban area inevitably find their way to the agency most willing to accept them.

For example, consider the officer assigned to a specific neighborhood with a broad mandate to improve service. Within a very short period of time, that officer will be overwhelmed by the need for services that—despite the greatest creativity and resourcefulness—far exceeds his or her capacity to deliver.

Very often the police *can* do more to satisfy citizen needs. They can identify problems and take actions that result in mitigating or solving them when they are given the time and license to do so. But in the larger scheme of things the need to reduce public expectations is every bit as important as the need to broaden the police function—not simply to make limited resources fit the demand, but for more complex reasons. Many of the most troublesome aspects of policing stem from the pressure that has been exerted on the police to appear omnipotent, to do more than they are authorized, trained, and equipped to do.

Police tend to like challenges. But the challenge to fill needs, to live up to expectations, can lead to the taking of shortcuts, the stretching of authority and, as a consequence, the potential for abuse of that authority. It is demoralizing to the thoughtful, dedicated officer to create the expectation that he or she can do more than take the edge off some of the more intractable problems that the police confront.

The new policing seeks to make the police job more achievable by realigning what the police do and do not do by giving higher priority to some tasks and lower priority to others, by reducing public expectations and leveling with the public about police capacity, by engaging the public in taking steps to help themselves, and by connecting with other agencies and the private sector in ways that ensure that citizens referred to them will be helped. There is a need to invest much more, in our individual communities, in working through the questions that arise in trying to achieve this better alignment.

Getting Involved in the Substance of Policing

A common theme in initiatives under the community policing umbrella is the emphasis on improving relationships with the citizenry. Such improvement is vital in order to reduce tensions, develop mutual trust, promote the free exchange of information, and acquaint officers with the culture and lifestyle of those being policed.

Improved relationships are important. They would constitute a major advance in some cities. But many would argue that they merely lay a groundwork and create an environment in which to strive for more. When citizens ask if community policing works, they are not so much interested in knowing if the community likes the police or if the police are getting along with the community. Rather, they usually want to know if the community policing initiative has had an impact on the problems of concern to them: their fear of using the streets, the abandoned cars in the neighborhood, the gang that has been intimidating them. If the initiatives that have been taken do not go beyond improving relationships, there is a risk that community policing will become just another means by which police operate without having a significant, demonstrable impact on the problems the police are expected to handle.

This tendency in policing to become preoccupied with means over ends is obviously not new. It was this concern that gave rise to the work on problem-oriented policing. The police must give more substance to community policing by getting more involved in analyzing and responding to the specific problems citizens bring to their attention. This calls for a much heavier investment by the police in understanding the varied pieces of their business, just as the medical field invests in understanding different diseases. It means that police, more than anyone else, should have a detailed understanding of such varied problems as homicides involving teenage victims, drive-by shootings, and carjackings. And it means that a beat officer should have in-depth knowledge about the corner drug house, the rowdy teenage gang that assembles at the convenience store on Friday night, and the panhandler who harasses passersby on a given street corner. Analyzing each of these quite different problems in depth leads to the realization that what may work for one will not work for the other, that each may require a different combination of different responses. That is the beginning of wisdom in policing: One size clearly does not fit all.

Problem-solving is being integrated into community policing initiatives in many jurisdictions. It dominates the commitment to change in some jurisdictions. Conference and training sessions for police have, with increased frequency, focused on such problems as the homeless, family violence, high-risk youth, child abuse, and school violence.

More of the momentum associated with community policing must be focused on these and similar problems. Smarter policing in this country requires a sustained effort within policing to research substantive problems, to make use of the mass of information and data on specific problems accumulated by individual police agencies, to experiment with different alternative responses, to evaluate these efforts, and to share the results of these evaluations with police across the nation. It would be useful to do more to reorient the work of research and development units in police departments, and to entice some of the best minds in the field of criminology and related specialties to assist in these efforts. The police should not only make greater use of research done by others; they should themselves be engaged in research.

Rethinking the Relationship Between the Police and the Criminal Justice System

Buried in all of the rhetoric relating to community policing is the fact that, with little notice and in subtle ways, the longstanding relationship between the police and the criminal justice system is being redefined. This is a radical change, but it is given scant attention in the literature on community policing. And the full consequences of the changes—and their relationship to some of the developments most commonly associated with community policing—have not been adequately explored.

The enforcement of criminal law is inherent in the police role. The great emphasis on enforcement affects the shape of their organizations, the attitudes and priorities of their personnel, and their relationship with the community. Significantly, police officers are referred to as "law enforcement officers." The [perceived] need for objectivity and neutrality in law enforcement often results in the police being characterized as having no discretion. And the commitment to enforcement encourages the police to act in ways designed to inflate the public's impression of their capacity to enforce the law in the hope that their image alone will reduce crime and disorder.

Advanced forms of community policing reject many of the characteristics stemming from the emphasis on enforcement. A neighborhood police officer, for example, is expected to have a much broader interest than simply enforcing the criminal law, to exhaust a wide range of alternatives before resorting to arrest for minor offenses, to exercise broad discretion, and to depend more on resourcefulness, persuasion, or cajoling than on coercion, image, or bluff.

Reconciling these different perspectives has always been difficult. Some would even argue the two postures are incompatible. Simplistically, they are often distinguished as the "hard" and "soft" approaches in policing. But as a result of a sequence of developments in the past decade, the difference between the two approaches has been diminished.

What has happened? So long as the police were intricately intertwined with the criminal justice system, they came to depend more heavily on the system. Thus, as violence and, especially, crimes associated with drugs increased, the police made more and more arrests of serious offenders. And to deal with disorder on the streets they arrested thousands of minor offenders as well, often stretching their authority somewhat (as police are pressured to do) in order to restore order. Predictably, the criminal justice systems in most large urban areas, and many smaller ones as well, have been overwhelmed to the point that it is no longer possible for the system to accept some serious offenders, let alone minor offenders.

The consequences of recognizing that the capacity of the criminal justice system has limits are more far-reaching than is commonly recognized. Police can no longer use arrest, as they so freely did in the past, to deal with a wide variety of ambiguous situations. Moreover, the aura of authority on which the police have so heavily depended for getting so much of their job done, rooted in the capacity to arrest, has been greatly diminished. Police officers today simply do not appear as powerful and threatening to those who most frequently come in contact with them because they can no longer use the criminal justice system as they once did.

What does this mean for some of the central themes under the community policing umbrella? It means that there are new, pragmatic reasons for searching intensively for alternatives to the criminal justice system as the way in which to get the police job done.

It also means that there is now an added incentive to cultivate positive relationships with the community. The police need to replace the amorphous authority that they previously derived from the criminal justice system and on which they depended so heavily in the past. What better way to do this than arm themselves with what Robert Peel characterized in 1829 as that most powerful form of authority, the "public approval of their existence, actions, and behavior?"

The congested state of affairs in the criminal justice system means, too, that the police must conserve their use of that system for those situations in which it is most appropriate and potentially most effective. This latter need should lead the police and others committed to community policing to . . .[speak] out for a more sensible national criminal justice policy that curbs the indiscriminate overuse of a system that will, if not checked, draw scarce funds away from the police and away from preventive programs where those funds can do more good.

Searching for Alternatives

The diversification of policing—the move from primary dependence on the criminal law to the use of a wide range of different responses—is among the most significant changes under the community policing umbrella. It enables the police to move away from having to "use a hammer (the criminal justice system) to catch a fly"; it enables them to fine-tune their responses. It gives them a range of options (or tools) that in number and variety come closer to matching the number and variety of problems they are expected to handle. These may include informal, common sense responses used in the past but never formally authorized.

The primary and most immediate objective in authorizing the police to use a greater range of alternatives is to improve police effectiveness. Quite simply, mediating a dispute, abating a nuisance, or arranging to have some physical barrier removed—without resorting to arrest—may be the best way to solve a problem.

But there are additional benefits in giving police officers a larger repertoire of responses. Currently, for example, one of the greatest impediments to improvement in policing is the strength of the police subculture. That subculture draws much of its strength from a secret shared among police: that they are compelled to bend the law and take shortcuts in order to get their job done. Providing the police with legitimate, clear-cut means to carry out their functions enables them to operate more honestly and openly and, therefore, has the potential for reducing the strength and, as a consequence, the negative influence of the police subculture.

The diversification of options is also responsive to one of the many complexities in the staffing of police agencies. It recognizes, forthrightly, the important role of the individual police officer as a decision-maker—a role the officer has always had but one that has rarely been acknowledged. Acknowledging and providing alternatives contribute toward redefining the job of a police officer by placing a value on thinking, on creativity, and on decisionmaking. It credits the officer with having the ability to analyze incidents and problems and gives the officer the freedom to choose among various appropriate responses.

Changing to a system in which so much responsibility is invested in the lowest level employee, one who already operates with much independence on the streets, will not occur quickly or easily. And absent sufficient preparation, the results may be troublesome. This is especially so if officers, in their enthusiasm, blend together community support and their desire to please the community to justify using methods that are either illegal or improper. And implementation in a department that has a record of abuse or corruption is obviously much more problematic. Those concerned about control, however, must recognize that the controls on which we currently depend are much less effective than they are often thought to be. Preparations for the empowerment of officers requires changes in recruitment standards and training, establishing guidelines for the exercise of discretion, and inculcating values in officers that, in the absence of specific directions, guides their decision-making. Meeting these needs in turn connects with the fifth and final dimension of change.

Changing the Working Environment in a Police Agency

If new forms of policing are to take hold, the working environment within police agencies must change. Much has been written about new management styles supportive of community policing. But with a few remarkable exceptions, relatively little has actually been achieved. And where modest changes have been made, they are often lost when a change in administration occurs or when the handling of a single incident brings embarrassment, resulting in a reversion to the old style of control.

"Working environment" means simply the atmosphere and expectations that superiors set in relating to their subordinates. In a tradition-bound department, managers, supported by voluminous, detailed rules, tend to exercise a tight, paramilitary, top-down form of control—perhaps reflecting the way in which they have historically sought to achieve control in the community.

The initiatives associated with community policing cannot survive in a police agency managed in traditional ways. If changes are not made, the agency sets itself up for failure. Officers will not be creative and will not take initiatives if a high value continues to be placed on conformity. They will not be thoughtful if they are required to adhere to regulations that are thoughtless. And they will not aspire to act as mature, responsible adults if their superiors treat them as immature children.

But properly trained and motivated officers, given the freedom to make decisions and act independently, will respond with enthusiasm. They will grasp the concept, appreciate its many dimensions, and skillfully fill their new roles. These officers will solve problems, motivate citizens to join together to do things for themselves, and create a feeling of security and goodwill. Equally important, the officers will find their work demanding but very satisfying. In rank and file officers, there exists an enormous supply of talent, energy, and commitment that, under quality leadership, could rapidly transform American policing.

The major impediment to tapping this wellspring has been a failure to engage and elicit a commitment from those having management and supervisory responsibilities. It is disheartening to witness a meeting of the senior staff of a police agency in which those in attendance are disconnected and often openly hostile to changes initiated by the chief executive and supported by a substantial proportion of the rank and file. It is equally disheartening to talk with police officers on the street and officers of lower supervisory rank who cite their *superior officer* as their major problem, rather than the complexity of their job.

Because the problem is of such magnitude, perhaps, some bold—even radical—steps by legislative bodies and municipal chief executives may be necessary. Perhaps early retirement should be made more attractive for police executives who resist change. Perhaps consideration should be given to proposals recently made in England that call for the elimination of unnecessary ranks, and for making continuation in rank conditional on periodic review.

But before one can expect support for such measures, the public will need to be satisfied that police executives have exhausted whatever means are available to them for turning the situation around. When one looks at what has been done, it is troubling to find that a department's investment in the reorientation of management and supervisory personnel often consisted of no more than "a day at the academy"—and sometimes not even that. How much of the frustration in eliciting support from management and supervision stems from the fact that agencies have simply not invested enough in engaging senior officers, in explaining why change is necessary, and in giving these supervisors and managers the freedom required for them to act in their new role?

Some efforts to deal with the problem have been encouraging. The adoption of "Total Quality Management" [TQM] in policing has demonstrated very positive results and holds much promise. It ought to be encouraged. An important lesson can be learned from experiences with TQM. Training to support changes of the magnitude now being advocated in policing requires more than a one-shot effort consisting of a few classroom lectures. It requires a substantial commitment of time in different settings spread over a long period, a special curriculum, the best facilitators, and the development of problems, case studies, and exercises that engage the participants. It requires the development of teamwork in which subordinates contribute as much as superiors. And it requires that the major dimension of the training take the form of conscious change in the day-to-day interaction of personnel—not in a training setting, but on the job.

CONCLUSION

Dwelling on complexity is risky, for it can be overwhelming and intimidating. It is difficult. It turns many people off. But for those who get involved, the results can be very rewarding.

There have been extraordinary accomplishments in policing in the past two decades by police agencies that have taken on some of these difficult tasks. There is an enormous reservoir of ability and commitment in police agencies, especially among rank and file officers, and a willingness on the part of individual citizens and community groups at the grass roots level to engage with the police and support change. Viewed collectively, these achievements should be a source of optimism and confidence. By building on past progress and capitalizing on current momentum, change that is deeper and more lasting can be achieved.

But there is an even more compelling, overriding incentive to struggle with these complexities. We are being challenged today to commit ourselves anew to our unique character as a democracy, to the high value we as a nation place on diversity, ensuring equality, protecting individual rights, and guaranteeing that all citizens can move about freely and enjoy tranquil lives. The social problems that threaten the character of the nation are increasing, not decreasing. It will take major changes—apart from those in the police—to reduce these problems. In this turbulent period it is more important than ever that we have a police capacity that is sensitive, effective, and responsive to the country's unique needs, and that, above all else, is committed to protecting and extending democratic values. That is a high calling indeed.

Chapter 9

Contemporary Policing in a Community Era

by Quint C. Thurman

Whether the problem for a community is youths out too late, speeding cars, or drive-by shootings, the ability of the police to respond to issues raised by citizens is constrained by legal, social, and political considerations. By law, the police are limited in the amount of force they can apply and by the policies and procedures they must follow in any particular situation. Similarly, citizen expectations may further reduce what the police can do according to what citizens believe is acceptable police behavior. In addition, police leaders may have to consider their possible actions in terms of the support or resistance from certain interested and organized groups.

Economic forces also interact with legal, social, and political systems to play an important role in the delivery of criminal justice services. On the one hand there is poverty, which Aristotle once referred to as the "parent of revolution and crime." On the other hand, there are expectations about the economic standards of living that we as American should aspire to regardless of our financial circumstances. Americans seem to believe that the United States is the land of opportunity and that anyone who wants to can succeed economically. But when poverty, lack of education, or other social conditions block access to jobs and salaries that can support a desired standard of living, people may be tempted to resort to illegal means to gain highly valued goods.

Americans have greater access to material goods than most other nationalities have and are more constantly being encouraged through marketing and advertising to believe that life is not complete unless we drive the best cars, wear the best clothes, or vacation in the most exotic places. Unfortunately, all this emphasis on material success comes without much attention being paid to the price of success in terms of rules and legal obligations. The result is that Americans seem to have incredibly large appetites for enjoying themselves, a large menu from which to choose, and the ability to ignore the known complications that result from making unwise or illegal choices. Thus, the individual freedoms that we enjoy as citizens of the United States also give rise to perplexing social problems. For example, such freedom of choice lends itself to greater opportunity for crime in a variety of ways—more things to steal, more people to steal from, and more people willing to consider stealing as an appropriate way to obtain the things they want.

AMERICA IS ORGANIZED FOR CRIME

Steven Messner and Richard Rosenfeld have suggested that American society in partic-ular is organized for crime and disorder.[1] At no other time in the history of this country have civil liberties been so high, extending through nearly all age groups. At no other time have people felt that it is their right as American citizens to enjoy life and all that it may offer in terms of expressing themselves and feeding their appetites for material goods. Simultaneously, Messner and Rosenfeld note that Americans are all too willing to down-play the means that people use to get what they want. So not only are many Americans organized for crime, they also are relatively unorganized for controlling it. This makes policing more difficult in the United States than in many other countries.

Traditionally, ensuring that people obey the law has been attended to by instruction from families, churches, schools, friends, and co-workers. People learn what to do and what not to do from those who are closest to them during their adolescent years, when they are being socialized. However, when they do not receive adequate instruction from these institutions, their unruly behavior may attract disapproval and, ultimately, police attention.

Public expectations about who should take the lead in handling crime and crime-related matters have not changed all that much over time, except for one subtle difference. Although American citizens still fundamentally believe that it is the police who can make people obey the law by issuing citations or using arrests or punishments if they refuse, the public also has begun to recognize that the police cannot solve crime problems alone. Both the public and police departments around the world are starting to realize that by working together they can do more to improve the quality of life in their communities than when the police concentrate only on basic law enforcement.

COMMUNITY POLICING: A SENSIBLE RESPONSE TO SOCIAL PROBLEMS

Sometimes social problems are best solved by bringing the public and the police together to work on them. For example, in the case of Mountlake Terrace, Washington, the police first began working on the youth gang delinquency problem by getting residents older than 17 years to endorse the traditional law enforcement response of a curfew (the police chief actually went to the high school and asked 18-year-olds what they thought about keep-ing 17-year-olds and younger teens off of the streets after 10 P.M.). But as the idea of a curfew was debated around town, this not-so-typical chief began to see that local residents were taking a harder look at the problem. They seemed determined to try to reach its root cause rather than just allow the police to employ a typical police response that only dealt with one symptom of the larger problem. Researchers David Mueller and Cary Heck describe what happened next.

> Instead of resorting to a quick-fix solution to the problem, Chief Turner decided to hold pub-lic meetings on the issue to allow residents to vent their frustrations and air their opinions about possible alternatives. Out of these meetings arose the idea that perhaps a better way to con-trol juvenile delinquency would be to involve area youth in a sports-related program that would simply keep them busy and off public streets on weekend nights when problems seemed to be at their worst. The idea was that youths would be forced to choose between attending

the late-night program or being escorted home after curfew by the local police department. But would a 'midnight basketball program' really produce the outcomes that local residents were hoping for? After holding several of these meetings, the suggestion was made to offer the participants free food to increase their participation and turnout. Slowly, but surely, a grassroots movement was set in motion that eventually led to the establishment of the Mountlake Terrace Community Action Resource Team (CART). Rather than dealing with the symptoms of juvenile problems in a revolving-door fashion, Chief Turner and CART sought solutions that would get at the root of juvenile crime and gang delinquency.

After reviewing a number of alternative strategies in various cities around the nation, Turner and CART established a collaborative, nontraditional crime prevention program in Mountlake Terrace in June 1992, called the Neutral Zone. As originally designed, the Neutral Zone was created to: (1) reduce the likelihood of youth involvement in, as victims or as perpetrators, crimes or violence on Mountlake Terrace streets specifically during the most active portions of the week; (2) make inroads into the youth gang culture for purposes of prevention, intervention, and suppression of youth gang activity; (3) provide an arena where recreation and services were available to high-risk youth during the most crucial hours; and (4) allow youth, community volunteers, police, and other helping professionals to work together in seeking more positive outcomes for high-risk youth.

Designed and implemented as a community-based response to the problem of youth crime, the Neutral Zone offers juvenile participants, ages 13 to 20, an alternative environment in which to more productively pass their time during the most crime-prone hours of the weekend on Fridays and Saturdays from 10:00 P.M. to 2:00 A.M. Though originally designed to act as a late-night sports program, the Neutral Zone has since evolved into an educational and social services–oriented outreach program that has substantially reduced juvenile crime in the area (by some estimates, as much as 63 percent).[2]

DEFINING COMMUNITY POLICING

Many definitions of community policing exist. In one of the earliest versions of this concept, John Angell coined the term democratic policing to distinguish current practices of the time from those which he thought would better fit the American political system.[3] Angell suggested that American policing had become too far removed from its initial purpose of creating a safe society that would maximize freedom regarding the exchange of ideas, movement across jurisdictions, and religious practices. He called for a change from police who are the crime experts, solely oriented toward enforcing criminal laws to a situation where citizens have a voice in deciding how police services should be carried out in the community. After all, it is the citizens who pay the taxes that support policing services and the public has a right to expect accountability from the police whenever tax dollars are spent.

Perhaps the most frequently used definition of community policing is the one that was developed by the late Robert Trojanowicz and Bonnie Bucqueroux. For these authors, community policing, unlike previous attempts to reform the police, is a set of values rather than a complete package of strategies. In their book, *Community Policing: A Contemporary Perspective*, they offer this definition of community policing:

> [A] new philosophy of policing, based on the concept that police officers and citizens working together in creative ways can help solve contemporary community problems related to crime, fear of crime, social and physical disorder, and neighborhood decay.[4]

More recently, William A. Geller and Guy Swanger's views have expanded the definition of community policing even further to clarify not only what community policing is but also what it is not:

> Community policing is a reorientation of policing philosophy and strategy away from the view that police alone can reduce crime, disorder and fear. The strategy is based on the view that police don't help their communities very much by placing primary reliance on random preventive patrolling, rapid response to calls for service irrespective of their urgency, post-incident investigations to identify and arrest offenders, and other primarily reactive criminal justice system tactics.[5]

Perhaps the definition that explains community policing in the fewest words is one expressed by a former police superintendent of Edmonton, Canada. Police Superintendent Chris Braiden defines community policing in light of the golden rule for getting along well with other people: "Police others as you would have them police you."[6]

DEFINING COMMUNITY POLICING ACCORDING TO FOUR DIMENSIONS

Despite some of the best efforts to define the concept of community policing, there remain differences of opinion about what exactly community policing is or is not. As Gary Cordner points out, "Community policing remains many things to many people."[7] He observes that four major dimensions help to identify the shape of community policing.[8]

First, the philosophical dimension of community policing contains the values of the department and what its membership thinks it ought to be doing. Central ideas and beliefs about the role of citizen input, the police mission, and how best to serve the public say a lot about a department's philosophy. Community-oriented police departments value citizen input, define their mission more broadly than just law enforcement, and believe that policing must be tailored to the needs of the community.[9]

Second, the strategic dimension represents a more "operational" version of a department's philosophy. The strategic dimension has to do with translating the philosophical side into practice through planning. Here the department thinks through how best to reorient its operations, geographic focus, and emphasis on crime prevention. Reexamining the way it investigates crimes, assigning officers to cover beats rather than neighborhoods, and allocating resources to prevent crimes in the first place are examples of issues addressed strategically.[10]

The third dimension is tactical, concerned with that part of the department involving daily operations that currently are in place. Moving from ideas to planning to daily operations indicates a clear progression from the abstract to the concrete, from what the department might imagine to what it actually does to what the public actually sees. Community-oriented police departments will stand out from more traditionally focused departments in that the former emphasize positive citizen interactions, police-community partnerships, and problem-solving activities.[11]

The fourth and final dimension is organizational. It concerns the structure of the department and its personnel, the department's management practices, and how the department maintains and distributes information related to evaluating employees, policies, and procedures. Cordner points out that community policing favors a work environment where employee input is highly valued, mentoring is encouraged, and systematic evaluation methods are in place.[12]

PERF'S FIVE PERSPECTIVES OF COMMUNITY POLICING

A closer look at the various definitions of community policing and the police programs that are said to be community oriented reveals common features. For example, the Police Executive Research Forum (PERF) categorizes the various approaches to community policing it has observed according to five perspectives.[13] First, is the *deployment* perspective, that is, community policing is seen as a way to move officers closer to citizens on the streets, whether by foot patrol, police substations, or some other means that increases the familiarity of officers with the persons and places they police. As citizens and police get to know each other better, levels of trust between them should rise and there should be more sharing of information.

A second perspective identified by PERF is *community revitalization*. This view focuses on preventing neighborhood decay and fighting the fear of crime by eliminating those features of a neighborhood setting that cause people who live there to feel afraid. This approach fits well with the idea that turning a neighborhood or community around, or preventing it from going downhill in the first place, requires maintaining the upkeep of property so that residents seem to be keeping a watchful eye on the area. Allowing things to run down to a state of disrepair or neglect invites crime and disorder, since those who sell illegal drugs or engage in other criminal activity will view such places as uncontrolled space that can readily be used to carry out illegal acts. This view fits James Q. Wilson and George L. Kelling's notion of "broken windows":

> That link [between order maintenance and crime prevention] is similar to the process whereby one broken window becomes many. The citizen who fears the ill-smelling drunk, the rowdy teenager, or the importuning beggar is not merely expressing his distaste for unseemly behavior, he is also giving voice to a bit of folk wisdom that happens to be a correct generalization—namely, that serious street crime flourishes in areas in which disorderly conduct goes unchecked. The unchecked panhandler is, in effect, the first broken window. Muggers and robbers, whether opportunistic or professional, believe they reduce their chances of being caught where potential victims are already intimidated by prevailing conditions. If the neighborhood cannot keep a bothersome panhandler from annoying passersby, the thief may reason, it is even less likely to call the police to identify a potential mugger or to interfere if the mugging actually takes place.[14]

PERF identifies *problem solving* as a third perspective. In this view, community policing may be seen as a focused approach to a crime problem that involves both the police and the community in identifying a problem, analyzing its scope, developing a proactive response, and then assessing how well their solution worked. This approach, which readers might recognize from the previously cited example of Mountlake Terrace's Neutral Zone, was developed by Herman Goldstein as "problem-oriented policing."[15]

A fourth perspective recognized by PERF is the *customer*; which emphasizes the importance of listening to the needs of citizens. Citizen priorities would help determine the importance that police leadership places upon the various crime and crime-related issues that the community would like addressed before any others. An important feature of this perspective is the emphasis on open lines of communication with local residents, frequently involving the use of citizen advisory groups and citizen surveys to provide feedback on police performance and insight into the priorities that the public assigns to various problems.

The fifth and final perspective recognized by PERF is *legitimacy*, which emphasizes establishing the credibility of the police as a fair and equitable public-service organization that dispenses resources evenly and effectively throughout the community. Of particular importance for this perspective is the just treatment of the concerns of racial minorities and other groups that historically have suffered from poor police-community relations.

A NEW DEFINITION OF COMMUNITY POLICING

Some scholars believe that community policing should remain a loosely defined concept. For example, Mark Moore suggests that concepts such as community policing and problem-oriented policing should be viewed "not as new programmatic ideas or administrative arrangements but as ideas that seek to redefine the overall goals and methods of policing."[16] Moore suggests that such ambiguity allows police departments more flexibility to try any of a wide variety of "community-policing" approaches they think might work to control and prevent crime. As long as the public approves of the community policing concept, virtually anything that police departments try that they might label community policing is bound to be given some initial community support.

> In short, it is partly the ambiguity of the concept that is stimulating the wide pattern of experimentation we are observing. In this sense, it is important that the concept mean something, but not something too specific. Ambiguity is a virtue.[17]

For our purposes here, community policing might be defined as *the guiding philosophy for the delivery of police services that relies upon positive interactions among police, other public servants, and community representatives to serve local needs regarding crime control, crime prevention, and crime-related quality-of-life issues*. This definition stresses three elements.

POSITIVE INTERACTIONS

First, it emphasizes *positive interactions* between the police and others who are not specially equipped to deal with the problems of crime in society. Crime is seen as a problem that is larger than the police can handle by themselves. Greater resources than the police can muster by themselves must be brought to bear to deal with crime and related issues.

Positive interactions, as the term is used here, also implies a partnership of an unusual or extraordinary nature. A key partnership that can be expected from community policing is between the police department and the public it serves, who do not necessarily have any policing expertise at all. Such a role for the public is unusual because citizen involvement in policing during the professional era was limited to that of victim, bystander, or criminal.[18] Community policing gives ordinary citizens a primary role that does not require them to become involved in a criminal matter until the police can show interest in their concerns, their ideas about what to do, and their willingness to participate in a solution. Citizens who wish to be involved with helping the police in this way can be proactive before any particular crime occurs, just like police who might invest time in crime prevention strategies rather than waiting to react to crimes that already have occurred.

Community policing changes the very nature of usual interactions between police and residents of the communities they patrol. Consider officers assigned to the 11:00 P.M. to 7:00 A.M., or "graveyard," shift. They have little opportunity to meet the average, law-abiding citizens whose homes, businesses, and streets they protect. Instead, the graveyard officers usually receive calls for service that mainly involve domestic violence, public drunkenness, and bar fights. Exposed to the worst side of human nature, they run the risk of losing sight of the good citizens they serve.

Similarly, the kinds of situations that face patrol officers assigned to high-crime areas can lead to poor police perceptions of the public. William Bratton, a former police commissioner in Boston and New York City, writes that "A cop will try to stay within the bounds of acceptable behavior, but sometimes, when he gets immersed in the job, he begins to identify more with the people in the street than with his own family and friends."[19] When frequent and negative interactions with the public become the norm, it is the "bad guys" who become a police officer's reference point for judging all of society. "In high-crime precincts, cops spend a lot of their time dealing with hard-core criminals, sociopaths, and psychopaths."[20] As a result, Bratton concludes that these negative experiences encourage officers to develop a "street morality" when dealing with citizens, that in turn creates public mistrust of the police. And the police can ill afford to risk further mistrust by its citizens in light of sensational accounts of brutality and excessive force in 1990s cases such as those of Abner Louima and Amadou Diallo.

Bratton has argued that policing in New York City could not succeed without public support. This same statement applies just as well outside New York. Negative experiences with the public can reinforce impressions of the public as untrustworthy and fickle and create barriers to police-citizen partnerships and problem solving. It is through positive interactions with the great majority of law-abiding citizens who appreciate police services that the police are brought into favorable contact with those persons who they are called upon to "protect and serve."

CONTACTS WITH OTHER GROUPS

The second element in the definition is contact between the police, who ordinarily are seen as the experts in criminal matters, and other groups in the community. Sometimes this contact may mean the involvement of other public service agencies such as the courts, social-welfare agencies, and sanitation departments, depending on the role that each might contribute to helping a police-community partnership work through a crime or crime-related problem. Effective contact requires the participation of local citizens who either formally or informally represent identifiable groups or the community-at-large in a deliberate effort to resolve crime or crime-related matters that affect the local quality of life.

The way citizens are included in a police-community partnership is an important issue that may distinguish community policing from more traditional policing approaches that are passed off as community policing in smaller towns and jurisdictions. Although "small-town" police administrators may be practicing community policing by virtue of their familiarity with the needs of the citizens whom they police, a genuine effort to implement community policing requires the inclusion of a broad representation of all the citizens of a community. Coffee shop discussions with mayors, business leaders, and close friends in order to keep a pulse on the needs of the community do not by themselves provide a good foundation for forming police-community partnerships. Representation from all (or as many as possible) of the diverse ethnic, social, and economic groups that make up the community has to be undertaken in a systematic and deliberate way. Obtaining input from the broad cross section of people who live in a community and then getting them involved in police-community partnerships is a continuous challenge for police departments that are committed to community policing.

EXPANDED MISSION

The third element in the definition is an expanded mission of the police to include whatever issues the community believes are crimes or related to crime. Instead of the police deciding what are the most significant issues of the day, they set priorities in consultation with the public about what their concerns are. Research shows that the police believe that most citizens share their concern for better protection against serious and violent crimes that occur fairly infrequently. When asked directly, however, about what issues cause them most concern or which crimes make them most fearful, citizens, according to surveys, are more interested in controlling the less serious law violations that occur more frequently. In most communities, it is barking dogs, noisy neighbors, and speeding cars that trouble citizens the most, because these are the "crimes" that citizens usually see.

When the police begin asking citizens about which issues deserve more police attention, they also create an opportunity to begin discussions with citizens about what steps should be taken to develop likely solutions. Without this type of interaction, police departments can be out of touch with citizen concerns and unaware of how citizens might be willing to participate in finding a solution. Similarly, the public cannot understand the perspective of the police or the police's lack of awareness of the everyday problems that concern most citizens. The public also will not know the limitations of the police in terms of their resources or how the public might contribute to problem solving. Keeping citizens and the police apart only ensures that understanding will not occur, needs will go unheard, and problem solving partnerships will not develop. In short, without these partnerships, crime control will prove more difficult.

LIMITATIONS IN DEFINING COMMUNITY POLICING

One drawback of such a broad definition of community policing as the one just proposed is that it is not particularly useful for telling students how to do community policing. A simpler definition may be to move from the abstract, conceptual level to one that is more concrete or operational. For example, the Community Policing Consortium identifies two key components of community policing: community engagement and problem solving.

Refining these terms, David Bayley suggests that the police must consult with communities to understand their needs, mobilize resources that address citizen concerns, and pay particular attention to the underlying conditions that cause crime and its symptoms to occur.[21] A third key component of community policing is organizational change.

One might conclude that the definition of community policing is still evolving and that no one definition will be agreeable to everyone. Whatever the definition, however, it is clear that community policing remains a popular alternative to the professional model of policing. The research literature suggests that "While community policing can be many things to many people, the fuzziness of this concept has not slowed the enthusiasm for it among law enforcement executives in the United States."[22] Results from a recent National Institute of Justice study indicate that "over 80 percent of the police chiefs surveyed were either practicing community policing or had plans to do so in the near future. The problems begin when agencies start asking what it looks like, how to do it, and where to start."[23]

CRITICISMS OF COMMUNITY POLICING

Community policing also has its critics. For example, Roy Roberg and Jack Kuykendall question whether community policing is truly a welcome change or is just seen by police administrators as a continuation of the public relations campaigns begun by the police in the 1950s and 1960s that ultimately led to the introduction of team policing in the 1970s.[24] At that time, team-policing strategies were based on the ideas of decentralizing police forces throughout a jurisdiction and having officers assigned to a beat provide personalized services to the citizens with whom they came into contact. Team policing, like community policing, assumed that more familiarity between officers and citizens would result in officers developing a greater sense of responsibility for what went on in a neighborhood. In turn, increased trust and cooperation with the police would make neighborhood residents want to do more on their own to prevent crime.

Summarizing the studies of team policing, Moore concluded that this "first modern model of what is becoming community policing" showed many positive results, including favorable reactions to it by both citizens and the police, decreases in crime, and improvements in the quality of neighborhood life."[25] Nevertheless, team policing died out by the late 1970s. Although there may be many reasons, one likely explanation is that team policing failed because it required too much change in the formal and informal organization of the police. Critics of community policing wonder if it too expects policing to change in too many ways.

Other criticisms of community policing can be found in Jack Greene and Stephen Mastrofski's book *Community Policing: Rhetoric or Reality?*[26] Several contributors to that book questioned whether or not community policing actually exists, whether or not it has really been tried, and whether or not it really works. Mastrofski notes that it is difficult in modern cities to even identify what a community is in the first place.[27] Similarly, Peter Manning asks about the nature of police-community partnerships and questions how we can know them to be real.[28] Still other criticisms raised in Greene and Mastrofski's book draw attention to the potential for resistance to community policing by the police subculture, the possibility that closer ties with the public might result in illegal policing or corruption, and the difficulty of controlling the discretionary behavior of officers who are authorized to do community policing. Finally, there remain some questions as to whether all neighborhoods within a community actually want increased contact with the police[29] or if those who do will necessarily get it.[30]

The criticisms found in Greene and Mastrofski's book raise many valid questions. Undoubtedly for some police departments, community policing may be little more than a popular fad that police chiefs seem to support for the sake of good public relations. For many other police departments, community policing may simply represent a goal that will not be quickly realized. Still, quite a few departments can be held up as examples where great progress is being made.

THE FUTURE OF COMMUNITY POLICING

All good ideas generally meet with skepticism in the beginning. Wesley Skogan notes that the rhetorical nature of community policing is a necessary preliminary step to becoming a reality. First, community policing reflects a new philosophy for conducting police business that differs from the professional approach departments usually employ. For community policing to be accepted by police personnel it must be presented to them as a desirable alternative that offers them attractive features. Second, community policing has to draw favorable support from the taxpayers whose dollars pay for it. For the public to accept it, community policing must benefit the community in ways that they ordinarily would not experience if policing styles remain unchanged.

Viewed in another way, however, one might conclude that if everyone were happy with a professional model of policing, then there would be little room for the rhetoric of community policing. Community policing by its nature necessarily must start out as rhetoric that promises something new and different from the old way of enforcing laws. If change were not needed, then the rhetoric of community policing would not appear so promising. As always, we must wait on history, and to some extent our historians, to determine the ultimate success of community policing.

ENDNOTES

1. Steven F. Messner and Richard Rosenfeld, *Crime and the American Dream* (Belmont, CA: Wadsworth, 1994).
2. David G. Mueller and Cary Heck, "The Neutral Zone as One Example of Police-Community Problem Solving," in *Community Policing in a Rural Setting*, eds. Quint C. Thurman and Edmund F. McGarrell (Cincinnati: Anderson, 1997), pp. 115–121.
3. John E. Angell, "Toward an Alternative to the Classic Police Organizational Arrangement: A Demographic Model," *Criminology* 8 (1971): 185–206.
4. Robert Trojanowicz and Bonnie Bucqueroux, *Community Policing: A Contemporary Perspective* (Cincinnati: Anderson, 1990).
5. Quotation appearing in William A. Geller and Guy Swanger, *Managing Innovation in Policing: The Untapped Potential of the Middle Manager* (Washington, DC: Police Executive Research Forum, 1995).
6. *Ibid.*
7. Gary W. Cordner, "Community Policing: Elements and Effects," in *Critical Issues in Policing: Contemporary Readings*, 3rd ed., ed. Roger Dunham and Geoffrey Alpert (Prospect Heights, IL: Waveland, 1997), pp. 451–468.
8. Gary W. Cordner, "Elements of Community Policing," in *Policing Perspectives: An Anthology*, eds. Larry K. Gaines and Gary W. Cordner (Los Angeles: Roxbury, 1999), pp. 137–149.
9. *Ibid.*
10. *Ibid.*
11. *Ibid.*
12. *Ibid.*
13. Police Executive Research Forum, *Themes and Variations in Community Policing* (Washington, DC: Police Executive Research Forum, 1996).

14. James Q. Wilson and George L. Kelling, "Broken Windows: The Police and Neighborhood Safety," *Atlantic Monthly* (March, 1982): 29–38, [p. 33].
15. Herman Goldstein, "Improving Policing: A Problem-Oriented Approach," *Crime and Delinquency* 25 (1979): 236–258.
16. Mark H. Moore, "Problem Solving and Community Policing," in *Modern Policing*, vol. 15, eds. Michael Tonry and Norval Morris (Chicago: University of Chicago Press, 1992), pp. 99–158.
17. Mark H. Moore, "Research Synthesis and Policy Implications," in *The Challenge of Community Policing*, ed. Dennis Rosenbaum (Thousand Oaks, CA: Sage, 1994), pp. 258–299.
18. Quint C. Thurman, "The Police as a Community-Based Resource," in *Reinvesting Human Services: Community and Family-Centered Practice*, eds. Paul Adams and Kristine Nelson (New York: Aldine de Gruyter, 1995), pp. 175–187.
19. William Bratton and Peter Knobler, *Turnaround: How America's Top Cop Reversed the Crime Epidemic* (New York: Random House, 1998), p. 241.
20. *Ibid.*
21. David H. Bayley, *Police for the Future* (New York: Oxford University Press, 1994).
22. Quint C. Thurman and Edmund F. McGarrell, "Community Policing in a Rural Setting: Innovations and Organizational Change," in *Community Policing in a Rural Setting*, eds. Quint C. Thurman and Edmund F: McGarrell (Cincinnati: Anderson, 1997), pp. 1–8 [p. 1].
23. *Ibid.*
24. Roy R. Roberg and Jack Kuykendall, *Police Organization and Management: Behavior, Theory, and Process* (Pacific Grove, CA: Brooks/Cole, 1990).
25. Moore, "Problem Solving and Community Policing."
26. Jack R. Greene and Stephen D. Mastrofski, *Community Policing: Rhetoric or Reality?* (New York: Praeger, 1988).
27. Stephen D. Mastrofski, "Community Policing as Reform: A Cautionary Tale," in *Community Policing: Rhetoric or Reality?* eds. Jack R. Greene and Stephen D. Mastrofski (New York: Praeger, 1988), pp. 47–68.
28. Peter K. Manning, "Community Policing as a Drama of Control," in *Community Policing: Rhetoric or Reality?* eds. Jack R. Greene and Stephen D. Mastrofski (New York: Praeger, 1988), pp. 27–46.
29. Michael E. Buerger, "The Limits of Community Policing," in *The Challenge of Community Policing: Testing the Promises*, ed. Dennis P. Rosenbaum (Thousand Oaks, CA: Sage, 1994), pp. 270–273.
30. Hubert Williams and Patrick V. Murphy, "The Evolving Strategies on Policing: A Minority View," in *The Police and Society: Touchstone Readings*, ed. Victor E. Kappeler (Prospect Heights, IL: Waveland), pp. 29–52.

Chapter 10

Police Shootings

Myths and Realities

by Roger G. Dunham and Geoffrey P. Alpert

Police use of deadly force has been a controversial topic for members of the public and police administrators since the beginning of policing. Misuse of force has dominated our concerns about the police because the consequences of deadly force in general and firearms specifically are so serious and irrevocable. In today's world, we readily accept the officers' right to use force to protect lives, control crime, and keep the peace. At the same time, however, citizens must maintain control over police use of force and sometimes restrict how that force is used (Alpert and Smith, 1994a).

The most prevalent examples of excessive force are those in which officers act too quickly or inappropriately against a perceived threat. That is, an officer may react to a suspect without knowing the situation or he may place himself in a situation where deadly force is used in self-defense (See Geller and Scott, 1992; and Note, 1988). Other, less frequent but more outrageous examples include the use of force to suppress a minority group, to express hatred for an individual, or to maintain the illegitimate interests of the powerful (United States Civil Rights Commission, 1981).

The natural tension between the need to authorize the legitimate use of force for policing and the fear of abuse of that right has created a great dilemma. How can we as citizens authorize the police to use force in order to protect lives and maintain control in our neighborhoods and communities, and at the same time regulate that authority so that it is not used inappropriately or repressively against us? This dilemma is manifest whenever the police use any type of force, but becomes especially troublesome when the police use deadly force with a firearm, which is viewed as the ultimate use of force.

POLICE USE OF DEADLY FORCE: DISPELLING A FEW MYTHS

Critical questions concerning police use of firearms include: (1) how often do the police shoot citizens; (2) under what conditions do the police find it necessary to fire their weapons; (3) how often do the police hit their intended target; (4) how often do they hit innocent bystanders, someone's property, or another police officer; and (5) what are the rules for when to shoot and when not to shoot? These questions, among others, have been the focus of several studies on police shootings. The purpose of this chapter is not to review all the information available on police shootings, but to use some general information on the use of firearms to answer these questions and then to describe findings

Roger G. Dunham and Geoffrey P. Alpert. Prepared especially for this volume—1996.

from a recent study conducted in a major metropolitan police department over a ten-year period. First, we will address briefly several myths of policing and the amount of force used in a normal tour of duty.

Most of us get our ideas of what police officers do during a normal tour of duty from the mass media. We read about police activities in the newspapers and magazines, and we see depictions of the police on television and in the movies. These portrayals generally show the police in action-packed confrontations with dangerous criminals, constantly firing their weapons, fighting with offenders in difficult take-downs, and shooting at suspects in high-speed vehicle chases. In some cases, the confrontations that are presented in the electronic media include multiple officers and multiple suspects in massive shootouts. This, of course, makes exciting entertainment but creates an unrealistic view of police work. This type of high adventure seldom occurs in real-life situations. In fact, most police officers complete an entire career in police work without involvement in these types of confrontations with offenders. Even when such encounters occur, they seldom are of the type depicted in the media. In many cases, these portrayals would be good examples of what police officers should *not* do. A professional analysis of many of these accounts would reveal numerous laws and policies being broken by the police.

If potential recruits are interested in police work mainly for the crime-fighter image and envision themselves spending most of their time apprehending and arresting dangerous criminals, they will be greatly disappointed when they finally get on the job. Most of their time will be spent in peace-keeping or order-maintenance activities (and report writing) that have no contact with dangerous criminals. They will find that their image of police work greatly overemphasizes the amount of police violence, especially the use of firearms.

POLICE USE OF DEADLY FORCE: SOME EMPIRICAL FINDINGS

Having addressed some of the myths of police work concerning the use of force, the next step is to look at some of the facts and figures from studies of police discharge of weapons. Our design is to introduce an area of concern, create a general understanding of the issue with some information from other studies, and then report specific information from a recent ten-year study of the Metro-Dade Police Department in south Florida. The decision to focus on data from one agency over time rather than to report information from a variety of departments of different sizes that operate in different environments is to create an understanding of one agency's experiences (Alpert and Dunham, 1995). Metro-Dade police officers are required to fill out a special report each time they discharge a weapon. This includes all discharges except those occurring at the shooting range. Accidental discharges, shooting at animals that were threatening an officer or citizens, and shots that hit nothing at all are included. The figures presented here are generated from these reports.

It is important to recognize that the Metro-Dade Police Department is a large agency that has approximately 2,700 sworn officers today [1996], but operated with a sworn force of less than 2,000 when the study began in 1984. Also, the department operates in a very high crime area with one of the most liberal gun laws in the country. It is hard to imagine any area of the country with greater danger to police officers performing their duties. The area is a major conduit for illegal drugs coming into the country. It suffers from serious immigration problems and experiences continual ethnic conflict, which occasionally erupts into race riots. The following statistics truly represent one of the most extreme social contexts for the use of force by police officers. While we would expect a great amount of force in such an atmosphere, it is surprising how little deadly force is actually used.

HOW MANY SHOOTINGS?

The first thing we learn from agency statistics is how infrequently officers fire their weapons, and when they do, how infrequently they hit their intended target! Police officers actually killing a suspect is even less frequent. Larry Sherman and his associates compiled statistics for U.S. cities with over 250,000 people (Sherman et al, 1986:1). They concluded:

> Police in all cities kill rarely, but at widely varying rates. The average Jacksonville police officer would have to work 139 years before killing anyone. In New York City, the wait would be 694 years. It would be 1,299 years in Milwaukee and 7,692 years in Honolulu, all based on 1980–84 rates of killing.

They also found that the rates declined over the years they studied. While every incident is tragic, this picture is very different from the media portrayals.

In the Metro-Dade County (Florida) study, there were 511 discharge of firearm incidents during the 10-1/2 year period studied (see Table 1).

This is far fewer than one would expect from reading about the crime rate, the riots that occurred in Miami, and watching television shows such as *Miami Vice*. In fact, only 240 or 47% of the firearm discharge incidents were purposeful shootings involving suspects. This figure reveals that, on average, there were slightly less than twenty-three incidents per year. One hundred fifty-five of the other discharges were at animals, usually dogs threatening an officer or a citizen. One hundred four were accidental discharges, and the remaining twelve incidents were officers shooting out lights and discharging their weapons for other, miscellaneous reasons. It is obvious then that shooting at a suspect . . . [does not occur] nearly as frequent[ly] as most people imagine. In this large metropolitan department, which serves in a high-crime environment, officers shoot at suspects on the average less than *twice* per month. If this rate of shooting at suspects appears high to some, and if one is fearful that this contributes to a dangerous environment, one need only to look at the hit and fatality rates to feel a little more comfortable.

TABLE 1.   Overview of Weapon Discharges (Metro-Dade Police Department, 1984–1994)

Total discharges	511	
Purposeful, involving suspects	240	47%
Purposeful, involving animals	155	30%
Accidental	104	20%
Miscellaneous, not involving suspects	012	02%

HIT RATES AND FATALITY RATES

To give a more current description of the details of shooting incidents from the Metro-Dade Study, we will use the most recent data (over a 7-1/2 year period), as reported in the final report entitled *Metro-Dade Police Department Discharge of Firearm Study 1988–1994*. These data are not only the most current, but are more complete than the earlier data.

Most officers (64%) who did fire their weapons fired only one or two shots per incident, and very few fired more than four shots per incident (18%). Most of the time officers *did not* hit their intended target (68%). In only 41 of the 146 purposeful shootings during this time period, or 28% of the time, did the officer hit a suspect. Twenty-five of these suspects died. On the average, then, between six and seven suspects were shot by an officer per year, and between three and four died per year. This confirms the study cited earlier and the information presented that it is very unusual for an officer to shoot a suspect and even less likely to kill one. Of course, this is not meant to trivialize the shooting or to infer that police should not try to minimize the use of deadly force in enforcing the law. It does, however, give us a very different picture of police work than what we learn from the media.

ACCIDENTS: POLICE SHOOTING POLICE

An ironic finding of this study and other studies of police shooting is the frequency with which police personnel unintentionally shoot themselves or other officers. Several studies conducted in New York City and Chicago revealed that an alarming proportion of the police officers who were shot were shot either by themselves (accidental discharge or suicides) or by other police officers (accidental discharges or accidentally hitting another officer) (Geller and Scott, 1991). Over a ten-year period, 43% of the officers who were shot were shot by themselves or by other officers. The researchers conclude that "It is the armed robber and, paradoxically, the armed policeman who are the threats to the life of the police" (1991:453). In our study, almost as many officers were shot in accidental discharge as were shot by offenders. According to the *Sourcebook of Criminal Justice Statistics—1993*, (pp. 401, 405) during the period between 1984 and 1992 a total of 1,260 law enforcement officers (including federal, state, and local) were killed in the United States and its territories. Exactly 50% were killed feloniously and 50% accidentally. Most of the accidental deaths involved motor vehicles (86%), while only 8% involved accidental shootings. These data indicate that it is about as dangerous for officers to be on the road as it is to face dangerous criminals.

REASONS FOR SHOOTINGS

The most frequent circumstances precipitating a purposeful shooting incident involved the police stopping someone for committing a felony (35%), stopping someone who was suspicious or driving a suspicious car (29%), or trying to arrest someone in the midst of committing a felony (19%). The remainder involved drug-related arrests (7%), traffic stops (5%), domestic calls (3%), and activities of the Special Response Teams (2%). In almost all cases, there was resistance by the suspect (97%), and most of the time the suspect had a weapon of some type (89%). About half of the suspects had a gun. In a little more than one-third (34%) of the cases, the suspect actually shot at the police. Suspects verbally threatened to use the weapon on the police in 46% of the cases, and the remainder (20%) involved pushing, hitting, or grabbing the police officer.

It is obvious that in nearly all of these incidents, officers shoot because they are themselves threatened by a suspect. In fact, this was supported in several studies questioning whether officers discriminate against African-Americans and other minorities (see Dempsey, 1994:253). The data indicate that almost 80% of police killings involve minority suspects, which seems to imply discrimination. In fact, several studies reveal that when the police shoot unarmed suspects, African-Americans are greatly overrepresented. Other studies, though, indicate that it is when the suspect engages in violent crime or violent confrontations with the police that police are most likely to shoot. The disparity between black and white shooting victims disappeared when participation in violent crime was considered. Police officers are most likely to shoot suspects who are armed and engage in violent confrontations with the police. When these factors are considered, racial differences in the police use of deadly force become insignificant (see Dempsey, 1994). This is not to say that specific instances of extreme racial and ethnic bias do not happen. Obviously they do, and they are of tremendous concern. In general, however, precipitating events tend to account for most racial disparities in police shooting incidents. This conclusion is supported by the Metro-Dade Police Study. Discharging a weapon at the police was more likely to be a precipitating incident in police shooting at African-American suspects (43%) than when compared to Anglo (32%) or Hispanic (35%) suspects. This was true whether the officer discharging the weapon was Anglo, Hispanic, or African-American.

CHARACTERISTICS OF OFFICERS

Officers involved in purposeful shooting incidents are mostly male (93%) and young. Females comprise 20% of the sworn officers and only 7% of the shootings. The average age of officers discharging their weapons was 33 years. The majority of the officers involved in shooting are on uniform patrol (54%) and plainclothes patrol (15%), with an average of 8 years on the force.

Fifty-two percent of the shootings involved Anglo officers, 34% Hispanic officers, and 14% African-American officers. This is just about identical to the ethnic breakdown of the sworn officers in the department. However, African-American officers are slightly underrepresented in the shooting incidents, and Hispanic officers are a little overrepresented. It is informative to analyze the ethnic matches between the officers and suspects involved in shooting incidents. In Table 2 an analysis of the ethnicity of the officer and of the suspect illustrates an almost complete absence of African-American officers shooting Anglo or Hispanic suspects. African-American officers shot only 3 non-black suspects over a 6-1/2 year period. It is hard to interpret this finding because it is impossible to estimate exactly how many situations there were in which African-American officers encountered threatening non-black suspects. Also, it is true that African-American officers are more likely to be assigned in African-American neighborhoods. However, in spite of this, it is striking how unlikely it is for an African-American officer to shoot non-black suspects. We asked a high-ranking African-American officer who had been in the police department for 35 years to help us interpret these findings. He was not surprised by the findings and gave two explanations for them. First, he reminded us of how relatively recent it has been that African-Americans were permitted to join the police department, and

TABLE 2.   Ethnic Background of Officers and Suspects in Shooting Incidents (Metro-Dade Police Department, 1988–1994)

Officer ethnicity	Suspect ethnicity			Total
	Anglo	African American	Hispanic	
Anglo	18	44	10	**72**
Total percent	13	32	7	**52**
African-American	2	13	1	**16**
Total percent	1	10	>1	**12**
Hispanic	10	29	9	**48**
Total percent	7	21	7	**35**

that initially African-American officers were not given the authority to arrest whites. When these laws changed, there was still an unwritten rule that African-Americans do not use force against white suspects. He said that much of the enforcement of these unwritten rules was by other African-American officers. If they were aware of an African-American officer using force against a white, they would pull him aside and straighten him out because such incidents would make life harder for all of them. Even though all this happened some time ago, today some of these informal norms still linger, making African Americans less likely to use force against whites. He said that African-American officers will find other options to make an arrest.

Another reason the African-American administrator gave for African-American officers being underrepresented in shootings is that they are more likely to come from lower income, high-crime neighborhoods, which has given them more exposure to and experience with the types of conflict officers encounter. He thought the African-American officers, on the average, feel less threatened by these types of situations and are less likely to overrespond and use excessive force. They are more likely than other officers to find ways to deal with confrontations without using force.

CHARACTERISTICS OF SUSPECTS

Suspects at whom the police shoot are almost all males (97%) and tend to be young. The mean age of suspects in the Metro-Dade study is 27 years. Also in the Metro-Dade study, 60% of the suspects the police shot were African American; 22% were Anglos; 14% Hispanic; and [in] 4% ethnicity was unknown. Most of the suspects had criminal histories. Sixty-two percent had criminal histories involving felonies, 6% had misdemeanor or traffic offenses, and 11% had no criminal history. In the remainder of the cases, the criminal history was unknown. Almost all of the suspects resisted the police in some manner (97%). In one well-regarded study, it was concluded that despite some diversity in findings, most studies over the past three decades support the following broad generalization: "The most common type of incident in which police and civilians shoot one another in urban America involves an on-duty, uniformed, white, male officer and an armed black, male civilian between the ages of 17 and 30 in a public location within a high-crime precinct at night in connection with a suspected armed robbery or a 'man with a gun' call" (Geller and Scott, 1991:453).

LAWS AND POLICE POLICY REGARDING DISCHARGE OF WEAPONS

There are two fundamental authorities that guide the appropriate use of deadly force by the police. These are laws and policies. First and foremost, the United States Supreme Court in *Tennessee v. Garner*, 471 U.S. 1(1985), established the minimum legal standard: Deadly force cannot be used against a non-dangerous fleeing felon. That is, the Supreme Court created the standard that police agencies and officers cannot violate. Of course, police agencies can create policies that are more restrictive than what the Supreme Court requires and can limit officers from using deadly force except under very specific conditions. These policies establish the second authority by which police officers can use deadly force.

The *Garner* decision has become a very important decision for the police. First, it ruled that police shootings must be evaluated as seizures under the Fourth Amendment of the U.S. Constitution. Under this type of analysis, all purposeful shootings by police that hit the target are considered seizures. Seizures that are reasonable do not violate anyone's Constitutional rights but seizures that are unreasonable are illegal. Determining the reasonableness of a shooting is a difficult task. The Court in *Graham v. Conner* (490 U.S. 386, 396 [1989]) acknowledged that:

> the test of reasonableness under the Fourth Amendment is not capable of precise definition or mechanical application, however, its proper application requires careful attention to the facts and circumstances of each particular case, including the severity of the crime at issue, whether the suspect poses an immediate threat to the safety of officers or others, and whether he is actively resisting or attempting to evade arrest by flight. . . The reasonableness of a particular use of force must be judged from the perspective of a reasonable officer on the scene, rather than by 20/20 hindsight (citations omitted).

The Court has left the understanding of an appropriate use of force application to the "reasonable officer" or, stated in a different way, would a reasonable officer believe the force used was necessary? Unfortunately, what is reasonable and what is necessary are terms that were not defined precisely and were left open for interpretation (Alpert and Smith, 1994b).

To assist officers in understanding the limits of the application of deadly force, police departments promulgate their policies based upon the information presented in *Garner*. A wide range of policies exist, and some agencies adopt language taken directly from *Garner* without any definition or explanation, while others provide specific direction to their officers. This range of policies includes what is referred to as: (1) *Garner* or forcible felony policies; (2) defense of life policies; and (3) protection of life policies. These three types of policies differ on the type of shooting that is permitted. For example, under the *Garner*, or forcible felony, policies, shootings are justified if there is a substantial risk that a person who is escaping will cause death or serious bodily harm to someone if his arrest is delayed. This is the policy with the fewest restrictions and departments that adopt it will have the greatest number of shootings (Geller and Scott, 1992). A middle ground policy is what is known as a defense-of-life policy. Agencies operating under this type of policy limit the use of deadly force to situations where someone's life is in imminent peril. The defense-of-life policies include components that require officers to "plan ahead and consider alternatives" to the use of deadly force and to use deadly force "only as a last resort." Agencies operating under this type of policy will have the fewest number of shootings (Alpert and Fridell, 1992).

POLICE USE OF DEADLY FORCE: A CONCLUDING COMMENT

Police use of deadly force is a controversial topic that needs serious attention by law enforcement professionals and members of the public. The reform movements of the 1970s and 1980s have resulted in a change of philosophy within law enforcement. The authority for police officers to take the life of any felon who would not stop at the officer's command is over. However, departments operate under a wide variety of rules and regulations, some asking officers to use their discretion and some restricting the use of firearms to very specific situations. The data presented here, that of the Metro-Dade Police Department in Miami, reveal the nature and extent of discharges in one large metropolitan area. As demonstrated, police shootings do not resemble what is portrayed by the media. In real life, a shooting is a traumatic event for all concerned. Most officers go through a career without having taken a life or firing a weapon at a suspect. Hopefully, this trend will continue to improve and police officers will not be the judge, jury, and executioner of those they attempt to apprehend.

REFERENCES

Alpert, Geoffrey and Roger Dunham, *Metro-Dade Police Department Discharge of Firearm Study, 1988–1994*. Final report prepared for Dade County, Florida, March 1995.

Alpert, Geoffrey and Lorie Fridell, *Police Vehicles and Firearms: Instruments of Deadly Force*. Prospect Heights, IL: Waveland Press, 1992.

Alpert, Geoffrey and William Smith, "Developing Police Policy: An Evaluation of the Control Principle." *American Journal of Police* 13:1–20 (1994a).

Alpert, Geoffrey and William Smith, "How Reasonable is the Reasonable Man: Police and Excessive Force." *Journal of Criminal Law and Criminology* 85:481–501 (1994b).

Bureau of Justice Statistics, *Sourcebook of Criminal Justice Statistics—1993*. U.S. Department of Justice, Washington, D.C.: U.S. Government Printing Office, 1994.

Dempsey, John S. *Policing: An Introduction of Law Enforcement*. St. Paul, MN: West Publishing Company, 1994.

Geller, William A. and Michael S. Scott, *Deadly Force: What We Know*. Washington, D.C.: Police Executive Research Forum, 1992.

Geller, William A. and Michael S. Scott, "Deadly Force: What We Know." In *Thinking About Police: Contemporary Readings*. Edited by Carl B. Klockers and Stephen D. Mastrofski, 2nd ed., New York: McGraw-Hill, 1991.

Note, "Police Liability for Creating the Need to Use Deadly Force in Self-Defense." *Michigan Law Review* 86:1982–2009 (1988).

Sherman, Lawrence W., Ellen G. Cohen, Patrick R. Gratin, et al, *Citizens Killed by Big City Police, 1970–1984*. Washington, D.C.: Crime Control Institute, 1986.

United States Civil Rights Commission, *Who Is Guarding the Guardians*? Washington, D.C.: United States Civil Rights Commission, 1981.

Chapter 11

What We Know About Police Use of Force

by Kenneth Adams

Ambrose Bierce, a social critic known for his sarcasm and wit, once described the police as "an armed force for protection and participation."[1] In this pithy statement, Bierce identifies three critical elements of the police role. First, by describing the police as "armed," their ability to coerce recalcitrant persons to comply with the law is emphasized. Because police carry weapons, it follows that the force they use may have lethal consequences. The capacity to use coercive, deadly force is so central to understanding police functions, one could say that it characterizes a key element of the police role.

Second, the primary purpose of police is protection, and so force can be used only to promote the safety of the community. Police have a responsibility for safeguarding the domestic well-being of the public, and this obligation even extends in qualified ways to protecting those who violate the law, who are antagonistic or violent toward the police, or who are intent on hurting themselves. In dealing with such individuals, police may use force in reasonable and prudent ways to protect themselves and others. However, the amount of force used should be proportional to the threat and limited to the least amount required to accomplish legitimate police action.

Third, the concept of participation emphasizes that police and community are closely interrelated. Police are drawn from the community, and as police they continue to operate as members of the community they serve. The community, in turn, enters into a solemn and consequential relationship with the police, ceding to them the power to deprive persons of "life, liberty, and the pursuit of happiness" at a moment's notice and depending on them for public safety. Without police, the safety of the community is jeopardized. Without community support, police are dispossessed of their legitimacy and robbed of their effectiveness.

This three-element definition of police makes it easy to understand why abuse of force by police is of such great concern. First, there is the humanitarian concern that police are capable of inflicting serious, even lethal, harm on the public. Second, there is the philosophical dilemma that in "protecting" the whole of society, some of its constituent parts, meaning its citizens, may be injured. Third, there is the political irony that police, who stand apart from society in terms of authority, law, and responsibility, also are part of society and act on its behalf. Thus, rogue actions by a few police, if condoned by the public, may become perceived as actions of the citizenry.

From Kenneth Adams, "Use of Force by Police: Overview of National and Local Data," *National Institute of Justice Research Report*, October, 1999.

Recent developments in policing have elevated concerns about police use of force beyond ordinarily high levels. In particular, community policing, which is becoming widespread as a result of financial incentives by the federal government, and "aggressive" policing, which is becoming widely adopted as a solution to serious crime problems, have come to the fore as perspectives of choice by policing experts. Community policing emphasizes the role of the community as "coproducers" of law and order in conjunction with the police. Communities naturally vary in attributes, and they vary in how they are defined for the purposes of community policing. Consequently, some communities look to add restrictions on police use of force, while others are satisfied with the status quo, and still others seek to ease current restrictions. Regardless of the community's orientation on this issue, community policing means increased levels of accountability and responsiveness in key areas, such as use of force. Increased accountability hinges on new information, and new information stimulates debate.

The other emerging perspective is "aggressive" policing, which often falls under the rubric of broken windows theory, and, as a strategic matter, is concerned with intensifying enforcement against quality-of-life and order maintenance offenses. The influence of aggressive policing can be seen in the proliferation of "zero tolerance" enforcement strategies across the nation. The concern is that the threat posed by petty offenders may be exaggerated to the point that use of force becomes more commonplace and abuses of force more frequent.

The Violent Crime Control and Law Enforcement Act of 1994 mirrored congressional concern about excessive force by authorizing the Civil Rights Division of the U.S. Department of Justice (DOJ) to initiate civil actions against police agencies when, among other conduct, their use of force reaches a level constituting a pattern or practice depriving individuals of their rights. DOJ exercised that authority when, for example, it determined that an urban police department engaged in such conduct and negotiated a consent decree that put in place a broad set of reforms, including an agreement by the department to document its use of force and to implement an early warning system to detect possible abuses.[2]

Use-of-force concerns also are reflected in the attention the media give to possible instances of police abuse. An accumulation of alleged abuse-of-force incidents, widely reported in the media, encourages over-generalization by giving the impression that police brutality is rampant and that police departments across the nation are out of control. For example, Human Rights Watch states, "Allegations of police abuse are rife in cities throughout the country and take many forms."[3]

Before considering the details of recent research efforts on police use of force, it is useful to summarize the state of our knowledge.[4] We know some details about police use of force with a high degree of certainty. These items represent "facts" that should frame our understanding of the issues. Other details about police use of force we know in sketchy ways, or the research is contradictory. These items should be subject to additional research using more refined methods of inquiry. Finally, there are some aspects of police use of force about which we know very little or next to nothing. These items represent critical directions for new inquiry.

As is often the case with important policy questions, the information that we are most confident of is of limited value. In many cases, it does not tell us what we really need to know, because it does not focus squarely on the important issues or is subject to competing interpretations. Conversely, the information that is most critical for policy decisions often is not available or is very difficult to obtain. Such is the case with police use of force. The issues that most concern the public and policymakers lack the kinds of reliable and solid information that advance debate from the realm of ideological posturing to objective analysis. Nonetheless, it is important to take stock of our knowledge so that it is clear which issues can be set aside and which should be the target of efforts at obtaining new knowledge.

What, then, is the state of knowledge regarding police use of force? We begin with issues about which we have considerable information and a high degree of confidence in our knowledge. Discussed next are issues where knowledge is modest and considerably more research is merited. Finally, we conclude with issues that are critical to debates over police use of force and about which little knowledge exists.

WHAT WE KNOW WITH SUBSTANTIAL CONFIDENCE ABOUT POLICE USE OF FORCE

Police use force infrequently

Whether measured by use-of-force reports, citizen complaints, victim surveys, or observational methods, the data consistently indicate that only a small percentage of police-public interactions involve the use of force. As Bayley and Garofalo observed, police-citizen encounters that involve use of force and injury are "quite rare."[5]

Because there is no standard methodology for measuring use of force, estimates can vary considerably on strictly computational grounds. Different definitions of force and different definitions of police-public interactions will yield different rates[6] (see "Working definitions" on page 134). In particular, broad definitions of use of force, such as those that include grabbing or handcuffing a suspect, will produce higher rates than more conservative definitions. The Bureau of Justice Statistics' (BJS) 1996 pretest of its Police-Public Contact Survey resulted in preliminary estimates that nearly 45 million people had face-to-face contact with police over a 12-month period and that approximately 1 percent, or about 500,000 of these persons, were subjected to use of force or threat of force.[7] When handcuffing is included in the BJS definition of force, the number of persons increases to 1.2 million.

Expanding and contracting definitions of "police-public" interactions also work to affect use-of-force rates but in an opposite way from definitions of force. Broad definitions of police-public "interactions," such as calls for service, which capture variegated requests for assistance, lead to low rates of use of force. Conversely, narrow definitions of police-public interactions, such as arrests, which concentrate squarely on suspects, lead to higher rates of use of force.

The International Association of Chiefs of Police (IACP) is in the process of compiling statistics on use-of-force data being submitted by cooperating agencies. These data indicate that force is used in less than one-half of 1 percent of dispatched calls for service. From this point of view, one might well consider police use of force a rare event. This figure is roughly consistent with the preliminary estimate reported by BJS, although the IACP figure is subject to the reporting biases that may exist in police agency data. Furthermore, IACP data are not yet representative of the national picture because of selection bias; the estimate is based on a small percentage of police departments that voluntarily report information on use of force.

Garner and Maxwell found that physical force (excluding handcuffing) is used in fewer than one of five adult custody arrests. While this figure hardly qualifies as a rare event, it can be considered low, especially in light of the broad definition of force that was used.

In characterizing police use of force as infrequent or rare, the intention is neither to minimize the problem nor to suggest that the issue can be dismissed as unworthy of serious attention. Society's ends are best achieved peaceably, and we should strive to minimize the use of force by police as much as possible. However, it is important to put police use of force in context in order to understand the potential magnitude of use-of-force problems. Although estimates may not completely reassure everyone that police are doing everything they can to minimize the use of force, the data do not support the notion that we have a national epidemic of police violence.

Another purpose for emphasizing the infrequent nature of police use of force is to highlight the methodological challenges of trying to count or study infrequent events. In this regard, methodological approaches can vary considerably in terms of cost efficiency, reliability, and precision of information obtained. In BJS's 1996 pilot household survey of 6,421 persons, 14 respondents, or roughly 1 in 450, said that they were subjected to use of force or threat of force by police over a year's time. The household survey approach has the benefit of providing national-level estimates based on data that are free of police agency reporting biases. However, as noted by BJS, the preliminary estimates derived from such a small number of respondents are subject to a wide margin of error. This issue is particularly important if one is interested in tracking changes over time, because a very small change in reporting can have a very large impact on estimates. In the survey's continuing development, the next pilot test will use a sample about 10 times the size of the 1996 pilot test as well as involve a redesigned questionnaire.

Police use of force typically occurs at the lower end of the force spectrum, involving grabbing, pushing, or shoving

Relatively minor types of force dominate statistics on police use of force. Garner and Maxwell observed that police use weaponless tactics in roughly 80 percent of use-of-force incidents and that half the time the tactic involved grabbing the suspect. Alpert and Dunham found that in Miami 64 percent of use-of-force incidents involved grabbing or holding the suspect. In the BJS pilot national survey, it was estimated, preliminarily, that about 500,000 people were "hit, held, pushed, choked, threatened with a flashlight, restrained by a police dog, threatened with or actually sprayed with chemical or pepper spray, threatened with a gun, or experienced some other form of force."[8] Three-fifths of these situations, however, involved only holding. Finally, Pate and Fridell's survey of law enforcement agencies regarding use of force and civilian complaints also confirms that minor types of force occur more frequently than serious types.[9]

As a corollary finding, when injuries occur as a result of use of force, they are likely to be relatively minor. Alpert and Dunham observed that the most common injury to a suspect was a bruise or abrasion (48 percent), followed by laceration (24 percent). The kinds of police actions that most captivate the public's concerns, such as fatal shootings, severe beatings with fists or batons that lead to hospitalization, and choke holds that cause unconsciousness or even death, are not typical of situations in which police use

Working Definitions

Police use of force is characterized in a variety of ways. Sometimes, these characterizations are functionally interchangeable so that one can be substituted for another without doing injustice to the factual interpretation of a statement. At other times, however, differences in terminology can be very consequential to a statement's meaning. For example, "deadly force" refers to situations in which force is likely to have lethal consequences for the victim. This type of force is clearly defined and should not be confused with other types of force that police use.

In contrast, "police brutality" is a phrase used to describe instances of serious physical or psychological harm to civilians, with an emphasis on cruelty or savageness. The term does not have a standardized meaning; some commentators prefer to use a less emotionally charged term.

In this report, the term "excessive force" is used to describe situations in which more force is used than is allowable when judged in terms of administrative or professional guidelines or legal standards. Criteria for judging excessive force are fairly well established. The term may also include within its meaning the concept of illegal force.

Reference also is made to "excessive use of force," a similar, but distinctly different, term. Excessive use of force refers to high rates of force, which suggest that police are using force too freely when viewed in the aggregate. The term deals with relative comparisons among police agencies, and there are no established criteria for judgment.

"Illegal" use of force refers to situations in which use of force by police violated a law or statute, generally as determined by a judge or magistrate. The criteria for judging illegal use of force are fairly well established.

"Improper," "abusive," "illegitimate," and "unnecessary" use of force are terms that describe situations in which an officer's authority to use force has been mishandled in some general way, the suggestion being that administrative procedure, societal expectations, ordinary concepts of lawfulness, and the principle of last resort have been violated, respectively. Criteria for judging these violations are not well established.

To varying degrees, all of the above terms can be described as transgressions of police authority to use force.

force. These findings reassure us that most police exercise restraint in the use of force, even if one has concerns over the number of times that police resort to serious violence.

From a police administrator's point of view, these findings are predictable. Officers are trained to use force progressively along a continuum, and policy requires that officers use the least amount of force necessary to accomplish their goals.

Another affiliated finding is that police rarely use weapons. According to Garner and Maxwell, 2.1 percent of adult custody arrests involved use of weapons by police. Chemical agents were the weapons most frequently used (1.2 percent of arrests), while firearms were the weapons least often used (0.2 percent of arrests). Most police departments collect statistics on all firearm discharges by officers. These data consistently show that the majority of discharges are accidental or are directed at animals. Only on infrequent occasions do police use their firearms against the public. One implication of these findings is that increased training in how to use standard police weapons will be of little value in dealing with day-to-day situations that involve use of force. Training, if it is to be effective in reducing the use of force, needs to focus on how to gain compliance without resorting to physical coercion.

Use of force typically occurs when police are trying to make an arrest and the suspect is resisting

Research indicates that police are most likely to use force when pursuing a suspect and attempting to exercise their arrest powers. Furthermore, resistance by the public increases the likelihood that police will use force. These findings appear intuitively sound given the mandate that police have regarding use of force. Police may use force when it is necessary to enforce the law or to protect themselves or others from harm. The findings also seem logical in view of police training curriculums and departmental regulations. Alpert and Dunham find that police almost always follow the prescribed sequence of control procedures they are taught, except when suspect resistance is high, in which case they tend to skip the intermediate procedure.

The conclusion that police are most likely to use force when dealing with criminal suspects, especially those who are resisting arrest, is based on four types of data: arrest statistics, surveys of police officers, observations of police behavior, and reports by the public about their encounters with police.

Arrest statistics show that resisting-arrest charges often are involved in situations in which officers use force. The interpretation of this finding is ambiguous, however, because officers may bring such charges in an attempt to justify their actions against a suspect. Some commentators would even argue that resisting-arrest charges are a good indication that police officers acted inappropriately or illegally. Because we are relying on official reports by officers who are involved in use-of-force incidents, and because they have self-interest in presenting the situation in the most favorable light possible, we cannot rely on arrest records alone in determining what happened.

Fortunately, other research is available to help clarify the situation. The pilot national household survey by BJS included a series of questions about the respondent's behavior during contact with police.[10] The preliminary analysis revealed that of the 14 respondents in the sample who reported that police used or threatened force against them, 10 suggested that they might have provoked the officer to use force. The provocative behaviors reported by suspects include threatening the officer, assaulting the officer, arguing with the officer, interfering with the arrest of someone else, blocking or interfering with an officer's movement, trying to escape, resisting being handcuffed, and resisting being placed in a police vehicle.

Research by Alpert and Dunham confirms that criminal suspects are not always cooperative when it comes to arrest. In almost all (97 percent) cases in which police officers used force in a Florida jurisdiction, the suspect offered some degree of resistance. In 36 percent of use-of-force incidents, the suspect actively resisted arrest, and in one-quarter of the incidents the suspect assaulted the officer. The researchers observed that the most common type of suspect force was hitting or striking a police officer (44 percent).

Garner and colleagues, after using statistical controls for more than 50 characteristics of the arrest situation, the suspect, and the police officer, found that forceful action by suspects was the strongest and most consistent predictor of use of force by police.[11]

Furthermore, they found that while 22 percent of arrests involved use of force by police, 14 percent of arrests involved use of force by suspects. Police officers in Phoenix completed a use-of-force survey after each arrest to generate these data.

Finally, Bayley and Garofalo tallied 36 instances of force used by police or suspects out of 467 police-public encounters observed firsthand by researchers.[12] They found that in 31 incidents police used force against suspects and in 11 incidents suspects used force against police.

One implication of the research is that the decision to use some level of force probably has legal justification in most cases. Force is likely to be used when suspects resist arrest and attempt to flee. Also, in a significant number of instances, suspects use force against the police. These findings leave open the issue of *excessive* force, since issues of proportionality are not clearly addressed. However, the findings do suggest that many debates over excessive force will fall into gray areas where it is difficult to decide whether an officer acted properly, because there is credible evidence that the use of force was necessary.

WHAT WE KNOW WITH MODEST CONFIDENCE ABOUT POLICE USE OF FORCE

Use of force appears to be unrelated to an officer's personal characteristics, such as age, gender, and ethnicity

A small number of studies suggest that use of force by police is not associated with personal characteristics, such as age, gender, and ethnicity. Bayley and Garofalo concluded that use of force is not related to age, although it may be related to experience.[13] Worden, in an analysis of observational data on 24 police departments in 3 metropolitan areas, concluded that the personal characteristics of police officers do not have a substantively significant effect on use of force.[14]

Likewise, Garner and colleagues reported that the race of suspect and officer is not predictive of use of force.[15] However, they found that incidents involving male police officers and male suspects are more likely to involve force. Alpert and Dunham found that officer characteristics are of little utility in distinguishing between force and nonforce incidents.

Hence, gender and ethnicity appear unrelated to use of force. Given the limited research in this area, these conclusions should be accepted with caution and additional verification of these findings is needed.

It is widely accepted in criminology that violence, along with a wide variety of other risk-taking and norm-violating behaviors, is a young man's game. Thus, we should expect that young, male police officers should use force more than their female colleagues or older officers. The fact that this is not clearly the case seems surprising.

A lack of relationship between age and gender, on the one hand, and use of force, on the other, may be a function of police hiring and deployment practices. Retirement plans keep the age of police officers lower than that of most other occupations, and seniority, which is derivative of work experience, often brings more choice in work assignments, including duties that limit one's contact with criminal suspects on the street. Both these tendencies serve to constrain variation in the age of police officers who are exposed to potentially violent situations. This may attenuate the relationship between age and use of force. However, it is equally plausible that young male officers are assigned to high-crime areas where frequent use of force is necessary to gain compliance. Finally, it is possible that exposure to the police culture works to encourage the use of force, thus counterbalancing the decline in aggressivity that comes with age as demonstrated in criminological studies. More research is needed to disentangle these relationships.

The finding that an officer's race is unrelated to the propensity to use force runs counter to the argument that racial animosity lies at the heart of police abuse. Indeed, Alpert and Dunham's research indicates that officers are more likely to use force against suspects of their own race. The lack of relationship between race and use of force, as well as between gender and use of force, is probably disheartening to those who argue that integration of police agencies along racial and gender lines will do much to reduce the incidence of police violence. Again, more research is needed to understand the situation of minority and female police officers with regard to their use of force.

Use of force is more likely to occur when police are dealing with persons under the influence of alcohol or drugs or with mentally ill individuals. More research is needed

Police come across a wide variety of situations in their work. They encounter problems that range from relatively minor to serious to potentially deadly. They also interact with people exhibiting various mental states, including persons who are hysterical, highly agitated, angry, disoriented, upset, worried, irritated, or calm.

Two situations that often give police officers cause for concern are when suspects appear to be under the influence of alcohol or drugs and when civilians appear to suffer from serious mental or emotional impairments. The concern stems from the fact that in such situations a person's rational faculties appear impaired. In dealing with problem situations, officers most often talk their way, rather than force their way, into solutions. For this reason, when a civilian is in a highly irrational state of mind, the chances of the police officer having to use force presumably increase and the possibility of injury to both officer and civilian increases as well.

Research carried out for the President's Commission on Law Enforcement and Administration of Justice observed that alcohol use by either a suspect or an officer increased the chances that force will be used.[16] Garner and colleagues found that alcohol impairment by suspects was a consistent predictor of police use of force, while drug impairment predicted increased use of force for some but not all measures of use of force.[17] In contrast, Alpert and Dunham observed that alcohol or drug impairment of suspects was unrelated to police use of force or subsequent injury. That finding is interesting because, although impaired civilians did not demonstrate an increased propensity to resist an officer's actions, when they did resist they were more inclined to do so by actively resisting or assaulting the officer.

Part of the disparity in findings between the President's Commission's research and more recent studies may be attributed to the fact that police officers today are better trained in how to deal with impaired civilians. Most police officers now receive training in a variety of violence reduction techniques, and this development is partly attributable to concerns over the President's Commission's findings and over the frequency with which police now are called to respond to large-scale violence, such as riots.

Questions about how police deal with civilians who appear to have impaired mental states are important from administrative and practical points of view. Police officers are expected to exercise restraint in dealing with impaired civilians, while at the same time they need to be cautious about protecting their safety as well as the safety of other civilians. This puts them in a precarious situation, one in which mistakes of judgment or tactics can have grave consequences.

From a practical standpoint, police regularly encounter civilians with impaired mental states, which makes the problem more than academic. Alpert and Dunham found that in 42 percent of use-of-force situations, suspects appeared to be under the influence of alcohol or drugs. Overall, the research on whether police use force more frequently in relation to civilians with impaired mental states is inconsistent. Further investigation, with an emphasis on implications for training, could reduce the risk of force and injury for both police officers and civilians.

A small proportion of officers are disproportionately involved in use-of-force incidents. More research is needed

We often are told that a small number of people are responsible for most of the productive or counterproductive work in an organization. For example, we hear about the 80/20 rule in organizational management. That is, 20 percent of the workers account for 80 percent of the work. Policing has its counterpart explanation for deviant or illegal behavior. It is called the rotten apple or rogue officer theory, and it is often used to explain police corruption. Recently, a variation of this theory has become the principal explanation for use-of-force problems in police departments. In this context, we speak of "violence prone" police officers and we point to these individuals as the reason why a department has problems with the use of force.[18]

People with extraordinary work performance, either good or bad, are noticeable when compared with their colleagues, and their salience leads us to think that their work is highly consequential to the good fortunes or misfortunes of an organization. The utility of this perspective for police managers attempting to deal with illegitimate use of force lies in the presumed concentration of problem behaviors in the work force. If only a handful of police officers accounts for most of the abuses, then effective solutions targeted at those individuals should deal with the problem. The nature of the solution, be it employee selection, training, oversight, or discipline, is less important than its degree of effectiveness and its ability to be directed at the problem group of employees.

The Christopher Commission, which investigated the Los Angeles Police Department subsequent to the Rodney King incident, highlighted the "violence prone" officer theory.[19] The Commission, using the department's database, identified 44 officers with 6 or more civilian allegations of excessive force or improper tactics in the period 1986 through 1990. For the 44, the per-officer average for force-related complaints was 7.6, compared with 0.6 for all officers identified as having been involved in a use-of-force incident for the period January 1987 through March 1991. The 44 officers were involved in an average of 13 use-of-force incidents compared with 4.2 for all officers reported to be using force.

Put another way, less than one-half of 1 percent of the department's sworn officers accounted for more than 15 percent of allegations of excessive force or improper tactics.

The degree of disproportion (30:1) is striking and suggests that focusing efforts on a handful of officers can eliminate roughly 1 out of 7 excessive force incidents. This finding has led many police departments to implement early warning systems designed to identify high-risk officers before they become major problems. Most of these systems use administrative records, such as disciplinary records and citizen complaints, to monitor officer performance for possible problems.

The concept of an early warning system for risk management of problem police officers is not new. In the early 1980s, a report on police practices by the United States Commission on Civil Rights found that "'(e)arly warning' information systems may assist the department in identifying violence-prone officers."[20] Consequently, it was recommended that "(a) system should be devised in each department to assist officials in early identification of violence-prone officers."[21]

Until recently, these systems received limited acceptance, owing in part to concerns over possible abuses. The abuses include use of inaccurate information, improper labeling of officers, misuse of confidential records regarding discipline and other personnel matters, and social ostracism by peers and community for officers identified as problematic. There also were concerns about limited resources and about increased legal liability for the organization and individual officers.

As Toch observes, the violence-prone officer paradigm often is based on a variety of loosely articulated theories of violent behavior.[22] The theories include concepts such as racial prejudice, poor self-control, and ego involvement. Furthermore, these theories often overlook the possibility that greater-than-average use of force may be a product of situational or organizational characteristics.

For example, an officer's work assignment may involve a high-crime area that contains a high proportion of rebellious offenders. Also, divisive, dehumanizing views of the world, such as "us-them" and "good guy–bad guy," that facilitate violent behavior may be supported by the organizational culture. Further, administrative views of work roles and products, communicated formally or informally, that emphasize crime control through aggressive police behavior may encourage confrontational tactics that increase the chances of violent behavior by either civilian or police officer. Unless the reasons for violence propensity are accurately identified, the effectiveness of interventions targeted at violent police officers is a hit-or-miss proposition.

Of the 44 officers identified by the Christopher Commission in 1991, 14 subsequently left the department as of October 1997. Of the 30 remaining officers, two had a use-of-force complaint that was sustained after review between 1991 and 1997.[23] This low number may be due to a variety of reasons, such as difficulties in sustaining citizen complaints, reassignment of work duties, negative publicity leading to a change in behavior, or greater circumspection when engaging in misconduct. However, the finding also may reflect regression to the mean. This is a statistical phenomenon postulating that extreme scores gravitate toward the mean or average score, thereby becoming less extreme over time.

For example, groups of police officers who receive many citizen complaints, or who are disproportionately involved in the use of force, or who frequently are given poor performance ratings, will tend to become "better" over time, in the sense of statistically looking more like the "average" officers, even if nothing is done about these problems. Statistical regression represents a serious threat to the validity of early warning systems based on the assumption that extreme patterns of behavior persist over extended periods of time.

WHAT WE DO NOT KNOW ABOUT POLICE USE OF FORCE

The incidence of wrongful use of force by police is unknown. Research is critically needed to determine reliably, validly, and precisely how often transgressions of use-of-force powers occur

We do not know how often police use force in ways that can be adjudged as wrongful. For example, we do not know the incidence of excessive force, even though this is a very serious violation of public trust. We could pull together data on excessive force using police disciplinary records and court documents, for example, but the picture would be sketchy, piecemeal, and potentially deceiving. When it comes to less grave or less precise transgressions, such as "improper," "abusive," "illegitimate," and "unnecessary" use of force, the state of knowledge is even more precarious.

In discussing this issue, we will concentrate on excessive force, because these transgressions are of utmost concern to the public and because well-established professional and legal criteria are available to help us evaluate police behavior. Notwithstanding a generally agreed-upon terminology, we should recognize that developing a count of excessive force that is beyond all dispute is an unworkable task. This is so because difficult judgments are involved in deciding whether use of force fits the criteria for these categories in a given situation, and reasonable people will disagree in such judgments. We clearly need more accurate, reliable, and valid measures of excessive force if we are to advance our understanding of these problems.

Academics and practitioners both tend to presuppose that the incidence of excessive force by police is very low. They argue that, despite their shortcomings, agency statistics provide a useful picture of the use-of-force problem. These statistics show that most officers do not engage in force on a regular basis, that few people are injured by police use of force, that only a small number of people complain about police misconduct involving use of force, and that only a handful of these complaints are sustained.

The argument has appeal. We believe that the vast majority of police officers are professionals who respect the law and the public. If use of force is uncommon, civilian complaints are infrequent, and civilian injuries are few, then excessive force by police must be rare. That conclusion may indeed be correct, but to the extent that it hinges on official police statistics, it is open to serious challenge.

Current indicators of excessive force are all critically flawed. The most widely available indicators are civilian complaints of excessive force and civil lawsuits alleging illegal use of force. Civilian complaints of excessive force are infrequent, and the number of substantiated complaints is very low. These figures are consistent with the argument that excessive force is sporadic. However, complaint mechanisms are subject to selection and reporting biases, and the operation of complaint systems, which typically is managed by police, wields considerable influence on whether people will come forward to complain.

Civil lawsuits against police are exceedingly rare relative to the number of times that police use force. Because the legal process is highly selective in terms of which claims get litigated, lawsuits are a very unreliable measure of illegal use of force. With both civilian complaints and lawsuits, small changes in administrative practices can have a large impact on the magnitude of the problem measured in these ways.

The difficulties in measuring excessive and illegal force with complaint and lawsuit records have led academics and practitioners to redirect their attention to all use-of-force incidents. The focus then becomes one of minimizing all instances of police use of force, without undue concern as to whether force was excessive. From this perspective, other records, such as use-of-force reports, arrest records, injury reports, and medical records, become relevant to measuring the incidence of the problem.

From a theoretical perspective, understanding all use-of-force incidents helps us to put wrongful use of force in perspective. However, because political, legal, and ethical issues are very serious when we are dealing with excessive force, pressures to know the incidence and prevalence of these events with precision will always be present.

As a corollary of our current inability to measure excessive force, we cannot discern with precision changes in the incidence of these events over time and across places. This means that we can neither determine whether excessive force problems are getting better or worse nor determine the circumstances under which those problems are more or less severe.

The impact of differences in police organizations, including administrative policies, hiring, training, discipline, and use of technology, on excessive and illegal force is unknown. Research is critically needed in this area

A major gap in our knowledge about excessive force by police concerns characteristics of police agencies that facilitate or impede this conduct. Although many of the conditions that arguably lead to excessive or illegal force by police seem obvious, or appear to be a matter of common sense, we still greatly need systematic research in this area. We need to know, for example, which organizational characteristics are most consequential, which characteristics take on added significance in various environments, and which characteristics are redundant or derivative of other characteristics.

Many formal aspects of the organization—such as hiring criteria, recruit training, in service programs, supervision of field officers, disciplinary mechanisms, operations of internal affairs, specialized units dealing with ethics and integrity, labor unions, and civilian oversight mechanisms—plausibly are related to levels of officer misconduct. It makes sense that poorly educated, badly trained, loosely supervised, and inadequately disciplined officers are likely to be problematic, and that when such officers are in the majority, the organization is on the road toward disaster. Yet, we lack research that systematically addresses these questions.

Less formal aspects of police organizations—officer morale, administrative leadership, peer culture and influence, police-community relations, relations with other government agencies, and neighborhood environments—also plausibly have a part in levels of officer misconduct. Alienated officers who do not have a clear vision of their role and responsibilities and who are working in disorganized agencies and interacting with the public under stressful circumstances probably are more likely to abuse their authority, including their authority to use force. Research that systematically addresses these questions is lacking.

Methodological investigation of relations between organizational elements and use-of-force transgressions will help explain police misconduct at a theoretical level. More importantly, research on these questions will allow us to deal effectively with police misbehavior. Faced with serious misconduct problems in a police agency, we need to focus scarce resources on those aspects of police organizations that are most clearly related to ensuring proper conduct of officers with regard to use of force. Generalized efforts to reform police organizations that are expected to reduce misconduct problems tend to be inefficiently focused and thus appear clumsy, inadequate, and misinformed.

Research must focus on establishing the relative cost-effectiveness of various strategies to reduce or eliminate police misconduct. Furthermore, only strategies that are solidly grounded in theory, practice, and empirical research will provide reliable solutions with predictable costs and benefits.

Influences of situational characteristics on police use of force and the transactional nature of these events are largely unknown. More research is necessary

Research on police-citizen encounters reveals that use of force by police is situational and transactional. That is, police respond to circumstances as they first encounter them and as they unfold over time. For example, Bayley and Garofalo observed that the situations most likely to involve police use of force are interpersonal disturbance and violent personal crime.[24] Beyond this, however, we do not know much about the types of events that enhance the likelihood that police will use force.

Similarly, we have noted that when suspects attempt to flee or physically resist arrest police are more likely to use of force. We also noted that in many cases both police and suspects use force against each other. However, these findings do not address the transactional nature of police-public encounters in that they do not describe the step-by-step unfolding of events and interactions. Knowing that police use force if suspects physically resist arrest, it matters if police use force without provocation and the suspect responds by resisting or vice versa.

A variety of situational elements plausibly are related to police use of force. If police are called to a scene where there is fighting, they may have to or believe they have to use force to subdue the suspects. If they are called to a domestic dispute where emotions are running high, they may have to or believe they have to use force to gain control of the situation. If they are called to intercede with a civilian who is recklessly brandishing a weapon, they may have to or believe they have to use force to protect themselves and others. Use of force in such circumstances may be justifiable, but to the extent that it is predictable, we can prepare officers for these encounters and devise alternative strategies that minimize or eliminate the use of force.

Some situational factors may increase the chances that force of questionable legitimacy will be used. For example, officers sometimes use force on the slightest provocation following a high-speed car chase, when adrenaline levels are high. They may use force more frequently when they are alone, because they feel more vulnerable or believe that they can get away with it. They may use force more frequently as a way of emphasizing their authority when suspects are disrespectful or when there is a hostile audience to the encounter. At this point, however, knowledge about the types of police-citizen encounters in which police are likely to use force is rudimentary.

Police-public encounters are transactional in the sense that all the actors in a situation contribute in some way to its development and outcome. Understanding the transactional nature of police use of force is important because it emphasizes the role of police actions in increasing the chances that force will be used.

From this perspective, it is possible to minimize the use of force by modifying the behavior and tactics of police officers. By understanding the sequences of events that lead police to use force, we can gain a greater degree of control over those situations and possibly redirect the outcome. But we have only a basic understanding of the transactional nature of use-of-force situations, despite the fact that sequences of actions and interactions are highly germane to determining whether use of force was excessive or illegal. . . .

REFERENCES

Joel H. Garner and Christopher D. Maxwell, "Measuring the amount of force used by and against its police in six jurisdictions." In *Use of Force by Police,* National Institute of Justice–Research Report (Washington DC: U.S. Department of Justice) October 1999 pp. 25–44.

Geoffrey P. Alpert and Roger G. Dunham, "The Force Factor." In *Use of Force by Police,* National Institute of Justice–Research Report. (Washington DC: U.S. Department of Justice) October 1999 pp. 45–60.

NOTES

1. Bierce, Ambrose, *The Devil's Dictionary*, New York: Dover, 1958: 101.
2. "Justice Department Consent Decree Pushes Police to Overhaul Operations," *Pittsburgh Post-Gazette*, March 1, 1998, C-1.
3. Based on an investigation in 14 cities, Human Rights Watch described the brutality situation as follows: "(p)olice officers engage in unjustified shootings, severe beatings, fatal chokings, and unnecessarily rough physical treatment in cities throughout the United States, while their police superiors, city officials and the Justice Department fail to act decisively to restrain or penalize such acts or even to record the full magnitude of the problem." Human Rights Watch, *Shielded from Justice: Police Brutality and Accountability in the United States*, New York: Human Rights Watch, 1998: 1, 27.
4. A previous summary of research on police use of force can be found in McEwen, Tom, *National Data Collection on Police Use of Force*, Washington, DC: U.S. Department of Justice, Bureau of Justice Statistics and National Institute of Justice, April 1996, NCJ 160113.
5. Bayley, David H., and James Garofalo, "The Management of Violence by Police Patrol Officers," *Criminology*, 27(1)(February 1989): 1–27; and Bayley, David H., and James Garofalo, "Patrol Officer Effectiveness in Managing Conflict During Police-Citizen Encounters," in *Report to the Governor*, Vol. III, Albany: New York State Commission on Criminal Justice and the Use of Force, 1987: B1-88.
6. Adams, Kenneth, "Measuring the Prevalence of Police Abuse of Force," in *And Justice For All: A National Agenda for Understanding and Controlling Police Abuse of Force*, ed. William A. Geller and Hans Toch, Washington, DC: Police Executive Research Forum, 1995: 61–97.
7. Greenfeld, Lawrence A., Patrick A. Langan, and Steven K. Smith, *Police Use of Force: Collection of National Data*, Washington, DC: U.S. Department of Justice,

Bureau of Justice Statistics and National Institute of Justice, November 1997, NCJ 165040.

8. Ibid.

9. Pate, Anthony M., and Lorie A. Fridell, with Edwin E. Hamilton, *Police Use of Force: Official Reports, Citizen Complaints, and Legal Consequences*, Vols. I and II, Washington, DC: The Police Foundation, 1993.

10. Greenfeld, Lawrence A., Patrick A. Langan, and Steven K. Smith, *Police Use of Force: Collection of National Data*.

11. Garner, Joel, John Buchanan, Tom Schade, and John Hepburn, *Understanding Use of Force By and Against the Police*, Research in Brief, Washington, DC: U.S. Department of Justice, National Institute of Justice, November 1996, NCJ 158614.

12. Bayley, David H., and James Garofalo, "The Management of Violence by Police Patrol Officers"; and Bayley, David H., and James Garofalo, "Patrol Officer Effectiveness in Managing Conflict During Police-Citizen Encounters."

13. Ibid.

14. Worden, Robert, "The 'Causes' of Police Brutality," in *And Justice For All: A National Agenda for Understanding and Controlling Police Abuse of Force*, 31–60.

15. Garner, Joel, John Buchanan, Tom Schade, and John Hepburn, *Understanding Use of Force By and Against the Police*.

16. Reiss, Jr., Albert J., *Studies on Crime and Law Enforcement in a Major Metropolitan Area*, President's Commission on Law Enforcement and Administration of Justice, Field Survey No. 3, Washington, DC: U.S. Government Printing Office, 1967.

17. Garner, Joel, John Buchanan, Tom Schade, and John Hepburn, *Understanding Use of Force By and Against the Police*.

18. Toch, Hans, "The 'Violence-Prone' Police Officer," in *And Justice For All: A National Agenda for Understanding and Controlling Police Abuse of Force*, 99–112.

19. Independent Commission on the Los Angeles Police Department, *Report of the Independent Commission on the Los Angeles Police Department*, Los Angeles, CA: Independent Commission on the Los Angeles Police Department, 1991.

20. United States Commission on Civil Rights, *Who's Guarding the Guardians? A Report on Police Practices*, Washington, DC: United States Commission on Civil Rights, 1981: 159.

21. Ibid.

22. Toch, Hans, "The 'Violence-Prone' Police Officer," 112.

23. Office of the Inspector General, Los Angeles Police Commission, "Status Update: Management of LAPD High-Risk Officers," Los Angeles: Los Angeles Police Commission, 1997.

24. Bayley, David, H., and James Garofalo, "Patrol Officer Effectiveness in Managing Conflict During Police-Citizen Encounters."

Chapter 12

Learning Police Ethics

by Lawrence Sherman

There are two ways to learn police ethics. One way is to learn on the job, to make your moral decisions in haste under the time pressures of police work. This is by far the most common method of learning police ethics, the way virtually all of the half-million police officers in the United States decide what ethical principles they will follow in their work. These decisions are strongly influenced by peer group pressures, by personal self-interest, and by passions and emotions in the heat of difficult situations.

There is another way. It may even be a better way. You can learn police ethics in a setting removed from the heat of battle, from the opinions of co-workers, and from the pressures of supervisors. You can think things through with a more objective perspective on the issues. You should be able to make up your mind about many difficult choices before you actually have to make them. And you can take the time to weigh all sides of an issue carefully, rather than making a snap judgment.

The purpose of this article is to provide a basis for this other, less common way of learning police ethics by making the alternative—the usual way of learning police ethics—as clear as possible. This portrait of the on-the-job method is not attractive, but it would be no more attractive if we were to paint the same picture for doctors, lawyers, judges, or college professors. The generalizations we make are not true of all police officers, but they do reflect a common pattern, just as similar patterns are found in all occupations.

LEARNING NEW JOBS

Every occupation has a learning process (usually called "socialization") to which its new members are subjected. The socialization process functions to make most "rookies" in the occupation adopt the prevailing rules, values, and attitudes of their senior colleagues in the occupation. Very often, some of the existing informal rules and attitudes are at odds with the formal rules and attitudes society as a whole expects members of the occupation to follow. This puts rookies in a moral dilemma: should the rookies follow the formal rules of society or the informal rules of their senior colleagues?

These dilemmas vary in their seriousness from one occupation and one organization to the next. Young college professors may find that older professors expect them to devote most of their time to research and writing, while the general public (and their students) expects them to devote most of their time to teaching. With some luck, and a lot of work, they can do both.

Lawrence Sherman, "Learning Police Ethics" (as appeared in *Criminal Justice Ethics*, Volume 1, Number 1, [Winter/Spring 1982] pp. 10–19). Reprinted by permission of The Institute for Criminal Justice Ethics, 555 West 57th Street, Suite 601, New York, NY, 10019-1029.

Police officers usually face much tougher dilemmas. Like waiters, longshoreman, and retail clerks, they may be taught very early how to steal—at the scene of a burglary, from the body of a dead person, or in other opportunities police confront. They may be taught how to commit perjury in court to insure that their arrests lead to conviction, or how to lie in disciplinary investigations to protect their colleagues. They may be taught how to shake people down, or how to beat people up. Or they may be fortunate enough to go to work in an agency, or with a group of older officers, in which none of these violations of official rules is ever suggested to them.

Whether or not rookie police officers decide to act in ways the wider society might view as unethical, they are all subjected to a similar process of being taught certain standards of behavior. Their reactions to that learning as the years pass by can be described as their *moral careers*: the changes in the morality and ethics of their behavior. But the moral career is closely connected to the *occupational career*: the stages of growth and development in becoming a police officer.

This article examines the process of learning a new job as the context for learning police ethics. It then describes the content of the ethical and moral values in many police department "cultures" that are conveyed to new police officers, as well as the rising conflict within police agencies over what those values should be. Finally, it describes the moral career of police officers, including many of the major ethical choices officers make.

BECOMING A POLICE OFFICER

There are four major stages in the career of anyone joining a new occupation:[1]

- the *choice* of occupation
- the *introduction* to the occupation
- the first *encounter* with doing the occupation's work
- the *metamorphosis* into a full-fledged member of the occupation

Police officers go through these stages, just as doctors and bankers do. But the transformation of the police officer's identity and self-image may be more radical than in many other fields. The process can be overwhelming, changing even the strongest of personalities.

Choice

There are three aspects of the choice to become a police officer. One is the *kind of person* who makes that choice. Another is the *reason* the choice is made, the motivations for doing police work. The third is the *methods* people must use as police officers. None of these aspects of choice appears to predispose police officers to be more or less likely to perform their work ethically.

Many people toy with the idea of doing police work, and in the past decade the applicants for policing have become increasingly diverse. Once a predominantly white male occupation, policing has accepted many more minority group members and attracted many more women. More college-educated people have sought out police work, but this may just reflect the higher rate of college graduates in the total population.

What has not changed, apparently, is the socioeconomic background of people who become police. The limited evidence suggests police work attracts the sons and daughters of successful tradespeople, foremen, and civil servants—especially police. For many of them, the good salary (relative to the educational requirements), job security, and prestige of police work represent a good step up in the world, an improvement on their parents' position in life.

The motivation to become a police officer flows naturally from the social position of the people who choose policing. People do not seem to choose policing out of an irrational lust for power or because they have an "authoritarian personality"; the best study on this question showed that New York City police recruits even had a *lower* level of authoritarian attitudes than the general public (although their attitudes become more authoritarian as they become adapted to police work, rising to the general public's level of authoritarian attitudes).[2] Police applicants tend to see police work as an adventure, as a chance to do work out of doors without being cooped up in an office, as a chance to do work that is important for the good of society, and not as a chance to be the "toughest guy on the block." Nothing in the motivation to apply for a police position seems to predispose police officers towards unethical behavior.

Nor do the methods of selecting police officers seem to affect their long-term moral careers. There was a time when getting on the force was a matter of bribery or political favors for local politicians, or at least a matter of knowing the right people involved in grading the entrance examinations and sitting on the selection committees. But in the 1980s, the selection process appears to be highly bureaucratic, with impersonal multiple-choice tests scored by computers playing the most important role in the process.

To be sure, there are still subjective background investigations, personal interviews, and other methods that allow biases to intrude upon the selection process. But these biases, if anything, work in the direction of selecting people who have backgrounds of unquestioned integrity. Combined with the high failure rate among all applicants—sometimes less than one in twenty is hired, which makes some police departments more selective in quantitative terms than the Harvard Law School—the selection process probably makes successful applicants feel that they have been welcomed into an elite group of highly qualified people of very high integrity.

Introduction

But this sense of high ideals about police work may not last for long. The introduction to policing provided by most police academies begins to convey folklore that shows the impossibility of doing things "by the book" and the frequent necessity of "bending the rules."

Police recruit training has changed substantially over the past thirty years. Once highly militaristic, it has recently taken on more of the atmosphere of the college classroom. The endurance test-stress environment approach, in which trainees may be punished for yawning or looking out the window, may still be found in some cities, but it seems to be dying out. Dull lectures on the technical aspects of police work (such as how to fill out arrest reports) and the rules and regulations of the department are now often supplemented by guest lectures on theories of crime and the cultures of various ethnic groups.

But the central method of *moral* instructions does not appear to have changed. The "war story" still remains the most effective device for communicating the history and values of the department. When the instructor tells a war story, or an anecdote about police work, the class discipline is relaxed somewhat, the interest and attention of the class increase, and an atmosphere of camaraderie between the class and the instructor is established. The content of the war story makes a deep impression on the trainees.

The war stories not only introduce police work as it is experienced by police officers—rather than as an abstract ideal—they also introduce the ethics of police work as something different from what the public, or at least the law and the press, might expect. Van Maanen recounts one excerpt from a police academy criminal law lecture that, while not a "story," indicates the way in which the hidden values of police work are conveyed:

> I suppose you guys have heard of Lucky Baldwin? If not, you sure will when you hit the street. Baldwin happens to be the biggest burglar still operating in this town. Every guy in this department from patrolman to chief would love to get him and make it stick. We've busted him about ten times so far, but he's got an asshole lawyer and money so he always beats the rap. . . . If I ever get a chance to pinch the SOB, I'll do it my way with my thirty-eight and spare the city the cost of a trial.[3]

Whether the instructor would actually shoot the burglary suspect is open to question, although he could do so legally in most states if the suspect attempted to flee from being arrested.* More important is the fact that the rookies spend many hours outside the classroom debating and analyzing the implications of the war stories. These discussions do help them decide how they would act in similar circumstances. But the decisions they reach in these informal "bull" sessions are probably more attributable to peer pressure and the desire to "fit in" to the culture of the department than to careful reflection on moral principle.

Encounter

After they leave the academy, the rookies are usually handed over to Field Training Officers (FTOs). In the classic version of the first day on patrol with the rookie, the FTO says, "Forget everything they taught you in the academy, kid; I'll show you how police work is really done." And show they do. The rookie becomes an observer of the FTO as he or she actually does police work. Suddenly the war stories come alive, and all the questions about how to handle tough situations get answered very quickly and clearly, as one police veteran recalls:

> On this job, your first partner is everything. He tells you how to survive on the job . . . how to walk, how to stand, and how to speak and how to think and what to say and see.[4]

The encounter with the FTO is only part of the rookie's "reality shock" about police work. Perhaps even more important are the rookie's encounters with the public. By putting on the uniform, the rookie becomes part of a visible minority group. The self-consciousness about the new appearance is heightened by the nasty taunts and comments the uniform attracts from teenagers and others.[5] The uniform and gun, as symbols of power, attract challenges to that power simply because they are there.[6] Other people seek out the uniform to manipulate the rookie to use the power on behalf of their personal interests. Caught frequently in the cross fire of equally unreasonable citizen demands, the

---

*Editor's note: The U.S. Supreme Court in *Garner v. Tennessee* (1985) severely limited the officer's right to shoot a fleeing felon.

rookie naturally reacts by blaming the public. The spontaneous reaction is reinforced by one of the central values of the police culture: the public as enemy.[7]

This is no different from the way many doctors view their patients, particularly patients with a penchant for malpractice suits. Nor is it different from the view many professors have of their students as unreasonable and thick-headed, particularly those who argue about grades. Like police officers, doctors and professors wield power that affects other people's lives, and that power is always subject to counterattack. Once again, Van Maanen captures the experience of the rookie:

> [My FTO] was always telling me to be forceful, to not back down and to never try to explain the law or what we are doing to a civilian. I really didn't know what he was talking about until I tried to tell some kid why we have laws about speeding. Well, the more I tried to tell him about traffic safety, the angrier he got. I was lucky just to get his John Hancock on the citation. When I came back to the patrol car, [the FTO] explains to me just where I'd gone wrong. You really can't talk to those people out there, they just won't listen to reason.[8]

It is the public that transforms the rookie's self-conception, teaching him or her the pains of exercising power. The FTO then helps to interpret the encounters with the public in the light of the values of the police culture, perhaps leading the rookie even further away from the values of family and friends about how police should act.

The FTO often gives "tests" as he or she teaches. In many departments, the tests are as minor as seeing if the rookie will wait patiently outside while the FTO visits a friend. In other departments, the test may include getting the rookie involved in drinking or having sex on duty, a seriously brutal slugfest against an arrestee, or taking bribes for nonenforcement. The seriousness of the violations may vary, but the central purpose of the test does not: seeing if the rookie can keep his or her mouth shut and not report the violations to the supervisors. A rookie who is found to be untrustworthy can be, literally, hounded and harassed from the department.

Finally, in the encounter stage, the rookie gets the major reality shock in the entire process of becoming a police officer. The rookie discovers that police work is more social work than crime fighting, more arbitration of minor disputes than investigations of major crimes, more patching of holes in the social fabric than weaving of webs to catch the bigtime crooks. The rookie's usual response is to define most of the assignments received as "garbage calls," not *real* police work. Not quite sure whom to blame for the fact that he or she was hired to do police work but was assigned everything else, the rookie blames the police executive, the mayor and city council, and even previous U.S. presidents (for raising public expectations). But most of all the rookie blames the public, especially the poor, for being so stupid as to have all these problems, or so smart to take advantage of welfare and other social programs.

Metamorphosis

The result of those encounters is usually a complete change, a total adaptation of the new role and self-conception as a "cop." And with that transformation comes a stark awareness of the interdependence cops share with all other cops. For all the independence police have in making decisions about how to deal with citizens, they are totally and utterly dependent on other police to save their lives, to respond to a call of an officer in trouble or need of assistance, and to lie on their behalf to supervisors to cover up minor infractions of the many rules the department has. This total change in perspective usually means that police accept several new assumptions about the nature of the world:

- loyalty to colleagues is essential for survival
- the public, or most of it, is the enemy
- police administrators are also the enemy
- any discrepancy between these views and the views of family and friends is due simply to the ignorance of those who have not actually done police work themselves

These are their new assumptions about the *facts* of life in police work, the realities which limit their options for many things, including the kinds of moral principles they can afford to have and still "survive," to keep the job, pay the mortgage, raise the kids, and vest the pension. This conception of the facts opens new police officers to learning and accepting what may be a new set of values and ethical principles. By the time the metamorphosis has been accomplished, in fact, most of these new values have been learned.

CONTENT OF POLICE VALUES TEACHING

Through the war stories of the academy instructor, the actions and stories of the FTO, the bull sessions with other rookies and veterans, and the new officer's encounters with the public, a fairly consistent set of values emerges. Whether the officer accepts these values is another question. Most students of police work seem to agree that these are the values (or some of them) that are taught:

1. Discretion A: *Decisions about whether to enforce the law, in any but the most serious cases, should be guided by both what the law says and who the suspect is.* Attitude, demeanor, cooperativeness, and even race, age, and social class are all important considerations in deciding how to treat people generally, and whether or not to arrest suspects in particular.

2. Discretion B: *Disrespect for police authority is a serious offense that should always be punished with an arrest or the use of force.* The "offense" known as "contempt of cop" or P.O.P.O. (pissing off a police officer) cannot be ignored. Even when the party has committed no violation of the law, a police officer should find a safe way to impose punishment, including an arrest on fake charges.

3. Force: *Police officers should never hesitate to use physical or deadly force against people who "deserve it," or where it can be an effective way of solving a crime.* Only the potential punishments by superior officers, civil litigation, citizen complaints, and so forth should limit the use of force when the situation calls for it. When you can get away with it, use all the force that society should use on people like that—force and punishment which bleeding-heart judges are too soft to impose.

4. Due Process: *Due process is only a means of protecting criminals at the expense of the law-abiding and should be ignored whenever it is safe to do so.* Illegal searches and wiretaps, interrogation without advising suspects of their Miranda rights and, if need be (as in the much-admired movie, *Dirty Harry*), even physical pain to coerce a confession are all acceptable methods for accomplishing the goal the public wants the police to accomplish: fighting crime. The rules against

doing those things merely handcuff the police, making it more difficult for them to do their job.

5. Truth: *Lying and deception are an essential part of the police job, and even perjury should be used if it is necessary to protect yourself or get a conviction on a "bad guy."* Violations of due process cannot be admitted to prosecutors or in court, so perjury (in the serious five percent of cases that ever go to trial) is necessary and therefore proper. Lying to drug pushers about wanting to buy drugs, to prostitutes about wanting to buy sex, or to congressmen about wanting to buy influence is the only way, and therefore a proper way, to investigate these crimes without victims. Deceiving muggers into thinking you are an easy mark and deceiving burglars into thinking you are a fence are proper because there are not many other ways of catching predatory criminals in the act.

6. Time: *You cannot go fast enough to chase a car thief or traffic violator, nor slow enough to get a "garbage" call; and when there are no calls for service, your time is your own.* Hot pursuits are necessary because anyone who tries to escape from the police is challenging police authority, no matter how trivial the initial offense. But calls to nonserious or social-work problems like domestic disputes or kids making noise are unimportant, so you can stop to get coffee on the way or even stop at the cleaner's if you like. And when there are no calls, you can sleep, visit friends, study, or do anything else you can get away with, especially on the midnight shift, when you can get away with a lot.

7. Rewards: *Police do very dangerous work for low wages, so it is proper to take any extra rewards the public wants to give them, like free meals, Christmas gifts, or even regular monthly payments (in some cities) for special treatment.* The general rule is: take any reward that doesn't change what you would do anyway, such as eating a meal, but don't take money that would affect your job, like not giving traffic tickets. In many cities, however, especially in the recent past, the rule has been to take even those rewards that do affect your decisions, as long as they are related only to minor offenses—traffic, gambling, and prostitution, but not murder.

8. Loyalty: *The paramount duty is to protect your fellow officers at all costs, as they would protect you, even though you may have to risk your own career or your own life to do it.* If your colleagues make a mistake, take a bribe, seriously hurt somebody illegally, or get into other kinds of trouble, you should do everything you can to protect them in the ensuing investigation. If your colleagues are routinely breaking the rules, you should never tell supervisors, reporters, or outside investigators about it. If you don't like it, quit—or get transferred to the police academy. But never, ever, blow the whistle.

THE RISING VALUE CONFLICTS

None of these values is as strongly or widely held as in the past. Several factors may account for the breakdown in traditional police values that has paralleled the breakdown of traditional values in the wider society. One is the increasing diversity of the kinds of people who join police departments: more women, minorities, and college graduates. Another is the rising power of the police unions which defend individual officers who get into trouble—sometimes even those who challenge the traditional values. A third factor is the rise of investigative journalism and the romantic aura given to the "bucking the system" by such movies as *Serpico*. Watergate and other recent exposés of corruption in high places—especially the attitude of being "above the law"—have probably made all public officials more conscious of the ethics of their behavior. Last but not least, police administrators have increasingly taken a very stern disciplinary posture towards some of these traditional police values and gone to extraordinary lengths to try to counteract them.

Consider the paramount value of loyalty. Police reformer August Vollmer described it in 1931 as the "blue curtain of secrecy" that descends whenever a police officer does something wrong, making it impossible to investigate misconduct. Yet in the past decade, police officers in Cincinnati, Indianapolis, New York, and elsewhere have given reporters and grand juries evidence about widespread police misconduct. In New York, police officers have even given evidence against their colleagues for homicide, leading to the first conviction there (that anyone can recall) of a police officer for murder in the line of duty. The code of silence may be far from breaking down, but it certainly has a few cracks in it.

The ethics of rewards have certainly changed in many departments over the past decade. In the wake of corruption scandals, some police executives have taken advantage of the breakdown in loyalty to assign spies, or "field associates," to corruption-prone units in order to detect bribe-taking. These officers are often recruited for this work at the police academy, where they are identified only to one or two contacts and are generally treated like any other police officer. These spies are universally hated by other officers, but they are very hard to identify. The result of this approach, along with other anti-corruption strategies, has been an apparent decline in organized corruption.[9]

The ethics of force are also changing. In the wake of well-publicized federal prosecutions of police beatings, community outrage over police shootings, and an explosion in civil litigation that has threatened to bankrupt some cities, the behavior and possibly the attitude of the police in their use of force have generally become more restrained. In Los Angeles, Kansas City, Atlanta, New York, Chicago, and elsewhere, the number of killings of citizens by police has declined sharply.[10] Some officers now claim that they risk their lives by hesitating to use force out of fear of being punished for using it. Even if excessive use of force has not been entirely eliminated, the days of unrestrained shooting or use of the "third degree" are clearly gone in many cities.

The increasing external pressures to conform to legal and societal values, rather than to traditional police values, have generated increasing conflict among police officers themselves. The divide-and-conquer effect may be seen in police officers' unwillingness to bear the risks of covering up for their colleagues, now that the risks are much greater than they have been. Racial conflicts among police officers often center on these values. At the national level, for example, the National Organization of Black Law Enforcement Executives (NOBLE) has been battling with the International Association of Chiefs of Police (IACP) since at least 1979 over the question of how restrictive police department firearms policies should be.

These conflicts should not be over-emphasized, however. The learning of police ethics still takes place in the context of very strong communication of traditional police values. The rising conflicts are still only a minor force. But they are at least one more contingency affecting the moral choices police officers face as they progress through their careers, deciding which values to adopt and which ethical standards to live by.

THE POLICE OFFICER'S MORAL CAREER

There are four major aspects of moral careers in general that are directly relevant to police officers.[11] One is the *contingencies* the officer confronts. Another is the *moral experiences* undergone in confronting these contingencies. A third is the *apologia*, the explanation officers develop for changing the ethical principles they live by. The fourth and most visible aspect of the moral careers of police officers is the *stages* of moral change they go through.

Contingencies

The contingencies shaping police moral careers include all the social pressures officers face to behave one way rather than another. Police departments vary, for example, in the frequency and seriousness of the rule-breaking that goes on. They also vary in the openness of such rule-breaking, and in the degree of teaching of the *skills* of such rule-breaking. It is no small art, for example, to coax a bribe offer out of a traffic violator without directly asking for it. Even in a department in which such bribes are regularly accepted, a new officer may be unlikely to adopt the practice if an older officer does not teach him or her how. In a department in which older officers explicitly teach the techniques, the same officer might be more likely to adopt the practice. The difference in the officer's career is thus shaped by the difference in the contingencies he or she confronts.

The list of all possible contingencies is obviously endless, but these are some of the more commonly reported ones:

- the values the FTO teaches
- the values the first sergeant teaches
- the kind of citizens confronted in the first patrol assignment
- the level of danger on patrol
- whether officers work in a one-officer or two-officer car (after the training period)
- whether officers are assigned to undercover or vice work
- whether there are conflicts among police officers over ethical issues in the department
- the ethical "messages" sent out by the police executive
- the power of the police union to protect officers from being punished
- the general climate of civic integrity (or lack of it)
- the level of public pressure to control police behavior

Contingencies alone, of course, do not shape our behavior. If we were entirely the products of our environment, with no freedom of moral choice, there would be little point in writing (or reading) books on ethics. What contingencies like these do is push us in one direction or another, much like the waves in the ocean. Whether we choose to swim against the tide or flow with the waves is up to each of us.

Moral Experiences

The moral experience is a major turning point in a moral career. It can be an agonizing decision about which principles to follow or it can be a shock of recognition as you finally understand the moral principles implicit in how other people are behaving. Like the person asleep on a raft drifting out to sea, the police officer who has a moral experience suddenly discovers where he or she is and what the choices are.

Some officers have had moral experiences when they found out the system they worked for was corrupt: when the judge dismissed the charges against the son of a powerful business executive, or when a sergeant ordered the officer not to make arrests at an illegal after-hours bar. One leading police executive apparently went through a moral experience when he was first assigned to the vice squad and saw all the money that his colleagues were taking from gamblers. Shocked and disgusted, he sought and obtained a transfer to a less corrupt unit within a few weeks.

Other officers have had moral experiences in reaction to particular incidents. One Houston police rookie was out of the academy for only several weeks when he witnessed a group of his senior colleagues beat up a Mexican American, Joe Campos Torres, after he resisted arrest in a bar. Torres drowned after jumping or being pushed from a great height into a bayou, and no one knew how he had died when his body was found floating nearby. The officer discussed the incident with his father, also a Houston police officer, and the father marched the young officer right into the Internal Affairs Division to give a statement. His testimony became the basis of a federal prosecution of the other officers.

Other officers may have a moral experience when they see their ethics presented in public, outside of the police culture. New York City police captain Max Schmittberger, for example, who had been a bagman collecting graft for his superiors in New York's Tenderloin district, was greatly moved by the testimony of prostitutes he heard at the hearings of the Lexow Committee investigating police corruption in 1893. He told muckraking reporter Lincoln Steffens that the parade of witnesses opened his eyes to the reality of the corruption, so he decided to get on the witness stand himself to reveal even more details of the corruption.

No matter what contingencies occur to prompt a moral experience, the police officer faces relatively few choices about how to react. One option is to drift with the tide, letting things go on as they have been. Another option is to seek an escape route, such as a transfer, that removes the moral dilemma that may prompt the moral experience. A third option is to leave police work altogether, although the financial resources of police officers are not usually great enough to allow the luxury of resigning on principle. The fourth and most difficult option is to fight back somehow, either by blowing the whistle to the public or initiating a behind-the-scenes counterattack.

Not all moral experiences are prompted by criminal acts or even by violations of rules and regulations. Racist jokes or language, ethnic favoritism by commanders, or other issues can also prompt moral experiences. With some officers, though, nothing may ever prompt a moral experience; they may drift out to sea or back to shore, sound asleep and unaware of what is happening to them.

Apologia

For those officers with enough moral consciousness to suffer a moral experience, a failure to "do the right thing" could be quite painful to live with. "Even a bent policeman has a conscience," as a British police official who resigned on principle (inadequate police corruption investigations in London) once observed.[12] In order to resolve the conflict between what they think they should have done and what they actually did, officers often invent or adopt an acceptable explanation for their conduct. The explanation negates the principle they may have wished they actually had followed, or somehow makes their behavior consistent with that principle.

Perhaps the most famous apologia is the concept of "clean graft": bribes paid to avoid enforcement of laws against crimes that don't hurt people. Gambling and prostitution bribes were traditionally labeled as "clean graft," while bribes from narcotics pushers were labeled "dirty graft." (As narcotics traffic grew more lucrative, however, narcotics bribes were more often labeled "clean.")

The apologia for beating a handicapped prisoner in a moment of anger may draw on the police value system of maintaining respect for authority and meting out punishment because the courts will not. The apologia for stopping black suspects more often than white suspects may be the assumption that blacks are more likely to be guilty. No matter what a police officer does, he or she is apt to find *situationally justified* reasons for doing it. The reasons are things only the officer can understand because only the officer knows the full story, all the facts of the *situation*. The claim of situational expertise, of course, conveniently avoids any attempt to apply a general moral principle to conduct. The avoidance is just as effective in the officer's own mind as it would be if the apologia were discussed with the officer's spouse, clergyman, or parents.

Perhaps the most important effect of the apologia is that it allows the officer to live with a certain moral standard of behavior, to become comfortable with it. This creates the potential for further apologias about further changes in moral standards. The process can clearly become habit-forming, and it does. The progression from one apologia to the next makes up the stages of moral change.

Stages

The stages of moral change are points on a moral continuum, the different levels of moral improvement or of the "slippery slope" of moral degeneration. Such descriptions sound trite and old-fashioned, but they are commonly used by officers who get into serious trouble—such as being convicted for burglary—to account for their behavior.

The officers caught in the Denver police burglary ring in 1961, for example, appear to have progressed through many stages in their moral careers before forming an organized burglary ring:

1. First they suffered moral experiences that showed them that the laws were not impartially enforced and that judges were corrupt.
2. Then they learned that other police officers were dishonest, including those who engaged in "shopping," i.e., stealing goods at the scene of a nighttime commercial burglary, with the goods stolen by the police thus indistinguishable from the goods stolen by others.
3. They joined in the shopping themselves and constructed an apologia for it ("the insurance pays for it all anyway").
4. The apologia provided a rationale for a planned burglary in which they were burglars ("the insurance still pays for it").
5. The final stage was to commit planned burglaries on a regular basis.

These stages are logically available to all police officers. Many, perhaps most, officers progress to Stage 3 and go no further, just as most professors steal paper clips and photocopying from their universities, but not books or furniture. Why some people move into the further stages and others do not is a problem for the sociology of deviance, not ethics. The fact is that some officers do move into the more serious stages of unethical conduct after most officers have established the custom in the less serious, but still unethical, stages.

Each aspect of police ethics, from force to time to due process, has different sets of stages. Taken together, the officer's movement across all the stages on all the ethical issues makes up his or her moral career in police work. The process is not just one-way; officers can move back closer to legal principles as well as away from them. But the process is probably quite connected across different issues. Your moral stage on stealing may parallel your moral stage on force.

LEARNING ETHICS DIFFERENTLY

This article has treated morality as if it were black and white, i.e., as if it consisted of clear-cut principles to be obeyed or disobeyed. Many issues in police ethics are in fact clear-cut, and hold little room for serious philosophical analysis. One would have a hard time making a rational defense of police officers stealing, for example.

But what may be wrong with the way police ethics is now taught and learned is just that assumption: that all police ethical issues are as clear-cut as stealing. They are not. The issues of force, time, discretion, loyalty, and others are all very complex, with many shades of gray. To deny this complexity, as the formal approaches of police academies and police rule books often do, many simply encourage unethical behavior. A list of "dos" and "don'ts" that officers must follow because they are ordered to is a virtual challenge to their ingenuity: catch me if you can. And in the face of a police culture that has already established values quite contrary to many of the official rules, the black-and-white approach to ethics may be naive.

As indicated above, an alternative approach may be preferred. This would consider both clear-cut and complex ethical issues in the same fashion: examining police problems in light of basic moral principles and from the moral point of view. While there may be weaknesses in this alternative approach, it may well be the sounder road to ethical sensitivity in the context of individual responsibility.

ENDNOTES

1. See John Van Maanen, "On Becoming a Policeman," in *Policing: A View from the Street*, Peter Manning and John Van Maanen, eds. (Santa Monica, Calif.: Goodyear, 1978).
2. See John McNamara, "Uncertainties in Police Work: The Relevance of Recruits' Backgrounds and Training," in *The Police: Six Sociological Studies*, David J. Bordua, ed. (New York: Wiley, 1967).
3. Van Maanen, "On Becoming a Policeman," p. 298.
4. Ibid., p. 301.
5. See William Westley, *Violence and the Police* (Cambridge, Mass.: M.I.T. Press, 1970), pp. 159–60.
6. See William Westley Ker Muir, Jr., *Police: Streetcorner Politicians* (Chicago: University of Chicago Press, 1977).
7. See Westley, *Violence*, pp. 48–108.

8. Van Maanen, "On Becoming a Policeman," p. 302.

9. See Lawrence Sherman, "Reducing Police Gun Use" (Paper presented at the International Conference on the Management and Control of the Police Organizations, Breukelen, The Netherlands, 1980).

10. Ibid.

11. Cf. Erving Goffman, "The Moral Career of the Mental Patient," in *Asylum: Essays on the Social Situation of Mental Patients and Other Inmates* (Garden City, NY: Anchor Books, 1961), pp. 127–69.

12. See Sherman, "Reducing Police Gun Use."

Chapter 13

Police Officer Sexual Misconduct

A Field Research Study

by Allen D. Sapp

INTRODUCTION

Police officer misconduct is a complex phenomenon that varies widely in scope, intensity, duration, and incidence (Barker & Carter, 1994; Cooksey, 1992; Holden, 1992; Kevlin, 1986; Lundman, 1980; Myron, 1992; Simpson, 1977, among others). Much of the literature on police misconduct has focused on graft and corruption (see, for example, Barker and Roebuck, 1974; Goldstein, 1975; Lundman, 1980; Meyer, 1976; Sherman, 1974, among others). More recently, additional areas of officer misconduct have been studied. Barker and Carter (1990) focused on police lying and evidence tampering as a form of police misconduct. Carter reported on police brutality (1985) and offered a typology of police drug-related corruption (1990). Drug-related corruption has been the focus of a number of studies (Carter, 1990; Kraska & Kappeler, 1988; Police ethics, 1991; Sechrest and Burns, 1992, among others).

Shering (1981) studied police misconduct from an organizational perspective and identified a number of areas of organizational deviance and misconduct. Others have focused on sexual misconduct (Sapp, 1994), police and prostitutes (Kevlin, 1986), professional courtesies as misconduct (Kleinig & Gorman, 1992), and departmental rules violations (Sapp, Kappeler, & Carter, 1992).

Concern for control of police misconduct continues to be evident in the literature. Almost all of the studies cited above include some form of prescriptive recommendations to control or reduce police misconduct. Williams (1986) argues that effective maintenance of police integrity requires strong leadership by the chief of the law enforcement agency, coupled with significant changes in the organizational structure, procedures, and environment. He also suggests that changes are needed in the way police officers are selected and socialized. Goldman and Puro (1987) suggest that decertification of police officers and a national exchange of information about decertified officers would help to control corruption and other forms of police misconduct. Sykes (1985) argued that reforms that attempt to subordinate police officer discretion to bureaucratic due process were unsuccessful and produced an appearance of change without any change in the fundamental status of police misconduct.

Allen D. Sapp. Prepared especially for this Volume—1996.

RESEARCH METHODOLOGY

This report presents preliminary findings from a research project intended to make some sense of an area of human behavior that is not easily quantified or understood. The nature of the problem of police sexual misconduct cannot easily be studied through survey or experimental research. In an attempt to gain an understanding of the behavior, field research methods were used. In the fourteen years since the project began, hundreds of discussions, interviews, and conversations with law enforcement officers at all levels, from municipal to federal, have been held. Many of the discussions and interviews took place in patrol cars, while others were in the home or office of the officers. Still others took place during coffee breaks or meals during duty hours of the officers.

The conversations were not initially directed to the subject of sexual misconduct but efforts were made to direct the interview into that area of discussion. Often, data collection was simply a matter of listening and watching officers at work and noting the behaviors evidenced and discussed. Whenever possible, the anecdotal material was verified through other sources. The overall methodology followed the model suggested by Polsky (1967) for collection and analysis of field data. Similarities, differences, and norms of behavior were identified and modified throughout the process.

Ultimately, this study began to focus on the deviations from the norm. In turn, those deviations from the norm were classified into a listing of types of behavior. The reported behaviors then were added to the classification of closest proximity. That listing then became the basis for the typology offered in this report. Typologies may be the best mechanism for understanding the behavior of groups and members of groups (Weber, 1947). By using ideal typologies, a form of working hypotheses for further investigation are created.

A TYPOLOGY OF SEXUAL MISCONDUCT BY POLICE

It is likely that no other occupation or profession offers the opportunities for sexual misconduct like the police occupation. Police officers frequently work alone, usually without direct supervision, in activities that involve frequent contact with citizens. When those contacts are made, usually in relative isolation, the police officer may use his authority inappropriately. The combination of the authority of the officer and isolated contacts with female citizens creates an opportunity for inappropriate sexually motivated behaviors by the officer.

It is evident that many police officers do not engage in such behaviors, but it is also evident that many do. The problem seems to be pervasive in police departments from the smallest to the largest, in all areas of the United States, and at all levels of law enforcement, from federal to local. Since the problem is widely distributed, it is worthy of study. While the opportunity for female officers to commit similar behavior does exist (see, for example, Female deputy, 1992), occurrences are much fewer and much less likely to occur. It also is possible for same-sex activities to take place, but such occurrences are likely to be few in number. In this study, the focus is solely on male police officers who commit inappropriate sexual behaviors with female citizens.

The typology of sexually motivated behaviors by police officers offered below is preliminary. Eight categories of sexually motivated behaviors are suggested:

1. sexually motivated nonsexual contacts
2. voyeuristic contacts

3. crime victims contacts
4. offender contacts
5. juvenile female contacts
6. sexual shakedowns
7. citizen-initiated sexual contacts
8. sex crimes by police officers

The eight types are discussed below.

Sexually Motivated Nonsexual Contacts

This type of sexual misconduct involves officer-initiated contacts with female citizens without probable cause or any legal basis. The behavior is sexually motivated but does not involve direct sexual actions or even inferences of sexual motivation or actions. The impropriety of the officer's action usually is not recognized by the female citizen nor is she likely to understand the motivations behind the officer's actions.

A subtle form of sexual misconduct involves computer license checks of female drivers for the purpose of obtaining names and addresses for possible later contacts by the officer. In many police departments, dispatchers note that certain officers have a habit of running license checks on cars driven by females much more often than those with male drivers.

In a large municipal police department, a one-month review of license numbers checked without an accompanying traffic stop was conducted. Of the forty-two male traffic officers, six had more than 80 percent returns on female drivers. One dispatcher noted that some officers almost never ran license checks on cars driven by males. When the officers ran a license and it came back to a male, they often followed up with a traffic stop and a driver's license check of the female driver.

> Well, when you see a young chick driving a car, it is usually her own car and registered in her name, and if it isn't, then you know she's probably married or her old man loaned her a car. If you really want to know who she is, then you pull her over and check her license. It's also okay to ask her who owns the car and that way you learn whether she's married and all that. (Interview: Patrolman, Medium Municipal Police Department.)

In a medium-sized sheriff's department, a dispatcher/computer operator offered odds on certain deputies running a woman's license on their next license check. In one medium-sized police department, one officer ran license checks on women drivers 83 percent of the time, with only 3 percent of those checks followed by a traffic stop. In the 17 percent of checks that reflected a male owner of the car, traffic stops followed 74 percent of the time. However, over 50 percent of the subsequent driver's license checks from those stops reflected female drivers. After the review of the records, the officer was transferred to non-traffic duties.

Another variation of this type of sexual misconduct is the traffic stop made without a valid reason. Officers may also stop a female pedestrian to initiate a conversation or to get her identification with similar motivations. It is rare for a citizen to complain about these incidents since they received no citation and the sexual motivation is not obvious. However, when a female citizen is stopped repeatedly for no apparent reason, she may complain and the resultant complaint reveal the officer's motives. A recent disciplinary case involved an officer whose chief received several complaints about his repeated traffic stops of female drivers. The officer was disciplined when his only reason given was "to look them over."

> You can stop almost any female and she will be so shook up that she doesn't even question whatever you tell her. I usually say that the turn signal didn't work or the brake lights are out and they buy that. It gives me a chance to check out the driver and any passenger. A lot of times they are so glad that I just give them a warning that they invite me to a party or to call them sometimes. Other times I see them somewhere and they remember me and that leads to something. Usually, to tell you the truth it is just another traffic stop and that's all it is but those other times have been pretty good as far as picking up women. (Interview: Traffic Officer, Large Municipal Police Department.)

Voyeuristic Contacts With Citizens

Some officers spend time engaged in voyeuristic behavior while on duty. The officers seek opportunities to view unsuspecting women partially clad or nude. Other officers seek out parked cars on "lovers lane" in hopes of observing sexual activities by the occupants of the cars.

> I'll never forget my first night on the street after the Academy. I was all fired up to go out and fight crime. I was assigned to a twelve-year veteran for on the street training. As soon as we left the station, he drove over to a side street behind the college dorms and parked in the middle of the block. He even had a pocket-type telescope in his briefcase and proceeded to check out the dorm windows while telling me all about the college girls he had seen. He pointed out two windows that were usually "good hunting." After checking the dorms for 15–20 minutes, he drove over into a residential area to show me three houses where "on a good night, you'll get an eyeful." Around two o'clock, he drove into another patrol district and into a parking lot to check the windows in an apartment building where "several barmaids and go-go dancers live." He said it was a "waste of time to get there before two o'clock because they don't get home before then." I rode with him for two months and he spent most of every shift looking for women undressing in front of windows. (Interview: Patrolman, Patrol Division, Large Municipal Department.)

Officers who spend their time looking for women to view are rarely noted by the citizens who may be the target of their peeping. Women who discover a patrol car on the street are likely to blame themselves for leaving the curtains open or the blinds undrawn rather than to complain. As long as the officer responds to his service calls and does not leave the patrol vehicle to carry out his voyeuristic activities, he is unlikely to be caught and reported. Even if the officer is caught in a yard or behind a house, he can always claim to be checking out a call about a prowler.

More overt voyeurism is practiced by some officers who leave their cars and walk quietly to check parked cars in lovers' lane areas. These officers seek to observe and interrupt couples engaged in sexual activities in the parked automobiles.

> Joe and I used to hit the local parking places where the high school and college kids go to make out every weekend. Friday and Saturday nights were the best. Lots of times we sneaked up and watched the kids. You wouldn't believe some of the things we saw! [Several sexually graphic examples deleted.] Some of the girls would just really take their time getting their clothes back on like they enjoyed having us watch them. We never took anybody in—just made them get dressed while we watched and moved them on. We did arrest a couple of [homosexual males] once when we caught them. (Interview: Sergeant, Patrol Division, Large Municipal Department.)

Officers engaged in overt voyeuristic activities similar to those discussed above are rarely the subject of a complaint since the citizens being harassed are engaged in illicit activities and would likely be embarrassed to file a complaint. Unless other officers complain or unless the officer goes beyond voyeurism, the offending officer usually is not detected.

The first two classifications dealt with citizen-police contact with police initiation of the contact. The next category is one where the potential victim of sexual harassment contacts the police. The authority of the police becomes a major factor in such contacts.

Contacts With Crime Victims

Victims of crime are particularly susceptible to sexual harassment by police officers. The victims are often emotionally upset and turn to the police for support and assistance. The officer is at the scene at the request of the citizen, who is fully aware of the authority of the police officer. A wide variety of sexually motivated misbehavior may occur. Unnecessary callbacks to the residence of female victims are one of the common forms of police misconduct.

> When you drop in a few times to check on the victim or to tell her that you are still working on her case, you kind of establish a connection there. She will offer a cup of coffee or a drink. When one of them offers a drink, I usually tell them I can't drink on duty but I'll take a rain check. I get invited back a lot after hours and that sometimes leads to something. You can't do this with everyone, but if you pick them carefully, it gets me a lot of action. (Interview: Detective, Burglary Squad, Large Municipal Department.)

Sex crime victims are also susceptible to sexual harassment by officers. Some of the harassment is unintentional and results from a lack of sensitivity and knowledge on the part of the officer. Victims of sex crimes should be interviewed by well-trained officers who are knowledgeable of the psychological needs of sex crime victims. When an officer questions victims of sex offenses beyond the depth of details needed for investigation purposes, the questioning becomes a form of sexual harassment.

Many victims of rape and sexual assault have complained of being raped again by the criminal justice system. This "second rape" often starts with questioning by insensitive officers who insist on graphic details and who ask judgmental questions. Some officers have insisted on examining the victim for signs of physical injury that may involve partial disrobing by the victim. Such forms of questioning and examination are unnecessary and constitute a form of sexual harassment.

Two officers were fired by a sheriff's department in a southern state for unnecessary bodily contact with accident victims. The officers were accused of fondling or touching the breasts and genitals of accident victims on two separate occasions. Behavior of this type is likely to be reported unless the victim is unconscious. Other officers who observe such behavior may also be a source of reporting.

Contacts With Offenders

Police officers have relatively frequent opportunities for sexual harassment and sexual contact with offenders. Offenders are not only aware of the authority of the officer but are also in a position where their complaints may be disregarded or played down.

You bet I get (sex) once in a while by some broad who I arrest. Lots of times you can just hint that if you are taken care of, you could forget about what they did. One of the department stores here doesn't like to prosecute, but they always call us when they catch a shoplifter. Usually, we just talk to them and warn them and let them go. If it's a decent looking woman, sometimes I'll offer to take her home and make my pitch. Some of the snooty, high class broads turn on real quick if they think their friends and the old man doesn't have to find out about their shoplifting. I never mess around with any of the kids, but I know a couple of guys who made out with a couple of high school girls they caught on a B and E. (Interview: Detective, Theft Squad. Large Municipal Department.)

In addition to sexual demands placed on offenders, officers may also sexually harass female offenders by conducting body searches, frisks, and pat-downs. Although departmental rules and regulations require the female suspects be frisked and searched by female officers or jail matrons, officers in the field often feel justified in making a pat-down for weapons. Offenders who resist arrest may also become involved in unnecessary bodily contact. One state police officer stated: "Whenever a female starts to hassle or fight me, I just grab a [breast] and twist. That quiets them down quick."

Officials of a large metropolitan county in a midwestern state have been the subject of a civil rights suit over body searches and strip searches by officers of a different sex than the offenders. Although mostly all of the cases cited have involved female officers strip searching offenders returning from work-release programs, apparently there is a possibility for male officers to conduct similar searches for female offenders. As a result, the county has agreed to avoid opposite sex strip searches whenever possible. Interestingly, the county justified its actions by reference to a previous civil suit that resulted in a court order requiring the county to assign identical duties to male and female corrections officers.

Offenders who are in detention are in a position where sexual harassment behaviors can take place with relative impunity. Most jails are not constructed to provide privacy for inmates. Female inmates often can be seen in their cells, showers, toilets, or during searches by jail matrons. Some officers apparently seek out opportunities to observe females in various degrees of undress.

Look at the women? Hell, you can't help but look at the women in here. The showers don't have any doors on them and you can't always wait until the showers are empty to go into the cell block. Some of the women try to show their bodies off to you, too. We don't have air conditioning and when the weather is hot, they lay around their cells with just underwear or even buck naked most of the time. I see so many naked women that after a while you just don't even notice it anymore. Now once in a while, we get a really built one in and the guys will make it a point to catch her in the shower or dressing, but most of those we get are really pigs, not worth looking at. (Interview: Sheriff's Detention Officer, Large Sheriff's Department.)

Female inmates in smaller jails particularly are sometimes exposed to sexual demands by their guardians. In many small jails, only one or two officers are on duty during the evening hours and their behavior is largely unsupervised.

Over in a county west of here, they tell that a sheriff will sometimes grab a hooker working one of the truck stops or the rest areas on the Interstate (highway) over there and keep her in jail over the weekend. He works out some kind of a deal where he turns them loose without any charges or anything and they put out for the sheriff and the deputies that might be interested. I've heard this from several officers and I believe it's true. Now I don't go for that kind of stuff at all. Seems to me that the sheriff over there is really asking for trouble over this kind of thing. It is different if some woman in the jail wants to have a party or whatever with some of the deputies or the sheriff but to go out and arrest one and then make the deal is too much. (Interview: Patrolman, Working as Jailer at Medium Municipal Jail.)

Contact With Juvenile Offenders

Younger females may also be the subject of sexual harassment by police officers. Runaways, truants, and delinquents are in a position similar to that of adult offenders in relation to police authority and lack of credibility. Juvenile females may be highly impressionable and easily influenced by the police officer. They are much less likely to be "street wise" and to understand the limits of police authority and proper police behavior. A former juvenile squad sergeant in Louisiana was the subject of a recent television program after he failed to appear for trial on charges that he sexually molested a 12-year-old girl that he was "counseling" after earlier abuse by someone else.

Several of the officers interviewed for this chapter were aware of sexual contact between officers and underage females but all declined to discuss details or to have their comments recorded. In a Texas city, an officer assigned to a junior high school as a school liaison officer was fired after disclosure of his sexual involvement with several female students.

> I tell you, it takes a really crazy guy to go after the San Quentin quails. Some of the juvenile girls look like 21 and some act like 35 but it just ain't worth the trouble if you get caught. Some of the girls fall in love or think they are in love if you [have sex with] them and they can really cause trouble calling you and writing notes and all that teenage stuff. I knew a guy that chased after the young girls all the time and he claims he got a lot of action, and he probably did because they were always calling him. He was single and I guess that helped him not get caught but it is really not worth it. (Interview: Patrol Officer, Large Municipal Police Department.)

Of the officers interviewed for this study, none admitted to having such contact themselves. This may be the rarest of the various forms of sexual misconduct because of the possible penalties.

Sexual Shakedowns

Demanding sexual service from prostitutes, homosexuals, or other citizens involved in illegal or illicit activities is one of the more severe forms of sexual harassment. Actual sexual activities are involved with an unwilling citizen who yields solely on the basis of the police authority to arrest and prosecute.

> I know several dozen guys who have worked vice in the ten years I've been assigned to the vice squad. I believe everyone of them has gone beyond the rules on sex with prostitutes. You see, when you are assigned to the prostitute detail, you have to get the female subject to offer specific sexual acts and then state a price for those sex acts. Once you have that, you have a case and are supposed to identify and arrest. Sometimes the officer goes ahead and has sex and then makes the arrest and files a report saying he followed the procedures. If the whore claims otherwise, no one believes her anyway since they think she is just trying to get her case tossed out. Have I ever done that? Well, I'm not saying I did but I've been in this business ten years so you draw your own conclusion. Everyone I know does it at one time or another. The

prostitute squad isn't the only way vice officers get action. I've been offered, and I'm not saying I took up the offers, understand, but I've been offered sexual services from barmaids, gamblers, narcotic addicts, and dealers, and damn near every other kind of case you run into. Most of those cases are just between you and the suspect and they will do almost anything to avoid the arrest. Guys that would never even consider taking money will take (oral sex or intercourse) from a good looking woman. I don't know if the guys who are oversexed get assigned to vice or if being exposed to so much of it makes the vice squad oversexed, but it seems to me there is more going on in vice than anywhere else. (Interview: Vice Squad Sergeant, Large Municipal Department.)

Police officers who exchange preferential treatment for sexual favors are not limited to those with the vice squad. Officers on traffic details, patrol, or other investigative squads may also offer differential treatment in exchange for sexual services.

When I first went on patrol, I was surprised to hear some of the other officers talking about the sex they got on duty or as a result of on-duty calls. Seems like everyone talked about it. I really didn't have any offers or even really think about it until I was assigned to a one-man car and one night I stopped a female subject for running a traffic light. She was really first class and the way she acted I just kind of hinted that maybe we could reach an understanding and she picked right up on it. Well, she had enough moving violations that another one could take her license and I guess she didn't want that to happen. Anyway, I met her later that night and had a wild session. I called her again a few days later and she wouldn't even talk to me. Yeah, I've had a few similar type experiences since but I'm real careful. It really isn't worth it if you get caught. There is plenty of opportunities without pressuring someone or taking a chance on someone filing on you. (Interview: Patrol Officer, Patrol Division, Medium Municipal Department.)

I worked traffic for a couple of years in (another city) before I quit and came here. I tell you, it was a rare night when I didn't get the batted eyes and tears and the "officer, I'll do anything" routine. My zone was close to the college and lots of the college girls were afraid that their old man would take their cars away, I guess, if they got tickets. We used to refer to traffic duty around the college as "fox hunting." It was quite an experience but after a while you get tired of it. Some of them would really give you a come-on and then later when it got right down to the nitty-gritty they wanted to back out or play kid games. You know, petting and no serious sex. One guy was supposed to meet one girl after the shift and when he showed up, her boyfriend came along. Man, that kind of stuff is weird and too risky. Naw, I didn't take up very many of them on the offers. I guess you could say that a couple of times I let it be known that maybe we could negotiate, but most always they made the offers. (Interview: Former Traffic Officer, Medium Municipal Department.)

Officers engaged in various forms of sexual shakedowns are engaged in activities that clearly are illegal and subject to severe penalties. While sexual shakedowns of prostitutes may be less risky, shakedowns of other citizens could easily become the subject of complaints.

Citizen-Initiated Sexual Contacts

Some sexual contacts between law enforcement officers and female citizens are initiated by citizens rather than by the police officer. It is a rare police department that does not have stories about "police groupies," females, often young, who are attracted sexually to the uniform, weapons, or power of the police officer. Officers in many departments have been disciplined and/or dismissed for participating in sexual activities with "groupies."

Another form of citizen-initiated sexual contact is the call from lonely or mentally disturbed women who seek attention and affection from an officer. Most law enforcement officers are familiar with these service calls when a citizen calls for an officer and has no real reason for doing so other than to have someone with whom to talk. Some women offer sex in exchange for the officer's time and attention. Officers who take the offered sexual services often are dealing with a person who needs other forms of professional attention. These citizens may become well-known throughout the department.

> We have several of the women who will call once or twice a week, always late at night to report a prowler or an attempted break-in or some other reason. We have to dispatch an officer when we get calls like that but everyone knows the addresses now and we warn our officers to avoid any situation where they would be compromised. We have orders to the dispatchers to always send a two-man unit or else send two units. These women are sick in my opinion because all they want when the officers get there is to talk and have the officers stay for a while. Some of them will offer sex or money or whatever just to keep the officers around for a while. I don't think we have any of our troops engaging in sex with any of these that we know about. Everyone knows what is going on when we get a call from them. I'm sure they aren't the only ones around and maybe there are others I don't know about. I guess some of the officers might not recognize that these subjects are sick but I don't know. (Interview: Captain, Patrol Division, Large Municipal Department.)

> There are three or maybe four addresses here in town that everyone knows when a car is dispatched that it's another call from one of the "lonely hearts" club. Everyone laughs but no one really wants the call because every time you make one of those runs everyone kids about whether you took care of the lady and so forth. You know, some guys never seem to know when an old joke is enough. You know what I mean? They just keep it up and no one is going to mess around with those women even though one of them is pretty young and fairly good-looking. She always answers the door in a nightgown that is nearly see-through and is scared or pretends to be so scared that she wants you to stay for a while. I answered one call, not one of the known addresses, and the woman just had a towel around her and she claimed someone was trying to get into her window while she was taking a shower. Well, when we looked the place over, the bathroom wasn't wet, the bed had been slept in and this was three o'clock in the morning. She just got lonely and wanted a man. I'll admit, she looked pretty good in that towel and she wasn't real careful, you know, about keeping it closed up and all. If I was there by myself I might of been tempted. My partner and I laughed about it but I'm sure other calls like that happen. The brass really stresses the known addresses and we have all been warned about them. They don't know about others though. (Interview: Patrolman in Captain's Division—see above.)

A third type of sexual contact initiated by the citizen is the offer of sexual services in return for favors, preferential treatment, or additional protection. This form of sexual contact is differentiated from officer-initiated contacts by the citizen making the offer without any prior indication from the officer that such an offer might be considered. Obviously, law enforcement officers who accept such offers in exchange for favors or preferential treatment are engaged in illegal use of police authority.

> I answered a call one day about a suspicious person out in one of the better neighborhoods. When I got there the woman, she was really a fox, about 35, and anyway, she wanted to know if it would be possible for me to come by her house several times a shift because her old man and her had split and he was harassing her by coming by and pounding on the door and such. I told her she would have to file a complaint and then she said that she was willing to "take

care of me" if I would just watch her house when I could. She said that she would "screw my brains out" if I would just drive by a few times. It was tempting but I figured it would probably cause me trouble if I went for the deal so I hadda turn her down. Sure hated to but you know how it is. (Interview: Deputy Sheriff, Patrol Division, Medium County Sheriff's Department.)

Even though most police officers do not misuse their authority or take advantage of the numerous opportunities for sexual harassment of female citizens, some do and the result is that exploitation of citizens by law enforcement officers lessens the respect for the department involved and all other law enforcement agencies and officers. Control of officers who sexually harass citizens is extremely difficult to achieve but it is a task that should receive attention from police administrators.

Sex Crimes by Police Officers

A number of cases of sexual assaults on jail inmates have been documented in recent years. Recently, a former sheriff in a border state was indicted on fifteen counts of rape and sodomy where the victims were inmates in his jail. At the time of the latest indictments, he was serving a sentence in a federal prison for earlier conviction based on similar behavior. A patrol officer was convicted in a major southern city after his arrest and subsequent rape of a citizen. Other jurisdictions have had similar cases where police officers on duty committed a serious sex crime. While a number of officers interviewed for the study indicated they were aware of such things happening, none were willing to admit to such activities.

SUMMARY AND CONCLUSIONS

The sample size and the limitations of the field research methods (Babbie, 1992) preclude conclusions that the observed behavior represents the universe of police sexual misconduct. The use of anecdotal data included cases where officers related stories about other officer behavior. Self-reports are also subject to exaggeration and embellishment. The results cannot be generalized beyond the officers studied. Therefore, the typology is offered as a heuristic finding that may aid further research to the topic.

Sexual harassment and sexual misconduct as part of law enforcement must not be acceptable in any law enforcement agency. This problem is similar to many others; by accepting some level of misconduct, the department invites such conduct. Only when administrators and supervisors make it clear to every member of the department that sexual misconduct and sexual harassment will not be tolerated in any form or any degree is the behavior likely to decrease. Police officers should be educated about sexual misconduct and its effect upon the department and the public. Sexual misconduct and sexual harassment of female citizens by male law enforcement officers can be reduced or eliminated only by a concerted effort of police administrators and supervisors. Apathy towards sexual misconduct and harassment must be reduced, both on the part of police officials and the general public. As long as the "boys will be boys" attitude prevails, sexual harassment will not receive the attention it deserves.

The secrecy surrounding sexual harassment and other forms of police misconduct must be removed. As long as misconduct of any type is hidden and thus largely invisible, the misconduct will continue. If the general public and the police officers are fully aware of the appropriate limits on police contacts with female citizens, the shroud of secrecy is torn and the misconduct is identified. Once police misconduct involving sexual harassment or sexually motivated behavior and activities is identified, appropriate disciplinary action must be taken. The disciplinary action should be fair, firm, and appropriate for the degree and type of misconduct. Dismissal and/or criminal charges are certainly within the range of appropriate responses to some of the more serious forms of sexual harassment and misconduct. On a broader scale, sexual misconduct in all occupations will not be eliminated until such time as we make basic changes in society and in our views of sex roles.

REFERENCES

Babbie, E. (1992). *The Practice of Social Research*, 6th ed. Belmont, CA: Wadsworth.

Barker, T. and Roebuck, J.B. (1974). *An Empirical Typology of Police Corruption: A Study in Organizational Deviance*. Springfield, IL: Charles C. Thomas.

Barker, T. (1978). "An Empirical Study of Police Deviance Other than Corruption," *Journal of Police Science and Administration*, 6(3), 264–272.

Barker, T. and Carter, D. L., eds. (1994). *Police Deviance*, 3rd ed. Cincinnati: Anderson.

Barker, T. and Carter, D. L. (1990). "Fluffing Up the Evidence and Covering Your Ass: Some Conceptual Notes on Police Lying." *Deviant Behavior*, 11(1) 61–75.

Brady, D. H. (1992). "Police Corruption and Community Actions: Community Policing," *Police Studies*, 15(4), 178–183.

Carter, D. L. (1990). "Drug-related Corruption of Police Officers: A Contemporary Typology," *Journal of Criminal Justice*, 18(2) 85–98.

Carter, D. L. (1985). "Police Brutality: A Model for Definition, Perspective, and Control," in A. Blumberg and E. Niederhoffer, eds., *The Ambivalent Force: Perspectives on the Police*, 3rd ed. New York: Holt, Rinehart & Winston.

Cooksey, O. E. (1992). "Corruption: A Continuing Challenge for Law Enforcement," *FBI Law Enforcement Bulletin*, 60(9), 5–9.

"Female Deputy Fired for Sexually Harassing Males." (December 15, 1992). *Law Enforcement News*, 18, 3.

Goldman, R. and Puro, S. (1987). "Decertification of Police: An Alternative to Traditional Remedies for Police Misconduct," *Hastings Constitutional Law Quarterly*, 15(1) 45–80.

Goldstein, H. (1975). *Police Corruption: A Perspective on Its Nature and Control*. Washington, D.C.: Police Foundation.

"Harassment in the Workplace: A Proactive Approach." (1991). *The Police Chief*, 58(12), 29–30.

Holden, R. N. (1992). *Law Enforcement: An Introduction*. Englewood Cliffs, NJ: Prentice Hall.

Kevlin, T. A. (1986). "Police Corruption and Prostitution in the United States: The Historical Background," *Journal of Police and Criminal Psychology*, 2(2), 24–38.

Kleinig, J. and Gorman, A. J. (1992). "Professional Courtesies: To Ticket or Not to Ticket," *American Journal of Police*, 11(4), 97–113.

Kraska, P. B. and Kappeler, V. E.(1988). "Police On-Duty Drug Use: A Theoretical and Descriptive Examination," *American Journal of Police*, 7(1), 1–28.

Lundman, R. J., ed. (1980). *Police Behavior*. New York: Oxford University Press.

Meyer, J. C., Jr. (1976). "Definitional and Etiological Issues in Police Corruption: Assessment and Synthesis of Competing Perspectives," *Journal of Police Science and Administration*, 4(1), 46–55.

Myron, P. (1992). "Crooks or Cops: We Can't be Both," *The Police Chief*, 59(1) 23–25.

"Police Ethics: Building Integrity and Reducing Drug Corruption." (1991). *The Police Chief*, 58(1), 1.

Polsky, N. (1967). *Hustlers, Beats, and Others*. Chicago, IL: Aldine.

Sapp, A. D. (1994). "Sexual Misconduct by Police Officers," in T. Barker and D. L. Carter, eds. *Police Deviance*, 3rd ed. Cincinnati: Anderson Publishing Company.

Sapp, A. D., Kappeler, V. E. and Carter, D. L. (1992). "Police Officer Higher Education, Citizen Complaints, and Departmental Rule Violations," *American Journal of Police*, 11(2), 37–54.

Sechrest, D. K. and Burns, P. (1992) "Police Corruption: The Miami Case," *Criminal Justice & Behavior*, 19(3), 294–313.

Shearing, C. D., ed. (1981). *Organizational Police Deviance: Its Structure and Control*. Toronto, Canada: Butterworth.

Sherman, L. W., ed. (1974). *Police Corruption: A Sociological Perspective*. New York: Doubleday.

Simpson, A. E. (1977). *The Literature of Police Corruption*, Vol. 1. New York: John Jay Press.

Sykes, G. W. (1985). "The Myth of Reform: The Functional Limits of Police Accountability in a Liberal Society," *Justice Quarterly*, 2(1), 51–65.

Weber, M. (1947). *The Theory of Social and Economic Organization*. New York: Oxford University Press.

Williams, H. (1986). "Maintaining Police Integrity: Municipal Policing in the United States," *Police Studies*, 9(1), 27–31.

Chapter 14

Public Attitudes Toward Police Pursuit Driving

What Do Studies on Attitudes Toward Police Pursuit Reveal?

by John M. MacDonald
Department of Criminal Justice and Criminology
University of Maryland

Geoffrey P. Alpert
College of Criminal Justice
University of South Carolina

INTRODUCTION

Studies of police vehicle pursuits include information from official agency forms, officers and even suspects (Alpert, 1997; Lucadamo, 1994; Alpert and Fridell, 1992; Falcone, Wells, and Charles, 1992). Although empirical studies have reported the risks and benefits of pursuit driving, as well as the attitudes of law enforcement personnel, little is known about the public's perception of pursuit. The research on pursuit policy development, pursuit outcome, and civil liability has identified four critical factors important to police in reaching a pursue/don't pursue decision (Alpert and Fridell, 1992; Alpert, 1997):

1. known violation,
2. area in which the chase occurred,
3. traffic conditions, and
4. weather conditions.

A fifth consideration should be the public's understanding of and support for pursuit. This study reports information on the public's support for pursuit.

Previous Research on Attitudes Toward Pursuit

It was not until the 1960s that police pursuit was considered a critical issue for either the police or the public. During that decade, two juxtaposed positions became the focus of the pursuit debate: the benefit of pursuit, or need to enforce laws and apprehend violators; and the risk of pursuit, or the importance of public safety. While these two concerns have been the cornerstone of the pursuit argument and the courts have balanced them in their opinions, precious little information has been collected on the views of officers or the public on the issue.

During the late 1960s, an effort was made to determine the public's response to pursuit driving. A small public opinion survey was conducted to measure the support for police pursuit driving. According to Fennessy et al. (1970:11), a random sample of the driving population of Fairfax County, Virginia, was questioned about pursuit driving and penalties for fleeing from the police. Each subject was given a short scenario in which a motorist did not stop when signaled by a police officer's emergency signals. Sixty-four percent of the subjects agreed that the police should chase the fleeing suspect, 33 percent responded that they should not chase the suspect, and 3 percent did not reply. In addition, members of the driving public were asked to indicate whether a fleeing motorist should be sent to prison, lose his license, receive a heavy fine, or receive a light fine. Almost 11 percent responded that the fleeing motorist should be sent to prison and almost 63 percent reported that the motorist should lose his license. Twenty-six percent wanted the law violator fined heavily, and no one reported a light fine as an appropriate punishment. From the data reported in the survey, it certainly appears that the public in the late 1960s was less than unanimous in its support for pursuit driving, but regarded fleeing from a police officer as a serious law violation deserving relatively heavy sanctions.

Unfortunately, this early survey provided only one scenario. It did not ask those surveyed about other offenses for which the suspect might have been chased. Similarly, the research did not address risk factors associated with pursuit driving; however, the study was important as a first step in determining the level of the public's support for pursuit as a police tactic.

Although the focus of this study is on the public's perception of pursuit, the lack of research on attitudes toward pursuit permits the review of all attitudinal research, including studies of both public and officers' opinions. Eight studies were found that analyzed attitudes toward pursuit. Each had some methodological imperfection, but, nonetheless, contributed to a knowledge of pursuit. The first study, conducted in 1991 by the University of Utah for the Salt Lake City Police Department, measured the public's attitude toward chasing. In a state-wide survey of residents (805 subjects), 28 percent reported that police should routinely pursue suspects. Fifty-six percent said that police should only pursue in cases involving forcible felonies and 8 percent reported that police should not pursue suspects at all. Five percent reported other answers and 3 percent reported "don't know" (Reese, 1991).

The second study was conducted by Falcone, Charles, and Wells (1994). Falcone has been a leader in the design, collection, and analysis of officers' attitudes and beliefs about pursuit. His research included a sample of officers and agencies in Illinois. The data from this research included opinions from almost all of the responding officers that pursuits are "somewhat" or "absolutely essential" for controlling crime and maintaining order (Falcone, Wells, and Charles, 1992:104–5). Further, Falcone and his colleagues reported that the respondents had different opinions about the offense categories that would justify pursuit. The categories ranged from traffic offenses to driving under the influence (DUI), and included misdemeanors, felonies, drug offenses, and forcible felonies (Falcone, Wells, and Charles, 1992:73). The authors acknowledged that there appeared to be an attitudinal split between law enforcement officers in some areas. Some officers admitted the risks of pursuit and avoided pursuing suspects, while others considered that the benefits outweighed the risks. These officers readily pursued suspects (Falcone, Wells, and Charles, 1992:73).

Although differences existed among the respondents in Falcone's research, several consistent themes emerged. As one would expect, the seriousness of the offense was positively and strongly correlated to the need to pursue. Most officers reported (in declining order) that reasons to terminate a pursuit included traffic conditions, certain speed zones, dangerousness of offense and weather conditions. More than 84 percent reported that a pursuit should be permitted for a forcible felony (Falcone, Wells, and Charles, 1992:106). Most officers reported that they did not believe that the majority of citizens would run from them if their agency had a no-pursuit policy. Falcone, Wells, and Charles (1994:150–51) concluded the following:

> Actually, officers thought that somewhere between five and 15% of the population would be so encouraged. . . . Most officers also mentioned that many of the would-be offenders would probably attempt to elude them despite the presence of a no-pursuit policy.

Insight into why officers continue pursuits was provided by the research of Falcone, Wells, and Charles (1992:81):

> Most officers interviewed agreed that it became difficult to call off a pursuit once they became involved in such an activity. Not only did they report that the chase often became a personal challenge requiring them to win over the violator, but they frequently admitted to a high state of excitement that often shaded their good judgment.

This view has also been presented by other research (Homant and Kennedy, 1994a:116):

> All too often, an officer becomes so personally involved in the capture of a suspect that the safety of others is forgotten. The chase then becomes a matter of professional pride in driving skill: the officer concentrates only on winning.

While the officers reported general resentment on any limitation to pursue aggressively, it was acknowledged that "discretionary pursuit behaviors are not institutionally rewarded, are not given clear support by the majority of their peers [and] are not part of their public safety mandate inherent in their departmental mission" (Falcone, Charles, and Wells, 1994:152). Perhaps the most important conclusion drawn from these data reflects on the response to restricting officers' discretionary pursuit actions. In a comparative analysis of police agencies, Falcone, Charles, and Wells (1994:154) reported: "The data suggest that civilian departments which discourage pursuit policies experience no increase in attempts to elude and show that actual pursuits were lower than in departments with more permissive policies."

The third study, conducted by Britz and Payne (1994), was designed to determine if attitudes toward pursuit policies differed between line officers and administrators. The researchers surveyed police officers in a state agency. The officers reported serious deficiencies in the language of their pursuit policy, as well as problems with training (Britz and Payne, 1994:115, 131). Specifically, the results of this study indicated that 38 percent of the officers found the pursuit policy difficult to understand (and implement); 80 percent of the supervisors reported that no training on pursuit was provided to their patrol officers; and 35 percent of the officers had been in pursuits that were not reported. As expected, there were significant differences among the ranks concerning "perceptions of policy, supervisory support, the adequacy of training, liability issues and discretionary issues regarding police pursuit" (Britz and Payne, 1994:131).

In a fourth study, conducted by Picolo (1994), a mall intercept method and a quota sample were used to investigate the public's attitude toward pursuit driving. This innovative study also examined whether exposure to information about risks influenced attitudes toward pursuit. Picolo approached and received permission to interview 200 males and 200 females of age twenty-one years or older (50 percent White and 50 percent Black) and who were randomly assigned to control and experimental groups. Members of the "control" group were provided with only a standard definition of pursuit. Members of the "experimental" group were provided the same definition, as well as a series of risk statistics from Alpert and Dunham's (1990) study of pursuit driving. Finally, each subject was given a nineteen-item survey concerning attitudes toward pursuit under adverse conditions. Picolo reported that there was, generally, only moderate support for pursuit and quite low support for the most risky scenarios. Further, Picolo concluded:

> [W]hite men seem to be exceptionally different from white women, black men and black women in their attitudes toward the use of hot pursuits. Over and over again, white males are overwhelmingly more supportive of pursuits regardless of the seriousness of a criminal offense, the road and weather conditions, and the locations in which they occur (1994:77).

White males were the group most affected by the introduction of risk factors. While the other racial and gender comparisons revealed insignificant attitudinal differences based upon introduction to the risk factors, the white male "experimental" group was the only one that reported significantly less support for a continued pursuit and more support to terminate a chase. Picolo attributes these differences to the crime control orientation of White males and the relative importance of the knowledge about risks.

The fifth study, by Homant and Kennedy (1994a), involved a survey of registered voters in a suburb of approximately 80,000 people near Detroit. The researchers mailed out survey instruments to their sample and received a 40 percent return. The members of the public who responded reported that police officers use good judgment in deciding whether to engage in a high-speed pursuit (76 percent). Interestingly, 60 percent reported that the police should be allowed to engage in a high-speed pursuit only to prevent the escape of someone known to be a dangerous criminal. Although it is not clear, this could suggest that 36 percent of the respondents did not support a pursuit for even a dangerous felon. Fifteen percent of the respondents reportedly would be tempted to elude if it was known that the police would not follow in pursuit. The authors report that the 15 percent plus a 6 percent "unsure" response is a low estimate because registered voters may be more prosocial than nonregistered voters.

The sixth study, also by Homant and Kennedy (1994b), was designed to examine pursuit tendencies among patrol officers from departments with different policies. Officers from seven state agencies completed the questionnaires and formed the sample for this study. One part of the study asked officers to respond to scenarios by indicating their willingness to pursue. The researchers reported, "As predicted, states with the most permissive policies had officers who were most inclined to pursue, while the more restrictive states had officers that were less inclined" (Homant and Kennedy, 1994b:103).

A seventh study conducted, by Steele (1995), explored officers' attitudes toward pursuit as a police tactic. More than 200 officers from a suburban county were surveyed to determine their attitudes toward pursuit and to determine if knowledge of risks associated with pursuit affected these attitudes. The methods of this study incorporated the same concepts and measures as Picolo's (1994) research discussed above. Steele's research found that experienced officers were more likely to terminate a pursuit than officers with less experience; exposure to risk had little to do with the formulation of their attitudes.

In the eighth study, Alpert and Madden (1994) reported the attitudes of students majoring in criminal justice, police recruits, and police supervisors. Groups of subjects were provided a set of pursuit scenarios. Each scenario contained four bits of information depicting the environment of a pursuit: the need to immediately apprehend the suspect (known offense), area in which the chase occurred, traffic, and weather conditions (risk factors). The results demonstrated that supervisors were most likely, and the students were least likely, to support a general decision to pursue. Police supervisors weighed the need to immediately apprehend a suspect as more important than the risks to the officers and the public. Law enforcement was given a higher priority than public safety. Students ranked the risk factors as more important than the need to immediately apprehend criminal suspects: public safety was ranked higher than the apprehension of offenders. It was anticipated that police recruits would support pursuit driving to a greater degree than the students; however, their responses were in between the other two groups. Thus, the dilemma of pursuit as a police tactic was underscored. Police supervisors, who can terminate a pursuit, viewed the tactic differently from a group of young citizens studying criminal justice and a group of young citizens learning to become police officers.

Summary of Research Findings

The information gleaned from these eight studies provides insight into the attitudes held by officers and the public concerning pursuit driving. Together, this information indicates that pursuit driving is a controversial tactic that is viewed differently by various groups or samples. Previous research showed that officers resented having their discretion reduced or controlled; policies were not understood; training was not received or remembered; and officers got caught up in the heat of the chase. Despite these facts, many of these same officers realized the need for restrictions and placed public safety over the need to immediately apprehend certain suspects. It may be that the officers who most resented the institutional control engaged in pursuit driving, but did not always report it. The little these studies learned about the public's attitudes toward pursuit indicated that citizens view pursuit with a cautious eye and provide only limited support. There is a great deal the public does not know about the benefits or costs of pursuit.

METHODOLOGY

The present study examined attitudes toward police pursuit held by citizens in Aiken County, South Carolina; Omaha, Nebraska; and Baltimore, Maryland. The survey instrument presented pursuit scenarios by creating categories that corresponded to the existing empirical information affecting officers' decisions to engage in pursuit driving (Alpert and Fridell, 1992). The benefits of pursuit or the *need to immediately apprehend* included eight levels of potential law violations, under high-risk and low-risk conditions. The potential costs or *risks to the public* included three categories: area of pursuit, traffic, and weather conditions. The area in which the chase occurred had four levels. The traffic and weather conditions each had two levels (see Table 1).

Subjects were asked to imagine that the police had initiated a traffic or felony stop and that the suspect refused to pull over and actively attempted to flee and avoid apprehension. Consistent with prior research and discussions with officers after pretesting the instrument, subjects were asked not to rank the aggressiveness or degree of pursuit, but to respond with a simple "yes" or "no" dichotomy. The factors and levels are presented in Table 1.

Systematic sampling was used in Aiken County and Omaha to generate a random probability sample. For a probability sample, each sampling unit must have some known nonzero chance of being selected and, before sampling takes place, every possible sample of a given size must be capable of being specified from the population. The primary advantage of a probability sample is that it allows statistical inferences of the results to the target population.

Interviewers were given the following instructions for sample selection: (1) Select the bottom name in the first column for each page in the telephone listing pages received;

TABLE 1.   Factors Influencing the Decision to Pursue

Need to apprehend

Traffic offense
Property misdemeanor
DUI
Stolen vehicle
Nonviolent felony other than stolen vehicle
Violent felony, no reported death
Violent felony with reported death
Officer shot

Risk factors

---

1. Chase area
     Freeway
     Commercial
     Inner-city
     Residential
2. Weather conditions
     Wet
     Dry
3. Traffic Conditions
     Congested
     Noncongested

---

and (2) If there is no answer, the line is busy, or it is a business or inoperative number, dial the number directly above.

To ensure that the sample was representative of households with unlisted as well as listed numbers, the plus-one dialing method was used by the interviewers. In this method, the interviewer adds one to the last digit of the phone number selected through the systematic sampling method, and then dials that number. (For example, if the telephone number of the last name in the first column is 777-6074 the interviewer dialed 777-6075.) In Aiken County, a sample of 255 residents was interviewed. According to the most recent census data for Aiken County, the sample interviewed was similar to the population according to age, gender, and geographic area.

In Omaha, 300 telephone surveys with randomly selected Omaha residents were conducted in the same way as those administered in Aiken County. The interview schedule and training guide included the same questions and instructions as the one used in Aiken County. As in Aiken County, the sample interviewed was representative of the population in Omaha.

In Baltimore, the survey was conducted from a sample of all residents, eighteen years and older. A random sample of phone numbers was purchased from Survey Sampling, Inc. of Connecticut. Each phone number was called twice to obtain a response. Four hundred and forty-four numbers purchased from Survey Sampling were appropriate for the study. Out of these 444 eligible numbers, 275 refused to answer the survey. As a result of these methods, the final sample of respondents was 169, which represented a 38 percent response rate. Similar to the Aiken County and Omaha samples, the Baltimore sample overall was representative of the city's population.[1]

Two survey instruments were administered in Baltimore. The first instrument was similar to the one used in the other two areas. The second survey instrument provided citizens with some general statistical information about the outcome of pursuits and then asked for responses to specific questions. Specifically, respondents were told that approximately 40 percent of pursuits result in accidents, 20 percent of the pursuits result in injuries, and 1 percent of the pursuits result in a death. Additionally, respondents were told that nationwide, there are between 350 and 400 people killed per year as a result of police pursuit, and the police have no way to stop a fleeing vehicle without setting up a roadblock, ramming the car, or shooting it. The first instrument that did not provide information to the subjects was completed by ninety-two citizens (54 percent). The second instrument that provided the information about pursuits was completed by seventy-seven of the subjects (46 percent).

FINDINGS

The data presented below include results from all three jurisdictions and are presented for comparison, but are limited to the high-risk, low-risk level questions. The first analysis includes responses to questions concerning general support for pursuits under high-risk conditions.[2] Second, responses to questions concerning general support for pursuit under low-risk conditions are presented.[3] Finally, the differences in responses of Baltimore residents to the instrument that provided results of pursuit driving and the one that provided no information is presented under low-risk conditions.

High-Risk Conditions

The data for high-risk conditions are presented in Table 2. Under high-risk conditions involving traffic violations, approval for police pursuits was given by 13 percent of the respondents from Omaha, 30 percent of the respondents from Aiken County, and 27 percent of respondents from Baltimore. Property crime—misdemeanor pursuits were approved by only 21 percent of Omaha respondents, 38 percent of the respondents from Aiken County, and 36 percent of those from Baltimore. Property crime—felony pursuits (other than those involving stolen vehicles) were supported by 48 percent of the respondents from Omaha, 61 percent of those from Aiken County, and 50 percent of those from Baltimore. When a vehicle was stolen, 44 percent of respondents from Omaha, 77 percent of respondents from Aiken County, and 48 percent of those respondents from Baltimore supported the police when pursuing the suspect. Seventy-one percent of Omaha respondents, 77 percent of Aiken County respondents and 70 percent of Baltimore respondents approved pursuits for DUI. Violent felony—no reported death pursuits were approved by 88 percent of Omaha respondents, 74 percent of Aiken County respondents, and 68 percent of Baltimore respondents. Violent felony—reported death pursuits were approved by 96 percent of those from Omaha, 90 percent of those from Aiken County, and 83 percent of those from Baltimore. The difference between all three samples was statistically significant at the .05 level. Cases in which a police officer was shot were approved by 97 percent of those Omaha, 91 percent of those from Aiken County, and 86 percent of those from Baltimore.

At this high level of risk conditions, the least serious offenses received one of the largest differences among respondents. A pursuit for a traffic offense was supported by 13 percent of the Omaha respondents and 30 percent of those from Aiken County. Incidents involving property crimes—misdemeanors received 38 percent support from Aiken County respondents and 21 percent support from respondents in Omaha. Sixty-one per-

TABLE 2. High-Risk Conditions: Percent of Respondents Approving Pursuit for Specified Offenses

	Aiken county (n = 255)	Baltimore (n = 169)	Omaha (n = 300)
Traffic violation	30	27	13
Property crime—misdemeanor	38	36	21
Property crime—felony (other than stolen car)	61	50	48
Stolen vehicle	77	48	44
DUI	77	70	71
Violent felony—no reported death	74	68	88
Violent felony—reported death	90[a]	83[a]	96[a]
Police officer shot	91	86	97

[a]All three categories were statistically significant at the $P < 0.05$ level.

cent of respondents from Aiken County supported pursuit, while 48 percent of respondents from Omaha supported pursuit for incidents involving property crime felonies. Incidents involving stolen vehicles received 62 percent support from respondents in Aiken County and 44 percent support from respondents in Omaha.

Low-Risk Conditions

The data on low-risk conditions are presented in Table 3. Under low-risk conditions involving traffic violations, approval for a police pursuit was given by 47 percent of the respondents from Omaha, 68 percent of the respondents from Aiken County, and 81 percent of respondents from Baltimore. Property crime—misdemeanors pursuits were approved by only 50 percent of respondents from Omaha, 66 percent of those from Aiken County, and 62 percent of those from Baltimore. In property crime—felony pursuits (other than those involving stolen vehicles), approval for a pursuit was given by 83 percent of respondents from Omaha, 84 percent of those from Aiken County, and 73 percent of those from Baltimore. In stolen vehicle pursuits, 84 percent of Omaha respondents, 83 percent from Aiken County, and 91 percent from Baltimore approved. In Omaha, 93 percent of respondents approved DUI pursuits, with approval coming from 88 percent of those in Aiken County and 82 percent of those in Baltimore. Violent felonies with no reported death were approved by 97 percent of the respondents from Omaha, 91 percent of those from Aiken County, and 85 percent of those from Baltimore. One hundred percent of respondents from Omaha, 99 percent of those from Aiken County, and 83 percent of those from Baltimore approved pursuits for violent felonies with a reported death. Ninety-nine percent of respondents from Omaha, 98 percent from Aiken County, and 80 percent for Baltimore approved of a pursuit when a police officer was shot. A striking finding in the Baltimore sample is that approximately the same percentage of respondents approved of pursuits involving traffic violations (81 percent, $n = 137$) as for the shooting of a police officer (80 percent, $n = 135$).

TABLE 3.   Low-Risk Conditions: Percent of Respondents Approving Pursuit for Specified Offenses

	Aiken county (n = 255)	Baltimore (n = 169)	Omaha (n = 300)
Traffic violation	68[a]	81[a]	47[a]
Property crime—misdemeanor	66	62	50
Property crime—felony (other than stolen car)	84	73	83
Stolen vehicle	83	91	84
DUI	88	82	93
Violent felony—no reported death	91	85	97
Violent felony—reported death	99	83	100
Police officer shot	98	80	99

[a]All three categories were statistically significant at the $P < 0.05$ level.

As under the high-risk conditions, the largest differences were in the least-serious offense categories, including traffic and property crimes. A pursuit for a traffic offense received support ranging from 81 percent of the respondents in Baltimore to 47 percent of the respondents in Omaha. The differences across all three samples were statistically significant at the 0.05 level. Property crime—misdemeanor received 66 percent support from Aiken County respondents and 50 percent support from Omaha respondents. Pursuits for property crimes involving felonies were supported by 84 percent of Aiken County respondents as compared to 73 percent of the Baltimore respondents.

Educating the Public on Pursuit Risks

The final set of analyses includes the differences of opinions reported by citizens of Baltimore who were provided with some information concerning the outcome of pursuit and those who were not. The citizens were asked to respond to the questions assuming low-risk conditions. The term "information" indicates that the respondents were given information concerning possible outcomes of police pursuits prior to responding to a set of questions. The term "no information" indicates that the respondents received no information about possible outcomes of police pursuits before answering questions.

Respondents gave less support for police pursuits when given information about possible outcomes. The differences are presented in the last column of Table 4. When given no information on pursuit outcomes, respondents approved police pursuits by a higher percentage across all offenses than when given information of pursuit outcomes.

Pursuits for traffic violations received approval from 87 percent of Baltimore respondents who received no information about the hazards of pursuit. In contrast, 73 percent of the Baltimore respondents gave approval when informed about the outcome of pursuit driving. Sixty-five percent of Baltimore respondents gave approval of a police pursuit for incidents involving a property crime—misdemeanor when no information about pursuit was provided compared to 58 percent approval when these dangers were explained. Baltimore respondents gave 75 percent approval to a police pursuit for a property crime—felony when no information of the hazards was provided compared to

TABLE 4. Low-Risk Conditions: Percent of Respondents Approving Pursuit for Specified Offenses

	No information	Information	Difference
Traffic violation	87	73	14
Property crime—misdemeanor	65	58	7
Property crime—felony (other than stolen car)	75	70	5
Stolen vehicle	95	87	8[a]
DUI	83	80	3
Violent felony—no reported death	88	82	6
Violent felony—reported death	88	77	11[a]
Police officer shot	85	74	11[a]

[a] Significant at the $P < 0.05$ level (1-tailed).

70 percent approval when information of pursuit outcome was provided. When a vehicle was stolen, respondents with no explanation of pursuit dangers gave 95 percent approval compared to 87 percent approval of those who were given some information of the likelihood of an accident, injury, or death. Eighty-eight percent of respondents approved of a police pursuit for a violent felony—no reported death when no information was provided, while 82 percent of those approved of a pursuit after information of pursuit outcome was provided. Support for pursuits in a crime involving a violent felony—death reported was given by 88 percent of those who received no information about pursuits and 77 percent of the respondents supported pursuit after information of the possibility of a negative outcome was provided. When a police officer shooting occurred, 85 percent of those respondents approved of pursuit when given no information on pursuit hazards, while 74 percent approved of pursuit after being told about possible pursuit outcomes.

The largest differences were reported in the least serious offense category. Incidents involving a traffic violation reflected a 14 percent difference among respondents who were provided information about pursuit outcomes and those who were not told about the dangers of pursuit driving. This difference was statistically significant at the 0.05 level. There were also differences between those who had been told about pursuit outcomes and those who had not been informed when respondents expressed opinions about property crime felonies (5 percent), property crime misdemeanors (7 percent), and a stolen car (8 percent). Additionally, for the most serious offenses (a police officer shot and a violent felony with a reported death), there was an 11 percent difference between groups who had been told about pursuit outcomes and those who had not been informed.

CONCLUSION

The impact of public perceptions on officers' performance generally has the potential to improve compliance with departmental policy and individual accountability. The analysis of citizens' responses to police pursuit scenarios demonstrates public reaction to this dangerous practice. The results of this research suggest that the public overwhelmingly supports pursuits for serious criminal offenses. This support echoes the results of earlier public opinion research on pursuit driving. The data presented here, however, also show a clear trend in which the public's support for pursuits diminishes with the seriousness of the offense for which the pursuit was initiated. This general trend across sites is supported, although regional and site-specific differences are reported.

This study did not focus on police officers' attitudes, however, it is worth noting the similarities between officers and members of the public. The general trend of support appears to be similar from each group and controlled by the seriousness of the offense. Support for pursuits is strong and criticism is minimal, if it exists at all when a police officer is shot or a felony committed. Support is minimal, especially under high-risk conditions, when a traffic violator is pursued.

The public opinion surveys conducted in Aiken County, Baltimore, and Omaha demonstrated that citizens support the police trying to capture suspects of serious crimes; but, the support diminishes when the nature of the offense is not as serious. In addition, public support for pursuit decreases when information about the dangers of pursuit is presented. The findings suggest that an informed public is less likely to accept the necessity of police use of pursuit for less serious offenses. If the public becomes more knowledgeable of these dangers, police departments may have to develop stricter pursuit policies.

In making those decisions, however, it is also important to recognize two potential benefits of pursuit as well as the costs. First, many suspects who attempt to flee the police will be arrested for crimes unrelated to the underlying violation that caused the pursuit. Suspects are sometimes arrested for outstanding felony warrants, possession of drugs or weapons, as well as offenses related to reckless driving (Alpert and Dunham, 1990). The question remains, how many arrests will be made for serious felonies? Second, the question of deterrence must be considered. That is, if the police do not pursue, how many people will be encouraged to drive recklessly because they know the police will not follow? Similarly, how many drunk drivers will stop if they are not chased by police? The critical question is this: Will more injuries and deaths occur if the police decide not to chase instead of continuing to chase?

Although there is no clear empirical evidence, the police in some areas where pursuits have been restricted to violent felonies report that there has been no change in crime because of the change in pursuit policy. There also has not been a change in the number of suspects who attempt to flee the police.[4] Clearly, future research should address those issues.

ACKNOWLEDGEMENTS

Support for this research has been provided, in part, by the National Institute of Justice Grant #93-IJ-CX-0061. Opinions stated in this paper are those of the authors and do not necessarily represent the official positions of the National Institute of Justice.

NOTES

1. Whites in the Baltimore sample were overrepresented by 9 percent according to census figures.
2. High-risk conditions were defined as a pursuit that takes place on congested inner-city streets at night in wet weather.
3. Low-risk conditions were defined as a pursuit that takes place on a noncongested roadway during the day in clear weather.
4. These comments were made by Tom Arnold, Deputy Director, Metro-Dade Police Department, at the Police Executive Research Forum (PERF) 20th Anniversary Meeting, May 1997. Interestingly, similar comments were made by former Tampa police Chief Eddie Gonzales at the PERF annual meeting in 1994.

REFERENCES

Alpert, G. P. (1997). Pursuit driving: Planning policies and action from agency, officer, and public information. *Police Forum* 7:1–12.

Alpert, G. P., and Dunham, R. G. (1990). *Police pursuit driving: Controlling responses to emergency situations*. Westport, CT: Greenwood Press.

Alpert, G. P., and Fridell, L. A. (1992). *Police vehicles and firearms: Instruments of deadly force*. Prospect Heights, IL: Waveland Press, Inc.

Alpert, G. P., and Madden, T. (1994). Police pursuit driving: An empirical analysis of critical decisions. *American Journal of Police* 4:23–45.

Britz, M., and Payne, D. (1994). Policy implications for law enforcement pursuit driving. *American Journal of Police* 13:113–42.

Falcone, D., Charles, M., and Wells, E. (1994). A study of pursuits in Illinois. *The Police Chief* 61:59.

Falcone, D., Wells, E., and Charles, M. (1992). *Police pursuit in pursuit of policy: The empirical study*. Vol. 2. Washington, DC: AAA Foundation for Traffic Safety.

Fennessy, E., Hamilton, T., Joscelyn, K., and Merritt, J. (1970). *A study of the problem of hot pursuit by the police*. Washington, DC: U.S. Department of Transportation.

High-speed pursuits: Police officers and municipal liability for accidents involving the pursued and an innocent third party. (1986). *Seton Hall Law Review* 16:101–26.

Homant, R., and Kennedy, D. (1994a). The effect of high-speed pursuit policies on officers' tendencies to pursue. *American Journal of Police* 13:91–111.

Homant, R., and Kennedy, D. (1994b). Citizen preferences concerning police pursuit policies. *Journal of Criminal Justice* 22:415–58.

Homant, R., Kennedy, D., and Howton, J. (1993). Sensation seeking as a factor in police pursuit. *Criminal Justice and Behavior* 20:293–305.

Lucadamo, T. (1994). *Identifying the dimensions of police pursuit*. Master's Thesis, University of Maryland.

Picolo, S. (1994). *Attitudes toward the use of hot pursuits by the police*. Master's Thesis, University of Maryland.

Reese, R. (1991). *Results of hot pursuit poll*. Memorandum to Salt Lake City Police Department, University of Utah, August 14.

Steele, L. T. (1995). *The standard of care: Police attitudes on hot pursuit policy*. Master's Thesis, University of Maryland.

Chapter 15

Race-Based Policing
Alternatives for Assessing the Problem

by Brian L. Withrow, Ph.D., and Henry Jackson, B.A.
Wichita State University

INTRODUCTION

Recently, serious charges of racism have been leveled against some of the nation's largest police departments. There is a growing perception that some police officers and/or their departments are highly, and inappropriately, influenced by the race of the driver when making a decision to stop a vehicle and then, subsequent to the stop, conduct a search of the vehicle. Preliminary evidence suggests that at least a correlation exists between the race of the driver and the probability of being stopped and searched, but not necessarily receiving a citation to appear in court.

We routinely compare the racial proportions of eligible workers against the hiring and promotion records of companies within a community. These comparisons provide us with evidence of any disparate effect in hiring and promotion and serve as an important component of active affirmative action programs. In fact, substantial discrepancies are considered *prima facie* evidence of a disparate effect. While these comparisons are useful in a court of law, they do not provide very much scientific insight into the causes of institutional racism. Many states and the federal government are considering requiring police officers to routinely record the race of all citizens they contact in an official capacity. Presumably, if the proportions of minorities stopped and/or searched by the police were higher than the proportional representations of minorities within the community, then race would appear to play a key role in this form of police officer decision-making.

We are strongly critical of the use of proportional comparisons alone to determine whether or not police officers and/or their departments are improperly influenced by race when making individual enforcement or administrative decisions. Similarly, we believe that requiring the police to record the race or ethnicity of citizens they contact in an official capacity may, for several reasons, not provide valid information on whether or not race is a primary factor in this realm of police decision-making.

The purpose of this paper is to offer a cautionary note and some methodological recommendations for researchers interested in this issue. We begin with a survey of the available literature on racial profiling and race-based policing. Following this, we discuss the results of our own content analysis of scenarios describing officer/citizen contacts

Brian L. Withrow and Henry Jackson. Prepared especially for this volume—1996.

wherein the citizens perceive that race was the primary factor leading to the officer's decision to stop them and/or subsequently search their vehicle. We conclude with a series of suggestions for researchers on various methodological strategies.

A REVIEW OF THE LITERATURE

There is a small but compelling body of literature supporting the assertion that race plays an important role in a police officer's decision to stop and/or search a motorist. Most of the evidence in support of this assertion is either anecdotal or relies on statistical comparisons of the disparity between the proportions of minorities in a population and those stopped by the police and/or subjected to a vehicle search. These studies indicate that the proportion of minorities stopped by the police, and/or subjected to a vehicle search, are higher than their proportional representation in the community or among licensed drivers (see Harris, 1999; Harris, 1997; Norris, Fielding, Kemp & Fielding, 1992; Roberts, 1999).

Comparisons between the racial proportions of licensed drivers and those actually issued tickets, and/or convicted for violating traffic laws, do not appear to indicate a wide disparity. For example, throughout the state of Florida, Blacks represent 11.7% of the driving-age population and 15.1% of all drivers actually convicted of traffic violations (ACLU, 1999). These researchers do not report whether or not this difference is statistically significant. More convincingly, in a *rolling survey* of motorists over a 42-hour period on a defined stretch of Interstate 95 in Maryland, researchers were able to identify the race of 96.8% of the drivers in the 5,741 cars observed. White drivers represented 75.6% and Black drivers represented 16.9% of the drivers. The researchers observed 93.3% of all drivers committing a bona fide traffic violation and thus were eligible to be stopped by the Maryland State Police. Of the total number of motorists actually issued citations during the study period, 74.7% were White and 17.5% were Black (Harris 1999). We conclude from this that, even though some disparity exists between the proportions of minority drivers and those actually issued citations for bona fide violations of the traffic law, this disparity does not appear to be substantial.

Of more concern is the apparent disparity between racial groups with respect to the probability of being stopped, and once stopped, being subjected to a vehicle search. For example, the minority population in Valkyrie, Illinois, is 8% Hispanic and 15% Black. Hispanics and Blacks take fewer than 3% and 10% of the personal vehicle trips in Illinois, respectively. However, Hispanic and Black motorists are subjected to 27% and 23%, respectively, of vehicle searches conducted by Valkyrie police officers pursuant to a traffic stop (ACLU, 1999). A similar study in Florida indicates that while Blacks and Hispanics account for only 5% of the drivers on a Volusia County stretch of Interstate 95, minority drivers operated more than 70% of the vehicles stopped. In addition, Blacks and Hispanics were detained at the side of the road for longer periods of time than White drivers. Overall, the police searched about half of all vehicles stopped. However, 80% of the vehicles stopped that were operated by Black drivers were searched (Harris, 1999). The Maryland State Police reports that between January 1995 and September 1996, of the 823 motorists searched pursuant to a bona fide traffic stop on I-95 north of Baltimore, 80.3% were racial minorities (ACLU, 1999).

Similar disparities are evident in Great Britain. When compared to their proportions of the population, Whites were stopped at 90% of the expected rate, Asians at less than 20%, and Blacks were stopped at 280% of the expected rate. The British researchers conclude that Blacks, particularly young Blacks, are substantially more likely to be stopped and for more "speculative reasons" than Whites or Asians (Norris, Fielding, Kemp and Fielding, 1997:222). From this evidence we conclude that race plays a relatively small role in a police officer's decision on whether or not to issue a citation to a motorist. More importantly, it appears that race plays a greater role in a police officer's initial decision to stop and/or search a vehicle.

CHARACTERISTICS OF PERCEIVED RACIALLY MOTIVATED TRAFFIC STOPS AND SEARCHES—A QUALITATIVE ANALYSIS

Our content analysis of fifty scenarios from citizens alleging racism in police decision-making reveals patterns consistent with the previous research. These reports came from various newspapers and other media sources and have in common the perception of racism on the part of the motorists. The motorists believe that the police considered the race of the driver and/or occupants of the vehicle when deciding on whether or not to stop and/or search the vehicle. In short, these citizens are accusing the police officers of racism, or at the very least race-based policing (see Table 1).

In forty-seven (47) of the fifty (50) scenarios, (94%) the police articulated a bona fide reason for stopping the motorists. Most were stopped for relatively minor traffic violations. A few officers stated that either the motorists, occupants of the car, or the vehicle itself fit the description of individuals or vehicles used in other crimes. Considered alone, this is a rather benign finding. It is reasonable to expect that most police officers would routinely inform a motorist of the reason for the stop. However, only thirteen (13) of the fifty (50) stops (26%) resulted in the issuance of a citation or the arrest of the

TABLE 1. Reported Characteristics of Perceived Racially Motivated Traffic Stops (N = 50)

Reported characteristic	Frequency
The officer articulated a bona fide justification for stopping the motorist	47
The officer(s) neither issue a ticket nor arrested the motorist	37
Physical confrontation or the threat of violence	14
The motorist, passengers and vehicle were searched	10
The citizen/officer contact lasted an inordinately long period of time	8
The officer either drew a weapon or placed his/her hand on a weapon without provocation	8
Minority motorist in an expensive car	7
The citizen was handcuffed during the contact	6
The officers damaged the citizen's vehicle and other personal property	6
Multiple officers involved	6
Vehicle occupants were different race/ethnic groups	4
The motorists reported being stopped numerous times	4
The officers delivered racial epithets	3
The motorist was followed for an inordinately long period of time	3
Minority driver in 'wrong' neighborhood	3

motorists. These two findings, considered together, suggest a pattern of police behavior consistent with the previous research. At the very least, one should be curious as to why the officers in these situations are engaging in a potentially high-risk and time-consuming activity that does not produce an indicator of measurable performance. Although there is no generally accepted standard defining an appropriate ratio between citations issued and vehicles stopped, it would seem that slightly more than one in four would not be a very efficient use of resources, much less a deterrent against traffic law violations.

In fourteen (14) of the fifty (50) scenarios (28%), the citizen/officer contact included actual or threatened physical confrontation. The percentage of citizen/officer contacts that result in actual or threatened physical confrontation nationally is unclear. However, more than one in four seems alarmingly high. In eight (8) of the fifty (50) scenarios (16%), the officer either drew a weapon or placed his or her hand on a weapon without provocation. The authors are aware that some police officers routinely rest their hands and arms on their weapons during a routine traffic stop. This practice, albeit ill advised, could be misinterpreted by a motorist as an offensive or threatening gesture. As a result, the authors were very careful to record this as a factor only when the citizen actually reported that he or she considered it as a threat. Finally, in three (3) of the fifty (50) scenarios (6%), the officers uttered derogatory racial comments or epithets. These three findings considered together suggest a substantially more violent and threatening type of police/citizen contact than what is perceived to be the norm.

In ten (10) of the fifty (50) scenarios (20%), the motorists, passengers and/or vehicle were searched. This seemingly high rate of vehicles searched would explain why in eight (8) of the fifty (50) scenarios (16%) the citizens reported that the contact lasted an inordinately long period of time and why in six (6) of the fifty (50) scenarios (12%) there were multiple officers involved. Collectively, these findings are consistent with previous research indicating that minority drivers are subjected to more frequent searches and longer detainments at the side of the road.

Because this sample of scenarios was not collected randomly, the findings presented above are not intended to be inferential. Our intent is not to develop a profile or 'typical' case of a racially motivated traffic stop. Rather, we present this information to illustrate the point that there are important qualitative and subjective elements of traffic stops that appear to lead some motorists to believe that the enforcement action was based on something other than their lack of compliance with traffic regulations, specifically race. These qualitative elements would not be evident in research relying solely on disparate effect comparisons using racial proportions. Further, once documented, these elements will assist policing administrators with developing training programs that are more sensitive to the cultural differences among people. Police officers that are more cognizant of these differences will be in a better position to avoid misunderstandings and misperceptions of their motives.

POTENTIAL EXPLANATIONS OF DISPARATE EFFECT

The most salient question, once a disparate pattern of this nature is identified, is to ask why it is occurring so regularly and consistently? We propose three potential explanations. By presenting these we make no value statement regarding their plausibility. Instead, consistent with the overall purpose of this article, these explanations are simply intended to encourage rigorous scientific inquiry and to enhance the creativity of subsequent researchers.

First, racial disparity in this form of police decision-making may be the result of institutionalized racism within the police organization. Predictably, police administrators would be quick to dismiss this as a plausible explanation. However, there are several examples in the literature suggesting that some police administrators have encouraged, through policy or other directives, individual officers to target racial minorities for enforcement. An official document that surfaced during the litigation of a lawsuit alleging racial profiling within the Maryland State Police Department encouraged troopers to watch for drug dealers and traffickers who are "predominately black males and females" (Harris, 1999:565). In the late 1980s, the Eagle County (Colorado) Sheriff's Department established a highway drug interdiction unit. This unit was issued, and instructed to use, a drug courier profile that included twenty-two (22) "indicators" of likely drug couriers. Race, based on "intelligence information from *other law enforcement agencies*", was among these indicators (Harris, 1999:568, emphasis ours). Finally, Governor Christine Todd Whitman dismissed Carl Williams, New Jersey's Chief of Troopers, when he defended race-based profiling by alleging that "mostly minorities" trafficked in marijuana and cocaine (ACLU, 1999:4).

Second, racial disparity in this form of police decision-making might be explained by the use of drug courier profiles that include race as a key indicator. Profiling is not new to policing. Even relatively inexperienced police officers learn very quickly to respond to hunches and "suspicious" behavior. One may legitimately argue that certain subjective behaviors are consistent with potentially dangerous situations or are "typical" of some types of criminality. Men are more likely to commit crime than women. Teenagers commit more crime than senior citizens. Abusive spouses tend to maintain a pattern of abusive behavior. For the most part, profiles serve a legitimate purpose by improving the efficiency of police officer decision-making, and in many respects improve officer safety.

The War on Drugs has for at least two decades heightened our awareness of the dangers of illicit drugs. Police departments are motivated by a sincere desire, and intense public support, to substantially reduce the supply of drugs. This desire became even more intense when civil forfeiture laws enabled police departments to benefit financially from aggressive drug enforcement through the seizure of large quantities of cash and valuable assets from convicted drug couriers. In their zeal to "get tough on drug dealers" many departments have developed or are using profiles to assist officers in identifying potential drug couriers and traffickers. While this can be a legitimate enforcement option, the very real potential exists for abuse, particularly when the indicators used are either not consistent with the realities of drug trafficking or are, in this case, based inaccurately on the race of the suspect. According to ACLU, Blacks constitute 13% of all drug users, 37% of those arrested on drug charges, 55% of those convicted and 74% of drug offenders sentenced to prison (ACLU, 1999:7). The very fact that the vast majority of drug offenders sentenced to prison are Black could lead an otherwise misinformed individual to believe that the nation's drug couriers are predominantly Black. As a result, when considering who, or what, to target for aggressive drug interdiction, Blacks would appear to be the logical choice. This is a classic example of how a limited knowledge of the intricacies of the criminal justice system can be dangerous.

In 1996, the United States Supreme Court validated a long-standing police practice commonly referred to as pretextual stops (see *Whren v. U.S.*). A pretextual stop occurs when a police officer observes and then follows a "suspicious" person (e.g., an individual meeting a drug courier profile) until he violates a traffic law. When this occurs the officer then has the necessary probable cause to stop the individual. Once stopped, the officer may then conduct a plain-view search of the vehicle and its occupants. In addition, the officer may ask the driver's permission to search the vehicle. A surprisingly large percentage of drug traffickers will consent to a search. If no drugs, large amounts of cash or drug paraphernalia are found then, more often than not, the motorist is released without receiving a citation.

Finally, racial disparity in this form of police decision-making may be the result of the differential deployment of policing resources. Police officers are not purposely deployed with respect to the racial representation within a city. Rather, police administrators routinely concentrate policing resources in high-crime areas, densely populated portions of the city, to reduce response times and various other workload type measures (Tsai, 1995). Unfortunately, in most American cities some of these areas are also predominately minority. All officers, regardless of their particular beat assignment, are subject to the same performance standards. Given this, one would expect that in areas of highly concentrated police resources the per capita number of enforcement actions would routinely exceed that of the lower crime areas or less densely populated portions of the city. In short, a disparity in enforcement actions, with respect to race, may be due to the department's deployment strategy.

RECOMMENDATIONS FOR FURTHER RESEARCH

The following recommendations are intended to engage members of the scientific and policing communities and individuals interested in this issue in an honest attempt to develop a prudent research strategy for this difficult issue. We are not proposing that these recommendations are the only, or even the best, way for conducting this type of research. Instead we offer these suggestions so that the results of research in this area will be more useful for developing effective enforcement policies.

- The pattern of disparity may be differential with respect to the context of the enforcement objective.

Drug interdiction on the interstate highway system is a different type of police operation than routine patrol in an urban setting. It appears that racial profiling may be more useful as an explanation for disparity arising from interstate highway or drug interdiction enforcement, while deployment may be more useful for urban settings. Of course, it would be unwise to limit inquiry to a single explanation. Racial profiles may also be evident in routine patrol decision-making.

- Data generated from police department self-reports may lack sufficient validity because of potential reactivity.

The most prominent contemporary recommendation for collecting data on race-based policing involves requiring police departments to record the race or ethnicity of all individuals they contact in an official capacity. Harris (1999) believes these data should include the reason for the stop; the race, ethnicity, and other identifying information concerning the person stopped; whether or not the driver received a citation or warning and for what; whether a search followed the stop; the basis for the search; whether a dog was used as part of the procedure; whether contraband was found, and if so what kind; and whether any property was seized under forfeiture laws.

For many years, researchers have known that individuals behave differently when cognizant of an observer. Asking the police to routinely report the race or ethnicity of all individuals they contact will undoubtedly generate questions from officers on how the information will be used, as if they won't already know. An honest response will leave officers with the perception that should the data reveal a disparate pattern in enforcement decision-making, then they or their departments may be subjected to public scrutiny and even disciplinary action. This has the potential for influencing the data-gathering exercise by threatening the validity of the information. Individual responses could include incomplete reporting, outright deception and/or the failure of an officer to make a legitimate contact out of fear that it may be perceived to be racially motivated. We hasten to deny even the suggestion that the typical police response would necessarily be untruthful. Rather, we raise the reactivity issue precisely because critics of the research might consider the resulting data invalid and thereby dismiss important findings.

- Conclusions drawn solely from proportional comparisons may not produce complete information regarding the dynamics of racial discrimination.

Proportional comparisons may be useful for determining whether or not an overall enforcement program results in a disparate effect. However, they provide little insight into the subjective characteristics of a contact that might lead a citizen to believe that his or her race motivated an officer's attention. If a disparate effect is found, then it may easily be explained away by differential deployment. Furthermore, the courts have recently been reluctant to restrict the police discretion in this activity. The primary research question, whether or not the police are racially biased in their decision-making, cannot be answered completely on the basis of proportional comparisons alone.

Unfortunately, there are no tests that can, with an acceptable level of reliability, determine whether or not an individual is prejudiced. Perceptions of racism or prejudice are largely based on the victim's perspective. Admittedly, an individual's perception may not be objectively accurate. All of us develop perceptions of other persons based on misunderstandings or miscommunications. However, regardless of their lack of objective reliability, perceptions can and do affect an individual's behavior and eventually become an important element of public opinion. Because of this we recommend that researchers include qualitative measures of the perceptions of motorists as part of a comprehensive investigation into the dynamics of race-based policing. This can be achieved through the use of either general or follow-up "quality control" surveys that ask questions relating to officers' demeanor. The results of our content analysis provide an initial set of indicators that appear to lead a citizen to perceive the officer's motivation is prejudiced.

- Proportional comparisons should be based on the appropriate sampling frame.

The racial distribution of a general population is not necessarily the same as the racial distribution of its subsets. For example, the racial proportion of adults, licensed drivers or actual users of the roadways may be different than that of the general population. The sampling frame of any research relating to race-based policing should not include individuals that are not eligible to drive or otherwise not within the purview of police supervision. Ideally, research of this type should only include those individuals that *actually* drive or are observed by the police. The Maryland study (see Harris, 1999) is an example of this type of inquiry.

CONCLUSION

Confidence in government is critical to a free democracy. When we lack confidence in agencies of government the effectiveness of those agencies is, at the very least, compromised. Americans are inherently distrustful of government, and some are particularly distrustful of the police. We find it especially repugnant when the police, the most visible symbol of government, are perceived to violate the very principles upon which this nation is founded. As a result, every police department in America has a vested interest in the outcome of research on race-based policing.

However, the importance of this issue should not be overshadowed by its rhetoric. Precisely because this issue is so important, we should be particularly careful in designing our methodological strategy. This article is not intended to be a definitive treatise on race-based policing. Instead our purpose is to offer first a caution against limiting our inquiry to one methodological approach and second, to provide a series of suggestions for the consideration of subsequent researchers. We sincerely hope these suggestions will be received in the spirit of communalism and will ultimately enhance the quality of research.

REFERENCES

American Civil Liberties Union. (1999). http://www.aclu.org/profiling/reoirt.index.html.

Harris, D. A. (1997). Driving while black and all other traffic offense: The supreme court and pretextual stops. *Journal of Criminal Law & Criminology*. 87, 544–582.

Harris, D. A. (1999). Driving while black: Racial profiling on our nation's highways. American Civil Liberties Union. http://www.aclu.org/profiling/reoirt.index.html.

Norris, C., Fielding, N., Kemp, C., & Fielding, J. (1992). Black and blue: An analysis of the influence of race on being stopped by the police. *British Journal of Sociology*. 43, 207–224.

Roberts, B. L. (1999). Race, ethnicity and the influence it has on stop and seizure. http://cs.sau.edu/~broberts/stops.htm.

Whren v. U.S. 116 S. Ct. 1769 (1996).

Tsai, T. J. (1995). Patrol allocation. *TELEMASP Bulletin*, 2, 9. Bill Blackwood Law Enforcement Management Institute of Texas, Huntsville, Texas.

Chapter 16

The Future of Policing in a Community Era

by Jihong Zhao

Where is policing headed in the twenty-first century? A similar question was asked at the start of the twentieth century when modern policing was in its infancy. Predicting the future of any occupation or organization is a formidable task that is fraught with difficulty. For example, many innovations in the criminal justice system that once were predicted to have far-reaching effects have failed to do so. In his book, *Sense and Nonsense About Crime*, noted scholar Samuel Walker studied the impact of 20 such innovations proposed by either liberals or conservatives and found that very few of them met with expectations.[1]

In that light, it might be wiser not to speculate about the future of American policing. However, aside from the fact that the author finds this challenge irresistible, two other reasons for doing so are compelling. First, I believe that a fairly accurate forecast of police departments over the next five years is possible because a new style of policing known as community policing is well underway. The concept of community policing and its implementation has a history that spans two decades if the pilot studies on foot patrol in Flint, Michigan, and Newark, New Jersey, are considered.[2]

A second reason that prediction is warranted is that the implementation of community policing has been accompanied by a strong emphasis on research evaluation, especially over the past five years. The results from several studies might be drawn upon to inform predictions based upon information that is both theoretical and practical.

WHERE POLICING IS NOW AND WHERE IT IS GOING

Before any prediction can be made, it is important to familiarize ourselves with the pattern of change in community policing to date. Three stages of organizational change proposed by Robert Yin are noteworthy in this regard.[3] The first stage involves initiation, that is, the implementation of innovative activities. In this stage, an organization tries a variety of innovations and then assesses their respective utility. Effective innovations are retained, while ineffective ones are discontinued.

Note: Adapted from Chapter 13 of *Contemporary Policing in a Community Era: An Introduction and Exploration* (2001) by Quint C. Thurman, Jihong Zhao, and Andrew Giacomazzi. (Roxbury: Los Angeles, CA).

James Thompson notes that during the initiation stage, innovative programs are isolated from the core of an operation.[4] This means that innovations are not deliberately integrated into the formal organizational structure. In addition, they are evaluated by organizational rationality based upon social recognition rather than by technical rationality based on a cost-and-benefit analysis, even though the latter is more certain.

The pattern of change in community policing is similar to what Thompson predicted about the initiation stage of organizational change. In particular, the change process always starts with the adoption of innovative programs. The number of programs will differ depending on the size and location of a police department. For example, the New York Police Department may implement more programs than a medium-sized police department because it is much larger and is located in a very dynamic environment.

Innovative programs such as foot patrols and storefront police substations are generally set up by a designated unit, which, to a large extent, is isolated from core police operations such as patrol and criminal investigations. This isolation allows police administrators to have better control of new programs before they can decide to expand the scope, change the focus, or even terminate the programs without disturbing the normal operations of the department.

A review of the community policing literature suggests that a majority of innovative programs are rarely implemented more widely than by a special unit.[5] The primary means of evaluating innovative programs is customer satisfaction. This evaluation is usually done by conducting a variety of citizen surveys and interviews about their contacts with beat police officers. The effectiveness of these programs is then determined according to organizational rationality. Does this program generate social recognition? Do residents like the program?

After 20 years of community policing, there has been no irrefutable evidence that it significantly reduces crime in a community. This means that technical rationality based upon a cost-and-benefits analysis cannot be applied to community policing innovations. The bottom line is this—despite some 20 years of efforts, community policing as a form of organizational change still remains largely at the initiation stage.

Most of the research in policing suggests that community policing is the future model for American policing in the twenty-first century. It is expected then that community policing should progress naturally toward the second stage identified by Yin, the institutionalization of change.

Institutionalization has several important aspects. One key issue is organizational structure. To institutionalize community policing, the structure of police departments needs to be modified so that innovations may be integrated. Innovative units must become a formal part of patrol operations or criminal investigations rather than remain as isolated units. Another primary concern is that the evaluation of community policing should move beyond simply measuring citizen satisfaction. Although it is extremely valuable to learn what local communities think of a police program, technical rationality must be achieved, and clearly defined measures to facilitate institutionalization should be developed. Following this, the third aspect of change involves the widespread acceptance and adoption of changes by the policing culture itself.

The next sections present the positive, negative, and uncertain forces that likely will affect the institutionalization of community policing.

POSITIVE FORCES

In order to predict whether or not the institutionalization of community policing will be the future of American policing, it is necessary to examine the competing forces of change and evaluate possible outcomes. Four specific forces seem to favor the change to community policing.

More Community Policing Programs

First, community policing programs are very popular with police executives, other community leaders, and the public as evidenced by the considerable increase in these programs over the past five years. Recent studies show that community policing is widespread, having been adopted not only in a few large police departments but also in medium and small departments that traditionally have followed the winds of change.[6] In addition to the expansion of community policing, there also is a wider variety of community policing programs in place compared to the previous five years.

In the 1980s, the primary focus of community policing programs was to reduce citizen fear of crime and social disorder. For example, an important factor behind the implementation of the foot-patrol program in the Houston Police Department was to reduce the fear of crime; an evaluation of the program found that it was effective in reducing public fear of crime.[7] At that time, only a handful of community policing programs were identified as such, including foot patrol, special units, and neighborhood watch.[8] Recent developments have substantially expanded the variety of programs available.[9] The Resolving Conflict Creatively Program (RCCP) implemented in the New York City and the Boston Police Youth Corps are examples.[10]

The expansion of community policing programs makes organizational change in policing more visible to the public and the news media. It seems fair to say that the longer police departments can keep up the momentum of innovation, the more likely it is that innovations will be institutionalized.

Strong Support From the Federal Government Since 1994

The second positive force behind institutionalization of community policing has been the very strong endorsement of the federal government after the passage of the Violent Crime Control and Law Enforcement Act in 1994. This statute represents "an investment of more than $30 billion over six years . . . . [It] is the largest Federal anti-crime legislation in the Nation's history."[11] As a direct result of this legislation the federal government is actively involved in the national implementation of community policing. In addition, this act subsidized the hiring of an additional 100,000 officers who must promote community policing goals in their departments. A key example of this effort includes the establishment of Community Oriented Policing Services (COPS). A primary goal of COPS is to ensure the institutionalization of community policing innovations in police departments across the country. COPS coordinates and supervises federally subsidized community policing programs and oversees evaluations. The creation of 35 community policing regional training institutes across the nation is another important step taken to expand the scope of implementation.[12]

Similarly, as a direct result of the 1994 Crime Act, there has been more money available for research and evaluation than at any other time in the history of American policing. Many of COPS' grants to local departments, for example, include provisions for research and evaluation. There has been a substantial increase in research activities to document the progress of community policing. In sum, the direct involvement of the federal government, particularly the Clinton administration, provides much-needed funding and technical support for the implementation of community policing.

The Use of Technology

A third positive force for change is the increase in the use of advanced technology in community policing. Since the early 1990s, community policing innovations have extended to the use of hi-tech tools for combating urban crimes and reducing social disorder. Computerized statistics (CompStat) is a good example of this development. Police departments in several large cities such as Boston, Indianapolis, and Chicago have used CompStat and computer-mapping technology to disseminate information to all the ranks of officers to make them all accountable for fighting crime. The best-known use of CompStat was in New York in 1993 under the leadership of then police commissioner William Bratton. During his brief tenure, Bratton chided his sworn personnel: "No one ever lost his job over not having the right answers. No one gets into trouble for crime being up in their precinct. People got in trouble if they didn't know what the crime was and had no strategy to deal with it."[13]

As the first step in CompStat, personnel from each of the 76 New York City precincts, nine police service areas, and 12 transit districts compiled a statistical summary of the week's crime incidents. Next, the information on arrests, summons activity, use of firearms, and victims was forwarded to central headquarters. These data included the specific times, locations of the crimes, and police activities. The CompStat unit in the department loaded the information into a citywide database for an analysis of crime patterns. A weekly CompStat report was then generated to present a concise summary of crime incidents and other important performance indicators.

The next step in CompStat involved crime strategy meetings attended by senior administrators, all the precinct commanders, and supervisors of specialized investigative units. These meetings were usually convened every two weeks from 7 A.M. to 10 A.M. in the command and control center. Every commander was expected to be called on at random to make his or her presentation approximately once a month. During the presentation, the commander had to analyze the pattern of crime incidents in the area, potential problems, and the strategies adopted or planned to deal with them. The presentation was aided with a computerized "pin mapping" technology that displayed crimes, arrests, and quality-of-life data in a series of visual formats including charts, graphs, and tables. During the presentation, the senior administrators frequently asked commanders questions and looked for solutions.[14]

The significance of using CompStat is that the precinct commanders and supervisors were held accountable for an increase or decrease in local crimes and social disorder. Therefore, they were forced to develop new strategies to reduce neighborhood crimes. At the same time, the lower level of management also was held responsible for their respective areas because the "pin mapping" was able to display crime patterns at the street level. CompStat became the crucial link that demanded accountability at every level of the department.

As New York City mayor Rudolph Giuliani observed:

CompStat transformed the Department from an organization that reacted to crime to a Department that actively works to deter offenses. Before CompStat, the Department's 76 precinct commanders were isolated from the Department's top executives. Under the CompStat system, precinct commanders meet with the Police Commissioner and other high-ranking members of the Department at semi-weekly meetings to identify local crime patterns, select tactics, and allocate resources. Arrests are no longer the measure of effective policing—commanders are now responsible for deterring crime.[15]

Similarly, the Chicago Police Department adopted the Information Collection for Automated Mapping (ICAM) computer program. This program has two primary features. First, it can produce a map of reported offenses of a particular type in an area, or it can generate a list of the 10 most frequently reported offenses in a patrol beat. Second, it can generate a map and conduct a search of a particular type of offense. The unique part of the ICAM program is that the computer terminals can be installed at the district level, and supervisors and patrol officers can have access to ICAM. In essence, the availability of this high-tech program facilitates the problem-solving efforts in the department. The ICAM program has been well-received in Chicago. It is estimated that 20 percent of all officers use ICAM regularly, and 60 percent use it occasionally. From June 26 to July 25, 1995, a total of 6,689 queries were requested in the department, or 223 queries per day.[16]

The Crime Rate Is Down

The fourth positive force for change is that crime rates are down. No matter what happens, police departments are essentially evaluated by the local crime rate because the public believes that crime is the most important component of their job description. It is one thing for a police department to establish a few outreach programs and improve the quality of life in a community, but it is another if the crime rate remains the same or rises. When this happens, pressure falls on the police to respond appropriately.

A primary reason for the police to move toward community policing is that, for most of the 1960s and 1970s, the rates for both violent and property crimes were up significantly. Since the early 1990s, however, the crime rate has been declining. According to the *Uniform Crime Report*, for example, the crime index rate fell for the sixth straight year in 1997 and was down almost 17 percent from 1991. In addition, the violent crime rate declined 7 percent, continuing the downward trend since 1994.[17] In nearly all major cities, including New York, Los Angeles, and Chicago, the number of murders has dropped significantly. In turn, the continuing decline of crime rates has captured the attention of almost all major news networks and received extensive coverage. American cities are becoming safer.

Who should be given the credit for this declining crime rate? Unquestionably, the implementation of community policing has received much of the praise. In a recent public address, President Clinton stated, "In 1997, crime decreased for the sixth straight year thanks in part to community policing. Our commitment to American's law enforcement officers is working to keep our streets and communities safe."[18] To date, law enforcement agencies have added more than 88,000 community policing officers to patrol the streets, and the public seems to have responded favorably to this trend. Although other factors, such as the aging of the baby boomer generation, might also account for declining crime rates, community policing is widely perceived to be at least partially responsible.[19]

Even at the local level, the reduction of crime has been attributed to community policing innovations. Since 1993, overall crime was down more than 43 percent in New York City. The city's murder rate at the time was at its lowest level since the late 1960s, and Mayor Giuliani gave much of the credit to the NYPD and its new methods for dealing with crime and incivilities: "A very critical component of the success of the New York City Police Department has been an innovative style of police management called CompStat."[20] Although some might debate whether or not CompStat and community policing are synonymous, this New York style of meeting the public-safety needs of its citizens has been credited with achieving miraculous results.

Similarly, in Boston, the police and juvenile probation officers joined hands and created an innovative program, Operation Night Light, to prevent juvenile probationers from getting into trouble again and again. At night, police and juvenile probation officers visited each probationer's residence to make sure the person stayed at home. Since the inception of the program, the number of juveniles killed by gunfire has greatly diminished. In fact, from July 1995 to December 1997, not a single boy or girl in the city was murdered. Much of this success has been attributed to Operation Night Light.

In sum, the decline of crime has provided the police with a favorable external environment. They can show the nation that community policing is working and that people are benefitting from these innovative programs. All four of these positive forces keep the momentum of community policing moving forward toward institutionalization.

NEGATIVE FORCES

Ambiguity About COP

The first negative force that impedes change concerns the ambiguity surrounding the definition of community policing. What is community policing anyway? Police administrators and quite a few scholars have a hard time defining the term despite the popularity of community policing across the nation. John Eck and Dennis Rosenbaum argue that, "One reason for its popularity is that community policing is a plastic concept, meaning different things to different people."[21] Furthermore, Mark Moore has suggested that, "It is important that the concept mean something, but not something too specific . . . the ambiguity is a virtue."[22] However, it is exactly the virtue of looseness as a concept that may act as an impediment to its institutionalization.[23]

Today it is difficult to reject community policing as a welcome reform because every program implemented in a police department can be labeled a community policing innovation of one type or another. At the same time, it is difficult to accept it as a legitimate reform movement as long as its definition remains largely elusive. For example, after almost two full decades of implementation, there is not a single department that can claim to have implemented community policing completely, to have institutionalized its principles throughout the department. Community policing remains a loosely defined concept, with definitions that vary from broad abstraction to narrow specificity.

. . . Three distinctive theories might explain the institutionalization of the police during the professional era. They are: (1) scientific management articulated by Taylor, focusing on one best way and technical rationality; (2) the "ideal-type" of bureaucracy suggested by Weber, emphasizing the structural rationality of management; and (3) Gulick's organizational-supervision approach that proposes a chain of command and span of control. In the previous era, the institutionalization of a bureaucratic style of policing was guided by a clearly developed theoretical framework for a specific structural arrangement.

Community policing, however, lacks this theoretical refinement. The theoretical framework continues to remain relatively undefined or "plastic," as more new programs labeled community policing are added nearly every day. The author believes that this confusion at the theoretical level threatens to impede the institutionalization of community policing.

The Largely Unchanged Organizational Structure

The second negative force that might impede the institutionalization of community policing concerns structural change in police departments. In general, organizational structure can be defined as "the enduring characteristics of an organization reflected by the distribution of units and positions within the organization and their systematic relationships with each other."[24] This definition suggests that an organizational structure is relatively permanent. Unlike innovative programs that can easily be modified or dropped, the structure of an organization, especially the core structure, is not very easy to change over a short period of time.

Peter Blau has identified two dimensions of organizational structure based on a study of 53 public employment security agencies.[25] The horizontal dimension has two components: spatial differentiation and occupational differentiation. Spatial differentiation is the extent to which an organization's tasks are divided among subordinate units, for example, the number of different units in a police department. Occupational differentiation is the number of different specialties available in an organization, that is, the extent of the division of labor. The number of specialists (e.g., crime lab specialists and computer analysts) is greater in the New York Police Department, for example, than in the Omaha Police Department.

The vertical dimension, or hierarchy, concerns the distribution of authority, reflecting the degree of managerial control. In a police department, organizational hierarchy can be assessed by the number of ranks from police officer at the bottom to the chief at the top. It is assumed that the more levels in the hierarchy, the more formalized the organizational structure. The more formal the structure, the less likely it is to institutionalize innovations.

Three anthologies published since 1994 have focused on community policing.[26] They contain many examples of influential research, but only a few of these refer to the relationship between structural change and the institutionalization of community policing. Among these few, there is a consensus that organizational hierarchy impedes innovations.[27] Little research is available on the relationship between reducing organizational hierarchy and community policing innovations. Research is very limited on how to incorporate community policing programs into the formal structure of a police department. Very little has been written on the need to increase the horizontal structure of a police department and flatten the vertical structure if community policing is to be institutionalized. Studies on this topic tend to focus on evaluation of community policing programs.

UNCERTAIN FORCES

The Increase in Paramilitary Policing Units

About three decades ago, Egon Bittner argued that the use of force is the defining feature of American police.[28] Therefore, he argued, crime control will always be the core function of police work. This view of American policing seems to rule out any substantial deviation from the bureaucratic or professional model because community policing promotes the idea of police community partnerships to produce order. In addition, community policing recommends a reprioritization of police functions to make controlling social disorder and provision of services more important.

The purpose of a paramilitary policing unit (PPU) or Special Weapons and Tactics (SWAT) unit in a police department is straightforward. These highly trained law enforcement bodies can be swiftly deployed with an impressive use of force. During the last 10 years when students of American policing were focusing mostly on an expansion of community policing, there also has been a less noticeable trend toward the militarization of some components of the American police. Peter Kraska and Louis Cubellis conducted a survey of police departments serving small jurisdictions of 25,000 to 50,000 citizens.[29] The 40 items of the survey were designed to collect data on the formation, prevalence, and activities of PPUs in small cities that had not previously had a paramilitary emphasis. More than half of the departments completed and returned the survey. Kraska and Cubellis noted three important findings. First, they found a rapid expansion of PPUs in these departments between 1985 and 1995 (an increase of 157 percent). More and more departments have established PPUs to call on for hostage situations, acts of terrorism, civil disturbances, and high-risk search and arrests—infrequent activities in small cities. Second, the establishment of a PPU was not linked to worsening conditions because there was no increase in crime rates, drug use, fear of crime or the economic problems in these small cities. Third, in Kraska and Cubellis's opinion, the emergence of the PPU represents a pent-up desire to return to an earlier era that was characterized by the war on drugs and crimes. In the light of these findings, one might conclude that rather than becoming more open and progressive, the police culture may be returning to a more paramilitaristic orientation and one that proved largely ineffective in dealing with the conditions and causes of crime in the 1970s . . . .

The author believes that the growth of PPUs constitutes an uncertain force affecting the institutionalization of community policing because any incident involving the police use of force can lead to conflict between police and residents in a community, particularly minority residents. The history of police-community relations in this country is replete with examples of peaceful demonstrations turning violent because of an inappropriate police action or because a controversial court decision appeared to exonerate police misconduct. The fact that PPUs are being established in small cities, not as a result of an increase in crimes or social disorder but as an appeasement to a paramilitary culture, suggests a grave error may be in the making. It could force a showdown between factions who embrace a community problem-solving approach and factions who wish to return to the narrower mission of law enforcement and reactive policing.

The Role of the Police Unions

Research in community policing is almost completely silent on the relationship between police unions and organizational change. Police unions have played an important role in the history of American policing. In general, unions are not advocates for change. Unions tend more toward fighting for the benefits of ordinary employees and for power sharing with management.[30]

Unions operating in the public sector have similar interests to those in the private sector. Labor relations often take on the character of intense and tough "battles" with management to settle a host of issues connected primarily to the economic interests of employees.[31] In the recent history of police unions in America, there has been a tough "war" between the management and unions concerning economic benefits and management discretion.[32] Recent research confirms that the collective bargaining by police unions does produce economic benefits for police officers.

In police departments that use collective bargaining, a number of management issues such as the allocation of manpower and structural change need the approval of police unions. In addition, any new department policies concerning disciplinary actions and employee benefits usually involve the participation of police unions. If unions are to play an important role in such managerial issues, then they might be expected to be heavily involved in the process of structural and operational changes brought about by community policing. For example, community policing encourages police officers to know their beats and interact with local residents, which could mean a longer shift assignment for individual officers. At this point, however, there is little information about the role of police unions in the implementation of community policing. The role of PPUs and police unions in the institutionalization of community policing will be determined over time.

THE FUTURE DIRECTION OF COMMUNITY POLICING

If organizational change can be represented as a continuum between the bureaucratic style of policing during the professional era at one end and the community policing style of the community era at the other end, American policing might be described as making some progress away from the bureaucratic style toward the community policing style. Movement in such a direction does not mean, however, that community policing has been fully institutionalized.

Considering the positive, negative, and uncertain forces affecting the institutionalization of community policing, the author predicts that in the next five years community policing will neither be institutionalized in all American police departments nor abandoned. Probably, it will continue to be somewhere in the middle. The following text suggests what students of policing might expect to see over the next few years:

Community policing innovations will continue to expand in police departments across the United States. Police departments will continue to explore new ways of doing things as long as the external environment remains dynamic, which is likely. More demands concerning crime, social disorder, and quality of life will force police departments and their leaders to respond and change. Community policing innovations are a good way to demonstrate that police departments are responsive to the needs of the community. There is little risk for a local chief of police to implement outreach programs such as citizen academy, block watch, and storefront stations. These programs have been around for several years, and the public seems to like them. Programs that target crime reduction, such as weed and seed programs, also are well received. *Weed and seed* is a federally funded program that is divided into two parts. The *weed* part is strong law enforcement. Police target high-crime areas and officers intensify their law enforcement activities. The *seed* part focuses on community rebuilding, crime prevention, etc. The popularity of two types of program—crime-focused or prevention-focused—may depend on local crime trends. If the crime rate in a community has increased significantly, the crime-focused program will be given a high priority and vice versa. Either way, the police stand to lose little and gain the support of the public by trying innovative solutions.

The author also expects that *change in the organizational structure of police departments will occur at a very slow pace.* Structural changes involve greater risks than programmatic changes because of the high investment of personnel in the current way of doing things. For example, to reduce the rank structure by eliminating the rank of lieutenant would take some time to get through city politics, rewrite job descriptions for sergeants and captains, develop new policies, and relocate the lieutenants. Modifying the span of organizational control and chain of command is always perceived as risky. Throughout police history, the structural arrangements in police departments have been relatively stable. Consequently, there is little reason to believe that substantial structural change will take place at a rapid pace any time in the near future.

Nevertheless, it is important to acknowledge the necessity of change. American society is changing and so are . . . public-service agencies. Seen in this perspective, community policing is a part of broader social change. The current round of change in public-service agencies began in the late 1980s. The National Commission on the Public Service highlights the need for organizational change in public service by calling for a return to a public-service ethic:

> The central message of this report of the Commission on the Public Service is both simple and profound, both urgent and timeless. In essence, we call for a *renewed sense* of commitment by all Americans to the highest traditions of the public service—to a public service responsive to the political will of the people and also protective of our constitutional values.[33]

Some scholars emphasize the need to change public-service practices, a theme commonly referred to as "reinventing government." In their book, David Osborne and Ted Gaebler provide a forceful argument that American public service is in crisis and that a fundamental change is essential for its survival:

> And then, in 1990, the bottom fell out. It was as if all our government had hit the wall, at the same time. Our states struggled with multibillion-dollar deficits. Our cities laid off thousands of employees. Our federal deficit ballooned toward $350 billion.[34]

The economic turnaround in the 1990s has changed much of the political landscape in America. Municipal governments have enjoyed a considerable economic surplus, and the economy remains strong across the country. Change is continuous and will surely affect police departments.

Crises, like social turmoil and rising crime rates, breed change in policing. This was the case for American policing during the late 1960s and 1970s when crime rates rose to an astonishing level, and the professional-style means to control crime proved to be ineffective. Today, police departments across the nation are in a much better position than they were 25 years ago. Seen from this perspective, there really is no compelling reason why police departments should make broad and sweeping organizational changes, as long as external sources are not beckoning their leadership to do so.

Unless police executives and employees share the same vision for how organizational change can serve both police personnel and the public, the future of substantial organizational change in American policing is likely to be slow. The future of community policing remains uncertain, at least in terms of the important dimension of organizational change. The author thinks that although police departments will continue to make programmatic responses to the need for change that the external environment demands, community policing still has a way to go before it is institutionalized. However, it does appear to be headed in a forward direction.

ENDNOTES

1. Samuel Walker, *Sense and Nonsense About Crime* (Monterey CA: Brooks/Cole, 1985).
2. Robert Trojanowicz and Bonnie Bucqueroux, *Community Policing: A Contemporary Perspective* (Cincinnati: Anderson, 1990). For a discussion of theoretical framework, see Herman Goldstein, *Policing a Free Society* (Cambridge, MA: Ballinger, 1977); and John Angell, "Toward an Alternative to the Classic Police Organizational Arrangement: A Democratic Model," *Criminology* 8 (1971): 185–206.
3. Robert Yin, *Changing Urban Bureaucracies* (Lexington, MA: Lexington Books, 1979).
4. James Thompson, *Organizations in Action* (New York: McGraw-Hill, 1967).
5. There is very little research on the relationship between a change in organizational structure and Community Oriented Policing (COP) innovations. To a large extent, there has been limited effort to change the structural arrangements of a police department in order to make COP programs permanent. Please also see Jack Greene, William Bergman, and Edward McLaughlin, "Implementing Community Policing: Cultural and Structural Change in Police Organizations," in *The Challenge of Community Policing: Testing the Promises*, ed. Dennis Rosenbaum (Thousand Oaks, CA: Sage, 1994), pp. 92–109.
6. Please see two books on this topic: Dennis Rosenbaum, *The Challenge of Community Policing: Testing the Promises* (Thousand Oaks, CA: Sage, 1994); and Quint Thurman and Edmund McGarrell, *Community Policing in a Rural Setting* (Cincinnati, OH: Anderson, 1997).
7. Mary Ann Wycoff, "The Benefits of Community Policing: Evidence and Conjecture," in *Community Policing: Rhetoric or Reality?* eds. Jack Greene and Stephen Mastrofski (New York: Praeger, 1988), pp. 103–120.
8. Please see the discussion in Jack Greene and Stephen Mastrofski, *Community Policing: Rhetoric or Reality?* (New York: Praeger, 1988). The programs were the early phase of implementation of community policing.
9. Quint C. Thurman, Jihong Zhao and Andrew Giaconazzi, Community Policing in a Community Era: An Introduction and Explanation, Roxbury: Los Angeles, 2001.
10. William DeJong, *Building the Peace: The Resolving Conflict Creatively Program (RCCP)* (Washington, DC: National Institute of Justice, 1994).

11. National Institute of Justice, *Criminal Justice Research Under the Crime Act—1995 to 1996* (Washington, DC: U.S. Department of Justice, 1997), p. 2.

12. Office of Community Oriented Policing Services, *Community Cops* (Washington, DC: U.S. Department of Justice, February/March, 1997).

13. William Bratton, *Turnaround: How America's Top Cop Reversed the Crime Epidemic* (New York: Random House, 1998), p. 239.

14. This information is obtained on the website of the New York Police Department at (www.ci.nyc.nyus/html/nypd/html/).

15. New York Police Department News Release #268-97 (May 13, 1997). "Mayor Giuliani Delivers Keynote Address at the International CompStat Conference:"

16. The discussion about the ICAM program is adapted from Thomas Rich, "The Chicago Police Department's Information Collection for Automated Mapping (ICAM) Program," *Program Focus* (Washington, DC: National Institute of Justice, 1996).

17. Bureau of Justice Statistics, *Crime and Victims Statistics* (1998). Data were obtained from the Bureau of Justice Statistics website at www.ojp.usdoj.gov/bjs/cvict.htm.

18. The Office of Community Oriented Policing Services, "American's Law Enforcement to Receive Community Policing Boost," *Press Release* (Wednesday, November 25, 1998).

19. See Alfred Blumstein and Richard Rosenfeld, "Assessing the Recent Ups and Downs in U.S. Homicide Rates," *National Institute of Justice Journal* (Washington, DC: U.S. Department of Justice, October, 1998).

20. New York Police Department News Release #268-97 (May 13, 1997).

21. John Eck and Dennis Rosenbaum, "The New Police Order: Effectiveness, Equity and Efficiency in Community Policing," in *The Challenge of Community Policing*, ed. Dennis Rosenbaum (Thousand Oaks, CA: Sage, 1994), pp. 3–26.

22. Mark Moore, "Research Synthesis and Policy Implications," in *The Challenge of Community Policing*, ed. Dennis Rosenbaum (Thousand Oaks, CA: Sage, 1994), pp. 285–299.

23. Jayne Seagrave, "Defining Community Policing;" *American Journal of Police* 15 (1996): 1–22.

24. Lawrence James and Allan Jones, "Organizational Structure: A Review of Structural Dimension and Their Conceptual Relationships With Individual Attitudes and Behavior," *Organizational Behavior and Human Performance* 16 (1976): 74–113.

25. Peter Blau, "A Formal Theory of Differentiation in Organizations," *American Sociological Review* 35 (1970): 201–218.

26. The three books are Dennis Rosenbaum, *The Challenge of Community Policing: Testing the Promises* (Thousand Oaks, CA: Sage, 1994); Peter Kratcoski and D. Dukes, *Issues in Community Policing* (Cincinnati: Anderson, 1995); and Geoffrey Alpert and Alex Piquero, *Community Policing: Contemporary Readings* (Prospect Heights, IL: Waveland, 1998).

27. For a discussion see: Farimorz Damanpour, "Organizational Innovation: A Meta-Analysis of Effects of Determinants and Moderators," *Academy of Management Journal* 34 (1991): 555–590.

28. Egon Bittner, *The Functions of Police in Modern Society* (Washington, DC: National Institute of Mental Health, 1970).

29. Peter Kraska and Louis Cubellis, "Militarizing Mayberry and Beyond: Making Sense of American Paramilitary Policing," *Justice Quarterly* 14 (1997): 607–629.

30. Samuel Walker, *A Critical History of Police Reform* (Lexington, MA: D. C. Heath, 1977).

31. T. Chandler and R. Gely "Union and Management Organizational Structure for Bargaining in the Public Sector," in *Handbook of Public Sector Labor Relations*, eds. Jack Rabin, Thomas Vocino, W. Bartley Hildreth, and Gerald Miller (New York: Marcel Dekker, 1994).

32. For a discussion on the history of police unions and management relations please see International Association of Chiefs of Police, *Critical Issues in Police Labor Relations* (Gaithersburg, MD: 1ACP, 1974); Steven Rynecki and Michael Morse, *Police Collective Bargaining Agreements: A National Management Survey* (Washington, DC: Police Executive Research Forum, 1981); and David Carter and Allen Sapp, "A Comparative Analysis of Clauses in Police Collective Bargaining Agreements as Indicators of Change in Labor Relations," *American Journal of Policing* 12 (1992): 17–46.

33. Volcker Commission, "Leadership for America: Rebuilding the Public Service," cited in *Classics of Public Personnel Policy*, ed. Frank Thompson, (Pacific Grove, CA: Brooks/Cole, 1991), pp. 386–390.

34. David Osborne and Ted Gaebler, *Reinventing Government: How the Entrepreneurial Spirit Is Transforming the Public Sector, From Schoolhouse to City Hall to the Pentagon* (Reading, MA: Addison-Wesley, 1992), p. 1.

QUESTIONS FOR THOUGHT AND DISCUSSION

Chapter 7: "The Development of American Police: An Historical Overview," by Craig D. Uchida

1. What are some current issues in policing that have their roots in earlier epochs of policing history? Are we making any progress in those areas?
2. How is the concept of community policing traced to the colonial period and to medieval England?
3. What problems within police departments were discovered by President Johnson's Kerner Commission?

Chapter 8: "The New Policing: Confronting Complexity," by Herman Goldstein

1. Why is it so important to involve the community in policing? What are some accomplishments being made in this area?
2. What are some of the changes being made in defining the police function and public expectations?
3. What is diversification of policing? What are some benefits and problems of diversification?

Chapter 9: "Contemporary Policing in a Community Era," by Quint C. Thurman

1. Exactly what is community policing?
2. What are PERF's five major perspectives used to define community policing?
3. How do police officers balance community policing ideals with law enforcement duties? Are the two mutually exclusive?

Chapter 10: "Police Shootings: Myths and Realities," by Roger G. Dunham and Geoffrey P. Alpert

1. Why do most citizens have an exaggerated view of the amount of police violence involved in typical police work?
2. What are the three types of policies regarding police shooting at suspects?
3. What are some things that can be done to reduce the number of inappropriate shootings by the police?

Chapter 11: "What We Know About Police Use of Force," by Kenneth Adams

1. According to the author, what are the realities about police use of force?
2. Under what circumstances is the use of force by the police most likely to occur?
3. Are an officer's personal characteristics related to the use of force?
4. What do we know about the incidence of wrongful use of force by the police?

Chapter 12: "Learning Police Ethics," by Lawrence Sherman

1. How does the police value of loyalty to each other conflict with living up to the code of ethics?
2. According to Sherman, what are the two main ways of teaching police ethics? Which one do you think is the most effective?
3. How can we be more effective in ensuring that police officers abide by the Code of Ethics?

Chapter 13: "Police Officer Sexual Misconduct: A Field Research Study," by Allen D. Sapp

1. What are some of the types of sexual misconduct regarding the police? What aspects of the police role facilitate each type of misconduct?
2. Can departments control this type of misconduct? If so, what can they do to control it?

Chapter 14: "Public Attitudes Toward Police Pursuit Driving" by John M. McDonald and Geoffrey P. Alpert

1. What are your views concerning police pursuit driving?
2. Does the public limit the use of police pursuit?

Chapter 15: "Race-Based Policing: Alternatives for Assessing the Problem," by Brian L. Withrow and Henry Jackson

1. Are police substantially more likely to ticket a person of color than a white motorist?
2. Are police more likely to stop and/or search the car of a person of color than a white motorist?
3. How do we determine these facts? What are some alternative methods and strategies for discovering if racial profiling exists?

Chapter 16: "The Future of Policing in a Community Era," by Jihong Zhao

1. How has technology transformed community policing from its original conception?
2. Does the overreliance of technology threaten community policing? Is it antithetical to its original philosophy?
3. What are some positive and negative forces impacting community policing?
4. What is the future of community policing?

Section 3

Adjudication and Sentencing

INTRODUCTION

The courts are at the core of the criminal justice system. They are among the most controversial, most powerful, and perhaps the least understood and least studied components of the criminal justice system. In this section, we examine the roles of some of the key players in the judiciary process and analyze some of the major issues.

This section opens with "Facts About Courts." Here statistics from the Bureau of Justice Statistics are organized in such a way as to provide the reader with basic information about the court system in America. Both state and federal courts are discussed as well as a brief look at sentencing practices nationwide.

In Chapter 17, "Adversarial Justice," Professor Franklin Strier presents a cogent essay tackling the issue and nature of justice in our judicial system. Strier focuses on pretrial abuse, the inherent corruption of the adversarial system, abuse on the part of attorneys (i.e., the prosecutor and defense), witness tampering or coaching, and problems with the jury system. Possible solutions for reform are presented.

In Chapter 18, "Talking on Testilying: The Prosecutor's Response to In-Court Police Deception," Larry Cunningham from Georgetown University Law Center discusses the problem of perjury and other forms of in-court deception by police officers, labeled by Cunningham as *testilying*. What is unique about this manuscript is that it is from a prosecutor's perspective. Mr. Cunningham offers an overview of police perjury, steps the judicial system (i.e., the prosecutor's office) can initiate to prevent such illegal action, and professional and personal obligations court representatives have in addressing such behavior.

Chapter 19, "Capital Murder: A Prosecutor's Personal Observations on the Prosecution of Capital Cases," by Ronald J. Sievert provides the reader with a candid representation of the inner workings of a prosecutor's office. Specifically, he details the emotional process behind the prosecution of capital cases. Considering the political ideology that is traditionally associated with the death penalty, Sievert provides the reader with a personal assessment of the topic as it relates to finding "justice."

In Chapter 20, "Why Prosecutors Misbehave," Bennett L. Gershman analyzes the issue of misconduct by prosecutors. The authors argue that the temptation to cross over the allowable ethical limit must often seem irresistible in that it provides a distinct advantage in assisting the prosecutor in winning his or her case. This reading is important because the prosecutor's role provides the link between law enforcement and adjudicatory processes.

In Chapter 21, "The Criminal Lawyer's 'Different Mission': Reflections on the 'Right' to Present a False Case," Harry I. Subin, writing for the *Georgetown Journal of Legal Ethics*, discusses dilemmas encountered in his representation of a client in a rape case. Ethical and practical issues are raised to just how far a defense attorney should go in representing a client. This reading raises fundamental issues for defense attorneys concerning clients and the role that "truth" should play in a defense strategy.

Chapter 22, "How to Improve the Jury System," by Judge Thomas F. Hogan, Judge Gregory E. Mize, and senior analyst Kathleen Clark, presents several key recommendations for modernizing the jury system. This piece is more than a theoretical argument. It represents policy initiatives relevant to legal scholars, researchers, the judiciary, and the lay person summoned to serve.

In Chapter 23, "Should Juries Nullify Laws They Consider Unjust or Excessively Punitive?", Clay S. Conrad, an appellate attorney, and Nancy King, a law professor at Vanderbilt University, debate a controversial issue currently plaguing the courts. The issue of jury nullification is not a simple one nor is it one that can be easily ignored. Although on opposing sides, the authors abandon rhetoric for substance as each outline the substantive issues at hand.

Chapter 24, "Truth in Sentencing in State Prisons," presents a statistical portrait of states adopting new sentencing guidelines. This Bureau of Justice Statistics report offers the current figures relating to the amount of time criminal offenders can expect to serve and the type of criminal offender (i.e., substance or violent offender) currently being sentenced and imprisoned. The reader can draw conclusions as to the impact such new sentencing guidelines have on corrections as a whole.

In Chapter 25, "The Impact of Sentencing Guidelines," Dale Parent, Terence Dunworth, Douglas McDonald, and William Rhodes present an overall assessment of presumptive sentencing guidelines. The authors argue that such guidelines have led to improved sentencing neutrality, increased sentence uniformity and proportionality, unchanged plea negotiations, and more flexibility for states that are obligated to control their prison levels.

In Chapter 26, "Therapeutic Jurisprudence and the Emergence of Problem-Solving Courts," David Rottman and Pamela Casey outline the potential for courts to work in real collaborative relationships with corresponding communities: therapeutic jurisprudence. Their guiding theoretical framework is not unlike that of community oriented policing. Rather than being guided by the legal premise of disposition, the overall mandate of therapeutic jurisprudence is resolution. The authors offer several recommendations for this new type of legal work.

In Chapter 27, entitled "Restoring the Balance: Juvenile and Community Justice," Gordon Bazemore and Susan E. Day describe an alternative approach to juvenile justice—one which focuses on the interests of multiple justice clients. This approach is referred to as restorative justice. Restorative justice focuses on repairing the harm done to society by attempting to determine who is responsible for the harm and what can be done to make amends.

FACTS ABOUT COURTS

Summary Findings

- Courts and Judges
- Judicial Selection and Service
- The Judicial Branch
- State Appellate Court Systems
- Specialized Courts
- The Jury
- The Sentencing Context

Courts and Judges

In 1998—
There were 208 statewide general and limited jurisdiction trial court systems in the United States, the District of Columbia, and Puerto Rico. About 9,065 full-time authorized judges served in the 71 statewide trial court systems of general jurisdiction alone. There were 132 courts of appeal, including the U.S. Supreme Court and U.S. Courts of Appeal. The combined full-time federal and state appellate bench had a reported 1,474 members. About 75% or 1,108 appellate judges served on intermediate appellate courts.

Judicial Selection and Service

Twenty-one (42%) of the 50 states selected their appellate judges through a gubernatorial appointment and 3 by legislative appointment in 1998. An additional 14 states used nonpartisan elections, 8 partisan elections and 4 retention elections. Initial/pre-bench education for general jurisdiction judges was required in 30 states (including Puerto Rico), for limited jurisdiction judges in 31 states, and in 9 states for appellate judges. Continuing education for general jurisdiction judges was required in 44 states, for limited jurisdiction judges in 42 states, and for appellate judges in 38 states.

The Judicial Branch

Every state has a judicial branch which is headed by the court of last resort in 13 states, the Chief Justice of the court of last resort in 36 states, and in 1 state, Utah, the Judicial Council. In the majority of states (33), the head of the judicial branch is established by the state constitution. In the remaining states, authority is established either by state statute or some combination of both.

Source: http://www.ojp.usdoj.gov/bjs/stssent.htm.

State Appellate Court Systems

Appellate courts implement various strategies to make their workload more efficient. For example, by 1998, 37 states had some expedited briefing procedures in their appellate court systems. Eighteen states had accelerated or special calendars in some courts for specific case types, and all but 12 states had some limitation on oral arguments in criminal and/or civil cases.

Specialized Courts

There were 327 drug courts across 43 states, the District of Columbia, and Puerto Rico in 1998. The majority of drug courts were established between 1992 and 1996. During 1998, drug courts were established in Maine and Mississippi. By 1998, all but 17 states had family courts that served some number of counties, districts, or were statewide. These courts typically had jurisdiction over domestic and marital matters such as divorce, child custody and support, and domestic violence.

There are currently over 450 tribal justice forums among the 556 federally recognized Native American tribes in the United States. Sixteen states have assumed mandatory or optional jurisdiction over tribal lands, pursuant to Public Law 280.

The Jury

In most states, the minimum age to serve on a jury was 18. The minimum age in Missouri and Montana, however, was 21 years of age. There was some residency requirement to serve on a jury in all states, and literacy and/or language requirements in all but 8 states.

Grand jury indictments for all felony prosecutions were required in 14 states and in an additional 4 states for capital and/or life imprisonment cases. The size of grand juries ranged from 6 members in Indiana to 23 members in Maryland and Massachusetts.

The Sentencing Context

In non-capital felony cases, original sentences were set by a jury in 46 states, the District of Columbia, and Puerto Rico, and by a judge in 6 states. The judge can alter the jury sentence or recommendation in 4 states: Arkansas, Indiana, Kentucky, and Missouri.

Of the 37 states with the death penalty in capital felony cases during 1998, original sentences were set by a jury in 23 states, by a judge in 5 states, and by a judge with the recommendation of the jury in 7 states.

In 1998, collateral consequences for felony convictions were in place in all states. In most states, a felony conviction was associated with the restriction of voting rights, parental rights, public employment, jury duty service, and firearm ownership.

Summary Findings

Between 1994 and 1996, the number of felony convictions increased 14% in state courts and 11% in federal courts.

State courts convicted almost 998,000 adults of a felony in 1996, an average growth of approximately 5% every year since 1988 (667,366).

From 1988 to 1996, the number of felony convictions increased faster than the number of arrests.

Sixty-nine percent of those convicted in 1996 were sentenced to incarceration.

Almost two-thirds of defendants charged with a felony in the 75 most populated counties in May 1996 were released from jail pending disposition of their case.

Thirty-one percent of those who were released were rearrested for a new offense or did not show up for a court date or violated some other condition of their pretrial release.

1996 was the first year state and federal courts convicted a combined total of over 1 million adults of felonies. State convictions totalled 997,970 adults and federal convictions totalled 43,839 adults (accounting for 4% of the national total.)

In 1996, 69% of all convicted felons were sentenced to a period of confinement—38% to state prisons and 31% to local jails. Jail sentences are for short-term confinement (usually for a year or less) in a county or city facility, while prison sentences are for long-term confinement (usually for over a year) in a state facility.

State courts sentenced 38% of convicted felons to a state prison, 31% to a local jail, and 31% to straight probation with no jail or prison time to serve.

Felons sentenced to a state prison in 1996 had an average sentence of 5 years but were likely to serve almost half (45%) of that sentence—or just over 2 years—before release, assuming that 1996 release policies continue in effect.

The average sentence to local jail was 6 months. The average probation sentence was about 3-1/2 years.

Besides being sentenced to incarceration or probation, 32% or more of convicted felons also were ordered to pay a fine, pay victim restitution, receive treatment, perform community service, or comply with some other additional penalty. A fine was imposed on at least 20% of convicted felons.

TABLE 1.   Lengths of Felony Sentences Imposed by State Courts, 1996

Most serious conviction offense	Average maximum sentence length (in months) for felons sentenced to:			
	Incarceration			Probation
	Total	Prison	Jail	
All offenses	38	62	6	41
Violent offenses	78	105	7	48
Property offenses	30	49	6	40
Drug offenses	28	51	6	42
Weapons offenses	29	45	5	35
Other offenses	24	42	6	40

Note: Means exclude sentences to death or to life in prison. Sentence length data were available for 997,906 incarceration and probation sentences.

Felony Defendants

An estimated 54,579 felony cases were filed in the state courts of the nation's 75 largest counties during May 1996.

About one-fourth of these felony defendants were charged with a violent offense, usually assault (11.4%) or robbery (7.1%). Murder (0.9%) and rape (1.5%) defendants accounted for a small percentage of defendants.

About two-thirds of defendants were charged with a nonviolent felony. The most frequently charged nonviolent offenses were drug trafficking (18.5%), other drug offenses (18.2%), theft (12.3%), and burglary (8.1%).

About 3 in 8 defendants had an active criminal justice status at the time of the current charged offense, including 16% who were on probation, 13% on pretrial release, and 6% on parole.

Fifty-five percent of all defendants were convicted of a felony, and 15% were convicted of a misdemeanor.

The highest felony conviction rates were for defendants charged with a drug trafficking (68%), murder (62%), burglary (62%), or a driving related (61%) offense.

The lowest felony conviction rate was found among assault defendants (33%).

Ninety-four percent of convictions occurring within 1 year of arrest were obtained through a guilty plea. About 5 in 6 guilty pleas were to a felony.

Murder defendants (35%) were the most likely to have their case adjudicated by trial. Seventy-seven percent of trials resulted in a guilty verdict, including 86% of murder trials.

Overall, 67% of the defendants whose most serious conviction charge was a felony were sentenced to incarceration. Nearly all of the remaining convicted defendants received a probation sentence.

Juvenile Defendants in:

Criminal Courts

Under certain circumstances, juveniles (as defined by state law) can be tried in criminal court. An estimated 7,110 juvenile defendants were charged with felonies in the state criminal courts of the nation's 75 largest counties during May 1990, May 1992, and May 1994.

These juvenile felony defendants who were handled as adults in criminal courts represented about 1% of all felony defendants.

Two-thirds of the juvenile felony defendants handled in adult court were charged with a violent offense.

Most (67%) of the juvenile felony defendants were either 16 or 17 years of age at the time of arrest.

Fifty-nine percent of juveniles handled in adult court were convicted of a felony, and about half (52%) of those convicted of a felony were sentenced to prison.

Juvenile Courts

An estimated 24% of the 370,000 sampled defendants in juvenile courts in the nation's 75 largest counties from 1990, 1992 and 1994 were referred for violent offenses, 46% for property offenses, about 18% for public order offenses, and 13% for drug-related offenses.

More than half (55%) of the juvenile defendants formally processed in juvenile courts in the nation's 75 largest counties were adjudicated delinquent.

Among juvenile defendants adjudicated delinquent, 40% received a disposition of residential placement and 50% received formal probation.

Chapter 17

Adversarial Justice

by Franklin Strier

We take it as axiomatic that our trial courts dispense justice. The very legitimacy of the courts depends on that expectation. Yet the reliance we place on our adversarial trial court system to deliver just decisions is a misguided leap of faith. This is neither a radical nor novel perspective. Consider, for example, this observation by the eminent jurist Karl Llewellyn:

> The adversary trial seems from outside like back-handedness or trickery which approaches a travesty on justice; a dragging, awkward, unreliable machinery at best; at worst, one which is manipulated. In consequence . . . there is not one sole excrescence of trial machinery that will find one sole jot of support from any person in the court except the lawyer.[1]

Several inherent flaws of the adversary trial system support Llewellyn's assessment, but none more forcefully than the system's weakness in exposing the truth. In a trial, justice without truth is serendipitous. Benjamin Disraeli said, "Justice is truth in action." The U.S. Supreme Court has concurred, frequently stating that the central purpose of the trial is the determination of truth. The sobering reality is that our trials, especially jury trials, are decidedly fickle vehicles to the truth. Justice is the casualty.

Paradoxes and false presumptions suffuse the theories and concepts undergirding our trial system. One such presumption is sometimes referred to as the *fight theory*, which holds that truth is best revealed in the courtroom through the clash of opposing views, rather than through investigation by the judge or other neutral third parties. Adversary theory presumes that the personal motivation of attorneys will generate the most assiduous search for favorable evidence. Essentially, this is the legal version of the "invisible hand" theory: Each party pursuing his or her own self-interest will adduce the most favorable evidence and generate the best arguments, yielding the fairest possible trial and a just result. By the same token, statements of the opposition will be vigorously monitored. Because the parties (rather than the judge) control the proceedings, rigorous cross-examination of adverse testimony is assumed.

The problem with the fight theory is that it is neither logically supportable nor empirically verifiable. Federal judge Jerome Frank, former chairman of the SEC and an oft-quoted critic of the adversary system, challenged the fight theory. His premise was simple: "The partisanship of the opposing lawyers blocks the uncovering of vital evidence or

This article appeared in the July 1998 issue and is reprinted with permission from *The World & I*, a publication of the Washington Times Corporation, © 1998.

leads to a presentation of vital testimony in a way that distorts it."[2] He concluded: "To treat a lawsuit as, above all, a fight, surely cannot be the best way to discover facts. Improvement in fact-finding will necessitate some considerable diminution of the martial spirit in litigation."[3]

Other critics disparage the fight theory. Judge Marvin Frankel, a leader in the movement to give truth a greater value in trials, was shocked by the wanton leap of logic necessary to subscribe to the fight theory. After noting that other truth seekers do not use adversary means, he observed:

> We . . . would fear for our lives if physicians, disagreeing about the cause of our chest pains, sought to resolve the issue by our forms of interrogation, badgering, and other forensics. But for the defendant whose life is at stake—and for the public concerned the defendant is a homicidal menace—this is thought to be the perfect form of inquiry. We live, at any rate, as if we believe this.[4]

Commenting on the implausibility of the truth-from-fight assumption, Thurman Arnold wrote in *The Symbols of Government:*

> Bitter partisanship in opposite directions is supposed to bring out the truth. Of course no rational human being would apply such a theory to his own affairs. . . . Mutual exaggeration of opposing claims violate(s) the whole theory of rational, scientific investigation. Yet in spite of this most obvious fact, the ordinary teacher of law will insist (1) that combat makes for clarity, (2) that heated arguments bring out the truth, and (3) that anyone who doesn't believe this is a loose thinker.[5]

Our use of the fight theory results in a paradox: Trial procedure assigns exclusive responsibility for presenting the evidence to those with no legal or professional obligation to seek the truth—the attorneys. Their goal is victory, not enlightenment. Studies show that attorneys often spend more time trying to hide or distort facts than revealing them. In every trial, at least one attorney usually tries to suppress or cloud unfavorable evidence.

A tenet of the adversary system is that each side's attorney will fight as hard as he can. Thus the attorney's duty of "zealous advocacy" is prescribed in the various professional codes that purport to delineate ethical conduct for attorneys. But this makes adversarial excess endemic to the system. And although we expect attorneys to adhere to the rules of evidence and confine their strategies to the ethical boundaries of the rules, they often bend the rules and stretch the strategies.

PRETRIAL ABUSE

Attorney abuses begin before the trial, during the discovery process. Under discovery, a litigant may request of the opposing party any relevant information (not protected by privilege) which that party has or to which that party has access. One objective was to do away with the element of unfair surprise in a trial. Initially, discovery was hailed as a boon to truth seeking, fairness, and the expedited disposition of cases. No longer. Discovery abuses now constitute the single greatest source of dispute, delay, cost, and trickery in the adversary system. Excessive discovery tactics either bully the opposition into submission or limit and distort the flow of information. Either result defeats the principal purposes for which discovery was designed.

Attorneys often use written interrogatories as tactical weapons by smothering a relatively impecunious adversary with extensive discovery demands and resultant costs. A survey of Chicago litigators found widespread use of another discovery tool, the deposition (direct questioning of a party or witness), as an aggressive weapon. The idea, said one respondent, is to "see if you can get them mad," to put them "through the wringer, through the mud," so that "they are frightened to be a witness and . . . are a much worse witness."[6] Responding attorneys employ an equally mischievous array of tactics. These include creating false, diversionary leads; providing the bare minimum of information; and making the acquisition of that information as difficult and expensive as possible.

In criminal cases, the prosecution always has the constitutional duty to disclose exonerating evidence. But many states now make pretrial discovery a "two-way street," requiring that the defense grant similar discovery rights to the prosecution. California is one of the states to recently mandate reciprocal discovery. The intentional breach of this duty by the defense in the Simpson case may bear heavily on the outcome. During his opening statement, defense attorney Johnnie Cochran flagrantly broke the discovery law by referring to intended witnesses and their prospective testimonies without first disclosing their identities and/or statements to the prosecution for discovery. These witnesses, Cochran said, would offer testimony exculpating Simpson or casting great doubt upon the prosecution's evidence. Cochran further suggested that the prosecution had hidden this evidence.

The prosecution expostulated convulsively. The government was unaware of some of the new witnesses. How could it hide that of which it was unaware? The other new witnesses were known miscreants or felons and thus were completely unreliable.

When the prosecution asked for sanctions against the defense, Judge Lance Ito found himself in an extremely delicate situation. Some sanctions were clearly in order, yet they could not be so severe as to produce bias against the defendant and create grounds for appellate reversal. After all, it was the defense attorney, not the defendant, who was the misfeasor in this procedural breach. The judge mulled it over for a day, then imposed two sanctions: First, he granted the prosecution ten minutes of "reopening" statements—in essence, a rebuttal; second, he admonished the jury to disregard the defense counsel's opening statements as they pertained to six of the potential witnesses.

Significantly, the judge did not mention what the testimony of these potential witnesses was to be. Thus, the jury does not know what weight to attach to the admonition. The warning will, therefore, have little corrective impact on the effect of the defense's opening statements (save suggesting to the jury that the defense counsel is somewhat untrustworthy). The ultimate effect of this gambit by the defense may never be known, but it is likely to be an affordable "cost of doing business."

Discovery abuse epitomizes the adversary system. Indeed, some attorneys argue that adversarial professionalism *commands* the use of such devices whenever they offer significant advantages. Whatever the validity of this contention, the intense competitive pressures of the adversary system make resort to obstructionist discovery devices a constant temptation and a common occurrence.

Pretrial adversarial excesses continue during voir dire (jury selection), a fertile area for trial attorneys to ply their trade. Attorneys may dismiss prospective jurors by challenges. Those whose responses to the voir dire questions indicate probable bias are challenged for *cause*. Attorneys may perceive that other prospective jurors would not view their client's case favorably but are not sufficiently biased to challenge for cause. Such individuals can be removed by *peremptory* challenges. Unlike challenges for cause, peremptory challenges require no stated reason by the requesting attorney; however, they are limited in number—a common number is six for each side. But in cases of serious crimes, the number may be twelve or more. (There were twenty in the Simpson case.) Because of their limited availability, a premium is put on the attorney's skill in using peremptory challenges.

Statute and case law require the panel from which the jury is selected to be drawn from a representative cross section of the community in which the case is filed. To this end, courts use voter registration lists as the primary source for jury panels. Theoretically, the varying views within the community, if represented on the jury, make for vigorous and salutary debate. The hope is that conflicting prejudices will cancel each other out.

By strategic use of peremptory challenges, an attorney tries to assemble a jury receptive to his case. As candid practitioners readily admit, lawyers conduct voir dire not to get unbiased jurors but to get jurors favorably biased. Attorneys also seek competitive advantage by attempting to influence prospective jurors while interviewing them. Their tactics are designed to *create* bias in prospective jurors—via indoctrination, education, and socialization—rather than merely detect it.

Trial advocacy tracts (some even appearing in law school textbooks) are replete with advice on achieving an illegitimate goal: gaining adversarial advantage during voir dire. Several studies support the conclusion that the vast majority of the attorney's efforts during voir dire are indeed undertaken for gaining adversarial advantage rather than screening for bias. For example, one survey found that over 80 percent of attorneys' time during voir dire was used to indoctrinate prospective jurors. These findings were confirmed by an extensive survey of Los Angeles jurors (hereafter "the Los Angeles survey") that I conducted in 1987–88. (With over 3,800 jurors responding, it was the largest of its kind.)[7] More than one-third of the jurors agreed that "one or both attorneys were trying to persuade me in addition to probing for bias." This suggests that numerous attorneys are using voir dire for inappropriate didactic purposes.

TRUTH CORRUPTION

Once trial begins, tricks by attorneys can escalate—thanks in large part to the bench's historically lax enforcement of professional conduct rules. When infractions occur, they are routinely winked at by judges and bar association ethics committees. As a result, trial lawyers ostensibly enjoy a unique privilege in plying their trade: They are largely unanswerable to society for behavior that would be morally questionable elsewhere. This led the venerable jurist Felix Cohen to lament: "How the edifice of justice can be supported by the efforts of liars at the bar and ex-liars on the bench is one of the paradoxes of legal logic which the man on the street has never solved."

Space does not permit even a modest catalog of truth-corrupting tactics, but mention of a few common artifices will suffice:

Coaching witnesses.   A standard practice is for attorneys to interview their witnesses in preparation for testimony. The practice is known by a variety of sobriquets—"rehearsing," "horse shedding," "prepping," and "sandpapering"—but the most common term is "coaching." The dangers of coaching are substantial: An attorney who knows the testimony of all friendly witnesses can orchestrate a common story that can avoid contradictions. In the course of coaching their witnesses, attorneys suggest "better" answers that, if not clearly contravening the witness' intended answer, subtly but effectively shade, dissemble, or distort the truth. The Simpson prosecutors continued to accuse the defense counsel of coaching those defense witnesses whose changed stories benefited the defendant.

Attorney statements.   Judges frequently tell jurors that attorney statements are not evidence. That is not enough. Jurors should also be informed that *attorneys are not under oath and do not have to believe their own statements*. Few jurors appreciate this. That is why attorneys are so effective when they (permissibly) impeach the credibility of witnesses they know to be telling the truth.

Similarly effective is the presumptuous question, one of the more insidious tools in the cross-examining attorney's arsenal. The presumptuous question implies a serious charge against the witness for which the attorney has little or no proof. An example: "Isn't it true that you have accused men of rape before?" Such innuendos are particularly effective against expert witnesses. A recent study found that by merely posing these questions, an attorney could severely diminish an expert's credibility, *even when the witness denied the allegation and his attorney's objection to the charge was sustained*. This clearly indicates that the presumptuous cross-examination question is a dirty trick that can sway jurors' evaluations of a witness' credibility.

Explanations for the effectiveness of this tactic vary. Communications research suggests people believe that when a speaker offers a premise, he has an evidentiary basis for it. With their pristine mind-sets, jurors assume that the derogatory premise of an attorney's question is supported by information. Another explanation lies in the possible confusion of jurors as to the sources of their information. The longer the trial, the less likely jurors will be able to distinguish information suggested by an attorney's presumptuous question from that imparted by the witness' answer.

Witness abuse.   Cross-examining attorneys often regard witnesses as if they were open garbage cans and treat them accordingly. Early in the Simpson trial, for example, the defense resorted to hardball tactics against witnesses. Recall the derisive browbeating of police detectives by defense counsel. And when Simpson's friend, Ron Shipp, testified that O.J. had disclosed his dream of killing Nicole, the defense counsel on cross-examination accused Shipp of being an alcoholic, a deadbeat, an ingrate, and a perfidious grasper who knowingly betrayed his friend to advance his own aspirations as an actor.

Emotional appeals.   In the Los Angeles survey, two-fifths of the jurors felt "one or both attorneys were trying harder to distort or selectively hide facts rather than seeking to reveal the truth so the jury could make an informed judgment." Jurors rank ordered the tactics used to accomplish this obfuscation. "Appeals to the emotions of the jurors" and "repeated interruptions and disruptive tactics" came in first and second, respectively.

An emotional appeal to the jury, of course, is the time-honored ploy of the trial attorney with a weak case. How it will "play with the jury" becomes the overarching consideration in presenting evidence. Surely one of the most emotional moments in the Simpson trial appears to have been skillfully choreographed by the prosecution to have maximum impact on the jury. Assistant District Attorney Christopher Darden questioned Denise Brown, the sister of Nicole Brown Simpson, on the first Friday afternoon of the trial. After recounting O.J.'s past physical abuses of Nicole, Denise dissolved in tears. Darden then immediately asked for and received a recess, knowing that the jurors would carry that last compelling tableau with them over the entire weekend.

Adversarial trials conduce such drama because they are staged like theatrical performances. The show is the action taking place in the arena, bounded on the jury's right by the witness stand and judge's bench, and on the left by the attorneys' tables. Indisputably, the attorneys are the performers. Only they are allowed to walk freely in the arena, to and from the witness stand, the bench, and the jury box. They gesture, flail, and point. But mostly they talk: They bluster, blather, harangue, sermonize, and beguile. They laugh, cry, and bristle; they make the jurors laugh, cry, and bristle. Bar associations unabashedly offer "courtroom acting" classes to attorneys that satisfy continuing-education requirements. It is the greatest show in town because it involves real people with real problems and high stakes: prison or freedom; child custody or childlessness; recompense for serious bodily injury or destitution and welfare. Should matters of such consequence be resolved by a process that elevates showmanship over dispassionate and rational inquiry?

Dumb shows. The "repeated interruptions and disruptive tactics" referred to in the Los Angeles survey can come in many forms. Sometimes referred to as "dumb shows," this category consists of indecorous behavior intended to distract or mislead the jury, such as dropping books or making bogus objections. The legendary Clarence Darrow used a novel subterfuge. Before trial, he would insert a nearly invisible wire in his cigar. When his opponent began interrogating a witness, Darrow would smoke the cigar. Eventually, all eyes would follow the cigar ash, which, magically, never dropped.

Changing the story. In the unique, "fact-finding" inquiry that is the trial, attorneys selectively present evidence only to the extent that it furthers their version of the facts. The objective is to craft a credible story for the jury. In developing its story, the Simpson prosecution team chose an interesting strategy. Knowing it had to tarnish an American icon, the prosecution eschewed the conventional wisdom of beginning its case with evidence of the murder in favor of presenting evidence of antecedent wife beating.

Sometimes the attorneys' stories change as the trial progresses. An Arizona trial judge offers his impression of how this happens:

> The sporting lawyer's concern is whether the story is convincing, whether it adequately meets the opposing story, not whether it is true or false. Thus it is not at all unusual to hear a courtroom story unfold like a novel, changing as the trial proceeds. Sometimes the story becomes clearer, sometimes fuzzier, sometimes contradicted as it is orchestrated by the lawyer-maestros. As one side crafts a story, the other side expresses outrage at the opponent's fiction and responds by fictionalizing its own story. The story is not as dismaying as the attorney's acquiescence in it. In this sort of liar's paradise, truth ceases to be a Heideggerian revelation; instead, trial evidence becomes a progressive sedimentation, with new layers of lies overlaying the original ones.[8]

The defense's story certainly changed in the Simpson trial. Defense counsel Robert Shapiro initially said O.J. was asleep at the alleged time of the murder. Later, defense counsel Johnnie Cochran claimed O.J. was swinging golf clubs in his yard at that time. We can only speculate as to why the story changed. We know the change occurred after the judge ruled that O.J.'s exercise videotape—recorded shortly before the murders—could be shown to the jury. This evidence would obviously refute the claim that O.J. was so racked with arthritis at the time as to be incapable of a double murder with a knife. Once the arthritis claim was dropped, there was no disadvantage in maintaining O.J. was swinging golf clubs at the time of the murder. Further, it helped explain why O.J. was outside his house when he called his girlfriend on his cellular phone.

Partisan expertise.   Will technological advances improve trial truth seeking? Even with the advent of more accurate fact-finding techniques such as DNA testing, the adversarial process will continue to subvert the truth by subordinating it to competing values. Peter Sperlich, who writes on the use of scientific evidence, says: "The adversary system maximizes the opportunities to obscure the facts, coopt the experts, and propagandize the judge . . . . The greatest single obstacle to complete and accurate scientific information . . . is the adversary system."[9]

When expert witnesses are pushed into advocacy roles, attorneys and the system corrupt the value of the witness' expertise. Attention is too often focused on the personal characteristics of expert witnesses instead of the quality of their evidence. In a 1987 book compiling papers and comments on social research and the courts, the authors reached consensus on these points: (1) scientists serving as expert witnesses must expect to be used (and misused) for partisan purposes; and (2) the adversary system is not a reliable means of bringing all the relevant scientific data to the adjudicator's attention or of separating valid research from unwarranted conclusions.

With judges being generally passive, the scope of zealous advocacy trial tactics is limited only by the often-fertile imaginations of the litigation attorneys. Censuring individual practitioners or even the entire litigation bar for this state of affairs misses the source of the problem. After all, trial lawyers merely play their assigned roles within the adversary system. We should not condemn the attorney for engaging in morally questionable but nevertheless permissible trial tactics. Rather, we should decry the system that sanctions such tactics.

PROBLEMS WITH THE JURY SYSTEM

Any discussion of the adversary system is incomplete without considering the impact of the jury. Juries became enshrined in the Constitution because they were our bulwark during colonial times against the arbitrary and unjust decisions of the local judges appointed by the English Crown. Now we have representative democracy and many other constitutional protections against government encroachment. (Instructively, the courts of most other democracies do not use juries as we know them; none, including England, use them as extensively.) So the primary purpose of the jury is no longer protection against the government. Rather, it is a vehicle to attainment of an ideal: integration of community values, via the perspectives of common citizens, into the administration of justice. To this end, the law seeks juries composed of a representative cross section of the community where the trial is held.

Whether the jury system achieves or even approximates this ideal is highly debatable. Exemptions from service routinely afforded professionals and other potentially competent jurors both dilute the quality of juries and remove the very individuals particularly able to inject the community values that the law seeks. Most important, juries are usually selected partly or fully by the attorneys. It would betray great naïveté to contend that, in any given trial, the trial attorney's allegiance to the ideal of a representative, impartial jury is more than coincidental.

The main focus, however, should not be the jurors themselves. We should instead vet the jury system. Specifically, does current jury procedure facilitate or inhibit the realization of the ideal? And does this procedure make sense within the context of an adversarial trial?

The jury is called the trial's "fact finder." But unlike fact-finding in any other inquiry, the jury does not find, or investigate, any facts. Instead, it is the passive recipient of information, called evidence, introduced by the partisan attorneys. Although no appellate court has ruled that questions from jurors are forbidden, the vast majority of courts do not allow them or do not inform jurors of the right to ask questions. Incredibly, juries enter deliberations without the opportunity to fill in missing information or clarify uncertainties.

The restriction on questions is only the overture to a litany of ill-founded constraints imposed on jurors. No matter how lengthy or complex the evidence, most courts do not allow jurors to take notes or do not advise them of the right if it is permitted. Nor do they permit jurors to see a transcript of the testimony or a notebook of exhibits. Trials operate under the myth of perfect juror recall—yet another blatantly erroneous presumption.

There's more: Our trials litigate everything at once. All evidence on all possible issues is heard in one continuous trial. Evidence on any issue can be introduced at any time between opening and closing statements. No juror-friendly, logical order to the presentation of witnesses or evidence is required. As a consequence of this implausible scheme of "fact-finding," jurors tend to forget evidence or apply it to the wrong issue. Historian Carl Becker's commentary on the jury system resonates with truth: "Trial by jury, as a method of determining facts, is antiquated and inherently absurd—so much so that no lawyer, judge, scholar, prescription-clerk, cook, or mechanic in a garage would ever think for a moment of employing that method for determining the facts in any situation that concerned him."[10]

Being laypersons rather than experts, jurors are frequently overwhelmed by technical or complex evidence. This would include the DNA evidence that expert witnesses hired by the opposing sides "explained" in the Simpson jury. Unfortunately, these experts often compound instead of ease the jury's task: How is a juror to know if the most persuasive expert is the most authoritative? Also troubling is the potential degree to which the experts' hefty fees may flavor their testimonies.

Equally confounding the jury's search for truth is all the relevant evidence that they *cannot* hear. Because nontruth values such as individual dignity and privacy coexist with truth in the philosophical underpinning of our trial system, large gobs of highly probative evidence can be withheld from the fact finder. As illustration, the sanctity of the family dictates that spouses need not reveal spousal communications. The judge also has great discretion to exclude relevant evidence if he believes its probative value is outweighed by the danger of unfairly prejudicing, confusing, or misleading the jury.

But substantially more evidence is kept inadmissible by exclusionary rules based on erroneous presumptions. These exclusions both compromise the search for truth and profoundly beggar the justice of the final decision. For instance, a procedural rule intentionally blindfolds jurors as to whether civil-case defendants carry insurance. (It is presumed that such information would unduly influence the jury's award.) The problem is that juries go ahead and make their own assumptions anyway, thereby unwittingly corrupting the decision-making process even more.

Simpson case watchers will note the magnitude of relevant evidence that may be excluded by the grand-daddy of all exclusions, the hearsay rule. A historical distrust of jurors' ability to properly discount hearsay forms the basis of the exclusion. Yet no empirical consensus supports this contention. That is why legal scholars since Jeremy Bentham have advocated that hearsay be excluded only when more direct proof is available.

Jury problems in divining the facts pale in comparison with understanding the judge's instruction on the law to be applied. *Most judicial instructions are worthless.* Rather than explain or clarify the law, the judge's instructions usually confuse the jurors with jargon-laden, incomprehensible language. That is because they are worded to avoid appellate reversal, not to educate the jurors. Consequently, jurors commonly deliberate and vote in ignorance of the law, referring instead to their personal values and biases or succumbing to the emotions evoked by the pandering of the attorneys.

Let us pause to reassess the two preeminent features of the adversarial trial. First, we have the partisan opposing attorneys. With the qualified exception of prosecutors, they have no obligation to the truth but do have an overriding professional and financial incentive to do all they can to win within the decidedly loose bounds of zealous advocacy. Second, we have the lay jury. It cannot independently investigate but must rely exclusively on the staged, colored, and filtered versions of the facts presented by the attorneys.

This relationship profoundly affects trial outcomes. *The adversary and jury systems combine to deliver a witch's brew of trial justice.* Crafty attorneys have long prevailed in contravention of the merits of the cases they tried before juries by employing superior forensic skills or tricks or pandering to the basest of the jurors' emotions. Not only does the legal profession condone these tactics, it instructs in their use through law school courses and practitioner seminars. Over one-third of the Los Angeles survey jurors believed that the outcome of the case they sat on was dictated by a disparity in skills between the opposing attorneys. Two-fifths said the skills disparity was partly or completely responsible for a "wrong" decision with respect to the verdict or size of an award. These findings are unsurprising in light of adversary system theory, which holds that the optimal benefits of the system are realizable only in the presence of a supposition of epic proportions: Opposing litigants will be represented by competent attorneys of roughly equal skills. No more reason exists to believe this myth than to believe that opposing litigants will have roughly equal resources.

The mismatched attorney phenomenon is not entirely random. The wealthier the litigant, the better the available legal representation. I refer not only to better attorneys, but also to more persuasive expert witnesses and to other litigation support services that help "scientifically" select the most favorably disposed jurors. These factors have certainly benefited wealthy litigants, such as William Kennedy Smith. It is no small curiosity that our legal system espouses equality of treatment (equal justice); yet our trial mechanism, more than any other, skews trial outcomes in favor of the side with the better attorney and more money.

REFORMS

Although failing, the trial system is not irreparable. I list below a few reform proposals.[11] The aim of all of them is to distribute some of the powers now wielded exclusively by attorneys to the judge and jury. As the impartial players in the trial, they are best suited to seek justice; the attorneys are not. Writes University of Chicago law professor Albert Alschuler:

> Although the adversary system may need a watchman, the task need not be assigned to the watched. Lawyers are simply not the appropriate figures to correct the defects of our adver-

sary system. Their hearts will never be in it, and more importantly, it is unfair to both their clients and themselves to require them to serve two masters.[12]

Action from judges is the key to reform. Few people realize how extensive the judge's inherent authority is. All that is required for its exercise is the courage to impose rationality on the system.

If we are going to continue assigning weighty responsibilities to juries for little pay and much disruption of their lives, let's at least facilitate their task. All exclusionary evidence rules should be reevaluated to test whether their underlying presumptions correspond with reality. If we truly value the jury system, we should dare to embrace the revolutionary notion that jurors can actually be trusted with hearsay and other evidence commonly excluded, if the judge provides appropriate cautionary instructions. On balance, is justice really served by completely barring potentially decisive evidence because some jurors may ignore these instructions? Jurors should also be allowed to ask questions. When attorney incompetence leaves critical questions unasked, thereby threatening a possible miscarriage of justice, the judge should ask the questions.

The judge can order that all evidence on the same issue be presented at the same time by both sides. Imagine how much more lucid and judicable a trial would be with the following procedures. Witnesses with opposing testimony—including expert witnesses— would testify consecutively. Jurors would have a qualified opportunity to ask them questions. If helpful, the judge could call *neutral* expert witnesses to testify. At the end of each day and during deliberations, jurors could retrieve any or all of the testimony plus pictures of the exhibits from computers in the jury room. In order to provide a framework for processing the evidence, written copies of the judge's instructions would be simplified and given to the jurors *before* as well as after hearing the evidence.

Two important reforms should be made in jury selection. First, trial venues should no longer be changed because of pretrial publicity. In the age of mass media and instant communications, everyone hears about a high-profile case immediately. Deadly riots followed the first Rodney King trial because it had been moved from a minority community to a predominantly white one; the resulting jury had no African Americans. Now it has been bruited about that Los Angeles District Attorney Gil Garcetti moved the Simpson trial from the west side of Los Angeles (predominantly white) to the more mixed downtown area because he felt a conviction by a predominantly white jury would lack credibility. This may be a valid political judgment, but it has little to do with the law. It certainly contravenes the ideal of a jury representing a cross section of the community where the crime occurred.

Many experts believe most trials are won during jury selection. This militates in favor of the second jury selection reform—eliminating peremptory challenges. (Peremptories remove prospective jurors for reasons other than overt bias.) Inevitable disparities in the jury selection skills of attorneys probably skew the final jury more in a particular direction than the full panel from which it has been drawn. Now, the advent of expensive jury consultants gives an unfair advantage to wealthy clientele both in jury selection and in strategy suggestions during trial.

These and other reforms will be vigorously opposed. Who gains the most by preservation of the status quo? Not the judges. A recent extensive survey I conducted of the California judiciary confirms the earlier findings of a nationwide Harris survey that judges favor many trial reform proposals. Narrowing further the search for the antireform interests, contemplate who is most adversely affected by an obviously projury reform—videotaped testimony. Prerecorded testimony (i.e., before jury selection) would have the following benefits for juries and the quality of trial justice:

- Jurors would not be inconvenienced by interruptions for sidebar conferences, attorney objections, witness delays, and so forth.
- The resulting compression of evidence presentation time would give the jurors a more comprehensive view of the entire case.
- The court no longer need resort to the absurd fiction that jurors can actually follow the judge's instructions to disregard what they have already heard ("unringing the bell").
- All improper attorney questions and bogus objections intended solely for effect could be eliminated from the jury's purview.

Note that by virtue of the last benefit, any inappropriate nonverbal behavior (gestures, facial expressions) by attorneys or their clients could also be eliminated. Is there any remaining doubt as to who wants to keep trial procedure as is?

NOTES

1. Karl Llewellyn, *Jurisprudence: Realism of Theory and Practice* (Chicago: University of Chicago Press, 1962), 446–47.
2. Jerome Frank, *Courts On Trial* (Princeton, N. J.: Princeton University Press, 1949), 81.
3. Frank, *Courts*, 102.
4. Frank, *Courts*, 102.
5. Thurman Arnold, *The Symbols Of Government* (New York: Harcourt, Brace & Co., 1962), 183–85.
6. Wayne Brazil, "Civil Discovery: Lawyers' Views on Its Effectiveness, Its Principal Problems and Abuses," *American Bar Foundation Research Journal* 787 (1980).
7. Franklin Strier, "Through the Jurors' Eyes," *ABA Journal*, October 1988, 78–81.
8. R. J. Gerber, "Victory vs. Truth: The Adversary System and Its Ethics," 19(3) *Arizona State Law Journal* 3, 19 (1987).
9. Peter Sperlich, "Scientific Evidence in the Courts: The Disutility of Adversary Proceedings," *Judicature* 66(10) (May 1983), 472, 474, 475.
10. Quoted in Frank, *Courts*, 124.
11. For a full discussion of proposed reforms, see Franklin Strier, *Reconstructing Justice: An Agenda for Trial Reform* (Westport, Conn.: Quorum Books, 1994), chapter 7.
12. Albert Alschuler, "The Preservation of Clients' Confidences: One Value among Many or a Categorical Imperative?" 52 *University of Colorado Law Review*, 349, 354 (1981).

Chapter 18

Taking on Testilying

The Prosecutor's Response to In-Court Police Deception

by Larry Cunningham

INTRODUCTION

In this article, I examine the problem of "testilying"—perjury and other forms of in-court deception by police officers—from the prosecutor's point of view. What are the prosecutor's legal and ethical duties and obligations? What, if anything, should he or she do to combat the problem? These questions, and others, are important to ask, discuss, and answer because a judicial "system" that is supposed to adjudicate guilt and innocence yet permits lies—no matter how small or infrequent—is no system at all. Under our adversarial system of justice, competing, zealous advocates argue their causes before neutral and impartial arbiters.[1] Implicit in such a system is the belief that those zealous advocates should fight fairly. Using lies does not promote justice; it distorts it.[2]

In this article, I give a detailed overview of the problem of testilying. I demonstrate that it is a real, but by definition unmeasurable, problem. Precisely because the problem is so impervious to quantitative measurement, I spend a significant portion of this article explaining the problem. I examine how prosecutors have and have not dealt with the problem. I show what the federal subornation of perjury statute and the Model Rules of Professional Responsibility require prosecutors to do in response to testilying. I identify what steps, above and beyond laws and rules of ethics, prosecutors should take to combat the crime of police perjury. Finally, I address criticisms of my approach.

THE TESTILYING PROBLEM

The term "testilying" was coined by police officers in New York City.[3] It usually refers to perjury committed by police officers. However, it has also been used to describe other forms of in-court deception.[4] As I demonstrate in the following review of the frequency, nature, and reasons for police perjury, testilying is an amorphous problem, not easily understood or fixed, but nevertheless a real one in our criminal justice system.

Larry Cunningham, "Taking on Testilying: The Prosecutors Response to In-Court Policee Deception (as appeared in Criminal Justice Ethics, Vol. 18 No. 1, (Winter/Spring, 1999) pp 26-40). Reprinted with permission of The Institute for Criminal Justice Ethics, 555 West 57th St., Suite 601, New York, NY 10019-1029. I would like to thank Leslie Griffin, Erin O'Hara, and John Kleinig for their helpful comments and suggestions.

What is Testilying?

The problem with defining "testilying" is that it is a new term to describe a concept that is not easily definable or understandable. The Mollen Commission was the first to report the use of the term by police officers in New York City. Officers coined the phrase most probably to persuade themselves that what they were doing was morally acceptable. When an officer is deceptive in court, the rationale goes, he is "not quite lying" but "not quite testifying truthfully and completely" either. Testilying is seen as a middle ground between pure honesty and pure dishonesty. Officers feel that they can tread ethically within this middle ground because they feel that they have society's best interests at heart: the conviction of the guilty.

This alleged "ethical middle ground" is perhaps the best evidence of the ethical problems with testilying. Officers invented a word in part to avoid acknowledging that testilying sometimes involves committing perjury and other illegal acts. The fact that they do not call their actions perjury or deception or some other term with clearly unethical implications evinces their belief that testilying—whatever form, illegal or legal—is somehow justified. If they believed their actions were clearly wrong, there would be no need to create a new word. Lying, perjury, and deceit all characterize deception negatively. Testilying is seen as morally acceptable, however, because it is deception used against someone (the defendant) who is himself morally blameworthy. Testilying is viewed as a small moral compromise that can prevent a larger moral wrong, the non-conviction of a guilty defendant. The question of what is testilying, therefore, needs to be understood within its proffered Machiavellian justification.[5]

To address its legitimacy, it is appropriate that we start with considering what forms of in-court deception *police officers* consider to be ethically "questionable" yet ultimately justifiable. This inquiry is subjective because most lawyers and ethicists would probably agree that aside from pre-charge interrogations and investigations, all forms of police testimonial deception are unjustifiable. That does not help to define testilying. Testilying is unique to policing and deserves a police-oriented definition. Accordingly, testilying should not be limited to provable cases of perjury. Although most would probably agree that perjury—a material lie made under oath[6]—is always testilying because deceiving a court is virtually always wrong, officers themselves consider other forms of deception, such as false swearing to affidavits, to fall under the category of "testilying," even though those deceptive statements are not made on the witness stand. At the same time, most people—officers and lay persons alike—would agree that it is acceptable for a police officer to deceive a suspect in custody in order to secure a true and voluntary confession, for example, by telling the suspect that the police have his fingerprints on the murder weapon when in fact they do not.[7]

Testilying, I believe, has both a locus component and a deception component. I define 'testilying' in part as any *in-court* deception by a police officer, whether made at trial, at a hearing, or in written documentation (for example, affidavits in support of search warrants). The second part of this inquiry is: What amount of "deception" is serious enough to warrant moral condemnation? Not all wrongful acts of deception are necessarily outright lies. In fact, many observers believe that testilying usually involves "shading" testimony or failing to disclose material facts—not necessarily outright lies.[8] The question of definition is critical in examining this problem from the prosecutor's point of view because, as I will show, his ethical and legal duties depend in part on whether he knows or has good reason to know that the police officer will "lie."

What is a "lie"? In the recent impeachment of President Clinton, many legal observers stated that Mr. Clinton was "legally accurate" when he stated that he did not have "sexual relations" (as that term was defined in the deposition) but was nonetheless deceptive.[9] Even some of the President's strongest supporters stated that he should have volunteered more information so as not to mislead the court. In the police context, "shading" can occur when, for example, officers draw conclusions about the reliability of informants. An officer may say that an informant is "reliable" even though he or she has information that the informant may not be 100 percent reliable. A lie? Perhaps not. Deceptive? Probably. Worthy of moral condemnation? I think so—and certainly so would the magistrate who approved the warrant based on the affidavit as well.

Circumstances

Testilying may take many different forms. For example, during the O.J. Simpson murder trial, evidence surfaced that Mark Fuhrman had once stated:

> [If] you find a [needle] mark [on a drug suspect] that looks like three days old, pick the scab. Squeeze it. Looks like serum's coming out, as if it were hours old. . . . That's not falsifying a report. That's putting a criminal in jail. That's being a policeman.[10]

Testilying may involve the creation of a confidential informant to obtain a search warrant,[11] lying about the circumstances of a search to justify a warrantless arrest of a perpetrator,[12] planting evidence on a suspect ("flaking"),[13] increasing the quantity of drugs found on a suspect ("padding"),[14] or even, as the above-quoted statement from Mark Fuhrman illustrates, manufacturing evidence of a crime.[15]

Most testilying occurs at the investigative and pretrial stages of the criminal justice system,[16] especially in suppression hearings.[17] "Because the government has the initial burden in hearings on warrantless searches, including *Terry* stops and frisks, the police officer's testimony serves as the beginning point for a trial court's consideration of the constitutionality of the police action."[18] Testilying occurs most often in cases involving drugs or guns[19] in high-crime areas.[20] Narcotics and weapons cases often rely exclusively on police testimony and involve little corroborative evidence.[21]

Judge Irving Younger, in *People v. McMurty*, described the problem of "dropsy" testimony, a prevalent form of testilying in suppression hearings.[22] The prototypical dropsy case usually involves the following boilerplate testimony:

> I observed defendant X acting suspiciously at the corner of Main and Spruce Streets. He appeared nervous. He had a small white package in his hands. When I crossed the street, he dropped the package and ran away from me. I apprehended him, picked up the package, and determined that the substance inside was cocaine. I arrested the defendant and read him his *Miranda* rights.

Judge Younger noted, "Usually the very language of the testimony is identical from [one] case to another."[23] The problem with dropsy cases is that it is impossible to tell who is lying in an individual case—the defendant who claims the officer conducted an illegal search, or the police officer who claims that the defendant dropped the incriminating evidence.

"The difficulty arises," Judge Younger concluded, "when one stands back from the particular case and looks at a series of cases. It then becomes apparent that policemen are committing perjury at least in some of them, and perhaps in nearly all of them."[24] Because judges are relegated to deciding cases based on the testimony of individual officers and defendants, however, they usually have no choice but to find a police officer more credible than the accused.[25] Indeed, that was the result in *McMurty*: Judge Younger reluctantly denied the defendant's motion to suppress because he found no direct evidence that the police officer in that specific case was lying.[26] "Were this the first time a policeman had testified that a defendant dropped a packet of drugs to the grounds," Judge Younger stated, "the matter would be unremarkable."[27] The problem is that testilying becomes apparent only when one looks for patterns in police testimony.

Frequency

Part of the problem with testilying is that we know very little about how often—if it all—police deceive the courts. Kevin Reitz, who argues that police perjury should be treated like any other crime, states, "Compared with many other offenses, the crime of testilying has been poorly measured, and we should be suspicious of claims that its incidence is known or its causes understood."[28] This lack of knowledge can be attributed, in part, to the fact that perjury is by definition perpetrated secretively. Like deception generally, it is something kept quiet.

It is even more difficult to study deception in the police context. Officers are not generally willing to break their *esprit de corps* to speak candidly with a researcher about corruption.[29] Also known as the "blue wall of silence" or the "code of silence," this *esprit de corps* prevents officers from being candid with researchers, even under conditions of anonymity.[30] Although similar to subcultures in other professions, the police subculture is more pronounced because police officers operate under distinctively high amounts of stress, discretion, and danger, often with low pay, benefits, and societal gratitude.[31]

Even with these problems of studying police perjury, many observers have concluded that it is a widespread problem. At one extreme, Alan Dershowitz claims, "Almost all police lie."[32] Given that Mr. Dershowitz is a criminal defense attorney, his sweeping generalization can probably be understood as an exaggerated by-product of years of frustration with a few corrupt officers. It is quite possible that all of the police that Mr. Dershowitz has observed on the witness stand have testilied. But one cannot logically induce that because some police lie, all police must therefore lie.

This is not to say that I think police are always honest. Police are human, and I think it is reasonable to assume that *some* police lie *some* of the time. The question is where to draw the line: at the high, middle, or low end of the spectrum. Nicholas Zales concludes that testilying is a problem and is in fact growing. "The evidence is clear," he writes, "that police perjury is, if not pervasive, at least a serious cancer invading our criminal justice system."[33] If so, it would be helpful, as Kevin Reitz urges, to conduct a study measuring the long-term trends of testilying.[34]

There are a handful of researchers and judges who disagree with the assertion that testilying is widespread; they view it as rare and exceptional. As a rule, they say, the police are honest. In *People v. Berrios*, the New York Court of Appeals declined to adopt a rule that would have put the burden of proving the legality of a warrantless search on prosecutors.[35] In the process, the court concluded, "[T]here is no valid proof that all members of law enforcement or that all other citizens who testify are perjurers."[36] Similarly, a special commission of the American Bar Association, chaired by Samuel Dash, surveyed judges, prosecutors, and defense lawyers, and concluded that police perjury was an isolated occurrence.[37] Of the three groups the commission surveyed, only members of the defense bar believed that police perjury was widespread.[38] This may indicate either an anti-police bias by defense attorneys or a pro-police bias by judges and prosecutors.

The research in this area has been scant and largely anecdotal. One study, conducted by Myron Orfield, surveyed a few dozen judges, defense attorneys, and prosecutors in Chicago.[39] Its results are problematic because the small sample size in the study makes them statistically unreliable.[40] In an earlier study, Orfield interviewed roughly two dozen narcotics officers from the Chicago Police Department about their perceptions of the Exclusionary Rule.[41] Nearly all of the officers admitted that some of their colleagues commit perjury, although they disagreed on the frequency.[42] However, because the officers' statements were not self-serving, they are somewhat indicative of a serious problem. We simply do not know whether their responses are typical of all law enforcement officers, of all Chicago police officers, or even of all Chicago narcotics officers.

Anecdotally, several defense attorneys and judges have spoken about what they perceive to be a vast number of cases of police perjury. As noted above, Alan Dershowitz, who has practiced as a defense attorney for several decades (including as a member of the "Dream Team" for O.J. Simpson, a case which featured its own allegations of testilying by Detectives Philip Vanatter and Mark Fuhrman), has written many times that he believes virtually all police lie.[43] David Wolchover estimated that London police lie in approximately thirty percent of trials.[44] Irving Younger, as both a defense attorney[45] and later as a judge on the New York City Criminal Court,[46] concluded that testilying was a vast and underestimated problem. In 1970, he estimated that "hundreds, perhaps thousands, of cases" involved police perjury.[47]

In the early 1990s, Milton Mollen chaired a commission charged with investigating corruption in the New York City criminal justice system. The so-called Mollen Commission summarized the problem of testilying in the NYPD by stating that, "[a]s with other forms of corruption, it is impossible to gauge the full extent of police falsifications. Our investigation indicated, however, that this is probably the most common form of public corruption facing the criminal justice system."[48]

Given the problems of studying police perjury and the continuing reports of its existence, it is probably reasonable to conclude that testilying does occur in a significant number of cases. At the very least, many people believe it is a serious problem; that perception in and of itself is worthy of study. More scientific studies, robustly designed, need to be conducted to determine the frequency and trends of police perjury.

Why Does Testilying Occur?

"Police, like people generally," Christopher Slobogin observes, "lie in all sorts of contexts for all sorts of reasons."[49] The most common reason cited is a Machiavellian one: Police view perjury as a necessary means to achieve the ends of justice.[50] Constitutional rules—particularly the Exclusionary Rule[51]—are viewed as technicalities that "[let] the criminal . . . go free because the constable has blundered."[52] A study by students at Columbia

Law School found that immediately after *Mapp v. Ohio*[53] was handed down, when police officers told the truth, many cases were dismissed because judges found that key pieces of evidence were the products of illegal searches or seizures.[54] The study found that within a short time after cases had started to be dismissed, police began to lie in order to keep valuable evidence from being excluded.[55]

Ironically, police say they lie in order to serve the "truth."[56] Truth-seeking, to them, means making sure that a guilty person goes to jail at whatever cost. Police see only the day-to-day effects of the Exclusionary Rule: good cases against known criminals being dismissed because police erred.[57] Most do not recognize or value the broad purpose of the Exclusionary Rule which is to encourage lawful searches and seizures.[58] As Alan Dershowitz correctly states, "If the only goal of the adversary system were to find 'the truth' in every case, then it would be relatively simple to achieve. Suspects could be tortured, their families threatened, homes randomly searched, and lie detector tests routinely administered."[59] Machiavellian police ignore the fact that the criminal justice system is not designed just to find and convict the guilty, but to find and convict the guilty in a way that comports with fairness, justice, and equity. Testilying, in the long run, destroys citizens' trust in government,[60] particularly since citizens have the most contact with police officers, as compared to other government agents.[61]

Machiavellianism is also problematic because testilying often involves lying about matters that are "outcome determinative in . . . litigation."[62] They are not "little white lies." They go to the heart of a defendant's guilt or innocence. Guilt in drug- and gun-possession cases often hinges solely on the outcome of search-and-seizure suppression hearings.[63] An argument can be made in response that truth is not undermined by testilying in these instances because the guilty are punished. One small deception is made so a larger deception (a guilty person being let go) is not. This utilitarian argument fails to account for the policy behind the Exclusionary Rule. The purpose of our justice system is not just to convict, but to convict in a fair manner. When the Exclusionary Rule mandates that key evidence be suppressed because of a police officer's error, the very release of the possibly guilty defendant is meant to deter police from committing constitutional errors in future cases.

Furthermore, the win-at-all-costs attitude assumes that police are more accurate at guilt-finding than other entities, such as prosecutors, judges, or juries.[64] Our justice system is not inquisitorial: We do not vest truth-finding in one person or group. Ours is an adversarial system, in which the truth is arrived at through zealous advocacy before an impartial and neutral arbiter.[65]

It is for these reasons that the Machiavellian justification for testilying is unpersuasive. There are, however, other reasons—not justifications, but explanations—for why police lie. Some lie to cover up the corruption or incompetence of other officers, or themselves.[66] Others lie in order to get extra overtime processing arrests and testifying in court (what the Mollen Commission reported as "collars-for-dollars").[67] Some fabricate cases in order to appear busy and to increase conviction statistics.[68]

The problem also persists because police are allowed to get away with lying in other instances. For example, most ethicists accept that police may lie during the pre-trial investigation stage of a case.[69] Lying, therefore, is not viewed as something that is *absolutely* wrong. Instead, lying's morality or immorality depends on the circumstance. Of course, the circumstances are very different when a police officer lies to a suspect and when he lies to a court.[70]

There is a final explanation for testilying: the "blue wall of silence."[71] Police view the criminal justice system with an "us versus them" attitude that develops from the extreme stress that they face every day from many directions. Family members worry about their safety, complain about their low pay, and often fail to understand the on-the-job stresses that they undergo. Supervisors bombard them with useless paperwork. Defense attorneys undermine their credibility through insulting cross-examination. Judges dismiss cases seemingly because of "legal technicalities." When cases go wrong, prosecutors blame the police. And, of course, criminals try to thwart their every attempt to keep or restore law and order. Consequently, police believe that the odds are stacked against them. Society isolates them, so they turn inward to the only people who understand them: fellow officers. Camaraderie is a positive effect of stress. When camaraderie goes too far, however, it can lead to a distorted perception of morality. Police lie because they view themselves as guardians of right and wrong, the only people in the criminal justice system who have the best interests of society and victims at heart. Lying to serve a noble end (truth seeking) is thus a natural outgrowth of the police psychology of isolation and silence.[72]

PROSECUTORS' (NON)RESPONSE

Perhaps the most persuasive reason why police officers commit perjury is because other players in the criminal justice system—judges and prosecutors, in particular—let them get away with it. Alan Dershowitz recounted the following story:

> I once asked a policeman, "Why do cops lie so brazenly in search-and-seizure cases?" He responded with a rude macho joke: "Why do dogs lick their balls?" To which the answer is "Because they can." In short, police know they can get away with certain kinds of common lies.[73]

I start with the assumption that some prosecutors know about testilying and in fact tolerate it (some out of sympathy or subscription to the Machiavellian justification for testilying, and some out of an inability to do anything about the problem).[74] In a survey of a small sample of prosecutors, judges, and defense attorneys,[75] Myron Orfield found that prosecutors "frequently" tolerate testilying, and sometimes encourage it.[76] More than half of the survey respondents believed that at least half the time the prosecutor knows about evidence fabrication or perjury.[77] However, forty-eight percent believed that prosecutors discourage testilying.[78] Some prosecutors said they would refuse to prosecute a case they knew would be based on perjured police testimony.[79]

Prosecutors' tolerance and (at times) encouragement of testilying is explained by several factors. When prosecutors aggressively prepare police witnesses for their testimony, officers receive overt or subtle suggestions to lie.[80] While interviewing officers, some prosecutors will tell them what the law will require that he, the prosecutor, establish through his witnesses. The officer-witness will then parrot back those requirements, making his testimony fit the requirements of the law.[81]

Prosecutors' widespread acceptance of plea bargains subtly encourages testilying.[82] Because most cases end with guilty pleas,[83] there is a lesser chance of perjury being detected through pre-trial discovery and vigorous cross-examination in a public trial.[84] Prosecutors are also less zealous in their pursuit of police perjury because they are afraid that testiliars will "blow the whistle" on their accomplices in the district attorney's office.[85]

Prosecutors also experience the same obstacle that police whistleblowers face: the "blue wall of silence." It is difficult to prosecute testilying because there is no corroborative evidence. The dispute is limited to the defendant's word against the officer's.[86] The problem is complicated by the small investigative staffs in most prosecutors' offices.[87] Most prosecutors' offices are reactive, not proactive. Even if they are fortunate enough to have detectives to perform prosecutor-initiated investigations, those detectives are often on detail from the very police department that the prosecutor is investigating.[88]

For some prosecutors, the "blue wall of silence" may not be an obstacle at all. Some may be fully behind the wall itself: They may share the police officers' Machiavellian justification/excuse for testilying.[89] They may not like the fact that officers are testilying, but they tolerate it. Most draw a line, however, at planting evidence. Testilying is tolerable, framing an innocent person is not.[90]

That is not to say that prosecutors have taken no action against testilying. The Manhattan District Attorney's Office has been the most visible in prosecuting testiliars. In 1971, District Attorney Hogan argued that prosecutors should bear the burden of proof in suppression hearings.[91] Other area district attorneys took the opposite view. In 1992, the Mollen Commission reported that Manhattan District Attorney Robert Morgenthau had prosecuted several police officers for perjury.[92] This included Barry Brown, the principal informer for the Commission. Police Commissioner Bratton and District Attorney Morgenthau forced Brown to resign in order to send a "message that lying under oath is unacceptable no matter what the circumstances."[93] Some district attorneys have also implemented structural changes in their offices to combat the testilying problem. In Queens County, New York, assistant district attorneys receive training on how to prepare police officers properly for trial. The training includes mock trials with real officer-witnesses. One Queens County assistant reported, "People think the police and prosecutors are sleeping in the same bed, but we're not."[94] In Manhattan, grand jury prosecutors are urged to interview police officers separately if there is any possibility that they may be fabricating evidence or about to testilie.[95]

LEGAL AND ETHICAL STANDARDS

Against this background of the extent and nature of the testilying problem, I now turn to the law of police perjury from the prosecutor's perspective. In this section, I do not articulate any particular strategy for how prosecutors could or should proactively reduce police perjury. Instead, I set forth the minimum requirements of prosecutors: what they *must* do, not what they *should* do. I consider first the criminal law. Prosecutors, like all other citizens, must obey the law. Second, I consider the special obligations of prosecutors, as lawyers, under the Model Rules of Professional Conduct.

Suborność of Perjury

When a police officer—like any witness—lies under oath, he does not commit the crime in a vacuum. The attorney (here, prosecutor) who calls him to the stand could also be exposed to criminal liability. Under certain circumstances, a lawyer could be liable for putting a witness on the stand who later commits perjury. Here I delineate the bounds of that criminal liability vis-à-vis prosecutors and deceptive police witnesses.

Consider the federal suborność of perjury statute; 18 U.S.C. §1622 provides: "Whoever procures another to commit any perjury is guilty of suborność of perjury. . ." The elements of the offense are thus (1) procurement (2) of another (3) to commit perjury.

Mere knowledge that a witness is about to testify falsely is not subornation of perjury unless the suborner induces or procures the false testimony.[96] A subpoena *ad testificandum* would probably qualify as inducement or procurement since prosecutors, like all attorneys, willfully choose which witnesses they will call to the stand. Subornation includes situations in which the suborner "should have known or believed or have had good reason to believe that testimony given would be false."[97] This imposes a negligence standard. If a reasonable prosecutor *should have known* that the testimony would be false, then there is criminal liability. Subornation of perjury, of course, requires a perjurious statement to be made. Perjury under federal law is a false statement made under oath about a material matter.[98] If a witness tells the literal truth, he cannot be convicted of perjury[99] and, consequently, the attorney who calls him to the witness stand cannot be convicted of subornation of perjury.

Consider a situation, however, in which a prosecutor actively encourages a police officer to commit perjury. Under federal law, the prosecutor would clearly be guilty of subornation of perjury because he knew that the police-witness would lie, he was responsible for that perjury (by the encouragement and by his subpoena to the officer), and the police-witness himself knew that the testimony he was to give would not be the truth. However, if a prosecutor discovers that a police-witness lied after the witness's testimony, the prosecutor would not be guilty of a crime because subornation of perjury requires some *ex ante* procurement and knowledge. This does not mean, necessarily, that the prosecutor does not have an ethical obligation to make a disclosure to the court if he discovers *ex post* that a witness had lied.[100]

What if instead of the prosecutor actually telling the officer to lie, the prosecutor simply knows that the officer will lie yet calls him anyway? The prosecutor would still be guilty of subornation. This would include situations in which the prosecutor knows for sure that the police officer will lie (for example, he tells him to lie), knows he has a strong tendency to lie (for example, based on prior boilerplate testimony), or he has "good reason" to know that he might lie in the present case. In *Tedesco v. Mishkin*,[101] for example, an attorney was convicted of subornation of perjury after the witness practiced his testimony in front of the attorney, the attorney knew that the testimony was false, but yet he still called and examined the witness and elicited the false testimony. When in doubt, the subornation statute seems to require that the prosecutor confront the witness and find out for sure whether the police-witness will testify truthfully.

A particular police department's history of in-court deception may be relevant to the determination of whether the prosecutor had *good reason* to believe that the officer will lie. What is a "good reason": a 25 percent chance, 50 percent, 75 percent? That is a question of fact for a jury to decide. Even though the fact that an officer comes from a police department with a high testilying rate might not be enough to convict a prosecutor of subornation, it might be enough to impose a duty on the prosecutor to investigate the officer's credibility beforehand. In *Petite v. United States*,[102] the Fourth Circuit held that if a defendant "should have known" that the testimony he or she procured was false, he or she can be liable for subornation. Thus a prosecutor might not know for sure that an officer may give false testimony but may still be held criminally liable if he *should have known* that it would be false. When should a prosecutor know that an officer will give false testimony? It seems logical to conclude that an officer from a department with a great deal of testilying is more likely to be a testiliar himself, based on pure probability.

All of this is not to say that I think we should start zealously prosecuting prosecutors for subornation of perjury. It is simply an illustration that testilying can have legal consequences not only for the officer-witness, but also for the prosecutor who subpoenas the officer knowing or having reason to believe that the officer will lie. The problem though—and this is true in most public integrity prosecutions—is that members of one group (prosecutors) are not going to be eager to go after one of their own. This is true in police corruption, securities fraud, or any type of internal corruption: People will simply not "rat out," let alone prosecute, one of their colleagues unless they have good reason to do so.

In a jurisdiction in which prosecutors are within the police blue wall of silence,[103] it may be necessary for a higher-ranking prosecutor's office (the U.S. Attorney general, state attorney general, or a special prosecutor) to investigate and prosecute widespread subornation of perjury by local prosecutors.[104] The problem with independent, outside investigations is that they break the *esprit de corps*, they are perceived as witch-hunts, and they cause fewer, good, ethical people to join prosecutors' offices. There is an argument, however, that all of those consequences are good things. The *esprit de corps* is what undermined the system in the first place. By cleaning up a given locale's justice system, it will encourage good people to become prosecutors, not scare them away.

On balance, however, the sheer cost—in terms of money, resources, reputations, and confidence—of using special prosecutors to prosecute local prosecutors makes such a solution infeasible as a way to eliminate testilying across-the-board. It punishes a peripheral, yet important, player in the testilying scheme but does not get to the core of the problem. It should therefore be reserved for situations in which prosecutors and police are so involved in corrupt activities, such as testilying, that there is no hope for change from within. In those cases, independent investigations and prosecutions may be necessary.

Ethical Rules

Prosecutors are also subject to rules of ethics, as promulgated by state bar associations, courts, legislatures, and their employers. Violations of these rules can lead to disciplinary sanctions, including termination or suspension from the practice of law.

The Model Rules of Professional Conduct, drafted by the American Bar Association, are in effect in a number of states, and therefore are a useful starting point. Model Rule 3.3 provides in pertinent part: "A lawyer shall not knowingly . . . offer evidence that the lawyer knows to be false."[105] If a lawyer does not *know* the evidence is false, but "*reasonably believes* [it] is false," he or she has the *option* whether or not to offer it.[106] Interestingly enough, the Model Rules are less strict than the subornation statute.[107] Under federal law, subornation occurs even when the suborner "should have known or believed or . . . had good reason to believe that the testimony given would be false."[108] The Model Rules impose an obligation not to offer evidence only when the attorney has *knowledge* that the witness will lie. Federal criminal law seems to go further and prohibit introduction of evidence that the attorney *should know* or *has good cause to know* will be perjurious. For jurisdictions with similar subornation statutes, the good cause standard applies, not the Model Rules' knowledge requirement.

Assume for the moment we are in a jurisdiction that requires knowledge under both the criminal law and the rules of ethics. When does one *know* that testimony will be false? Where a prosecutor is encouraging a police officer to lie, not only is the act illegal as subornation of perjury (under either the knowledge or good cause standard), it is also violative of Model Rule 3.3 because the prosecutor is introducing evidence which he knows is false. The same result occurs when the prosecutor does not encourage an officer to testilie (aside from the necessary subpoena *ad testificandum*), but knows that the officer will commit perjury. If, on the other hand, the prosecutor knows that an officer has a propensity to lie under oath, but does not know that *in this case* he or she will lie, Model Rule 3.3 would appear to allow the prosecutor to get away with calling the officer to the stand because the prosecutor does not "know" for sure that the testimony is false. He is *permitted*, however, not to call the officer because he could have a reasonable belief that the officer would lie based on the officer's past behavior.[109] A similar result occurs in cases in which the prosecutor's suspicions are based on the testilying rate in an officer's police department. Model Rule 3.3's knowledge requirement excludes only testimony a prosecutor knows *for sure* will be perjurious.

The Model Rules ignore the reality of police perjury. Testilying is not an overt, openly talked about phenomenon. It is by definition clandestine. Furthermore, there is rarely direct evidence that a particular officer will lie in a particular case because the dispute boils down to the word of a police officer versus the word of an accused. Testilying becomes apparent only when one takes a macro-level view of an officer's history or the institutional nature of his department's police subculture. Cases in which prosecutors suspect testilying—either based on inklings about a particular officer (that he *might* testilie in this case, but the prosecutor is not sure) or based on the rate of testilying in a particular department—represent the heartland of testilying cases. The Model Rules leave cases of mere suspicion up to the discretion of the prosecutor.[110] Prosecutors will often fail to exercise their discretion not to call a police witness. They may not want to lose a case because "the constable has blundered."[111] They may share judges' concerns that it is unfair to disregard a police officer's testimony when it is only controverted by the self-serving statement of the accused. They may even share the officers' belief that it is acceptable to deceive the court in order to convict truly guilty defendants. Therefore, the Model Rules, as they are presently framed, do little to reduce testilying.

This epistemological dilemma—when does one know when one knows?—has been examined most prolifically in the hypothetical case of a criminal defendant who tells his lawyer that he wants to testify falsely.[112] Little attention has been paid to prosecutors' obligations, though, because prosecutors are not in lawyer-client relationships with their police witnesses.[113] Even so, some of the same problems and issues arise as to the epistemological problem.

Monroe Freedman describes the ethical quandary of a defense attorney as a "trilemma."[114] A defense attorney is required to know everything about his client's case,[115] he must keep his client's communications in confidence,[116] but he must reveal those confidences to the court if the client insists on testifying falsely.[117] Some defense attorneys adopt an ostrich-head-in-the-sand approach. They simply ignore the first prong of the trilemma. They purposefully shield themselves from the Model Rule 3.3 prohibition against using perjured testimony by not asking their clients key questions about the alleged crime.[118]

Can a prosecutor get away with such a tactic? It is doubtful, since the ostrich approach is usually shunned even for defense counsel.[119] Surely the standards are higher for prosecutors, since "[they are] the representative[s] not of an ordinary party to a controversy, but of a sovereignty whose obligation to govern impartially is as compelling as its obligation to govern at all; and whose interest, therefore, in a criminal prosecution is not that it shall win a case, but that justice shall be done."[120]

I argue that in light of the prosecutor's heightened duty to seek justice, the good cause standard of the crime of subornation should be adopted by the ABA. A prosecutor has the duty, in my opinion, to determine the veracity and truthfulness of all of his other witnesses, police officer or not. Specifically, I believe the ABA should adopt a new subsection to Model Rule 3.8, Special Responsibilities of a Prosecutor, as follows:

The prosecutor in a criminal case shall: . . .

(h) prior to an adjudicative proceeding in which the prosecutor will examine a witness under oath, investigate the truthfulness of the witness's intended testimony. Upon discovering that the witness intends to lie, the prosecutor's duties shall be governed by Model Rule 3.3 and the requirements of justice. As to the testimony of a police officer, the prosecutor shall consider the frequency and nature of institutionalized perjury, if any, by the police officer in the past or in the officer's police department in determining whether the officer is likely to commit perjury.

This explicit approach essentially codifies the requirements of the federal subornation statute while taking into account the reasons and nature of police perjury. It is an expansion on Comment 5 to Model Rule 1.1: "Competent handling of a particular matter includes inquiry into and analysis of the factual . . . elements of the problem . . . ."[121]

If a prosecutor determines before a trial or hearing that his or her police witness intends to commit perjury, the prosecutor has several courses of action. He should first try to dissuade the officer from lying. If the officer still persists in testifying falsely, or if he or she refuses to acknowledge that his or her testimony will be false (but the prosecutor believes otherwise), the prosecutor should either not call the officer at all (if the necessary testimony can be established using another witness) or limit the questioning to areas in which the officer will not lie. If the necessary testimony can be obtained only by asking the police officer a question to which the prosecutor knows the officer will lie, the prosecutor should so warn the officer. If the officer does in fact lie, the prosecutor should notify the court and opposing counsel accordingly.[122]

GOING BEYOND THE MINIMUMS

In [the previous section], I established that prosecutors have a duty to investigate the purported testimony of their police witnesses and not to allow perjured testimony to enter into the record of judicial proceedings. In this section, I examine how prosecutors can go beyond these minimum requirements and take a proactive role in combating police perjury, like any other crime. I propose that prosecutors adopt a multi-tiered, graduated approach in dealing with testilying. The proper response will be dictated by the officers involved, the nature and frequency (if at all) of testilying in a given jurisdiction, and the resources of the prosecutor's office.

The Duty to Educate

First and foremost, prosecutors should participate in the training of police officers. This is a preemptive step; it aims to stop testilying before it even begins. Because testilying occurs most often in search and seizure hearings,[123] prosecutors should be actively involved in educating officers about how to investigate crimes constitutionally.[124] This includes giving specific information about the various exceptions to the warrant and probable cause requirements of the Fourth Amendment. The instructions should be practical, not theoretical. As new developments in search and seizure law occur, prosecutors should be involved in the retraining of officers.

Part of the instruction should be how to testify properly. The Queens County District Attorney's Office accomplishes this through mock trials. While mock trials are a good starting point, they cannot be the be-all-and-end-all of the prosecutorial response to testilying. There should be frank, open discussion from prosecutors—and maybe even former jurors—about the professional, legal, and ethical consequences of perjury. Prosecutors must impress on officers that they will lose cases if they commit perjury. They should be warned that guilty defendants will go free. They should also be warned that prosecutors will not protect them. At the same time, police should be praised when they testify truthfully. Prosecutors should not place blame on police for losing a case unless it is in a constructive fashion. The point should be to educate, not to complain.

The Duty to Counsel

When a prosecutor develops knowledge that a particular officer is a testiliar or is planning on testilying in one of the prosecutor's cases, the prosecutor's first response should be to dissuade the officer from committing perjury. This is the approach recommended by the Model Rules[125] and by the Supreme Court.[126] The prosecutor should calmly explain the consequences of perjury and other forms of in-court deception. The officer should know that the prosecutor will not protect him if he lies. He should be forcefully told that if he does commit perjury he will be prosecuted. The same no-tolerance stance that has been so effective in combating street crime should be used to address testilying.[127]

Conversely, if an officer testifies truthfully, the prosecutor should show appreciation, even if valuable evidence was excluded because of the officer's blunder. Such a case should be used as a learning tool. The officer should leave the courtroom or the prosecutor's office knowing what went wrong in the search and how to prevent a repeat occurrence. The prosecutor should not place blame on the officer or try to divert blame to the judge or on a "legal technicality." Above all else, the officer must leave the situation knowing that he or she did the right thing by testifying truthfully. Yes, it is somewhat perverse to say that we need to reward police officers for being honest. That should be a given. But given the reality today of police perjury, it is not. Prosecutors are in an excellent position to shape the outlook of individual officers through their role as quasi-judicial superiors.

The Duty Never to Subpoena a Particular Officer

It is possible to imagine a situation in which a veteran prosecutor, having dealt with police officers from a particular jurisdiction for many years, knows that a particular officer has a habit of testilying. In those cases, it is possible that the prosecutor could conclude that he or she can never trust that particular officer, at least not without corroborative evidence. In cases that rest solely on the results of search and seizure suppression hearings, the prosecutor may have no choice but to dismiss the charges against the defendant. If a police officer's testimony can never be relied on because he testilies so often, the prosecutor will have no way of knowing whether or not a particular search was legal or not. If the legality of a search or seizure is in question, a defendant's actual guilt may be in question as well. Some testilying involves fabrication of evidence—"frame-ups."[128] Ethical standards forbid a prosecutor from "permit[ting] the continued pendency of criminal charges when the prosecutor knows that the charges are not supported by probable cause."[129]

Such a significant step as losing *complete* confidence in an officer's honesty is a very serious one. It should be reserved for cases in which the prosecutor, after consultation with superiors and other attorneys who have worked with the officer, is convinced that the police officer in question is a chronic liar about dispositive issues in cases. The personal consequences of such an action for the officer may be strong. The prosecutor's ethical decision not to call a particular officer to the stand may be akin to an adverse personnel decision for the officer. He may be forced into desk duty by his superior officers because the prosecutor has said that his uncorroborated testimony cannot be trusted. The responsibility will be on the testiliar to earn the trust of the prosecutor back. Either that, or he might resign or be terminated.

The Duty to Prosecute

If despite extensive training, counseling, and lost cases, a particular officer persists in testilying in future cases, the prosecutor may have no choice but to prosecute the officer for perjury, obstruction of justice, or other crimes. Because prosecution of police officers will lower morale, increase police-prosecutor distrust,[130] and undermine public confidence in the justice system, this action should be taken only after discussion at the highest levels of the prosecutor's office. It should be reserved for particularly corrupt officers. For others who will not change, forced resignation may be more appropriate.

The Duty Never to Subpoena an Entire Police Department

A similarly draconian measure is one that, to my knowledge, has never been undertaken. If testilying is systemic and ingrained in a particular police department or other law enforcement agency, the prosecutor's office may have no choice but never to offer the testimony of any officer in that department or agency. This is such a drastic step that it should be taken only after all of the other steps in this section have been tried. Even then, fair warning should be given to the department so it can reform itself. The ultimate decision to implement such a policy should rest solely with the head of the prosecutor's office after extensive consultation with senior trial counsel, elected officials, judges, and police officials. This is the ultimate last resort. It signifies that testilying is so bad in a department that the prosecutor has lost all trust and confidence in anything the department produces. As a practical matter, cases will have to be investigated by the prosecutor's office's in-house detectives, if they exist. If not, state police or special deputies will need to be used.

This approach is so severe that it will probably never be used. It should not have to be. But it signifies the seriousness of police perjury. If police officers lie, their results cannot be trusted. If their results cannot be trusted, judges and juries will be making their decisions of guilt or innocence based on misinformation. Such arbitrary and capricious results cannot be used to send potentially innocent people to jail. In a society that values due process, they cannot be used to send the guilty to jail either.

CRITICISMS OF MY APPROACH

Before concluding, I pause briefly to consider some potential problems with my argument. First, one could argue that testilying does not exist or at least is not as bad as I (or others) make it seem. That may be true. But assuming that is true—that testilying is not a real problem—is there any harm in what I propose? The first step in my graduated approach to testilying is education. It cannot hurt police to learn more about the Fourth Amendment. It does not hurt prosecutors or police to have the former investigate the latter's testifying record. Or does it? Surely my approach of using prosecutors as a way to reduce testilying will cause some antagonism if a prosecutor believes he or she has uncovered testilying. But what if the prosecutor does not find any wrongdoing? Where is the harm?

Prosecutors and police are usually on the same side of a criminal case: They want to send guilty people to jail. My approach argues that there are legal and ethical consequences for prosecutors who know or should reasonably know that their witnesses will lie. The result is that prosecutors may choose not to investigate police officers' histories, may not engage in sufficient trial preparation, and may simply stick their proverbial ostrich heads in the proverbial sand. The result would be to push testilying further behind the blue wall of silence. Worse yet, prosecutors who are fearful of their own legal and ethical jeopardy may decline to prosecute cases where guilt hinges completely on police testimony. The result is that guilty defendants will go free.

My response to that argument is that it is acceptable to let a few guilty defendants go free in order to ensure that the process of determining guilt is fair. If we impose heightened ethical standards on prosecutors to be more cautious and not to believe *without question* the testimony of police officers, society could be assured that its criminal justice system is fair and is convicting guilty people and acquitting the innocent.

Another criticism is that academic pontifications about how prosecutors should behave are useless in the "real world." After all, who will keep tabs on the prosecutors? Surely there are special prosecutors, state attorneys general, the Department of Justice, and others that can prosecute the prosecutors. But is that the answer I am proposing? Not necessarily. In our legal system, we tend to put our faith in laws, not necessarily in the people who enforce them. If academia can set the bar or the moral compass for prosecutors—even knowing that it may be difficult for all prosecutors to always resist the temptations of accepting testilying—at least then we promote awareness of the problem.

CONCLUSION

My attempt here was not to argue that all police are perjurers or otherwise dishonest. Probably most are not. But the evidence is sufficiently strong to suggest that police officers, as a whole, commit perjury or other forms of testimonial deception more often than most of us are comfortable with. The question is what to do about it. In fashioning solutions to problems that involve people's livelihoods, it is critical that moderation guide our approach. Members of the defense bar, especially, have an understandable tendency to translate the misdeeds of a handful of police officers and prosecutors into an indictment of the entire system. A better approach is for each element of the criminal justice system—police, prosecutors, defense counsel, and judges—to work together to solve this problem. That is why the first step in my graduated approach is education. If search-and-seizure law is considered a "legal technicality" because it is too complicated to understand, prosecutors need to clarify it. Officers should learn from their mistakes and receive appropriate rewards for following the rules. The public prosecutor is in a perfect position to deal with testilying. In most jurisdictions, cases cannot be brought to court without a prosecutor initiating charges. Prosecutors can exercise their discretion in the charging stage to decline to prosecute cases that they feel were based on unconstitutional evidence. In preparing police witnesses for trial, they can insure that officers do not misunderstand their preparation as a go-ahead for perjury through boilerplate testimony. When a prosecution team loses a case because a police officer testified truthfully but key evidence was excluded, the prosecutor can make sure that the officer does not come away with the wrong message. The prosecutor is in a constant war against the win-at-any-cost attitude that often permeates the police subculture.

In the end, however, prosecutors should not and cannot tolerate testilying, no matter how small the lie or infrequent the occurrence. Perjury is a fraud perpetrated on the court. It deprives the accused of his right to a fair trial. It distorts results. It makes a mockery of our justice system.

The Mollen Commission, investigating police corruption in the New York City Police Department in the 1990s, began the section of its report on testilying with a quote from Sir Walter Scott: "Oh what a tangled web we weave when first we practice to deceive."[131] If anything, members of the criminal justice system need to bring this topic to the forefront, so we can all better understand the complexity of the dynamics of testilying.

NOTES

1. *See* Trial of Queen Caroline 8 (J. Nightingale ed. 1821) ("[A]n advocate, in the discharge of his duty, knows but one person in all the world, and that person is his client."); *see also* S. Gillers, Regulation of Lawyers 345–368 (5th ed. 1998) (outlining the debate about the adversary system).
2. Some police officers attempt (erroneously) to justify testilying by arguing that the use of lies to convict those they "know" are guilty promotes truth seeking because then the guilty are not set free. *See infra* notes 49–72 and accompanying text.
3. *See* Commission to Investigate Allegations of Police Corruption and the Anti-Corruption Practices of the Police Department, City of New York, Commission Report § 4, at 36–43 (1994) (Milton Mollen, Chair) [hereinafter cited as Mollen Commission Report].
4. *See infra* notes 10–27.
5. *See infra* notes 49–72 and accompanying text for further discussion of how some officers justify testilying.
6. *See* Black's Law Dictionary 1139 (6th ed. 1990).
7. *See infra* note 69 and accompanying text.
8. *See* Barker & Carter, *"Fluffing Up the Evidence"* and *"Covering Your Ass"*: *Some Conceptual Notes on Police Lying*, 11 Deviant Behavior 61 (1990).
9. *See, e.g.*, Rosen, *The Perjury Trap*, New Yorker, Aug. 10, 1998, at 28.
10. A. M. Dershowitz, Reasonable Doubts: The O. J. Simpson Case and the Criminal Justice System 55 (1996) [hereinafter cited as A. Dershowitz, Reasonable Doubts].
11. *See* Slobogin, *Testilying: Police Perjury and What To Do About It*, 67 U. Colo. L. Rev. 1037, 1043 (1996); *see, e.g.*, Commonwealth v. Lewin, 542 N.E.2d 275 (Mass. 1989).

12. *See* Chin & Wells, *The "Blue Wall of Silence" As Evidence of Bias and Motive to Lie: A New Approach to Police Perjury*, 59 U. Pitt. L. Rev. 233 (1998); *see, e.g.*, People v. Berrios, 270 N.E.2d 709 (N.Y. 1971); People v. McMurty, 314 N.Y.S.2d 194 (N.Y.C. Crim. Ct. 1970).
13. *See* J. Kleinig, The Ethics of Policing 146 (1996).
14. *See id.*
15. *See* A. Dershowitz, Reasonable Doubts, *supra* note 10, at 55.
16. *See* Slobogin, *supra* note 11, at 1042.
17. *See* Harris, *Frisking Every Suspect: The Withering of Terry*, 28 U.C. Davis L. Rev. 1, 32 (1994).
18. *Id.*
19. *See* Mollen Commission Report, *supra* note 3, at 38; Sexton, *Jurors Question Honesty of Police*, N.Y. Times, Sept. 25, 1995, at B3.
20. *See* Mollen Commission Report, *supra* note 3, at 38.
21. *See* Sexton, *supra* note 19, at B3 (noting that "[i]n Brooklyn, nearly 40 percent of criminal prosecutions involve drug or gun cases, and the vast majority of those cases are built exclusively on the testimony of police").
22. 314 N.Y.S.2d 194, 195 (N.Y.C. Crim. Ct. 1970) ("For several years now, lawyers concerned with the administration of criminal justice have been troubled by the problem of 'dropsy' testimony.").
23. *Id.* at 196.
24. *Id.*
25. *See id.*
26. *Id.* at 198.
27. *Id.* at 195.
28. Reitz, *Testilying as a Problem of Crime Control: A Reply to Professor Slobogin*, 67 U. Colo. L. Rev. 1061 (1996); *see also* Wolchover, *Police Perjury in London*, 136 New L.J. 181 (1986).
29. *See* Wolchover, *supra* note 28, at 181.
30. *See id.*
31. *See generally* J. Kleinig, *supra* note 13, at 67–80.
32. A. M. Dershowitz, The Best Defense, at xxi (1982) [hereinafter cited as A. Dershowitz, The Best Defense].
33. Zales, *Reasonable Doubts: The O. J. Simpson Case and the Criminal Justice System*, 69 Wis. Law. 37 (Dec. 1996) (book review).
34. *See* Reitz, *supra* note 28, at 1065.
35. 270 N.E.2d 709 (N.Y. 1971).
36. *Id.* at 713.
37. Special Comm'n on Criminal Justice in a Free Soc'y, Criminal Justice Section, American Bar Ass'n, Criminal Justice in Crisis: A Report to the American People and the American Bar on Criminal Justice in the United States: Some Myths, Some Realties, and Some Questions for the Future 21 (1988) (Samuel Dash, Chair).
38. *See id.*
39. Orfield, Jr., *Deterrence, Perjury, and the Heater Factor: An Exclusionary Rule in the Chicago Criminal Courts*, 63 U. Colo. L. Rev. 75 (1992).
40. *See* Reitz, *supra* note 28, at 1063.

41. *See* Orfield, Jr., Comment, *The Exclusionary Rule and Deterrence: An Empirical Study of Chicago Narcotics Officers*, 54 U. Chi. L. Rev. 1016 (1987).

42. *See id.* at 1051.

43. *See, e.g.*, A. Dershowitz, Reasonable Doubts, *supra* note 10; A. Dershowitz, The Best Defense, *supra* note 32; Dershowitz, *Is Legal Ethics Asking the Right Questions?*, 1 J. Inst. Study Legal Ethics 15 (1996) [hereinafter Dershowitz, *Right Questions*]; Dershowitz, *Controlling the Cops: Accomplices to Perjury*, N.Y. Times, May 2, 1994, at A17 [hereinafter Dershowitz, *Accomplices*].

44. *See* Wolchover, *supra* note 28.

45. *See, e.g.*, Younger, *The Perjury Routine*, The Nation, May 8, 1967, at 596–97.

46. *See, e.g.*, People v. McMurty, 314 N.Y.S.2d 194 (N.Y.C. Crime. Ct.1970).

47. *Id.* at 195–96.

48. Mollen Commission Report, *supra* note 3, at 36.

49. Slobogin, *supra* note 11, at1059.

50. *See* A. Dershowitz, Reasonable Doubts, *supra* note 10, at 42; A. Dershowitz, The Best Defense, *supra* note 32, at xxi; J. Kleinig, *supra* note 13, at 146; Mollen Commission Report, *supra* note 3, at 37; Slobogin, *supra* note 11, at 1044.

51. *See* Taylor, Jr., *For the Record*, American Lawyer, Oct. 1995, at 72 ("[The Exclusionary Rule] sets up a great incentive for people to lie.") (quoting Judge Alex Kozinski, U.S. Court of Appeals for the Ninth Circuit).

52. People v. Defore, 150 N.E. 585, 587 (1926) (Cardozo, J.).

53. 367 U.S. 643 (1961). *Mapp* held that evidence illegally obtained by state law enforcement officers must be excluded from trial. It was an application of the Exclusionary Rule that had been in force in federal court since *Weeks v. United States*, 232 U.S. 383 (1914).

54. *See* Comment, *Effect of Mapp v. Ohio on Police Search and Seizure Practices in Narcotics Cases*, 4 Col. J. Law & Soc. Probs. 94 (1968).

55. *See id.*

56. *See* A. Dershowitz, Reasonable Doubts, *supra* note 10, at 42.

57. *See* Slobogin, *supra* note 11, at 1044.

58. *See* A. Dershowitz, Reasonable Doubts, *supra* note 10, at 42.

59. *Id.* One of the dangers of such draconian means of law enforcement is that innocent people will falsely confess.

60. *See* Slobogin, *supra* note 11, at 1038–39.

61. *See* Neuhard, *Foreward: The Right to Counsel: Shouldering the Burden*, 2 T. M. Cooley J. Prac. & Clinical Law 169, 169 (1998).

62. Cloud, *The Dirty Little Secret*, 43 Emory L.J. 1311 (1994) [hereinafter cited as Cloud, *Dirty Little Secret*].

63. *See* Sexton, *supra* note 19, at B3.

64. *See* Slobogin, *supra* note 11, at 1038–39.

65. *See generally* S. Gillers, *supra* note 1.

66. *See* Mollen Commission Report, *supra* note 3, at 35.

67. *See id.* at 29.

68. *See* Chin & Wells, *supra* note 12, at 246–47.

69. *See* Green v. Scully, 850 F.2d 894 (2d Cir. 1988) (verbal deception in confessions is not unconstitutional). *But see* Florida v. Cayward, 552. So. 2d 971 (Fla.

App. 1989) (creation of fake documentary evidence for use in confession unconstitutional).

70. *See* J. Kleinig, *supra* note 13, at 149.

71. *See generally id.* at 68–70.

72. *See id.* at 147.

73. A. Dershowitz, Reasonable Doubts, *supra* note 10, at 50

74. *See id.* at 48; J. Kleinig, *supra* note 13, at 148 ("Although the courtroom may be an alien environment for the police officer, it can be made easier by a friendly prosecutor. Police and prosecutors are often on the same side, and it can sometimes be as important to the prosecutor as it is to the police that a conviction is secured. . . . [P]ressure or encouragement to engage in some form of testimonial deception may come from the prosecutor's office."); Mollen Commission Report, *supra* note 3, at 42 ("Members of the law enforcement community, and particularly defense attorneys, told us that the same tolerance is sometimes exhibited among prosecutors. Indeed, several former and current prosecutors acknowledged—'off the record'—that perjury and falsifications are serious problems in law enforcement that, though not condoned, are ignored."); Chin & Wells, *supra* note 12, at 261 ("Police criminality, including police perjury, even where guilt is clear, has not traditionally been dealt with aggressively by prosecutors."); Cloud, *Dirty Little Secret*, *supra* note 62, at 1311–12 ("[P]rosecutors . . . know that police officers lie under oath."); Cloud, *Judges, "Testilying," and the Constitution*, 69 S. Cal. L. Rev. 1341, 1353 (1996) ("Others are responsible for dealing with the problem as well. Prosecutors are duty-bound to take steps to insure that their police witnesses obey the law, and not to sponsor witnesses who commit perjury.") [hereinafter cited as Cloud, *Judges*]; Dershowitz, *Right Questions*, *supra* note 43, at 23 ("The time has come to shift the focus back to prosecutors. The time has come for the courts to understand that they are a serious part of the problem."); Hentoff, *When Police Commit Perjury*, Wash. Post, Sept. 5, 1985, at A21; Rudovsky, *Why It Was Hands Off on the Police*, Phila. Inq., Aug. 28, 1995, at A7.

    This is also the case in London. *See* Wolchover, *supra* note 28, at 183 (". . . the casual and matter of fact way in which the Bar tends to refer to police perjury. It was regarded as a commonplace. Indeed, it is almost as if this state of affairs is not in the least regretted since it provides so much of their bread and butter.").

75. *See* Orfield, *supra* note 39. His results, although criticized scientifically by other authors, remain alarming.

76. *Id.* at 109.

77. *See id.*

78. *See id.* at 112.

79. *See id.*

80. *See* Dershowitz, *Police testilying must not be tolerated*, Boston Globe, Nov. 15, 1995, at A27 (paraphrasing NYPD Commissioner William F. Bratton, "When a prosecutor is really determined to win, the trial prep procedure may skirt along the edge of coercing or leading the police witness. In this way, some impressionable young cops learn to tailor their testimony to the requirements of the law."). *But see* Krauss, *Bratton Announces Plan to Train Officers to Testify*, N.Y. Times, Nov. 15, 1995, at B3 (comparing comment by Staten Island Assistant District Attorney David W. Lehr

that police learn to testilie from aggressive trial preparation by prosecutors who will win at any cost with response by Queens District Attorney Brown, "I don't believe that happens in Queens County, and I would not tolerate it from any assistant working for me.").

81. *See* Orfield, *supra* note 39, at 111; *see also infra* note 23 and accompanying text for discussion of use of boilerplate testimony.

82. *See* Mollen Commission Report, *supra* note 3, at 37.

83. *See* American Bar Ass'n, Standards Relating to Pleas of Guilty 1–2 (1st ed. 1968).

84. *See* Mollen Commission Report, *supra* note 3, at 37.

85. A. Dershowitz, Reasonable Doubts, *supra* note 10, at 57 (police perjurers have an "ace in the hole" —"[t]hey can testify against the very prosecutor's office that is empowered to arrest them. That is why so few cops are ever indicted for perjury.").

86. *See* Chin & Wells, *supra* note 12, at 261–62.

87. *See id.* at 263.

88. *See id.*

89. *See id.*

90. *See* Dershowitz, *Right Questions*, *supra* note 43, at 17.

91. *See* Berrios, 270 N.E.2d at 709. The New York Court of Appeals disagreed and put the burden on the defendant.

92. *See* Mollen Commission Report, *supra* note 3, at 42.

93. Krauss, *supra* note 80, at B3.

94. Sexton, *supra* note 19, at B3.

95. *See id.*

96. *See* Petite v. United States, 262 F.2d 788 (4th Cir. 1959), *remanded on other grounds*, 361 U.S. 529 (1960).

97. *See id.*

98. 18 U.S.C. § 1621 (1994).

99. *See* Bronston v. U.S., 409 U.S. 352 (1973).

100. *See infra* Section IV(b).

101. 629 F. Supp. 1474 (S.D.N.Y. 1986).

102. 262 F.2d 788 (4th Cir. 1959), *remanded on other grounds*, 361 U.S. 529 (1960).

103. *See* discussion *supra* note 89 and accompanying text, describing instances in which prosecutors may be so close to the police that they too share the Machiavellian justification for testilying.

104. This is the solution that Richard Hemley, of the New York Civil Liberties Union, advocated. *See* Hentoff, *supra* note 74, at A21.

105. Model Rules of Professional Conduct Rule 3.3(a) (1983); *accord* American Bar Ass'n, Standards for Criminal Justice, Standard 3-5.6(a) (1992) ("A prosecutor should not knowingly offer false evidence, whether by documents, tangible evidence, or the testimony of witnesses, or fail to seek withdrawal thereof upon discovery of falsity.").

106. Model Rules of Professional Conduct Rule 3.3(c) (1983) (emphasis added).

107. *See* 18 U.S.C. 1622 (1994).

108. *Petite*, 262 F.2d at 794.

109. *See* Model Rules of Professional Conduct Rule 3.3(c) (1983).

110. *See id.*

111. *Defore*, 150 N.E. at 587.

112. *See* S. Gillers, *supra* note 1, at 376 ("[T]he paradigmatic example has been the perjury of a criminal defendant.").
113. *See* Dershowitz, *Right Questions*, *supra* note 43, at 20.
114. *See* M. Freedman, Lawyers' Ethics in an Adversary System (1975). He concludes that a defendant's right to counsel trumps the prohibition against using perjured testimony and that defense counsel should be allowed to put a criminal defendant on the stand, examine him in a normal fashion, and permit the introduction of perjury before the court. *See id.* Some states are in agreement as a matter of state constitutional law. *See* Model Rules of Professional Conduct Rule 3.3 cmt.12 (1983). As a matter of federal constitutional law, a defendant does not have the right to testify falsely. *See* Nix v. Whiteside, 475 U.S. 157 (1986).
115. *See* American Bar Ass'n, Standards for Criminal Justice Standard 4-3.26(a) (1992).
116. *See* Model Rules of Professional Conduct Rule 1.6 (1983).
117. *See id.* Rule 3.3(a)(4).
118. The ABA does not support the use of this tactic. *See* American Bar Ass'n, Standards for Criminal Justice, Standard 4-3.2(b) ("Defense counsel should not instruct the client or intimate to the client in any way that the client should not be candid in revealing facts so as to afford defense counsel free rein to take action which would be precluded by counsel's knowing of such facts."). There is no corresponding duty for prosecutors.
119. *See, e.g., id.*
120. Berger v. United States, 295 U.S. 78, 88 (1935).
121. Model Rules of Professional Conduct Rule 1.1 cmt. 5 (1983).
122. *See id.* Rule 3.3, cmts. 4–6.
123. *See supra* note 63 and accompanying text.
124. The ABA Standards for Criminal Justice are in accord: Standard 3-3.4 requires prosecutors to take "reasonable care" that their investigators are "adequately trained" in Fourth Amendment law. The Standard recommends that investigators should consult with prosecutors in "close or difficult cases." *See* American Bar Ass'n, Standards for Criminal Justice, Standard 3-3.4(a) (1992).
125. *See* Model Rules of Professional Conduct Rule 3.3, cmt.11 (1983).
126. *See Nix*, 475 U.S. at 171.
127. Ironically, however, zero-tolerance policies themselves may be partially to blame for an increase in perjury and other in-court deception. The pressure from superiors to make arrests may be translating into pressure to lie and fabricate evidence.
128. *See supra* note 15, and accompanying text.
129. American Bar Ass'n, Standards for Criminal Justice, Standard 3-3.9(a) (1992).
130. Prosecutors and police are often in an uneasy working relationship; neither quite trusts the other. My impression in talking to police officers is that they consider many prosecutors to be naive kids with little world experience, their only "qualification" being a J.D. degree. Perhaps that stereotype is true in some cases. Regardless the fact that these "kids" could be prosecuting police officers—the "good guys"—could only worsen whatever feelings of resentment prosecutors and police feel for each other.
131. Mollen Commission Report, *supra* note 3, at 36.

Chapter 19

Capital Murder

A Prosecutor's Personal Observations on the Prosecution of Capital Cases

by Ronald J. Sievert*

I prosecuted four of the cases contained in the descriptive index of persons who have been on death row in Texas. It has been many years since I tried those cases and I have often looked back on them with the greater perspective that comes from the passage of time. My experience, I believe, was typical of most death penalty prosecutors. We as a class of trial lawyers understand that experience, but we also feel that, given the often perceived bias of the media and the prevalence of defense attorneys as instructors at most law schools, that neither the public at large nor law students accurately comprehend our thoughts and motivations as we go through the process.

When I applied for a position as an Assistant District Attorney, I was interviewed by a six-person team of senior assistants, one of whom asked whether or not I believed in the death penalty. My answer, although sincere, was far from hardline. I told them that I was not excited about it, that it might be appropriate if it proved to be a deterrent, but that to my knowledge that had not been established. In my own mind, it was still an open question. I found out later that the office with whom I interviewed ranked third in the State in capital cases. Nevertheless, despite the moderate attitude demonstrated by my answer, I was hired to begin my career as a prosecutor.

CONVERSION

After approximately one year trying juveniles and misdemeanors I was asked by a felony attorney if I wanted to help try a "dog" murder case (that is, one which is very difficult but nevertheless had to be tried). In preparing for that case I had to study for the first time actual photos of a real murder victim—an innocent human being with a family suddenly and unexpectedly killed for no reason other than the malice of the defendant. Because of technical problems in the case I also had to become thoroughly familiar with all the nuances of the autopsy report. This document discussed in cold detail the damage caused to the victim's body and revealed, without much imagination, the agonies of his death. I felt tremendous inner anger towards the perpetrator of the crime as I reviewed this evidence and that anger drove me throughout the trial until the defendant was convicted and duly punished.

Ronald J. Sievert, Essay, Capital Murder; A Prosecutor's Personal Observations on the Prosecution of Capital Cases, 27 *Am. J. Crim. L.* 105 (1999). Reprinted with permission.

That anger was to recur throughout the year as I subsequently tried a number of defendants who had committed crimes of equal magnitude. Although I was known in the office as an attorney who was capable of having compassion for some defendants, at the time I had little for this particular class of criminals. Wasn't life hard enough without having to worry about whether your wife or friends would survive a trip to the mall or the local 7–11? Could people not even go to sleep at night in their own home in safety? What type of animals were these men who attacked and greatly hurt so many decent good folk in our society on a continuous basis with absolutely no remorse or hint of feeling bad about what they did? You have heard similar statements, but if you reread them and take a minute to reflect on their basic truth in today's society it is easy to understand a prosecutor's conversion. Were these defendants not domestic terrorists who posed a greater threat to security in America from the inside than any foreign country did from the outside? Terrorists who were having their way because America in the last 30 years had lost the will to punish.

Before long, approximately two years out of U.T. law school, I was assigned my first capital case. I was suddenly engaged in devoting all of my energy to accomplishing a goal which a short time before I had publicly and seriously questioned.

It is not the purpose of this article to discuss the law and the facts of the capital cases I tried. I believe it is sufficient to point out that there were five: Walter Bell, Maurice Andrews, Elliot Rod Johnson, Laura Goode, and Lester Leroy Bower. The four men received the death penalty; the female, a motivator and a co-conspirator, but a non-shooter, received life. Johnson has been executed, the impact of which I'll address later. Andrews was killed on death row. The rest are on appeal. I am saddened by all of these cases, by the atrocities perpetrated on the victims, by the fact that human beings exist who could do these things, and with the thought that they too may now need to be executed for the good of society. I would discuss the particular details and the character of each defendant with anyone who has the need to know. I think the readers would be better served, however, if I utilize these pages to disclose from personal experience the prosecution's inner thinking and planning as they approach and try a capital case.

SELECTION OF DEFENDANTS

There were a number of crimes committed in our jurisdiction which would legally justify the death penalty under Section 19.03 of the Texas Penal Code. When these offenses were committed, there was often an immediate flare in public opinion against the defendant which would lead the elected district attorney to heatedly demand an indictment for capital murder. Our first duty as trial assistants was to calm him down and try to impose a rational order to the process by which some of the eligible defendants were selected for capital indictment and others were indicted on simple murder charges.

Upon obtaining a hearing in the front office, we would first review all of the facts (regardless of technical admissibility) to the point where we were certain in our own mind beyond any possible doubt that the defendant was guilty. We would hold ourselves to this standard in every criminal case because the last thing any honorable prosecutor would ever want to do, popular fiction and *Sixty Minutes* to the contrary, is convict an innocent man. All of us took very seriously our oath and statutory duty "to see that justice is done." If we were convinced of the defendant's guilt, we would then simultaneously analyze the case from two aspects. First, how strong was the admissible evidence and second, did the case "cry out" for the death penalty.

Regarding the strength of the case, law students, civil lawyers, and others who have not been educated or are not intimately familiar with prosecution often have no concept of the difficulties of proving guilt in a criminal trial or how much office debate will arise over the courtroom merits of a specific prosecution. The truth is that most prosecutors must work very hard for long hours before trial so that a case will look relatively easy when it is presented and so that the ultimate conclusion will appear inescapable. Juries and observers do not realize that the state's attorneys routinely deal with lost evidence, tests that have not been completed, witnesses who have not been interviewed, witnesses who are undesirable characters or who have short memories and almost no powers of observation, mistakes made in the investigation, and numerous other problems before they can ever put a case together. When that is done they then must think of every conceivable defense and how to counter it.

While preparing, prosecutors are also thinking about the fact that they are going to have to meet the highest burden of proof in our system of law for all twelve jurors. They know that during the course of the trial that all close evidentiary rulings are likely to go for the defense because they can appeal and the prosecution cannot. Finally they understand that every point they make is likely to be disputed by a dedicated, articulate, persuasive defense attorney who often may have the capacity to confuse the issues and obliterate the truth. It is often much easier for him to shoot holes in the wall than it is for the prosecutor to build it.

We would examine every case with these thoughts in mind and the result was often lively discussion among the attorneys. But in capital cases our analysis of the admissible evidence was even more intense because we knew that the jury was going to subconsciously hold us to the highest possible imaginable burden of proof before they would feel justified in assessing the death penalty. In addition, the trial courts had told us repeatedly that they would bend over backwards to make these cases "clean." This meant that we could not count on any imaginative theories to support our attempts to admit evidence and the defense attorney was going to have his way even more than he might in other cases. Lastly, despite reports I have read from other sections of the country, our judges, and I believe that most courts in Texas, appointed only the very best attorneys to defend capital cases. They were motivated and highly skilled. They were also well compensated by the county for their work and we joked with them more than once about the fact that they were being paid more money by the government for a month's work than we received for a year. We sometimes bitterly wondered why this was so when we were trying to protect society from the defendant and they were working hard to free him which would allow him to once again be a threat to the public safety.

The second question was, did the circumstances of the crime and the defendant's record "cry out" for the death penalty? As was the case with guilt, we had to first be certain in our hearts that this person should die for what they did before we would proceed. There was of course no set rule for that determination and it depended greatly on the individual beliefs of the prosecutor. For me, the crime and the likely death of an innocent victim had to be contemplated in advance, and the history of the defendant had to be such that it was clear he or she was a truly dangerous (and evil) human being. In my own mind, it was now enough that I could deter this one defendant from criminal acts regardless of whether his death would deter others. At the same time, the old fashioned concept of public retribution was beginning to make more sense.

Once we as trial attorneys were personally convinced the defendant should be executed, we would then look at the evidence in light of our theory that it would be best if the community and all potential jurors knew that the District Attorney's office asked for the death penalty only when absolutely necessary. We felt that the way to get that message across was to have the death penalty assessed every time we asked for it. Therefore, we convinced the DA (most of the time) to seek a capital indictment only when the facts of the crime were horrendous, such as multiple execution style murder or where the defendant had a history of prior violent acts which were admissible in court. With this evidence, the jury would have no problem answering yes in response to the critical second question, "Was there a probability that the defendant would commit future violent acts?" In those few instances where the DA did not follow our criteria and bowed to political or police pressure or his own emotions, it seemed that the jury invariably provided the proper balance and the defendant was not sentenced to death.

IMPACT OF RACE

There has been much written about the disproportionate number of African Americans who have been selected for prosecution for capital murder and who have received the death penalty. Our office had a good mix of attorneys from around the state and a few were classic "good old boys." It would be inaccurate to say there was absolutely no animosity towards black defendants. But although this was many years ago, in our discussions this attitude was rarely, if ever, supported by thinking and arguments that echoed the prejudice and bigotry associated with the Old South. Rather, it always came across as an outgrowth of the fact that these attorneys considered themselves crime fighters and statistics, reenforced by daily observations at docket call, established that a very large percentage of the violent crime, for whatever reason, was being committed by members of the county's minority population. A few prosecutors were thus angry at that segment of the population and I believe they would have had similar feelings whether the defendants were mostly Irish, Italian, Polish, Arab, or African Americans. In subsequent conversations with law enforcement officials from other nations I have often observed remarkably similar reactions against whatever "group" was considered responsible for a significant portion of the crimes committed in their country, regardless of whether the group came from virtually the same ethnic background as the officials.

Most importantly, I can unequivocally state that race was never a factor in our debates and analysis regarding which cases to select for capital prosecution. It was not discussed and I never saw the slightest hint that it was even subconsciously considered. The only matters debated were those that I have mentioned above regarding the strength of the case and the character of the defendant as reflected by his crime and his prior record.

Prosecutors were, of course, aware of race during jury selection. Despite the lengthy interviews characteristic of capital voir dire, attorneys do not really get to know a prospective juror before they have to make the decision whether or not to strike them. Because of this lack of knowledge, there is always the potential for stereotypes (valid or not) to have an influence. Some believe that members of the venire with a Nordic background are highly practical, Mediterraneans are thought to be emotional, elderly people are considered more forgiving, and social workers verboten because of a real or imagined predisposition to rehabilitation rather than punishment and so on. Along these lines, some people have theorized that African Americans may not be good prospective jurors in a capital case because they have historically been persecuted as a race and would therefore sympathize with the prosecuted defendant. In addition, some believe that many blacks have probably been the victims of, or observed, rough treatment in their neighborhoods by the police and that accordingly they would resent police officers regardless of the merits of the case.

Despite these stereotypes and the temptation to follow them, from my observation attorneys did not strike black members from the venire unless there were actual objective signs that a potential black juror did indeed sympathize or psychologically identify with the defendant, was anti-police, or would not follow the law. Even then, prosecutors were aware that they would be open to criticism for any strikes of minorities. But the prevalent attitude was that we were sworn to do justice, which meant convict the guilty and secure the proper punishment. It was not our job while prosecuting these cases to be social engineers. If an attorney honestly believed that there was a significant chance that a black or white venire person was not going to be fair and follow the law, based on whatever reasons, then that attorney did not want to put that person on the jury and risk a verdict which would result in the guilty defendant going free or a retrial of a month-long case. That was the practical logical approach of many prosecutors.

I must admit that after a time many of us started to go out of our way to look for blacks to put on the jury. We might have an honest fear that a particular minority juror might not be fair but we now resolved that conflict in favor of achieving highly integrated juries. When we had numerous black jurors in the case of a black defendant we might be apprehensive for all the reasons noted above but also felt good about doing what we believed was "right." From personal experience and observation, I can attest that in the last few years *Batson*[1] has accelerated this tendency in prosecutors. As a general principle, I do not like court decisions that interfere with an attorney's discretion in making peremptory challenges. But there is no question that *Batson* has forced honest attorneys to set aside stereotypes, overcome objective fears, and strike only when there are clear, race-neutral reasons to justify their actions.

TRIAL

Individual voir dire and the punishment phase are the two aspects of capital trials that are unique in death penalty cases so I will devote most of my attention to these areas.

The procedure by which each individual juror is brought to the witness stand and interviewed by each side for thirty minutes, at the end of which the government and then the defense must strike or accept, was, I believe, one of the most fascinating exercises in the legal system. Many of us felt that the skill, instincts, guesswork, moves, and countermoves were so challenging that the whole process could almost be packaged and sold as a parlor game if the subject was not so serious and consequential. Our goal was to obtain a jury composed entirely of bedrock solid citizens with common sense who would follow the law. The defense, in our opinion, was looking for people who were against the system, might not relate well with their fellow jurors and would be guided by their emotions instead of the court's instructions. The fact that we were seeking to achieve opposite results often led to a seemingly endless series of individual battles.

We generally started with a panel of approximately sixty jurors and fifteen peremptory strikes. Both prosecution and defense knew from review of the lengthy jury information forms that they were going to have to eliminate far more than the fifteen allotted if they were going to get the jury they desired. This placed a premium on the ability to draw out a juror's true beliefs to the point where they could be struck for cause. Equally important was the knowledge of how to subtly prepare the juror to withstand the defense's efforts to strike them for cause. In practice, this meant that we would utilize the jury questionnaire and the first ten minutes of questioning to determine if we wanted the juror, and then spend the next twenty minutes either trying to "save" or strike them. It was often incongruous, and the venire persons must have sometimes wondered if we really worked for the D.A. If we liked the juror, we found ourselves saying, "Now you could give probation in a murder case couldn't you?" When they said no, we would come up with the most sympathetic murderer you could imagine until they realized that if the facts warranted they could give probation. And so it went through a myriad of vulnerabilities that the defense might attack. On the other hand, if we decided that we wanted to strike the juror, you would then really have to get close to and empathize with the juror, and get them to acknowledge their real bias. So we would say something like

> I noticed you hesitated when I asked you how you felt about the death penalty. I understand many people feel it is against God's law, and that this law is higher than what the legislature in Austin might happen to pass one year. If that's the way you feel, if you feel you must obey what you believe to be God's laws and not just go along with what those folks in the state capital are saying, just tell us.

This was "straight forward" voir dire. On its own, it was an incredible study of human beings and practice in human relations. But the contest of wits with the defense went far beyond the "saves" and "strikes for cause" to the point where each side often "faked" or held its breath and gambled throughout the entire two week long period. Thus, if we did not like the juror and believed we could not get them for cause, but wanted to preserve our peremptory strikes, we might go into a save routine to convince the defense attorney we really wanted them, all with the hope that the defense would then strike. If while going through the save routine, we spotted an opening in one of the answers, we might quickly switch and try to strike them for cause, knowing we had only a few minutes left on the clock to get them to admit they could not follow the law in this particular area. At the same time, with jurors we wanted, we would occasionally make an apparent effort to strike for cause, trying to convince the defense attorney we were really worried about them for some secret reason so that they might leave them on the jury, while at the same time hoping we were not completely alienating the potential juror in the process.

This was the intense, high pressure game of capital murder jury selection as it was played in our jurisdiction and others with experience. Fifty or sixty little "mini trials" with each member of the venire that left the attorneys exhausted before we even started the guilt or innocence stage of the trial. I have not done it in years, but I imagine it is still practiced in much the same way. Some may question the maneuvering and apparent attempts at manipulation, but I am convinced that in every case the end result was a truly fair and impartial jury.

The guilt phase of a capital case contains all the drama of a murder case, heightened somewhat by the knowledge that a finding that the defendant is guilty means at least a life sentence and possibly death. Nevertheless, the procedure in the trial at this stage is not unique and I will not dwell on it. The punishment phase was the state's moment, as it should be if the DA was genuinely attempting to get the death sentence only on those who really deserved to be executed. It was always interesting to watch the reactions of the jurors when we produced the penitentiary packet listing multiple felony convictions. The jurors who had been strong for guilt during the first phase deliberations would look at whoever had been weak and nod their heads. You could count on the fact that the juror who had just finished strongly arguing for the defendant would not be such an effective advocate during punishment. In addition to the pen pack, we would also present psychiatric testimony, if needed, and often two or three reputation witnesses of unquestioned stature. If the defense attorney attempted to balance this with his own reputation witnesses, we would quickly turn the tables by asking if the witness had heard about all of the arrests and bad acts of the defendant which could not otherwise be admitted.

The death penalty argument, however, was the ultimate highlight of a state prosecutor's career. It was his job to convince a jury to make the supreme decision, the decision to take someone's life. Technically, you are just trying to tell the jury that the defendant acted deliberately and that there was a probability of future violent acts, but we all knew it was more than that. After reviewing the evidence to show the defendant's intent and logically demonstrating the likelihood of future violence based on the defendant's criminal history and character, you then talked about the need to assess the death penalty. There were some excellent "standard" arguments to support it which had circulated around the Texas District Attorney's Offices that you could adopt, insert your personal interpretation, and make your own. Such were the "they" argument ("You hear about this type of crime and wonder why they don't do something about it. The police and prosecutors have done their jobs. Did you ever wonder who they are? The 'they' who can do something about this crime right now is you.") and the forgiveness argument ("It is not up to you to forgive this defendant, only Mr. and Mrs. Jones, the victims he killed, could do that"),[2] as well as the innumerable references to God and the Bible that were spun by prosecutors with a religious bent.

But although the words and thoughts behind these formulations were good, what was probably far more effective was the moral force you brought with you to the argument. Part of this was anger. I had come from being doubtful about the death penalty to the point that as I personally approached the defendant in some of these cases, reciting what horrible acts he had done, I was filled with such outrage that I sometimes felt that if I had a weapon I might have executed him right then and there. But there was more. You were the avenging voice of the community, the one speaking representative of a just society. At the height of your argument you felt this emanate from your very being as if you were somehow spiritually connected with the county's 600,000 people and you were energetically, persuasively, thunderously speaking *their* words. You were an instrument. I cannot overstate this feeling, yet words cannot adequately reflect it. It is a very powerful moment. The jury could not help but get the message.

When the first capital case was over and the defendant had been assessed a death sentence, I recall getting very intoxicated with my co-counsel and friends in the office. It was not purely celebration, although there was some of that. We were moved, awed, permanently affected. I tried to explain it to my wife afterwards. "We have just spent thirty days of our life working unbelievably hard to kill a man, don't you understand? Someday its going to happen, because of what we did." She did not understand, nor will anybody who has never prosecuted a capital case.

The impact of that case was lasting, but it is also true that by the fourth one I was no longer as deeply affected as I had been. To me that was an indication that I should probably move on to the broader challenges of the U.S. Attorney's Office. It was there, several years later, working in clean new offices and surrounded by the financial records of crooked bankers and drug defendants, that I received a call from a friend in the District Attorney's office. "The Attorney General's office would like to know if you would awfully mind if they executed Elliot Rod Johnson tomorrow night?" I did mind. I was stunned because I had not thought about this for years. I told him I would call him back, shut my door, had my secretary hold my calls, and thought about Elliot Rod Johnson. I did not want him to die. I did not want anybody to die. But I forced myself to mentally go through the evidence, slowly, as if I had never heard it. There was no question he was guilty. I reviewed his prior record of assaults and robberies. I relived the facts surrounding the murders of jeweler Joe Granado and his assistant, Arturo Mendez, and, for a long time, thought of the wonderful family they had left behind. I felt great sorrow, and I still do today, but I nevertheless called the DA and said "I have no objection." God, make me an instrument of your peace.

During the last few years members of Congress have sought to include the death penalty as punishment for at least thirty-four additional federal crimes. The current procedures for a federal death penalty case, however, are both complicated and confusing while those in the Texas Code are simple and straightforward. The fact is, the number of federal death penalty cases will probably always be limited. The State of Texas, on the other hand, is leading the nation in executions for violations of State law. It is reality for the lawyers here. Each of us must constantly ask ourselves: should we continue with capital punishment in our state?

Recent allegations of "actual innocence" in capital cases certainly cause any objective person to seriously reconsider whether it should ever be invoked. But past charges of wrongful conviction have usually involved, upon thorough examination, procedural as opposed to factual errors. Those who claim failure to match DNA as proof of innocence are somewhat suspect because they are the same people who claim improper collection and analysis when DNA proves their client guilty. Their motives and interpretation of evidence must be closely scrutinized in each case. This is not to say that the goal of the criminal justice system in all cases, and especially in capital cases, should not be absolute certainty of the defendant's guilt. It is hard to object to moratoriums or major changes in procedure in any state which has not met that goal.

No sane person can "like" the death penalty. This is a different matter than supporting its implementation for the overall public good. My mind is always open on the subject, but currently I still support the death penalty in Texas if it is a deterrent to others. I know it is apparently impossible to scientifically determine one way or another if it is a deterrent, but logic as well as anecdotal evidence, dictates that it does restrain at least some people and therefore protects some innocent lives. But it will probably never have the deterrent effect it should have unless individuals know that if they commit a capital crime they will be identified, convicted, and punished. Our efforts at reform, therefore, should continue to be directed at, first, verifying that we have convicted the right person and, second, insuring that potential defendants know that if they commit the crime they will be appropriately punished as soon as the legal system can confirm that the conviction and sentence are just.

NOTES

1. Batson v. Kentucky, 476 U.S. 79 (1985).
2. In reviewing one of my transcripts, I found the following which is a typical verbatim argument in a death penalty case:

> Our job is a little bit different—my job and [the defense attorney's]. We don't represent the criminal defendant. We represent the people of the State of Texas and [this] County. All the people. People who want to live in a clean and decent society. The people who want to live in a society in which they can say good-by to their wives or their husbands in the morning and know at the end of the day they're going to see them again. And not see them the next time laying on a concrete floor with a bullet through their head, or in some ditch, or someplace else dead. Those are the people that we represent.
>
> I am going to try to tell it to you as straight and logical as I can, because I feel that's my job. . . .
>
> I don't know—Do some of you feel like I do? That maybe in twentieth century America, we've gotten away from the basic concepts and basic values that punishment is a right thing and a just thing in our society? That we have listened to the sociologists and the psychologists so long that we feel that no man is responsible for his crime, and we always find an excuse for them and let them off much lighter than we should?
>
> I'm telling you, our fathers, our grandfathers, knew the value of punishment. And we had a better society for it. We didn't have to worry about people like [the co-defendant]—as much like this as it is today—roaming the streets and the highways of the countryside.
>
> We believe that the United States of America is the best country on earth. And in many ways, it is. But, I can tell you right now, there are countries in this world where they don't have to have neighborhood watches set up. They don't have to have burglar bars on their windows. They don't have to worry about it when wives leave to go to the store, or when husbands leave to go to work. There are countries where you don't have to worry about that, because they wouldn't tolerate something like this. And for some reason, in the last ten or twenty years, we've got to the point where we are scared to punish. And what we get out of it, is that man. (Indicating)
>
> Justice has only been half served in this case. We're only half way there. Criminals don't fear guilt, they fear punishment. That's what it has to be. That's what they fear.
>
> [The defense] talked a lot about law and society. And the law is there to make sure that every man gets his due. What is this man due after what he did to those people?

Chapter 20

Why Prosecutors *Misbehave*?

by Bennett L. Gershman

The duties of the prosecuting attorney were well-stated in the classic opinion of Justice Sutherland fifty years ago.[1] The interest of the prosecutor, he wrote, "is not that he shall win a case, but that justice shall be done. As such, he is in a peculiar and very definite sense the servant of the law, the twofold aim of which is that guilt shall not escape or innocence suffer. He may prosecute with earnestness and vigor—indeed, he should do so. But, while he may strike hard blows, he is not at liberty to strike foul ones."[2]

Despite this admonition, prosecutors continue to strike "foul blows," perpetuating a disease which began long before Justice Sutherland's oft-quoted opinion. Indeed, instances of prosecutorial misconduct were reported at least as far back as 1897,[3] and as recently as the latest volume of the *Supreme Court Reporter*.[4] The span between these cases is replete with innumerable instances of improper conduct of the prosecutor, much of which defies belief.

One of the leading examples of outrageous conduct by a prosecutor is *Miller v. Pate*,[5] where the prosecutor concealed from the jury in a murder case the fact that a pair of undershorts with red stains on it, a crucial piece of evidence, were stained not by blood but by paint. Equally startling is *United States v. Perry*,[6] where the prosecutor, in his summation, commented on the fact that the "defendants and their counsel are completely unable to explain away their guilt."[7] Similarly, in *Dubose v. State*,[8] the prosecutor argued to the jury: "Now, not one sentence, not one scintilla of evidence, not one word in any way did this defendant or these attorneys challenge the credibility of the complaining witness."[9] At a time when it should be clear that constitutional and ethical standards prevent prosecutors from behaving this way,[10] we ought to question why prosecutors so frequently engage in such conduct.

Much of the above misconduct occurs in a courtroom. The terms "courtroom" or "forensic misconduct" have never been precisely defined. One commentator describes courtroom misconduct as those "types of misconduct which involve efforts to influence the jury through various sorts of inadmissible evidence."[11] Another commentator suggests that forensic misconduct "may be generally defined as any activity by the prosecutor which tends to divert the jury from making its determination of guilt or innocence by weighing the legally admitted evidence in the manner prescribed by law."[12] For purposes of this analysis, the latter definition applies, as it encompasses a broader array of behavior which can be classed as misconduct. As will be seen, prosecutorial misconduct can occur even without the use of inadmissible evidence.

From Bennett Gershman, "Why Prosecutors Misbehave," in M. Braswell, B.R. McCarthy, and B.J. McCarthy, *Justice, Crime, and Ethics*. Cincinnati, OH: Anderson Publishing Company, 1991. Used with permission of the publisher.

This article will address two aspects of the problem of courtroom misconduct. First, it will discuss why prosecutors engage in courtroom misconduct, and then why our present system offers little incentive to a prosecutor to change his behavior.

WHY MISCONDUCT OCCURS

Intuition tells us that the reason so much courtroom misconduct by the prosecutor[13] occurs is quite simple: it works. From my ten years of experience as a prosecutor, I would hypothesize that most prosecutors deny that misconduct is helpful in winning a case. Indeed, there is a strong philosophical argument that prosecutorial misconduct corrupts the judicial system, thereby robbing it of its legitimacy. In this regard, one would probably be hard pressed to find a prosecutor who would even mention that he would consider the thought of some form of misconduct.

Nonetheless, all of this talk is merely academic, because, as we know, if only from the thousands of cases in the reports, courtroom misconduct does occur. If the prosecutor did not believe it would be effective to stretch his argument to the ethical limit and then risk going beyond that ethical limit, he would not take the risk.

Intuition aside, however, several studies have shown the importance of oral advocacy in the courtroom, as well as the effect produced by such conduct. For example, the student of trial advocacy often is told of the importance of the opening statement. Prosecutors would undoubtedly agree that the opening statement is indeed crucial. In a University of Kansas study,[14] the importance of the opening statement was confirmed. From this study, the authors concluded that, in the course of any given trial,[15] the jurors were affected most by the first strong presentation which they saw. This finding leads to the conclusion that if a prosecutor were to present a particularly strong opening argument, the jury would favor the prosecution throughout the trial. Alternatively, if the prosecutor were to provide a weak opening statement, followed by a strong opening statement by the defense, then, according to the authors, the jury would favor the defense during the trial. It thus becomes evident that the prosecutor will be best served by making the strongest opening argument possible, and thereby assist the jury in gaining a better insight into what they are about to hear and see. The opportunity for the prosecutor to influence the jury at this point in the trial is considerable, and virtually all prosecutors would probably attempt to use this opportunity to their advantage, even if the circumstances do not call for lengthy or dramatic opening remarks.[16]

An additional aspect of the prosecutor's power over the jury is suggested in a University of North Carolina study.[17] This study found that the more arguments counsel raises with respect to the different substantive arguments offered, the more the jury will believe in that party's case. Moreover, this study found that there is not necessarily a correlation between the amount of objective information in the communication and the persuasiveness of the presentation.

For the trial attorney, then, this study clearly points to the advantage of raising as many issues as possible at trial. For the prosecutor, the two studies taken together would dictate an "action packed" opening statement, containing as many arguments that can be mustered, even those which might be irrelevant or unnecessary to convince the jury of the defendant's guilt. The second study would also dictate the same strategy for the closing argument. Consequently, a prosecutor who, through use of these techniques, attempts to assure that the jury knows his case may, despite violating ethical standards to seek justice,[18] be "rewarded" with a guilty verdict. Thus, one begins to perceive the incentive that leads the prosecutor to misbehave in the courtroom.[19]

Similar incentives can be seen with respect to the complex problem of controlling evidence to which the jury may have access. It is common knowledge that, in the course of any trial, statements frequently are made by the attorneys or witnesses, despite the fact these statements may not be admissible as evidence. Following such a statement, the trial judge may, at the request of the opposing counsel, instruct the jury to disregard what they have heard. Most trial lawyers, if they are candid, will agree that it is virtually impossible for jurors realistically to disregard these inadmissible statements. Studies here again demonstrate that our intuition is correct and that this evidence often is considered by jurors in reaching a verdict.

For example, an interesting study conducted at the University of Washington[20] tested the effects of inadmissible evidence on the decisions of jurors. The authors of the test designed a variety of scenarios whereby some jurors heard about an incriminating piece of evidence while other jurors did not. The study found that the effect of the inadmissible evidence was directly correlated to the strength of the prosecutor's case. The authors of the study reported that when the prosecutor presented a weak case, the inadmissible evidence did in fact prejudice the jurors. Furthermore, the judge's admonition to the jurors to disregard certain evidence did not have the same effect as when the evidence had not been mentioned at all. It had a prejudicial impact anyway.

However, the study also indicated that when there was a strong prosecution case, the inadmissible evidence had little, if any, effect.[21] Nonetheless, the most significant conclusion from the study is that inadmissible evidence had its most prejudicial impact when there was little other evidence on which the jury could base a decision. In this situation, "the controversial evidence becomes quite salient in the jurors' minds."[22]

Finally, with respect to inadmissible evidence and stricken testimony, even if one were to reject all of the studies discussed, it is still clear that although "stricken testimony may tend to be rejected in open discussion, it does have an impact, perhaps even an unconscious one, on the individual juror's judgment."[23] As with previously discussed points, this factor—the unconscious effect of stricken testimony or evidence—will generally not be lost on the prosecutor who is in tune with the psychology of the jury.

The applicability of these studies to this analysis, then, is quite clear. Faced with a difficult case in which there may be a problem of proof, a prosecutor might be tempted to sway the jury by adverting to a matter which might be highly prejudicial. In this connection, another study[24] has suggested that the jury will more likely consider inadmissible evidence that favors conviction.[25]

Despite this factor of "defense favoritism," it is again evident that a prosecutor may find it rewarding to misconduct himself in the courtroom. Of course, a prosecutor who adopts the unethical norm and improperly allows jurors to hear inadmissible proof runs the risk of jeopardizing any resulting conviction. In a situation where the prosecutor feels there is a weak case, however, a subsequent reversal is not a particularly effective sanction when a conviction might have been difficult to achieve in the first place. Consequently, an unethical courtroom "trick" can be a very attractive idea to the prosecutor who feels he must win.[26] Additionally, there is always the possibility of another conviction even after an appellate reversal. Indeed, while a large number of cases are dismissed following remand by an appellate court, nearly one half of reversals still result in some type of conviction.[27] Therefore, a prosecutor can still succeed in obtaining a conviction even after his misconduct led to a reversal.

An additional problem in the area of prosecutor-jury interaction is the prosecutor's prestige; since the prosecutor represents the "government," jurors are more likely to believe him.[28] Put simply, prosecutors "are the good guys of the legal system,"[29] and because they have such glamour, they often may be tempted to use this advantage in an unethical manner. This presents a problem for the prosecutor in that the "average citizen may often forgive, yea urge prosecutors on in ethical indiscretions, for the end, convictions of criminals, certainly justifies in the public eye any means necessary."[30] Consequently, unless the prosecutor is a person of high integrity and is able to uphold the highest moral standards, the problem of courtroom misconduct inevitably will be tolerated by the public.

Moreover, when considering the problems facing the prosecutor, one also must consider the tremendous stress under which the prosecutor labors on a daily basis. Besides the stressful conditions faced by the ordinary courtroom litigator,[31] prosecuting attorneys, particularly those in large metropolitan areas, are faced with huge and very demanding case loads. As a result of case volume and time demands, prosecutors may not be able to take advantage of opportunities to relax and recover from the constant onslaught their emotions face every day in the courtroom."[32]

Under these highly stressful conditions, it is understandable that a prosecutor occasionally may find it difficult to face these everyday pressures and to resist temptations to behave unethically. It is not unreasonable to suggest that the conditions under which the prosecutor works can have a profound effect on his attempt to maintain high moral and ethical standards. Having established this hypothesis, one can see yet another reason why courtroom misconduct may occur.

WHY MISCONDUCT CONTINUES

Having demonstrated that courtroom misconduct may in many instances be highly effective, the question arises as to why such practices continue in our judicial system. A number of reasons may account for this phenomenon. Perhaps the most significant reason for the continued presence of prosecutorial misconduct is the harmless error doctrine. Under this doctrine, an appellate court can affirm a conviction despite the presence of serious misconduct during the trial. As Justice Traynor once stated, the "practical objective of tests of harmless error is to conserve judicial resources by enabling appellate courts to cleanse the judicial process of prejudicial error without becoming mired in harmless error."[33]

Although the definition advanced by Justice Traynor portrays the harmless error doctrine as having a more desirable consequence, this desirability is undermined when the prosecutor is able to misconduct himself without fear of sanction. Additionally, since every case is different, what constitutes harmless error in one case may be reversible error in another. Consequently, harmless error determinations do not offer any significant precedents by which prosecutors can judge the status of their behavior.

By way of illustration, consider two cases in which the prosecutor implicitly told the jury of his personal belief in the defendant's guilt. In one case, the prosecutor stated, "I have never tried a case where the evidence was so clear and convincing."[34] In the other case, the prosecutor told the jury that he did not try cases unless he was sure of them.[35] In the first case the conviction was affirmed, while in the second case the conviction was reversed. Interestingly, the court in the first case affirmed the conviction despite its belief that the "prosecutor's remarks were totally out of order."[36] Accordingly, despite making comments which were "totally out of order," the prosecutor did not suffer any penalty.

Contrasting these two cases presents clear evidence of what is perhaps the worst derivative effect of the harmless error rule. The problem is that the stronger the prosecutor's case, the more misconduct he can commit without being reversed. Indeed, in the *Shields* case, the court stated that "the guilt of the defendant was clearly established not only beyond a reasonable doubt, but well beyond any conceivable doubt."[37] For purposes of our analysis, it is clear that by deciding as they do, courts often provide little discouragement to a prosecutor who believes, and rightly so, that he does not have to be as careful about his conduct when he has a strong case. The relation of this factor to the amount of courtroom misconduct cannot be ignored.

Neither can one ignore the essential absurdity of a harmless error determination. To apply the harmless error rule, appellate judges attempt to evaluate how various evidentiary items or instances or prosecutorial misconduct may have affected the jury's verdict. Although it may be relatively simple in some cases to determine whether improper conduct during a trial was harmless, there are many instances when such an analysis cannot properly be made but nevertheless is made. For example, consider the situation when an appellate court is divided on whether or not a given error was harmless. In *United States v. Antonelli Fireworks Co.*,[38] two judges (including Judge Learned Hand) believed that the prosecutor's error was harmless. Yet, Judge Frank, the third judge sitting in the case, completely disagreed, writing a scathing dissent nearly three times the length of the majority opinion. One wonders how harmless error can be fairly applied when there is such a significant difference of opinion among highly respected members of a court as to the extent of harmfulness of trial errors. Perhaps even more interesting is the Supreme Court's reversal of the Court of Appeals for the Second Circuit's unanimous finding of harmless error in *United States v. Berger*.[39] As noted, *Berger* now represents the classic statement of the scope of the prosecutor's duties. Yet, in his majority opinion for the Second Circuit, Judge Learned Hand found the prosecutor's misconduct harmless.

The implications of these contradictory decisions are significant, for they demonstrate the utter failure of appellate courts to provide incentives for the prosecutor to control his behavior. If misconduct can be excused even when reasonable judges differ as to the extent of harm caused by such misbehavior, then very little guidance is given to a prosecutor to assist him in determining the propriety of his actions. Clearly, without such guidance, the potential for misconduct significantly increases.

The *Shields* case presents yet another factor which suggests why the prosecutor has only limited incentive to avoid misconduct. In *Shields*, the court refused to review certain "potentially inflammatory statements" made by the prosecutor because of the failure of the defense to object.[40] Although this approach has not been uniformly applied by all courts, the implications of this technique to reject a defendant's claim are considerable. Most important, it encourages prosecutors to make remarks that they know are objectionable in the hope that defense counsel will not object. This situation recalls the previous discussion, which dealt with the effect of inadmissible evidence on jurors. Defense counsel here is in a difficult predicament. If he does not object, he ordinarily waives any appealable issue in the event of conviction. If he does object, he highlights to the jury the fact that the prosecutor has just done something which some jurors may feel is so damaging to the defendant that the defense does not want it brought out.

The dilemma of the defense attorney in this situation is confirmed by a Duke University study.[41] In that study, jurors learned of various pieces of evidence which were ruled inadmissible. The study found that when the judge admonished the jury to disregard the evidence, the bias created by that evidence was not significantly reduced.[42] Consequently, when a prejudicial remark is made by the prosecutor, defense counsel must act carefully to avoid damaging his client's case. In short, the prosecutor has yet another weapon, in this instance an arguably unfair aspect of the appellate process, which requires preservation of an appealable issue.[43]

A final point when analyzing why prosecutorial misconduct persists is the unavailability or inadequacy of penalties visited upon the prosecutor personally in the event of misconduct. Punishment in our legal system comes in varying degrees. An appellate court can punish a prosecutor by simply cautioning him not to act in the same manner again, reversing his case, or, in some cases, identifying by name of the prosecutor who misconducted himself.[44] Even these punishments, however, may not be sufficient to dissuade prosecutors from acting improperly. One noteworthy case[45] describes a prosecutor who appeared before the appellate court on a misconduct issue for the third time, each instance in a different case.

Perhaps the ultimate reason for the ineffectiveness of the judicial system in curbing prosecutorial misconduct is that prosecutors are not personally liable for their misconduct. In *Imbler v. Pachtman*,[46] the Supreme Court held that "in initiating a prosecution and in presenting the state's case, the prosecutor is immune from a civil suit for damages under Section 1983."[47] Furthermore, prosecutors have absolute rather than a more limited, qualified, immunity. Thus, during the course of a trial, the prosecutor is absolutely shielded from any civil liability which might arise due to his misconduct, even if that misconduct was performed with malice.

There is clearly a need for some level of immunity to be accorded all government officials. Without such immunity, much of what is normally done by officials in authority might not be performed out of fear that their practices [would] later [be] deemed harmful or improper. Granting prosecutors a certain level of immunity is reasonable. Allowing prosecutors to be completely shielded from civil liability in the event of misconduct, however, provides no deterrent to courtroom misconduct.

CONCLUSION

This analysis was undertaken to determine why the issue of misconduct seems so prevalent in the criminal trial. For the prosecutor, the temptation to cross over the allowable ethical limit must often be irresistible because of the distinct advantages that such misconduct creates in assisting the prosecutor to win his case by effectively influencing the jury. Most prosecutors must inevitably be subject to this temptation. It takes a constant effort on the part of every prosecutor to maintain the high moral standards which are necessary to avoid such temptations.

Despite the frequent occurrences of courtroom misconduct, appellate courts have not provided significant incentives to the prosecutor to avoid misconduct. It is not until the courts decide to take a stricter, more consistent approach to this problem that inroads will be made in the effort to end it. One solution might be to impose civil liability on the prosecutor who misconducts himself with malice. Although this will not solve the problem, it might be a step in the right direction.

NOTES

1. *Berger v. United States*, 295 U.S. 78 (1935).
2. Id. of 88.
3. See *Dunlop v. United States*, 165 U.S. 486 (1897), where the prosecutor, in an obscenity case, argued to the jury "I do not believe that there are twelve men that could be gathered by the venire of this court. . ., except where they were bought and perjured in advance, whose verdict I would not be willing to take. . ." Id. at 498. Following this remark defense counsel objected, and the court held that statement to be improper.
4. See *Caldwell v. Mississippi*, 105 S. Ct. 2633 (1985) (improper argument to capital sentencing jury): *United States v. Young*, 105 S. Ct. 1038 (improper argument but not plain error).
5. 386 U.S. 1 (1967). In this case, the Supreme Court overturned the defendant's conviction after the Court of Appeals for the Seventh Circuit had upheld it. The Court noted that the prosecutor "deliberately misrepresented the truth" and that such behavior would not be tolerated under the Fourteenth Amendment. Id. at 67.
6. 643 F.2d 38 (2d Cir. 1981).
7. Id. at 51.
8. 531 S.W.2d 330 (Texas 1975)
9. Id. at 331. The court noted that the argument was clearly a comment on the failure of the defendant to testify at trial.
10. See *Griffin v. California*, 380 U.S. 609 (1965), where the Supreme Court applied the Fifth Amendment to the states under the Fourteenth Amendment.
11. Alschuler, "Courtroom Misconduct by Prosecutors and Trial Judges," 50 Tex L. Rev. 627, 633 (1972).
12. Note, "The Nature and Function of Forensic Misconduct in the Prosecution of a Criminal Case," 54 Col. L. Rev. 946, 949 (1954).
13. Of course, there is also a significant amount of defense misconduct which takes place. In this respect, for an interesting article which takes a different approach than this article, see Kamm. "The Case for the Prosecutor," 13 U. Tol. L. Rev. 331 (1982), where the author notes that "courts carefully nurture the defendant's rights while cavalierly ignoring the rights of the people."
14. Pyszczynski, "The Effects of Opening Statement on Mock Jurors' Verdicts in a Simulated Criminal Trial," II *Journal of Applied Soc. Psychology* 301 (1981).
15. All of the cited studies include within the report a caveat about the value of the study when applied to a "real world" case. Nonetheless, they are still worthwhile for the purpose of this analysis.
16. In some jurisdictions, attorneys may often use the voir dire to accomplish the goal of early influence of the jury.
17. Calder, "The Relation of Cognitive and Memorial Processes to Persuasion in a Simulated Jury Trial," 4 *Journal of Applied Soc. Psychology* 62 (1974).
18. See *Model Code of Professional Responsibility* EC 7–13 (1980) ("The duty of the prosecutor is to seek justice.")
19. Of course, this may apply to other attorneys as well.
20. Sue, S., R.E. Smith, and C. Caldwell, "The Effects of Inadmissible Evidence on the Decisions of Simulated Jurors—A Moral Dilemma," 3 *Journal of Applied Soc. Psychology* 345 (1973).

21. Perhaps lending validity to application of the harmless error doctrine, which will be discussed later in this article.
22. Sue, note 20 *supra* at 351.
23. Hastie, *Inside the Jury* 232 (1983).
24. Thompson, "Inadmissible Evidence and Jury Verdicts," 40 *Journal of Personality & Soc. Psychology* 453 (1981).
25. The author did note that the defendant in the test case was very sympathetic and that the results may have been different with a less sympathetic defendant.
26. Of course, this begs the question: "Is there a prosecutor who would take a case to trial and then feel that he didn't have to win?" It is hoped that, in such a situation, trial would never be an option. Rather, one would hope for an early dismissal of the charges.
27. Roper, "Does Procedural Due Process Make a Difference?" 65 *Judicature* 136 (1981). This article suggests that the rate of nearly 50 percent of acquittals following reversal is proof that due process is a viable means for legitimatizing the judiciary. While this is true, the fact remains that there is still a 50 percent conviction rate after reversal, thereby giving many prosecutors a second chance to convict after their original misconduct.
28. See *People v. McCoy*, 220 N.W.2d 456 (Mich. 1974), where the prosecutor, in attempt to bolster his case, told the jury that "the Detroit Police Department, the detectives in the Homicide Bureau, these detectives you see in court today, and myself from the prosecutor's office, we don't bring cases unless we're sure, unless we're positive." Id. at 460.
29. Emmons, "Morality and Ethics—A Prosecutor's View," *Advanced Criminal Trial Tactics* 393–407 (P.L.I. 1977).
30. Id.
31. For an interesting article on the topic, see Zimmerman, "Stress and the Trial Lawyer," 9 *Litigation* 4, 37–42 (1983).
32. For example, the Zimmerman article suggests time off from work and "celebration" with family and friends in order to effectively induce relaxation.
33. R. Traynor, *The Riddle of Harmless Error*, 81 (1970).
34. *People v. Shields*, 58 A.D.2d 94, 96 (N.Y.), aff'd, 46 N.Y.2d 764 (1977).
35. *People v. McCoy*, 220 N.W.2d 456 (Mich. 1974).
36. *Shields*, 58 A.D.2d at 97.
37. Id. at 99.
38. 155 F.2d 631 (2d Cir. 1946).
39. 73 F.2d 278 (1934), rev'd, 295 U.S. 78 (1935).
40. *Shields*, 58 A.D.2d at 97.
41. Wolf, "Effects of Inadmissible Evidence and Level of Judicial Admonishment to Disregard on the Judgments of Mock Jurors," 7 *J. Applied Soc. Psychology* 205 (1977).
42. Additionally of note is the fact that if the judge rules the evidence and did not admonish the jury, then the biasing effect of the evidence was eliminated. The authors of the study concluded that by being told not to consider certain evidence, the jurors felt a loss of freedom and that in order to retain their freedom, they considered it anyway. The psychological term for this effect is called reactance.
43. Of course, this does not mean that appeals should always be allowed, even in the absence of an appealable issue. Rather, one should confine the availability of these appeals to the narrow circumstances discussed.

44. See *United v. Burse*, 531 F.2d 1151 (2d Cir. 1976), where the Court named the prosecutor in the body of its opinion.
45. *United States v. Drummond*, 481 F.2d 62 (2d Cir. 1973).
46. 424 U.S. 409 (1976).
47. Id. at 431. 42 U.S.C. § 1983 authorizes civil actions against state officials who violate civil rights "under color of state law."

Chapter 21

The Criminal Lawyer's
"Different Mission"

Reflections on the "Right" to Present a False Case

by Harry I. Subin

About fifteen years ago I represented a man charged with rape and robbery. The victim's account was as follows: Returning from work in the early morning hours, she was accosted by a man who pointed a gun at her and took a watch from her wrist. He told her to go with him to a nearby lot, where he ordered her to lie down on the ground and disrobe. When she complained that the ground was hurting her, he took her to his apartment, located across the street. During the next hour there, he had intercourse with her. Ultimately, he said that they had to leave to avoid being discovered by the woman with whom he lived. The complainant responded that since he had gotten what he wanted, he should give her back her watch. He said that he would.

As the two left the apartment, he said he was going to get a car. Before leaving the building, however, he went to the apartment next door, leaving her to wait in the hallway. When asked why she waited, she said that she was still hoping for the return of her watch, which was a valued gift, apparently from her boyfriend.

She never did get the watch. When they left the building, the man told her to wait on the street while he got the car. At that point she went to a nearby police precinct and reported the incident. She gave a full description of the assailant that matched my client. She also accurately described the inside of his apartment. Later, in response to a note left at his apartment by the police, my client came to the precinct, and the complainant identified him. My client was released at that time but was arrested soon thereafter at his apartment, where a gun was found.[1] No watch was recovered.

My client was formally charged, at which point I entered the case. At our initial interview and those that followed it, he insisted that he had nothing whatever to do with the crime and had never even seen the woman before.[2] He stated that he had been in several places during the night in question: visiting his aunt earlier in the evening, then traveling to a bar in New Jersey, where he was during the critical hours. He gave the name of a man there who would corroborate this. He said that he arrived home early the next morning and met a friend. He stated that he had no idea how this woman had come to know things about him such as what the apartment looked like, that he lived with a woman, and that he was a musician, or how she could identify him. He said that he had no reason to rape anyone, since he already had a woman, and that in any event he was

From Harry I. Subin, "The Criminal Lawyer's "Different Mission": Reflections on the "Right" to Present a False Case, *Journal of Legal Ethics*, Volume 1 (1987), pp. 125–136. Reprinted with permission of the publisher, © 1988 Georgetown Journal of Legal Ethics & Georgetown University.

recovering from surgery for an old gun shot wound and could not engage in intercourse. He said he would not be so stupid as to bring a woman he had robbed and was going to rape into his own apartment.

I felt there was some strength to these arguments, and that there were questionable aspects to the complainant's story. In particular, it seemed strange that a man intending rape would be as solicitous of the victim's comfort as the woman said her assailant was at the playground. It also seemed that a person who had just been raped would flee when she had the chance to, and in any case would not be primarily concerned with the return of her watch. On balance, however, I suspected that my client was not telling me the truth. I thought the complaining witness could not possibly have known what she knew about him and his apartment, if she had not had any contact with him. True, someone else could have posed as him, and used his apartment. My client, however, could suggest no one who could have done so.[3] Moreover, that hypothesis did not explain the complainant's accurate description of him to the police. Although the identification procedure used by the police, a one person "show up," was suggestive, the woman had ample opportunity to observe her assailant during the extended incident. I could not believe that the complainant had selected my client randomly to accuse falsely of rape. By both her and my client's admission, the two had not had any previous association.

That my client was probably lying to me had two possible explanations. First, he might have been lying because he was guilty and did not see any particular advantage to himself in admitting it to me. It is embarrassing to admit that one has committed a crime, particularly one of this nature. Moreover, my client might well have feared to tell me the truth. He might have believed that I would tell others what he said, or, at the very least, that I might not be enthusiastic about representing him.

He also might have lied not because he was guilty of the offense, but because he thought the concocted story was the best one under the circumstances. The sexual encounter may have taken place voluntarily, but the woman complained to the police because she was very angry at my client for refusing to return the valued wrist watch, perhaps not stolen, but left, in my client's apartment. My client may not have been able to admit this, because he had other needs that took precedence over the particular legal one that brought him to me. For example, the client might have felt compelled to deny any involvement in the incident because to admit to having had a sexual encounter might have jeopardized his relationship with the woman with whom he lived. Likewise, he might have decided to "play lawyer," and put forward what he believed to be his best defense. Not understanding the heavy burden of proof on the state in criminal cases, he might have thought that any version of the facts that showed that he had contact with the woman would be fatal because it would simply be a case of her word against his.

I discussed all of these matters with the client on several occasions. Judging him a man of intelligence, with no signs of mental abnormality, I became convinced that he understood both the seriousness of his situation, and that his exculpation did not depend upon maintaining his initial story. In ensuring that he did understand that, in fact, I came close enough to suggesting the "right" answers to make me a little nervous about the line between subornation of perjury and careful witness preparation, known in the trade as "horseshedding." In the end, however, he held to his original account.

At this point the case was in equipoise for me. I had my suspicions about both the complainant's and the client's version of what had occurred, and I supposed a jury would as well. That problem was theirs, however, not mine. All I had to do was present my client's version of what occurred in the best way that I could.

Or was that all that was required? Committed to the adversarial spirit . . ., I decided that it was not. The "different mission" took me beyond the task of presenting my client's position in a legally correct and persuasive manner, to trying to untrack the state's case in any lawful way that occurred to me, regardless of the facts.

With that mission in mind, I concluded that it would be too risky to have the defendant simply take the stand and tell his story, even if it were true. Unless we could create an iron-clad alibi, which seemed unlikely given the strength of the complainant's identification, I thought it was much safer to attack the complainant's story, even if it were true. I felt, however, that since my client had persisted in his original story I was obligated to investigate the alibi defense, although I was fairly certain that I would not use it. My students and I therefore interviewed everyone he mentioned, traveled and timed the route he said he had followed, and attempted to find witnesses who may have seen someone else at the apartment. We discovered nothing helpful. The witness my client identified as being at the bar in New Jersey could not corroborate the client's presence there. The times the client gave were consistent with his presence at the place of the crime when the victim claimed it took place. The client's aunt verified that he had been with her, but much earlier in the evening.

Because the alibi defense was apparently hopeless, I returned to the original strategy of attempting to undermine the complainant's version of the facts. I demanded a preliminary hearing, in which the complainant would have to testify under oath to the events in question. Her version was precisely as I have described it, and she told it in an objective manner that, far from seeming contrived, convinced me that she was telling the truth. She seemed a person who, if not at home with the meanness of the streets, was resigned to it. To me that explained why she was able to react in what I perceived to be a nonstereotypical manner to the ugly events in which she had been involved.

I explained to my client that we had failed to corroborate his alibi, and that the complainant appeared to be a credible witness. I said that in my view the jury would not believe the alibi, and that if we could not obtain any other information, it might be appropriate to think about a guilty plea, which would at least limit his exposure to punishment. The case, then in the middle of the aimless drift towards resolution that typifies New York's criminal justice system, was left at that.

Some time later, however, my client called me and told me that he had new evidence; his aunt, he said, would testify that he had been with her at the time in question. I was incredulous. I reminded him that at no time during our earlier conversations had he indicated what was plainly a crucial piece of information, despite my not too subtle explanation of the elements of an alibi defense. I told him that when the aunt was initially interviewed with great care on this point, she stated that he was not with her at the time of the crime. Ultimately, I told him that I thought he was lying, and that in my view even if the jury heard the aunt's testimony, they would not believe it.

Whether it was during that session or later that the client admitted his guilt I do not recall. I do recall wondering whether, now that I knew the truth, that should make a difference in the way in which the case was handled. I certainly wished that I did not know it and began to understand, psychologically if not ethically, lawyers who do not want to know their clients' stories.

I did not pause very long to ponder the problem, however, because I concluded that knowing the truth in fact did not make a difference to my defense strategy, other than to put me on notice as to when I might be suborning perjury. Because the mission of the defense attorney was to defeat the prosecution's case, what I knew actually happened was not important otherwise. What did matter was whether a version of the "facts" could be presented that would make a jury doubt the client's guilt.

Viewed in this way, my problem was not that my client's story was false, but that it was not credible, and could not be made to appear so by legal means. To win, we would therefore have to come up with a better theory than the alibi, avoiding perjury in the process. Thus, the defense would have to be made out without the client testifying, since it would be a crime for him to assert a fabricated exculpatory theory under oath. This was not a serious problem, however, because it would not only be possible to prevail without the defendant's testimony, but it would probably be easier to do so. Not everyone is capable of lying successfully on the witness stand, and I did not have the sense that my client would be very good at it.

There were two possible defenses that could be fabricated. The first was mistaken identity. We could argue that the opportunity of the victim to observe the defendant at the time of the original encounter was limited, since it had occurred on a dark street. The woman could be made out to have been in great emotional distress during the incident.[4] Expert testimony would have to be adduced to show the hazards of eyewitness identification. We could demonstrate that an unreliable identification procedure had been used at the precinct. On the other hand, given that the complainant had spent considerable time with the assailant and had led the police back to the defendant's apartment, it seemed doubtful that the mistaken identification ploy would be successful.

The second alternative, consent, was clearly preferable. It would negate the charge of rape and undermine the robbery case.[5] To prevail, all we would have to do would be to raise a reasonable doubt as to whether he had compelled the woman to have sex with him. The doubt would be based on the scenario that the woman and the defendant met, and she voluntarily returned to his apartment. Her watch, the object of the alleged robbery, was either left there by mistake or, perhaps better, was never there at all.

The consent defense could be made out entirely through cross-examination of the complainant, coupled with arguments to the jury about her lack of credibility on the issue of force. I could emphasize the parts of her story that sounded the most curious, such as the defendant's solicitude in taking his victim back to his apartment, and her waiting for her watch when she could have gone immediately to the nearby precinct that she went to later. I could point to her inability to identify the gun she claimed was used (although it was the one actually used), that the allegedly stolen watch was never found, there was no sign of physical violence, and no one heard screaming or any other signs of a struggle. I could also argue as my client had that even if he were reckless enough to rob and rape a woman across the street from his apartment, he would not be so foolish as to bring the victim there. I considered investigating the complainant's background, to take advantage of the right, unencumbered at the time, to impeach her on the basis of her prior unchastity.[6] I did not pursue this, however, because to me this device, although lawful, was fundamentally wrong. No doubt in that respect I lacked zeal, perhaps punishably so.

Even without assassinating this woman's character, however, I could argue that this was simply a case of a casual tryst that went awry. The defendant would not have to prove whether the complainant made the false charge to account for her whereabouts that evening, or to explain what happened to her missing watch. If the jury had reason to doubt the complainant's charge, it would be bound to acquit the defendant.

How all of this would have played out at trial cannot be known. Predictably, the case dragged on so long that the prosecutor was forced to offer the unrefusable plea of possession of a gun. As I look back, however, I wonder how I could justify doing what I was planning to do had the case been tried. I was prepared to stand before the jury posing as an officer of the court in search of the truth, while trying to fool the jurors into believing a wholly fabricated story, i.e., that the woman had consented, when in fact she had been forced at gunpoint to have sex with the defendant. I was also prepared to demand an acquittal because the state had not met its burden of proof when, if it had not, it would have been because I made the truth look like a lie. If there is any redeeming social value in permitting an attorney to do such things, I frankly cannot discern it.

Others have discerned it, however, and while they have been criticized, they seem clearly to represent the majority view. They rely on either of two theories. The first is that the lawyer cannot possibly be sufficiently certain of the truth to impose his or her view of it on the client's case. The second is that the defense attorney need not be concerned with the truth even if he or she does know it. Both are misguided.

ENDNOTES

1. The woman was not able to make a positive identification of the gun as the weapon used in the incident.
2. A student working on the case with me photographed the complainant on the street. My client stated that he could not identify her.
3. The woman had indicated that her assailant opened the door with a key. There was no evidence of a forced entry.
4. This would be one of those safe areas in cross-examination, where the witness was damned no matter what she answered. If she testified that she was distressed, it would make my point that she was making an unreliable identification; if she testified that she was calm, no one would believe her. . . .
5. Consent is a defense to a charge of rape. e.g., N.Y. Penal Law § 130.05 (McKinney 1975 & Supp. 1987). While consent is not a defense to a robbery charge, N.Y. Penal Law § 160.00–.15 (McKinney 1975 & Supp. 1987), if the complainant could be made out to be a liar about the rape, there was a good chance that the jury would not believe her about the stolen watch either.
6. When this case arose it was common practice to impeach the complainant in rape cases by eliciting details of her prior sexual activities. Subsequently the rules of evidence were amended to require a specific showing of relevance to the facts of the case. *N.Y. Crim. Proc. Law* § 60.42 (McKinney 1981 & Supp. 1987).

Chapter 22

How to Improve the Jury System

by Thomas F. Hogan, Gregory E. Mize, and Kathleen Clark

The subject of the American jury system raises conflicting cultural sentiments. While the jury trial is revered as the most democratic institution in our society, a summons for jury service is dreaded as an unwelcome intrusion into our lives. Jury verdicts, respected because they are reached by a group of peers, are also ridiculed in recent high-profile trials.

Amid this cultural cognitive disconnect, however, there is no major movement to abolish the right to a trial by jury. Rather, across the country, communities and their courts are joining forces to fix the system. Recent efforts in Washington, D.C., Arizona, California, Colorado, New York, and other states have all focused on modernizing the jury system by making it more convenient, democratic, and educational for the jurors.

The ongoing jury reform experience in Washington, D.C., provides a look at jury service through the eyes of the juror and reveals that community-wide collaboration may be the most effective way to reconnect our actions and our values about the duty to serve.

In late 1996, the Council for Court Excellence assembled a committee and charged it with recommending improvements to the jury systems in Washington, D.C. Then, in February 1998, after a full year of study, the D.C. Jury Project published its comprehensive research report, which includes 32 specific recommendations to the bench and bar on how to modernize jury trials in the local and federal courts.

In the District of Columbia, where well-intentioned committees addressing worthy problems are hardly uncommon, nothing unusual has happened. Or has it? This report, entitled *Juries for the Year 2000 and Beyond*, may not become another denizen of the library shelf after all.

What makes the D.C. Jury Project's recommendations worthy of thoughtful consideration by the local and national legal communities? First and foremost, the quality of analysis regarding an impressive number of important issues in *Juries for the Year 2000 and Beyond* renders it both readable and well worth reading.

The revered constitutional institution of the jury trial, under recent media attack, deserves a renewed opportunity to thrive. Modernization efforts such as this could be a good opportunity. Besides offering rather mundane and unexceptionable recommendations, such as improving the quality and scope of the juror source list and providing comfortable facilities for jurors, the report probes deep into the history of the jury selection process and takes a stand on the complex issue of peremptory challenges.

Second, the courts and the bar should consider the message in this report because of who the authors are. The 36 diverse members of the D.C. Jury Project, collaborating in

Improving the Jury System

There is national movement to modernize the jury system and reconnect our actions and our values about the duty to serve.

Recommendations include improving the quality and scope of the juror source list and providing comfortable facilities for jurors.

Jurors need practical training and easier access to information about the particulars of the cases before them.

a way not previously experienced by these authors, were able to avoid the typical chasm that exists between the legal and civic communities. When jurors, lawyers, and judges take the time to actually listen to one another, then their conclusions deserve special attention.

Substantive recommendations aside for a moment, one of the most gratifying and productive aspects of the D.C. Jury Project was the makeup of the committee. Instead of assembling a generic group composed entirely of like-minded lawyers and judges, the Council for Court Excellence actively recruited citizens with jury service experience as well as academicians with an interest in the field. Additionally, attorneys and businesspeople from a variety of backgrounds and viewpoints were called upon. Federal and local trial judges were included. Court administrators and jury officers rounded out the group.

The diversity of professional experience and personal background among Jury Project members was not an effort to have token representatives on the committee. Rather, the wide range of viewpoints enhanced the effectiveness of the collaborative effort. Each member was respected for his own perspective, but everyone understood that the purpose was to reach common/higher ground for the good of the overall system.

Not unlike a jury deliberation, we went about our work methodically, setting aside, when our convictions allowed, personal interests or biases that would impede true progress. It was clear at the outset that the citizen-juror members of the group were the real experts among us.

Also like deliberating jurors, committee members accepted the challenge with honesty and integrity. They struggled at times with controversial issues and differences of opinion yet continued to search for the right answers—overcoming the destructive chasm that so often divides the civic and the legal communities. Because this uncommon level of commitment and vision came from such a diverse committee and because former jurors contributed so significantly to the conclusions, the bench and bar need to listen to their consumers by giving careful consideration to all of the recommendations in *Jurors for the Year 2000 and Beyond*.

PEREMPTORY CHALLENGES

One lesson learned from this collaborative effort involves group dynamics. Since the committee comprised people who often sit opposite one other in the courtroom, perspectives and theories were bound to collide. Over time, though, committee members developed a sense of trust and respect for one another. Improper gamesmanship, cynicism, and distrust were replaced by year's end with a refreshing dose of candor and a willingness to listen. At no point in the process was this lesson in group dynamics more evident than in our discussion of jury selection and peremptory challenges.

Many members of the D.C. Jury Project believe that peremptory challenges should be abolished, and an overwhelming majority believe that if not eliminated, they should be drastically reduced.

Several two- or three-hour meetings were devoted to this topic, and the discussions were both enlightened and forthright. After much study, soul-searching, and listening to our juror colleagues, a majority of the Jury Project reached the conclusion that the peremptory challenge is inconsistent with the fundamental precepts of an impartial jury.

In *Batson v. Kentucky* (1986) and subsequent decisions over the past decade, the Supreme Court has affirmed the constitutional principle that peremptory strikes of jurors may not be exercised in our nation's trial courts to discriminate against jurors based on their race or gender, and that parties are not constitutionally entitled to peremptory strikes. Justice Thurgood Marshall, concurring in the *Batson* decision, forcefully advocated ridding trials of peremptory strikes. "The decision today will not end the racial discrimination that peremptories inject into the jury-selection process," he wrote. "That goal can be accomplished only by eliminating peremptory challenges entirely. . . . Misuse of the peremptory challenge to exclude black jurors has become both common and flagrant."

Indeed, in the experience of most trial judges on the Jury Project, attorneys in both civil and criminal cases continue to exercise peremptory strikes in a manner that, at a minimum, suggest the appearance that prospective jurors are being peremptorily stricken on the grounds of race, gender, or both. The District of Columbia Court of Appeals, as well as numerous state and federal appellate courts throughout the nation, repeatedly have found that such discrimination routinely occurs.

It is important to note that the use and abuse of peremptory challenges leaves prospective jurors and the public in general with the perception that people are being arbitrarily and discriminatorily denied the opportunity for jury service. Such a perception inevitably undermines confidence in our courts and the administration of justice.

In *The Future of Peremptory Challenges*, the Court Manager 16 (1997), G. Thomas Munsterman, director of the Center for Jury Studies of the National Center for State Courts, writes:

> The peremptory challenge is a curious feature of our jury system. Starting with randomly selected names from broadbased lists, we work hard to assemble a demographically representative panel from which to select a jury. We defend every step of the process used to arrive at that point. Then comes the swift sword of the peremptory challenge, cutting jurors from the panel with nary an explanation.

No one has recently written more thoroughly or compellingly of the need to eliminate peremptory challenges than Judge Morris Hoffman, a state trial judge in Denver, Colorado.

In *Peremptory Challenges Should Be Abolished: A Trial Judge's Perspective*, 64 U. Chi. L. Rev. 809 (1997), Hoffman carefully traces the history of the peremptory challenge and demonstrates that it is not rooted in principles of fairness, impartiality, or protection of the rights of the accused; rather, it stems from "the now meaningless and quite undemocratic concept of royal infallibility," having been "invented two hundred years before the notion of jury impartiality" was conceived.

He also observes that "the Supreme Court has consistently and unflinchingly held that the peremptory challenge is neither a constitutionally necessary component of a defendant's right to an impartial jury, nor even so fundamental as to be part of federal common law."

Indeed, there was no discussion whatsoever of peremptory challenges in the *Federalist* papers or during the Constitutional Convention, and the Constitution is "utterly silent" on the matter. As Hoffman forcefully demonstrates, efforts to subvert constitutional rights, *not* to defend them, have invigorated and sustained the practice of peremptory challenges as the "last best tool of Jim Crow" in American trials. Such challenges provide "an incredibly efficient final racial filter" to keep African Americans off juries in the South and throughout the United States.

Against this background, Hoffman shows that peremptory challenges have never had a legitimate purpose and have none today. Their genesis in England was to serve as a basis to excuse jurors for *cause*. Peremptory challenges are "decidedly undemocratic," are "susceptible to significant abuse by authorities," and are "inherently irrational." There is evidence that, notwithstanding the *Batson* decision and its progeny, they are used "in the same old way" they always have been used, "save for some nominal and meaningless extra hoops now required by *Batson*."

Judge Hoffman concludes, as do many members of the D.C. Jury Project, that the peremptory challenge is inconsistent with fundamental precepts of an impartial jury because (1) it reflects an inappropriate distrust of jurors, causing "perfectly acceptable, perfectly fair and perfectly impartial prospective jurors to be excluded in droves" and to become frustrated and cynical about the justice system; (2) it improperly shifts the focus on jury selection from the individual to the group; and (3) it injects an inappropriate level of adversariness into the jury selection process, tending to result in the selection not of impartial jurors but of jurors who are biased for one side or the other.

The foregoing considerations have persuaded a substantial majority of the D.C. Jury Project that peremptory strikes should be eliminated or drastically reduced in the District of Columbia. The project is also persuaded, however, that if peremptory strikes are eliminated, it is vital to improve the ability to ascertain grounds for strikes of jurors for cause. Relevant information about jurors should be obtained by (1) using a written questionnaire completed by all jurors and given to the court and parties upon the jury panel's arrival in the courtroom and (2) requiring that each juror be examined at least once during the voir dire process and attorneys be given a meaningful opportunity to ask follow-up questions of all jurors.

The process should be conducted so that no jurors will be called to the bench more than once. Moreover, to assure to the extent possible that prospective jurors who may be biased or partial are in fact stricken for cause, an expanded legal standard governing for-cause strikes should be established. It should mandate that when a prospective juror's demeanor or substantive response to a question during voir dire presents *any* reasonable doubt as to whether the juror can be fair and impartial, the trial judge shall strike the juror for cause at the request of any party, or on the court's own motion.

Throughout the report, the primary theme is that jurors need more institutionalized respect. When jurors arrive in a courtroom, we thank them for coming and remind them of their importance in the trial process. They are, we say with sincerity, the "other judges." Then, in more than a handful of instances, jurors and their needs are promptly forgotten. Our other actions—from the jury selection process throughout deliberations—send quite a different message about how important jurors really are.

No longer treated like judges, jurors are expected to endure a jury selection process that insults their intelligence and infects the entire judicial process with the stench of unfairness. They will likely spend countless hours waiting in the lounge or the jury room, often with no word of when they will be needed. During trial, we ask them to absorb complex and contradictory information, many times without the appropriate tools they need to fully understand and retain such information.

As Stephen Adler wrote in *The Jury*, "To build a better jury system, we need to grant jurors the perquisites of power: reasonable creature comforts, practical training in the nature of their endeavor, and easier access to information about the particulars of the cases before them." Fortunately, many judges in the District of Columbia and around the country have found ways to do this. In searching for ways to enhance the jury service experience and improve the quality of justice, the Jury Project learned from these judges.

For years, jurors have been viewed as passive recipients of often complex information. Recently, however, increasing numbers of judges and attorneys across the nation have recognized the juror education that takes place during trial.

Jurors, like students, need appropriate tools to make informed and rational decisions. We wouldn't send our children to school without pencils and paper. Why should jurors not have basic tools to do their important job? The Jury Project recommends that jurors be allowed to take notes and submit written questions for witnesses, that judges minimize sidebar conferences while the jury is in the room, that the court provide exhibit notebooks and interim summations in extended trials, and that judges offer to assist a jury that reports itself at an impasse.

How to efficiently incorporate these procedures into trials can be a part of every judge's training. What jurors want and need to do their job effectively is for such practices to be uniform throughout the court system. A citizen should have the same treatment no matter whose courtroom he reports to for jury service.

We recognize that receptivity to these recommendations will vary among those who read and ponder their contents. A recommendation may strike one person as unremarkable and a long-accepted custom, while another recommendation may appear radical or unreachable. The prime audience for one recommendation may be a juror administrator or data system designer. In other instances, a recommendation will be most relevant to a newer member of the bench or to a continuing legal education coordinator.

In any event, whether you are a jurist, policymaker, barrister, or citizen, we hope that you will engage yourself in this continuing project. In so doing, we believe, you will experience what we have: an opportunity to revisit important first principles of our jury system, join hands with a broad and talented spectrum of Washingtonians, and seek to make a genuine difference in the administration of justice in our courts. Welcome aboard.

Chapter 23

Should Juries Nullify Laws They Consider Unjust or Excessively Punitive?

by Clay S. Conrad and Nancy King

YES: JURIES CAN AND SHOULD CORRECT THE OVERLY BROAD USE OF CRIMINAL SANCTIONS

Jury nullification occurs when a criminal-trial jury refuses to convict a defendant despite proof of guilt because the jurors believe the law is unjust or is being unjustly applied. According to studies, 3 to 4 percent of jury criminal trials involve jury nullification. There is no way to prevent jury nullification because juries never can be ordered to convict or be punished for acquitting someone. A jury acquittal, under the Constitution, is final.

Juries rarely nullify irresponsibly. Consider the acquittal of Sam Skinner, a California AIDS patient prosecuted for using marijuana. The marijuana helped counteract the devastating side effects of the drug AZT and kept Skinner from wasting away. Although Skinner admitted to the facts, the jury found him not guilty because they believed the prosecution was fundamentally unjust.

Sometimes juries find defendants guilty only of lesser offenses when they believe the punishment for the charged offense is excessive. In earlier times, British law made theft of 40 shillings or more a capital offense. Juries often undervalued property so as to spare the life of the accused—including one case in which a jury found ten £10 notes to be worth 39 shillings. Jack Kevorkian's latest trial involved just that sort of amelioration. The jury found him guilty of second-degree murder despite the facts because they believed a conviction for first-degree murder would be too great.

Alternatively, it often is argued that race and prejudice lead to jury nullification more often than do considerations of justice. As common as that argument is, it doesn't hold water. During the 1960s in the trials of some who participated in crimes against civil-rights workers in the Deep South, it is true that juries returned "not guilty" verdicts. However, it also is true that sometimes prosecutors regularly refused to pursue those cases, police refused to investigate or testify honestly in them, and judges eviscerated the cases through discretionary rulings. The juries rarely were given cases justifying conviction—and then were scapegoated for failings elsewhere in the system.

These contentions are proved by the fact that federal prosecutions for violations of civil-rights laws, involving the same cases, regularly ended in convictions—before juries selected from the same communities. Different judges, prosecutors and investigators—but the same jury pool. Obviously, any racist acquittals must be explained by something other than the juries.

A recent *National Law Journal* poll revealed that three in four Americans would nullify if they believed the court's instructions would lead to injustice. That only 3 to 4 percent of jury trials end in nullification verdicts shows that, in most cases, the law is just and justly applied. In exceptional, marginal or divisive cases, however, jurors often acquit in the interests of justice—just as the Founders of this country intended.

The Founders on both sides of the ratification debate believed trial by jury was necessary to prevent governmental overreaching. Thomas Jefferson said it was the only way to anchor government to constitutional principles. Alexander Hamilton said it was the surest protection of the people's liberties. Theophilus Parsons, first chief justice of Massachusetts, said in the Constitutional Convention: "The people themselves have it in their power effectually to resist usurpation, without being driven to an appeal to arms. An act of usurpation is not obligatory; it is not law; and any man may be justified in his resistance. Let him be considered as a criminal by the general government, yet only his fellow-citizens can convict him; they are his jury, and if they pronounce him innocent, not all the powers of Congress can hurt him; and innocent they certainly will pronounce him, if the supposed law he resisted was an act of usurpation."

Many important colonial trials ended in nullification. American jurors knew they could refuse to enforce unjust laws. Early jurors routinely were informed by courts of their right to try the law as well as the fact, and lawyers regularly argued the merits of the law to the jury. The independent role of juries was well-accepted in early American law.

It was not until the mid-19th century that courts began to question the jury's independent voice. Judges attempted to bind juries to their instructions and began prohibiting lawyers from arguing law to the jury. The Supreme Court allowed such practices to stand, and today many judges wrongly believe they are forbidden to allow jury nullification to be discussed in court.

American courts have not always been so reluctant to trust the conscientious judgments of juries. In the early years of this country, the Supreme Court itself occasionally heard cases with a jury. In 1794, Justice John Jay, for a unanimous Supreme Court, instructed a jury: "It may not be amiss, here, gentlemen, to remind you of the good old rule, that on questions of fact, it is the province of the jury, on questions of law, it is the province of the court to decide. But it must be observed that by the same law, which recognizes this reasonable distribution of jurisdiction, you have nevertheless a right to take upon yourselves to judge of both, and to determine the law as well as the fact in controversy. On this, and on every other occasion, however, we have no doubt, you will pay that respect, which is due to the opinion of the court: For, as on the one hand, it is presumed, that juries are the best judges of fact; it is, on the other hand, presumable, that the courts are the best judges of the law. But still both objects are lawfully within your power of decision."

These instructions meticulously delineate the roles of bench and jury. The court instructed the jury on a general rule, which allowed for exceptions. They admonished the jury to take their instructions with respect, yet acknowledged that the jury could not be bound by them. These instructions fostered juror independence and responsibility, not jury lawlessness or wanton disregard for the rights of the parties. Similar instructions could assist jurors in delivering fair, just verdicts today—making sure the law is applied in a manner in which the citizens of this country approve and giving us a legal system of which again we could be proud. The Fully Informed Jury Association, a Section 501(c)(3) [tax-exempt] educational organization with a mission to inform potential jurors of their right to nullify unjust laws, has provided model initiatives to allow for just such instructions. These initiatives have been introduced by legislators in more than a dozen states.

What would be the result of informing jurors about their power to nullify the law in the interests of justice? Perhaps better questions would be: [Was] the criminal law applied more or less fairly in 1999 than it was in 1799? Is it more or less a source of social divisiveness and tension? Has the criminal sanction been wrested from providing social protection to become a tool for social engineering?

Criminal law often is a divisive factor in society. The nonsensical distinctions between powder and crack cocaine; enormous penalties for many minor crimes; unfair sentencing favoritism given to snitches (who serve a small fraction of the time given their underlings); criminalization of "wetlands" violations; regulatory, licensing and administrative infractions; and the often-mechanical application of law favored by prosecutors have resulted in a hodgepodge of injustices strung together without rhyme or reason. Apologists who claim a society must have rules miss the point—a just society has to have just rules. Juries, by refusing to enforce unjust rules, can help improve the law and the society it governs.

Courts usually pretend injustices under law cannot occur. They can and too often do. As Judge Thomas Wiseman noted, "Congress is not yet an infallible body incapable of passing tyrannical laws." Occasionally, jurors follow their instructions, then leave court in tears, ashamed of their verdict.

This sort of thing is not supposed to happen in America. It isn't justice. If being a juror means anything, it should mean never having to say you're sorry. If the law is just and justly applied, jurors should be proud of their verdict and confident that any sentences meted out are well-deserved. Then we will engender respect for the law because, as Justice Louis Brandeis observed, for the law to be respected it first must be respectable.

What happens when a jury nullifies a law? One factually guilty person is acquitted in the interests of justice. If a particular law frequently is nullified, the legislature should bring the law into conformity with the judgment of the community. If the law is being misapplied, the legislature may make the law more specific or prosecutors may quit applying it overbroadly. The law is improved, and injustices are prevented.

Does jury nullification lead to anarchy—or is it democracy in action, allowing citizens to participate in the administration of justice? The concept that jury nullification is anarchy has been bandied about without analysis or justification in the face of juries being given nullification instructions for the first century of this country's existence without collapse into anarchy. Jury nullification does not eliminate law—it regulates it, allowing the people's perception of justice, not the government's, to prevail. It takes a true authoritarian to call such vital citizen participation in governmental decisionmaking "anarchy."

Trial by jury, according to the Supreme Court, exists to prevent oppression by government. It is easy to see that an occasionally oppressive government does not like to have its powers limited. However, those of us who someday may find ourselves on the other side of the equation should be grateful that the Founders of this country had the foresight and wisdom to install this safety valve, this elegant and time-tested mechanism to anchor our government to the principles of its Constitution. It would be a disgrace to those same Founders to be unwilling to utilize this safety valve today, when circumstances indicate it would be appropriate to do so.

NO: DON'T GIVE SOCIETY'S MAVERICKS ANOTHER TOOL TO SUBVERT THE WILL OF THE PEOPLE

Inviting jurors to acquit regardless of what the law says is a tempting cure-all for the law's ills. But cultivating jury nullification is a mistake. Like the peddler's elixir, jury nullification is just as likely to produce unpleasant side effects as it is to bring relief. The most compelling reasons to be wary of the practice of jury nullification are the very arguments its advocates trot out in its defense—history, democracy, fairness, political change and the Constitution itself.

One does not have to look back far into history to find a good reason for discouraging jury nullification. True, the colonists embraced the jury's power as a weapon against the king's oppressive laws. And, we're reminded, juries bravely blocked prosecutions of those who resisted the Fugitives Slave Act, Prohibition, and the Vietnam War draft. But jury nullification has not been neatly confined to the rejection of "bad" law or the release of "good" defendants. A much less appealing pattern of jury lawlessness is also prominent in our nation's history. For generations juries have refused to convict or punish those who clearly are guilty of violence against unpopular victims, particularly African-Americans. The Klan Act, barring Ku Klux Klan sympathizers from juries after the Civil War, was passed because juries were exercising their "independence" to ignore civil-rights statutes. In Texas after the Civil War, prosecutors had to strike from juries those who "believe, morally, socially, politically, or religiously, that it is not murder for a white man to take the life of a [N]egro with malice aforethought." This is not a proud legacy. We should not assume that refusal to punish those who harm members of less popular groups is entirely behind us just because some juries, in some places, are more racially diverse than they used to be.

Racism, of course, is not the only risk. To invite nullification is to invite jurors to devise their own defenses to criminal charge. All three branches of government may have labored to eliminate similar considerations from the assessment of guilt. Juries have acquitted defendants in rape cases after concluding that the victims deserved to be raped because of the way they dressed or acted. Jurors may acquit protesters who trespass, damage property or harm others if they conclude the defendants were right to bypass lawful means of redress. Jurors may believe that reasonable doubt is not a strong-enough burden of proof and require fingerprints or eyewitnesses before convicting. They may decide that certain conduct by the police should be a complete defense, oblivious of efforts by legislators and judges to craft remedies and regulations for police misconduct. Now, as in the past, encouraging "good" nullification inevitably means encouraging "bad" nullification as well, because there is no way to second guess a jury's acquittal once delivered.

It is not feasible to try to separate "good" nullification from "bad." Even nullification advocates cannot agree on what type of nullification is acceptable. One supporter would require nullification instructions only in cases involving non-violent acts of civil disobedience where the defendant had "given serious thought" to legal means of accomplishing the same objective. Another would encourage jury pronouncements on the law only when the issue was the constitutionality of a criminal statute. A third insists that "true" nullification is limited to decisions "based on conscientious grounds." In a recent survey, college students were asked whether jury nullification included any combination of a set of possible reasons for acquittal, all of which the researchers believed were valid reasons for juries to nullify, such as, "The police wrongfully assaulted the defendant after he was arrested." When only 13 percent of those surveyed agreed that nullification included all of the reasons listed, the researchers concluded their subjects had a lot to learn about nullification. The response should suggest something else—that it is wishful thinking to assume that legislators or judges will be able to agree when jurors should ignore the law and when they should not.

One might support expanding the lawmaking role of the jury if one believes juries are an essential feature of our democracy, better at assessing whether a law is "just" or "unjust" than democratically elected legislators. But juries probably are much worse at this task. Unlike legislators or electors, jurors have no opportunity to investigate or research the merits of legislation. Carefully stripped of those who know anything about the type of case or conduct at stake, juries are insulated from the information they would need to make reliable judgments about the costs and benefits, the justice or the injustices, of a particular criminal prohibition. Nor can jurors seek out information during the case. The so-called "safety valve" of jury nullification, which exempts a defendant here and there from the reach of a controversial law, actually reduces the pressure for those opposed to a truly flawed statute to lobby for its repeal or amendment and deprives appellate courts of opportunities to declare its flaws.

Nullification's supporters point out that legislatures cannot anticipate unfair applications of the laws they enact, so jury nullification is needed for "fine-tuning." But jurors are not in any better position than judges or prosecutors to decide which defendants should be exempted from a law's reach. Again, jurors probably are much worse at this function because they lack critical information. Any juror who actually knows the defendant is excused from the jury. Jurors only can speculate on the penalty that would follow from their verdict: Unless the defendant testifies (and most defendants do not), the jury will never hear him explain his side of the story nor learn whether he has a prior record. They may never learn of evidence suppressed because it was illegally obtained or because of other errors on the part of the prosecution. More importantly, because jurors decide only one case, they cannot compare the culpability of different defendants or assess the relative importance of enforcing a particular prohibition against a particular defendant. No doubt about it: Juries are excellent fact finders and lie detectors. But when facts are not in issue and guilt is clear, the ability of jurors to reach sound decisions about when the law should be suspended and when it should be applied is questionable at best.

Jury nullification sometimes is touted as an effective political tool for those who have failed at the voting booth and on the legislative floor. There are two problems with this argument. First, if a group is not influential enough to obtain favorable legislation, it is not likely to secure a majority in the jury box. At most, jurors with dissenting views succeed in hanging the jury. But hung juries are a political dead end. The defendant is not spared; he can be tried again and convicted. More importantly, as a recent recommendation in California demonstrates, rising hung-jury rates inevitably lead to proposals to eliminate the unanimity requirement, proposals that if adopted would shut down minority viewpoints more effectively than any instruction against nullification ever could.

Even if a politically unsuccessful group finds strength in some local jury boxes, should we really be heartened by the prospect of being stuck with the decision of 12 people who have been encouraged to ignore the pronouncements of the state or nation's elected representatives? If there is a concentrated population of homophobes, racists, or anti-Semites in my state, I, for one, do not want judges and lawyers encouraging jurors drawn from these communities to apply their own standards—standards that may vary with the victim's sexual orientation, race or religion. Local dissent, of course, is not limited to group-based views. People disagree strongly about a variety of laws—laws against possessing weapons, euthanasia, driving after a couple of drinks, the use of marijuana, slapping one's wife or children around or the dumping of paint or oil. There are places well-suited for resolving these disagreements: the legislature and the polling booth. Our democratic process should not be jettisoned arbitrarily by an unelected group of citizens who need never explain themselves.

Finally, the Constitution does not support an enhanced law-making role for juries. Jurors have no personal constitutional right to disregard the law—otherwise, they would not be required to take an oath to obey it. Nor do defendants have constitutional right to insist that jurors be given the opportunity to disregard the law. True, judges cannot overturn a conviction or acquittal without the consent of the defendant (through appeal, motion or otherwise). But this rule is in place not because the Constitution considers the jury a superior lawmaker but because the Fifth Amendment prohibits the government from putting the defendant in jeopardy of life or limb more than once for the same offense. Judges also are barred from directing verdicts of guilt, but only because the Sixth Amendment guarantees to the defendant a jury's assessment of the facts.

Beyond what is necessary to protect these important interests of the accused, our refusal to tolerate jury nullification must not stray. Judges, for example, should continue to avoid seating jurors who cannot or will not promise to follow the judge's instructions; continue to prohibit argument and deny instructions concerning defenses not supported by the evidence; continue to instruct jurors about the law and require them to follow these instructions; and continue to prohibit nullification advocates from approaching jurors with nullification propaganda (just as they bar prosecution sympathizers from lobbying the jury for conviction). Although each of these practices is designed to prevent jury nullification, each is constitutional because the Constitution does not protect jury nullification itself. It protects a defendant's right to fact-finding by a jury and to the finality of a verdict.

Legislators and judges so far steadfastly have rejected repeated proposals to lower barriers to jury nullification because they understand that the costs of such changes would far outweigh any benefits they may bring. Other fundamental changes in our jury system, such as the Supreme Court's decision to ban race-based peremptory challenges as a violation of the equal-protection rights of potential jurors, have been preceded by sustained social, political and legal critique of the status quo. A similar groundswell to cede more power to those who sit in jury boxes in criminal cases has never existed and, fortunately, probably never will.

Chapter 24

Truth in Sentencing in State Prisons

by Paula M. Ditton and Doris James Wilson, BJS Statisticians

The amount of time offenders serve in prison is almost always shorter than the time they are sentenced to serve by the court. Prisoners released in 1996 served on average 30 months in prison and jail or 44% of their sentence. Many states have recently enacted a truth-in-sentencing law which requires offenders to serve a substantial portion of their sentence and reduces the discrepancy between the sentence imposed and actual time served in prison.

In the early 1970s, states followed an indeterminate sentencing model in which a parole board decided when an offender would be released from prison. Pressure for longer sentences and uniform punishment led to mandatory minimums and sentencing guidelines in the 1980s. However, prison crowding, good-time sentence reductions for satisfactory prison behavior, and earned-time resulted in the early release of prisoners.

To assure that offenders serve a large portion of their sentence, the U.S. Congress authorized funding for additional state prisons and jails through the Violent Crime Control and Law Enforcement Act of 1994. In 1998, incentive grants were awarded to 27 states and the District of Columbia that met the eligibility criteria for the truth-in-sentencing program. Another 13 states have adopted a truth-in-sentencing law requiring certain offenders to serve a specific percentage of their sentence.

Data were compiled from multiple sources

The findings in this report are based primarily on data from the Bureau of Justice Statistics [BJS], National Corrections Reporting Program (NCRP), and data collected through the Violent Offender Incarceration and Truth-in-Sentencing (VOI/TIS) Incentive Grants program, administered by the Office of Justice Programs Corrections Program Office.

Since 1983, BJS has compiled the NCRP data series that collects individual inmate records for prison admissions and releases and parole discharges. It is the only national level data base with information on sentence length, time to be served in prison, actual time served by released prisoners, time served on parole, type of parole discharge, and offense composition of inmates entering and exiting prison and parole. The annual series includes prison population movement data and parole population data, providing a comprehensive description of offenders as they enter and exit correctional custody and supervision.

During the 1990s between 35 and 41 states have participated in NCRP. In 1996, 37 states and the California Youth Authority reported 469,650 admissions that represented 91% of all admissions to state prisons, based on data from the BJS National Pris-

Source: *Bureau of Justice Statistics* Special Report, January 1999

Highlights

Three decades of sentencing reform—1970s through 1990s

- *Intermediate sentencing:* Common in the early 1970s, parole boards have the authority to release offenders from prison.
- *Determine sentencing:* States introduced fixed prison terms which could be reduced by good-time or earned-time credits.
- *Mandatory minimum sentences:* States added statutes requiring offenders to be sentenced to a specified amount of prison time.
- *Sentencing guidelines:* States established sentencing commissions and created ranges of sentences for given offenses and offender characteristics.
- *Truth in sentencing:* First enacted in 1984, truth-in-sentencing laws require offenders to serve a substantial portion of their prison sentence. Parole eligibility and good-time credits are restricted or eliminated.

- Violent offenders released from prison in 1996 were sentenced to serve an average of 85 months in prison. Prior to release they served about half of their prison sentence or 45 months.
- Under truth-in-sentencing laws requiring 85% of the sentence, violent offenders would serve an average of 88 months in prison based on the average sentence for violent offenders admitted to prison in 1996.
- Nearly 7 in 10 state prison admissions for a violent offense in 1997 were in states requiring offenders to serve at least 85% of their sentence.
- By 1998, 27 states and the District of Columbia met the federal Truth-in-Sentencing Incentive Grants program eligibility criteria. Eleven states adopted truth-in-sentencing laws in 1995, 1 year after the 1994 Crime Act.

oner Statistics data collection. The releases reported (427,627) represented 91% of all releases from state prison in 1996.

All 50 states and the District of Columbia reported data through the VOI/TIS Incentive Grants program as part of the data collection for determining grant eligibility. The VOI/TIS data provide an additional state-level indicator of time served with a common definition of violent offenses. For each year between 1993 and 1997, states reported the number of admissions and releases for Part 1 violent offenses and sentence length and time served by released violent offenders. Part 1 violent crimes include murder/nonnegligent manslaughter, rape, robbery, and aggravated assault.

Sentencing reforms parallel "get tough on crime" attitude

Sentencing reform policies have paralleled the mood of the country on crime and punishment, shifting between requiring a fixed prison time prior to release or allowing discretionary release of offenders by judges, parole boards, or corrections officials. Over the last two decades, sentencing requirements and release policies have become more restrictive, primarily in response to widespread "get tough on crime" attitudes in the nation. (See References on pages 306-307 for sources on sentencing reform.)

In the early 1970s, states generally permitted parole boards to determine when an offender would be released from prison. In addition, good-time reductions for satisfactory prison behavior, earned-time incentives for participation in work or educational programs, and other time reductions to control prison crowding resulted in the early release of prisoners. These policies permitted officials to individualize the amount of punishment or leniency an offender received and provided means to manage the prison population.

Such discretion in sentencing and release policies led to criticism that some offenders were punished more harshly than others for similar offenses and to complaints that overall sentencing and release laws were too soft on criminals. By the late 1970s and early 1980s, states began developing sentencing guidelines, enacting mandatory minimum sentences, and adopting other sentencing reforms to reduce disparity in sentencing and to toughen penalties for certain offenses, specifically drug offenses (as part of the "war on drugs"), offenses with weapons, and offenses committed by repeat or habitual criminals.[1]

Washington State enacted the first truth-in-sentencing law in 1984

States continued to increase the severity of sentencing laws (primarily for violent offenders) by enacting restrictions on the possibility of early release, which became known as truth in sentencing. Truth-in-sentencing laws require offenders to serve a substantial portion of the prison sentence imposed by the court before being eligible for release. Previous policies which reduced the amount of time an offender served on a sentence, such as good-time, earned-time, and parole board release, are restricted or eliminated under truth-in-sentencing laws. The definition of truth in sentencing varies among the states, as do the percentage of sentence required to be served and the crimes covered by the laws. Most states have targeted violent offenders under truth in sentencing.

A few states, such as Florida, Mississippi, and Ohio, require all offenders to serve a substantial portion of the sentence before being eligible for release. The percentage of sentence required to be served under truth in sentencing in general spans from 50% to 100% of a minimum sentence (table 1).

Most truth-in-sentencing states require offenders to serve 85% of the prison sentence

In response to prison crowding and public dismay with the early release of prisoners, the U.S. Congress authorized incentive grants to build or expand correctional facilities through the Violent Offender Incarceration and Truth-in-Sentencing Incentive Grants program in the 1994 Crime Act (Pub.L. No. 103-322, 108 Stat. 1796 [1994]). To qualify for the truth-in-sentencing grants, states must require persons convicted of a Part 1 violent crime to serve not less than 85% of the prison sentence. Along with other exceptions, states may qualify by demonstrating that the average time served in prison is not less than 85% of the sentence.[2]

Twenty-seven states and the District of Columbia qualified for the federal grant program in 1998 (table 1). Five states (Delaware, Minnesota, Tennessee, Utah, and Washington) adopted truth in sentencing prior to the 1994 Crime Act. Arizona, California, Missouri, and North Carolina enacted truth in sentencing in 1994, and 11 states enacted laws in 1995, 1 year after the Crime Act (Connecticut, Florida, Georgia, Kansas, Maine, Michigan, Mississippi, New York, North Dakota, Oregon, and Virginia).

Several states have not adopted the federal 85% standard. Maryland and Texas have a 50%-requirement for violent offenders. Nebraska and Indiana require all offenders to serve 50% of the sentence. Arkansas requires certain offenders to serve 70%. Colorado

TABLE 1.   Truth-in-Sentencing Requirements, by State

Meet federal 85% requirement		50% requirement	100% of minimum requirement	Other requirements
Arizona	Missouri	Indiana	Idaho	Alaska[c]
California	New Jersey	Maryland	Nevada	Arkansas[d]
Connecticut	New York	Nebraska	New Hampshire	Colorado[e]
Delaware	North Carolina	Texas		Kentucky[f]
District of Col.	North Dakota			Massachusetts[g]
Florida	Ohio			Wisconsin[h]
Georgia	Oklahoma[b]			
Illinois[a]	Oregon			
Iowa	Pennsylvania			
Kansas	South Carolina			
Louisiana	Tennessee			
Maine	Utah			
Michigan	Virginia			
Minnesota	Washington			
Mississippi				

[a] Qualified for federal funding in 1996 only.
[b] Effective July 1, 1999, offenders will be required to serve 85% of the sentence.
[c] Two-part sentence structure (2/3 in prison; 1/3 on parole); 100% of prison term required.
[d] Mandatory 70% of sentence for certain violent offenses and manufacture of methamphetamine.
[e] Violent offenders with 2 prior violent convictions serve 75%; 1 prior violent conviction, 56.25%.
[f] Effective July 15, 1998, offenders are required to serve 85% of the sentence.
[g] Requires 75% of a minimum prison sentence.
[h] Effective December 31, 1999, 2-part sentence: offenders serve 100% of the prison term and a sentence of extended supervision at 25% of the prison sentence.

requires violent offenders with two prior violent convictions to serve 75% and with one prior violent conviction, 56%. Massachusetts requires 75% of a minimum prison sentence.

14 states have abolished parole board release for all offenders

Fourteen states have abolished early release by discretion of a parole board for all of-fenders. Seven states abolished parole board release within the last 10 years. Eight states abolished parole board release during the same year a truth-in-sentencing law was passed (Arizona, Delaware, Kansas, Mississippi, Ohio, Virginia, Washington, and Wisconsin). Parole boards still have discretion over inmates who were sentenced for crimes commit-ted prior to the effective date of the law that eliminated parole board release.

A few other states have abolished parole board release for certain violent or felony of-fenders (Alaska, New York, Tennessee, and Virginia) or for certain crimes against a per-son (Louisiana). California allows discretionary release by a parole board only for offenders with indeterminate life sentences. In general, states restrict the possibility of parole board release based on the offender's criminal history or the circumstances of the offense.

Abolished Discretionary Parole Board Release for All Offenders[a]

State	Year
Arizona	1994
Delaware	1990
Florida[b]	1983
Illinois	1978
Indiana	1977
Kansas[c]	1993
Maine	1975
Minnesota	1980
Mississippi	1995
North Carolina	1994
Ohio[d]	1996
Oregon	1989
Washington	1984
Wisconsin	1999

Note: California allows discretional release by a parole board only for offenders with indeterminate life sentences. New Mexico's parole board has limited discretion to approve release plans.
[a] For offenses committed after the effective date of the law.
[b] In 1995 parole eligibility was abolished for offenses with a life sentence and a 25-year mandatory term.
[c] Excluded a few offenses, primarily first-degree murder and intentional second-degree murder. Truth in sentencing passed in 1993; it was amended in 1995 to meet the 85% requirement.
[d] Excluded murder and aggravated murder.

While discretionary release from prison by a parole board has been eliminated by some states, post-release supervision still exists and is generally referred to as community or supervised release. Parole boards, in various forms, have the responsibility to set conditions of release for offenders under conditional or supervised release, the authority to return an offender to prison for violating the conditions of parole or supervised release, and the power to grant parole for medical reasons.

Between 1990 and 1997 the number of offenders in state prison increased 7% annually

As a result of truth-in-sentencing practices, the state prison population is expected to increase through the incarceration of more offenders for longer periods of time. One purpose of the VOI/TIS incentive grants is to enable states to manage prison capacity by providing funds to increase prison beds for violent offenders.

On average, between 1990 and 1997 the prison population grew by 7% annually. State prison inmates totaled 1,100,850 in 1997, up from 689,577 in 1990 (table 2). Most of the growth occurred among violent offenders who accounted for 50% of the total increase in State prison inmates. Drug offenders comprised about 19% of the growth and property offenders, 16%.

TABLE 2.   **Trends in State Prison Population and Admissions, 1990–97**

Year	Year-end population[a]	Number of admissions[b]
1990	689,577	460,739
1991	732,914	466,285
1992	780,571	480,676
1993	857,675	475,100
1994	936,896	498,919
1995	1,001,359	521,970
1996	1,048,004	512,618
1997	1,100,850	540,748

Note: Includes only offenders with a sentence of more than 1 year.
[a] Sentenced prisoners under state jurisdiction.
[b] Excludes escapees, AWOLs returned, and transfers to other jurisdictions.

State prison admission rates have dropped

While the number of inmates held in state prisons increased 60% since 1990, the number admitted to prison increased about 17%. In 1997, 540,748 offenders were admitted to state prison, up from 460,739 in 1990. The number of admissions relative to the number of inmates in prison dropped from 73 per 100 state prisoners in 1990 to 52 per 100 in 1997.

During this period the source of admissions to prison also changed. New court commitments to state prison, or offenders admitted to prison under a new sentence, increased slightly between 1990 and 1997 (from 323,069 to 334,630), while parole violators represented an increased portion of prison admissions.

The most recent data on admissions by offense type reveal that offenders incarcerated for violent offenses increased, up from 86,600 in 1990 to 96,300 in 1996 (table 3). New court commitments for property and drug offenders decreased between 1990 and 1996.

TABLE 3.   **Sentenced Prisoners Under State Jurisdiction and New Court Commitments to State Prison, By Offense, 1990 and 1996**

Offense	Sentenced prisoners under state jurisdiction		New court commitments to state prison	
	1990	1996	1990	1996
Total	689,577	1,048,004	323,069	326,547
Violent	315,900	495,400	86,600	96,300
Property	175,000	240,000	104,400	94,800
Drug	149,700	237,600	102,400	98,700
Public-order	45,800	71,300	26,000	34,600

Note: Sentenced prisoners under state jurisdiction by offense were estimated. See "Methodology" on page 304 for details.

Over a Third of Prison Admissions in 1997 were Parole Violators

The percentage of prison admissions who were returned for a parole violation has steadily increased since 1985. Parole violators accounted for 23% of prison admissions in 1985, 29% in 1990, 34% in 1994, and 35%, by 1997.

Two-thirds of parole violators were drug or property offenders: 31% of parole violators were drug offenders, and 16% were burglary offenders. Violent offenders accounted for 25% of those returned to prison on a parole revocation; nearly 11% were originally sentenced to prison for robbery.

Year	Percent of admissions to State prison	
	New court commitments	Parole violators
1985	76.1%	23.4%
1990	70.1	29.1
1991	68.0	30.5
1992	69.5	29.5
1993	66.9	30.8
1994	64.7	33.8
1995	64.7	33.7
1996	63.7	33.7
1997	61.9	34.5

Note: Includes only offenders with a sentence of more than 1 year. Excludes escapees, AWOLs returned, and transfers to other jurisdictions.

Most serious offense	Percent of admissions to state prison, 1996	
	New court commitments	Parole revocations
All offenses	100.0%	100.0%
Violent offenses	29.5%	24.5%
Murder/nonnegligent manslaughter	2.7	1.4
Rape	1.9	1.4
Other sexual assault	4.1	2.4
Robbery	9.1	10.9
Assault	8.7	6.7
Property offenses	29.0%	35.1%
Burglary	12.0	15.7
Larceny/theft	7.5	9.7
Motor vehicle theft	2.1	3.7
Drug offenses	30.2%	31.0%
Possession	8.0	7.0
Trafficking	17.2	16.1
Public-order offenses	10.6%	8.1%

Note: Includes only offenders with a sentence of more than 1 year. Detail may not add to total.

The commitment rate for murder rose from 460 per 1,000 arrests in 1990 to 613 per 1,000 in 1996

In contrast to the increase in the number of incarcerated violent offenders and the slight increase in admissions overall, arrests for the major violent crimes (except for aggravated assault) actually declined between 1990 and 1996. Arrests for murder dropped 19%; rape, 18%; other sexual assault, 13%; and robbery, 16%. There was also a sharp decline in burglary arrests (21%) (table 4).

At the same time, the commitment rate, or the number of new court commitments to state prison relative to the number of arrests, increased for most violent offenses between 1990 and 1996. The number of admissions to state prison for murder per 1,000 arrests rose from 460 in 1990 to 613 in 1996, almost reaching the high of 621 admissions per 1,000 arrests in 1980.

The likelihood of going to prison upon arrest for drug offenses substantially increased between 1980 and 1990 as the commitment rate soared from 19 per 1,000 arrests to 103 per 1,000. The rate dropped to 77 commitments per 1,000 arrests in 1996. For property offenders the commitment rate also increased between 1980 and 1990 and remained relatively constant between 1990 and 1996.

TABLE 4. Adult Arrests and New Court Commitments to State Prison Per 1,000 Arrests, by Offense, 1980, 1990, And 1996

Most serious offense	Number of adult arrests			Number of new court commitments to state prison per 1,000 arrests		
	1980	1990	1996	1980	1990	1996
Violent offenses						
Murder	18,200	19,800	16,100	621	460	613
Rape	26,700	33,300	27,400	182	229	219
Other sexual assault	55,600	90,500	78,600	61	112	177
Robbery	102,200	127,400	106,700	245	233	277
Aggravated assault	236,600	410,800	445,005	45	56	62
Property offenses						
Burglary	282,800	290,000	229,700	107	160	165
Larceny/theft	745,300	1,088,700	983,900	14	24	27
Motor vehicle theft	75,600	119,800	102,600	40	72	72
Fraud	358,800	382,100	565,400	19	24	24
Drug offenses	471,200	1,008,300	1,294,700	19	103	77
Weapons Offenses	141,200	181,000	163,400	11	34	55

Note: Arrest data were obtained from the FBI's Uniform Crime Reporting program. Data on new court commitments by offense were estimated and include offenders with a sentence of more than 1 year. See "Methodology" on page 304 for details.

The implementation of truth-in-sentencing laws

The phase-in of truth-in-sentencing requirements, or the number of offenders sentenced under the new law, may vary considerably by state. Differences in the effective date of the law, court backlogs, case processing, and the type of offenders covered under the law (violent offenders versus all offenders) may affect the number of prison admissions sentenced under truth in sentencing.

Monthly data on the percentage of prison admissions sentenced under truth-in-sentencing laws in Nevada, New York, and Virginia demonstrate the lag between the effective date of truth in sentencing and the subsequent admission of offenders to prison covered under the new law.

At 12 months, 57% of New York's violent felony prison admissions were under truth in sentencing

Under a truth-in-sentencing law which became effective October 1, 1995, New York requires repeat violent felony offenders to serve at least 85% of the sentence. The law requires first-time violent felony offenders to serve 85% based on a presumptive sentence set at [two-thirds] of the maximum.

By August 1998, 3 years after the effective date, 94% of violent felony offenders admitted to prison were sentenced under the 1995 truth-in-sentencing law. A more recent law, effective September 1, 1998, requires first-time violent felons to serve 85% of a determinate sentence.

In Nevada nearly 80% of prison admissions were under truth-in-sentencing requirements, 3 years after implementation of the law

Effective for crimes committed after July 1, 1995, Nevada's truth-in-sentencing law requires all offenders to serve 100% of the minimum prison term prior to becoming eligible for parole release. Offenders are allowed to earn good-time reductions off the maximum prison sentence, but not the minimum. Six months after the effective date, 28% of offenders admitted to Nevada's prisons were sentenced under the truth-in-sentencing law. After 1 year the number increased to 43%, and after 2 years, 60%. After 3 years, 79% of prison admissions were sentenced under truth in sentencing.

Virginia estimates 100% truth-in-sentencing admissions by yearend 1999

Virginia implemented a truth-in-sentencing law on January 1, 1995, requiring all felony offenders to serve 85% of the sentence. A year after the effective date, 74% of prison admissions were sentenced under truth in sentencing; 39% were admitted under truth in sentencing only and about 35% under both truth in sentencing and the old parole system. These offenders were returned for a new offense sentenced under truth in sentencing and a prior offense under the parole system (old law). Five years after implementation, or yearend 1999, Virginia estimates 100% of admissions will be sentenced under truth in sentencing.

Nearly 40% of all female, black, and Hispanic prison admissions were drug offenders

Thirty-seven percent of black offenders, 40% of Hispanics, and 39% of females admitted to prison in 1996 had committed a drug offense. Black and Hispanic inmates were nearly twice as likely as white inmates to be admitted to prison for a drug offense.

Women were most likely to be admitted to prison for a drug offense (39%) or property offense (36%). Almost 31% of all men admitted to prison in 1996 had committed a violent offense, compared to 17% of women. Slightly less than a third of admissions in each racial and ethnic group had committed a violent offense. White offenders were more likely to be admitted to prison for a property offense (38%), particularly burglary (16%).

New Court Commitments to State Prison, 1996: Offense, by Sex, Race, and Hispanic Origin

	Male	Female	White*	Black*	Hispanic
All offenses	100%	100%	100%	100%	100%
Violent offenses	30.8%	17.3%	28.7%	29.5%	30.2%
Murder/nonnegligent manslaughter	2.9	2.2	2.3	2.9	3.3
Negligent manslaughter	1.1	1.4	1.4	1.0	0.9
Rape	2.1	0.2	2.9	1.3	1.4
Other sexual assault	4.5	0.5	6.7	2.0	4.3
Robbery	9.6	5.0	5.4	12.2	8.9
Assault	9.0	6.0	7.9	8.8	9.7
Other violent	1.7	1.9	2.2	1.4	1.7
Property offenses	28.3%	36.0%	38.1%	24.9%	20.0%
Burglary	12.6	5.9	16.1	9.5	9.7
Larceny/theft	6.8	13.6	9.0	7.3	4.1
Motor vehicle theft	2.2	1.0	2.2	1.7	2.7
Fraud	3.1	12.8	6.0	3.5	1.3
Other property	3.6	2.8	4.8	2.9	2.2
Drug offenses	29.3%	39.1%	18.7%	36.8%	39.7%
Possession	7.7	11.2	6.1	9.9	8.0
Trafficking	17.0	19.3	9.1	20.8	26.8
Other/unspecified drug	4.6	8.6	3.6	6.1	5.0
Public-order offenses	11.0%	6.8%	13.7%	8.2%	9.3%
Other offenses	0.6%	0.7%	0.8%	0.5%	0.8%

Note: Includes only offenders with a sentence of more than 1 year. Detail may not add to total.
*Excludes inmates of Hispanic origin.

Nearly 7 in 10 violent offenders are in a state that requires 85% of the sentence be served

Based on data reported through the VOI/TIS program, state facilities reported that 78,917 new court commitments were admitted to prison for a Part 1 violent offense in 1997. About two-thirds (54,023) of those admissions were in a truth-in-sentencing state that met the federal standard, requiring violent offenders to serve at least 85% of their sentence prior to release. Over 90% of Part 1 violent offenders admitted to prison in 1997 were in a state that had passed a law requiring at least 50% of the sentence be served prior to release.

Despite the large proportion of offenders being admitted in states with truth-in-sentencing laws, not all of these offenders were sentenced under truth in sentencing. Due to the time lag between commission of the offense, arrest, and conviction, some offenders entering prison in 1997 committed the offense prior to the effective date of recently enacted truth-in-sentencing laws. In 1997, an estimated 42% of all Part 1 violent offenders admitted to prison were actually sentenced under a truth-in-sentencing law that met the federal standard requiring at least 85% of the sentence be served in prison.

Offenders admitted to prison in 1996 for robbery were expected to serve 7 months longer than in 1990

Although recent sentencing reforms are linked to increasing time served, the average (or mean) sentence length imposed on offenders entering prison decreased, from 72 months in 1990 to 68 months in 1996 (table 5). Consistent with sentencing policy change, the projected minimum time expected to be served by persons entering prison increased slightly. If parole eligibility requirements, good-time credits, and early release policies are taken into account, persons entering state prisons in 1996 were expected to serve a minimum of 42 months in prison, up from 40 months in 1990.

For violent offenders the average imposed sentence decreased from 107 months in 1990 to 104 months in 1996, while the expected time to be served increased. On aver-

Table 5.   New Court Commitments to State Prison, 1990 and 1996: Average Sentence Length and Minimum Time to be Served

Most serious offense	Mean maximum sentence length[a]		Mean minimum time to be served[b]	
	1990	1996	1990	1996
All offenses	72 mo	68 mo	40 mo	42 mo
Violent offenses	107 mo	104 mo	67 mo	70 mo
Murder/nonnegligent manslaughter	233	253	176	215
Negligent manslaughter	106	117	63	61
Rape	153	140	90	72
Other sexual assault	97	107	62	64
Robbery	101	101	53	60
Assault	74	72	49	46
Other violent	96	82	70	54
Property offenses	62 mo	54 mo	31 mo	30 mo
Burglary	75	67	37	37
Larceny/theft	50	43	24	25
Motor vehicle theft	51	41	27	29
Fraud	54	47	23	22
Drug offenses	63 mo	57 mo	30 mo	32 mo
Possession	62	51	24	30
Trafficking	66	62	33	34
Public-order offenses	41 mo	44 mo	26 mo	25 mo
Number of admissions	278,417	266,705	129,489	128,863

Note: Includes only offenders with a sentence of more than 1 year. Excludes sentences of life without parole, life plus additional years, life, and death.

[a] Maximum sentence length an offender may be required to serve for the most serious offense.

[b] Minimum time to be served is the jurisdiction's estimate of the shortest time each admitted prisoner must serve before becoming eligible for release.

age, violent offenders admitted to prison in 1996 were expected to serve about 3 months longer than those admitted in 1990 (or a minimum term of 70 months versus 67 months).

By offense, the average sentence length for murder (excluding offenders sentenced to life) showed the largest increase between 1990 and 1996, up from 233 months to 253 months. Offenders admitted to prison in 1996 for murder, without a life sentence, were expected to serve about 40 months longer (215 months) than offenders admitted in 1990 (176 months). Just over a third of offenders admitted to prison in 1996 for murder/non-negligent manslaughter were sentenced to life in prison. Another 6% were sentenced to life without parole, and about 2% were sentenced to death.

Both the average sentence length and minimum time to be served in prison decreased for rape offenders admitted between 1990 and 1996. The average sentence length for rape dropped from 153 months to 140 months. The minimum time to be served for rape offenders decreased, from 90 months in 1990 to 72 months in 1996.

Offenders admitted to prison in 1996 for drug law violations were sentenced to an average of 57 months in prison, a 6-month decrease from 1990. Drug offenders were expected to serve 2 months longer in prison (32 months in 1996 versus 30 months in 1990).

Violent offenders admitted to prison in 1996 were expected to serve about half of their sentence

Based on the average sentence length and minimum time to be served, violent offenders admitted to prison in 1996 were expected to serve at minimum 51% of their sentence. Drug and property offenders were expected to serve about 46% of their sentence in prison prior to release. Public-order offenders were expected to serve 49% of their sentence.

Because many states are unable to report the minimum time to be served by offenders admitted to prison, estimates of minimum time to be served and percentage of sentence to be served were calculated with data from 26 states or about half of state prison admissions. The projected percentage of sentence to be served is expected to increase as the number of offenders entering prison who were sentenced under recently enacted truth-in-sentencing laws continues to grow.

Percent of Sentence to be Served by New Court Commitments to State Prison, 1996*

Most serious offense	Percent
All offenses	49
Violent	51
Property	46
Drug	46
Public-order	49

*Based on total sentence length.

Truth-in-sentencing laws would increase the minimum prison term by 15 months for violent offenders

Under a truth-in-sentencing law requiring 85% of the sentence, violent offenders would be expected to serve an estimated 15 months longer than the projected average minimum time to be served by offenders entering prison in 1996 (table 6). Assuming the average sentence length for those sentenced under truth in sentencing remains the same as that for new court commitments to state prison in 1996, violent offenders required to serve 85% of their sentence would serve a minimum of 88 months in prison prior to becoming eligible for release.

Offenders in prison for murder (excluding offenders sentenced to life) are projected to serve about the same amount of time in prison under an 85% requirement, compared to the current projected minimum prison term for 1996 (215 months). Offenders in prison for rape are estimated to serve a minimum of 119 months in prison if sentenced under an 85% requirement, or 47 months longer than the 1996 projected minimum term of 72 months.

Based on the maximum sentence length of offenders entering prison for robbery, a minimum 86-month prison term would be expected under an 85% requirement, compared to the current 60-month projected minimum prison term for 1996.

Violent offenders would serve about 10 months less under a 75%-requirement than an 85%-requirement

Assuming sentence length remains constant, violent offenders would be expected to serve on average 78 months in prison under a 75% requirement, or 10 months less than offenders under an 85% truth-in-sentencing requirement. Under a 50% truth-in-sentencing requirement, violent offenders would serve on average a minimum of 52 months in prison prior to becoming eligible for release.

TABLE 6. Estimated Average Time to be Served Under Truth-in-Sentencing Laws

Most serious offense	New court commitments, 1996		Estimated time to be served		
	Maximum sentence length	Minimum time to be served	85% of sentence	75% of sentence	50% of sentence
Selected violent offenses	104 mo	73 mo	88 mo	78 mo	52 mo
Murder/non-negligent manslaughter	253	214	215	190	127
Rape	140	72	119	105	70
Robbery	101	60	86	76	51
Assault	72	45	61	54	36

Note: Includes only offenders with a sentence of more than 1 year.
Excludes sentences of life without parole, life plus additional years, life, and death.

For releases, average time served in prison increased from 22 months in 1990 to 25 months in 1996

State prisoners released for the first time on their current offense served on average 30 months, or 25 months in prison and 5 months in jail in 1996 (table 7). Offenders released in 1990 served on average 28 months, or 22 months in prison and 6 months in jail.

Between 1990 and 1996, total time served by released prisoners increased for every offense, except robbery, which decreased slightly from 48 months in 1990 to 46 months in 1996, and a small category of other violent offenses, which dropped from 38 months in 1990 to 35 months in 1996. Violent prisoners released in 1996 served on average 45 months in prison and jail, or about 50% of the average sentence prior to release, up from 44% in 1990. Offenders released from prison for rape in 1996 served a total of 66 months, up from 62 months for those released in 1990. Offenders released for other sexual assault offenses in 1996 served 45 months, or 9 months longer than those released in 1990. Offenders released for assault also served longer in 1996 compared to 1990 (33 months versus 30 months).

Offenders released for motor vehicle theft during 1996 served on average 24 months in prison and jail, a 4-month increase from those released in 1990. Drug offenders released in 1996 served nearly 6 months longer in prison than offenders released for a drug offense in 1990 (20 months versus 14 months).

Overall, offenders released from prison in 1996 served about 44% of their sentence, up from 38% in 1990. Drug offenders served the smallest percentage of their sentence, about 40% for those released in 1996, up from 33%.

Time served by released Part 1 violent offenders increased in 38 States between 1993 and 1997

Data on the average time served reported to the VOI/TIS Incentive Grants program vary from the NCRP data because of differences in the definition of violent crimes. NCRP time-served statistics for violent offenders include Part 1 violent crimes and a number of other violent crimes, such as kidnaping, simple assault, sexual assault, and reckless endangerment.

VOI/TIS data generally include only Part 1 violent crimes (murder/nonnegligent manslaughter, rape, robbery, and aggravated assault). Some states used an alternative definition of violent crime approved through the grant program, based on the NCRP definition.

Through the VOI/TIS program, 38 states reported an increase in the average time served by released Part 1 prisoners between 1993 and 1997 (table 8). Vermont reported the largest increase in time served (up 50 months) between 1993 and 1997, followed by Florida (22 months) and North Dakota (16 months). Overall, time served for released Part 1 violent offenders increased from 43 months in 1993 to 46 months in 1995 and 49 months by 1997. The average time served for Part 1 violent offenders released in 1997 ranged from 35 months in Minnesota to 87 months in Kentucky.

Part 1 violent offenders released in 1997 served between 25% and 87% of their sentence

Among prisoners released in 1997, the average sentence for a Part 1 violent crime was about 93 months, and the average time served in prison and jail was 49 months, or 54%

TABLE 7.   Mean Sentence Length and Time Served for First Releases from State Prison, 1990 and 1996

Most serious offense	Mean maximum sentence length[a]		Mean time served for first releases						Percent of sentence served[d]	
			Jail[b]		Prison		Total time served[c]			
	1990	1996	1990	1996	1990	1996	1990	1996	1990	1996
All offenses	69 mo	62 mo	6 mo	5 mo	22 mo	25 mo	28 mo	30 mo	38.0%	44.4%
Violent offenses	99 mo	85 mo	7 mo	6 mo	39 mo	39 mo	46 mo	45 mo	43.8%	49.6%
Murder[e]	209	180	9	11	83	84	92	95	43.1	50.9
Negligent manslaughter	88	97	5	6	31	41	37	47	41.0	46.6
Rape	128	116	7	6	55	61	62	66	45.5	52.6
Other sexual assault	77	81	5	5	30	39	36	45	43.8	51.7
Robbery	104	92	7	6	41	40	48	46	42.8	47.0
Assault	64	61	6	6	23	28	30	33	43.9	51.7
Other violent	80	67	6	6	33	29	38	35	43.5	48.9
Property offenses	65 mo	56 mo	6 mo	5 mo	18 mo	22 mo	24 mo	26 mo	34.4%	43.0%
Burglary	79	68	6	5	22	26	29	31	33.9	42.2
Motor vehicle theft	56	45	7	5	13	19	20	24	33.1	49.1
Fraud	56	51	6	4	14	18	20	22	33.2	38.2
Other property	55	48	4	4	18	20	22	24	37.6	46.1

Drug offenses	57 mo	57 mo	6 mo	5 mo	14 mo	20 mo	20 mo	24 mo	32.9%	39.8%
Possession	61	55	6	4	12	17	18	22	29.0	37.6
Trafficking	60	62	6	5	16	22	22	26	34.8	39.3
Other/unspecified drug	42	45	4	5	12	17	16	23	34.8	46.7
Public-order offenses	40 mo	41 mo	5 mo	4 mo	14 mo	17 mo	18 mo	21 mo	42.6%	45.9%
Other offenses	51 mo	50 mo	6 mo	6 mo	16 mo	19 mo	23 mo	25 mo	39.2%	45.6%
Number of releases	212,166	252,238	174,161	203,167	214,871	254,217				

Note: Includes only offenders with a sentence of more than 1 year released for the first time on the current sentence. Excludes prisoners released from prison by escape, death, transfer, appeal, or detainer. Data were reported on maximum sentence length for 93.4% of the 227,100 first releases reported to NCRP in 1990 and 97.6% of the 258,480 first releases reported in 1996. Data were reported on time served in jail for 76.7% in 1990 and 78.6% in 1996, and time served in prison for 94.6% in 1990 and 98.4% in 1996.

[a] Maximum sentence length an offender may be required to serve for the most serious offense. Excludes sentences of life without parole, life plus additional years, life, and death.
[b] Average time spent in jail credited toward the current offense.
[c] Based on mean time served in jail and mean time served in prison by offense.
[d] Based on the mean total time served and mean total sentence length by offense. Details may not add to total because of rounding.
[e] Includes nonnegligent manslaughter.

TABLE 8. Part 1 Violent Offenders Released from State Prison, 1993, 1995, and 1997

	1993			1995			1997		
	Mean maximum sentence[a]	Mean time served	Percent of sentence served[b]	Mean maximum sentence[a]	Mean time served	Percent of sentence served[b]	Mean maximum sentence[a]	Mean time served	Percent of sentence served[b]
All states[c]	98 mo	43 mo	47%	95 mo	46 mo	51%	93 mo	49 mo	54%
Alabama	—	—	—	—	—	—	—	—	—
Alaska	115 mo	65 mo	57%	95 mo	61 mo	64%	83 mo	55 mo	67%
Arizona	69	43	62	66	43	65	70	52	74
Arkansas	131	35	27	137	38	28	150	38	25
California[d]	58	33	57	62	35	57	62	36	58
Colorado	98	39	40	99	51	52	97	50	51
Connecticut	71	38	54	71	45	64	77	53	68
Delaware[e]	—	41	—	—	43	—	—	44	—
Florida[d]	67	28	42	71	40	56	84	50	59
Georgia[d]	150	63	42	134	64	48	110	68	62
Hawaii	138	64	47	139	66	48	134	61	46
Idaho	104	59	57	119	72	61	104	51	49
Illinois	91	40	44	90	40	45	106	46	44
Indiana	108	54	50	109	57	52	115	55	48
Iowa[e,f]	192	39	20	155	40	26	130	49	38
Kansas[e,f]	—	29	—	—	31	—	—	41	—
Kentucky[f]	242	77	32	210	80	38	180	87	49
Louisiana[d,e]	104	67	64	113	65	58	117	59	51
Maine[d]	—	43	—	—	35	—	—	49	—
Maryland[d]	118	63	53	110	61	55	108	60	56
Massachusetts[d]	123	51	42	119	59	50	99	58	58
Michigan	—	46	—	—	50	—	—	54	—
Minnesota	50	34	68	54	36	66	50	35	69
Mississippi[d,e]	105	45	43	117	54	46	122	57	46
Missouri	92	72	78	87	68	78	82	71	86

Montana[e]	163	54	33	117	43	37	105	49	47
Nebraska[e]	118	55	47	109	52	48	134	60	45
Nevada	—	—	—	—	—	—	83	37	45
New Hampshire[e]	98	36	37	98	37	38	95	42	44
New Jersey	121	47	39	123	50	41	102	46	45
New Mexico[e]	70	37	54	62	38	61	67	38	57
New York	94	50	53	94	52	55	96	57	60
North Carolina	136	33	24	127	39	31	117	47	40
North Dakota	47	31	66	34	26	77	74	47	64
Ohio	237	61	26	230	68	29	192	63	33
Oklahoma	104	34	33	106	38	36	98	42	43
Oregon	111	43	39	64	38	60	60	38	63
Pennsylvania	117	54	46	115	59	51	108	64	59
Rhode Island	80	44	55	72	45	63	70	46	66
South Carolina	100	44	44	102	46	45	91	46	51
South Dakota	101	36	35	78	37	47	88	41	47
Tennessee	130	48	37	121	54	45	127	56	44
Texas[d]	150	52	35	142	61	43	114	59	52
Utah[e]	121	43	36	111	51	46	109	46	43
Vermont[e]	93	32	34	107	44	41	94	82	87
Virginia	107	41	38	91	44	49	105	55	52
Washington	41	31	76	47	33	70	49	36	74
West Virginia[e]	171	76	44	175	80	46	160	65	41
Wisconsin	83	41	49	84	41	49	87	48	55
Wyoming[d,e]	140	69	49	76	43	56	124	54	44

Note: Data were obtained from the Violent Offender Incarceration and Truth-in-Sentencing Incentive Grants program. Includes only offenders with a sentence of more than 1 year released for the first time on the current sentence. Excludes persons released from prison by escape, death, transfer, appeal or detainer. Part 1 violent crimes include murder/nonnegligent manslaughter, rape, robbery, and aggravated assault.

—Not reported.

[a]Excludes sentences of life or death.

[b]Based on states which reported both mean maximum sentence and mean time served.

[c]Mean sentence length, mean time served, and percent of sentence served are weighted averages.

[d]Used broader definition of violent crime approved for the grant program.

[e]Jail time not included in time-served data.

[f]Time served includes released offenders sentenced to life or death.

295

of the average total maximum sentence. Overall, the average percentage of sentence served increased from 47% in 1993 to 51% in 1995, and by 1997 released Part 1 violent offenders had served 54% of the average sentence.

The percentage of sentence served by released violent offenders varied widely among reporting states, ranging from 25% in Arkansas to 87% in Vermont for 1997. Variations in the percentage of sentence served are due to state differences in both time served and the maximum sentence length of released offenders. The average sentence length of re-

---

**Black offenders released in 1996 served
2 months longer than white offenders**

Black offenders released in 1996 served about 41 months in prison for a violent offense, compared to 38 months for white offenders. For murder white offenders served 90 months, compared to 86 months for black offenders and 76 months for Hispanics. Black offenders sentenced to prison for rape served about 14 months longer than whites (70 months versus 56 months).

Females released in 1996 served an average of 8 months less than males. Females served 9 months less than males for a violent offense, about 8 months less for a property offense, and 4 months less for a drug offense.

Mean Time Served in Prison by First Releases from State Prison, by Sex and Race, 1996

	First releases from state prison				
	Male	Female	White*	Black*	Hispanic
All offenses	26 mo	18 mo	24 mo	26 mo	23 mo
Violent offenses	39 mo	30 mo	38 mo	41 mo	33 mo
Murder/nonnegligent manslaughter	86	67	90	86	76
Rape	61	48	56	70	51
Robbery	41	28	42	42	30
Assault	28	23	25	30	27
Property offenses	23 mo	15 mo	21 mo	23 mo	22 mo
Burglary	27	18	25	29	26
Larceny/theft	19	15	18	19	19
Motor vehicle theft	19	14	19	21	17
Drug offenses	20 mo	16 mo	18 mo	20 mo	20 mo
Possession	18	15	15	18	21
Trafficking	22	18	20	22	21
Public-order offenses	17 mo	15 mo	16 mo	18 mo	15 mo

Note: Data were obtained from the National Corrections Reporting Program. Includes only offenders with a sentence of more than 1 year released for the first time on the current sentence. Excludes persons released from prison by escape, death, transfer, appeal, or detainer.
*Excludes inmates of Hispanic origin.

leased violent prisoners ranged from 49 months in Washington to nearly 4 times that in Ohio (192 months).

Part of the variation in sentence length and percent of sentence served is due to differences between determinate and indeterminate sentencing. Offenders in indeterminate sentencing states may be sentenced to a relatively long maximum prison term and a short minimum term, compared to the fixed sentence of a determinate sentencing state. Variations by state in the percentage of sentence served may also reflect other state-specific sentencing practices, a differing mix of the type of violent offenders being released, and changing release policies.

Prisoners released in four States served over 70% of the sentence

Part 1 violent offenders released in Vermont, Missouri, Washington, and Arizona during 1997 served on average over 70% of the average sentence. Time served in these four states ranged from an average of 36 months for offenders released in Washington to 82 months for prisoners released in Vermont. Part 1 violent offenders released from Kentucky served the longest amount of time in prison and jail (87 months), which represented 49% of the average maximum sentence.

Nearly 18% of released offenders served their entire prison sentence

About 81% of prisoners released in 1997 were conditionally released to community supervision (table 9). The remaining 19% were released into the community without further correctional supervision, up from 14% in 1990.

Consistent with recent trends in requiring longer portions of the sentence to be served, more released prisoners in 1997 served their entire prison term (18%), compared to 1990 (13%). Also, more offenders were released to mandatory parole (release supervision mandated by law rather than granted by a parole board) during 1997, compared to 1990 (41% versus 30%).

Top 10 states, by percent of sentence served, 1997		
	Time served	Percent of sentence
Vermont	82 mo	87
Missouri	71	86
Washington	36	74
Arizona	52	74
Minnesota	35	69
Connecticut	53	68
Alaska	55	67
Rhode Island	46	66
North Dakota	47	64
Oregon	38	63

TABLE 9.   Type of Release from State Prison, 1990, 1993–97

	1990	1993	1994	1995	1996	1997*
Conditional releases	86.0%	86.0%	85.9%	84.1%	81.4%	81.4%
Parole	40.5	39.9	36.1	33.4	31.5	29.3
Mandatory	29.6	32.5	36.8	40.2	39.4	41.2
Other	15.9	13.7	13.0	10.5	10.5	10.9
Unconditional releases	14.0%	14.0%	14.1%	15.9%	18.6%	18.6%
Expiration of sentence	13.0	12.2	12.9	15.0	17.4	17.5
Other	1.0	1.8	1.2	0.9	1.2	1.1

Note: Data were obtained from the National Prisoner Statistics data collection.
*Preliminary.

Time served increased for parole board releases
between 1990 and 1996

Parole boards have followed the trend toward increasing the amount of time offenders serve in prison. The average time served among offenders released by a parole board increased from 23 months in 1990 to 24 months in 1994 and 25 months in 1996 (table 10). The time served for those released under nondiscretionary mandatory parole also increased from 20 months in 1990 to 23 months in 1995 and 24 months in 1996.

Violent offenders released by parole boards
served 4 months longer than other
conditional releases

During 1996 violent offenders released by the discretion of a parole board served 42 months, while other conditional releases (mandatory parole and other nondiscre-

TABLE 10.   Time Served in Prison for First Releases from State Prison, by Release Type, 1990–96

	Release type		
Year	Parole board	Mandatory parole	Expiration of sentence
1990	23 mo	20 mo	27 mo
1991	23	20	27
1992	23	19	22
1993	23	19	23
1994	24	20	26
1995	24	23	25
1996	25	24	26

Note: Includes only offenders with a sentence of more than 1 year released for the first time on the current sentence. Excludes persons released from prison by escape, death, transfer, appeal, or detainer.

tionary conditional releases) served 38 months in prison (table 11). Offenders released by a parole board who were in prison for murder/nonnegligent manslaughter served 21 months longer than other conditional releases (96 months versus 75 months). Offenders serving time for assault who were released by a parole board served 30 months, or 5 months longer than other conditional releases (25 months).

Property offenders served about 22 months under both types of release. Drug offenders released by a parole board served 21 months, and other conditional releases served about 19 months in prison. Persons in prison for a public-order offense served about the same amount of time whether released by a parole board (16 months) or other conditional releases (17 months).

TABLE 11.   Sentence Length, Time Served, and Percent of Sentence Served, for First Releases, by Offense and Release Type, 1996

Most serious offense	Maximum sentence		Time served in prison		Percent of sentence served in prison	
	Parole board	Other conditional*	Parole board	Other conditional*	Parole board	Other conditional*
All offenses	79 mo	47 mo	25 mo	25 mo	29.1	47.0
Violent offenses	113 mo	65 mo	42 mo	38 mo	34.0	53.2
Murder/ nonnegligent manslaughter	229	138	96	75	35.6	52.3
Rape	157	94	65	64	37.6	57.2
Other sexual assault	117	75	44	41	35.5	50.0
Robbery	118	63	42	40	32.4	56.9
Assault	81	45	30	25	35.1	51.5
Property offenses	73 mo	43 mo	23 mo	22 mo	28.0	45.7
Burglary	88	50	27	28	28.3	49.3
Larceny/theft	59	39	18	19	27.9	43.3
Motor vehicle theft	61	36	19	18	28.7	41.8
Drug offenses	74 mo	40 mo	21 mo	19 mo	25.6	41.8
Possession	66	42	18	18	24.5	39.6
Trafficking	80	42	22	21	25.3	44.4
Public-order offenses	47 mo	36 mo	16 mo	17 mo	29.9	42.8
Other offenses	60 mo	33 mo	20 mo	14 mo	31.2	36.5

Note: Data were obtained from the National Corrections Reporting Program. Includes only offenders with a sentence of more than 1 year released for the first time on the current sentence. Excludes persons released from prison by escape, death, transfer, appeal, or detainer.
*Includes mandatory parole releases and other nondiscretionary conditional releases for selected states.

Parole board releases served 29% of the sentence, and other conditional releases, 47%

Offenders released by a parole board during 1996 served a smaller percentage of their sentence than other conditional releases (29% versus 47%). Offenders in prison for a violent offense who were released by a parole board served 34% of their sentence, and other conditional releases served 53% of their sentence. The difference between the two release types in percentage of sentence served was the result of longer sentences for offenders who were eligible for discretionary parole board release. Offenders released in 1996 by a parole board had an average sentence of 79 months, 32 months longer than other conditional releases (47 months).

Prisoners are serving more time than release data indicate

The average time-served data reported for released prisoners understate the actual time that will be served by persons entering prison. The numbers reflect the time served by prisoners actually released without accounting for those who will never be released. In addition, prisoners with extremely long sentences will not show up in the release statistics for many years.

Current time-served data are based on released offenders who were generally sentenced under past or "old law" sentencing policies. Offenders sentenced under recently implemented truth in sentencing or "new laws" requiring large portions of the sentence to be served do not show up in current release statistics.

State prison population growth is linked to increasing time served

The state prison population dramatically increased between 1990 and 1997. Since 1990 the state prison custody population has increased by 57%, reaching a high of 1,075,052 inmates in 1997, up from 684,544 in 1990. The growth has not been entirely the result of more offenders entering state prison. The number of offenders admitted each year has remained fairly constant in recent years. Admissions to state prisons have increased by about 17% since 1990, up from 460,739 to 540,748 in 1997. An increasing amount of time served by offenders is contributing to the growth in state prison populations. (See Blumstein and Beck, 1999.)

The sentences of released offenders decreased between 1990 and 1996

Another indicator of increasing time served is a shorter average sentence length of those actually released from prison. As a result of changes in sentencing and release policies, the more serious offenders with long sentences are being held in prison, and less serious offenders with shorter sentences make up an increasing fraction of the released prisoners.

Overall, the average sentence length of offenders released from prison in 1996 was 62 months, down from 65 months in 1990 (table 12). The average sentence length of violent offenders released in 1996 was 10 months shorter than those released in 1990 (84 months versus 94 months). Property offenders released in 1996 had a 5-month shorter average sentence length. Offenders with long sentences for violent and property offenses may be serving longer periods of time in prison.

TABLE 12.   Mean Sentence Length of First Releases from State Prison, 1990–96

Year	Mean maximum sentence length				
	All offenders	Violent	Property	Drug	Public-order
1990	65 mo	94 mo	61 mo	54 mo	37 mo
1991	66	92	63	59	38
1992	60	89	53	53	35
1993	66	90	61	61	39
1994	64	85	60	60	42
1995	61	84	56	57	39
1996	62	84	56	57	40

Note: Includes only offenders with a sentence of more than 1 year released for the first time on the current sentence. Excludes persons released from prison by escape, death, transfer, appeal, or detainer.

The release rate for rape offenders dropped from 24 per 100 to 15 per 100 state prison inmates

While the actual number of prisoners released each year continues to increase, the rate of release (or the number of releases relative to the number of inmates in prison) dropped. In 1996 an estimated 467,200 offenders were released from prison, up from 405,400 in 1990 (table 13). However, the release rate dropped from 37 per 100 state prisoners in 1990 to 31 per 100 in 1996.

The overall decline in the release rate was also due to a declining rate of release for violent and property offenders. The violent offender release rate dropped from 25 per 100 state prisoners in 1990 to 19 per 100 in 1996. The release rate for murder showed the most dramatic decline, cut nearly in half from about 10 per 100 in 1990 to 5 per 100 in 1996. Robbery and assault decreased from a release rate of 32 per 100 in 1990 to about 25 per 100 in 1996. The release rate for property offenders decreased from 47 per 100 state prisoners in 1990 to 39 per 100 in 1996. The rate for drug and public-order offenses decreased slightly from about 41 per 100 prisoners in 1990 to 39 per 100 in 1996.

Few offenders admitted under truth-in-sentencing laws are being released from prison

Through the VOI/TIS program 15 federally funded truth-in-sentencing states and 3 non-federally funded states reported 1997 admission and release data on offenders sentenced under truth in sentencing (table 14). Three states reported that none of the offenders admitted under a truth-in-sentencing law was released from prison during 1997 (Illinois, Iowa, and Missouri). Four states reported fewer than 10 offenders were released (Connecticut, North Dakota, South Carolina, and Tennessee).

Among the reporting states, prisoners admitted under truth in sentencing and released from prison during 1997 had both short sentences and prison terms. The average sentence of released offenders ranged from 9 months in Ohio, where offenders served 9 months in prison, to 43 months in Nevada, where offenders served 18 months. Since the small number of truth-in-sentencing prisoners who were released during 1997 had short

TABLE 13.   Rate of Release From State Prison, by Offense, 1990 and 1996

Most serious offense	Number of releases		Release rate*	
	1990	1996	1990	1996
Total	405,400	467,200	37.0	30.9
Violent offenses	103,000	115,300	24.8	19.0
Murder/nonnegligent manslaughter	7,700	6,100	9.7	5.2
Negligent manslaughter	4,100	4,200	22.2	20.1
Rape	7,700	7,000	23.8	15.4
Other sexual assault	9,700	13,500	20.4	17.4
Robbery	46,600	44,800	31.8	23.9
Assault	23,900	33,100	31.6	25.4
Other violent	4,100	6,100	24.4	21.9
Property offenses	158,900	154,000	46.8	38.5
Burglary	75,800	65,800	45.8	36.2
Larceny/theft	42,200	41,100	53.2	43.9
Motor vehicle theft	11,400	14,000	44.2	38.9
Fraud	17,800	18,200	46.1	39.3
Other property	11,800	14,900	38.6	35.0
Drug offenses	105,800	148,900	41.6	38.8
Public-order offenses	30,000	44,800	40.6	38.8
Other offenses	7,700	4,200	71.8	54.9

Note: Releases exclude escapees, AWOLs, and transfers and include prisoners with a sentence of more than 1 year.

* Number of releases per 100 state prisoners. The prisoner count includes inmates at the beginning of each year plus those admitted during the year.

sentences, the average time served by these offenders is not comparable to national time-served data. Due to the estimated time to be served by offenders admitted under truth in sentencing, these offenders are not expected to be released from prison for many years.

Six states projected an average 10-year prison term under truth in sentencing

Both the sentence length and projected average time to be served by Part 1 violent offenders admitted to prison during 1997 under a truth-in-sentencing law vary greatly by state. Of the 17 states able to report data, the average maximum sentence length ranged from 46 months in Minnesota to 233 months in Iowa. Generally, the average maximum sentence of indeterminate sentencing states was longer than that of determinate sentencing states.

For the 12 states reporting data, the average projected time to be served for Part 1 violent offenders admitted under a truth-in-sentencing law during 1997 ranged from

TABLE 14.   Part 1 Violent Offenders Admitted and Released from State Prison Under Truth in Sentencing, for Selected States, 1997

	New court commitments			First releases			
	Number	Maximum sentence[a]	Average time to be served	Number	Maximum sentence	Time served	Percent of sentence served
Determinate							
Arizona	1,359	74 mo	64 mo	360	30 mo	27 mo	90
Connecticut	561	128	/	2	29	25	88
Delaware[b]	264	82	/	68	35	31	88
Florida[c,d]	3,720	72	61	465	19	15	80
Illinois[e,f]	936	208	192	0	—	—	—
Minnesota[g]	748	46	46	433	22	22	100
New York[d,h]	1,107	100	86	0	—	—	—
Ohio	2,660	54	/	165	9	9	100
Virginia	932	140	126	110	25	22	88
Indeterminate							
California[d]	5,277	123 mo	105 mo	/	/	/	/
Iowa	66	233	198	0	—	—	—
Massachusetts[d,e]	753	80	59	186	36	26	71
Missouri	464	201	171	0	—	—	—
Nevada[e]	483	173	/	48	43	18	42
New York[d,h]	1,805	64	54	98	24	19	80
North Dakota	29	92	/	4	21	19	88
South Carolina	515	183	160	2	18	15	83
Tennessee[i]	346	207	184	9	10	6	59

Note: Data were obtained from the Violent Offender Incarceration and Truth-in-Sentencing Incentive Grants program.
/ Not reported.
— Not applicable.
[a] Excludes prisoners sentenced to life or death.
[b] Jail time not included in time-served data.
[c] Releases serving less than 85% are the result of a judicial action impacting sentencing structure.
[d] Used a broader definition of violent crime.
[e] Not a federally funded truth-in-sentencing state.
[f] Includes only select violent crimes (primarily murder).
[g] Average executed sentence (which includes the maximum supervised release term) was 68 months for admissions and 33 months for releases.
[h] Under New York's 1995 truth-in-sentencing law, first felony offenders are given an indeterminate sentence; second felony offenders, a determinate sentence. For indeterminate cases the statutory presumptive release date is reported rather than the maximum sentence.
[i] All 9 releases were either judicially released or sentenced under a split confinement and released on probation.

46 months in Minnesota to 198 months in Iowa. Six of the twelve states projected that offenders admitted under a truth-in-sentencing law would serve on average over 10 years in prison prior to becoming eligible for release.

Seven states reported an average percentage of sentence served above 85%

Violent offenders sentenced and released under truth-in-sentencing requirements are serving a large portion of their sentence. For Part 1 violent offenders sentenced under a truth-in-sentencing law and released during 1997, seven states reported an average percentage of sentence served above 85% (Arizona, Connecticut, Delaware, Minnesota, North Dakota, Ohio, and Virginia). An additional four states reported an average percent of sentence served between 70% and 80% (Florida, Massachusetts, New York, and South Carolina).

As the number of offenders sentenced under truth in sentencing continues to grow, the national average percentage of sentence served by violent offenders should also continue to increase. Because truth-in-sentencing laws are relatively recent, however, the majority of offenders sentenced under them will not be released from prison for many years. Statistics based on current release data may underestimate changes in time served due to truth in sentencing.

METHODOLOGY

The National Corrections Reporting Program collects individual level data for persons admitted to and released from state prisons and offenders exiting parole supervision, by calendar year. The data cover prisoners admitted to or released from custody regardless of the jurisdiction where the prisoner was sentenced. While NCRP collects data on all offenders, this report includes data on prisoners with a total sentence of more than a year. The NCRP datasets are available from the National Archive of Criminal Justice Data at the University of Michigan and can be downloaded via the Internet. A codebook, explanatory notes, and sample SPSS and SAS statistical setup files are included with each dataset. The datasets for 1983 through 1995 are also available on a series of eight CD-ROMs.

Caution should be used for year-to-year comparisons of NCRP data to account for differences based on state participation and valid data reported. Variations in the ability of a state to report certain variables (such as sentence length and minimum time to be served) and in definitions used by participating jurisdictions are reported in the explanatory notes.

NCRP Participating States

The number of jurisdictions reporting data varies from year to year. In 1996, admissions and releases were reported by the following 37 states and the California Youth Authority: Alabama, Arkansas, California, Colorado, Florida, Georgia, Hawaii, Illinois, Iowa, Kentucky, Louisiana, Maine, Maryland, Michigan, Minnesota, Mississippi, Missouri, Nebraska, Nevada, New Hampshire, New Jersey, New York, North Carolina, North Dakota,

Ohio, Oklahoma, Oregon, Pennsylvania, South Carolina, South Dakota, Tennessee, Texas, Utah, Virginia, Washington, West Virginia, and Wisconsin. Except for Florida and Maine, these states and Massachusetts also reported in 1990.

Estimating the Admission and Release Rates by Offense

The admission and release rates for sentenced prisoners under state jurisdiction by offense were estimated using the year-end custody population derived through the forward and backward estimation procedure outlined in the BJS Bulletin *Prisoners in 1996* (NCJ 164619). Data from the BJS state and federal inmate surveys, conducted in March 1986 and August 1991, were used to estimate a custody population by type of offense for each year from 1986 through 1996.

To obtain the base year jurisdiction population, the proportion of the estimated 1989 and 1995 custody numbers by type of offense was applied to the sentenced jurisdiction population from the National Prisoner Statistics (NPS) collection. For the 1990 and 1996 admissions and releases, the offense distribution (in percentages) from NCRP were multiplied by the total number of admissions and releases of sentenced prisoners reported in NPS. The final estimates of the number of inmates by offense for 1990 and 1996 were calculated by adding admissions and subtracting releases from the 1989 and 1995 year-end jurisdiction estimates.

The admission rate was calculated by dividing all admissions during the year by the year-end population of the preceding year. The rate of release was calculated by dividing the number of inmates released during the year by the number in prison at the beginning of the year plus the number admitted during the year.

Truth-in-Sentencing Reform

BJS contacted each state for verification of all truth-in-sentencing state-level references in this report. Truth-in-sentencing laws vary from state to state on effective date, offenses covered by the law, and percentage of sentence required to be served prior to release, among other requirements. The Violent Offender Incarceration and Truth-in-Sentencing Incentive Grants program provided state-validated sentence length and time-served data. All 50 states reported data on admissions and releases with a common definition of Part 1 violent offenses.

Weighted averages were used to calculate the average sentence, time served, and percentage of sentence served from state-level VOI/TIS data. A weighted average for time served is calculated by multiplying the mean time served for each state by the number of releases in the state. The results were summed and divided by the total number of releases.

DEFINITION OF TERMS

New court commitments—persons entering prison directly from a sentence by a court and not from an unsuccessful period of community supervision (parole). Includes new court admissions, probation revocations, and admissions after the imposition of a suspended sentence.

Violent offenses—crimes involving personal injury, threat of injury, and theft of property or attempted theft by force or threat of force. Includes murder, manslaughter, rape, other sexual assault, robbery, assault, extortion, intimidation, criminal endangerment, child abuse, and other offenses involving confrontation, force, or threat of force.

Maximum sentence length—the sentence for the most serious offense, as determined by the offense with the longest sentence. Whenever a sentence had both a minimum and a maximum term, the maximum was used to define the sentence length.

Total sentence length—the longest time that an offender could be required to serve for all offenses.

Minimum time to be served—the jurisdiction's estimate of the shortest time that each admitted prisoner must serve before becoming eligible for release. Factors used in this estimate include minimum sentence length, good-time credits, earned-time credits, parole eligibility requirements, and early release requirements and allowances.

Life sentence—any prison sentence with a fixed or maximum term of life in prison, regardless of the possibility of parole.

First release from prison—anyone released for the first time on the current sentence. Excluded from first releases from prison are persons who had previously been conditionally released from prison for the same offense and then were returned to prison for violating the conditions of that release.

Subsequent release from prison—persons released from prison after having been admitted to prison for a violation of parole or other conditional release.

Conditional release—anyone released from prison into community supervision with a set of conditions for remaining on parole, which, if violated, can cause the person to be returned to prison. This subsequent incarceration can be for any of the remaining portion of the sentence the inmate may have on the current offense.

Unconditional release—anyone released from any further correctional supervision who cannot be returned to prison for any remaining portion of the sentence for the current offense.

Total time served—calculated by adding the average time spent in prison and the average time spent in jail.

NOTES

1. For the additional information on sentencing reform see the *1996 National Survey of State Sentencing Structures*, Bureau of Justice Assistance, NCJ 169270, September 1998.
2. For additional information on eligibility criteria and other program requirements, see *Violent Offender Incarceration and Truth-in-Sentencing Incentive Grants: Program Guidance and Application Kit, FY98*, Office of Justice Programs Corrections Programs Office, U.S. Department of Justice, Solicitation Number 244, NCJ 168942.

REFERENCES

Association of Paroling Authorities, International. *1997 Parole Board Survey*. St. Louis: APAI Publications, May 1998.

Blumstein, Alfred, and Allen J. Beck. "Factors Contributing to the Growth in U.S. Prison Populations," in *Crime and Justice: A Review of Research on Corrections*, Michael

Tonry and Joan Petersilia, eds. Chicago: University of Chicago Press, 1999.

Beck, Allen J., and Lawrence Greenfeld. *Violent Offenders in State Prison: Sentences and Time Served*. BJS Selected Findings, NCJ 154632, July 1995.

Bureau of Justice Assistance. *1996 National Survey of State Sentencing Structures*. Washington, D.C.: NCJ 169270, September 1998.

———, *The National Assessment of Structured Sentencing*. Washington, D.C.: NCJ 153853, February 1996.

Corrections Program Office, Office of Justice Programs. *Violent Offender Incarceration and Truth-in-Sentencing Incentive Grants: Program Guidance and Application Kit, FY98*. Washington, D.C.: U.S. Department of Justice, 1998.

General Accounting Office. *Truth in Sentencing: Availability of Federal Grants Influenced Laws in Some States*. Washington, D.C.: U.S. Congress, GAO/GGD-98-42, February 1998.

Gilliard, Darrell, and Allen J. Beck. *Prisoners in 1997*. BJS Bulletin, NCJ 170014, August 1998.

National Center for State Courts. *Sentencing Digest, Examining Current Sentencing Issues and Policies*. Williamsburg, Virginia: NCSC Publications, Number R-204, 1998.

National Institute of Corrections. *State Legislative Actions on Truth in Sentencing*. Washington, D.C.: U.S. Department of Justice, NCJ 157895, May 1995.

Tonry, Michael, ed. *Crime and Justice, A Review of Research*. Chicago: University of Chicago Press, 1992.

Wicharay, Tamasak. *Simple Theory, Hard Reality: The Impact of Sentencing Reforms on Courts, Prisons, and Crime*. New York: State University of New York Press, 1995.

Chapter 25

The Impact of Sentencing Guidelines

by Dale Parent, Terence Dunworth, Douglas McDonald, and William Rhodes

The use of sentencing guidelines has been growing in the United States and is generating a debate with respect to their effects on the criminal justice system in jurisdictions where they have been enacted. By 1996 nine states and the federal government had presumptive guidelines and eight states were creating them, while four states continued to use voluntary sentencing guidelines. This Research in Action discusses the predominance of presumptive guidelines over voluntary guidelines, the goals of presumptive guidelines, and their impact on sentencing practices and criminal justice operations.

DOMINANCE OF PRESUMPTIVE GUIDELINES

Voluntary sentencing guidelines were a precursor to today's presumptive guidelines. Of the four states that still have voluntary sentencing guidelines, only two implemented them after 1980, the year that the first state, Minnesota, initiated use of presumptive guidelines.

Voluntary guidelines sought to reduce sentencing disparity by making future sentencing decisions adhere more closely to past practice; they described past sentencing practices and used them as guidance. Usually, voluntary guidelines were created by committees of judges acting under the administrative authority of the courts. As the term suggests, voluntary sentencing guidelines have no enforcement mechanism. Rather, judges are encouraged to consider and apply the guidelines when sentencing offenders.

Presumptive sentencing guidelines differ from voluntary guidelines in important ways:

- They are developed by legislatively created sentencing commissions, whose members represent judges, prosecutors, defenders, law enforcement officials, correctional officials, the public, and (in some states) the legislature.
- Unlike voluntary guidelines, presumptive guidelines do not claim to *describe* past sentencing practices; rather, they *prescribe* policy that the officials ought to follow in the future.
- Presumptive guidelines contain enforcement mechanisms. If judges want to depart from the sentences recommended in the guidelines for a particular offender, they must hold a hearing to ascertain whether the facts warrant a departure, as well as issue a written finding stating why the departure is appropriate. In most states, departures can be appealed (providing a foundation for the development of sentencing case law).

Source: National Institute of Justice, November 1996.

- Although legislatures typically play no role in voluntary guidelines, presumptive guidelines do not go into effect without the legislature's consent.

GOALS OF PRESUMPTIVE SENTENCING GUIDELINES

The main goals of early presumptive sentencing guidelines systems were to inflict just punishment on convicted offenders. For punishment to be just, according to this view, it has to be proportional, uniform, and neutral. To be proportional, sanctions should vary with the seriousness of offenders' criminal conduct and their culpability—serious crimes should be punished more severely than minor crimes, and repeat offenders should be punished more severely than first-time offenders. To be uniform, punishment for similar offenders must be similar, and variations should be allowed only for demonstrably relevant reasons. To be neutral, sanctions should not vary by such factors as race, gender, and ethnicity, and preexisting differences in sentencing outcomes based on such factors should be diminished.

Role of the Commissions

The first commissions were created to develop guidelines to meet these goals. Early sentencing commissions were also directed to make their guidelines work within the limits of available correctional resources. Some later sentencing commissions sought to make sentences tougher as well as more uniform. The sentencing commissions that develop the guidelines maintain sentencing policy while ensuring that the legislatures retain ultimate control. Commissions routinely collect and analyze information on sentencing practices; the data they gather can be used to enhance policy decisionmaking. Commission members and staff also develop expertise that can help make policymaking more empirically based. For example, sentencing commissions can develop highly accurate forecasts of prison populations, allowing them to make precise estimates of the costs of implementing or amending the guidelines.

IMPACT OF GUIDELINES ON SENTENCING PRACTICES

Evaluations of early voluntary sentencing guidelines found that they did not make sentencing more uniform.[1] In addition, some scholars challenged the alleged descriptive basis of voluntary guidelines,[2] noting that researchers were able to explain only a small proportion of the variation in sentencing decisions.[3]

Most evaluations of presumptive guidelines have focused on earlier implementations. Where they have been evaluated, these guidelines have had a mixed, but generally positive, record of:

- Achieving adherence to the guidelines by judges and other justice system officials.
- Increasing sentencing uniformity and proportionality.
- Improving sentencing neutrality.
- Altering sentencing patterns in intended ways.

Effects on the operations of the criminal justice system include changes in prosecutor and plea negotiation practices, court workloads, and prison populations.

Achieving Conformance to Presumptive Guidelines

Studies show that judges, even those who publicly and stridently criticize the guidelines, adhere to them at a high rate.[4] Rates of conformity appear to be higher in systems that establish narrow grounds for departing from the guidelines and in states where case law strongly reinforces guideline policies.[5] Conformance also tends to be higher for guidelines that allow a wide range of presumptive practice; that is, place fewer restrictions on a practitioner's discretion.[6] Of course, precisely because they encompass a wider range of practice, these less restrictive guidelines are also less effective at increasing uniformity and proportionality.

Increasing Sentencing Uniformity and Proportionality

Virtually all studies of presumptive guidelines report sentencing uniformity and proportionality. Two caveats about before-and-after evaluations are necessary, however. First, studies that compare sentencing patterns before and after imposition of guidelines for offenders who fall into particular guideline categories are suspect. This is because officials are likely to change their charging or bargaining practices over time, thereby changing the characteristics of offenders who fall into those categories. Second, general sentencing practices change over time (in recent years, usually becoming harsher) for reasons unrelated to the guidelines. Hence, before-and-after sentencing comparisons become less relevant as time passes.

Despite these caveats, there is strong evidence that presumptive sentencing guidelines increase uniformity and proportionality, at least in the years just following implementation.[7] Three evaluations of Minnesota's guidelines support this conclusion.[8] No independent evaluations of other early sentencing commissions were conducted, but studies by commissions in Oregon, Pennsylvania, Washington, and Delaware all found increases in uniformity.[9]

At the federal level, the U.S. Sentencing Commission reported increased uniformity during the first 4 years of guideline operation.[10] However, three other studies offered more cautious interpretations, concluding that the question is open because the Commission's analysis was based on limited data.[11]

Improving Sentencing Neutrality

In Minnesota, the first state to implement presumptive guidelines, racial, ethnic, and gender differences in sentencing declined, even though minority defendants were more likely to be imprisoned via departures from the guidelines, and men were more likely to receive longer sentences than similarly situated women.[12] It is important to note that in jail sentences, which were *not* regulated by the guidelines, racial and ethnic differences did not change before and after the guidelines went into effect.[13] For women, movement toward neutrality meant movement toward the male norms; that is, toward a higher probability of confinement and longer confinement terms. A study of the Washington sentencing commission revealed that racial, ethnic, and gender differences in sentencing declined, but substantial differences by race, ethnicity, and gender persisted in the use of nonconfinement options.[14]

An analysis of U.S. Sentencing Commission guidelines found no compelling evidence of racial or ethnic bias in sentencing at the federal level. Independent of these guidelines, however, congressionally imposed mandatory minimum sentences for crack cocaine have resulted in substantially longer sentences for African Americans. This is largely because those convicted of crack trafficking in the federal courts are disproportionately African American, while those convicted of trafficking in powdered cocaine are mostly white or Hispanic.[15]

Altering Sentencing Patterns

Most presumptive guidelines sought to alter preexisting sentencing patterns and, hence, were prescriptive. Commissions in Minnesota, Oregon, and Washington intended to reduce imprisonment sentences for property offenders and increase them for violent offenders. In all three states, those outcomes were achieved.[16] At the federal level, the U.S. Sentencing Commission sought to increase use of imprisonment and decrease the use of probation—and succeeded in meeting these goals.[17]

One researcher has observed that modest changes in past practice tend to revert over time, as criminal justice practitioners modify their discretionary choices in response to the guidelines, whereas more radical changes tend to persist.[18] Minnesota's experience also suggests that when case law gives a green light to judicial departures from the guidelines, reversions to previous practice will be more pronounced.[19] Studies also show that as commissions amend guidelines (particularly to make sentences more severe), the severity of sentences given to offenders in the affected categories increases rapidly.[20]

IMPACT OF GUIDELINES ON CRIMINAL JUSTICE OPERATIONS

Effects on Plea Negotiations

Some critics expected presumptive guidelines to reduce rates of plea bargaining because they believed prosecutors would have less flexibility to offer inducements in return for guilty pleas. However, evaluations of state sentencing guidelines[21] have found that:

- In general, the total proportion of cases concluded by guilty pleas remained fairly constant.
- The proportion of guilty pleas resulting from plea bargains remained fairly constant.
- Guidelines for prison and nonprison sentences had different effects: offenders for whom prison was recommended were somewhat less likely to plead guilty, while those for whom nonprison sentences were recommended were more likely to plead guilty.
- Charge bargaining increased and became more targeted (that is, it achieved a desired result, such as dropping an offender to a lower seriousness level of the guide-

lines), while sentence bargaining declined (although it continued at a significant level in most states).

To date, no empirical studies of plea bargaining under the federal sentencing guidelines have been published.

Effects on Court Workload

Information on guidelines' impact on court workloads are limited to analyses of Minnesota and the U.S. sentencing guidelines. In general, increases in court workload were modest. In Minnesota the proportion of cases going to trial stayed about the same, and although they increased for some types of cases, they were offset by reductions for others.[22] Guideline requirements for such tasks as holding sentencing hearings, completing sentencing worksheets, and collecting monitoring data cause little delay or disruption. The lengths of time between charging and trial and between conviction and sentencing stayed about the same. However, review of sentences has added to the workload of the Supreme Court and triggered establishment of an intermediate court of appeals, a long-advocated reform. In general, appellate reviews were conducted expeditiously, but the additional cases may have delayed the disposition of other types of appellate cases.[23]

In the federal system, the amount of time from filing to disposition has increased slightly. Beyond that, the impact seems to have varied considerably from district to district. Over time there has been a substantial growth in sentencing appeals.[24]

Predictions of Effects on Prison Populations

The impact of guidelines on prison populations has tended to be predictable and relatively rapid. As expected, guidelines have made sentencing more certain and helped ensure that sentencing decisions are based on objective criteria. Therefore, simulation models that predict prison population levels with great accuracy can be developed. Such models were used in Minnesota, Oregon, and Washington to avert crowding in the short term and limit future maximum prison population levels (by modifying policy during initial development of the guidelines). The models were later used to assess the effects of proposed changes in the guidelines and in sentencing legislation on the prison population.

The U.S. Sentencing Commission accurately predicted that in the federal system, prison populations would (by design) increase under the guidelines because of the independent effects of the guidelines and concurrently enacted mandatory minimum sentences. Indeed, the Commission's 1987 simulation model predicted the 1991 federal prison population with almost perfect precision.[25] And the Commission used its simulation capacity to recommend a major federal prison construction program.

Evaluations of state guidelines conducted to date reveal that dispositional policies (rules specifying which offenders should and should not be imprisoned) generally have had a greater impact on prison population levels than policies on amount of time to be served. The reason is that sentencing commissions have generally chosen to change the categories of offenders who are to be imprisoned instead of changing the current average duration of imprisonment. In the federal system, guidelines on duration of confinement and congressionally mandated sentences for drug crimes have had a greater effect than have dispositional policies. Imprisonment rates have increased under the U.S. sentencing guidelines.[26] Across all guideline systems, effects on prison population resulting from changes in sentence duration take longer to emerge.

THE POTENTIAL OF GUIDELINES

State policymakers who were interviewed were deeply concerned about developing effective and affordable sentencing policies. While many felt compelled to respond to constituents' fear of crime and demands for tougher sanctions, they also recognized the need to limit spiraling correctional costs. In a time when voters want to cut costs of government, spending more on prisons means spending less on other important and worthwhile purposes.

Given these concerns, state legislators' interest in sentencing guidelines is understandable. Properly developed, presumptive sentencing guidelines can link the severity of punishment more rationally to the seriousness of crimes. They can modify the use of punishment so that available prison capacity is used for more serious and habitual offenders, and they can ensure that sanctions are applied more uniformly and more equitably.

NOTES

1. Carlson, K., *Mandatory Sentencing: The Experience of Two States*, Washington, D.C.: National Institute of Justice, U.S. Department of Justice, 1982; and Rich, W., P. Sutton, T. Clear, and M. Saks, *Sentencing Guidelines: Their Operation and Impact on Courts*, Williamsburg, VA: National Center for State Courts, 1980.
2. Because the early voluntary guidelines purported to analyze data on past sentencing to identify typical practices and to capture these practices as guideline policies, the argument went that if judges followed the guidelines, they would in effect be following their past practice more uniformly. Critics, however, noted that researchers typically could explain only about 35 percent of the sentencing variation observed to have occurred under the guidelines. With two-thirds of the variation unexplained by the guidelines, they contended it was misleading to claim that voluntary guidelines codified past practice.
3. Rich et al., *Sentencing Guidelines*.
4. Tonry, M., *Sentencing Matters,* Oxford, England: Oxford University Press, 1996.
5. Frase, R. S., "Sentencing Reform in Minnesota, Ten Years After: Reflections on Dale G. Parent's Structuring Criminal Sentences: The Evolution of Minnesota's Sentencing Guidelines," *Minnesota Law Review*, 75 (February 19910: 727–754; and Frase, R. S., "Implementing Commission-based Sentencing Guidelines: The Lessons of the First Ten Years in Minnesota," *Wake Forest Law Review*, 1993.
6. Tonry, M., *Sentencing Reform Impacts*, Washington, D.C.: U.S. Department of Justice, National Institute of Justice, 1987.
7. Tonry, *Sentencing Matters*.
8. Knapp, K. A., *The Impact of the Minnesota Sentencing Guidelines: Three Year Evaluation*, St. Paul: Minnesota Sentencing Guidelines Commission, 1984; Miethe, T . D., and C. A. Moore, "Socioeconomic Disparities Under Determinate Sentencing

Systems: A Comparison of Preguideline and Postguideline Practices in Minnesota," *Criminology*, 23 (1985):337–363; and Frase, R. S., "Implementing Commission-based Sentencing Guidelines."

9. Tonry, *Sentencing Matters*.

10. U.S. Sentencing Commission, *Federal Sentencing Guidelines: A Report on the Operation of the Guidelines System and Short-Term Impacts on Disparity in Sentencing, Use of Incarceration, and Prosecutorial Discretion and Plea Bargaining*, Washington, D.C.: U.S. Sentencing Commission, 1991.

11. Rhodes, W. M., "Sentence Disparity, Use of Incarceration, and Plea Bargaining: The Post-Guideline View from the Commission," *Federal Sentencing Reporter* 5 (1992); Weisburd, D., "Sentencing Disparity and the Guidelines: Taking a Closer Look," *Federal Sentencing Reporter* 5 (1992): 149–152; and McDonald, D. C., and K. E. Carlson, *Sentencing in the Courts: Does Race Matter? The Transition to Sentencing Guidelines, 1986–90*, Washington, D.C.: U.S. Department of Justice, Bureau of Justice Statistics, 1993.

12. Knapp, *The Impact of the Minnesota Sentencing Guidelines;* Parent, D. G., *Structuring Criminal Sentences*, Stoneham, MA: Butterworth Legal Publishers, 1988; and Frase, "Implementing Commission-based Sentencing Guidelines."

13. Knapp, *The Impact of the Minnesota Sentencing Guidelines*.

14. Washington State Sentencing Guidelines Commission, *A Decade of Sentencing Reform: Washington and Its Guidelines, 1981–1991*, Olympia, WA: Washington State Sentencing Guidelines Commission, 1992.

15. McDonald and Carlson, *Sentencing in the Courts: Does Race Matter?*

16. Knapp, *The Impact of the Minnesota Sentencing Guidelines;* Parent, *Structuring Criminal Sentences;* Washington State Sentencing Guidelines Commission, *Preliminary Evaluation of Washington State's Sentencing Reform Act*, Olympia, WA: Washington State Sentencing Guidelines Commission, 1986; and Ashford, K., and C. Mosbeck, *First Year Report on Implementation of Sentencing Guidelines: November 1989 to January 1991,* Portland, OR: Oregon Criminal Justice Council, 1991.

17. Tonry, M., "The Failure of the U.S. Sentencing Commission's Guidelines," *Crime and Delinquency*, 39 (April 1993).

18. Ibid.

19. Frase, "Implementing Commission-based Sentencing Guidelines."

20. Boerner, D., "The Legislature's Role in Guidelines Sentencing in 'The Other Washington,'" *Wake Forest Law Review*, 28 (1993):381–420; and Frase, "Implementing Commission-based Sentencing Guidelines."

21. Tonry, *Sentencing Reform Impacts*; Tonry, *Sentencing Matters*.

22. Parent, *Structuring Criminal Sentences*.

23. Ibid.

24. Dunworth, T., and C. D. Weisselberg, "Felony Cases and the Federal Courts: The Guidelines Experience," *Southern California Law Review*, 66 (November 1992):99–153.

25. Garry, J., "Why Me? Application and Misapplication of Section 3A1.1, the Vulnerable Victim Enhancement of the Federal Sentencing Guidelines," *Cornell Law Review,* 79 (November 1993):143–182.

26. McDonald and Carlson, *Sentencing in the Courts: Does Race Matter?*

Chapter 26

Therapeutic Jurisprudence and the Emergence of Problem-Solving Courts

by David Rottman and Pamela Casey

Individual judges, trial courts, and entire state court systems are adopting a new, problem-solving orientation to their work, one well removed from the traditional model of the "dispassionate, disinterested magistrate."[1] In doing so, courts, in many but not all respects, are taking a path previously cut by other components of the criminal justice system, where a problem-solving orientation first emerged as a reaction to the "management-dominated" concept of police reform of the 1970s and 1980s. In the new model, "problem" is defined expansively to include "a wide range of behavioral and social problems that arise in a community."[2] A series of executive sessions convened by the Kennedy School of Government refined this orientation into a community strategy of policing based on the "establishment of effective problem-solving partnerships with the communities they police."[3] Community policing, in turn, helped to shape the strategies of community prosecution, probation, and corrections.

Courts also are establishing problem-solving partnerships, but thus far lack a coherent strategy comparable to community policing. Various approaches are being tested across the country following a variety of principles, including those of therapeutic jurisprudence, which explore the role of the law in fostering therapeutic or antitherapeutic outcomes. Therapeutic jurisprudence attempts to combine a "rights" perspective—focusing on justice, rights, and equality issues—with an "ethic of care" perspective—focusing on care, interdependence, and response to need.[4]

Restorative justice and community justice are related approaches to problem solving that offer the field of therapeutic jurisprudence potential strategies for achieving therapeutic outcomes. In addition, court and community collaboration is a vehicle for implementing therapeutic jurisprudence. (See "Achieving Court and Community Collaboration.") These emerging partnerships are a response to forces pushing and pulling courts toward a more problem-solving and community-focused orientation.

THE ROAD TO THERAPEUTIC JURISPRUDENCE

The main push for this change came from the societal changes that placed courts in the frontline of responses to substance abuse, family breakdown, and mental illness. Courts cannot restrict the flow of such problems into the courtroom, and often such problems

Source: National Institute of Justice, July 1999.

Achieving Court and Community Collaboration

The following describes how courts can achieve a collaborative relationship with the community:

- Collaboration can be achieved by working with community organizations and the public to identify critical community problems and implement problem-solving strategies. The community can contribute in a variety of ways—for example, by providing paid and volunteer staff, assessment and sentencing options, and advice and support to the court.

- Court and community collaborations can problem-solve at both the community and the individual-case level. Such collaborations can address community wide problems in the aggregate, for example by engaging the court and community in programs designed to reduce the frequency of domestic violence, drug use, or juvenile delinquency.
- Collaboration means that the court is engaged with a cross-section of the community in an ongoing dialog that is expansive in scope.

Source: Rottman, D., H. S. Efkeman, and P. Casey, *A Guide to Court and Community Collaboration*, National Center for State Courts, 1998.

stand in the way of effective adjudication of cases.[5] Consequently, courts are struggling to create appropriate dispositional outcomes, including securing treatment and social services.

The push provided by rising caseloads coincided with demands from the public and individual communities for a more responsive and involved judiciary. In recent decades, the courts of most urban and many rural areas have become distant from the public, both physically and psychologically. The public lacks a sense of connection to the court system and views courts as irrelevant to solving the problems of greatest concern to most citizens—the breakdown of social and family support networks. Public opinion surveys indicate considerable dissatisfaction with the accessibility and relevance of the courts and low levels of trust and confidence in the judiciary.

Judges and courts also were pulled rather than pushed toward a problem-solving, proactive orientation. One pull came from a new model for judging that reshapes the nature of the judicial process across the board. (See "A Comparison of Traditional and Transformed Court Processes.") The Commission on Trial Court Performance Standards developed and published in 1990 a set of standards, several of which are relevant to this discussion. First, one standard recognizes an obligation on the part of courts to anticipate and adjust their operations to meet new conditions. Second, three standards hold courts responsible for their standing with the public. These standards acknowledge that objectively measured high performance is not enough if the public fails to perceive that high performance.[6]

THERAPEUTIC JURISPRUDENCE AND ITS APPLICATION

Therapeutic jurisprudence is one source of guidance as the judiciary thinks through the philosophical and practical issues associated with these changes in their role and public expectations. Formally, therapeutic jurisprudence is a relatively new and rapidly growing

A Comparison of Transformed and Traditional Court Processes

Traditional Process	Transformed Process
• Dispute resolution	• Problem-solving dispute avoidance
• Legal outcome	• Therapeutic outcome
• Adversarial process	• Collaborative process
• Claim- or case-oriented	• People-oriented
• Rights-based	• Interest- or needs-based
• Emphasis placed on adjudication	• Emphasis placed on postadjudication and alternative dispute resolution
• Interpretation and application of law	• Interpretation and application of social science
• Judge as arbiter	• Judge as coach
• Backward looking	• Forward looking
• Precedent-based	• Planning-based
• Few participants and stakeholders	• Wide range of participants and stakeholders
• Individualistic	• Interdependent
• Legalistic	• Common-sensical
• Formal	• Informal
• Efficient	• Effective

Source: Warren, Roger K., "Reengineering the Court Process," Madison, WI, Presentation to Great Lakes Court Summit, September 24–25, 1998.

area of academic inquiry. In essence, it "proposes the exploration of ways in which, consistent with principles of justice, the knowledge, theories, and insights of the mental health and related disciplines can help shape the law."[7] The fundamental principle underlying therapeutic jurisprudence is the selection of a therapeutic option—an option that promotes health and does not conflict with other normative values of the legal system.

Therapeutic jurisprudence claims that attending to the individuals as well as the issues involved in a case leads to more effective dispositions.[8]

> Legal rules, legal procedures, and the roles of legal actors (such as lawyers and judges) constitute social forces that, like it or not, often produce therapeutic or antitherapeutic consequences. Therapeutic jurisprudence proposes that we be sensitive to those consequences, and that we ask whether the law's antitherapeutic consequences can be reduced, and its therapeutic consequences enhanced, without subordinating due process and other justice values.[9]

Thus, the orientation underlying therapeutic jurisprudence directs the judge's attention beyond the specific dispute before the court and toward the needs and circumstances of the individuals involved in the dispute.

Within these broad parameters, therapeutic jurisprudence can be implemented on a continuum. First, therapeutic jurisprudence can be practiced by judges when interacting with the individuals involved in a particular case. Second, therapeutic jurisprudence may be practiced at the organizational level of the court by devising new procedures, information systems, and sentencing options and by establishing links to social service providers to promote therapeutic outcomes. Third, for some areas of law and court policy, the practice of therapeutic jurisprudence principles requires changes to State statutes or to court rules, policies, or procedures that apply across courts. The following real-life examples help to clarify the role of therapeutic jurisprudence at all three levels.

At the Individual Case Level

At the individual case level, therapeutic jurisprudence proposes that judges look for "psychojudicial soft spots"—areas in which judicial system actions could lead to antitherapeutic consequences—when interacting with individuals in the courtroom. In some cases, these "therapeutic moments," or opportunities to promote a more therapeutic outcome, are discovered simply by being attentive to the emotional dynamics of the courtroom. Consider a therapeutic moment described by Justice John Kelley of Australia at the London Conference on Criminal Law Reform.

It happened in a rape case in which Justice Kelley reports that he:

> . . . made a special effort to ensure that the victim felt vindicated. He had just sentenced the defendant to prison, but before calling the next case he asked the victim to approach the bench. Justice Kelley had watched the complainant throughout the proceedings, and it was clear that she was very distraught, even after the offender's conviction and sentencing. The justice spoke with her briefly and concluded with these words: "You understand that what I have done here demonstrates conclusively that what happened was not your fault." The young woman began to weep as she left the courtroom. When Justice Kelley called the family several days later, he learned that his words had marked the beginning of psychological healing for the victim. Her tears had been tears of healing.[10]

Most of the examples of therapeutic jurisprudence that have been discussed in the literature, however, reflect a systematic approach to identifying psychojudicial soft spots, which can be applied to more than one individual or case at a time, rather than ad hoc comments. Typically, the examples relate to decisions that the judge must make in a particular category of cases but has discretion in how she or he decides (e.g., accept a no contest plea). For example, research indicates that individuals who commit acts of domestic violence or sexual molestation frequently deny responsibility for or distort the seriousness of their acts.[11] Because such cognitive distortions are likely to lead to recidivistic behavior, attempts to restructure these individuals' cognitive distortions may prove beneficial for the effective disposition of their cases.

One approach for incorporating cognitive restructuring into the court process is to require defendants who enter guilty pleas to provide details about their offenses. After receiving a defendant's guilty plea, for example, one metropolitan court "requires the defendant to take the stand, under oath, and state that he did commit the crime and exactly how he committed it."[12] The defendant's acknowledgment and description of the offense may be helpful in convincing the defendant to participate willingly in treatment. In addition, the detailed description of the offense subsequently may be helpful during treatment if the offender relapses into denying participation in the offense. A related approach is to respond to offenders' denial and minimization of acts of domestic violence by explicitly sentencing them in the same way as offenders who attack strangers.[13]

Concepts associated with behavioral contracting can be adapted by courts to increase compliance with orders in a treatment setting. Behavioral contracting is used in some treatment settings to increase adherence to a treatment plan. In a court setting, it would be used to seek an offender's agreement to comply with the conditions of an order. Agreement is fostered by court efforts to involve the offender in the development of the conditions of the order.[14]

At the Court Level

In some jurisdictions, the therapeutic jurisprudence approach has been adopted at the organizational level in the form of special court programs or specialized courts. Drug treatment courts are the best known example of a court for which therapeutic jurisprudence arguably provides the underlying legal theory.[15] Such courts have five essential elements: (1) immediate intervention; (2) nonadversarial adjudication; (3) hands-on judicial involvement; (4) treatment programs with clear rules and structured goals; and (5) a team approach that brings together the judge, prosecutor, defense counsel, treatment provider, and correctional staff.[16] The therapeutic potential of the courtroom can be exploited in a drug treatment court through simple changes to procedures such as the court calendar. Scheduling new defendants to appear last allows them to observe the court in action, and thus learn what is expected and understand that participating in the program will take considerable effort but can succeed in turning their lives around.[17]

Although other specialized courts are not specifically founded on therapeutic jurisprudence principles, they reflect the same school of thought. For example, consider the following statement from the mission of the Jefferson County Family Court in Louisville, Kentucky:

> Cognizant of the fact that traditional legal approaches may create new barriers to relationships and exacerbate problems within families, the court encourages alternative dispute resolution, and, as appropriate, recommends or orders counseling, self-help, and other available, suitable governmental and community services.[18]

The court's advisory committee has established a subcommittee on the family court as social services delivery system to improve practice on all family court dockets and coordinate social services for all family cases.

A handgun intervention program was established in 1993 by a judge in the 36th district court in Detroit, Michigan, working with a group of volunteers, including court employees (probation officers, clerks, and translators); law enforcement officers; members of the clergy; and other community leaders. The program represents the potential of a special court to work collaboratively with a community to foster therapeutic outcomes for individuals, families, and the entire community.

The program requires that adults charged with felony firearm offenses attend a special 4-hour presentation on the dangers and consequences of gun violence before they are considered eligible for bail release. Juvenile defendants attend on referral. Other participants attend voluntarily, typically on referral from teachers, clergy members, social workers, parents, and past participants. The program, which is held weekly in a courtroom on Saturday mornings, features police officers, probation officers, and a judge who present a focused, fine-tuned message aimed at raising awareness. All of the presentations reinforce the basic message of the program: the need to make positive life choices and to take responsibility for one's own life and the life of one's community. The message is balanced by the availability of practical advice, as well as educational and employment resources.

It should be noted that although specialized courts may be optimal for practicing therapeutic jurisprudence for some categories of cases and defendants, the potential limitations associated with the establishment of specialized courts in general may prove them less optimal. For example, defining the subject matter of the specialized court can be a problem. If the specialization is too broad, it is diluted; if it is too narrow, the volume of cases may be too low to warrant a specialized court. And if the court shares jurisdiction of a particular subject matter, the court system becomes more complex for the user.

Another potential limitation is that specialized courts usually require some amount of judicial specialization. Although such specialization can result in improved precision and accuracy and more creative responses to complex problems, it can result in judicial stress and burnout. Specialized courts also are likely to afford fewer opportunities for judicial career advancement, and because specialized courts generally are viewed as less prestigious among members of the judiciary, it may be more difficult to attract high-quality judges to serve in these courts.

At the Policy Level

Although some therapeutic outcomes can be achieved at either the individual case level or at the court organizational level, some must be addressed at the policy level. For example, a judge may be able to reduce a sexual offender's minimization of an offense by using some of the cognitive restructuring and behavioral contracting ideas mentioned above. However, if the system routinely allows defendants to plead to a lesser offense or enter a nolo contendere or *Alford* plea, cognitive restructuring to overcome offense denial will be more difficult to achieve.[19] Therapeutic jurisprudence, then, would call into question the benefits of the plea bargaining policy, at least for certain offenses.

Examining the consequences of labeling individuals incompetent provides another example of using the therapeutic lens at the policy level. Labeling individuals "as incompetent and thereby depriving them of the opportunity for self-determining behavior induces feelings of helplessness, hopelessness, depression, and low self-esteem."[20] These antitherapeutic consequences suggest revisiting the definition of competency for the purpose of clarifying the concept and narrowing its application.

Another therapeutic issue for courts to consider at the policy level is the coordination of cases involving members of the same family. A family in crisis may come to the court(s) through a civil case (protection order), adult criminal case (assault), juvenile criminal case (delinquency), dependency case (child abuse or neglect), and/or domestic relations case (custody). Notwithstanding these complexities, coordination can be crucial for the physical and psychological well-being of a family. Without information about the family's legal history, such as former and pending cases involving intrafamilial matters, a judge could unknowingly add to the tragedy of a family crisis situation by, for example, awarding unsupervised visitation to a parent who has a juvenile court history of abusing the child. Also, the judge is unlikely to know what services, if any, have already been provided to family members and the impact of those services on the family. Thus, the development and evaluation of mechanisms to track these cases is a policy issue with considerable therapeutic consequences for courts to address.

ALTERNATIVE APPROACHES FOR IMPLEMENTING THERAPEUTIC JURISPRUDENCE

As noted, the practice of therapeutic jurisprudence principles can occur at any point on a continuum that ranges from one judge in one case to an entire state court system. Although individual judges and court staff may view the application of therapeutic jurisprudence principles as beneficial, they also may see it as resource- and time-intensive. Even modest efforts by an individual judge can be time-consuming as the judge begins the process of identifying problem areas and possible therapeutic strategies. Some support for experimenting with therapeutic jurisprudence principles may provide the incentive for individual judges to make the extra effort. For example:

- **Recognize the importance of therapeutic jurisprudence at the state level.** This will let judges know that their efforts in this area are welcomed and considered consistent with state judicial goals. This may be particularly important for judges who work in relative isolation or whose colleagues do not view therapeutic jurisprudence as a worthwhile endeavor.
- **Provide funding for therapeutic jurisprudence pilot projects.** Modest funding might be needed, for example, to support the administration of and incidental costs associated with a small working group of judges and court staff seeking to identify therapeutic strategies to address a specific problem, accessing relevant resources in the jurisdiction, or implementing a specific therapeutic jurisprudence project.
- **Offer training and information on therapeutic jurisprudence.** Educational programs may offer judges an effective and efficient forum for exploring the concept of therapeutic jurisprudence. A clearinghouse at the state level also could facilitate the transfer of therapeutic jurisprudence knowledge and experience from one jurisdiction to another and provide relevant materials and references to assist judges who are just learning about the concept.
- **Recognize innovative therapeutic jurisprudence programs.** The identification of therapeutic jurisprudence practices that work will showcase particular jurisdictions and facilitate the transfer of effective programs.
- **Provide opportunities for judges to share their experiences and ideas.** Judicial interaction can be accomplished at annual conferences and incorporated into judicial education programs, but it also can take place in more informal settings on a local level, such as the therapeutic jurisprudence discussion group in Kalamazoo, Michigan.[21] By continually describing and discussing the application of therapeutic jurisprudence, practitioners will increase their awareness of and sensitivity to therapeutic problems and potential strategies.[22]
- **Revise the code of judicial ethics.** The wording of state codes of judicial ethics may appear to discourage or place little value on problem-solving and court and community collaboration.

The California Judicial Council, working with the American Judicature Society, recently revised its code of judicial ethics to make involvement in problem-solving with the community an expectation. In California, "The question for judicial officers is not 'How to avoid community involvement to ensure compliance with the canons of ethics?' Rather, the question is 'How can judges most effectively balance their community leadership responsibilities within the appropriate limitations?' "[23]

NOTES

1. Zimmerman, Michael D., "A New Approach to Court Reform," *Judicature* 82(3) (November–December 1998). Justice Zimmerman offers a concise and coherent view of changes now occurring in the State courts in response to changes in societal conditions and public expectations of the courts.
2. Goldstein, Herman, "Improving Policing: A Problem-Oriented Approach," *Crime and Delinquency* 25(2) (April 1979):242. Goldstein's definition of a law enforcement problem is notable: "By problems I mean the incredibly broad range of troublesome situations that prompt citizens to turn to the police, such as street robberies, speeding cars, runaway children, accidents, acts of terrorism, even fear."
3. Kelling, George L., and Mark H. Moore, "The Evolving Strategy of Policing," *Perspectives on Policing* 4 (November 1988):1.
4. Janoff, S., "The Influence of Legal Education on Moral Reasoning," *Minnesota Law Review* 76 (1991):194–95.
5. Domestic relations cases in the United States grew by 77 percent and juvenile cases grew by 68 percent between 1984 and 1997. By contrast, the state courts' criminal caseloads grew by 45 percent, their civil caseloads by 34 percent, and the national population by 13 percent during the same time period. See Brian Ostrom and Neal Kauder, eds., *Examining the Work of State Courts, 1997: A National Perspective From the Court Statistics Project*, Williamsburg, Va.: National Center for State Courts, 1998.
6. Standard 4.5 Response to Change: The trial court anticipates new conditions and emerging trends and adjusts its operations as necessary. Commentary: "Effective trial courts are responsive to emergent public issues such as drug abuse, child and spousal abuse, AIDS, drunken driving, child support enforcement . . . ." Public trust and confidence is the fifth court performance area with standards such as "The public has trust and confidence that basic trial court functions are conducted expeditiously and fairly, and that court decisions have integrity." See Commission on Trial Court Performance Standards, *Trial Court Performance Standards With Commentary*, Washington, D.C.: U.S. Department of Justice, Bureau of Justice Assistance, 1997:20. The standards were approved by the Commission and first published in 1990.
7. Wexler, D. B., and B. J. Winick, eds., *Law in a Therapeutic Key*, Durham, N.C.: Carolina Academic Press, 1996:xvii.
8. Janoff, "The Influence of Legal Education on Moral Reasoning," 194–95.
9. Wexler and Winick, *Law in a Therapeutic Key*, xvii.
10. Van Ness, D. W., "New Wine and Old Wineskins: Four Challenges of Restorative Justice," *Criminal Law Forum* 4(252) (1993).
11. Simon, L. M. J., "A Therapeutic Jurisprudence Approach to the Legal Processing of Domestic Violence Cases," and Wexler, D. B., "Reflections on the Scope of Therapeutic Jurisprudence," in D. B. Wexler and B. J. Winick, eds., *Law in a Therapeutic Key*, Durham, N.C.: Carolina Academic Press, 1996:243–85 and 811–29.

12. The court's practice was included in a study by Donald Newman that is cited in Wexler, "Reflections on the Scope of Therapeutic Jurisprudence," 161.

13. Simon, "A Therapeutic Jurisprudence Approach to the Legal Processing of Domestic Violence Cases," 261–62.

14. Wexler, "Reflections on the Scope of Therapeutic Jurisprudence," 168.

15. Hora, Peggy Fulton, William G. Schma, and John T. A. Rosenthal, "Therapeutic Jurisprudence and the Drug Treatment Court Movement: Revolutionizing the Criminal Justice System's Response to Drug Abuse and Crime in America," *Notre Dame Law Review* 74(2) (January 1999):453.

16. Ibid., 453.

17. Ibid., 474.

18. *Kentucky Rules of Court, State*, St. Paul: West Publishing, 1997:429.

19. Wexler, "Reflections on the Scope of Therapeutic Jurisprudence," 159–60.

20. Winick, B. J., "The Side Effects of Incompetency Labeling and the Implications for Mental Health Law," in D. B. Wexler and B. J. Winick, eds., *Law in a Therapeutic Key*, 37.

21. Patry, M. W., D. B. Wexler, D. P. Stolle, and A. J. Tomkins, "Better Legal Counseling Through Empirical Research: Identifying Psycholegal Soft Spots and Strategies," *California Western Law Review* 34 (1998).

22. Wexler, D. B., "Practicing Therapeutic Jurisprudence: Psycholegal Soft Spots and Strategies," *Revista Juridica* 67, (1998):336–42.

23. Judicial Council of California, *Courts Reaching Out to Their Communities: A Handbook for Creating and Enhancing Court and Community Collaboration*, San Francisco: California Judicial Council, 6.1 (1999).

Chapter 27

Restoring the Balance

Juvenile and Community Justice

by Gordon Bazemore and Susan E. Day

The problem of crime can no longer be simplified to the problem of the criminal.

— Leslie Wilkins

Offender-based control strategies are incomplete, since they take a 'closed system' view of correctional interventions: change the offender and not the community.

— James Byrne

In a democratic society, citizens' expectations of government agencies are critically important. Unfortunately, within our juvenile justice system, community needs have been lost in the decade-long debate over the future of the juvenile court and the relative efficacy of punishment versus treatment. A number of politicians and policymakers argue for criminalizing our juvenile justice system through "get tough," adult sentences for juvenile offenders. Some even advocate abolishing the juvenile justice system and its foundation, the independent juvenile court.

On the other hand, many proponents of the juvenile court call for reaffirming the traditional treatment mission. Increasingly, the public and even many juvenile justice professionals perceive that treatment and punishment options are, as one judge aptly put it, "bad choices between sending kids to jail or sending them to the beach."

It is doubtful that either traditional treatment or criminalized retributive models can restore public confidence in the juvenile justice system. Only through extensive, meaningful citizen participation will public expectations and community needs be met. For most juvenile justice systems, achieving this level of involvement will require substantial restructuring.

This article describes an alternative approach to addressing juvenile crime that focuses on the interests of multiple justice clients. Alternatively referred to as restorative justice, the balanced approach, and balanced and restorative justice (BRJ), this model is viewed by a growing number of juvenile justice professionals as a way to reengage the community in the juvenile justice process.

From *Juvenile Justice*, December 1996, pp. 3–14. Reprinted by permission of the U.S. Department of Justice, Office of Juvenile Justice and Delinquency Prevention.

THE LIMITS OF CURRENT PARADIGMS

> Crime should never be the sole or even primary business of the State if real differences are sought in the well-being of individuals, families, and communities. The structure, procedures, and evidentiary rules of the formal criminal justice process coupled with most justice officials' lack of knowledge and connection to (the parties) affected by crime preclude the State from acting alone to achieve transformative changes. (Judge Barry Stuart)

> Worse still, we fear that even when something does work, it is seen to do so only in the eyes of certain professionals, while 'outside' the system, ordinary citizens are left without a role or voice in the criminal justice process. (John Braithewaite and Stephen Mugford)

Advocates of reaffirming treatment argue that the system is failing because it lacks adequate resources. Critics and defenders of juvenile justice, however, argue that juvenile justice systems have failed to articulate a vision of success. If juvenile justice is underfunded, it is also underconceptualized. As closed-system paradigms, the treatment and retributive models are insular and one-dimensional. They are insular because they are offender-focused and one-dimensional because they fail to address the community's diverse interests.

Although the punitive approach may appease public demand for retribution, it does little to rehabilitate or reintegrate juvenile offenders. Punishment is often used inappropriately, resulting in amply documented negative effects. Ironically, retributive punishment may encourage offenders to focus on themselves rather than on their victims. Even increasing its severity may have little impact if we have miscalculated the extent to which sanctions such as incarceration are experienced as punishment.[1]

In the public mind, punishment is at least somewhat related to offense. In contrast, treatment appears to address only the needs of the offender. Treatment programs often ask little of the offender beyond participating in counseling, remedial services, or recreational programs. Even when such programs "work," they make little difference in the lives of victims of juvenile crime, citizens concerned with the safety of their neighborhoods, or individuals who want young offenders held accountable for their actions.[2]

In fact, both punitive and treatment models focus little attention on the needs of victims and victimized communities. Neither model engages them as clients or as coparticipants in the justice process. Whether treatment or punishment is emphasized the offender is the passive and solitary recipient of intervention and service. Increasingly reliant on facilities, treatment programs, and professional experts, juvenile justice systems exclude victims and other community members from what could be meaningful roles in sanctioning, rehabilitation, and public safety.

Fortunately, treatment and retributive models are not the only options for juvenile justice. The alternative, a community-oriented system, would involve citizens in setting clear limits on antisocial behavior and determining consequences for offenders. Victims' needs for reparation, validation and healing would be at the core of a community justice system, which would work toward building crime-resistant communities whose residents feel safe. It would emphasize the need for building relationships and involving youth in work, service, and other roles that facilitate bonding with law-abiding adults. Finally, a community justice system would articulate more meaningful roles in rehabilitating offenders and improving community safety for employers, civic groups, religious communities, families, and other citizens.

TOWARD COMMUNITY JUVENILE JUSTICE:
A BALANCED AND RESTORATIVE APPROACH

> Government is responsible for preserving *order* but the community is responsible for establishing *peace*. (Daniel Van Ness)

- In inner-city Pittsburgh, young offenders in an intensive day treatment program solicit input from community organizations about service projects they would like to see completed in the neighborhood. They work with community residents on projects that include home repair and gardening for the elderly, voter registration drives, painting homes and public buildings, and planting and cultivating community gardens.
- In Florida, young offenders sponsored by the Florida Department of Juvenile Justice and supervised by The 100 Black Men of Palm Beach County, Inc., plan and execute projects that serve as shelters for abused, abandoned, and HIV-positive and AIDS-infected infants and children. In Palm Beach County, victim advocates train juvenile justice staff on sensitivity in their interaction with victims and help prepare victim awareness curicula for youth in residential programs.
- In cities and towns in Pennsylvania, Montana, Minnesota, Australia, and New Zealand, family members and other citizens acquainted with a juvenile offender or victim of a juvenile crime gather to determine the best response to the offense. Held in schools, churches, or other community facilities, these family group conferences are facilitated by a community justice coordinator or police officer and ensure that offenders hear community disapproval of their behavior. Participants develop an agreement for repairing the damage to victim and community and a plan for reintegrating the offender.
- In Minnesota, Department of Corrections staff collaborate with local police and citizen groups to establish family group conferencing programs and inform the community about offender monitoring and victim support. In Dakota County, a suburb [outside] Minneapolis, retailers and senior citizens whose businesses and homes have been damaged by burglary or vandalism call a crime repair hotline to request a work crew of probationers to repair the damage.
- In Deschutes County, Oregon, offender work crews cut and deliver firewood to senior citizens and worked with a local contractor to build a homeless shelter.
- In more than 150 cities and towns throughout North America, victims and offenders meet with volunteer mediators to develop an agreement for restitution. At these meetings, victims express their feelings about the crime and gain information about the offense.
- In several cities in Montana, college students and other young adults in the Montana Conservation Corps supervise juvenile offenders working on environmental restoration, trail building, and other community service projects. They also serve as mentors.

While many professionals have become demoralized as juvenile justice systems are threatened with extinction, others are seeking to create a new partnership between youth and victim advocates, concerned citizens, and community groups.

The balanced and restorative justice model is centered around community-oriented responses to crime.[3] Jurisdictions implementing it represent a diverse range of urban, suburban, and rural communities. These communities share a common commitment to restructuring juvenile justice on the basis of a new mission (balanced approach) and a new value framework (restorative justice).

RESTORATIVE AND COMMUNITY JUSTICE

From the perspective of restorative justice, the most significant aspect of crime is that it victimizes citizens and communities. The justice system should focus on repairing this harm by ensuring that offenders are held accountable for making amends for the damage and suffering they have caused. The most important issue in a restorative response to crime is not deciding whether to punish or treat offenders. Rather, as Howard Zehr suggests, the three primary questions to be answered are "What is the harm?" "What needs to be done to make it right?" and "Who is responsible?"[4]

A restorative system would help to ensure that offenders make amends to their victims. Juvenile justice cannot do this alone, however. Restorative justice requires that not only government but victims, offenders, and communities be actively involved in the justice process. In fact, some have argued that the health of a community is determined by the extent to which citizens participate in community decisions. An effective justice system strengthens the capacity of communities to respond to crime and empowers them to do so. As Judge Barry Stuart notes:

> When members fail to assume responsibility for decisions affecting the community, community life will be characterized by the absence of a collective sense of caring, a lack of respect for diverse values, and ultimately a lack of any sense of belonging. . . . Conflict, if resolved through a process that constructively engages the parties involved, can be a fundamental building ingredient of any relationship. As members increase their ability to resolve disputes creatively, the ability of the community to effectively sanction crime, rehabilitate offenders, and promote public safety increases.[5]

The most unique feature of restorative justice is its elevation of the role of victims in the justice system. Victim rights has become a popular slogan, but victim needs are addressed by the system only after the needs of judges, prosecutors, probation officers, treatment providers, and even offenders are considered. Restorative justice does not define victim rights as the absence of offender rights; it focuses on the needs of victim, community, and offender. To bring balance to the present offender-driven system, however, it is necessary to give priority to victims' needs for physical, material, and emotional healing.

THE BALANCED APPROACH MISSION

The balanced approach is a back-to-basics mission for juvenile justice that supports a community's need to sanction crime, rehabilitate offenders, and ensure public safety. Toward these ends, it articulates three goals for juvenile justice: accountability, public safety, and competency development.[6] Balance is attainable when administrators ensure that equitable resources are allocated to each goal.

- **Accountability.** Crime is sanctioned most effectively when offenders take responsibility for their crimes and the harm caused to victims, when offenders make amends by restoring losses, and when communities and victims take active roles in the sanctioning process. Because the offender's obligation is defined primarily as an obligation to his victims rather than to the state, accountability cannot be equated with responsiveness to juvenile justice professionals by obeying a curfew, complying with drug screening, or writing an essay. Nor can it be equated with punishment. It is easier to make offenders take their punishment than it is to get them to take responsibility for their actions.

- **Competency.** The most successful rehabilitation ensures that young offenders make measurable gains in educational, vocational, social, civic, and other competencies that enhance their capacity to function as productive adults. When competency is defined as the capacity to do something well that others value, the standard for achieving success is measured in the community. Competency is not the mere absence of bad behavior. It should increase the capacity of adults and communities to involve young people in work, service, dispute resolution, community problem solving, and cognitive skills building.

- **Public safety.** Assuring public safety requires more than mere incapacitation. Communities cannot be kept safe simply by locking up offenders. Locked facilities must be part of any public safety strategy, but they are the least cost-effective component. A balanced strategy invests heavily in strengthening a community's capacity to prevent and control crime. A problem-oriented focus ensures that the time of offenders under supervision in the community is structured around such activities as work, education, and service. Adults, including parents, are assigned clear roles in monitoring offenders. A balanced strategy cultivates new relationships with schools, employers, and other community groups to enhance the role of juvenile justice professionals as resources in prevention and positive youth development.

The principle behind BRJ is that justice is best served when victims, offenders, and communities receive equitable attention in the justice process. The needs of one client cannot be met unless the needs of other clients are addressed. Crime severs bonds between victims, offenders, and families. Although offenders must take full responsibility for their acts, the responsibility for restoring mutual respect, understanding, and support among those involved must be shared by the community.

SMALL CHANGES YIELD LARGE RESULTS

The change at the heart of BRJ is embodied in the community-building interventions described above. BRJ collaborators, including juvenile justice and other service professionals, have discovered that even small changes in how they conduct business can have immediate and lasting effects on the dynamics of community relationships.

Communities in the United States and across the globe are making dramatic policy changes on the basis of restorative priorities. In 1989, New Zealand began requiring that all juvenile offenders over age 14 (except in the most serious cases) be referred to a family group conference in which restorative goals are addressed in meetings that include victims, offenders, support groups, families, policy-makers, social workers, and others. The New Zealand law appears to have drastically reduced court work-loads and the use of incarceration.[7]

Fourteen states have enacted legislation adopting the balanced approach as the mission of their juvenile justice systems. A number of states have administrative rules or statewide policies that require case managers and other decision makers to consider the goals of the balanced approach in dispositional recommendations. In Pennsylvania and Montana, decision makers are using balanced approach criteria funding guidelines and have formed statewide groups to oversee the development of restorative justice efforts.

Balanced and restorative justice cannot be achieved by mandates or legislation alone. As the three jurisdictions that constitute the OJJDP-funded demonstration effort are learning, the new model cannot be implemented overnight. Working with different juvenile justice systems in diverse communities, administrators in Palm Beach County, Florida, Dakota County, Minnesota, and Allegheny County, Pennsylvania, are pursuing varied approaches to systemic change to build a restorative model from the ground up. These administrators have made significant progress but acknowledge that the kind of change envisioned by BRJ is quite different from past practices. This change is especially striking in the model's focus on citizen involvement, including restructuring juvenile justice agencies to more effectively engage the community.

BALANCED AND RESTORATIVE JUSTICE: NEW ROLES FOR CITIZENS AND PROFESSIONALS

> I'm glad to see somebody is finally trying to instill some responsibility in these kids. I'm happy to help when it's obvious that we're trying to make taxpayers out of these kids, rather than tax liabilities. (Community Member)

> In the mediation session I learned that the offender was just a little kid and not the threat I thought he was. I also learned he had some needs that weren't being met. . . . For the first time (I've been a victim before), it seemed like someone was responding to my needs and listening to me. (Youth Crime Victim)

> When I first walked into the conferencing meeting and saw the victim and her friends and then saw my grandfather there I wished I could have gone to jail instead. But once everybody had talked about the crime I began to realize that Mrs. B was really hurt and scared by what I had done. I had to work hard to earn the money to pay her back and to do the community service hours (but the work on the crew was pretty fun) and I thought it was fair after all. (Juvenile Offender)

> Now I know what my job is really about! As a manager, I have a better sense of how to allocate, or reallocate, our resources. And my staff are getting a better sense of what their role is and how this fits with my vision of what the community's role should be. We know we're really 'out of balance,' but for the first time we have a plan to move forward without chasing every fad and new program that comes along. We can also talk to the community about what we're doing in a way that they understand and want to help. (Manager of a Local Juvenile Justice System)

As a community justice model, balanced and restorative justice offers a new vision of how victims, offenders, and others can be involved in the juvenile justice process. As table 1 illustrates, this vision is best understood by examining how the model is viewed by its participants.

Balanced and restorative justice is a work in progress. No juvenile justice system is completely balanced or fully restorative. But if juvenile justice systems, including those most committed to the model, fail to meet the standards they have set for community and client involvement, it is not because the model is utopian. It is because administrators are constrained by management protocols designed to deliver services based on the treatment and retributive paradigms.

The innovation of balanced and restorative justice lies in its agenda for restructuring the juvenile justice system to make it community-focused rather than bureaucracy-driven. This agenda demands new values, clients, performance objectives, decision-making processes, program priorities, staff roles, and patterns of resource allocation. While most juvenile justice agencies determine intervention priorities on the basis of current staff roles and resource allocations, juvenile justice managers who adopt the balanced approach mission are committed to making their agencies and systems value- and client-driven and outcome-oriented. Decisions are based on the premise that pro-

---

TABLE 1.   The Participants in a Balanced and Restorative Juvenile Justice System

Crime victims

Receive support, assistance, compensation, information, and services.

Receive restitution or other reparation from the offender.

Are involved and are encouraged to give input at all points in the system as to how the offender will repair the harm done.

Have the opportunity to face the offenders and tell their story.

Feel satisfied with the justice process.

Provide guidance and consultation to juvenile justice professionals on planning and advisory groups.

Offenders

Complete restitution to their victims.

Provide meaningful service to repay the debt to their communities.

Face the personal harm caused by their crimes by participating in victim offender mediation or other victim awareness programs.

Complete work experience and active and productive tasks that increase skills and improve the community.

Are monitored by community adults as well as juvenile justice providers and supervised to the greatest extent possible in the community.

Improve decision-making skills and have opportunities to help others.

Citizens, families, and community groups

Are involved to the greatest extent possible in rehabilitation, community safety initiatives, and holding offenders accountable.

Work with offenders on local community service projects.

Provide support to victims.

Provide support to offenders as mentors, employers, and advocates.

Provide work for offenders to pay restitution to victims and service opportunities that allow offenders to make meaningful contributions to the quality of community life.

Assist families to support the offender in obligation to repair the harm and increase competencies.

Advise courts and corrections and play an active role in disposition.

grams are means to accomplish restorative outcomes that address community needs (see table 2).

From a community justice perspective, the value of a program and the quality of its implementation is gauged in large measure by the extent to which it involves community members at all levels of implementation.

CITIZEN INVOLVEMENT AND CLIENT FOCUS

In the total quality management (TQM) movement,[8] the concept of a client involves three components: a recipient of service, a target of intervention and change, and a coparticipant who must have input into the process and be involved to the greatest extent possible in decisionmaking.

The input of each client group is needed to stimulate and maintain community involvement. Currently few citizens are involved at significant levels in juvenile justice because they are seldom asked. Although many professionals would welcome community involvement and may work hard at collaboration and service brokerage, such efforts often fail to include employers, clergy, civic leaders, and neighborhood residents. Too often, juvenile justice agencies are unable to find appropriate roles for community members who are not social service professionals or time to support their efforts. Short-term involvement is often uninteresting because it is not linked to interventions that achieve significant outcomes for offenders or victims. When citizens are asked to participate, it is often on the basis of civic duty rather than personal commitment. As Braithwaite and Mugford observe, citizens are more willing to become involved if they have a personal interest in the offender, victim, or the family.[9]

Crimes typically evoke a community of concern for the victim, the offender, families and friends, and interested citizens and community groups. As the New Zealand experiment with family group conferencing illustrates, these personal communities can be a primary resource in resolving youth crimes. It is around such microcommunities that citizen participation in justice decisionmaking is being built.[10]

BRJ practices and programs invite a high level of citizen participation. Community involvement is never easy, but it is satisfying for citizens to help young offenders make restitution to their victims.

The more active roles for offenders, victims, and community in the juvenile justice process, noted in table 1, have implications for the roles of juvenile justice professionals. The most important and difficult challenge in moving toward balanced and restorative justice will be to alter the job descriptions and professional orientations of juvenile justice staff. For those accustomed to working with offenders individually or in programs and facilities, the role change implied by the need to engage victims and communities may be dramatic. Essentially, this change may be best understood as moving from direct service provider or service broker to community justice facilitator.[11]

As table 3 suggests, the new roles involve juvenile justice professionals in activities with each of the three justice clients. These activities include a variety of efforts to enhance preventive capacity and to help adults provide offenders with opportunities for competency development.

TABLE 2.   Outcome Measures and Priorities for Practice in the Balanced Approach

---

Competency development
Intermediate outcome

Measures	**Priorities for practice**
Proportion of youth on supervision completing successful work experience or employment (quality of experience?).	Structured work experience and employment programs.
Proportion of youth on supervision completing meaningful work/service project.	Service/active learning.
Extent of bonding between youth under supervision and community adults.	Cognitive and decisionmaking programs.
Increase in empathy and improvement in skills.	Dispute resolution training.
Demonstrated improvement in conflict resolution and anger management.	Intergenerational projects.
Measured increase in educational, interpersonal, citizenship, and other competencies.	Cross-age tutoring.
	Conservation and environmental awareness.

Accountability
Intermediate outcome

Measures	**Priorities for practice**
Proportion of offenders completing fair and appropriate restitution orders or agreements.	Restitution to victims.
Proportion of victims given input into the process.	Restorative community service.
Proportion of victims satisfied with the process.	Victim offender mediation.
Proportion of offenders showing measured increase in victim awareness and empathy.	Direct service to victims or surrogate victims.
Proportion of offenders and victims completing mediation or other resolution and community service.	Victim awareness panels or victim offender groups in treatment programs.
Proportion of offenders completing meaningful community service projects (number of such projects completed).	

Public safety
Intermediate outcome

Measures	**Priorities for practice**
Proportion of offenders reoffending while under juvenile justice supervision.	Structuring time of offenders being supervised in the community: work experience, community service, and alternative education.
Number of citizens involved in preventive and monitoring activities.	Effective use of natural surveillance and community guardians such as employers, relatives, churches, and mentors.
Decrease in community fear and increase in understanding of juvenile justice.	
Decrease in school violence and increase in school and community-based conflict resolution.	Continuum of graduated community-based sanctions and surveillance.
Increase in competency, empathy, and internal controls for offenders under supervision.	Prevention and capacity building in schools and other community groups.

TABLE 3.   New Roles in the Balanced and Restorative Justice Model

---

The coparticipants

Victim	Active participant in defining the harm of the crime and shaping the obligations placed on the offender.
Community	Responsible for supporting and assisting victims, holding offenders accountable, and ensuring opportunities for offenders to make amends.
Offender	Active participant in reparation and competency development.

Juvenile justice professional

Sanctioning	Facilitate mediation, ensure restoration, develop creative or restorative community service options, engage community members, and educate the community on its role.
Rehabilitation	Develop new roles for young offenders that allow them to practice and demonstrate competency, assess and build on youth and community strengths, and develop community partnerships.
Public safety	Develop incentives and consequences to ensure offender compliance with supervision objectives, help school and family control and maintain offenders in the community, and develop prevention capacity of local organizations.

GETTING THERE

> Some may say this [movement toward restorative justice] is Utopian. While this may be true, in a climate of failure and irrational extremism in the response to juvenile crime, there may be *nothing so practical as a good Utopia*. (Lode Walgrave)

Robert Fulcrum tells the story of a reporter visiting the cathedral in Chartres, France, during the cathedral's construction. Hoping to get a sense of how those working on this magnificent structure understood and experienced their contribution to its completion, the reporter began asking several workmen about their jobs. The first, a stonecutter, said that his job was simply to cut the stone into square blocks for someone else to use in the foundation; the job was monotonous, and he had been doing the same thing day in and day out. Next, the reporter asked a workman who was painting stone blocks on the front of the building about his job. "I just paint these blocks and nothing more," he said. "There is not much to it."

Frustrated that these workmen had little to say about the significance of working on this historical effort, the reporter moved to another part of the building and approached a man carefully cutting stained glass windows. Surely, this man felt that his work was the artistic opportunity of a lifetime. Once again the reporter was disappointed; the man said that he was very tired and somewhat bored with his task. Finally, as he walked out of the cathedral in despair, the reporter passed an elderly woman stooped and working rapidly to clean up the debris left from the stone and glass cutters, painters, and other artisans. He asked what it was that she was doing. Her answer was that she was building the most magnificent cathedral in the history of the world to the glory of God.

As this story illustrates, the key to progress toward restorative justice is viewing small steps as the building blocks of a more effective juvenile justice system.

Will balanced and restorative justice work? BRJ is not a treatment program but a model for system reform. It cannot be assessed by using traditional program evaluation technologies. The success of a restorative justice system should be measured not only by recidivism but also by victim satisfaction, offender accountability, competency development, and public safety.[12] The success of BRJ will depend on the consistency and integrity of implementation, how well its core philosophy is understood, how effectively it is adapted to local conditions, and whether restorative justice is given a chance. Although restorative justice may not lead to immediate reductions in recidivism, the standard of comparison should be the current system. As a First Nations Community Justice Coordinator in Yukon, Canada, reminds us:

> So we make mistakes. Can you—the current system—say you don't make mistakes? . . . If you don't think you do, walk through our community. Every family will have something to teach you. . . . By getting involved, by all of us taking responsibility, it is not that we won't make mistakes, we would be doing it together, as a *community* instead of having it done to us. . . . We need to make *real differences* in the way people act and the way we treat others. . . . Only if we empower them and support them can they break out of this trap.[13]

It is the failure of the current paradigms that has moved some policy-makers toward radical measures to abolish the juvenile justice system. Those who wish to preserve it see balanced and restorative justice as a means to do so by crafting a new system in which juvenile justice reflects community justice.

NOTES

1. For commentary on closed-system approaches to community corrections, see J. Byrne, "Reintegrating the Concept of Community in Community Corrections," *Crime and Delinquency* 35 (1989): 471–499; see also A. J. Reiss and M. Tonry, "Why Are Communities Important in Understanding Crime?" *Communities and Crime* (Chicago: University of Chicago Press, 1986). Like treatment, punishment will remain an essential component of any juvenile justice system. However, punitive measures focused primarily on incarceration represent only one limited approach to meeting community needs to sanction crime. For commentary on more educative and expressive approaches to setting tolerance limits for crime, see J. Braithewaite, *Crime, Shame and Reintegration* (Cambridge, England: Cambridge University Press, 1989); L. Wilkins, *Punishment, Crime and Market Forces* (Brookfield, VT: Dartmouth Publishing Company, 1991); and G. Bazemore and M. Umbreit, "Rethinking the Sanctioning Function in Juvenile Court: Retributive or Restorative Responses to Youth Crime," *Crime and Delinquency* 41 (1995): 296–316. The counterdeterrent effects of retributive punishment, including stigmatization, weakening bonds, and conventional peer and adult relations, are also well documented. Finally, empirical evidence that criminal justice decision makers typically overestimate the perceived punitive effects of incarceration is provided in M. Crouch, "Is Incarceration Really Worse? Analysis of Offenders' Preferences for Prison Over Probation," *Justice Quarterly* 10 (1993): 67–88.

2. The critique of the individual treatment model presented here is not premised on the largely discredited "nothing works" perspective, nor do we question the need for an effective rehabilitative model for juvenile justice. Rather, our criticisms of traditional counseling-based treatment are based primarily upon the very limited context of intervention in most treatment programs and on the deficit assumptions about offenders on which most of these programs are based. A more comprehensive agenda for rehabilitation and reintegration would focus more on relationship building and the development of roles for delinquent youth that allow them to demonstrate competency while forming bonds with conventional peers and adults. A competency development component of such a reintegrative and restorative agenda is outlined in G. Bazemore and P. Cruise, "Reinventing Rehabilitation: Exploring a Competency Development Model for Juvenile Justice Intervention," *Perspectives* 19 (1995): 4; and G. Bazemore and C. Terry, "Developing Delinquent Youth: A Reintegrative Model for Rehabilitation and a New Role for the Juvenile Justice System," *Child Welfare* (forthcoming).

3. Balanced and Restorative Justice (BRJ) is also the title of a national action research project funded through the Technical Assistance and Training Prevention division of the Office of Juvenile Justice and Delinquency Prevention. This project provides national training and information dissemination as well as support and assistance to demonstration projects currently implementing BRJ.

4. H. Zehr, *Changing Lenses: A New Focus for Crime and Justice* (Scottsdale, PA: Herald Press, 1990).

5. Judge B. Stuart, notes from presentation at the annual conference of the Society for Professionals in Dispute Resolution (Toronto, Canada, 1993): 7.

6. In a balanced system, programs and practices aimed at repairing harm to victims should, as Troy Armstrong has phrased it, "resonate with" practices aimed at rehabilitative and public safety objectives. Specifically, holding offenders accountable is a first step in the rehabilitative process. Developing capacities for competent behavior in offenders increases community safety by increasing connectedness and concern for others as well as life skills. Enhanced community safety is often necessary to carry out meaningful community sanctioning, offender reintegration, and victim support and restoration. For a detailed discussion of the balanced approach mission, see D. Maloney and G. Bazemore, "Rehabilitating Community Service: Toward Restorative Service in a Balanced Justice System," *Federal Probation* (1994); G. Bazemore, "On Mission Statements and Reform in Juvenile Justice: The Case of the Balanced Approach," *Federal Probation* (1992); G. Bazemore and C. Washington, "Charting the Future of the Juvenile Justice System: Reinventing Mission and Management," *Spectrum: The Journal of State Government* (1995). Table 2 of this paper provides a general summary of how performance objectives on each goal can be measured.

7. F.W.M. McElrae, "Restorative Justice—The New Zealand Youth Court: A Model for Development in Other Courts?" *Journal of Judicial Administration* 4 (1994), Australian Institute of Judicial Administration, Melbourne, Australia.

8. W. E. Deming, *Out of Crisis* (Cambridge, MA: MIT Center for Advanced Engineering, 1986); L. Martin, *Total Quality Management in Organizations* (Newbury Park, CA: Sage, 1993).

9. J. Braithewaite and S. Mugford, "Conditions of Successful Reintegration Ceremonies: Dealing with Juvenile Offenders," *British Journal of Criminology* (1995):

34. The authors give examples of how relatives, friends, and acquaintances of young offenders, victims, and their families become vital resources in restoring and meeting the needs of crime victims while also helping offenders when asked to participate in family group conferences.

10. For a more detailed description of the New Zealand and Australian models of family group conferencing, including research findings and critical concerns about implementation, see G. Maxwell and A. Morris, *Family, Victims, and Culture: Youth Justice in New Zealand* (Wellington, New Zealand: Social Policy Agency and Victoria University, Institute of Criminology, 1993); C. Alder and J. Wundersitz, *Family Group Conferencing: The Way Forward or Misplaced Optimism?* (Canberra, Australia: Australian Institute of Criminology, 1994); M. Umbreit and S. Stacy, "Family Group Conferencing Comes to the U.S.: A Comparison With Victim Offender Mediation," *Juvenile and Family Court Journal*.

11. The transformation from service provider to the facilitator role is used to describe changes in probation services in the Vermont Department of Corrections' restructuring of the State's probation system through Community Reparative Boards.

12. Answering the question "Does it work?" in a restorative community justice framework must give consideration to improvements in the capacity of community groups and citizens to prevent, sanction, and control crime. For example, the development of community support groups of nonprofessional citizens is generally not viewed as a success outcome, but such measures may be a more critical gauge of long-term community safety than reductions in recidivism of offenders in treatment programs.

13. Rose Couch, Community Justice Coordinator, Quanlin Dun First Nations, Yukon, Canada. As quoted in B. Stuart, "Sentencing Circles: Making 'Real Differences'," monograph, Territorial Court of Yukon, Whitehorse, Yukon, Canada.

SUPPLEMENTAL READING

Bazemore, G., and M. S. Umbreit, (1995). "Rethinking the Sanctioning Function in Juvenile Court: Retributive or Restorative Responses to Youth Crime." *Crime and Delinquency* 41(3): 296–316. This article proposes restorative justice as an alternative model for the juvenile courts to address limitations of sanctioning choices inherent in individual treatment and retributive justice paradigms. NCJ 156328

Bazemore, G., and M. S. Umbreit. (1994). *Balanced and Restorative Justice.* Washington, DC: U.S. Department of Justice, Office of Juvenile Justice and Delinquency Prevention. Community supervision of juvenile offenders based on the balanced and restorative justice approach is discussed in this examination of the Balanced and Restorative Justice Project being developed as an out-growth of the Office of Juvenile Justice and Delinquency Prevention's juvenile restitution training and technical assistance program. NCJ 149727

Cragg, W. (1992). *Practice of Punishment: Towards a Theory of Restorative Justice.* New York: Routledge. This book develops a theory of punishment in which the central function of law is to reduce the need to use force in the resolution of disputes. The author examines traditional approaches to punishment to determine why they have failed to provide a coherent and humane approach to sentencing and corrections. NCJ 143921

Umbreit, M. S. (1995). "Holding Juvenile Offenders Accountable: A Restorative Justice Perspective." *Juvenile and Family Court Journal* 46(2): 31–42. This article defines accountability for juvenile offenders as an intervention strategy within the context of the restorative justice paradigm, in which the meaning of accountability shifts from incurring a debt to society to incurring a responsibility for making amends to the victimized person. NCJ 156121

Umbreit, M. S., R. B. Coates, and B. Kalanj. (1994). *Victim Meets Offender: The Impact of Restorative Justice and Mediation*. Monsey, NY: Willow Tree Press. This book reports findings from a study of victim-offender reconciliation and mediation programs for juvenile offenders in California, Minnesota, New Mexico, and Texas. NCJ 147713

QUESTIONS FOR THOUGHT AND DISCUSSION

Chapter 17: "Adversarial Justice" by Franklin Strier

1. Why is the adversarial trial system such an integral part of American trial process?
2. What types of abuse are associated with the adversarial trial system?
3. Is reform of the American trial system realistic?

Chapter 18: "Talking on Testilying: The Prosecutor's Response to In-Court Police Deception," by Larry Cunningham

1. What is testilying?
2. Under what circumstances is testilying justified?
3. Does the adversarial trial system create the context for such behavior?

Chapter 19: "Capital Murder: A Prosecutor's Personal Observations on the Prosecution of Capital Cases," by Ronald J. Sievert

1. Does the author support or denounce the death penalty?
2. According to the author, is racial bias a problem in capital cases?
3. According to the author, what purpose does the death penalty serve?

Chapter 20: "Why Prosecutors Misbehave," by Bennet L. Gershman

1. In what ways can prosecutors gain distinct advantages for winning cases by crossing over ethical lines?
2. Which aspects of the prosecutor role create the most temptation to act unethically?
3. What are some ways to curb the misconduct of prosecutors?

Chapter 21: "The Criminal Lawyer's 'Different Mission': Reflection on the 'Right' to Present a False Case," by Harry I. Subin

1. How far should defense attorneys go in presenting a false case to represent a client, and when have they gone too far?
2. What are the arguments used to debate the "truth" theory versus the "fight" theory? With which do you agree?

Chapter 22: "How to Improve the Jury System," by Thomas F. Hogan, Gregory E. Mize, and Kathleen Clark

1. Are the recommendations made for improving the jury system practical?
2. What are some possible obstacles in implementing such changes to the jury system?

Chapter 23: "Should Juries Nullify Laws They Consider Unjust or Excessively Punitive?" by Clay S. Conrad and Nancy King

1. What is jury nullification? When is it justified?
2. What are the advantages and disadvantages of nullification?

Chapter 24: "Truth in Sentencing in State Prisons," by Paula M. Ditton and Doris James Wilson

1. What is the purpose of truth-in-sentencing guidelines?
2. How does truth in sentencing differ compared with other sentencing reforms?
3. What has been the short-term impact of such sentencing guidelines?
4. What are the long-term implications of such sentencing guidelines for correctional facilities?

Chapter 25: "The Impact of Sentencing Guidelines," by Dale Parent, Terence Dunworth, Douglas McDonald, and William Rhodes

1. What are the advantages and disadvantages of sentencing guidelines?
2. How have sentencing guidelines impacted the criminal justice system?

Chapter 26: "Therapeutic Jurisprudence and the Emergence of Problem-Solving Courts," by David Rottman and Pamela Casey

1. What are some of the steps for achieving therapeutic jurisprudence?
2. Is such an approach realistic given the adversarial system of justice? Explain.
3. How would such a model work in culturally diverse communities?

Chapter 27: "Restoring the Balance: Juvenile and Community Justice" by Gordon Bazemore and Susan E. Day

1. How does restorative justice differ from traditional juvenile justice strategies?
2. What do the authors mean by "the interests of multiple justice clients?"
3. What are some of the outcome measures critical to a restorative justice model?

Section 4
Jails, Prisons, and Community-Based Corrections

INTRODUCTION

As we begin a new century the number of adults under some form of correctional control in the United States has reached an all-time high of 6.3 million—just over 3% of the of all United States adult residents—in jail, prison, or under some form of community-based correctional supervision. The corrections system, overcrowded and seemingly ineffective, has been subject to a great deal of controversy, beginning with the Quaker-inspired prisons in Pennsylvania over 200 years ago and continuing today. This section analyzes the major components of the correctional system, examines the issues, and reviews alternatives to traditional prison and community-based correctional modalities.

This section opens with "Facts About Jails, Prisons, and Community Corrections." These data, derived from recent Bureau of Justice Statistics reports, allow the reader to gain a feel for the extent of the use of correctional strategies to control crime and to understand the various constituencies affected.

In Chapter 28, "Life on the Inside: The Jailers," Andrew Metz provides the reader with a rather unique personal perspective concerning life as a correctional officer. The misconception often held by the general public is that a correctional officer's job is rather mundane and routine. However, Metz takes the reader on an experiential journey by explicitly writing about the fears, apprehensions, and personal misgivings not usually associated with those in the profession.

In Chapter 29, "The Imprisonment of Women in America," Pauline Katherine Brennan reviews the current status of women in prison. Professor Brennan offers a critical yet balanced review of the issues pertinent to female offenders. Brennan offers the reader a candid description of such issues as substance abuse history, abuse experience (i.e., sexual, physical, domestic violence), HIV/AIDS, and mental illness. These factors provide a stark portrait of women currently under correctional supervision. Based on these factors, Professor Brennan offers specific social policy recommendations.

Chapter 30, Delores E. Craig-Moreland's contribution entitled, "The Needs of Elderly Offenders," is a brief but incisive view of the problems associated with elderly persons in our prisons and jails.

Chapter 31, entitled "Behind Bars: Substance Abuse and America's Prison Population," represents a three-year analysis by the National Center on Addiction and Substance Abuse at Columbia University concerning the impact substance use has had on the correctional system. The report assembles the latest statistical data concerning substance using inmates. The report presents a cost-benefit analysis of the advantages of improving drug treatment programs in correctional facilities.

Determining the effectiveness of boot camps has become an arduous task for researchers and practitioners alike. Chapter 32, "Rethinking the Assumptions About Boot Camps," is an attempt to ease this task. The authors, Dale Colledge and Jurg Gerber, provide an historical and programmatic outline of this extremely popular yet controversial corrections-based program. They provide the reader with a typology that can be used as a model for understanding differences in boot camp facilities and programmatic objectives, as well as evaluative research designs.

In Chapter 33, "A Decade of Experimenting With Intermediate Sanctions: What Have We Learned?" Professor Joan Petersilia offers a retrospective analysis of the effects of implementation of intermediate sanctions programs (ISPs) nationwide. Professor Petersilia focuses on the role of the community as the critical component to the successfulness of any ISP.

Chapter 34, "The Evolving Role of Parole in the Criminal Justice System," by Paul Cromwell looks at the various era of parole and how the practice has evolved from a purely rehabilitative correctional strategy to a means of controlling prison populations.

Drawn from Robert Johnson's Distinguished Faculty Lecture given at American University, Chapter 35 entitled, "This Man Has Expired: Witness to an Execution," presents a view of the death penalty seldom revealed. He describes the work of executioners as they prepare for and conduct an execution, and then raises a controversial question during a time when executions have been rapidly increasing.

Chapter 36, "Maxxing Out: Imprisonment in an Era of Crime Control," by Melissa E. Fenwick, presents a critical analysis of the correctional system in America. Leaving rhetoric aside, Ms. Fenwick presents a cogent argument layered with facts concerning a new trend in the corrections movement. This chapter raises some difficult but necessary questions concerning the current practices of correctional management.

Finally, Chapter 37, "Ophelia the CCW: May 11, 2010," by Rutgers criminologist Todd R. Clear, explores the changing nature of probation and parole, and uses a clever futuristic scenario to describe the future and how technology may directly affect the delivery of probation and parole services.

FACTS ABOUT JAILS, PRISONS AND COMMUNITY CORRECTIONS

Summary Findings

- Lifetime Likelihood of Going to State or Federal Prison
- Characteristics of State Prison Inmates
- Characteristics of Jail Inmates
- Comparing Federal and State Prison Inmates
- Recidivism
- Sex Offenders
- Child Victimizers
- Intimate Victimizers
- Use of Alcohol by Convicted Offenders
- Women Offenders

Lifetime Likelihood of Going to State or Federal Prison

If recent incarceration rates remain unchanged, an estimated 1 of every 20 persons (5.1%) will serve time in a prison during their lifetime.

Lifetime chances of a person going to prison are higher for:

- Men (9%) than for women (1.1%)
- Blacks (16.2%) and Hispanics (9.4%) than for whites (2.5%)

Based on current rates of first incarceration, an estimated 28% of black males will enter state or federal prison during their lifetime, compared with 16% of Hispanic males and 4.4% of white males.

Characteristics of State Prison Inmates

Women were 5% of the state prison inmates in 1991, up from 4% in 1986.

Sixty-five percent of prison inmates belonged to racial or ethnic minorities in 1991, up from 60% in 1986.

Sixty-eight percent of inmates were under age 35 in 1991, down from 73% in 1986.

About 4% of state prison inmates were not U.S. citizens.

Altogether, 59% of inmates had a high school diploma or its equivalent.

Two-thirds of inmates were employed during the month before they were arrested for their current offense; over half were employed full time.

Source: http://www.ojp.usdoj.gov/bjs/correct.htm.

Among the state prison inmates in 1991:

- fewer than half were sentenced for a violent crime
- one–fourth were sentenced for a property crime
- about a fifth were sentenced for a drug crime

Characteristics of Jail Inmates

Women were 10% of the local jail inmates in 1996, unchanged from 1989.

Forty-eight percent of jailed women reported having been physically or sexually abused prior to admission; 27% had been raped.

Sixty-three percent of jail inmates belonged to racial or ethnic minorities in 1996, up slightly from 61% in 1989.

Twenty-four percent of jail inmates were between the ages of 35 and 44 in 1996, up from 17% in 1989.

Over a third of all inmates reported some physical or mental disability.

About 8% of local jail inmates were not U.S. citizens.

Altogether, 54% of inmates had a high school diploma or its equivalent.

Thirty-six percent of all inmates were not employed during the month before they were arrested for their current offense—20% were looking for work; 16% were not looking.

Among the local jail inmates in 1996:

- A fourth were held for a violent crime
- A fourth were held for a property crime
- About a fifth were held for a drug crime

More than 7 of every 10 jail inmates had prior sentences to probation or incarceration.

A quarter of the jail inmates said they had been treated at some time for a mental or emotional problem.

Comparing Federal and State Prison Inmates

In 1991, federal inmates were more likely than state inmates to be:

- women (8% vs. 5%)
- Hispanic (28% vs. 17%)

- age 45 or older (22% vs. 10%)
- partly college educated (28% vs. 12%)
- noncitizens (18% vs. 4%)
- employed prior to their arrest (74% vs. 67%)

In 1991, an estimated 58% of federal inmates and 21% of state inmates were serving a sentence for a drug offense; about 17% of federal inmates and 47% of state inmates were in prison for a violent offense.

On average, federal inmates were expected to serve almost 6 1/2 years on a sentence of almost 10 1/2 years, and state inmates, 5 1/2 years on a sentence of 12 1/2 years.

Recidivism

Of the 108,580 persons released from prisons in 11 states in 1983, an estimated 62.5% were rearrested for a felony or serious misdemeanor within 3 years, 46.8% were reconvicted, and 41.4% returned to prison or jail.

Sex Offenders

On a given day in 1994, there were approximately 234,000 offenders convicted of rape or sexual assault under the care, custody, or control of corrections agencies; nearly 60% of these sex offenders are under conditional supervision in the community.

The median age of the victims of imprisoned sexual assaulters was less than 13 years; the median age of rape victims was about 22 years. An estimated 24% of those serving time for rape and 19% of those serving time for sexual assault had been on probation or parole at the time of the offense for which they were in state prison in 1991.

Child Victimizers

Offenders who had victimized a child were on average 5 years older than the violent offenders who had committed their crimes against adults. Nearly 25% of child victimizers were age 40 or older, but about 10% of the inmates with adult victims fell within that age range.

Intimate Victimizers

About 4 in 10 inmates serving time in jail for intimate violence had a criminal justice status—on probation or parole or under a restraining order—at the time of the violent attack on an intimate.

About 1 in 4 convicted violent offenders confined in local jails had committed their crime against an intimate; about 7% of state prisoners serving time for violence had an intimate victim.

About half of all offenders convicted of intimate violence and confined in a local jail or a state prison had been drinking at the time of the offense. Jail inmates who had been drinking prior to the intimate violence consumed an average amount of alcohol equivalent to 10 beers.

About 8 in 10 inmates serving time in state prison for intimate violence had injured or killed their victim.

Use of Alcohol by Convicted Offenders

Among the 5.3 million convicted offenders under the jurisdiction of corrections agencies in 1996, nearly 2 million, or about 36%, were estimated to have been drinking at the time of the offense. The vast majority, about 1.5 million, of these alcohol-involved offenders were sentenced to supervision in the community: 1.3 million on probation and more than 200,000 on parole.

Alcohol use at the time of the offense was commonly found among those convicted of public-order crimes, a type of offense most highly represented among those on probation and in jail. Among violent offenders, 41% of probationers, 41% of those in local jails, 38% of those in state prisons, and 20% of those in federal prisons were estimated to have been drinking when they committed the crime.

Women Offenders

In 1998, there were an estimated 3.2 million arrests of women, accounting for 22% of all arrests that year.

Based on self-reports of victims of violence, women account for 14% of violent offenders, an annual average of about 2.1 million violent female offenders.

Women accounted for about 16% of all felons convicted in state courts in 1996: 8% of convicted violent felons, 23% of property felons, and 17% of drug felons.

In 1998, more than 950,000 women were under correctional supervision, about 1% of the U.S. female population.

Use of Probation/Parole

Probationers include adult offenders whom courts place in community supervision instead of incarceration.

Parolees include those adults conditionally released to community supervision whether by parole board decision or by mandatory conditional release after serving a prison term. They are subject to being returned to jail or prison for rule violations or other offenses.

Nearly 4.5 million adult men and women were on probation or parole at the end of 1999, an increase of about 119,000 during the year.

From 1998 to 1999, the probation and parole population increased 2.7%, less than the 3.8% average annual growth rate since 1990.

On December 31, 1999, approximately 3,773,600 adults were under federal, state, or local jurisdiction on probation, and nearly 713,000 were on parole.

Among offenders on probation, slightly more than half (51%) had been convicted for committing a felony, 48% for a misdemeanor, and 1% for other infractions. Seventy-seven percent of probationers were being actively supervised at the end of 1999; 10% were inactive cases and 9% had absconded.

Nearly all of the offenders on parole (97%) had been sentenced to incarceration of more than 1 year.

Women made up about 22% of the nation's probationers and 12% of the parolees.

Approximately 63% of the adults on probation were white, and 35% were black. Fifty-five percent of parolees were white, 44% black.

Hispanics, who may be of any race represented 16% of probationers and 21% of parolees.

Chapter 28

Life on the Inside: The Jailers

In a Wary World, Battling Tension, Fear—and Stereotypes

by Andrew Metz

This is the job: One unarmed correction officer and 60 inmates, the jailer and the jailed, warily taking each other's measure, sparring for control. Right now, the officer is Cpl. William Roulis, and though it's only 6:30 in the morning, he's already on edge. Purple crescents hammock his eyes as he moves about a locked, windowed room in a second-floor cellblock at the Nassau County jail.

The inmates, men in orange jail jumpsuits, in on mostly drug and alcohol offenses, sluggishly walk through breakfast lines, picking up plastic trays of scrambled eggs, boxes of Fruit Loops, half-pints of milk, slices of white bread.

"Although we are charged with watching them, they watch us," Roulis says, studying through the glass one of the men who is using an empty peanut-butter jar as an oversized coffee cup. "They know what cologne you wear, the click of your heels."

Of all the things Roulis has learned over 10 years at the jail in East Meadow, the most important may be this: "You don't know what is going to happen, or when it is going to happen."

When two inmates will abruptly start brawling in front of the shower stalls, and he will have to order over the loud speaker, "lock in; everybody lock in *now*." Or when an inmate will barricade himself in his cell, and three officers will have to drag him out by the arms and legs. Or when an inmate will taunt him from behind the bars, "I'm going to ___ me a Greek boy."

So, the 44-year-old officer is cynical, always expecting to be had. And this constant tension, this nerve-wracking wait-and-see, imprisons him, too.

"You do 25 years, but a day at a time, a week at a time," he says, parting his lips in a faint smile. "When you come through the gates, you're in a different world."

There are about 1.8 million people in jails and prisons around the country, roughly 3,600 in Nassau and Suffolk awaiting trial or serving sentences of up to a year. But even as the public cheers the get-tough policing that fills correctional institutions, correction officers believe they are seen as brutes, only a shade better than the people behind bars.

This stigma is a sort of occupational hazard that is usually sloughed off. But for officers at the Nassau County Correctional Center, the past three months have brought the stereotype painfully close to home.

After an inmate was allegedly beaten to death by officers inside the jail in January, federal authorities stepped in to investigate the homicide and whether there is a pattern of brutality. And the whole situation has revealed a bevy of complaints and lawsuits brought by inmates with wide-ranging claims of mistreatment.

Inside lunch rooms and control rooms, in the trailers that function as the training academy and in dozens of posts throughout the facility, morale is dark. Officers say they have been wounded by recent headlines and newscasts.

They tell of being looked at askance by neighbors. Of wives being insulted in supermarkets. Of children confused by what they hear.

Few deny that abuses have occurred. But they insist any misbehavior is limited to rogues, to officers unable to rise above the depravity of jail culture.

"We spend our day with the kind of people you don't want next door," says Officer Bob Shanlin, 41, who in his 15 years at the jail has twice saved inmates who were trying to hang themselves with bedsheets. "We're like offensive linemen. You only hear our name when something goes wrong. . . . The vast majority of people here are not beating people. I wouldn't work with people that were."

One thousand and ten correction officers and commanders work at the jail, one of the largest county lockups in the country. In three shifts of around 120 officers each, they supervise and provide for about 1,800 inmates.

While keeping some of the jail off limits, including the building where the inmate allegedly was beaten in January, correction officials permitted closely monitored visits inside the jail in recent weeks. Days of observation and interviews—14 hours on one day—show just how complicated life on the inside can be. Locked in, officer and inmate move in a suspicious waltz, staking out positions, enduring the monotony, the indignities, the dependance.

One minute an officer is handing out toilet paper, the next he is explaining court papers. An officer is joking with two inmates playing checkers, and in an instant, he is ordering everyone to their cells.

This is the job: Put on a blue-and-gray uniform, pin a silver sheriff's badge to your shirt pocket and lace up black work shoes. Drive to a sprawling complex of concrete and metal, through 18-foot-high fences topped with thick coils of razor wire.

In a two-story building called the 832, bars open and seal shut behind you, and as you walk to the Muster Room to get your assignment, the odor of floor cleaner, the industrial kitchen and too many bodies carries you forward.

Soon you are locked inside a cellblock. You are outnumbered. Your only weapons are the wits you walked in with and the alarm on your waist. And when you set that off, officers come running, and more often than not it means inmates are swinging fists or throwing feces or food. For sure, they're yelling and swearing and refusing to lock down. Your life could be in danger.

You're enraged, and if you're honest, you're scared.

"Anytime a body alarm goes off, your adrenaline starts pumping because you are running into a situation and you don't know what it is going to be like and it could be a war," says Shanlin, who can't recall being assaulted in his career, but has had a jar of urine thrown at him and has been insulted and threatened countless times. "You're an idiot if you . . . are not scared."

But all-out violence is rare, and you know it as you settle down behind a desk at the center of the cellblock. You supervise the "feedings," keeping track of each meal tray because almost anything can be made into a weapon.

Usually, the closest you come to using force is an unequivocal command or a firm grip on an elbow. No one wants to be locked down. No one wants weightlifting canceled.

At least every half-hour, you get up and pace the dimensions of the dorm, peering into each cell and inserting a key in a slot to record your passage. You sock away the paychecks that don't ever seem fat enough, rack up the overtime when you can and push your union to get a 20-year retirement clause in your contract. Police have one, after all.

You bristle when you're called a guard because guards work at Macy's and banks and don't stop dead in their tracks when they hear, "Yo, C.O.!" as they leave a mall and see five former inmates behind them. At the end of a day, you decompress however you can, if you can, and tell yourself you're an integral part of the criminal justice system.

"The public doesn't want to know about them," Officer Robert Koplar, 35, who has worked at the jail for 14 years, says of the inmates. "After they are caught, they forget about the other part. Where are you supposed to store them? Not the Marriott.

". . . Someone has to watch them 24-7. Someone has to do it."

Few people actually plan on a career in corrections.

"I don't think you'll talk to anyone that says, 'Since I was 12 years old I wanted to be a correction officer,'" says Lt. Richard Plantamura, who is in charge of the jail's training academy.

Of the dozens of new officers who each year routinely join the Nassau County Sheriff's Department, Division of Correction, most say they were looking for a position as a police officer.

They had taken a slew of civil service exams, perhaps not scoring high enough to land a police job at first. Then the jail made an offer.

Some eventually move to the Suffolk or Nassau police departments, where salaries are significantly higher. The first year of employment at the jail, base pay is about $28,000. A rookie Suffolk police officer makes about $45,000. And after two years, so does a new officer in Nassau.

Still, jail officials say attrition is low, and for men and women shopping for a civil service job, a job that doesn't require any college and eventually promises salaries more than $50,000, thousands in overtime, security and benefits, corrections is a coveted career.

"I love what I do," says Officer Ronald Lanier, a former Army enlisted man, who was driving a Drake's delivery route in Brooklyn, when he was offered a post at the jail eight years ago.

Standing tall, his black oxfords reflecting like mirrors, Lanier is monitoring visiting hours. As inmates hug mothers and girlfriends and wives, the 35-year-old says he sees his work as a calling.

"A lot of these guys I went to school with," he says nodding his chin to the inmates. "I am here to do a job but I care."

One of roughly 150 black officers, Lanier says he is mentor for African-American inmates, who make up about half the jail population.

Lanier says he has been in only one physical tussle in his eight years and that was while breaking up a fight. Holding ground in a cellblock rarely comes down to force, he says. He lets the inmates know they're in his "house" now, and "this is how it's done."

"I don't go straight to C," he says. "I start at A and nine times out of 10 we end up at A."

And that, in the simplest sense, is the philosophy officers say they carry with them day to day: Force is supposed to be the last resort, and when it's doled out, it meant to be measured.

As a rule, officers are unarmed. Supervisors have a can of pepper spray. The greatest tools, officers say, are composure and communication.

"The way you present yourself to people, how you communicate with people is going to get you through 90 percent of the time," says Sgt. Daniel Dooley, who teaches recruits. "Your communication skills will get you through. It's the easiest way to go."

In a cavernous jail gymnasium, Officer Kenny Sellers says he puts this to the test every day. During a midmorning recreation period, 77 inmates are pumping iron and dribbling basketballs and jogging. Sellers mingles with them all, smiles a lot. In small groups, he tries to quell brewing discontent this day, because both basketball hoops are being repaired.

The inmates are disappointed, but "they don't want to fight because they know if they do, they will lose out," says Sellers, 41, who at 6-foot-2, 240 pounds is as rippled as they come.

During 12 years as an officer, he says, he has forged a respectful discourse with inmates, giving them space—and sometimes advice on how to bulk up.

"They respect me," he says. "They know me."

This is the job: A 40-year-old officer makes a patrol along a guardwalk one Christmas. He sees the lights and snow outside and thinks of his family. He passes cell after cell and is pinched by a sorrow that takes years for him to understand.

"I thought, just on the other side of the bars are people thinking the same things I am," Lt. Richard Levering recalls.

Now, more than two decades later, Levering describes what hit him as the "incarceration feeling." He wrote poetry to make some sense of it:

> *Lonely, I stare through barred windows,*
> *Watching the seasons go past.*
> *In "lock-step," they march in a circle*
> *And I can't tell the first from the last.*
> *I listen with cautious compassion,*
> *Keep my lamp of suspicion trimmed low*
> *Enough to reveal hidden dangers*
> *But not make me distrust those I know.*
> *My day is a structured chaos*
> *And the ominious slam of each gate*
> *Reminds me that I am a captive*
> *And the pleasures of freedom must wait.*
> *I'm not serving time for some victim*
> *To whom I brought pain, loss or fear.*
> *I serve time in these dungeons of justice*
> *For choosing a Correctional career.*

"We are all locked in here," says Levering, 66.

And that's a universal feeling for correction officers. Mel Grieshaber of Michigan, who is the immediate past president of the International Association of Correctional Officers, likens corrections to combat.

"You are there coaching Little League one moment, then you get up the next day, brush your teeth and go to this . . . 100-percent hostile environment," says Grieshaber. "A lot of jobs are stressful, however, this is the type of job where everything can be calm for periods of time, but you are always dealing with this little voice way deep down that says something could happen. So there is a certain edge all the time."

Up-to-date figures on the effects of corrections work are scarce and are more anecdotal than scientific. However, most correction experts agree that officers have excessively high rates of suicide, burn-out, divorce and alcohol abuse. Studies have shown they have heart attacks, hypertension and ulcers more than almost any other employment group. And a 1980s report by the American Federation of State and County Municipal Employees put their life expectancy at 59.

Nationally, officials estimate that seven died in the line of duty last year and more than 14,000 were seriously assaulted. At the Nassau jail, there were 38 assaults against officers last year, and two . . . in 1999. Inmates assaulted one another 39 times last year, and already 35 times this year.

"It's a hard life to grow up in," Levering says. "I have often thought that no one should come on this job before 28 or 30."

He has had to tell inmates that relatives were killed, separate a baby from a mother, cut down a prisoner trying to hang himself.

Mostly, officers hope for a humdrum day. "A good day for me is when none of my officers get hurt," says Cpl. Bob Zizza, 37, who in 12 years has been assaulted five times.

In 1971, two professors in California embarked on a study of the psychology of imprisonment. In what became known as the Stanford Prison Experiment, they cast a group of college students in the roles of correction officers and inmates for six days. The results, the authors, Craig Haney and Philip Zimbardo declared, were shocking and forced them to halt the experiment.

In under a week, they witnessed mock inmates and officers suffer trauma and stress. They watched many of the "officers," particularly those on the night shifts, harass and degrade and mistreat inmates. Others stood by and failed to report the abuses.

"You are talking about an environment that is constantly pushing against people" says Haney, a professor of psychology at the University of California at Santa Cruz. "This is really antithetical to what people are, and so prisoners are not at their best and not surprisingly correction officers aren't either."

And while the national corps of correction officers is more diverse, better educated and instructed than at any other time, according to experts, abuses persist.

Bob Gangi, head of the Correctional Association of New York, a nonprofit watchdog group, says that while the job breeds brutality, "correction officers have legitimate beefs that we as a society throw them down into the pits and ask them to do the dirty work and often don't really care about what goes on."

And so, correction officials and critics agree, in this field that constantly challenges moral bearings, rules and regulations are crucial compasses.

"You have to have structure for both the inmates and the officers," says Lt. Jerry Magnus, a supervisor who has worked in the Nassau jail for 27 years. He says the officers' rulebook is voluminous and "tells you how to do everything here except go to the bathroom."

Since the jailhouse death in January [1999] of Thomas Pizzuto and the federal probe, he says inmates are "thriving on the media," concocting accusations, even inflicting injuries on themselves and threatening to blame officers.

These are trying times, he says. "People have to put themselves in our place."

This is the job: Twelve hours after he first walked into his cellblock, Cpl. Roulis is in the same small bubble, monitoring the men in his charge.

It is 6:30 p.m. and the last feeding has finished. Inmates are talking on phones, talking to one another. Two TVs broadcast hazy images. A wiry, gray-haired inmate is sitting at a table, staring blankly at the floor.

"Look at that guy over there," says Roulis, a father of three. "He's done. He's left it all here."

A few minutes later, a mountainous man with thick hair bursting from his shirttop and a beard waits to be let inside the dorm. He is glowering and doesn't even turn his eyes as Roulis pushes a button to open the gate.

Roulis shakes his head. He says he "shudders to think if . . . [his children] ever got trapped in this world and couldn't get out."

In four hours, his double shift will be done. Then he'll drive home around 10:30 p.m. At 4 a.m., he'll pull himself out of bed again.

"Tomorrow's my last," before the weekend, he says, "and when I walk out of here, I'm running out of here. When I hit that parking lot, it's like I left the burden of the world behind me."

Chapter 29

The Imprisonment of Women in America

by Pauline Katherine Brennan, Ph.D.
University of North Carolina at Charlotte, Department of Criminal Justice

INTRODUCTION

In this chapter, an overview of the imprisonment of female offenders in the United States is provided. The discussion begins with an examination of female incarceration rates, how these have changed over time, and reasons for the increase. From that discussion, a profile of female inmate characteristics is provided and comparisons are made to males under correctional supervision. A general overview of correctional programs and issues for prison managers is provided in section four of this chapter. The chapter concludes with a discussion, where the need for community-correctional alternatives to incarceration is suggested.

STATISTICS PERTAINING TO THE INCARCERATION OF FEMALE OFFENDERS

Relative to the their male counterparts, the number of incarcerated females in the United States is quite small. Female inmates comprise approximately six percent of the nation's prison population and about 11 percent of the nation's jail population (Bureau of Justice Statistics [hereafter BJS], December 1999: 4, 6). Therefore, separate jails and prisons for female inmates are few. Indeed, most states have only one prison for female offenders. Prison and jail populations have increased tremendously over time, and overcrowding has increasingly become a concern of correctional management in both male and female institutions. However, across the country, the female-inmate population is growing at a much faster rate than the male-inmate population (see for example, BJS, April 2000, August 1999; Conly, 1998). In a recent report from the Bureau of Justice Statistics (1997), researchers noted that the number of men in the nation's jails and prisons doubled from 1985 to 1995, but the number of women tripled. Since 1990, female prison populations have increased, on average, 8.4 percent, which is higher than the 6.5 percent average annual rate of increase for male inmates (BJS, April 2000: 4). Reporting these figures somewhat differently, statisticians noted that the total number of male prisoners grew 67 percent from 1990 to 1998. Comparatively, the female-inmate population increased by 92 percent (BJS, August 1999: 5). What these figures forebode is that, over time, overcrowding will become especially pronounced in female correctional institutions.

Pauline Brennan. Prepared expressly for this edition.

These alarming rates of increase may be explained by the current "get tough on crime" ideology. For example, both male and female offenders across the country have been affected by stricter and tougher sentencing policies (e.g., "three-strikes-and-you-are-out" legislation, determinate sentencing, mandatory sentencing, sentencing guidelines). Thus, more and more offenders are being sentenced to serve time in jails and prisons, and many are given longer sentences as well. For females, that pattern is especially evident for drug crimes and property crimes (Illinois Department of Corrections, 1991: 1; Virginia State Crime Commission, 1993: 4). With regard to drug offenses in particular, the Bureau of Justice Statistics (March 1990: 4) reported that the number of arrests of women for drug violations increased at about twice the rate of men, over the decade of the 1980s.[1] Thus, it is not surprising for one to find that drug offenders make up a much larger percentage of the female, than male, prison population. In 1997, 35 percent of all female inmates incarcerated in state prisons were there because of a drug offense, compared with only 20 percent of all male inmates (BJS, August 1999: 10).

Other reasons for the increase in female prison populations may include lack of community resources for women offenders and/or a perception that programs in a prison setting better meet the multiple needs of the woman offender. To elaborate, and for example:

> "A comprehensive inventory of services and sanctions available to women offenders throughout Oregon revealed that there are few specifically designed for women offenders. Although there is a wide array of interventions, services and sanctions for offenders under community supervision, no sanctions were found that had an expressed emphasis on serving the needs of women offenders. While many countries have a specialized supervision caseload for women offenders, few resources exist to support this supervision through interventions, services or sanctions that take into account real differences between men and women in their learning and relationship styles and life circumstances. State prison facilities for women offer the most comprehensive array of gender-specific programs in Oregon. This may contribute to decisions to revoke community supervision for some women who are not endangering public safety, who cannot obtain services in the community" (Oregon Department of Corrections, 1995: 8).

There may also be less tolerance for technical violations of probation/parole conditions by women offenders. In support of the notion, in Oregon, from October 1992 through September 1992, 74 percent of all female admissions to prison were probationers revoked without conviction, compared with 52 percent of the male prison population (Oregon Department of Corrections, 1995: 16; see also Brennan & Belenko, 1999; Bloom & Steinhart, 1993: 15).

CHARACTERISTICS OF FEMALE INMATES

Offense Type

Most convictions for female offenders are for misdemeanors. Female misdemeanants are primarily charged with offenses involving prostitution, property, and/or drugs. Most female felons are also property and drug offenders. And, it is the drug offenders in particular who are increasingly making up a larger segment of the female prison population.

Only a small proportion of female offenders has committed an offense against a person. In 1998, less than four percent of all arrests for female offenders were for violent offenses, including murder, robbery, and aggravated assault (BJS, December 1999: 5).

While violent female offenders are few, they constituted 28 percent of the female state prison population in 1998 (BJS, December 1999: 6). A much larger percentage of males are incarcerated for violent offenses; in 1997, approximately 48 percent of male inmates were sentenced violent offenders (BJS, August 1999: 10).

As noted in the previous section of this chapter, drug offenses constitute the most common incarceration-offense category (approximately 35 percent) for women in prison. The remaining major offense categories are for property crimes (about 27 percent) and "public-order offenses," such as driving while intoxicated (roughly 10 percent total) (BJS, December 1999: 6).

More often than not, the crimes women commit stem from economic motivation/necessity, with retail fraud and bad checks being among the more common offense types (see for example Michigan Women's Commission, 1993: 19). And, as highlighted above, drug and/or alcohol related offenses are also prevalent among this population. Combined, it is not surprising that many female offenders acknowledge that they engage in crime in order to have money to support a drug habit (see for example, Michigan Women's Commission, 1993: 23).

Substance Abuse History

It is estimated that between 60 to 90 percent of all female offenders have drug or alcohol problems (Illinois Department of Corrections, 1991: 3; Michigan Women's Commission, 1993: 3, 77). Across the country, an estimated 84 percent of women inmates in state and federal prisons reported having used drugs at some point in their life (BJS, January 1999: 7). Rates were similarly high among the population of male inmates in 1997; 83 percent had previously used drugs (BJS, January 1999: 7).

With regard to differences in drug use between male and female prison inmates, women were more likely than men to have taken a drug in the month before they committed their offense; 62 percent of female inmates reported doing so, compared with 56 percent of the male inmates (BJS, January 1999: 7). Regular use of drugs, defined as once a week or more, was also more common among female inmates (BJS, January 1999: 7). Similarly, the Michigan Women's Commission (1993: 78) found that, relative to male jail inmates, more than twice as many incarcerated women in jail reported having used a major drug on a daily basis.

In addition to differences in the extent of drug use, there may also be differences in the number of drugs abused by male and female offenders under correctional supervision. Sheridan (1996) examined 81 male and female substance abusers serving sentences in a mid-Atlantic state. Although 86 percent of the total sample reported multiple drug use, the women reported significantly more drugs used. Moreover, significantly more women than men abused both alcohol and other drugs, rather than just one or the other. These data suggest that "the women may be more serious polysubstance abusers than are the men" (Sheridan, 1996: 426).

Victims of Abuse

Estimates from the Bureau of Justice Statistics (April 1999: 1) indicate that 57 percent of women who were incarcerated in state prisons across the United States in 1997 had previously been sexually or physically abused, compared with 16 percent of male prison inmates. Many of the incarcerated women were abused before the age of 18 years; approximately 26 percent of these women were sexually abused before their eighteenth birthday (BJS, April 1999: 1). The high rate of abuse among this population has been reported elsewhere. For example, a survey of women incarcerated in Michigan's county jails noted that 50 percent had been the victim of some form of abuse during their lifetime (Michigan Women's Commission, 1993: 2, 43, 49; see also Oregon Department of Corrections, 1995: 26; and Virginia State Crime Commission, 1993: 5).

Researchers have found that sexual, physical, and emotional abuse are often linked to chemical dependency (Oregon Department of Corrections, 1995: 8, 26). For example, Natarajan (1994: 1) found that 95 percent of the female offenders at Crossroads, an alternative incarceration program for substance abusers in New York City, had been the victims of child abuse, domestic violence, and/or incest. A Michigan study also reported that female substance abusers, in particular, frequently came from violent backgrounds. Specifically, 19 percent reported being severely beaten during their childhood and 15 percent reported being raped as children. As these women entered adulthood, the situation worsened; 70 percent indicated that they had been beaten as adults, usually by their husband or partner, and 21 percent reported that they had been raped as adults (Michigan Women's Crime Commission, 1993: 51, 82). These findings have implications for correctional drug-treatment policy, suggesting the greater need for such programs in female institutions, where issues of past physical abuse are simultaneously considered.

HIV/AIDS

The number of people infected with AIDS (Acquired Immunodeficiency Syndrome) across the country continues to grow. Heterosexuals, sexual partners of intravenous drug users, and people who have multiple sex partners are at the greatest risk (Lawson & Fawkes, 1993: 43). The number of women infected with HIV (the Human Immunodeficiency Virus that causes AIDS) has increased dramatically over time. Between 1982 and 1986, there was a 100 percent increase in the number of women infected by the virus. The number again increased by 100 percent between 1986 and 1992 (Lawson & Fawkes, 1993: 44). Among women with AIDS, the overwhelming majority were infected via either intravenous drug use (52%) or were exposed to HIV through heterosexual contact (30%) (Lawson & Fawkes, 1993: 43–44).

Data from 1997 showed that 23,548 inmates (or 2.2 percent) in state and federal prisons across the United States were HIV-positive (BJS, November 1999: 1). Of this number, there were 6,184 confirmed cases of AIDS (BJS, November 1999: 3). This represented a rate of 55 cases per 10,000 inmates, compared to a rate of 10 cases per 10,000 people in the general population (BJS, November 1999: 4). Thus, "the rate of confirmed AIDS in State and Federal prisons was five and one-half times higher than in the total U.S. population" (BJS, November 1999: 4). Also noteworthy is the finding that, from 1991 to 1997, the number of prison inmates with AIDS more than tripled (BJS, November 1999: 4). These numbers are expected to continue to increase over time, especially among female inmates.

Many female offenders have engaged in prostitution and/or have used drugs with infected needles. Consequently, the rate of HIV or AIDS is higher for these women than for women in the general population. Moreover, relative to their male counterparts, a higher percentage of women under correctional supervision are infected (Sheridan, 1996:

44). To illustrate that point, researchers from the Johns Hopkins School of Public Health and the Centers for Disease Control tested nearly 11,000 inmates entering ten prisons and jails between mid-1988 and mid-1989 and found that:

> "rates of HIV infection ranged from 2.1 percent to 7.6 percent for male inmates and from 2.5 percent to 14.7 percent among female inmates. At nine of the ten correctional facilities, women had higher rates of HIV infection than men" (Lawson & Fawkes, 1993: 44).

These figures are consistent with more recent data. At yearend 1997, 3.5 percent of female prison inmates nationwide were known to be HIV-positive, compared with 2.2 percent of male prisoners (BJS, November 1999: 5).

Criminal History (Recidivism)

Findings from past research indicate that the rate of recidivism varies, depending on how and when it is measured. Among those who have been released from prison (e.g., on parole), rates of rearrest are high. Pearl (1998) found that the length of parole supervision averaged a little over nine months for female offenders released from prison in 1989, 1990, and 1991. Approximately two-thirds of the women were successfully terminated from parole. Although that was the case, during a two-year follow-up period, nearly two-thirds of the parolees were arrested one time or more, with an average of 3.08 subsequent arrests (Pearl, 1998: 98).

Rates of reconviction are also high. For example, statistics compiled by the Michigan Women's Commission (1993: 34) for the period 1991-92 showed that 63.8 percent of the male jail inmates and 61.8 percent of the female jail inmates were recidivists, because they had a prior conviction. Consistent with these figures, among a sample of female parolees in Oregon, 63.9 percent had one or more prior convictions (Oregon Department of Corrections, 1995: 47). Although a substantial portion of the female offender population has a previous record of conviction, it is important for the reader to take note that male offenders are more likely to be recidivists. In 1998, among female inmates in state prisons across the country, approximately 65 percent had a history of prior convictions (BJS, December 1999: 9). In contrast, 77 percent of the male prisoners were found to have a prior record of conviction (BJS, December 1999: 9).

Reincarceration rates, another measure of recidivism, have also been examined. When using this indicator, the overall rate of recidivism has been found to be lower. For example, Pearl (1998: 98) found that her sample of Massachusetts parolees had an average of 12.85 prior arrests and had been incarcerated 1.15 times. Turning to the studies reporting percentage figures, researchers of one study showed that 15 percent of the women in a Wisconsin prison had served previous time in an adult institution and that 14 percent had spent time in a juvenile facility (Wagner, 1986: 5). Thus, it is clear that rates of recidivism appear comparatively lower when the measure of reincarceration is examined.

Race/Ethnicity

Minority women, particularly African-American women are over-represented in the criminal justice system, and especially so in female prison and jail populations (Bloom & Steinhart, 1993: 14; BJS, December 1999: 7). A 1998 examination of female offenders indicated that among state prisoners, 33 percent were white, 48 percent were black, and 15 percent were Hispanic (BJS, December 1999: 7). Race/ethnicity percentage breakdowns are similar among male inmates (BJS, April 2000: 10).

Age

Female prison populations are filled with relatively young offenders, with a large concentration between the ages of 25 through 29 years (Bloom & Steinhart, 1993: 14). Based on data gathered from prisoners across the country in 1998, statisticians reported that 55 percent of female prison inmates were 34 years of age or younger (BJS, December 1999: 7). Only 11 percent were 45 years old or older. Male prison inmates are similarly young (BJS, April 2000: 10).

Educational Attainment

Most women in prison or jail typically have less than a high school education (Bloom & Steinhart, 1993: 14; Oregon Department of Corrections, 1995: 27). In Michigan, for example, a survey of female jail inmates showed that 40 percent had never completed their high school education and that only eight percent had advanced schooling (Michigan Women's Commission, 1993: 30, 100). Nationally, statistics compiled on state female prison inmates in 1998 showed that 44 percent had not graduated from high school (BJS, December 1999: 7). Of the women who had not graduated from high school, seven percent had not advanced beyond the eighth grade. Percentage figures are similar for male inmates.

These figures, however, may be providing an inaccurate picture. Many inmates may not be functioning at their identified educational level. For example, in a study of females incarcerated at the Niantic Correctional Facility for Women in Connecticut, researchers discovered that many of the inmates scored only at the sixth-grade level in many subject areas. Specifically, test scores indicated that 26 percent of the female inmates were at the sixth-grade reading level; 47 percent were at that level in spelling; and 52 percent had not progressed beyond the sixth-grade level in mathematics (The Permanent Commission on the Status of Women in Connecticut, 1989: 9). Thus, many who report high school degrees and beyond may not possess math and reading skills at the twelfth-grade level.

Employment Status

Statistics compiled from state prisoners across the United States indicated that more than half of the females incarcerated in 1997 were not employed at the time of their arrest, compared with 73 percent of their male counterparts (BJS, August 2000: 10). The Virginia State Crime Commission, in 1993, also acknowledged that women who ultimately wound up in prison or jail were less likely to have been employed prior to arrest. Moreover, among those who were employed, the wages for females were, for the most part, lower than those found for their male counterparts (Virginia State Crime Commission, 1993: 6).

Marital Status

Few female offenders under correctional supervision are married (Bloom & Steinhart, 1993: 14; BJS, December 1999: 7). In general, statistics derived for female inmates, housed throughout the country in state prisons in 1998, revealed that only 17 percent were married (BJS, December 1999: 7). Close to 50 percent of the female inmates had never been married. The marital status of male prison inmates is similar.

Children and Children-to-Be

Although few female inmates report being married, the majority have children (Oregon Department of Corrections, 1995: 26; Virginia State Crime Commission, 1993; and BJS, August 2000: 1). Nationally, roughly two-thirds of all women in jail or in prison have children under the age of eighteen years (Bloom & Steinhart, 1993: 14; Michigan Women's Commission, 1993: 60). In addition to the large number of incarcerated women with children, it is also important for one to take note that a fair number will give birth while incarcerated.

A 1987 study conducted by the American Correctional Association found that six percent of females in prison and four percent of females in jails were pregnant (Bloom & Steinhart, 1993: 14). In a later study conducted by the National Council on Crime and Delinquency, nine percent of jailed and imprisoned women gave birth while incarcerated (Bloom & Steinhart, 1993: 14). State-specific figures coincide with these. Figures from Oregon, for example, showed that 10 percent of women were pregnant when they entered prison in 1994, and 15 percent were post-partum (Oregon Department of Corrections, 1995: 28).

For the year 1999, statisticians from the Bureau of Justice Statistics estimated that there were approximately 1.5 million children with at least one parent incarcerated in either a state or federal prison (BJS, August 2000: 1). The number is highest in California, where more than 200,000 children have an incarcerated parent (Bloom & Steinhart, 1993: 15). This reality has implications for prison-visitation policies.

Not surprisingly, given the number of incarcerated women who are not married, most reported having been the primary and sole caretaker for their children prior to incarceration (Illinois Department of Correction, 1991: 3). Given this finding, one may wonder what happens to the children of incarcerated women. Children are most often placed with a relative, often with a grandparent, rather than put into foster care (BJS, August 2000: 3; Oregon Department of Corrections, 1995: 27, 33; Illinois Department of Corrections, 1991: 3; and Michigan Women's Commission, 1993: 64).

In contrast to male inmates, few female inmates report that the other biological parent (i.e., father) is caring for the child (BJS, August 2000: 3). A 1997 survey of state prison inmates showed that only 28 percent of the female inmates said their child was living with the other parent, compared with 90 percent of the male inmates (BJS, August 2000: 3). Likewise, in an earlier study of female prisoners in 1986, only 22 percent of the mothers said their child was living with the father. In addition, fewer than 10 percent indicated that their child was living in foster care or in some other institutional setting (BJS, March 1990: 6).

Wherever the children go, one thing is certain—the relationship between the incarcerated female offender and her child is altered significantly, if not jeopardized. Many young children come to think of their female caretaker as their real mother, which may be agonizing for the inmate. Depending on the state, the inmate may even lose legal custody of the children.

A SNAP-SHOT OF CORRECTIONAL PROGRAMMING AND POLICY ISSUES INVOLVING FEMALE INMATES

As documented in the previous sections, female inmates are unique. Unlike their male counterparts, female offenders are more likely to have suffered from abuse over the course of their lifetime (e.g., sexual, physical, psychological). These inmates are also more likely to have had parental responsibilities prior to incarceration, been addicted to drugs, and used drugs on a daily basis. Moreover, relative to their male counterparts, female prisoners are more likely to suffer from mental illness (Morash et al, 1998: 1). In addition, some of the females who enter correctional supervision are pregnant, have health problems requiring immediate attention, and/or are HIV positive.

> "These different circumstances, together with the general rise in the management of women in prison and jail, point to the need for different management approaches as well as different programming to ensure parity and to provide interventions that reduce recidivism. To achieve greater gender parity in correctional programming, women must have the same range of opportunities as men, and their needs must be meet to the same extent that men's are. This standard is difficult to achieve because women make up just a fraction of the total inmate population. Their needs can easily be overlooked when programs are designed and resources allocated" (Morash et al, 1998: 2).

Many correctional institutions are ill-equipped, either in assessment, management, or in programming, to meet the special needs of female offenders.[2] In a number of state prisons and local jails, women inmates are not routinely assessed for needs that many of them are likely to share—those related to children or previous abuse.

In addition to employing strategies that seek to assess the special needs of female offenders, correctional administrators should also be cognizant that different management styles may be required for female, rather than male, inmates. Women offenders have been described as more concerned with interpersonal relationships and as likely to express their feelings differently from male offenders (Morash et al, 1998: 4). These differences carry over into skills necessary for staff to have when working with the female offender. Indeed, in their analysis of survey responses provided by prison administrators, Morash and colleagues (1998: 4) found that:

> " . . . seven in 10 correctional administrators believed that a different style of management was needed for women. Different management styles would involve a capacity to respond to expressions of emotions and a willingness and ability to communicate openly with offenders. A less authoritarian manner and a recognition that women had needs different from men were also cited as desirable characteristics of women's prison management. Skills such as active listening, patience in explaining rules and expectations, awareness of emotional dynamics, and the capacity to respond firmly, fairly, and consistently were also cited as important attributes of those who would manage women in prisons."

The difference in the day-to-day relationship between correctional staff and female offenders has implications for policy related to correctional programming. For example, training of correctional staff should aim to promote greater sensitivity to women offenders. In addition, some have suggested the "use of approaches that decentralize management decisions and involve offenders in carrying out selected responsibilities" (Morash et al, 1998: 4–5). Even with more adequate assessments and different management strategies, little is likely to change for the female offender if more program and treatment options are not provided. Across the country, programs and treatment options for female offenders are limited. To a certain extent, this is because correctional administrators often feel justified in providing more opportunities for the larger male offender segment. Indeed, disparity in available programming (e.g., vocational) and access to services (e.g., medical) for women offenders has been documented repeatedly (see for example, Fortune & Balbach, 1992: 114).

In addition, the development of programs for women has been restricted by limited correctional budgets across the country. Instead, the majority of correctional budgets have gone toward the building of new facilities (or expanding existing facilities) and/or the operating costs associated with overcrowding. Thus, in many jurisdictions, some correctional programs and services have been eliminated. This does not bode well for female offenders, who are likely to have multiple problems.

Education and Vocational Programs

The programming opportunities for female offenders have been criticized by observers as reinforcing the traditional roles of wife, mother, and homemaker, which are not viable for a population that, for the most part, is unmarried (Carp & Schade, 1993; Fortune & Balbach, 1992). In addition, given that female offenders are likely to come from backgrounds of poverty, underemployment, and limited education, it is unrealistic to presume that such women, upon termination of their correctional sentence, would be able to become stay-at-home wives and mothers. Nonetheless, the majority of available training programs concentrate on occupations consistent with stereotypical conceptions of the female role—sewing, cleaning, food service, and cosmetology (Carp & Schade, 1993: 38; Fortune & Balbach, 1992: 115). This is problematic, because these occupations are often low paying and, thus, of limited value for female offenders. Specifically,

> " . . . with traditional programs such as cosmetology and food services these women are not offered the diversity necessary to enable sufficient opportunities for employment when they leave prison. Contrast this with the myriad of training programs for men throughout the state prison system. This shortcoming is perhaps a result of the overcrowded conditions at the prison (and the fact that there is but a single facility for women). Nevertheless, it bodes badly for the opportunities of these women to break a cycle of behavior that resulted in their incarceration initially." (Virginia State Crime Commission, 1993: 6)

Thus, correctional administrators have advocated that:

> "Educational and vocational programs . . . must keep pace with the prison population growth in addition to the demands of the job market. Non-traditional career paths must be viable options for females. Raising the functional literacy level, providing program counseling services, assessing an inmate's capabilities and aptitude, as well as providing needed follow-up, will help promote employment for the female upon release" (Illinois Department of Corrections, 1991: 2).

The Permanent Commission on the Status of Women in Connecticut (1989: 22) also acknowledged the need for expansion of job programs for women, because training in traditional low-paying clerical and service sectors would be of limited assistance. Specifically, the Connecticut Commission recommended training in dental technology, industrial cleaning, plastics technology, carpentry, machining, plumbing, and electronics. It should be noted, however, that nurses' aide classes, typing, day care, and home economics continue to be the most popular programs among female inmates at the Niantic Correctional Facility for Women (The Permanent Commission on the Status of Women in Connecticut, 1989: 22). Indeed, the reality across the country is that female offenders are most attracted to occupations that support traditional sex roles (Fortune & Balbach, 1992: 115). Thus, correctional administrators need to encourage females under correctional supervision to participate in nontraditional vocational training.

In addition to providing women with specific types of vocational training, it is also important to provide classes on searching, obtaining, and retaining employment. For example, job interview training could aid in securing employment. Classes on appropriate dress in the work setting may also be beneficial. For many offenders, successful vocational training may be linked to educational programming. Obviously, functional literacy is important to one who is searching and applying for a job. Literacy skills, for example, are vital to success in a vocation that requires ability to read a technical manual. In addition, many employers require a high school diploma. Thus, it is not surprising to find that in many institutions across the country, education programs are in place. As an example:

> "At Niantic, every inmate who expresses an interest in a school program is tested. All inmates under the age of 21 are strongly encouraged to take part. Teachers are sent into the pre-trial and punitive segregation units. Others attend classes at the school facility. Inmates receive pay for school attendance at the same rate as on the majority of job assignments" (The Permanent Commission on the Status of Women in Connecticut, 1989: 22).

While this situation may appear ideal, when the average length of stay for female inmates is considered, one quickly realizes that achievement may not be possible. To elaborate, at Niantic and elsewhere, many women are released as soon as an educational plan can be drawn up for them, or they are released before the program can be completed. (The Permanent Commission on the Status of Women in Connecticut, 1989: 22). The same dilemma exists with vocational training.

In short, to facilitate the chances of success following correctional supervision, female offenders are clearly in need of both educational and vocational programs that increase the chances of post-release success in a modern society. In addition, for those who are released prior to program completion, a mechanism for continuation of the programs begun while incarcerated is needed in the community setting.

Substance Abuse

> "Drug-abusing women offenders constitute one of the fastest-growing segments within the criminal justice system, yet little is known about their unique needs, their multiple problems and treatment effectiveness" (Clement, 1997: 61).

As noted in an earlier section, many women under correctional supervision have a history of substance abuse. Female offenders are also likely to have a history of emotional problems linked to drug or alcohol abuse (Carp & Shade, 1993: 37; Morash et al, 1998: 7).

The Virginia State Crime Commission (1993: 6) reported that "if addiction to drugs is a common trait among female offenders, it is symptomatic of a life-style suggestive of low self-esteem and an inability to function as an individual in society." The Commission went on to state that the problem differs quantitatively and qualitatively from that found in the male offender population. Therefore, relative to treatment provided in exclusively male institutions, the treatment needs for female inmates are different.

Most alcohol and drug treatment programs were designed by men and for men (Michigan Women's Commission, 1993: 3, 77). This is unfortunate because female substance abusers [differ] from their male counterparts. Specifically, female substance abusers are more likely to have economic (e.g., lower incomes), social (e.g., poor relationships), psychological (e.g., lower self-esteem, depression, anxiety), and physical (e.g., effects of drugs/alcohol are different for women) problems than male substance abusers (Michigan Women's Commission, 1993: 81). Sexual, physical, and emotional abuse are the leading causes of chemical dependency among women (Oregon Department of Corrections, 1995: 8, 25).

Given the above, it is not surprising that Sheridan (1996: 430) found that, relative to their incarcerated male counterparts, incarcerated women reported significantly more reasons for their previous substance abuse.

> "Significantly more women than men reported abusing substances in order to 'block out painful feelings/events,' 'escape reality,' 'relax/reduce tension,' 'feel more normal,' and 'cope with physical pain'—all reasons that reflect a self-medicating function of substance abuse. Significantly more women than men also stated that they abused substances because they were 'unable to stop,' a reason that reflects a serious level of substance abuse dependency or addiction." (Sheridan, 1996: 430)

The above is important because many of the reasons noted, such as using chemical substances as a means of self-medicating emotional or physical pain, have been found to be associated with a high risk of relapse, if underlying issues are not resolved (Sheridan, 1996: 430). Females under correctional supervision may self-medicate because they have suffered from abuse during childhood and adulthood. These early childhood experiences often tie into the selection of a partner [who] is often a wrong choice. This is problematic because negative relationships with men are the leading cause of return to chemical use (Oregon Department of Corrections, 1995: 25).

As noted, a large portion of the female inmate population has problems of substance abuse. There is a relationship between substance abuse and crime. On a positive note, researchers have found that most drug users are able to reduce or eliminate their drug use and criminal behavior while in treatment (Michigan Women's Commission, 1993: 81). It also appears that treatment outcomes may be improved via a linkage between jail or prison-based programs and subsequent community supervision (Michigan Women's Commission, 1993: 81). However, across the country, there are not enough treatment programs to accommodate women who need them, or it is difficult to obtain access to these programs.

A recent report by Massachusetts' Task Force on Justice (1991) highlighted the limited treatment options for offenders (in general) with problems of drug and/or alcohol dependence. Specifically,

> "While incarceration gets the offender off the road [in cases of drunk driving], the county jails have little in the way of alcohol treatment. The state and county Sheriffs have established

three effective alcohol treatment centers (recidivism of 6.5% for the treatment centers vs. 15.9% for jail), but entrance to them is blocked to over half the convicted drunk drivers by waiting lists or narrow entrance criteria. . . . In state prisons, there is a dramatic increase in offenders serving long mandatory sentences. These commitments went from 55 in 1980 to 1,133 in 1989. As was found in these county jails, drug treatment before release is not available for these offenders. Indeed, drug abusers constitute over 80 percent of the state inmate population (6,700 of 8,380), yet treatment is available for only 400. Moreover, many of these offenders are sentenced under mandatory sentences that prohibit them from participating in effective reintegration programs." (Boston Bar Association and Crime and Justice Foundation, 1991: 15)

Among women offenders, results from a recent national survey of drug abuse treatment programs showed that many women who required services did not receive any (Wellisch et al, 1994). Moreover, of the programs found, many did not address the multiple problems of drug-abusing women offenders (Wellisch et al, 1994). This will become an increasingly important issue for criminal justice policymakers.

The Importance of the Family for Women Offenders, the Effect of Incarceration on Children, and Parenting Programs

Male and female offenders benefit from family contact while incarcerated. Moreover, there is evidence that offenders with stronger ties to their families are less likely to recidivate, either after release or while under community correctional supervision. The emphasis on family, however, differs between male and female offenders. Female inmates are more likely than their male counterparts to maintain regular family contact by visit, phone, or mail (BJS, August 2000: 1; Carp & Schade, 1993: 38). This may be because many female offenders report having been the primary caretakers for their child before incarceration. While they are incarcerated, separation from their child becomes one of their major concerns.[3] Specifically, the female offender worries about the loss of parental rights, which may be terminated during her period of incarceration. And it may be for these reasons that female inmates rely more heavily on a created family structure within an institution, which often manifests itself in the formation of play families.[4]

As indicated by statistical data, many women under correctional supervision are mothers. What the general data fail to show, however, is that many of these women do not know how to be effective parents. Therefore, parenting programs within a correctional setting are often designed with the purpose of creating "a mechanism by which communication and bonding can be fostered between parent and child" (Illinois Department of Corrections, 1991: 3). While one may imagine how such programs may be put in place for females who remain in the community, it may be difficult for one to imagine how or why correctional administrators should strive to develop such programs for females in prisons or jails. Specifically, one may wonder why incarcerated mothers should be allowed the opportunity to continue, strengthen, or better their relationship with their child during their period of incarceration.

There are many reasons why female inmates should be allowed the opportunity. First, such programs are important because data suggest that when women are released from prison their parental responsibilities resume (Illinois Department of Corrections, 1991: 3). In order to make the separation and eventual reunion less traumatic for both the parent and child, parenting programs are important. Second, there is evidence that maintaining family ties can assist in reducing the chances of recidivism upon release (Illinois

Department of Corrections, 1991: 3). Third, children of inmates have their lives disrupted, and possibly damaged by their separation from imprisoned mothers. Indeed, children of incarcerated parents have been found to suffer from a host of psychological disorders. These include fear of emotional closeness, aggression, anxiety, anger, depression, attention disorders, developmental regression, loss of identity, and guilt (Michigan Women's Commission, 1993: 2, 59, 64, 67, 74; Bloom & Steinhart, 1993: 16; and Hagan, 1996). These emotional problems may manifest in a variety of ways, including acting out, withdrawal, poor academic performance and/or attendance, teenage pregnancy, alcohol and drug abuse, and delinquency (Michigan Women's Commission, 1993: 67, 74; Bloom & Steinhart, 1993: 16, 25; and Hagan, 1996). Such problems are often the uncalculated costs of imprisonment. With regard to an increased propensity for criminal involvement, researchers have found that children of incarcerated parents are five to six times more likely to end up in jail or prison than the average child (Michigan Women's Commission, 1993: 70). Consistent with that finding, researchers from the Bureau of Justice Statistics reported that more than one-third of adult inmates had at least one family member who had been incarcerated (Michigan Women's Commission, 1993: 70).

Visitation with incarcerated parents may help children cope with the problems they are likely to face. The Center for Children of Incarcerated Parents, located in California, maintains that such visits are beneficial because they:

> " . . . allow children to express their emotional reactions to the separation, which may not be allowed elsewhere . . . Visitation allows children to see their parents realistically. Parent/child separation normally produces irrational feelings and fears within children about their parents; these children also entertain unrealistic fantasies when contact with their parent does not occur. Visits allow children to release these feelings, fears, and fantasies and replace them with a more realistic understanding of their parents' characteristics and circumstances . . . Visits allow parents to model appropriate interactions for children who react inappropriately, but understandably, to the circumstances of separation. This is particularly important for children who do not accept their new caregivers and/or whose reactive behaviors are difficult to manage." (as paraphrased by the Michigan Women's Commission, 1993: 71)

Although there are many reasons why we should allow inmates to visit with their children, some female correctional facilities do not allow children under the age of 17 to visit at all (Michigan Women's Commission, 1993: 2, 59). Correctional administrators who employ this strategy often argue that children are too difficult to control and/or that it is best for children not to see their parents in an incarceration setting (Michigan Women's Commission, 1993: 71). In addition, children may be a distraction from working on issues related to such things as chemical dependency and criminal behavior (Oregon Department of Corrections, 1995: 27).

In many of the institutions across the country that allow children to visit their mothers, visitation is often limited to non-contact. To illustrate that point, a study of female inmates in a number of county jails throughout Michigan found that, of the inmates who reported seeing their children during their period of incarceration (55%), the vast majority (88%) indicated that contact visitation was not allowed (Michigan Women's Commission, 1993: 61). These inmates further reported that not being able to have physical contact with their children was one of the most difficult consequences of being incarcerated, both for themselves and for their children (Michigan Women's Commission, 1993: 61). This may also be a reason why many female inmates report that their children never visit them while incarcerated. For example, in Oregon, 58.3 percent of women incarcerated at the Women's Correctional Center in July 1994 reported that none of their children had visited (Oregon Department of Corrections, 1995: 33). Findings from a national study of incarcerated women with children lend support to that finding. Specifically, the National Council on Crime and Delinquency (NCCD) found, after surveying incarcerated women in eight states and in the District of Columbia from 1991 to 1992, that 54 percent of inmate children had never visited their mothers in jail or in prison (Bloom & Steinhart, 1993: 26).

In addition to the lack of contact visitation in some facilities, another reason why visitation may be so infrequent is because most states have only one prison for female offenders. Thus, the distance that a child may have to travel may be quite far. Indeed, Bloom and Steinhart (1993: 26) noted that the main reason (43% of the reasons cited) reported by women inmates for infrequent or non-visitation of their children was the distance between the child and the correctional facility. Of the women inmates surveyed in a recent NCCD study, most (61.5%) were incarcerated at a distance of over 100 miles from their children (Bloom & Steinhart, 1993: 27). This is especially problematic when one considers that many of primary caretakers do not own automobiles and must, therefore, rely on public transportation. Taking children on long bus or train rides can be an ordeal. That situation may be compounded by institutional policy and staff attitudes. Caregivers may find that, upon arrival at the institution, that an inmate "cannot be cleared and presented in the visiting area for another two or three hours" (Bloom & Steinhart, 1993: 37, 51).

Recognizing the importance of mother-child visitation, there are some correctional institutions that have attempted to make such encounters less "institutional." Typically, this is accomplished by constructing children's playrooms and/or allowing visitation in a living-room atmosphere. However, only about 10 percent of jails and prisons have a "children's center" on their grounds (Bloom & Steinhart, 1993: 28). Another option is extended visitation. Some facilities, such as the one located in Lancaster, Massachusetts, allow inmate mothers and their children to have extended visits in trailers (Massachusetts Executive Office of Human Services, 1987: 10). It should be noted, however, that visitation policies such as this are rare. Bloom and Steinhart (1993: 28) noted that only 7.3 percent of the prisons and jails they studied allowed for overnight family visits.

Health Care Concerns

Turning to some physical health concerns, recall that some women under correctional supervision are pregnant. Although there is variation by state, high-risk pregnancies are predominant among incarcerated expectant mothers, primarily because of substance abuse and related problems. For example, in 1987, an estimated 80 percent of pregnant inmates in Massachusetts were at high-risk for medical complications during pregnancy (Massachusetts Executive Office of Human Services, 1987: 8). Women offenders also suffer from other health-related problems. Because many have been intravenous drug users and/or prostitutes, it is not uncommon for a female offender to have a sexually transmitted disease. For some of these diseases there is a cure, but for others, such as AIDS, there is only limited treatment.

Given that the female offender population is at high risk for HIV infection, it would also be wise for prison administrators to offer counseling on transmission of the virus and how to minimize risk. The Centers for Disease Control found that many women were unaware of their risks. The extent to which prevention programs are offered in a correctional setting is unknown (Lawson & Fawkes, 1993). The current literature also suggests the need for counseling in this area. Many correctional agencies do not provide pre- and post-test counseling for women who request an AIDS test (Lawson & Fawkes, 1993). In the years to come, correctional administrators will be faced with an increasing number of female offenders with HIV and AIDS. Policies related to housing, medical care, and counseling will need to be implemented. And, for women who die of AIDS while under correctional supervision, correctional administrators may also be required to contend with issues surrounding the placement of children who no longer have mothers.

DISCUSSION AND CONCLUSION

State and federal data show that the rate of incarceration for women is increasing at an alarming rate. Male prison populations also continue to grow, but the rate of growth has been more pronounced for female inmates. Female prison inmates resemble their male counterparts on many dimensions. More than half are black or Hispanic, most are young, few have ever been married, and most are undereducated. However, drug offenses, physical or sexual abuse history, substance abuse, lack of employment prior to incarceration, and parenthood are more common among female prisoners. These differences have implications for correctional programming. Unfortunately, what is often available in jails and prisons is not designed to address the specialized needs of female offenders. Thus, many have advocated for alternatives to incarceration for non-violent female offenders. A recent publication of results obtained from a national survey of responses from correctional administrators at both the state and local levels echoes that suggestion. Specifically,

> "Program administrators who worked most closely with offenders were asked whether their clients would be better served by more use of alternatives to incarceration. Regardless of whether their programs were in prison, jail, or in the community, nearly half of the program administrators felt that the use of alternatives to incarceration should be expanded." (Morash et al, 1988: 5)

Community-correctional alternatives make sense, for a variety of reasons. First, programs in the community typically cost less. Second, a woman with dependents makes community correction a more attractive alternative. Third, given the types of crimes women are likely to engage in (i.e., non-violent), women offenders pose little threat to the community.

Regardless of whether female offenders are placed in an institutional or community-correctional setting, programs must take on a "holistic approach." There must be opportunities to improve family skills and preserve the family unit. There must be gender-specific services that focus on the unique experiences and problems of women. Moreover, programs must be of sufficient duration and have an aftercare component to have a desired effect. This may be problematic considering that women are typically involved in the less serious types of crimes. Therefore, they are likely to be given a sanction whereby they are under supervision for too brief a time to fully benefit from interventions/treatment. This ties into the need for a concerted effort between the institutional system and other agencies or organizations in the community. Such connections are not only beneficial while the female offender is under correctional supervision, but may also assist her with prolonged successful re-entry into the community.

NOTES

1. "Between 1980 and 1989, there was a 307 percent increase in the number of women arrested for drug crimes, including possession, manufacturing, or sale of illegal drugs. Over the same period, arrests of men for drug violations increased 147 percent." (BJS, March 1990:4)

2. Some have argued that it is more than the differences in the numbers of male versus female inmates that leads to disparity. Rather, it is specifically a male-centered penal-management philosophy that creates problems in programming for female offenders. Arguing this point, Clement, for example (1997: 63) wrote:

   " . . . it is becoming apparent that women are being incarcerated in a system originally developed in philosophy and structure for men. The incidences of discrimination and disparity of services are increasing. The correctional system has long been male-oriented in rules, structured programs and standard operating procedures. The result is that men can be assigned to various prisons based upon the severity of their offense, security risk or rehabilitative needs. Most states, however, have only one prison for women, who are generally grouped together regardless of their special needs or problems."

   Morash and her colleagues (1998: 14) also noted that assessment procedures and classification are "often unrelated" to where female offenders are sent or to what programs they are referred to. Specifically, the program needs of a woman influenced her placement in only half the states with 500 or more women inmates. The proportion is even lower (one-third) in states with smaller female inmate populations (Morash et al, 1998: 14).

3. Psychologists have found that the complaints and concerns discussed by male inmates differ from those discussed by female inmates. Male inmates discuss their fears and problems about being incarcerated, particularly feelings of a loss of power and independence. In contrast, female inmates are more inclined to talk about family, especially their children and the associated guilt they feel over leaving them (Baruch, 1993: 102).

4. This manifestation has consistently been noted over time, and is something that occurs only in female institutions. As an example, in Baruch's (1993: 103) discussion of women housed in the 5-South Unit at the New York Metropolitan Correctional Center (a federal detention unit), she noted the following:

   "In an attempt to adjust to their isolation and emotional deprivation, some women form symbolic families in which they nurture other 'family' members. Other inmates actually take on the role of mother, father, sister, brother, or child, as well as extended 'family' members. This type of role playing—an unhealthy form of dependency—is unique to women's institutions."

REFERENCES

Baruch, Marcia (1993) "The 5-South Unit at MCC New York," in *Female Offenders: Meeting Needs of a Neglected Population*, pp. 101–104. Laurel, Maryland: American Correctional Association.

Bloom, Barbara and David Steinhart (1993) *Why Punish the Children? A Reappraisal of the Children of Incarcerated Mothers in America*. San Francisco, California: National Council on Crime and Delinquency.

Boston Bar Association and Crime and Justice Association (1991) *The Crisis in Corrections and Sentencing in Massachusetts: Report and Recommendations of the Task Force on Justice (Final Report)*. Boston, Massachusetts: Boston Bar Association and Crime and Justice Association.

Brennan, Pauline K. and Steven Belenko (1999) "Male and Female Prison Populations: Differential Effects of Probation and Parole Violations." Paper presented at the annual meeting of the American Society of Criminology, November 1999, Toronto, Canada.

Bureau of Justice Statistics (August 2000) *Incarcerated Parents and Their Children*. Washington, D.C.: U.S. Department of Justice, Office of Justice Programs, NCJ 182335.

———(April 2000) *Prison and Jail Inmates at Midyear 1999*. Washington, D.C.: U.S. Department of Justice, Office of Justice Programs, NCJ 181643.

———(December 1999) *Women Offenders*. Washington, D.C.: U.S. Department of Justice, Office of Justice Programs, NCJ 175688.

———(November 1999) *HIV in Prisons 1997*. Washington, D.C.: U.S. Department of Justice, Office of Justice Programs, NCJ 178284.

———(August 1999) *Prisoners in 1998*. Washington, D.C.: U.S. Department of Justice, Office of Justice Programs, NCJ 175687.

———(April 1999) *Prior Abuse Reported by Inmates and Probationers*. Washington, D.C.: U.S. Department of Justice, Office of Justice Programs, NCJ 172879.

———(January 1999) *Substance Abuse and Treatment, State and Federal Prisoners, 1997*. Washington, D.C.: U.S. Department of Justice, Office of Justice Programs, NCJ 172871.

———(1997) *Correctional Populations in the United States, 1995*. Washington, D.C.: U.S. Department of Justice, Office of Justice Programs, NCJ 163916.

———(March 1990) *Women in Prison*. Washington, D.C.: U.S. Department of Justice, Office of Justice Programs, NCJ 127991.

Carp, Scarlett V. and Linda S. Schade (1993) "Tailoring Facility Programming to Suit Female Offenders' Needs," in *Female Offenders: Meeting Needs of a Neglected Population*, pp. 37–42. Laurel, Maryland: American Correctional Association.

Clement, Mary (1997) "New Treatment for Drug-Abusing Women Offenders in Virginia," *Journal of Offender Rehabilitation* 25(1/2): 61–81.

Conly, Catherine (1998) *The Women's Prison Association: Supporting Women Offenders and their Families*. Washington, D.C.: U.S. Department of Justice, National Institute of Justice, NCJ 172858.

Fortune, Eddyth P. and Margaret Balbach (1992) "Project Met: A Community-Based Educational Program for Women Offenders," in Imogene L. Moyer, ed., *The Changing Roles of Women in the Criminal Justice System*, pp. 113–129 Prospect Heights, Illinois: Waveland Press, Inc.

Hagan, John (1996) "The Next Generation: Children of Prisoners." *Journal of the Oklahoma Criminal Justice Research Consortium* 3(August): 19–28.

Illinois Department of Corrections (1991) *Five-Year Plan for Female Inmates: Fiscal Year 1991 Update*. Springfield, Illinois: Illinois Department of Corrections, Illinois Bureau of Administration and Planning, Planning and Budget.

Lawson, Travis W. and Lt. Lena Sue Fawkes (1993) "HIV, AIDS, and the Female Offender," in *Female Offenders: Meeting Needs of a Neglected Population,* pp. 43–48. Laurel, Maryland: American Correctional Association.

Michigan Women's Commission (1993) *Unheard Voices: A Report on Women in Michigan County Jails.* Lansing, Michigan: Michigan Women's Commission.

Morash, Merry, Timothy S. Bynum, and Barbara A. Koons (1998) *Women Offenders: Programming Needs and Promising Approaches.* Washington, D.C.: National Institute of Justice, NCJ 171668.

Natarajan, Mangai (1994) *Crossroads: A Community-Based Outpatient and Alternative-to-Incarceration Program for Women Offenders in New York City.* Washington, D.C.: U.S. Department of Justice, National Institute of Justice. Grant 92-IJ-CX-K108.

Oregon Department of Corrections (1995) *Intermediate Sanctions for Women Offenders.* Salem, Oregon: Oregon Department of Corrections, Intermediate Sanctions for Women Offenders Policy Group.

Pearl, Natalie (1998) "Use of Community-Based Social Services by Women Offenders." *Journal of Offender Rehabilitation* 26(3/4): 91–110.

The Permanent Commission on the Status of Women (1989) *Task Force on Women, Children, and the Criminal Justice System: Summary of Findings and Recommendations.* Hartford, Connecticut: The Permanent Commission on the Status of Women.

Sheridan, Michael J. (1996) "Comparison of Life Experiences and Personal Functioning of Men and Women in Prison," *Journal of Contemporary Human Services* 77(7): 423–434.

Virginia Crime Commission (1993) *Report of the Virginia State Crime Commission on Special Needs and Conditions of Incarcerated Women to the Governor and the General Assembly of Virginia.* Richmond, Virginia: Virginia State Crime Commission, Virginia General Assembly.

Wagner, Dennis (1986) *Women in Prison: How Much Community Risk?* Madison, Wisconsin: Wisconsin Department of Health and Social Services, Division of Policy and Budget, Bureau of Evaluation.

Wellisch, Jean, Michael L. Prendergast, and M. Douglas Anglin (1994) *Drug-Abusing Women Offenders: Results of a National Survey.* Washington, D.C.: U.S. Department of Justice, National Institute of Justice.

Chapter 30

The Needs of Elderly Offenders

Delores E. Craig-Moreland, Ph.D.

The U. S. Census Bureau reports that the elderly are the fastest-growing segment of the population as a whole—a statistic worth considering in understanding the rapid growth of older inmates. A closer look at crimes by those over age 55 shows that these offenders are more often going to prison, and for lengthy sentences. Uniform crime reports by the FBI showed a 30% decline in arrest of those over age 55 in the period 1971–1992; during that same period there was an 84% increase in arrests of those over age 55 for violent crimes such as murder, forcible rape, and aggravated assault. These arrests associated with violent crimes are the most likely to lead to time in prison.

Another factor to consider in accounting for a growing number of inmates over age 55 is the increasing length of sentences. Longer sentences mean that more offenders will remain in prison into advanced age. The Corrections Yearbook (Camp & Camp, 1986-1995) showed that those sentenced to natural life (no parole), life, or 20 years or more went from 17% of state prisoners in 1986 to 25% by 1995. Aday (1994) has concluded that these sentencing changes mean that more inmates will finish their lives behind bars. This is reflected in the estimates that the correctional population in state prisons would reach as many as 125,000 in 2000; anywhere from 35,000 to 50,000 would be over the age of 65.

When consideration is given to the total correctional population in state and federal prisons, which approaches 1.25 million, it may be hard to get excited about this group of elderly inmates, a mere 10%. But these aging inmates make particular demands on already overburdened national correction institutions. Aging inmates require protection from the overall inmate population, have increasing health care needs, and may require a modified environment to deal with physical limitations.

ELDERLY INMATES

Consider the types of inmates which fall into the aging prison population. Many of these inmates aged 55 years or older will be first offenders. In a study of Kansas inmates over the age of 55 it was found that roughly one-fourth were first time offenders, mainly charged with sex offenses. It is easy to conclude that these individuals were maladjusted in society, and will present some management problems in the prison system. These inmates are a good argument for a segregated geriatric living unit within a prison of an appropriate security level.

Aging inmates that are chronic offenders composed 16% of the Kansas study. These inmates had a history of prior criminal convictions which did not result in prison time.

Delores Craig-Moreland. Prepared expressly for this edition.

Their commitment to prison at the later stages of their life appeared to be the progression of a crime career, where sentencing escalated mainly because of the previous convictions. The main adjustment for this group would be the adjustment to life in prison, since they have presumably already made the adjustment to being a criminal.

Prison recidivists, older offenders on a return visit to prison, were by far and away the largest group in the older inmate population, comprising 41% of the Kansas aged inmates. These inmates had previous time in prison, mainly for crimes against persons or for drug offenses. A search of individual cases showed that a typical such elderly offender would have previous prison time for drug related offenses, with an escalating trend to violence. The main problem for [these elderly inmates] is that their lifestyle may have led to major medical problems.

Inmates who have grown old in prison were 16% of the Kansas study. These inmates entered prison when they were less than 50 years of age for crimes with lengthy sentences. This is typically the person sentenced to life in prison because of a murder conviction.

When all four types are combined as a group solely on the basis of their age, the heterogeneous nature of elderly offenders is ignored. Lifestyle related to drug use makes some of these inmates old beyond their years. Others have actually benefitted from long years in the stable environment of prison. Some may have a heart condition based on genetics rather than a life of crime. The supportive environment of a geriatric living unit would serve well the needs of a first offender in fragile health, but would be unnecessary to the healthy inmate who has long ago made an adjustment to prison life. Let us review some of the predictable special needs for elderly offenders with respect to housing, activities, and medical care.

HOUSING

Correctional facilities not only come in different security levels, but different living quarters as well. Inmates can be housed in dormitories, group cells, or single cells. Prisons may be in urban areas, where support services such as medical are readily available, or in remote areas where access to services is a problem. For elderly inmates, housing needs may conflict. Inmates may wish to be near family, which may not place them in a facility that is well equipped to meet medical needs. Moving them into geriatric units, which are in limited supply, may mean taking them away from friends and family. For example, in Texas, there is a geriatric living unit in the Estelle unit near Huntsville, which serves medium security inmates. If an elderly inmate is from the western part of Texas, family visits would be a real hardship.

Other housing considerations include accessibility and safety. Ramps and subtle grades, with handrails where necessary, enhance access for older frail inmates. Levers can be used to replace knobs, making it easier to open doors. These are some of the ADA requirements which apply. These features improve physical safety of the inmates, as well as provide access. Safety also involves protection from other inmates who might view the older inmate as vulnerable to abuse and attack. Elderly inmates can be housed in dormitory settings because they are not typically a high security risk, but it should be a priority to place them with other older inmates, or low risk inmates. If older inmate are to be housed in a group cell with between one and three other inmates, they will need to avoid upper bunks which are difficult to access, and they will need to be provided safe cell mates.

ACTIVITIES

The activity range of an elderly inmate can be expected to vary greatly from inmate to inmate. In some states, inmates are classified by age and restricted in work assignment. In Texas, for example, inmates aged 50 to 55 receive a classification requiring lighter, slower duties. This can actually help to deal with limited job availability at some sites. Such a blanket approach to the activity needs of an elderly inmate does not bode well for their adjustment to prison life. Some meaningful way to spend time is a problem for every inmate, regardless of age. While some inmates are glad for any excuse not to work, jobs remain a key way to provide structure and meaning to the long days. In the words of one 82-year-old inmate, "I have worked all my life and expect to continue to the day I die, regardless of where I am."

Other activities such as crafts and any recreation should be encouraged for elderly inmates as a means to maintain good mental and physical health. This may require space in a geriatric unit for such activities, such as a day room which accommodates such group functions. Access to an outside recreational area for exercise also promotes healthy lifestyles for inmates. Care and attention to activity needs is not based on some altruistic ideal of prison life; it is very self-serving for prison administrators who wish to keep health care costs at a minimum.

HEALTH CARE

Just as health care costs in society have ballooned, so have these costs exploded as a part of the corrections budget. Some contributing factors include more special needs inmates with AIDS, mental health needs, and the growth in elderly inmates (Wall, 1998). But another factor is simply the increased cost of medical treatment. In a survey by Aday (1994), 30% of the states responding indicated that the rising cost of medical care was the most pressing concern related to elderly inmates.

Various strategies are in play to try and control health care costs. In Louisiana, many of the elderly inmates are moved to a special needs center. The special needs center is a renovated jail which houses 330 special needs inmates and an addition 225 other inmates who serve as a permanent work party to perform maintenance and other service functions. The center site is near a medical school and allied health care program, which provide consultants and medical components through contracts. Two other similar facilities are expected to become available soon.

In Texas, similar efforts are under way to control health care costs. Five of the state prisons also have regional medical centers, which are serviced by medical school personnel. They are run in a manner very similar to health maintenance organizations, with incentives for cost control. Texas prisons are also serviced by the largest pharmacy in the country. It makes daily shipments of prescriptions to all of the prisons within the system.

While these two states appear to be getting a handle on health care, there are numerous problems to be solved. Prison personnel are trained to handle security issues and the management of inmates. They are not necessarily versed in skills needed to deal with a greying population. Standard security measures may make it difficult for the EMT to respond to a heart attack suffered by an elderly inmate. Training inmates and staff in CPR could be beneficial, but may be logistically challenging.

Wall (1998) pointed out the value of proactive health care for elderly inmates. More frequent health screening, routine TB tests, and programs of inmate peer counseling on good health care practices are but a few efforts undertaken in Louisiana. Medical co-payments have been added to avoid abuse of health care services.

REFERENCES

Aday, Ronald H. (1994) Golden Years Behind Bars: Special Programs and Facilities for Elderly Inmates. *Federal Probation* 58(2): 47–54

Camp, George & Camp, Camille. (1986–1995) *The Corrections Yearbook*. South Salem, NY: Criminal Justice Institute.

Wall, Jean. (1998) Elder Care. *Corrections Today* 60(2): 136–138, 195.

Chapter 31

Behind Bars

Substance Abuse and America's Prison Population

National Center on Addiction and Substance Abuse, Columbia University

Substance abuse and addiction have fundamentally changed the nature of America's population. In the 21st century, state and federal prisons and local jails are bursting at the bars with drug abusers and addicts and those who sell illegal drugs. In America, crime and substance abuse are joined at the hip.

At the end of 1996, more than 1.7 million American adults were behind bars: 1,076,625 in state prisons, 105,544 in federal prisons, and 518,492 in local jails—more than three times the number incarcerated just 15 years earlier. Of the 1.7 million inmates, only 130,430 or 7.7 percent are women, but the female prison population is growing at a faster rate than the male population. The surge in the number of Americans behind bars—now a population the size of Houston, Texas, the nation's fourth largest city—and the rapidly escalating costs of building and maintaining prisons are unprecedented. More and more Americans are becoming aware of this situation. What few understand is why.

State prisons generally hold inmates who have been convicted of felony offenses under state law and sentenced to at least one year of incarceration. Federal prisons hold inmates convicted of violating federal laws. Local jails generally house individuals convicted of misdemeanors and sentenced to less than on year in prison and individuals who are awaiting trial. Most offenses related to illegal drug selling are felonies, while possession of drugs may be either a felony or misdemeanor depending on state law and the amount of drugs. Possession of small amounts of marijuana is typically treated as a misdemeanor or a lesser, noncriminal infraction.

The estimate of 1,700,661 is based on the most recent data available: year-end 1996 for state (1,076,625) and federal prisoners (105,544), midyear 1996 for jail inmates (518,492). Throughout this report, different years may be cited for different types of data. This is because different data sets and publications are available for various types of criminal justice data, and not all data are available for the same year. The data used are the most recent available. Adults are defined as more than 17 years of age.

For three years, The National Center on Addiction and Substance Abuse at Columbia University (CASA) has been examining and probing all available data on the people in prison, surveying and interviewing state and federal corrections officials, prosecutors and law enforcement officers, testing programs for substance-abusing offenders and reviewing relevant studies and literature in the most penetrating analysis ever attempted of the relationship of alcohol and drug abuse and addiction to the character and size of America's prison population.

Reprinted with permission from *Spectrum*, Winter 1999, pp. 8–13. © 1999 by The Council of State Governments.

The stunning finding of this analysis is that 80 percent of the men and women behind bars—some 1.4 million individuals—are seriously involved with drug and alcohol abuse and the crimes it spawns. These inmates number more than the individual populations of 12 of the 50 United States. Among these 1.4 million inmates are the parents of 2.4 million children, many of them minors.

SUBSTANCE-INVOLVED OFFENDERS

The overwhelming majority of those who have ever used drugs regularly used them in the month immediately before they entered prison—76 percent of state, 69 percent of federal, and 70 percent of local jail inmates who have regularly used drugs. Alcohol and drug abuse and addiction are implicated in assaults, rapes and homicides. Thousands of individuals incarcerated for robbery and burglary stole to support drug habits. Thousands more are imprisoned for violations of laws prohibiting selling, trafficking, manufacturing or possessing illegal drugs like heroin and cocaine, driving while intoxicated, and disorderly conduct while high or drunk. The bottom line is this: one of every 144 American adults is behind bars for a crime in which drugs and alcohol are involved.

The enormous prison population imposes a hefty financial burden on our nation. In 1996, America had more than 4,700 prisons—1,403 state, 82 federal and 3,304 local—to house an inmate population that is still growing. Americans paid $38 billion in taxes to build and operate these facilities: $35 billion for state prisons and local jails and $3 billion for federal prisons.

This report is an unprecedented effort to assess the relationship between drug and alcohol abuse and addiction and America's prison population and the implications of that relationship for our society—for public safety; state and federal criminal justice, public health and social service policies; taxes that Americans pay and the nation's economy. The first step in formulating sensible prison policies to protect the public safety in a cost-effective way is to understand the human, social and economic costs of substance abuse, crime and incarceration, how we got here and what we can do about it. The case for change is urgent and overwhelming: if rates of incarceration continue to rise at their current pace, one out of every 20 Americans born in 1997 will serve time in prison—one out of every 11 men, one of every four black men.

This CASA report targets America's prison and jail population. But prisons are the end game. Millions of children grow up in families wracked by drug and alcohol abuse and in neighborhoods and schools infested with illegal drugs and drug dealers—situations that General Colin Powell calls "training camps for America's prisons." There are 3.8 million individuals convicted of a crime who are on probation and parole, which brings the total to more than 5.5 million people currently under the supervision of state, federal and local criminal justice systems. That is a criminal population larger than the city of Los Angeles, the second largest city in the United States. The states monitor 3,146,062 individuals on probation and 645,576 on parole; the federal government, 34,301 on probation and 59,133 on parole. For most of these individuals, the road to prison, probation and parole is paved with alcohol and drug abuse.

How did America's prisons and jails come to be dominated by alcohol and drug abusers and those who deal drugs? Citizen concerns about crime and violence led federal, state and local officials to step up law enforcement, prosecution and punishment. As a result of such concern and the heroin epidemic of the 1970s and crack cocaine explosion in the 1980s, state and federal legislatures enacted more criminal laws, especially with respect to selling illicit drugs and related activities such as money laundering; agents of the Federal Bureau of Investigation and Drug Enforcement Administration and state and local police made more arrests for all kinds of crime; prosecutors brought more charges and indictments; judges and juries convicted more defendants; and judges imposed more prison sentences authorized or mandated by law. While in prison, little attempt was made to deal with the underlying inmate drug and alcohol addiction that led to so much criminal activity. Inmates who are alcohol and drug abusers and addicts are the most likely to be reincarcerated—again and again—and sentences usually increase for repeat offenders. The result has been a steady and substantial rise in the nation's prison population over the past generation. Between 1980 and 1996, the number of inmates in state and federal prisons and local jails jumped 239 percent, from 501,886 to 1,700,661: the number of men from 477,706 to 1,570,231, a 229 percent increase; the number of women from 24,180 to 130,430, a 439 percent increase.

The explosion of the inmate population is drug- and alcohol-related

Most offenders, whatever their crime, have a drug or alcohol problem. Alcohol and drugs are implicated in the increased rate of arrest, conviction and imprisonment of property, violent and drug law offenders, the three major groups of inmates.

Much of the growth in America's inmate population is due to incarceration of drug-law violators. From 1980 to 1995, drug law violators accounted for 30 percent of the total increase in the state prison population, and the proportion of offenders in state prisons convicted of drug-law violations rose from 6 percent to 23 percent. In federal prisons, drug law violators accounted for 68 percent of the total increase, driving the proportion of drug-law violators from 25 percent to 60 percent and making drug law violators by far the largest group of federal inmates. In local jails, drug law violators accounted for 41 percent of the increase in the total population between 1983 and 1989, and the proportion of drug-law violators rose from 9 percent to 23 percent. While the percentage of inmates convicted of property and violent crime declined, the number of such inmates increased, largely due to drug- and alcohol-related offenses.

Fast Facts . . .

At the end of 1996, more than 1.7 million American adults were behind bars: 1,076,625 in state prisons, 105,544 in federal prisons and 518,492 in local jails.

Of the nation's 1.7 million inmates only 130,430 (7.7 percent) are women.

Eighty percent of the men and women behind bars are seriously involved with drug and alcohol abuse and the crimes it spawns.

Americans paid $38 billion in taxes to build and operate prisons in 1996: $35 billion for state prisons and local jails and $3 billion for federal prisons.

In 1997, the Federal Bureau of Prisons spent $25 million on drug treatment—only 0.9 percent of the federal prison budget.

The more often an individual is imprisoned, the more likely that individual is a drug or alcohol addict or abuser

Substance use is tightly associated with recidivism. The more prior convictions an individual has, the more likely that individual is a drug abuser: in state prisons 41 percent of first offenders have used drugs regularly, compared to 63 percent of inmates with two prior convictions and 81 percent of those with five or more convictions. Only 4 percent of first-time offenders have used heroin regularly, compared to 12 percent of those with two prior convictions and 27 percent of those with five or more. Sixteen percent of first offenders have used cocaine regularly, compared to 26 percent of those with two prior convictions and 40 percent of those with five or more convictions. State prison inmates with five or more prior convictions are three times likelier than first-time offenders to be regular crack users.

Only 25 percent of federal inmates with no prior convictions have a history of regular drug use, but 52 percent of those with two prior convictions and 71 percent of those with five or more have histories of regular drug use. Among jail inmates, 39 percent with no prior convictions have histories of regular drug use, but 61 percent with two prior convictions and 76 percent with five or more convictions regularly used drugs.

The growing chasm in substance-abuse treatment: increasing inmate need and decreasing access

In state and federal prisons, the gap between available substance abuse treatment, inmate participation and the need for such treatment and participation is enormous and widening.

State officials estimate that 70 to 85 percent of inmates need some level of substance-abuse treatment. But in 1996, only 13 percent of state inmates were in any such treatment. The Federal Bureau of Prisons estimates that 31 percent of their inmates are hooked on drugs, but only 10 percent were in treatment in 1996. The proportion of jail inmates who need treatment has not been estimated, but given the similar alcohol and drug-abuse profiles of state prison and local jail inmates, it is likely to mirror the state estimate of 70 to 85 percent. Only eight percent of jail inmates were in treatment in 1992. As the number of inmates in need of treatment has risen in tandem with the prison population, the proportion receiving treatment has declined. Indeed, from 1995 to 1996, the number of inmates in treatment decreased by 18,360 as inmates in need of treatment rose by 39,578.

Not surprisingly given this lack of treatment, government spending on inmate drug and alcohol treatment is relatively small compared to the costs of imprisoning drug and alcohol addicts and abusers. CASA estimates that on average, states spend 5 percent of their prison budget on drug and alcohol treatment. In 1997, the Federal Bureau of Prisons spent $25 million on drug treatment—only 0.9 percent of the federal prison budget.

TREATMENT EFFECTIVENESS

Research in recent years indicates that well-designed prison-based treatment can reduce post-release criminality and drug and alcohol relapse, especially when combined with pre-release training and planning and community-based after care services, including assistance with housing, education, employment and health care.

Evaluations of prison-based treatment have focused on residential treatment programs and suggest that length of stay in treatment and the availability of aftercare following treatment are important predictors of success. Amity Rightum, a therapeutic community-based program at the R.J. Donovan medium-security prison in San Diego, for example, reduced reincarceration rates within one year of parole to 26 percent for Amity graduates who completed aftercare, compared with 43 percent for Amity graduates who did not participate in aftercare, 50 percent for Amity program dropouts and 63 percent for a matched comparison group.

Forever Free, a similar program operated by the California Department of Corrections for female inmates approaching their parole dates, reduced the rate of return to custody to 38 percent for all program graduates, compared with 62 percent for program dropouts. Participation in community-based treatment further increased the likelihood of successful outcomes—reducing the rate of return to custody to 28 percent for program graduates with some community treatment and 10 percent for graduates with at least five months of community treatment.

BEYOND TREATMENT

Substance-abuse treatment alone is not enough. Most inmates who are drug and alcohol addicts and abusers also need medical care, psychiatric help, and literacy and job training. Drug and alcohol-involved inmates tend to have ailments—cirrhosis, diabetes, high blood pressure, malnutrition, sexually transmitted diseases, HIV and AIDS—that require medical care. Some have never worked or worked so sporadically in such low-level jobs that they need not only to improve their reading, writing and math skills, but also to acquire levels of socialization that most Americans take for granted. Without help in prison acquiring these skills, once released these inmates have little chance of resisting a return to lives of drug and alcohol abuse and crime.

To appreciate the heavy baggage substance abusing inmates carry, consider the histories of inmates who were regular drug users:

- Fifteen percent in state prison, 9 percent in federal prison and 20 percent in jail have been physically and/or sexually abused.
- Sixty-one percent in state prison, 44 percent in federal prison and 48 percent in jail did not complete four years of high school.
- Thirty-six percent in state prison, 33 percent in federal prison and 39 percent in jail were unemployed in the month prior to their offense.

SUBSTANCE-ABUSE RELATED CRIME: IT RUNS IN THE FAMILY

Like substance abuse itself, substance-abuse related crime runs in the family. Children of substance-involved inmates are at high risk of addiction and incarceration. Inmates whose parents abused drugs and alcohol are much more likely to abuse drugs and alcohol themselves. In state and federal prison, regular drug users are twice as likely to have parents who abused drugs and alcohol than inmates who are not regular drug users.

Regular drug users in prison and jail are likelier than the general inmate population to have a family member who served prison time: 42 percent of regular drug users in both state prisons and local jails and 34 percent in federal prison have at least one family member who served time in prison or jail, compared to 37 percent of the general state prison population, 35 percent of the local jail population and 26 percent of the general federal prison population.

TOBACCO, ALCOHOL AND DRUGS IN PRISON

Prison policies regarding tobacco, alcohol and drugs set expectations and send important messages to inmates about official attitudes toward substance use. Unfortunately, not all prisons take advantage of this opportunity. While an estimated 29 percent of state and federal prisons are smoke-free, some state prisons provide free cigarettes to indigent inmates; a few provide free cigarettes to all inmates.

Although systematic evidence is lacking, anecdotal information suggests that drugs and alcohol are available in many prisons and jails. Current surveillance methods which occasionally test for drugs, at times with advance notice, are inadequate to eliminate drug dealing and use in prisons and to support treatment programs. Wider and more frequent random testing can help keep prisons drug-free, identify inmates in need of treatment and monitor those undergoing treatment.

THE COST OF DRUG- AND ALCOHOL-INVOLVED INMATES

Of the $38 billion spent on prisons in 1996, more than $30 billion dollars paid for the incarceration of individuals who had a history of drug and alcohol abuse, were convicted of drug and alcohol violations, were high on drugs and alcohol at the time of their crime, or committed their crime to get money to buy drugs. If current trends continue, by the year 2000, the nation will break the $100 million-dollar-a-day barrier in spending to incarcerate individuals with serious drug and alcohol problems.

Inmates who have abused alcohol or drugs often have special health needs that add expense to their incarceration. These include detoxification programs, mental and physical health care and AIDS treatment. State and federal inmates who regularly used drugs or abused alcohol are, on average, twice as likely as those who didn't to have history of mental illness.

In addition to incarceration, there are other criminal justice system costs for arresting and prosecuting substance abusers. For example, the bill for arresting and prosecuting the 1,436,000 DUI arrests in 1995 was more than $5.2 billion, exclusive of the costs of pretrial detention and incarceration.

PREVENTION

Prevention is the first line of defense against drug- and alcohol-related crime. The tremendous costs of incarcerating so many drug- and alcohol-abusing inmates underscores the vital importance of developing, implementing and evaluating large-scale prevention efforts that are designed for the populations at risk for substance abuse and criminal activity. Since most addicts begin using drugs while they are teens, efforts to give youngsters the will and skill to say no are critical to keeping them out of the criminal justice system. The difficulties of recovering from drug or alcohol addiction are enormous even for middle- or upper-class addicts. For those with family histories of substance abuse, living in poverty, with limited educational and vocational skills and health problems, the treatment process can be extraordinarily difficult. Developing effective drug-prevention programs for children and teens and making our schools drug-free are key elements in any effort to reduce drug- and alcohol-related crime.

MISSED OPPORTUNITY: REDUCING CRIME AND COSTS TO TAXPAYERS

Preventing drug and alcohol abuse and providing effective treatment for drug- and alcohol-abusing inmates hold the promise of significant savings to taxpayers and reductions in crime. CASA estimates that it would take approximately $6,500 per year, in addition to usual incarceration costs, to provide an inmate with a year of residential treatment in prison and ancillary services, such as vocational and educational training, psychological counseling, and aftercare case management.

However, if an addicted offender successfully completes the treatment program and returns to the community as a sober parolee with a job, then the following economic benefits will accrue in the first year after release:

- $5,000 in reduced crime savings (assuming that drug-using ex-inmates would have committed 100 crimes per year with $50 in property and victimization costs per crime);
- $7,300 in reduced arrest and prosecution costs (assuming that they would have been arrested twice during the year);
- $19,600 in reduced incarceration costs (assuming that one of those rearrests would have resulted in a one-year prison sentence);
- $4,800 in health care and substance abuse treatment cost savings, the difference in annual health care costs between substance users and nonusers;
- $32,100 in economic benefits ($21,400—the average income for an employed high school graduate—multiplied by the standard economic multiplier of 1.5 for estimating the local economic effects of a wage).

Under these conservative assumptions, the total benefits that would accrue during the first year after release would total $68,800 for each successful inmate. These estimated benefits do not include reductions in welfare, other state or federal entitlement costs, or foster care for the children of these inmates.

Given these substantial economic benefits, the success rate needed to break even on the $6,500 per inmate investment in prison treatment is modest. If only 10 percent of the inmates who are given one year of residential treatment stay sober and work during the first year after release, there will be a positive economic return on the treatment investment.

There are 1.2 million inmates who are drug and alcohol abusers and addicts (the other 200,000 of the 1.4 million substance-involved inmates are dealers who do not use drugs). If we successfully treat and train only 10 percent of those inmates—120,000—the economic benefit in the first year of work after release would be $8.256 billion. That's $456 million more than the $7.8 billion cost of providing treatment and training (at a cost of $6,500 each) for the entire 1.2 million inmates with drug and alcohol problems.

Thereafter, the nation would receive an economic benefit of more than $8 billion for each year they remain employed and drug- and crime-free. That's the kind of return on investment to capture the imagination of any businessman.

The potential for reduction in crime is also significant. Estimates of property and violent crimes committed by active drug addicts range from 89 to 191 per year. On a conservative assumption of 100 crimes per year, for each 10,000 drug-addicted inmates who after release stay off drugs and crime, the nation will experience a reduction of one million crimes a year.

Chapter 32

Rethinking the Assumptions About Boot Camps

by Dale Colledge and Jurg Gerber

HISTORY AND NATURE OF BOOT CAMPS

The relatively recent implementation of military-style correctional programs as an alternative sanction has elicited diverse opinions regarding their ethics, rehabilitative potential, and purpose. Commonly called "shock incarceration" or "prison boot camp" programs, these facilities employ strict discipline and military drill as key elements. For the purposes of this article, the term "boot camp" will be used to describe these programs because "shock incarceration" has been associated in much of the literature with other types of sanctions that cannot be defined as boot camp programs (Cronin, 1994, p. 1). In 1983, Georgia and Oklahoma opened the first modern prison boot camps. By 1994, a total of 29 states were operating 59 separate boot camp facilities (Cronin, 1994, p. 11). Current literature indicates that almost all state governments, along with many counties, are currently operating boot camp programs, have used them in the recent past, or are developing such a program (MacKenzie & Hebert, 1996, p. vii).

According to Parent (1989, p. xii), prison boot camps have a historical tie to earlier community corrections programs such as "Scared Straight" and "shock probation" and challenge programs such as "Outward Bound." For the purposes of this research, these types of programs will not be included since they differ significantly from present-day boot camp programs. The conditions that past researchers have established for a program to be considered a prison boot camp are not fulfilled by any of these programs.

Boot Camp Core Components

A general definition of boot camp facilities is problematic since programs differ in their basic components. This has caused confusion and debate among researchers as to what programs should be defined as boot camps:

> There is no widely accepted or official definition of the term "boot camp." Because boot camps have proven so popular with legislators and other potential backers, no doubt many program developers find it prudent to stretch the term to include as broad a range of programs as possible. (Cronin, 1994, p. 1)

From *Federal Probation*, June 1998, pp. 54-61.

The National Institute of Justice (1996, p. 3) solicited research that specifically addressed the question "What is a boot camp?"

These differences are often problematic for analysts because evaluative results of one boot camp program cannot be generalized to other facilities. The only component that almost all research has identified as being prerequisite for a program to be considered a boot camp is a military type of structure, regimen, and discipline. More generally, common elements of boot camp facilities cited by most researchers (MacKenzie, 1990, pp. 44–45; GAO, 1993, p. 11; Cronin, 1994, p. 1; and Parent, 1989, p. 11) are (1) a regimented military-style program, (2) strict discipline and rules, (3) young, first-time, nonviolent inmates, and (4) programs that are a shorter alternative to a prison sentence. The most recent and comprehensive publication on boot camps narrows that spectrum somewhat by removing the offender age and crime stipulations (MacKenzie & Hebert, 1996, p. viii). This softening of the classification requirements solves some of the dilemma in defining what constitutes a boot camp. However, it does little to address the complex issue of variation between facilities.

Program Goals and Objectives

The goals and objectives of prison boot camps have been the focus of much of the descriptive literature. A potential cause of the popularity of boot camp programs may be that they have multiple goals that can satisfy the objectives of different interest groups: "In a sense, shock incarceration is a program that can be—at least in perception—all things to all people" (Parent, 1989, p. xi). The actual or perceived goals provide a basis for analyzing the success or failure of boot camp programs. Most researchers agree (Parent, 1989, pp. 11–12; Osler, 1991, pp. 35–36; GAO, 1993; and Cronin, 1994, p. 6) on five basic goals: (1) incapacitation, (2) deterrence, (3) rehabilitation, (4) reduction of prison costs and crowding, and (5) punishment. Whether these goals are achieved successfully is an issue that directly affects correctional policy and critical analysis of these programs. Further, they provide a basis for determining success or failure of boot camp programs. Program goals or components may have to be altered to make them achievable.

General Accounting Office (1993, p. 20) statistics indicate that administrators vary in their support of these different goals for boot camp programs. Rehabilitation received the highest level of support among administrators, with more than 90 percent ranking it as of great or very great importance. The second most important goal according to administrators was reduction in costs. Nearly 87 percent ranked this goal of at least great importance. Reduction of crowding was ranked as of great or very great importance by more than 81 percent of respondents. More than 83 percent of administrators ranked protecting the public (incapacitation) as a goal of great or very great importance. Deterrence received far less support, with just over 35 percent ranking it of at least great importance. The lowest scoring goal among administrators surveyed was punishment, with only 20 percent of respondents ranking it of great or very great importance (GAO, 1993, p. 20).

Boot Camps at the Local and Federal Levels

Although most research on boot camps has focused on facilities operated at the state level, boot camps also are being operated by federal and local governments. Local governments have begun operating boot camp facilities as a method of diverting some of the jail population away from state correctional facilities. According to Cronin (1994, p. 32), the locally operated boot camp facilities are similar to the state facilities in their goals and services, but are less able to address crowding problems than state-operated boot camps. The jail boot camp programs surveyed by Austin, Jones, and Bolyard (1993, p. 3) were generally smaller and shorter in duration than state facilities. The first federal boot camp for men opened in 1990, and a facility for women opened in 1992. The federal program has a duration of 180 days (Cronin, 1994, p. 33; Klein-Saffran, Chapman, & Jeffers, 1993, pp. 13–14; GAO, 1993, p. 35; Klein-Saffran, 1991, pp. 2–3). Two noteworthy differences in the federal boot camp program are (1) its lack of summary punishments for minor infractions (Cronin, 1994, p. 33; Klein-Saffran, 1991, p. 4) and (2) a relatively intensive and extended aftercare supervision component (GAO, 1993, pp. 43–44).

Evaluative Research

Because boot camps have been operating only since 1983, evaluative research on this subject is somewhat limited. Of the 26 states surveyed by the General Accounting Office (1993, p. 22), only five reported having completed any formal evaluation. Moreover, several validity and reliability concerns have been raised regarding this body of research (Cronin, 1994; Salerno, 1994; GAO, 1988, 1993; Mack, 1992; Osler, 1991; MacKenzie, Gould, Riechers, & Shaw, 1990; and MacKenzie, 1990). Despite limited evaluation and understanding of the effects of boot camp programs on participants, these programs continue to be popular as new and innovative correctional options. MacKenzie (1994, p. 66) notes the need to "use science to help us decide whether boot camp prisons can achieve the desired goals or, if necessary, be redesigned to reach these goals."

Perhaps the most compelling problem for researchers is the applicability of the results of empirical research of one boot camp program to others. "These differences are expected to result in differences in the success or failure of programs in reaching their goals" (MacKenzie, 1990, p. 50). The validity of interagency comparison is at least questionable if not highly problematic (Mack, 1992, p. 145); however, this type of comparison has fueled the debate and has been used by both proponents and critics of boot camps to bolster their arguments (MacKenzie, 1990, pp. 44, 50–51).

MULTIPLE GOAL TYPOLOGY

This section describes a typology that seeks to explain the differences between boot camp programs as a function of their emphasis on different goals. The typology's theoretical foundation is provided by the work of MacKenzie (1990), who divided boot camp programs according to their level of emphasis on rehabilitation. Boot camps were classified as having a "high" or "low" focus on rehabilitation (programs were considered to have a high level of focus on rehabilitation if the amount of time spent in rehabilitative activities was equal to or greater than the number of hours spent working). Even if modified, this model entails numerous problems. Labor, physical exercise, military regimen, and drill could be considered as punishment (which MacKenzie did not address), but they may in fact have rehabilitative value. More importantly, though, this model only addresses two of the five commonly accepted goals of boot camp facilities (Colledge, 1996). The typology proposed here, the Multiple Goal Typology, addresses some of the shortcomings of MacKenzie's classification system.

Methods

From the 26 state facilities listed by the General Accounting Office (1993, pp. 56–58), the researchers contacted 25 boot camp administrators by telephone and asked them to participate in this study. One facility was not included in this solicitation as the researchers were unable to make telephone contact. The researchers asked the administrators to provide documentation that described their respective facilities. This information included policy manuals, inmate handbooks, internal and external evaluations, and mission statements. Fifteen administrators agreed to participate and sent information describing their respective facilities. This provided a response rate of 60 percent. The researchers used information in these documents to supplement existing descriptive statistics available in current literature (GAO, 1993; Cronin, 1994). Two locally operated boot camp facilities provided on-site interviews and tours in addition to descriptive information.

Constructing the Typology

The Multiple Goal Typology addresses the differences between boot camp programs with regard to their components and how those differences affect the five common goals: incapacitation, deterrence, rehabilitation, reduction of prison costs and crowding, and punishment (Parent, 1989, pp. 11–12; Osler, 1991, pp. 35–36; GAO, 1993, p. 20; and Cronin, 1994, p. 6). This spectrum of goals raises questions regarding what boot camps are truly designed to achieve, how greatly they differ in their emphases on these goals, the achievability of these goals (success or failure), and to what extent the programs' components reflect their stated goals. If boot camp programs differ in their stated goals, one should expect variation among program components (GAO, 1993; Cronin, 1994).

Achievability of Goals as a Function of Components

This section addresses the hypothetical relationships between various components and the five common goals of boot camp programs. Differences in program components reflect the focus on, and affect the achievability of, the separate goals. Fluctuations in one or more specific components may have different effects on the separate goals.

Previous research by MacKenzie (1990, p. 47) separated varying characteristics of boot camp programs into four distinct categories: selection decisions, community supervision upon release, program characteristics, and program location. MacKenzie recognized the fact that differences in boot camp program components may represent potential problems and benefits for goal achievement. This research seeks to build upon MacKenzie's work by presenting a more complete picture of hypothetical effects of variation in the multiple components of boot camps.

The multiple components of boot camp programs addressed in this research are broken into five categories similar to those used by MacKenzie (1990). The components will be grouped into selection criteria, participant selection controllers, program characteristics, capacity and location components, and community supervision issues. Table 1 presents these component categories and for each lists the relevant component variables, describes the type and range of variation of individual components, and identifies the hypothetical relationships between each component and the five goals. A positive (+) sign in the table indicates that inclusion of or increase in the component variable hypothetically has a positive effect on the achievability of the specific goal. A negative (−) sign indicates that inclusion of or increase in the component variable hypothetically has a negative effect on the specific goal's achievability. A zero (0) indicates that little or no effect is expected on the specific goal. In some cases, components may have multiple effects upon specific goals, which indicates that the relationship between the component and the specific goal may be conditional.

Selection Criteria Components

Selection criteria identify the range of possible offenders who could be placed in a boot camp program. Boot camp programs vary on selection components such as age, prior and violent offenses, physical and mental restrictions, sentence type, and original sentence length. Age-related components may have conditional relationships with all of the major goals by providing a larger group from which to select potential participants. Increases in minimum age restrictions can reduce the potential pool of offenders. Conversely, decreases in maximum age restrictions should have a similar diminishing effect on the potential offender pool.

Accepting offenders into boot camp programs with prior or violent offenses, who would ordinarily have been sent to a traditional prison facility, should reduce the ability of a program to achieve the goals of incapacitation, deterrence, rehabilitation, and punishment. A longer incarceration time may allow for greater rehabilitative potential for the offender if effective programs are available in prison. The absence of restrictions on the basis of prior offense(s) should increase the ability to achieve reduction in prison costs and crowding if the original incarceration length would have been longer.

Physical and mental restrictions may reduce the ability of boot camps to achieve all of the five major goals of boot camp programs by reducing the potential pool of offenders eligible for the program. However, the boot camp facility may realize indirect cost and crowding reductions by diverting offenders from the program who do not have the physical or mental ability to complete it and replacing them with more suitable candidates.

Sentencing components have multiple hypothetical effects upon goal achievement. If a boot camp is used as an alternative sentencing option that lengthens the actual time spent incarcerated, the goals of incapacitation, deterrence, rehabilitation, and punishment should be enhanced. Conversely, using boot camp as an alternative to probation should result in a net-widening effect (MacKenzie, 1990, p. 47), thus thwarting reductions in prison cost and crowding. Increasing minimum and maximum original sentence lengths will reduce incapacitation, deterrence, and punishment goals while increasing potential for realizing cost and crowding reductions. Effects of variation in original sentence length on rehabilitation will depend upon success of treatment programs available in prisons versus those in boot camps.

Participant Selection Controllers

The participant selection process also may affect the potential to achieve organizational goals. Selection decisions generally are controlled by the sentencing judge, the correctional authority operating the boot camp program, or a combination of the two entities (GAO, 1993; Cronin, 1994). Hypothetically, judges selecting boot camp participants

TABLE 1. Components of Boot Camp Programs and Hypothetical Relationships With Typology Goals

Selection criterion components

Component	Type	Range	Incapac-itation	Deter-rence	Rehabil-itation	Cost/Crowding	Punish
Min. Age	Age/Yrs	0–18yrs	–/0	–/0	–/0	–/0	–/0
Max. Age	Age/Yrs	22 yrs–No Max.	+/0	+/0	+/0	+/0	+/0
Prior Offense	Categorical	Yes/No	–	–	–/0	+	–
Physical Restrict.	Categorical	Yes/No	–/0	–/0	–/0	–/+	–/0
Mental Restrict.	Categorical	Yes/No	–/0	–/0	–/0	–/+	–/0
Violent Offenders	Categorical	Yes/No	–	–	–/0	+	–
Sentence Type	Categorical	Prison/Prob./Parole	–/+	–/+	–/+	–/+	–/+
Min. Sentence	No. of Years	0–2.5 Years	–	–	+/–	+	–
Max. Sentence	No. of Years	3.0–No Max.	–	–	+/–	+	–

Participant selection controllers

Component	Type	Range	Incapac-itation	Deter-rence	Rehabil-itation	Cost/Crowding	Punish
Correctional Authority Selects	Categorical	Yes/No	+/–	+/–	+/–	+/–	+/–
Judge Selects	Categorical	Yes/No	+/–	+/–	+/–	+/–	+/–
Selection by Judge and Corr. Auth.	Categorical	Yes/No	+/–	+/–	+/–	+/–	+/–
Voluntary In	Categorical	Yes/No	–	–	0	+	–
Voluntary Out	Categorical	Yes/No	–	–	0	+	–
Governing Authority	Government	Fed/State/Local	0	0	0	0	0

Program characteristics

Component	Type	Range	Incapac-itation	Deter-rence	Rehabil-itation	Cost/Crowding	Punish
Counseling	Hours/Day	0–24	0	0	+	–/0	0
Education	Hours/Day	0–24	0	0	+	–/0	0
Edu. Budget	Dollars	0–Unlimited	0	0	+	–	0
Vocational	Hours/Day	0–24	0	0	+	–/0	0
Military Regimen	Hours/Day	0–24	+/0	+/0	+/0	0	+/0

(continued)

TABLE 1.   (continued)

Component	Type	Range	Incapac-itation	Deter-rence	Rehabil-itation	Cost/Crowding	Punish
Summary Punishments	Categorical	Yes/No	0	+	0	0	+
Physical Labor	Hours/Day	0–24	+	+	0	+/0	+
Physical Training	Hours/Day	0–24	+/0	+	+/0	0	+
Community Service	Categorical	Yes/No	–	+/0	0	+	+/0
Restricted Privileges	Categorical	Phone, Visits	+	+	0	+/0	+
Induction Process	Categorical	Yes/No	0	+	0	0	+
Progressive Levels	No. of and Length	1–Unlimited	0	0	+/0	0	0
Demotion Possible	Categorical	Yes/No	+	+	0	–	+
Graduation Ceremony	Categorical	Yes/No	0	0	+	–	0
Summary Punishments	Categorical	Yes/No	0	+	+/–	0	+
Program Length	No. of Days	30–240	+	+	+	–	+

Program capacity and location components

Component	Type	Range	Incapac-itation	Deter-rence	Rehabil-itation	Cost/Crowding	Punish
Total Capacity	# of Beds	24–2773	0	0	0	+/–	0
Total Prison Population	Numeric	Unknown	0	0	0	–	0
Number of Security Staff	Numeric	1–No Limit	+	0	+/0	–	+/0
Number of Service Staff	Numeric	0–No Limit	0	0	+	–	0
Volunteer Staff	Numeric	0–No Limit	+/0	0	+/0	+	0
Multiple Use Facility	Categorical	Yes/No	0	0	+/0	+	0
On Existing Prison Site	Categorical	Yes/No	+	+	0	+	+
Capacity Male	No. of Beds Male	24–2623	0	0	0	+	0
Capacity Female	No. of Beds Female	0–150	0	0	0	+/–	0
Coed Facility	Categorical	Yes/No	0	0	0	+/–	0

Community supervision issues

Component	Type	Range	Incapac-itation	Deter-rence	Rehabil-itation	Cost/Crowding	Punish
Halfway House	Categorical	Yes/No	+	+	+/0	−	+
Job Assistance	Categorical	Yes/No	0	0	+	−/0	0
Training Programs	Categorical	Yes/No	0	0	+	−/0	0
Length Monitored Post-release	No. of Days	0–No Limit	+	+	+/0	−	+
Counseling	Categorical	Yes/No	0	0	+	−/0	0
Electronic Monitoring	Categorical	Yes/No	+	+	0	−	+
Intensity of Supervision	Categorical	Yes/No	+	+	+/0	−	+
Urinalysis	Categorical	Yes/No	0	+	+/0	−	+
Partial Confinement	Categorical	Yes/No	+	+	0	−	+

would be less interested in achieving cost and crowding reductions than correctional authorities would.

Other decision makers in the boot camp selection process are the potential participants themselves. We assume that potential boot camp participants would choose not to participate in a boot camp program if it means a longer period of incarceration. This leads to a negative relationship between voluntary participation components and the goals of incapacitation, deterrence, and punishment. Inversely, programs allowing inmate self-selection (voluntary participation) may realize reductions in prison cost and crowding as potential participants with longer original sentences opt for shorter boot camp incarceration. There is no significant information at this time linking the governing authority component to variation in achievability of goals; however, this does not preclude that such relationships might exist.

Program Characteristics

The next components to be addressed are those related to program characteristics. Hypothetically, increases in counseling, education, vocational training, and educational budgets should result in an increased ability to rehabilitate offenders. A negative relationship is predicted between these four components and cost and crowding reductions due to increased rehabilitative programming costs. This negative relationship may be mitigated by counseling, education, and vocational training provided by community organizations without charge to the boot camp facility. Both county boot camps that participated in the study reported that community organizations provided rehabilitative services to their programs without cost.

Increases in physical training, labor, and military regimen may have a positive effect upon the goals of incapacitation, deterrence, rehabilitation, and punishment. Boot camp facilities devoting more time to military regimen, physical training, and labor should have a greater ability to incapacitate offenders through increased monitoring and control. Likewise, increases in deterrence and punishment goals may be realized by increasing time spent in military drill, physical training, and labor.

The use of inmate labor for community service projects indirectly might reduce government costs by reducing labor costs to public and community organizations. Officials of one of the counties reported using inmate labor to assist low income and elderly members of the community with housing repairs, to restore a local area high school football field, and to perform several other community service projects.

Restricted privileges, induction processes, and possibility of demotion vary among boot camp facilities. Boot camps with extensive restrictions should realize increases in incapacitation, deterrence, and punishment while possibly decreasing costs to the facility. Induction processes, such as head shaving and verbal intimidation of new inmates, should increase levels of punishment and deterrence. Demotion for poor behavior or lack of progress, leading to a longer period of incarceration, should lead to increases in the goals of punishment, deterrence, and incapacitation while increasing cost and crowding.

The use of summary punishments for rule infractions is a relatively common element among boot camp programs (GAO, 1993, p. 18; Cronin 1994, p. 24). The extent to which facilities use these punishments varies. Federal boot camp programs do not use these types of punishments at all (Klein-Saffran, 1991, p. 4). The use of summary punishments are expected to have positive effects upon the goals of deterrence and punishment; however, the effect of these punishments upon rehabilitation are undetermined.

The existence of a graduation ceremony for inmates completing the boot camp program may have some rehabilitative effect on participants by reaffirming their accomplishment in completing the program. Additionally, it may instill confidence and a positive perception of the boot camp experience. We expect that a graduation ceremony will increase costs to some extent.

Maximum program length varies extensively among state-operated programs from a low of 30 days to a high of 240 days (GAO, 1993; Cronin, 1994). Both county boot camp programs included in this study reported lengths of 180 days. Increases in program length should improve all major goals with the exception of cost and crowding reductions. The increased program duration will directly increase cost and crowding levels.

Program Capacity and Location

Variations in total capacity of boot camp facilities directly affect the potential to achieve cost and crowding reductions. Increasing the capacity of a boot camp facility will increase cost and crowding reductions if the program admits offenders who would have been sentenced to a longer prison term. If the offenders would not have been sent to a correctional facility, or would have spent a shorter time incarcerated, increasing capacity will increase prison cost and crowding. Ability to reduce costs and crowding is mitigated by the total prison population of the jurisdiction. If the total prison population is extremely large in comparison to the total capacity of the boot camp facility, the number of offenders diverted may not have a significant effect on cost and crowding.

Staffing levels have some hypothetical effects upon achievement of boot camp goals. Increasing the number of security staff should lead to increased incapacitation levels by providing closer supervision. This also may increase the punishment and rehabilitation goals of boot camps depending on roles that security staff play (counseling versus control). Greater numbers of service staff should increase the rehabilitative capacity of a boot camp by increasing the number, quality, and intensity of training and rehabilitation programs. Increases in paid staff, however, will increase the costs of boot camp operation. Boot camp location within a multiple-use facility or on an existing prison site should reduce the cost of providing inmate services and programs. Placing a boot camp on an existing prison site should increase punishment and deterrence by providing a reminder of the possible result of future crime and increase incapacitation where greater levels of security are present.

Increasing capacity to house male inmates should reduce prison costs and crowding. Some different problems are presented for boot camp facilities that are designed to house female inmates. Including females in boot camps, especially coed facilities, may result in fraternization if inmates are not kept in check by closer supervision (resulting in possible higher staffing costs). Not admitting females into boot camp programs may present equal opportunity litigation problems (Klein-Saffran, Chapman, & Jeffers, 1993, p. 4).

Community Supervision

Community supervision issues make up the final set of component/goal relationships. Cowles and Castellano (1995, p. 121) note the importance of aftercare in successfully reintegrating offenders into the community. Placing released inmates in a halfway house or some other form of partial community confinement should increase incapacitation, deterrence, and punishment goals and may increase rehabilitation if treatment is continued at the new placement location. The operating expense of a halfway house facility will likely increase costs.

Post-release rehabilitative components such as job assistance, training programs, and counseling should increase the rehabilitative capacity of boot camp programs by extending treatment and easing transition into the community but also will increase costs. The effects of increased cost of post-release treatment and training programs are mitigated in instances where community organizations provide services without charge to boot camp graduates. Both county boot camp facilities reported that community organizations provided treatment and training services free of charge to participants upon release.

Increasing the length of time that inmates are monitored after release should increase the achievability of incapacitation, deterrence, punishment, and possibly rehabilitation while increasing costs. We anticipate that increasing the intensity of community supervision will have effects similar to extending the length monitored. The use of post-release sentencing options such as electronic monitoring and urinalysis should have positive effects on the goals of incapacitation, deterrence, and punishment, but have a negative effect on cost and crowding reductions. Urinalysis may positively affect the goal of rehabilitation if it helps the offender abstain from drug and alcohol use. Increasing the intensity of post-release supervision should have a positive effect on incapacitation, deterrence, and punishment. It also may increase rehabilitation where the restrictions assist inmates in their transition to life in the community. Increasing intensity of supervision likely will lead to increases in cost of post-release supervision and may increase crowding if it causes a higher level of revocations.

CONCLUSION

The Multiple Goal Typology presents a method of understanding differences in boot camp facilities based upon variation in components and the resulting differential emphasis on separate major goals. This preliminary typology provides a framework for understanding the relationship between components and goals. The components of boot camps clearly vary among different facilities. These component differences reflect each individual facility's focus upon specific goals and each facility's ability to achieve these separate goals.

The key to determining overall success or failure of boot camps lies in understanding the differences between them and the effect of these differences upon their goals. Program evaluation should be based upon the true goals. A facility scoring high on the deterrence and rehabilitation goals but low on the cost/crowding should be evaluated based upon recidivism rates rather than upon ability to reduce prison costs. Finally, the proposed typology leads to an increase in generalizability of evaluative research on boot camp facilities. Future research testing the multiple goal scale will be required to provide empirical evidence of the extent of similarity or dissimilarity between programs. Boot camps may be grouped in a rational manner based on real and measurable similarities, enabling generalizations of the results of evaluative studies of similar facilities.

REFERENCES

Austin, J., Jones, M., & Bolyard, M. (1993). *The growing use of jail boot camps: The current state of the art.* Washington, DC: U.S. Department of Justice.

Colledge, D. (1996). *A historical and content analysis of prison boot camps.* Thesis presented to the faculty of the College of Criminal Justice, Sam Houston State University.

Cowles, E., & Castellano, T. (1995). *"Boot camp" drug treatment and aftercare intervention: An evaluation review* (NCJ 153918). Washington, DC: National Institute of Justice.

Cronin, R. (1994). *Boot camps for adult and juvenile offenders: Overview and update.* Washington, DC: U.S. Department of Justice.

Klein-Saffran, J. (1991). Shock incarceration, Bureau of Prisons style. *Research Forum,* 1(3), 1–9.

Klein-Saffran, J., Chapman, D., & Jeffers, J. (1993, October). Boot camp for prisoners. *FBI Law Enforcement Bulletin,* 13–16.

Mack, D. (1992). Combining shock incarceration and remedial education. *Journal of Correctional Education,* 43(3), 144–150.

MacKenzie, D. (1990). Boot camp prisons: Components, evaluations, and empirical issues. *Federal Probation,* 54(3), 44–52.

MacKenzie, D., Gould, L., Riechers, L., & Shaw, J. (1990). Shock incarceration: Rehabilitation or retribution? *Journal of Offender Counseling, Services & Rehabilitation*, 14(2), 25–40.

MacKenzie, D. (1994). Results of a multisite study of boot camp prisons. *Federal Probation*, 58(2), 60–66.

MacKenzie, D., & Hebert, E. (Eds.). (1996). *Correctional boot camps: A tough intermediate sanction* (NCJ157639). Washington, DC: National Institute of Justice.

National Institute of Justice. (1996). *Boot camp research and evaluation for fiscal year 1996*. Washington, DC: Author.

Osler, M. (1991). Shock incarceration: Hard realities and real possibilities. *Federal Probation*, 55(1), 34–42.

Parent, D. (1989). *Shock incarceration: An overview of existing programs*. Washington, DC: U.S. Department of Justice.

Salerno, A. (1994). Boot camps: A critique and a proposed alternative. *Journal of Offender Rehabilitation*, 20(3/4), 147–158.

United States General Accounting Office. (1988). *Prison boot camps: Too early to measure effectiveness*. Washington, DC: Author.

United States General Accounting Office. (1993). *Prison boot camps: Short-term prison costs reduced, but long-term impact uncertain*. Washington, DC: Author.

Chapter 33

A Decade of Experimenting With Intermediate Sanctions

What Have We Learned?

by Joan Petersilia, Ph.D.
Professor of Criminology, Law, and Society
University of California, Irvine

This article reviews what has been learned during the past 10 to 15 years about the restrictions and costs of intermediate sanctions, those mid-range punishments that lie somewhere between prison and routine probation. Various intermediate sanctions programs (ISPs) that incorporate intensive supervision, home confinement, community service, boot camps, and day fines have been developed in recent years.

For those of us whose research has focused primarily on community corrections, the end of the 1990s marks an important landmark. We have witnessed the natural progression of ISPs, beginning in the mid-1980s with the media's enthusiastic portrayal of them as the panacea of corrections; through program design and implementation; to evaluation and testing; and finally to institutionalization, redesign, or abandonment. It is critical for scholars, policymakers, and practitioners to look back and reflect upon what has been learned during these years.

When looking at ISPs, there are three important questions to consider: First, what did the ISP experiment consist of—who did what, with whom, and for what purpose? Secondly, how did ISPs affect program costs, recidivism, and prison crowding? And, perhaps most important, how is the knowledge gained from this experience influencing current practice?

Several conclusions can be drawn from the evaluations of ISPs:

- In terms of sheer numbers and investments, the overall ISP experiment was more symbolic in its achievements than substantive.
- Specific components must be in place for these programs to work.
- Research findings currently influence the design of corrections programs and, more important, contribute to an emerging community justice model that promises to create a major paradigm shift in community corrections.

This article was originally prepared for the National Institute of Justice (NIJ) for use in its Crime and Justice Perspectives series and is reprinted with NIJ's permission.

From *Federal Probation*, December 1998, pp. 3-9. Reprinted by permission of the National Institute of Justice, National Criminal Justice Reference Service.

THE ISP EXPERIMENT BEGINS

In the mid-1980s, a broad-based consensus emerged as to the desirability of developing mid-range punishments for offenders for whom incarceration was unnecessarily severe and ordinary probation was inappropriately light. Three converging conditions and events drove the development of this consensus.

1. Crowded Southern prisons and a poor economy.   First, prison crowding in the Southern United States, coupled with a poor regional economy, created early pressures for tough community-based options. Federal courts found several overcrowded prisons in the South to be in violation of the eighth amendment prohibition against cruel and unusual punishment and mandated that these states either build new facilities or find some other way to punish offenders. Because these states did not have the funds to build new prisons (as other states experiencing prison population growth initially did), judicial pressure created an incentive for them to develop tough but inexpensive sentences, specifically those that did not require a prison cell. Because the voters were not about to endorse "soft" social programs, the new programs were presented to the public as punitive rather than rehabilitative. In fact, some of the older, first-generation intensive supervision programs (which provided intensive rehabilitation services) changed their names to "intensive surveillance" programs while programs originally called "alternatives to incarceration" were renamed "intermediate punishments."

The State of Georgia developed the first well-publicized intensive supervision program, the hallmark of which was the assignment of 25 offenders to a supervision team of two probation officers. The team consisted of a surveillance officer, whose main responsibility was to monitor the offender closely, and a probation officer, who provided counseling and had legal authority over the case. While on intermediate sanction, each probationer was seen five times a week, performed community service, paid a supervision fee, and had to be employed or in an educational program.

Georgia's self-evaluation showed that ISP participants had extremely low recidivism rates (less than 5 percent), and most offenders maintained employment and paid restitution to victims. In addition, the monthly supervision fee made the program self-supporting. In 1985, Georgia Corrections Commissioner David Evans claimed the ISP had saved the state the cost of building two new prisons.

A great deal of national publicity followed. The *Washington Post* and the *New York Times* ran major stories touting the program's success and called Georgia's program "the future of American corrections." Proponents suggested that intermediate punishments could relieve prison crowding, enhance public safety, and rehabilitate offenders—all at a cost saving. Probation staffs also were enthusiastic, saying intermediate sanctions programs gave them an opportunity to "do probation work the way it ought to be done."

Illinois, Massachusetts, New Jersey, and Florida, among other states, quickly followed suit, and the intermediate sanctions movement was born. It is important to be clear about the initial motivation: modern ISPs were developed in direct response to prison crowding, and without that pressure, we would not be here today reviewing their performance.

2. First indepth study of U.S. felony probation.   Research evidence produced at that time showed that the existing felony probation system was a failure in large urban areas. This evidence helped convince California and other large states that had not yet faced severe prison crowding that there were public safety risks in placing felons on routine probation. In 1983, the National Institute of Justice (NIJ) awarded a grant to the

RAND Corporation to conduct the first indepth study of felony probation in the United States. The final report, *Granting Felons Probation: Public Risks and Alternatives*, documented the fact that serious felons were being granted probation. Furthermore, because of limited (and often declining) community corrections resources, these offenders were ineffectively supervised, and the public safety consequences were severe. Two-thirds of the nearly 2,000 felony probationers who were tracked during this study were rearrested within 3 years, and more than half were reconvicted of serious offenses.[1]

The study also generated a great deal of public attention because it clearly showed that overburdened probation staff often were unable to closely supervise felons or hold them accountable for their crimes. The researchers, however, did not call for the abandonment of probation for felons or their incarceration in the future but rather something in between:

> The justice system needs an alternative, intermediate form of punishment for those offenders who are too antisocial for the relative freedom that probation now offers but not so seriously criminal as to require imprisonment. A sanction is needed that would impose intensive surveillance, coupled with substantial community service and restitution.

The study concluded that mid-range punishments—such as those instituted in Georgia—were needed not only to relieve prison crowding but to relieve probation crowding as well. The dissemination of the NIJ-RAND study became the second event to increase the acceptance of ISPs.

3. Morris and Tonry's book on the polarization of sentencing.   The third event that was critical in creating the impetus for the ISP movement was the publication of an influential book in 1990 by Norval Morris and Michael Tonry entitled *Between Prison and Probation: Intermediate Punishments in a Rational Sentencing System*.[2] Written by two of the nation's leading criminologists, this study acknowledged that U.S. judges faced a polarized choice between prison and probation, with a near vacuum of punishment options between these extremes. The study provided the needed conceptual framework for a more graduated sanctioning system that relied upon a range of sentences including fines, community service, house arrest, intensive probation, and electronic monitoring. Morris and Tonry argued that rigorously enforced intermediate punishments better serve victims and the justice system. A continuum that matches offenders to sanctions based on the seriousness of their crime is essential—regardless of any prison-crowding concerns—in creating a rational sentencing system, they wrote.

The ISP Concept Gains Strong Support

What existed, then, were program models that appeared to work, research to show that without these programs the public was at serious risk, and a compelling theoretical justification for moving forward. A ground-swell of support emerged for intermediate sanctions and, as one article noted about this period, "State legislators were virtually falling over each other" in an effort to sponsor legislation to implement these programs.[3]

The U.S. Department of Justice (DOJ) and several private organizations, particularly the Edna McConnell Clark Foundation, played a catalytic role in focusing this energy. In 1990, NIJ sponsored a national conference that brought together more than 300 federal, state, and local criminal justice administrators to explore the state of intermediate sanctions and their potential. In his keynote address, Attorney General Dick Thornburg emphasized the strong bipartisan support for developing intermediate sanctions. The Bureau of Justice Assistance (the "action" arm of DOJ) solicited agencies across the country to participate in a demonstration to test the costs and benefits of various types of ISPs. In addition, NIJ and the National Institute of Corrections (NIC) provided technical assistance, training, and research for a number of projects.

The 10 years between 1985 and 1995 could best be described as the period of ISP implementation and evaluation. Hundreds of programs were started, often with a great deal of ceremony. During this period, virtually every large probation or parole agency developed programs of intensive surveillance, electronic monitoring, house arrest, drug testing and, to a lesser extent, boot camps and day reporting centers.

A Closer Look Reveals Low ISP Participation and Shallow Funding

Most important, very few offenders, relatively speaking, participated in intermediate sanctions programs, and few dollars were spent on new ISP initiatives. Today, virtually every state and the federal government report having intensive supervision programs, but fewer than 6 percent of the 2.7 million adult probationers and parolees in the United States are estimated to be participating in them. (This number is, however, higher than anytime in the past.[4]) All 50 states report using electronic monitoring and, despite what has often been characterized as explosive growth, the number of probationers and parolees monitored electronically is now at its highest level ever—about 1 percent.[5] Although 35 states report operating boot camps, the combined daily census has never exceeded 10,000 participants.[6] Finally, although nearly 125 day reporting centers operate in the United States, their combined daily population is less than 15,000.[7]

It appears that, at most, 10 percent of adult probationers and parolees participate in ISPs—a figure that is probably higher than at any time in the past. It is safe to say that the ISP experiment has not touched the bulk of those for whom it might be appropriate, such as felons with increasingly serious prior records and a history of substance abuse who are granted probation.

Moreover, when offenders were assigned to ISPs, the intensity of services and surveillance fell short of what the initial program models prescribed—most likely because sufficient dollars were not invested. As best as can be calculated, less than $10 million was invested by the federal government in ISP research and demonstration projects between 1985 and 1995. This can be compared to the $10 million the federal government invests in evaluations of community-oriented policing each year.

In no way is this intended to offend those responsible for making these funding decisions. The boom in ISPs took place in 1994—the same time that DOJ and NIJ budgets for research and demonstration programs were declining to a 20-year low. Competition for those scarce dollars was fierce, and corrections research—particularly community corrections research—has never attracted major financial support. Fortunately, Congress has increased funding to the Bureau of Justice Assistance (BJA), the Bureau of Justice Statistics (BJS), and NIJ, and corrections research has again found support.

WHAT DID THE ISP EXPERIMENT REALLY CONSIST OF?

It is beyond the scope of this presentation to fully describe the nature of ISPs or their evaluations. For anyone interested in such details, the recently published University of Maryland report entitled *Preventing Crime: What Works, What Doesn't, What's Promising* is recommended.[8] However, I will briefly summarize the specifics of the more popular programs.

As mentioned earlier, intensive supervision programs were the first—and still remain—the cornerstone of the intermediate sanctions movement. ISPs initially were developed as a means to divert low-risk prisoners to the community or place higher-risk probationers on smaller caseloads with more restrictions. Concurrent with the emergence of ISPs was a developing technology to permit greater surveillance of offenders. As the cold war wound down, the defense industry along with the developing computer and electronic industries saw the community corrections clientele as a natural place to put its energies—a growing market. Electronic monitoring, voice verification systems, cheap on-site drug testing, breathalyzers through the phone—all allowed community corrections the option of becoming more surveillance-oriented and using the offender's home as a place of incarceration.

Jurisdictions could choose from a menu of bells and whistles, which included surveillance and services, and the goal came to be toughness in appearance. Jurisdictions adopted what they wanted, what they could afford, and applied such programs to whomever they wanted—so that a wide variety of ISPs got implemented—and the name "ISP" really has no commonly agreed upon definition as a result. It simply means "more than" what offenders in that location would have gotten in the absence of the ISP.

As noted earlier, most of the programs implemented were much less intensive than the original Georgia model had called for. Recall that the Georgia ISP model called for caseloads of 25:2, and two face-to-face contacts, minimally per week, and I know of no large urban probation department that was able to sustain that level of caseload size and contact level for its felony probationers. Even programs that began with multi-week visits displayed a strong tendency to "regress to the mean" of only one or two visits per month to a client. Suffice to say that for offenders who did participate, their level of *both* service and surveillance fell below the desired intensity.

Moreover, failure to comply with ISP conditions did not mean that you would be violated from probation. Patrick Langan of BJS studied a nationally representative sample of all adult probationers and discovered that nearly half of them were discharged from probation *without* having fully complied with their court-ordered sanctions.[9] More than a third of all offenders were successfully discharged from probation without completing court-ordered drug treatment, drug testing, house arrest, or day reporting programs. And 40 percent of those discharged had not paid their victim restitution or supervision fees. He concluded that "intermediate sanctions are not rigorously enforced." Still, something different *did* happen in those communities that implemented ISPs and several good evaluations were conducted.

PROGRAM COSTS, RECIDIVISM, AND PRISON CROWDING

Relative to the investment made, a tremendous amount was learned from these programs. Despite differences in the programs, the agencies that implemented them, and the characteristics of offenders who participated in them, three major findings are very consistent.

First, ISP participants, by and large, were not prison-bound but rather were high-risk probationers. In state after state, well-meaning program developers wrote guidelines for prison "diversions." Well-meaning judges and prosecutors ignored them and filled the programs with high-risk probationers. From the perspective of those who created these programs to save money and prison space, judges "misused" intermediate sanctions. From the perspective of judges, they had endorsed the concept of a continuum of sanctions and preferred to use these options to increase supervision and accountability for felony probationers. The ISP experiment was definitely "net widening," but given the laxity of current supervision of serious felons on probation, it is more accurate to characterize it as "net repairing."

Second, ISP offenders were watched more closely, but ISP supervision did not decrease subsequent arrests or overall justice system costs. Technical violations, however, increased. Offenders on intermediate sanctions, electronic monitoring, boot camps, day fines, and drug testing programs were watched more closely—as evidenced by a greater number of contacts—but the programs did not reduce new arrests.

For example, the ISP national demonstration evaluated by Susan Turner and me, which involved 14 counties in 9 states, found no difference in arrests after 1 year (38 percent for ISP participants and 36 percent for routine probationers), more ISP than control offenders with technical violations (70 percent and 40 percent, respectively), and, as a result, more ISP than control offenders returning to prison or jail by the end of 1 year (17 percent and 19 percent, respectively).[10]

Because it is doubtful that ISP offenders committed more violations, close surveillance probably uncovered more technical violations. Whenever this happened, many ISP managers took punitive action—often revocation to prison—to maintain the program's credibility in the eyes of the judiciary and the community. Programs that were started primarily to save money and avoid the costs of prison often cost their counties more over the long term.

These results bring into question two basic premises of intermediate sanctions, i.e., that increased surveillance acts as a constraint on the offender and that the likelihood of detection acts as a deterrent to crime. The University of Maryland project, which summarized evaluations across the full range of intermediate sanctions, concluded: "Except in a few instances, there is no evidence that these programs are effective in reducing crime as measured by official record data."[11]

Third, an important and tantalizing finding—consistent across all the evaluations regardless of program design—points to the importance of combining surveillance and drug treatment program participation. In the RAND ISP demonstration, offenders who participated in treatment, community service, and employment programs—prosocial activities—had recidivism rates 10 to 20 percent below that of those who did not participate in such additional activities.

Researchers have found similar results in Massachusetts, Oregon, and Ohio, and a recent meta-analysis of 175 evaluations of intermediate sanctions programs concluded that the combination of surveillance and treatment is associated with reduced recidivism.[12] Paul Gendreau and Tracy Little conclude, "In essence, the supervision of high-risk probationers and parolees must be structured, [be] intensive, maintain firm accountability for program participation, and connect the offender with prosocial networks and activities."

The empirical evidence regarding intermediate sanctions is decisive: Without a rehabilitation component, reductions in recidivism are elusive. In sum, the ISP evaluations show that programs were seldom used for prison diversion but rather to increase accountability and supervision of serious offenders on probation. In addition, programs did not reduce new crimes, but instead increased the discovery of technical violations and ultimately increased incarceration rates and system costs. However, programs that provided treatment and additional services obtained some reductions in recidivism, particularly for high-risk offenders and for drug offenders more specifically.

INFLUENCING CURRENT PRACTICE

How do ISP evaluations influence current practice? This is the most important of the three original questions because the ultimate goal of producing knowledge is to effect positive action. Still to be addressed are the same issues that motivated the intermediate sanctions movement—prison overcrowding, probation overload, insufficient resources, and public demand for accountability and punishment. How can this evidence be used to answer the central question, "If not prison, what?"

Researchers and policymakers cannot plead ignorance or abstain from the debate—because they know what is useful. Although they do not have all the answers, they have an obligation to engage in the debate and interject the known evidence because policy is made on these matters every day. It appears that this is happening in quiet but significant ways that may well result in a major paradigm shift for community corrections in the United States.

Program Redesign

First, the body of ISP evidence is being used to redesign programs that integrate surveillance with treatment opportunities. This is particularly true with juvenile justice programs but also with programs for adults, particularly drug offenders. The Office of Juvenile Justice and Delinquency Prevention Comprehensive Strategy for Youth endorses graduated sanctions and incorporates two principal components—increasingly strict supervision and a continuum of treatment alternatives.[13] Many states have adopted the Comprehensive Strategy. The California Legislature, for example, recently allocated $50 million to fund probation programs for delinquent youth and, drawing upon the evidence reviewed earlier, required that both surveillance and treatment be part of any funded program.

Other programs also have moved away from a singular focus on surveillance. Several boot camps, for example, are enhancing the therapeutic parts of their programs and shifting away from total reliance on physical, militaristic programming. UCLA's Mark Kleiman has proposed major funding for a national initiative labeled "coerced abstinence," which at its core will provide drug testing (a main ingredient in surveillance programs), plus treatment in and out of prison, followed by intensive aftercare upon release. A key component of his program is swift and certain response to drug-use violations.

One of the major recommendations of the recently published report by the Governor's Task Force on Sentencing and Corrections in Wisconsin, which draws heavily upon ISP experiences, calls for the elimination of probation for felons.[14] The task force recommends that felony probation be replaced with an arrangement named "community confinement and control" (CCC), which mandates electronic monitoring, urine testing, work or community service, and 18 to 20 contacts a month with a probation officer who has a caseload of no more than 17 offenders. CCC officers carry out "community-oriented probation" (similar to community-oriented policing), in which they provide active as opposed to passive supervision. They are required to engage the offender's family, employer, and neighborhood to create a support and supervision network. The Wisconsin Legislature has allocated the necessary resources to pilot the task force recommendation in two jurisdictions.

These are just a few of the ways in which ISP research results directly influence the design of future programs. It is safe to say that most corrections professionals are keenly aware of these findings. In terms of contributing to a cumulative body of knowledge about correctional programming, the ISP experiment can be considered a success.

Neighborhood Probation

The legacy of the intermediate sanctions experiment is likely to be far more important than simply the redesign of individual programs. ISPs have set the stage for an emerging model of community probation (also called community justice and neighborhood probation) in which probation officers partner with the police and community members to reduce public safety threats posed by offenders in their midst. Under this model, probation officers take an active role in community building and not just offender restraint. The probation and parole officers who are involved in ISP supervision programs are emerging as key players.

Interestingly, as community corrections officers move toward a tougher form of probation, which some liken to police work, police officers are embracing community-based policing, which some liken to probation or social work. Probation and police officers are getting out from behind their desks and out of their cars and into the community. "In your face" probation includes visiting the offender's home and work site and working with community agencies to develop and supervise community service obligations—a much more active type of probation.

Police, too, are getting out into communities, holding neighborhood meetings, and taking the pulse of neighborhoods they serve through comparatively well-funded community policing programs. One of the key goals of community policing is getting to know the people on the beat—offenders as well as law-abiding citizens. Police have heard repeatedly about residents' fear of offenders and the lack of justice and accountability for people who were arrested and placed on probation or released on parole. Victims felt crime was trivialized by a justice system that simply slapped the wrist of criminals and sent them home or imposed conditions that were not monitored. Repeat victimization was common, and the community wanted criminals who had committed serious offenses taken off its streets. Once that was done, community residents wanted programs to help the next generation become responsible citizens.

The police came to realize that to significantly reduce crime they had to get out in front of the problem and not merely react to reports of crime. They needed to be proactive rather than simply reactive. To be proactive, the police needed a variety of sources of information. Much of that information and—as it turns out—legal authority exists in the minds of the officers who operate intensive supervision programs in probation departments.

Historically, there has been animosity between police and probation officers—police believe they catch criminals, and probation lets them out. But this new "community justice" model creates a three-part collaborative between the police, probation, and members of the community.

Operation night light.   Let me illustrate this for you by describing briefly what is happening in Boston, in a formal police-probation partnership program, one component of which is called "Operation Night Light." President Clinton praised this program in his State of the Union address and called for its expansion nationwide. No one can remember a President ever mentioning "probation" in a national address, and that alone is seen as important since probation supervises two-thirds of all correctional clients in the U.S., yet few in the public know much about it. The originators of the Boston project describe it in *Community Corrections: Probation, Parole and Intermediate Sanctions.*[15]

Community meetings organized by community policing officers in Boston revealed that, as a result of ISP experiments and other local corrections programs, probation officers knew a lot about high-risk offenders and locations in their neighborhoods as well as community resources and programs. Moreover, these neighborhood discussions revealed that many of these lawbreakers were already on probation or parole, but probation officers simply did not have the resources to monitor them, serve warrants, locate absconders, or secure treatment and other programs that these offenders needed. Because these offenders were on probation, their movements in the community could be limited by court order as a condition of probation. In fact, many of them were under court-ordered conditions—for example, nighttime curfews and weapons restrictions—that, if enforced, could be extremely useful in reducing the community's fear.

Admittedly, police and probation partnerships in the past usually began as a way to increase surveillance of high-risk offenders in the community. There was such a partnership in Long Beach, California, as early as 1987. The new community justice partnerships look and feel different from earlier efforts. For example, the Boston project has expanded to include clergy, youth workers, school personnel, and parents. In addition, interesting trends have developed. Judges are expressing greater confidence that such probation terms as curfews and geographical restrictions might be enforced. Police now have information on conditions of probation and feel that they can count on the probation system to hold offenders accountable when they violate those terms. Finally, because warrants are being served, police are reporting violations to probation officers.

By combining police and probation resources, probation supervision has become a 24-hour-a-day, highly accountable reality. What was impossible for probation to do alone (even in the most intensive ISPs) has become possible under the partnership between the police and the community.

This effort has required a lot of cooperation and coordination. Initially, probation officers were reluctant to partner with the police, and the police did not want to connect with "social workers." Over time, however, each group began to realize that everyone has something to gain from each other. Police are learning from community corrections officers and others about community resources such as employment and school truancy prevention programs. Boston police officers attend joint training seminars, participate in strategic planning sessions with other organizations, and jointly participate in research projects. The police, probation, clergy, and lay people now attend monthly community meetings. Most recently, gang members and community mental health workers began to attend these meetings as well. The Boston program is expanding to incorporate new initiatives that employ the team approach. For example, police now help probation officers monitor high-risk, volatile domestic cases to reduce violence and school programs to reduce truancy. Probation absconders receive priority arrest status by police. The program has spread from Boston to a dozen other probation jurisdictions throughout Massachusetts.

Similar partnerships, now spreading across the nation, could not have been so easily forged without the ISP experiments of the past decade and the gradual acceptance by probation and parole staff of surveillance activities. Police and probation officers were moving in the same direction but did not realize it. Probation officers were getting out of their offices and monitoring offenders where they lived. Police officers were getting out of their cars and walking their beats, which allowed them to work with community members to identify problems and problem people. They stumbled onto one another; the collaborative prospects are exciting.

These programs are more than just surveillance, although admittedly surveillance plays a major role in some of them. Study after study has shown that probation and police officers, once they become familiar with individual communities and the people who live there, tend to develop less hardened attitudes. The following anecdote illustrates this.

Washington's SMART partnership.   The Washington State Supervision Management and Recidivist Tracking (SMART) Partnership for police and community corrections shares some of the characteristics of the Boston program.[16] One former director of corrections visited the community corrections field offices throughout the state annually to discuss priorities for the coming year. Each year, one particular field chief asked the director when probation officers would receive permission to carry weapons. This field chief complained at length about the personal risks he faced when making home visits to dangerous places and how drug use made offenders' behavior increasingly unpredictable and violent. However, the last time the former director saw this man, who had become an active participant in the SMART program, he said he did not need guns but needed more government funds to subsidize jobs for probationers. Clearly, a greater degree of community engagement occurs in these programs.

NO AGENCY IS AN ISLAND

The ultimate legacy of a decade of experimenting with intermediate sanctions is the strong message that no one program—surveillance or rehabilitation alone—and no one agency—police, probation, mental health, or schools alone—nor any of these agencies without the community can reduce crime or fear of crime on its own. Crime is a complex, multifaceted problem that will not be overcome by simplistic, singularly focused solutions—whether they be boot camps, electronic monitoring, or intensive probation. Workable, long-term solutions must come from the community and be embraced and actively supported by the community.

This message of community support and involvement is a lesson we learn repeatedly. If the ISP evidence lends any scientific support or credibility to that message or to practitioners and researchers who are involved in this experiment, the money invested in intermediate sanctions will have been exceedingly well spent.

NOTES

1. J. Petersilia et al, *Granting Felons Probation: Public Risks and Alternatives*. Santa Monica, CA: RAND Corporation, 1985.
2. N. Morris and M. Tonry, *Between Prison and Probation: Intermediate Punishments in a Rational Sentencing System*. New York: Oxford University Press, 1990.

3. T. Clear and P. Hardyman, "The New Intensive Supervision Movement," *Crime and Delinquency*, 36, pp. 42–61.
4. C. Camp and G. Camp, *The Corrections Yearbook*. South Salem, NY: Criminal Justice Institute, Inc., 1997.
5. Ibid, p. 143.
6. Ibid, p. 96.
7. D. Parent et al, *Day Reporting Centers*. Washington, DC: National Institute of Justice 1995.
8. L. Sherman et al, *Preventing Crime: What Works, What Doesn't, What's Promising*. College Park, MD: University of Maryland, 1997. See, in particular, Chapter 9, "Criminal Justice and Crime Prevention," by Doris L. MacKenzie.
9. P. Langan, "Between Prison and Probation: Intermediate Sanctions," *Science, 264*, 1994, pp. 791–794.
10. J. Petersilia and S. Turner, "Intensive Probation and Parole," in M. Tonry, ed., *Crime and Justice: An Annual Review of Research*. Chicago, IL: University of Chicago Press, 1993.
11. L. Sherman et al, *Preventing Crime: What Works, What Doesn't, What's Promising*, p. 21.
12. P. Gendreau and T. Little, *A Meta-analysis of the Effectiveness of Sanctions on Offender Recidivism*. Unpublished manuscript, University of New Brunswick, Saint John, B.C., 1993.
13. J. C. Howell, *Guide for Implementing the Comprehensive Strategy for Serious, Violent, and Chronic Juvenile Offenders*. Washington, DC: Office of Juvenile Justice and Delinquency Prevention, 1995.
14. Wisconsin Governor's Task Force on Sentencing and Corrections, *Governor's Task Force on Sentencing and Corrections*. Madison, WI: Author, 1996.
15. R. Corbett, B. Fitzgerald, and J. Jordan, "Boston's Operation Night Light: An Emerging Model for Police-Probation Partnerships," in J. Petersilia, ed., *Community Corrections: Probation, Parole, and Intermediate Sanctions*. New York: Oxford University Press, 1998.
16. T. Morgan and S. Marrs, "Redmond, Washington's SMART Partnership for Police and Community Corrections," in J. Petersilia, ed., *Community Corrections: Probation, Parole, and Intermediate Sanctions*. New York: Oxford University Press, 1998, pp. 170–180.

Chapter 34

The Evolving Role of Parole in the Criminal Justice System

by Paul Cromwell

Parole was first tried in the United States over a century ago. During the years that have intervened since its first official sanction at Elmira reformatory in 1876, its use has been expanded into all parts of the country and today has become one of the primary methods by which offenders are released from prisons and correctional institutions.

The motives for the development and spread of parole were mixed. They were partly humanitarian, to offer some mitigation of lengthy sentences; partly to control in-prison behavior by holding out the possibility of early release; and partly rehabilitative, since supervised reintegration into the community is more effective and safer than simply opening the gates.

However, even after a century of use, there is much misapprehension and misunderstanding about parole, and much of this arises from a confusion in terminology. The public often considers parole to be based on clemency or leniency and seldom distinguishes parole from probation and pardon. These three terms are used indiscriminately, not only by the public, but even by officials, judges, and in some states, statutes. Because of the confusion in terminology and administration, parole is often charged with all the shortcomings of other release procedures, for which it is in no way responsible. It is evident, therefore, that the prerequisite for an analysis of parole is a clear definition of the term: *Parole is the conditional release of a convicted offender from a penal or correctional institution, under the continued custody of the state, to serve the remainder of his or her sentence in the community under supervision.*

PAROLE DISTINGUISHED FROM PROBATION

Probation and parole are two different methods of dealing with offenders, although the two terms are often used interchangeably. While parole is a form of release granted to a prisoner who has served a portion of a sentence in a correctional institution, probation is granted to an offender without requiring incarceration. Parole is an administrative act of the executive or an executive agency, while probation is a judicial act of the court. In

Prepared expressly for this edition.

recent years the distinction between probation and parole has been further blurred by the development of the "split sentencing" schemes, such as shock probation, which mandates a brief period of incarceration followed by *probation* supervision.

PAROLE DISTINGUISHED FROM PARDON

One authoritative source distinguishes between pardon and parole as follows:

> Pardon involves forgiveness. Parole does not. Pardon is a remission of punishment. Parole is an extension of punishment. Pardoned prisoners are free. Parolees may be arrested and reimprisoned without a trial. Pardon is an executive act of grace; parole is an administrative expedient.[1]

In reality there is no similarity between pardon and parole, except that both involve release from an institution.

Parole has played a major role in the American correctional system. Once an offender is sentenced to prison, it is largely the parole authorities who determine when he or she will be released; under what conditions; and whether the offender's conduct after release warrants continued freedom.

PAROLE DECISIONMAKING

The decision to grant parole is a complicated one, and the consequences of the decision are of the gravest importance, both to society and for the inmate. A decision to grant parole results in conditional release prior to the expiration of the maximum term of imprisonment; a denial results in continued imprisonment. The parole release decision is often more important than the sentence of the court in determining how long prisoners actually spend incarcerated. In the absence of clear legislative or judicial guidelines for parole release decisionmaking, vast responsibility has been placed upon parole boards. Parole decisions traditionally have been considered matters of special expertise, involving observation and treatment of offenders and release under supervision at a time that maximizes both the protection of the public and offenders' rehabilitation. This idealistic correctional aim of protecting society and rehabilitating the offender has served as an additional justification for the broad discretionary powers vested in parole authorities.[2]

Statutes have usually directed parole boards to make decisions based upon one or more of the following criteria: (a) the probability of recidivism, (b) the welfare of society, (c) the conduct of the offender while in the correctional institution, and (d) the sufficiency of the parole plan. Traditionally, the hearing stage of parole decisionmaking was thought to provide decision makers with an opportunity to speak with and observe the prospective parolee, to search for such intuitive signs of rehabilitation as repentance, willingness to accept responsibility, and self-understanding. Parole decisions were not based upon formally articulated criteria or policies, but on the discretionary judgments of the individual decision makers.[3] This broad discretion has brought criticism upon the paroling authority for arbitrary, capricious, and disparate decisionmaking. The lack of fundamental fairness of such situations led to a search for more empirically based predictors of risk of recidivism.

DEVELOPMENT OF PAROLE GUIDELINES

In 1973, the U.S. Board of Parole (now the U.S. Parole Commission) initiated a system of parole guidelines, which made explicit the primary factors considered in parole selection. In so doing, the parole board provided judges, the public, and inmates with a clearer idea of the manner in which it intended to exercise its discretion (see box on page 408).

Research had shown that decisions could be predicted by using specific variables. Three variables were identified as explaining a large number of the board's decisions. These variables were: (1) the seriousness of the offense, (2) the risk posed by the inmate (probability of recidivism), and (3) the institutional behavior of the inmate (a variable that was relatively less important than the first two). The researchers produced a chart that linked seriousness of offense and risk of recidivism to suggested terms of imprisonment. Based on this chart, the parole board constructed a matrix by plotting the two dimensions—seriousness of offense and risk of recidivism—on a graph. Range of sentence length was determined by the position of both dimensions on the graph. This actuarial device was continually validated and evaluated over ten years and went through several changes. Known as the Salient Factor Score, it provided explicit guidelines for release decisionmaking based upon a determination of the potential risk of parole violation.

Following the lead of the federal parole system, other states adopted guidelines for use in release decisionmaking. While some states adopted a *matrix* guideline system similar to the Salient Factors, others adopted different types of guidelines. Most often, these involve a list of factors to be considered in making a parole release decision.

Regardless of the form parole release guidelines take, their goal is to structure the exercise of discretion. Parole boards are free to deviate from their guidelines, but generally must give reasons for doing so. Parole authorities are guided in their decisionmaking, while retaining broad powers; deviations from these guides are checked by the possibility of appeal.

Research indicates that guidelines have performed one of their intended functions, which is to even out obvious disparities and make prison time more predictable.

CRITICISMS OF PAROLE

Although parole has drawn support from many sources and generally has a history of consensual acceptance, it has on occasion been subject to vigorous criticism and reexamination. In the early years of the twentieth century, particularly after World War I, parole administration came under attack. Critics claimed that parole was not fulfilling its promise. Anti-parole groups believed that parole release was used primarily as a means of controlling inmates and that it failed to encourage changes in their behavior and attitudes after their release from prison.

Other critics pointed out that release was granted after only a cursory review of the records of inmates and that paroling authorities had no criteria by which rehabilitation could be measured and upon which release decisions could be based.

These criticisms led to two major changes in parole administration and organization. First, increasing emphasis was placed upon postrelease supervision of parolees, with a corresponding increase in the number of parole conditions. Second, there was a shift away from giving parole authority to prison personnel and toward parole boards, with independent authority and statewide jurisdiction.

The United States Parole Commission Parole Guidelines (Salient Factor Score)

Item A.   PRIOR CONVICTIONS/ADJUDICATIONS (ADULT OR JUVENILE) . . . . □
           None . . . . = 3
           One . . . . = 2
           Two or three . . . . = 1
           Four or more . . . . = 0

Item B.   PRIOR COMMITMENT(S) OF MORE THAN THIRTY DAYS
           (ADULT OR JUVENILE) . . . . □
           None . . . . = 2
           One or two . . . . = 1
           Three or more . . . . = 0

Item C.   AGE AT CURRENT OFFENSE/PRIOR COMMITMENTS . . . . □
           Age at commencement of the current offense:
           26 years of age or more . . . . = 2*
           20-25 years of age . . . . = 1*
           19 years of age or less . . . . = 0

           *EXCEPTION: If five or more prior commitments of more than
           thirty days (adult or juvenile), place an "x" here ___ and
           score this item . . . . = 0

Item D.   RECENT COMMITMENT-FREE PERIOD (THREE YEARS) . . . . □
           No prior commitment of more than thirty days (adult or
           juvenile) or released to the community from last such
           commitment at least three years prior to the commencement
           of the current offense . . . . = 1
           Otherwise . . . . = 0

Item E.   PROBATION/PAROLE/CONFINEMENT/ESCAPE STATUS VIOLATOR
           THIS TIME . . . . = □
           Neither on probation, parole, confinement, or escape status
           at the time of the current offense; nor committed as a
           probation, parole, confinement, or escape status violator
           this time . . . . = 1
           Otherwise . . . . = 0

Item F.   HEROIN/OPIATE DEPENDENCE . . . . = □
           No history of heroin/opiate dependence . . . . = 1
           Otherwise . . . . = 0

TOTAL SCORE . . . . □

Source: United States Parole Commission, 1997.

Score (SFS/81), it provides explicit guidelines for release decisions based on a determination of the potential risk of parole violation. The SFS measures six offender characteristics and assigns a score to each.

By the mid-1930s, the parole system was again being scrutinized as to its continuance as a viable part of the justice system. The Attorney General's Survey of Release Procedures, a monumental study of the correctional process, was essentially established to review the efficacy of parole.

The survey stated:

> While there has never been a time when the functions and purpose of parole have been clearly understood, at no period has the entire institution been the object of so much controversy and attack or viewed with as much suspicion by the general public as it has been during the past four or five years.[4]

Mounting prison population and rising recidivism rates aggravated the general uneasiness concerning early release via parole. Questions regarding the value of rehabilitation itself were making themselves heard, and without the philosophical underpinnings of reform and rehabilitation as a purpose of punishment, parole had no meaning in the criminal justice system.

Both the concept of rehabilitation and the practice of parole survived the criticism, and in 1940, President Franklin D. Roosevelt declared, "We know from experience that parole, when it is honestly and expertly managed, provides better protection for society than does any other method of release from prison."[5]

The years between World War II and 1970 witnessed the development and evolution of the so-called "medical," or rehabilitative, model of corrections. The belief that criminals could be changed if given the opportunity and if sufficient skills, funds, and personnel were available, was the central philosophy of this approach to corrections. By 1967 (at the height of the rehabilitation era), a Harris Poll, using a nationwide sample, found that 77 percent of the population believed that prisons should be *mainly corrective*, while only 11 percent believed prisons should be *mainly punitive*.[6] In this social context, parole was considered a viable and necessary aspect of the American system of corrections. By 1977, nearly three-quarters of those released from prison were released via parole.[7]

A PHILOSOPHICAL CHANGE

By the middle 1970s, with a suddenness remarkable in social change, there was a dramatic turnabout. Individualism, rehabilitation, sentence indeterminacy, and parole all seemed, once again, to fall from grace and appeared to be on their way out.[8]

The failure of the correctional system to reduce the steadily increasing crime rate and the system's obvious inability to reduce recidivism, rehabilitate offenders, or make predicative judgments about offenders' future behavior brought about public disillusionment, disappointment, and resentment. The pendulum began to swing, and by the late 1970s seemed to have moved 180 degrees from the rehabilitative ideal to a "just deserts" approach to criminal correction.

In contrast to the rehabilitative ideal, the just deserts, or "justice model," denies the efficacy of rehabilitation and changes the focus of the system from the offender to the offense. The general aim of those favoring determinate sentencing was to abolish, or at least tightly control, discretion. This included the discretion of the prosecutor to choose charges and plea bargain; the discretion of judges to choose any sentence within a broad range of time; the discretion of prison administrators to decide what kind of treatment a prisoner needed to become law-abiding; and the discretion of parole boards to release or not release prisoners without ever having to justify their decision or render their decisions consistent. Determinate sentencing was the reformers' answer to this problem.[9] The proposals of the mid-1970s called for clear, certain, uniform penalties for all crimes, either through legislative action or the promulgation of guidelines to which prosecutors, judges, and parole boards would be required to adhere.

The public attitude prevalent at the time seemed inevitably to point toward increasing determinacy in sentencing and, ultimately, abolishing parole as a release mechanism. Between 1976 and 1999, at least 17 states abolished parole or passed determinate sentencing legislation effectively eliminating parole as a release mechanism (see table 1). Other states increased penalties, passed mandatory sentencing and career criminal laws.

Table 1.   Jurisdictions Which Have Abolished Parole or Instituted Determinate Sentencing as of January 1999

	Abolished parole	Year abolished	Sentence Type Determinate
Alaska			X
Arizona	X	1994	X
Arkansas			X
Delaware	X	1990	X
Florida	X	1983	X
Illinois			X
Indiana			X
Kansas	X	1993	
Maine	X	1976	
Maryland			X
Minnesota	X	1982	
Mississippi			X
Nevada			X
North Carolina	X	1994	
North Dakota			X
Ohio	X	1996	
Oklahoma			X
Oregon	X	1989	X
Tennessee			X
Texas			X
Virginia	X	1995	
Washington	X	1984	X
Wisconsin	X	1999	
Federal	X	1984	X
Total	**13**	**1990**	**17**

Adapted from Camille Camp & George Camp, *The 1999 Corrections Yearbook*, pp. 60–61.

Although no model came to predominate, the impact on parole especially discretionary parole release, "was dramatic."[10] In some states both parole release and postrelease supervision were abandoned. In other states, parole release was abandoned but supervision was retained. In some jurisdictions, the legislature limited the releasing power of the parole board by requiring that prisoners serve a flat minimum or proportion of the maximum sentence before becoming eligible for parole. In other states parole guidelines were established to reduce and structure release decisionmaking.

A REPRIEVE AND A NEW ROLE FOR PAROLE: PRISON POPULATION CONTROL

The abolition of discretionary parole release did not prove to be the panacea that some expected. During the 1970s and 1980s, the nation's prison population grew dramatically—at least partly fueled by the reduction in parole discretion and the harsher sentences that came with determinate and mandatory sentencing. In 1970, there were 196,000 prisoners in state and federal prisons. The rate of incarceration was 96 per 100,000. By 1980 the prison population had increased to 315,000 and the incarceration rate had risen to 139 per 100,000. By 1990, the prison population had reached 755,000; the rate of incarceration was 289 per 100,000. At midyear 1999, the U.S. prison population had risen to 1,300,000 with an incarceration rate of 403 per 100,000.[11]

In some jurisdictions the rapid increase in prison populations brought about a reappraisal of the abolition decision. Maine, which abolished parole in 1976, has had to build four new prisons to handle the increased population. Other jurisdictions have faced similar problems. Colorado and Connecticut reinstated parole. North Carolina, which had placed severe limitations on the use of parole, has since given it more discretion. Florida, which adopted sentencing guidelines in 1983 and abolished parole, returned the function under a new name, "Controlled Release Authority."[12]

Parole boards have always been the "back-door keeper" of America's prisons, often serving as a safety valve to relieve crowded institutions. While this practice is not consistent with the philosophy of parole as a tool of rehabilitation, and most paroling authorities do not believe that the management of prison populations should be a primary responsibility, prison [population] management has become a de facto function of parole in many jurisdictions.[13]

Recent years have witnessed an institutionalization of this function. Some states have given legislative authority and direction to their parole boards to control prison population. Others have done so through informal agreements between the governor, director of corrections, and the parole board. Increasingly, through a variety of formal and informal methods, parole boards are being utilized in an effort to reduce and maintain the prison population—with varying and arguable degrees of success.

However, most authorities agree that it is not feasible, in the long term, to control prison populations by parole board action. The reductions achieved are at best, temporary—and have often achieved those results to the detriment of effective postrelease supervision due to escalating caseloads. It has become apparent that where parole boards are used as the "back-door" for overcrowded prisons, the prison population crisis is often simply transferred from the institutional component of corrections to the community component.

SUMMARY

Although the new millennium finds the criminal justice system embroiled in controversy, engaged in self-examination, and subjected to scrutiny by the public and the courts, the issues involved—overcrowding of prisons, the efficacy of parole, sentencing disparity, parole release decisionmaking, and indeed, the continued existence of parole—are not new, and neither are the proposed solutions. The inertia of the criminal justice system is as great as is its failure to learn the lessons of history. These same issues have been studied, scrutinized, rejected, embraced, modified, codified, outlawed, and reincarnated under new labels for over a century. Presidential commissions have alternatively recommended the extension of parole and indeterminacy of sentencing and the outright abolition of the same. The answer is not yet at hand. History has taught us that all too often the unenvisioned and unintended consequences of reform have aggravated rather than mitigated the problems leading to their enactment. Prudence in reform efforts is advisable, and such lessons that can be learned from past efforts should be carefully assessed. Parole, as it functions today, is an integral part of the total correctional process. As such, it is a method of selectively releasing offenders from the institution and placing them under supervision in the community, whereby the community is afforded continuing protection while the offender is making adjustments and beginning to contribute to society.

NOTES

1. Attorney General's Survey of Release Procedures, *Parole*, vol. 4. Washington, D.C.: Government Printing Office, 1939. p. 2.
2. William J. Grenego, Peter D. Goldberger, and Vicki C. Jackson, "Parole Release Decision Making and the Sentencing Process," 84 *Yale Law Journal*. 810, 1975.
3. 84 *Yale Law Journal*. 810, 820.
4. U.S. Department of Justice, *Parole, Vol. 4 of Attorney General's Survey of Release Procedures*, Washington, 1939.
5. Quoted by Sanford Bates in his speech, "The Next Hundred Years," at the Thirty-Fifth Annual Conference of the National Probation Association, Atlantic City, NJ, 1941.
6. Harris Poll, *Los Angeles Times*, Aug. 14, 1967.
7. Edward E. Rhine, William R. Smith, and Ronald W. Jackson, *Paroling Authorities: Recent History and Current Practice*. Laurel, MD: American Correctional Association, 1991, p. 26.
8. National Advisory Commission on Criminal Justice Standards and Goals, *A National Strategy to Reduce Crime*. Washington: Law Enforcement Assistance Administration, 1973.
9. David B. Griswold and Michael D. Wiatrowski, "The Emergence of Determinate Sentencing," *Federal Probation*, June 1983.
10. Rhine, et al., supra, p. 25 and Camille G. Camp and George M. Camp, *1999 Corrections Yearbook*, pp. 7, 16.
11. Camp and Camp, Id at 16.
12. Rhine et al, Supra at 26.
13. Id.

Chapter 35

"This Man Has Expired"

Witness to an Execution

by Robert Johnson

The death penalty has made a comeback in recent years. In the late sixties and through most of the seventies, such a thing seemed impossible. There was a moratorium on executions in the U.S., backed by the authority of the Supreme Court. The hiatus lasted roughly a decade. Coming on the heels of a gradual but persistent decline in the use of the death penalty in the Western world, it appeared to some that executions would pass from the American scene [cf. *Commonweal*, January 15, 1988]. Nothing could have been further from the truth.

Beginning with the execution of Gary Gilmore in 1977, over 100 people have been put to death, most of them in the last few years. Some 2,200 prisoners are presently confined to death rows across the nation. The majority of these prisoners have lived under sentence of death for years, in some cases a decade or more, and are running out of legal appeals. It is fair to say that the death penalty is alive and well in America, and that executions will be with us for the foreseeable future.

Gilmore's execution marked the resurrection of the modern death penalty and was big news. It was commemorated in a best-selling tome by Norman Mailer, *The Executioner's Song*. The title was deceptive. Like others who have examined the death penalty, Mailer told us a great deal about the condemned but very little about the executioners. Indeed, if we dwell on Mailer's account, the executioner's story is not only unsung; it is distorted.

Gilmore's execution was quite atypical. His was an instance of state-assisted suicide accompanied by an element of romance and played out against a backdrop of media fanfare. Unrepentant and unafraid, Gilmore refused to appeal his conviction. He dared the state of Utah to take his life, and the media repeated the challenge until it became a taunt that may well have goaded officials to action. A failed suicide pact with his lover staged only days before the execution, using drugs she delivered to him in a visit marked by unusual intimacy, added a hint of melodrama to the proceedings. Gilmore's final words, "Let's do it," seemed to invite the lethal hail of bullets from the firing squad. The nonchalant phrase, at once fatalistic and brazenly rebellious, became Gilmore's epitaph. It clinched his outlaw-hero image, and found its way onto tee shirts that confirmed his celebrity status.

Befitting a celebrity, Gilmore was treated with unusual leniency by prison officials during his confinement on death row. He was, for example, allowed to hold a party the night before his execution, during which he was free to eat, drink, and make merry with his guests until the early morning hours. This is not entirely unprecedented. Notorious English convicts of centuries past would throw farewell balls in prison on the eve of their executions. News accounts of such affairs sometimes included a commentary on the richness of the table and the quality of the dancing. For the record, Gilmore served Tang, Kool-Aid, cookies, and coffee, later supplemented by contraband pizza and an unidentified liquor. Periodically, he gobbled drugs obligingly provided by the prison pharmacy. He played a modest arrangement of rock music albums but refrained from dancing.

Gilmore's execution generally, like his parting fete, was decidedly out of step with the tenor of the modern death penalty. Most condemned prisoners fight to save their lives, not to have them taken. They do not see their fate in romantic terms; there are no farewell parties. Nor are they given medication to ease their anxiety or win their compliance. The subjects of typical executions remain anonymous to the public and even to their keepers. They are very much alone at the end.

In contrast to Mailer's account, the focus of the research I have conducted is on the executioners themselves as they carry out typical executions. In my experience executioners—not unlike Mailer himself—can be quite voluble, and sometimes quite moving, in expressing themselves. I shall draw upon their words to describe the death work they carry out in our name.

DEATH WORK AND DEATH WORKERS

Executioners are not a popular subject of social research, let alone conversation at the dinner table or cocktail party. We simply don't give the subject much thought. When we think of executioners at all, the imagery runs to individual men of disreputable, or at least questionable, character who work stealthily behind the scenes to carry out their grim labors. We picture hooded men hiding in the shadow of the gallows, or anonymous figures lurking out of sight behind electric chairs, gas chambers, firing blinds, or, more recently, hospital gurneys. We wonder who would do such grisly work and how they sleep at night.

This image of the executioner as a sinister and often solitary character is today misleading. To be sure, a few states hire free-lance executioners and traffic in macabre theatrics. Executioners may be picked up under cover of darkness and some may still wear black hoods. But today, executions are generally the work of a highly disciplined and efficient team of correctional officers.

Broadly speaking, the execution process as it is now practiced starts with the prisoner's confinement on death row, an oppressive prison-within-a-prison where the condemned are housed, sometimes for years, awaiting execution. Death work gains momentum when an execution date draws near and the prisoner is moved to the death house, a short walk from the death chamber. Finally, the process culminates in the death watch, a twenty-four-hour period that ends when the prisoner has been executed.

This final period, the death watch, is generally undertaken by correctional officers who work as a team and report directly to the prison warden. The warden or his representative, in turn, must by law preside over the execution. In many states, it is a member of the death watch or execution team, acting under the warden's authority, who in fact plays the formal role of executioner. Although this officer may technically work alone, his teammates view the execution as a shared responsibility. As one officer on the death watch told me in no uncertain terms: "We all take part in it; we all play 100 percent in it, too. That takes the load off this one individual [who pulls the switch]." The formal executioner concurred. "Everyone on the team can do it, and nobody will tell you I did it. I know my team." I found nothing in my research to dispute these claims.

The officers of these death watch teams are our modern executioners. As part of a larger study of the death work process, I studied one such group. This team, comprising nine seasoned officers of varying ranks, had carried out five electrocutions at the time I began my research. I interviewed each officer on the team after the fifth execution, then served as an official witness at a sixth electrocution. Later, I served as a behind-the-scenes observer during their seventh execution. The results of this phase of my research form the substance of this essay.

THE DEATH WATCH TEAM

The death watch or execution team members refer to themselves, with evident pride, as simply "the team." This pride is shared by other correctional officials. The warden at the institution I was observing praised members of the team as solid citizens—in his words, country boys. These country boys, he assured me, could be counted on to do the job and do it well. As a fellow administrator put it, "an execution is something [that] needs to be done and good people, dedicated people who believe in the American system, should do it. And there's a certain amount of feeling, probably one to another, that they're part of that—that when they have to hang tough, they can do it, and they can do it right. And that it's just the right thing to do."

The official view is that an execution is a job that has to be done, and done right. The death penalty is, after all, the law of the land. In this context, the phrase "done right" means that an execution should be a proper, professional, dignified undertaking. In the words of a prison administrator, "We had to be sure that we did it properly, professionally, and [that] we gave as much dignity to the person as we possibly could in the process. . . . If you've gotta do it, it might just as well be done the way it's supposed to be done—without any sensation."

In the language of the prison officials, "proper" refers to procedures that go off smoothly; "professional" means without personal feelings that intrude on the procedures in any way. The desire for executions that take place "without any sensation" no doubt refers to the absence of media sensationalism, particularly if there should be an embarrassing and undignified hitch in the procedures, for example, a prisoner who breaks down or becomes violent and must be forcibly placed in the electric chair as witnesses, some from the media, look on in horror. Still, I can't help but note that this may be a revealing slip of the tongue. For executions are indeed meant to go off without any human feeling, without any sensation. A profound absence of feeling would seem to capture the bureaucratic ideal embodied in the modern execution.

The view of executions held by the execution team members parallels that of correctional administrators but is somewhat more restrained. The officers of the team are closer to the killing and dying, and are less apt to wax abstract or eloquent in describing the process. Listen to one man's observations:

> It's a job. I don't take it personally. You know, I don't take it like I'm having a grudge against this person and this person has done something to me. I'm just carrying out a job, doing what I was asked to do. . . . This man has been sentenced to death in the courts. This is the law and he broke this law, and he has to suffer the consequences. And one of the consequences is to put him to death.

I found that few members of the execution team support the death penalty outright or without reservation. Having seen executions close up, many of them have lingering doubts about the justice or wisdom of this sanction. As one officer put it:

> I'm not sure the death penalty is the right way. I don't know if there is a right answer. So I look at it like this: if it's gotta be done, at least it can be done in a humane way, if there is such a word for it . . . The only way it should be done, I feel, is the way we do it. It's done professionally; it's not no horseplaying. Everything is done by documentation. One time. By the book.

Arranging executions that occur "without any sensation" and that go "by the book" is no mean task, but it is a task that is undertaken in earnest by the execution team. The tone of the enterprise is set by a team leader, a man who takes a hard-boiled, no nonsense approach to correctional work in general and death work in particular. "My style," he says, "is this: if it's a job to do, get it done. Do it and that's it." He seeks out kindred spirits, men who see killing condemned prisoners as a job—a dirty job one does reluctantly, perhaps, but above all a job one carries out dispassionately and in the line of duty.

To make sure that line of duty is a straight and accurate one, the death watch team has been carefully drilled by the team leader in the mechanics of execution. The process has been broken down into simple, discrete tasks and practiced repeatedly. The team leader describes the division of labor in the following exchange:

> The execution team is a nine-officer team and each one has certain things to do. When I would train you, maybe you'd buckle a belt, that might be all you'd have to do . . . And you'd be expected to do one thing and that's all you'd be expected to do. And if everybody does what they were taught, or what they were trained to do, at the end the man would be put in the chair and everything would be complete. It's all come together now.
>
> So it's broken down into very small steps. . . . *Very small*, yes. Each person has *one* thing to do. I see. What's the purpose of breaking it down into such small steps?
>
> So people won't get confused. I've learned it's kind of a tense time. When you're executin' a person, killing a person—you call it killin', executin', whatever you want—the man dies anyway. I find the less you got on your mind, why, the better you'll carry it out. So it's just very simple things. And so far, you know, it's all come together, we haven't had any problems.

This division of labor allows each man on the execution team to become a specialist, a technician with a sense of pride in his work. Said one man,

> My assignment is the leg piece. Right leg. I roll his pants leg up, place a piece [electrode] on his leg, strap his leg in . . . I've got all the moves down pat. We train from different posts; I can do any of them: But that's my main post.

The implication is not that the officers are incapable of performing multiple or complex tasks, but simply that it is more efficient to focus each officer's efforts on one easy task.

An essential part of the training is practice. Practice is meant to produce a confident group, capable of fast and accurate performance under pressure. The rewards of practice are reaped in improved performance. Executions take place with increasing efficiency, and eventually occur with precision. "The first one was grisly," a team member confided to me. He explained that there was a certain amount of fumbling, which made the execution seem interminable. There were technical problems as well: The generator was set too high so the body was badly burned. But that is the past, the officer assured me. "The ones now, we know what we're doing. It's just like clockwork."

THE DEATH WATCH

The death-watch team is deployed during the last twenty-four hours before an execution. In the state under study, the death watch starts at 11 o'clock the night before the execution and ends at 11 o'clock the next night when the execution takes place. At least two officers would be with the prisoner at any given time during that period. Their objective is to keep the prisoner alive and "on schedule." That is, to move him through a series of critical and cumulatively demoralizing junctures that begin with his last meal and end with his last walk. When the time comes, they must deliver the prisoner up for execution as quickly and unobtrusively as possible.

Broadly speaking, the job of the death watch officer, as one man put it, "is to sit and keep the inmate calm for the last twenty-four hours—and get the man ready to go." Keeping a condemned prisoner calm means, in part, serving his immediate needs. It seems paradoxical to think of the death watch officers as providing services to the condemned, but the logistics of the job make service a central obligation of the officers. Here's how one officer made this point:

> Well, you can't help but be involved with many of the things that he's involved with. Because if he wants to make a call to his family, well, you'll have to dial the number. And you keep records of whatever calls he makes. If he wants a cigarette, well he's not allowed to keep matches so you light it for him. You've got to pour his coffee, too. So you're aware what he's doing. It's not like you can just ignore him. You've gotta just be with him whether he wants it or not, and cater to his needs.

Officers cater to the condemned because contented inmates are easier to keep under control. To a man, the officers say this is so. But one can never trust even a contented, condemned prisoner.

The death-watch officers see condemned prisoners as men with explosive personalities. "You don't know what, what a man's gonna do," noted one officer. "He's liable to snap, he's liable to pass out. We watch him all the time to prevent him from committing suicide. You've got to be ready—he's liable to do anything." The prisoner is never out of at least one officer's sight. Thus surveillance is constant, and control, for all intents and purposes, is total.

Relations between the officers and their charges during the death watch can be quite intense. Watching and being watched are central to this enterprise, and these are always engaging activities, particularly when the stakes are life and death. These relations are, nevertheless, utterly impersonal; there are no grudges but neither is there compassion or fellow-feeling. Officers are civil but cool; they keep an emotional distance from the men they are about to kill. To do otherwise, they maintain, would make it harder to execute condemned prisoners. The attitude of the officers is that the prisoners arrive as strangers and are easier to kill if they stay that way.

During the last five or six hours, two specific team officers are assigned to guard the prisoner. Unlike their more taciturn and aloof colleagues on earlier shifts, these officers make a conscious effort to talk with the prisoner. In one officer's words, "We keep them right there and keep talking to them—about anything except the chair." The point of these conversations is not merely to pass time; it is to keep tabs on the prisoner's state of mind, and to steer him away from subjects that might depress, anger, or otherwise upset him. Sociability, in other words, quite explicitly serves as a source of social control. Relationships, such as they are, serve purely manipulative ends. This is impersonality at its worst, masquerading as concern for the strangers one hopes to execute with as little trouble as possible.

Generally speaking, as the execution moves closer, the mood becomes more somber and subdued. There is a last meal. Prisoners can order pretty much what they want, but most eat little or nothing at all. At this point, the prisoners may steadfastly maintain that their executions will be stayed. Such bravado is belied by their loss of appetite. "You can see them going down," said one officer. "Food is the last thing they got on their minds."

Next the prisoners must box their meager worldly goods. These are inventoried by the staff, recorded on a one-page checklist form, and marked for disposition to family or friends. Prisoners are visibly saddened, even moved to tears, by this procedure, which at once summarizes their lives and highlights the imminence of death. At this point, said one of the officers, "I really get into him; I watch him real close." The execution schedule, the officer pointed out, is "picking up momentum, and we don't want to lose control of the situation."

This momentum is not lost on the condemned prisoner. Critical milestones have been passed. The prisoner moves in a limbo existence devoid of food or possessions; he has seen the last of such things, unless he receives a stay of execution and rejoins the living. His identity is expropriated as well. The critical juncture in this regard is the shaving of the man's head (including facial hair) and right leg. Hair is shaved to facilitate the electrocution; it reduces physical resistance to electricity and minimizes singeing and burning. But the process has obvious psychological significance as well, adding greatly to the momentum of the execution.

The shaving procedure is quite public and intimidating. The condemned man is taken from his cell and seated in the middle of the tier. His hands and feet are cuffed, and he is dressed only in undershorts. The entire death watch team is assembled around him. They stay at a discrete distance, but it is obvious that they are there to maintain control should he resist in any way or make any untoward move. As a rule, the man is overwhelmed. As one officer told me in blunt terms, "Come eight o'clock, we've got a dead man. Eight o'clock is when we shave the man. We take his identity; it goes with the hair." This taking of identity is indeed a collective process—the team makes a forceful "we," the prisoner their helpless object. The staff is confident that the prisoner's capacity to resist is now compromised. What is left of the man erodes gradually and, according the officers, perceptibly over the remaining three hours before the execution.

After the prisoner has been shaved, he is then made to shower and don a fresh set of clothes for the execution. The clothes are unremarkable in appearance, except that velcro replaces buttons and zippers, to reduce the chance of burning the body. The main significance of the clothes is symbolic: they mark the prisoner as a man who is ready for execution. Now physically "prepped," to quote one team member, the prisoner is placed in an empty tomblike cell, the death cell. All that is left is the wait. During this fateful period, the prisoner is more like an object "without any sensation" than like a flesh-and-blood person on the threshold of death.

For condemned prisoners, like Gilmore, who come to accept and even to relish their impending deaths, a genuine calm seems to prevail. It is as if they can transcend the dehumanizing forces at work around them and go to their deaths in peace. For most condemned prisoners, however, numb resignation rather than peaceful acceptance is the norm. By the account of the death-watch officers, these more typical prisoners are beaten men. Listen to the officers' accounts:

> A lot of 'em die in their minds before they go to that chair. I've never known of one or heard of one putting up a fight. . . . By the time they walk to the chair, they've completely faced it. Such a reality most people can't understand. Cause they don't fight it. They don't seem to have anything to say. It's just something like "Get it over with." They may be numb, sort of in a trance.
>
> They go through stages. And, at this stage, they're real humble. Humblest bunch of people I ever seen. Most all of 'em is real, real weak. Most of the time you'd only need one or two people to carry out an execution, as weak and as humble as they are.

These men seem barely human and alive to their keepers. They wait meekly to be escorted to their deaths. The people who come for them are the warden and the remainder of the death watch team, flanked by high-ranking correctional officials. The warden reads the court order, known popularly as a death warrant. This is, as one officer said, "the real deal," and nobody misses its significance. The condemned prisoners then go to their deaths compliantly, captives of the inexorable, irresistible momentum of the situation. As one officer put it, "There's no struggle. . . . They just walk right on in there." So too, do the staff "just walk right on in there," following a routine they have come to know well. Both the condemned and the executioners, it would seem, find a relief of sorts in mindless mechanical conformity to the modern execution drill.

WITNESS TO AN EXECUTION

As the team and administrators prepare to commence the good fight, as they might say, another group, the official witnesses, are also preparing themselves for their role in the execution. Numbering between six and twelve for any given execution, the official witnesses are disinterested citizens in good standing drawn from a cross-section of the state's population. If you will, they are every good or decent person, called upon to represent the community and use their good offices to testify to the propriety of the execution. I served as an official witness at the execution of an inmate.

At eight in the evening, about the time the prisoner is shaved in preparation for the execution, the witnesses are assembled. Eleven in all, we included three newspaper and two television reporters, a state trooper, two police officers, a magistrate, a businessman, and myself. We were picked up in the parking lot behind the main office of the corrections department. There was nothing unusual or even memorable about any of this. Gothic touches were notable by their absence. It wasn't a dark and stormy night; no one emerged from the shadows to lead us to the prison gates.

Mundane consideration prevailed. The van sent for us was missing a few rows of seats so there wasn't enough room for all of us. Obliging prison officials volunteered their cars. Our rather ordinary cavalcade reached the prison but only after getting lost. Once within the prison's walls, we were sequestered for some two hours in a bare and almost shabby administrative conference room. A public information officer was assigned to accompany us and answer our questions. We grilled this official about the prisoner and the execution procedure he would undergo shortly, but little information was to be had. The man confessed ignorance on the most basic points. Disgruntled at this and increasingly anxious, we made small talk and drank coffee.

At 10:40 P.M., roughly two-and-a-half hours after we were assembled and only twenty minutes before the execution was scheduled to occur, the witnesses were taken to the basement of the prison's administrative building, frisked, then led down an alleyway that ran along the exterior of the building. We entered a neighboring cell block and were admitted to a vestibule adjoining the death chamber. Each of us signed a log, and was then led off to the witness area. To our left, around a corner some thirty feet away, the prisoner sat in the condemned cell. He couldn't see us, but I'm quite certain he could hear us. It occurred to me that our arrival was a fateful reminder for the prisoner. The next group would be led by the warden, and it would be coming for him.

We entered the witness area, a room within the death chamber, and took our seats. A picture window covering the front wall of the witness room offered a clear view of the electric chair, which was about twelve feet away from us and well illuminated. The chair, a large, high-back solid oak structure with imposing black straps, dominated the death chamber. Behind it, on the back wall, was an open panel full of coils and lights. Peeling paint hung from the ceiling and walls; water stains from persistent leaks were everywhere in evidence.

Two officers, one a hulking figure weighing some 400 pounds, stood alongside the electric chair. Each had his hands crossed at the lap and wore a forbidding, blank expression on his face. The witnesses gazed at them and the chair, most of us scribbling notes furiously. We did this, I suppose, as much to record the experience as to have a distraction from the growing tension. A correctional officer entered the witness room and announced that a trial run of the machinery would be undertaken. Seconds later, lights flashed on the control panel behind the chair indicating that the chair was in working order. A white curtain, opened for the test, separated the chair and the witness area. After the test, the curtain was drawn. More tests were performed behind the curtain. Afterwards, the curtain was reopened, and would be left open until the execution was over. Then it would be closed to allow the officers to remove the body.

A handful of high-level correctional officials were present in the death chamber, standing just outside the witness area. There were two regional administrators, the director of the Department of Corrections, and the prison warden. The prisoner's chaplain and lawyer were also present. Other than the chaplain's black religious garb, subdued grey pinstripes and bland correctional uniforms prevailed. All parties were quite solemn.

At 10:58 the prisoner entered the death chamber. He was, I knew from my research, a man with a checkered, tragic past. He had been grossly abused as a child, and went on to become grossly abusive of others. I was told he could not describe his life, from childhood on, without talking about confrontations in defense of a precarious sense of self—at home, in school, on the streets, in the prison yard. Belittled by life and choking with rage, he was hungry to be noticed. Paradoxically, he had found his moment in the spotlight, but it was a dim and unflattering light cast before a small and unappreciative audience. "He'd pose for cameras in the chair—for the attention," his counselor had told me earlier in the day. But the truth was that the prisoner wasn't smiling, and there were no cameras.

The prisoner walked quickly and silently toward the chair, an escort of officers in tow. His eyes were turned downward, his expression a bit glazed. Like many before him, the prisoner had threatened to stage a last stand. But that was lifetimes ago, on death row. In the death house, he joined the humble bunch and kept to the executioner's schedule. He appeared to have given up on life before he died in the chair.

En route to the chair, the prisoner stumbled slightly, as if the momentum of the event had overtaken him. Were he not held securely by two officers, one at each elbow, he might have fallen. Were the routine to be broken in this or indeed any other way, the officers believe, the prisoner might faint or panic or become violent, and have to be forcibly placed in the chair. Perhaps as a precaution, when the prisoner reached the chair he did not turn on his own but rather was turned, firmly but without malice, by the officers in his escort. These included the two men at his elbows, and four others who followed behind him. Once the prisoner was seated, again with help, the officers strapped him into the chair.

The execution team worked with machine precision. Like a disciplined swarm, they enveloped him. Arms, legs, stomach, chest, and head were secured in a matter of seconds. Electrodes were attached to the cap holding his head and to the strap holding his exposed right leg. A leather mask was placed over his face. The last officer mopped the prisoner's brow, then touched his hand in a gesture of farewell.

During the brief procession to the electric chair, the prisoner was attended by a chaplain. As the execution team worked feverishly to secure the condemned man's body, the chaplain, who appeared to be upset, leaned over him and placed his forehead in contact with the prisoner's, whispering urgently. The priest might have been praying, but I had the impression he was consoling the man, perhaps assuring him that a forgiving God awaited him in the next life. If he heard the chaplain, I doubt the man comprehended his message. He didn't seem comforted. Rather, he looked stricken and appeared to be in shock. Perhaps the priest's urgent ministrations betrayed his doubts that the prisoner could hold himself together. The chaplain then withdrew at the warden's request, allowing the officers to affix the death mask.

The strapped and masked figure sat before us, utterly alone, waiting to be killed. The cap and mask dominated his face. The cap was nothing more than a sponge encased in a leather shell with a metal piece at the top to accept an electrode. It looked decrepit and resembled a cheap, ill-fitting toupee. The mask, made entirely of leather, appeared soiled and worn. It had two parts, the bottom part covered the chin and mouth, the top the eyes and lower forehead. Only the nose was exposed. The effect of a rigidly restrained body, together with the bizarre cap and the protruding nose, was nothing short of grotesque. A faceless man breathed before us in a tragicomic trance, waiting for a blast of electricity that would extinguish his life. Endless seconds passed. His last act was to swallow, nervously, pathetically, with his Adam's apple bobbing. I was struck by that simple movement then, and can't forget it even now. It told me, as nothing else did, that in the prisoner's restrained body, behind that mask, lurked a fellow human being who, at some level, however primitive, knew or sensed himself to be moments from death.

The condemned man sat perfectly still for what seemed an eternity but was in fact no more than thirty seconds. Finally the electricity hit him. His body stiffened spasmodically, though only briefly. A thin swirl of smoke trailed away from his head and then dissipated quickly. The body remained taut, with the right foot raised slightly at the heel, seemingly frozen there. A brief pause, then another minute of shock. When it was over, the body was flaccid and inert.

Three minutes passed while the officials let the body cool. (Immediately after the execution, I'm told, the body would be too hot to touch and would blister anyone who did.) All eyes were riveted to the chair; I felt trapped in my witness seat, at once transfixed and yet eager for release. I can't recall any clear thoughts from that moment. One of the death watch officers later volunteered that he shared this experience of staring blankly at the execution scene. Had the prisoner's mind been mercifully blank before the end? I hoped so.

An officer walked up to the body, opened the shirt at chest level, then continued on to get the physician from an adjoining room. The physician listened for a heartbeat. Hearing none, he turned to the warden and said, "This man has expired." The warden, speaking to the director, solemnly intoned: "Mr. Director, the court order has been fulfilled." The curtain was then drawn and the witnesses filed out.

THE MORNING AFTER

As the team prepared the body for the morgue, the witnesses were led to the front door of the prison. On the way, we passed a number of cell blocks. We could hear the normal sounds of prison life, including the occasional catcall and lewd comment hurled at uninvited guests like ourselves. But no trouble came in the wake of the execution. Small protests were going on outside the walls, we were told, but we could not hear them. Soon the media would be gone; the protestors would disperse and head for their homes. The prisoners, already home, had been indifferent to the proceedings, as they always are unless the condemned prisoner had been a figure of some consequence in the convict community. Then there might be tension and maybe even a modest disturbance on a prison tier or two. But few convict luminaries are executed, and the dead man had not been one of them. Our escort officer offered a sad tribute to the prisoner: "The inmates, they didn't care about this guy."

I couldn't help but think they weren't alone in this. The executioners went home and set about their lives. Having taken life, they would savor a bit of life themselves. They showered, ate, made love, slept, then took a day or two off. For some, the prisoner's image would linger for that night. The men who strapped him in remembered what it was like to touch him; they showered as soon as they got home to wash off the feel and smell of death. One official sat up picturing how the prisoner looked at the end. (I had a few drinks myself that night with that same image for company.) There was some talk about delayed reactions to the stress of carrying out executions. Though such concerns seemed remote that evening, I learned later that problems would surface for some of the officers. But no one on the team, then or later, was haunted by the executed man's memory, nor would anyone grieve for him. "When I go home after one of these things," said one man, "I sleep like a rock." His may or may not be the sleep of the just, but one can marvel at such a thing, and perhaps envy such a man.

Chapter 36

Maxxing Out

Imprisonment in an Era of Crime Control

by Melissa E. Fenwick
University of South Florida

A prison confines, punishes, and hopefully deters. It is neither designed nor inclines to foster, cure or rehabilitate. (Hassine, 1999: 40)

INTRODUCTION

According to a recent report by the Bureau of Justice Statistics (2000), at yearend 1999 there were 6.3 million people under some form of correctional supervision including probation, in jail or prison, or on parole. Slightly over three percent of all U.S. adult residents were under some form of correctional control. Approximately ten percent of the U.S. prison population, both state and federal inmates, are confined in some form of isolation such as a super-maximum security prison or a control unit within a maximum security prison (Kerness, 2000).

By the end of 1999 American state and federal authorities had over one million "clients" in their facilities (BJS, 2000). In addition to the number of inmates held in state and federal prisons, local jails had a total of 687,973 persons under their supervision. This number includes both inmates serving sentences and pretrial detainees (BJS, 2000).

Within the past 9 years, from 1990 to 1999, the numbers of inmates in state, federal, and local facilities has grown an average of 5.7% annually (BJS, 2000). While the average population in all correctional facilities grew during this time period, there was a significant increase in the numbers of inmates in federal facilities. "The population in custody of Federal prison authorities rose by 13.4% (up 14,889 prisoners, the largest 12-month gain ever reported)" (BJS, 2000).

Changes in sentencing, such as the introduction of mandatory minimum sentences, three-strikes legislation, and sentencing guidelines, have greatly affected the numbers of inmates in local, state and federal facilities. Along with conservative ideology focusing on harsher sentences, the "war on drugs" has clearly had a tremendous impact on the increases in the correctional population. The media super-construction of the dangerous violent criminal has led citizens to be fearful. It is precisely this fear which has promoted politicians to jump on the "tough on crime," "truth in sentencing" bandwagon. One of the

Fenwick, Melissa E. "Maxxing Out-Imprisonment in an Era of Crime Control". Prepared expressly for this edition. Special thanks to Bonnie Kerness, Associate Director and Coordinator Prison Watch at the American Friends Service Committee, for all of her help and dedication to the elimination of super-max prisons.

best demonstrations of this emerging conservative rhetoric is evidenced in the construction of super maximum-security institutions and control units within maximum-security institutions.

THE HISTORY OF SUPER MAXIMUM-SECURITY FACILITIES AND CONTROL UNITS

In general, super-max prisons and control units are draconian places in which inmates are subject to cruel and degrading conditions. Inmates are subject to forced isolation for twenty-two or twenty-three hours per day. They are often subject to cold temperatures with only a blanket to keep warm. In addition, the light inside the cell shines brightly for sixteen hours a day and then dims for the next eight hours. Inmates claim that this dim light is bright enough to read by and therefore disturbs their sleep pattern (Human Rights Watch, 1999). This in and of itself is known to cause extensive psychological problems due to the interference in the normal sleep cycle (American Friends Service Committee, 1997). Visitation is restricted to two or three hours per month in a non-contact booth where the inmate and his visitors are separated by a Plexiglas window. Limited recreation activities are allowed. When allowed these consist of an hour of exercise, televised religious programming and GED classes which are also televised. Work programs are non-existent. Essentially the only times that inmates will leave their cell is for a visit, a shower, exercise, and a rare trip to the hospital. All other daily activities such as eating and routine medical care are brought to the inmate at his cell. However, although there is a lack of human contact, inmates are under constant surveillance through the use of video cameras and intercom systems. Inmates are not allowed to talk to each other and often can barely see the outside world through a tiny window in their cell. When inmates are moved around the facility they are shackled, handcuffed, and strip-searched before leaving their cell and upon return. A minimum of two correction officers will escort the inmates to their destination within the facility. This limited human contact is justified by prison officials as a security precaution. The deprivation of human contact and stimulation is one of the many reasons why human rights organizations and activist groups have lobbied to shut these facilities down (see American Friends Service Committee, Amnesty International and Human Rights Watch, etc.) The development of the super-max facility has been credited to the first extreme maximum security prison developed to house the hardest criminals in the United States—Alcatraz (NIC, 1999; Human Rights Watch, 1997). From 1934 to 1963, Alcatraz was considered the premiere facility in the United States for dealing with inmates with disciplinary problems. The closing of Alcatraz in 1963 marked a period in correctional ideology known as the rehabilitative period. However, this period was brief and soon gave way to a more conservative ideology known as crime control.

The first control unit came into existence when inmates at the federal prison in Marion, Illinois, killed two officers in 1983. Due to this incident, Marion became the first facility to go on permanent lockdown (NIC, 1999; American Friends Service Committee, 1997). All members of the inmate population were locked in their cell for 23 hours a day. This was the first facility in the United States to extend lockdown as a matter of facility protocol for all inmates. Previous to this incident, prisons used lockdown procedures only for disruptive inmates (known as the "hole") and for inmates who needed protective custody.

Since 1983 we have increased the number of facilities that have gone on permanent lockdown, also known as super maximum-security prisons. Today we have super-max institutions in at least forty states and the number is on the rise (American Friends Service Committee, 1997). The most widely known of these facilities is California's Pelican Bay facility and the super-max in Florence, Colorado.

What first started as an experiment by utilizing control units within maximum-security facilities has moved to whole penitentiaries built on the solitary ideal. This is a throwback to the solitary idea of Eastern State, which was one of the first penitentiaries in America built in 1826. Incidentally, the solitary system in Pennsylvania eventually was replaced by New York's congregate system, wherein inmates worked together during the day but were isolated at night. Researchers had found that inmates who remained in solitary confinement for their whole sentence became psychologically unstable. In this natural experiment prison officials saw the need for inmates to have human contact. Why are prison administrators blind to the detrimental effects of extended solitary confinement that is evidenced in our nation's penal history? The answer is simple— economics.

PRESENT USE OF CONTROL UNITS AND THE PRISON INDUSTRIAL COMPLEX

Today's prison boom is vested in the larger socio-political economy of America. The building of prisons has become big business, and with money to be gained in tax revenue and jobs by the proliferation of prisons, the expansion will continue. Intertwined with the corporatization of America, the very least of which is the corporatization of the American correctional system, is today's political climate, which epitomizes citizens' conservatism. In general, with the movement toward crime control ideology the super maximum-security prison is the natural progression and perhaps the end of the continuum. ". . .super-max prisons also play a symbolic role. Their highly restrictive nature is appealing in a conservative climate in which retribution is the principal response to crime" (Human Rights Watch, 1999: 7).

Super-max institutions violate the human rights of inmates to be free from torturous conditions and their constitutional right to due process. Inmates, once in the custody of the Department of Corrections, can be moved to a super-max facility as is deemed necessary by prison officials (Human Rights Watch, 1999). In addition, inmates can be kept in these facilities and control units for an indefinite period of time. Inmates often do not know what specific behaviors are necessary for them to be transferred to another less secure institution. Inmates have expressed concern that they have been moved to super-max units without a hearing, a violation of due process rights, to be held there indefinitely with no recourse (Sherman, Magnani & Kerness, 1999).

Not only do super-max prisons violate individual inmate rights but also the use of these institutions in the United States is in direct violation of international human rights documents that the United States has ratified. According to Human Rights Watch (1997), super-max prisons and the human rights violations that occur there are violations of the International Covenant on Civil and Political Rights (ICCPR). In addition, the United States is violating the international standards set in the United Nations Standard Minimum Rules for the Treatment of Prisoners (Standard Minimum Rules) adopted in 1957. The Standard Minimum Rules have been used in cases to establish "contemporary standards of decency" where an inmate's right to be free from cruel and unusual punishment as well as due process rights have been argued in a court of law (Human Rights Watch,

1997). Inmates have a right to be free from torture and cruelty as outlined by these documents as well as the Convention Against Torture and Other Cruel, Inhumane or Degrading Treatment or Punishment (CAT) which the United States has also ratified (Human Rights Watch, 1997; Sherman, Magnani & Kerness, 1999). The type of treatment and conditions found at super-max facilities is in direct violation of CAT and involves the use of abuse and torture (Sherman, Magnani & Kerness, 1999).

Madrid v. Gomez, a federal court case in 1995, serves as an excellent example of a super-max facility which had violated inmate constitutional rights. Inmates being held in the Security Housing Unit at Pelican Bay State Prison in California had been subject to numerous human rights violations, such as physical abuse of inmates by guards during cell extractions, and for punitive purposes which consisted of shackling inmates to toilets. In addition, violations of adequate medical and mental health care were cited and the use of physical torture was also found. In one case, Vaughn Dortch, a mentally ill inmate who had bitten an officer and wallowed in his own feces, was immersed in a bath of scalding water while his hands were handcuffed behind his back (Sherman, Magnani & Kerness, 1999; Welch, 1999). Mr. Dortch experienced third degree burns over a third of his body due to this incident. In addition, another inmate was shot at with a gas gun, beaten, and knocked unconscious because he refused to hand back his food tray (Sherman, Magnani & Kerness, 1999). Similar cases have been raised as to the conditions of confinement in which inmates are housed. Small windowless cells, deprivation of meaningful activities, deprivation of human contact, exposure to endless hours of light, and lack of adequate medical and mental health care have all been cited as violations of human rights.

OFFICIAL RHETORIC

The official premise behind the establishment of control units and super-maximum security facilities is custody. According to the National Institute of Corrections (1999),

> it appears that the purest intent of supermaxes around the country is to isolate inmates who through behavior—or threat of such behavior—are dangerous or chronically violent, have escaped or attempted escape form a high-security correctional facility, or have incited or attempted to incite disruption in a correctional facility.
>
> However, although the intention of such facilities was the housing of the chronically violent and disruptive, there is evidence that there are other populations being housed in these facilities that do not fit this description (Human Rights Watch, 1999). Super-max institutions hold mentally ill inmates, inmates in need of protective custody, bothersome inmates, and often political prisoners. Political prisoners have been held for indefinite periods of time based upon their political ideals and not for security purposes. According to Sondai Kamdibe, an inmate in California:
>
> Control units exist with their sole purpose being to crush the revolutionary spirit embodied within certain prisoners of consciousness aimed at crushing their resistance to fascist control and inevitably making them a tool of reaction for the state. The ideas of the state are embodied within the functions of the prison regime. (American Friends Service Committee, 1997: 27)

The question of whether these inmates are being appropriately held is one that scholars and prison administrators have recently begun to debate. One of the most controversial of these populations are mentally ill inmates.

MENTALLY ILL INMATES

According to Dr. Stuart Grassin:

> There is a notion in the popular mind that people who end up in solitary confinement are the most ruthless, kind of James Cagneys of the prisons system. In fact, what you often see there is the antithesis: they are very often the wretched of the earth, people who are mentally ill, illiterate, and cognitively impaired, people with neurological difficulties, people who really just can't manage their behavior at times. The prison system tends to respond to this by punishment. (American Friends Service Committee, 1997: 61–62)

Due to its recent development, the impact of super-max facilities and control units on mentally ill inmates has not been researched extensively (NIC, 1999). However, according to a recent report by Human Rights Watch (1999), at Red Onion State Prison, a super-max facility in Virginia, treatment for mentally ill inmates consists mostly of the distribution of psychotropic drugs. In this facility, psychological counseling for inmates consists of a visit once a week to the inmate wherein the mental health professional questions the inmate while standing outside his cell. Human Rights Watch concludes that the conditions present in control unit facilities will serve to exacerbate pre-existing mental conditions. It is still unclear what impact isolation, boredom, and constant surveillance have on the healthy inmate; however, researchers contend that the effect is detrimental to the inmate. Many inmates have reported adverse psychological symptoms as a result of confinement in isolation. Ronald Epps, an inmate in a super-max in Maryland writes:

> Steel and stone torture chambers where, absent various forms of social stimuli, the human mind can become so debased, so de-humanized, and sink so low that if one isn't careful, there is a tendency to adjust, conform, and accustom oneself to a standard of living that is lower than that which exists within the animal kingdom. This is the adverse effect of long-term Sensory Deprivation. It is a form of physical, social, and psychological torture, and it pushes many self-respecting, rational thinking, decent-minded men and women to a quest for excitement, acts of desperation, and to the most extreme points of paranoia. (American Friends Service Committee, 1997: 10)

LuQman Abdullah Hayes, an inmate in Pennsylvania reports, "sometimes this stress (of living in a control unit) leads to suicide drug addiction, and actively fights against discipline" (American Friends Service Committee, 1997: 29). Likewise, it is projected that these conditions would have even more devastating effects on the mentally ill inmate.

THE PRISON INDUSTRIAL COMPLEX

Although the official premise behind the emergence of the super-max institution is custody and security, criminologists are beginning to recognize the emerging connection between politics, economics, and the demonization of the criminal. All of these factors allow for the proliferation of super-max facilities.

The rise of the prison industry as an economic enhancement has become known as the prison industrial complex (Davis, 1997). Expenditure on prison construction and operation costs has reached an all time high. Clearly stated, the building of prisons bring with them jobs for local townspeople such as correctional officers, clerks in restaurants, hotels, and retail establishments needed to support incoming visitors; construction companies and contractors such as telephone companies; and food service industry employees that fight for contracts with the new facility. It is exactly this economic fervor that reproduces the cycle of building that is evidenced by today's growing expansion of the prison system. Succinctly stated, the corporatization of the prison system has perpetuated the building of more prisons and especially control units and super-max facilities, because these institutions are consistent with conservative ideals, fostered by the media, of both politicians and citizens.

FUTURE OF IMPRISONMENT IN THE UNITED STATES

Clearly the use of super-max facilities will continue to grow in the country as long as politicians and the media emphasize the need for such institutions. One must question the need for such facilities and whether the human rights violations that inmates are subjected to outweigh the necessity of these institutions. Understanding that the crime control ideology in America shows no evidence of waning, one must consider at the very least the modification of current super-max facilities to lessen the harm caused to inmates.

The National Institute of Corrections (1999: 22) raises the following questions for prison administrators interested in planning and building a super-max facility:

1. Do we want to risk the possible legal challenges that may accompany the expansion of placement criteria beyond what is absolutely necessary?
2. Do we want to incur the significant expense of placing inmates in extended control who do not actually require that level of control?
3. Do we want to subject inmates to the severe and rigid conditions of extended control if they do not clearly meet the narrow criteria for placement there?
4. Is a policy of "concentration" rather than "dispersal" in the best interest of our agency?

While all of these questions pose legitimate issues for the prison administrator, however, the first question concerning super-max prisons should address the need for such institutions. If we conclude that such institutions are necessary, then the next logical issue should be whether or not the current system subjects inmates to undue physical and psychological torture that is not necessary to maintain control. Currently, the super-max facility embraces the ideals of vengeance and torture, which most corrections experts would agree are not appropriate goals of the prison system.

The Human Rights Watch (1999) highlights several issues that need to be addressed in super-max facilities. Although specifically outlined in their report on Red Onion State Prison in Virginia, these recommendations can and should apply universally to all super-max prisons across the country (Human Rights Watch, 1999).

1. An independent agency of experts within the state should be assigned to evaluate the use of force within these institutions.
2. Strict guidelines need to be established as to who qualifies for a Level 6 super-max facility, not solely based on sentence length. Inmates who do not demonstrate these criteria need to be placed in institutions of lower security levels. In addition, inmates should be aware of the procedures that would allow them to be transferred to a less secure facility after a period of good conduct for one year.
3. The Department of Corrections should make available to the public statistical information about the inmates in their super-max facility.

4. Central administration should review the rationale for placing an inmate in a segregation facility. Central administrators, to reduce biases in the decision-making process, should also review decisions regarding release.

5. Educational, vocational, behavioral, substance abuse, and religious programming should be made available to inmates held within a super-max facility to eliminate boredom and allow for the demonstration of good behavior.

6. Inmates who suffer from mental illnesses should not be confined in super-max facilities. In addition, all inmates should receive proper mental health care while held at this facility.

7. Correctional officers should be trained in the proper handling of inmates with respect to verbal, physical, and mental abuse.

8. Public access through the media, citizens groups, and other members of the public should have access to the institution as long as the security of both the inmates and the guards are not violated.

What does the future hold for imprisonment in the United States? In order to answer this question, one must ask other broad-reaching, theoretical questions concerning the very nature of punishment and the usefulness or purpose of imprisonment itself. What purpose does punishment serve in today's society? The example of super-max facilities leads us to the conclusion that prisons serve as retribution. Clearly these facilities do not serve to rehabilitate or deter anyone. The research on deterrence based on punitive devices clearly shows that punishment does not deter [violence] and may in fact make inmates more violent. What, then, could we possibly be achieving by advocating control units that use sensory deprivation? Are we so concerned that these "worst of the worst," "hardest of the hard" will victimize our society or are we more concerned with separation of these people from society? Contrary to popular belief, the vast majority of the inmates that are being held in super maximum-security facilities will be released back into society. What purpose, other than vengeance, does it serve to keep inmates in such cruel and unusual circumstances that, once released back into society, these inmates have become so hardened and psychologically unstable? Who will deal with them then?

Do we not gain a sense of morality and elevate our social status by labeling individuals as deviant, criminal and, especially, forgotten by society? Super-max facilities are torturous, barbarous and cruel and unusual punishment.

Unfortunately, without human rights activists to stop the perpetual influx of inmates into the system, these prisons are going to proliferate. The tide of conservatism that has engulfed our country, limiting one's civil rights, will not sway any time soon. Activists who choose to give a voice to the invisible sectors of our society, such as the super-max confined inmates, serve as their only hope for the future. Until the elimination of these facilities, one can only help inmates learn to cope with the harsh realities of forced social isolation.

Perhaps Paul Redd, an inmate held in a super-max in California, said it best, ". . .your ability to know who you are as a people and your ability in thinking outside the walls take away these barbarians' control over your existence and your mind" (American Friends Service Committee, 1997: 22).

REFERENCES

American Friends Service Committee. 1997. *Survivors Manual*. Newark, NJ: American Friends Service Committee and The Human Rights Committee California Prison Focus.

Davis, Angela. 1997. *The Prison Industrial Complex*. (Recorded by AK Press) [CD]. Colorado College, Colorado Springs, CO: Alternative Tentacles Records.

Del Carmen, Alejandro. 2000. *Corrections*. Boulder, CO: Coursewise Publishing Co.

Kerness, Bonnie. 2000. *Torture in America: Abuse of Human Rights in the United States*. [Lecture] Simmons College, Boston, MA: American Friends Service Committee.

Hassine, Victor. 1999. *Life Without Parole: Living in Prison Today*. 2nd ed. Los Angeles, CA: Roxbury Publishing.

Human Rights Watch (HRW). 1999. *Red Onion State Prison: Super-Maximum Security Confinement in Virginia*. Available online at: http://www.hrw.org/reports/1999/redonion/index2.htm

Human Rights Watch (HRW). 1999. *Cold Storage: Super-Maximum Security Confinement in Indiana*. Human Rights Watch.

National Institute of Corrections (NIC). 1999. *Supermax Prisons: Overview and General Considerations*. Washington, DC: US Department of Justice.

Sherman, Mark, Magnani, Laura, and Bonnie Kerness. 1999. *Prison Conditions and the Treatment of Prisoners*. Available online at: http://www.omct.org/woatusa/projects/CATreport/prisons.htm

Welch, Michael. 1999. *Punishment in America: Social Control and the Ironies of Imprisonment*. Thousand Oaks, CA: Sage Publications.

Chapter 37

Ophelia the CCW

May 11, 2010

by Todd R. Clear

Ophelia Edison awakened gently, brought slowly to awareness by the vibrations of her massage bed. She opened her eyes to look at the ceiling of her bedroom, where the tele-inform displayed the time: 5:45 A.M. As she got up from her bed, the vibrations abruptly ceased, turned off by the body sensor, which felt her weight leave the bed's surface.

Walking to the lavatory center adjacent to the bedroom, she said in a firm tone, "Shower." Automatically, at the sound of her voice, the shower came on and the cascading water began to heat to a predetermined temperature. Because she wore no clothing to bed, she could walk right into the washing compartment of the lavatory, and she installed the VOICE-START system as a convenience. She loved their advert slogan: "A minute saved is a dollar earned."

Glancing back at the massage bed, she smiled slightly to herself, thinking it was one of her favorite indulgences. Actually, though, it was not an indulgence at all. Her union, the Middlesex Association of Community Control Workers, had negotiated them as part of last year's contract with COMCON, the firm that has the probation contract in her country. The COMCON contract specified merit bonuses for all employees whose performance scores were above the office average. Ophelia, who qualified easily, chose the massage bed instead of cash—inflation being what it was, it seemed a better investment.

Ophelia was a Community Control Specialist II, what used to be called a "probation officer" in the old days. She earned the "specialist" grade because she worked only with child sex offenders—it was her area of expertise. She was designated as "II" because she had been doing the work for five years, and every year her work performance scored out as "satisfactory"—within two standard deviations of the mean for the office.

She might not have said it publicly, but she was really glad she joined the union back when it first started up. Ever since COMCON got the contract for probation supervision services, there had been tension between the workers and the firm. COMCON was a wholly owned subsidiary of IBM, and it was in the money-making business. One way to make money, of course, was to keep salaries and wages down. In fact, the financial pressure to find ways to cut costs was worse now than in the old days, when government managed probation.

So no one could blame the CCWs (Community Control Workers) when they formed a union to protect their interests. After all, their work was difficult and dangerous, and they deserved to be well paid. Too bad the relations between the union and COMCON

From "Ophelia the C.C.W.: May 10, 2010," Todd R. Clear in J. Klofas and Stan Stojkovic, eds., *Crime and Justice in the Year 2010*, 1994, pp. 205–221. Belmont, CA: Wadsworth Publishing Company. Reprinted by permission of the publisher.

had been so vitriolic—there had been two strikes and a work slowdown in the first six months of the union. If the government hadn't stepped in and forced a settlement (by threatening to cancel the COMCON contract), things never would have calmed down.

She understood COMCON's problem very well, of course. With liability costs soaring (fighting civil suits and paying damage for lost suits had been more than 20 percent of last year's COMCON budget), the firm was even more pressed than ever. But the CCWs had the bosses between a rock and a hard place on this one: Suits were caused by failures to follow legally approved procedures and policy, and the slow-downs and strikes guaranteed more such failures.

"Let the management and union go after each other tooth and nail," she thought. "It doesn't bother me."

These were the sorts of things Ophelia pondered as she first showered, then dressed for work. She liked her job overall, and in the mornings it was good to reflect on that. The thoughts sort of warmed her up for the day ahead of her.

While drying her hair and dressing for the day, she turned on the audio news. "Good Morning America" was on, that old-time standard. The big news was the progress on talks of Ukraine and Mexico joining the United States, following Puerto Rico's lead. But this story interested her very little. She was waiting to hear about road conditions along the Eastern Seaboard, because today was a field day.

She chose her green flak-blouse for the day. It was hard to believe this stylishly cut material, which weighed only 2 pounds, could stop a bullet fired at point-blank range. All CCWs were required to wear flak-tops, ever since the massacre three years ago during a routine arrest and she certainly felt safer with one on. Typically, COMCON had resisted the policy, citing "absurd costs" of providing flak-clothes for everyone. In the end, the union won out by threatening to stop all arrests.

Strapped inside her field boots were a stun gun and an electric revolver. She checked to see that each was working. After finishing dressing, she pulled a breakfast tube from her pantry and microtoasted it. With coffee and orange juice it was a perfect 320 calories, just right to start the day but not too much for her exercise-health program guidelines.

When she walked out the door, the tele-inform said 6:05.

Ophelia needed to start early on field days. Policy standards required home contacts at certain intervals for offenders whose profiles fit the complicated criteria. It was good to start out early so she could catch as many as possible before they reported to work (or to their "service post" if they didn't have a job). On the normal working day—there were only five randomly scheduled field days a months—she would awaken at 8:30 A.M. and be at the office by 9:30. But the days when she was to be "in the field" were determined by the office computer in a random basis. Randomness prevented the offenders from being able to pick up a "routine" field time and arrange to be "out" when she came by. It also kept the bosses in charge of things, at least so she thought.

The way everything worked now, her entire daily schedule was handled by computer. This was a good thing, she felt, since she couldn't make heads or tails out of the supervision policies.

The whole thing ran on "profiles." Profiles were really a complicated, interlocking pattern of criteria that were applied to offenders to determine how they should be supervised. Some offenders were seen as often as daily in the field; these cases were handled by Community Control Specialist IIIs, who carried only the "intensive" cases. Since Ophelia's cases were sex offenders, she averaged seeing them fairly frequently, sometimes even twice weekly, depending on their profile.

According to what she had been told in her orientation training, the profiles were all determined by scientific research approaches called "actuarial tables" that predicted how offenders having certain backgrounds would behave and specified the best way to deal with them in order to prevent problems. She found the whole thing a bit confusing and a bit far-fetched, but the computer system made it all easy anyway, so she didn't mind. And they said it was based on literally thousands of case histories.

Stepping out into the sidewalk in front of her apartment building, Ophelia took a deep breath and looked around for the car she would be using. It was a company car and was in use nearly twenty-four hours a day. The carpool service would have delivered it to her street sometime in the night, after a night shift of CCWs had finished with it. It was never hard to find, since it was easily identifiable: military green, nondescript, and one of the few American-made cars on her street. She just looked around for a car nobody wanted to own. There it was, right across the street.

Getting into the car, she did a voice-start, saying simply, "Start." The engine softly hummed on, and the computer sitting under the dashboard engaged.

"Good morning," said the gender-neutral voice inside the machine. "Please identify yourself."

"Kiss my butt," said Ophelia with a sneer, as she punched in her ID. She knew this machine was deaf, and it amused her to be insolent to it.

"Good morning, Ophelia," the machine voice said. Ophelia winced and hit the function key that turned off the sound. The computer voice really annoyed her, and she preferred to read the instructions on the monitor rather than hear them.

On the monitor, the message appeared:

FIRST STOP: WALTER WILSON, 2721 LAKELAND BLVD., APT. 10G.

Ophelia remembered Wilson very well: He was on probation after being convicted of child sex abuse—fondling a neighbor's son. It was his first offense, but the profile indicated a "likelihood" of prior, unreported offenses. After meeting him, she thought the profile was dead-on.

These days he lived in an "iffy" neighborhood, and it made her uncomfortable to visit him there. He was a co-share case, and so she had only been out to see him a half-dozen times or so in the two years he had been on probation. A co-share case was one seen by more than a single CCW. Apparently, research had demonstrated that with certain cases, a joint-supervision approach was more effective, because one CCW might pick up on cues that another missed. She co-shared with Andy Rajandra, and about once a month or so the computer would set up a co-share conference between them to discuss this and other jointly supervised cases.

Ophelia liked sharing cases and she had a lot of respect for Andy's expertise. In the old days, a person had a caseload and was pretty much completely in charge of it. But this meant that offenders could learn officers' weaknesses and figure out ways to manipulate them—often with tragic consequences. Under joint supervision, she was paired with the other CCWs who specialized in sex offenders, and they reinforced each other's strengths while canceling out the weaknesses. She had grown so used to co-sharing her work that she didn't even think of herself as having a "caseload" anymore. She just had work assignments.

Today she was lucky. The first visit scheduled by the accountability system was along an "electric commuter" path from her apartment. She could let the transportation macrosystem drive the car for most of the way, and that would give her time to read the paper while in transit.

She used the computer to contact Transit and punched in her location and destination. Transit "accepted" her request (it almost always did, since government workers on duty had priority) and eased her into the morning traffic. She reached into the glovebox and pulled out the newspaper that was automatically printed there every morning. The front-page story made her chuckle: Congress had started the investigation of the report that thirty years ago three actors had impersonated Ronald Reagan during his presidency, because he had actually been secreted away in a coma off in some CIA basement room.

Twenty minutes later, she was across town and within a few blocks of Wilson's apartment. She reached down to the computer and hit the function key for "instructions." The monitor printed back:

WALTER WILSON, AGE: 53, ETHNICITY: WHITE.
PROFILE: SEX OFFENDER, TAPE A-2
DURING MOST RECENT CONTACT BY CCW
    RAJANDRA (MAY 3) SUSPICION OF ALCOHOL USE, BUT SKIN SCRATCH WAS
    NEGATIVE. PLEASE OBSERVE THE FOLLOWING PROTOCOL:

1. Take skin scratch.
2. Discuss job situation—supervision relations.
3. Check angela (daughter, age 9) for marks.
4. Talk to Myra (co-inhabitant, age 47).

CCW VIOLENCE RISK PROFILE, NEAR ZERO.

Ophelia made a mental note of the instructions, then took manual control of the car to drive up to Wilson's apartment. Moments later, she was facing him in his doorway.

"Good morning, Mr. Wilson," she began, "I hope I didn't awaken you."

"That's all right," he responded groggily. "Come on in."

Inside, they sat across from each other in the living room. Ophelia glanced about her, quickly taking in her whole surroundings. This was her habit, to see if anything struck her as amiss. It was a sixth sense she had developed about things and honed over her years on the job. This time her invisible antenna picked up nothing out of the ordinary.

Looking back at Wilson, she began. "I'd like to start with a skin scratch."

It was an abrupt way to start, she knew, and it made them both momentarily uncomfortable. But the computer system had been plain that this was the thing she would have to do, and if she deviated from specific instructions she would have to have a good reason, one her supervisor would accept. Her own preference would be to chat awhile before doing the test, but experience had taught her that a mere personal "preference" would not be enough to override "instructions," and then she would be liable for whatever happened.

And liability was a very big deal at COMCON. Workers who deviated from "instructions" too often or who did so without good, tangible reasons did not last long.

Wilson rolled up his sleeve. "Sure thing," he said. She pulled a styletometer from her bag and took a scratch. Three seconds later, the light on the styletometer showed green. A red or yellow reading would have required Wilson to give a full urine sample—a part of the job Ophelia disliked—and if that was positive, he would be arrested on the spot, since his violence profile was so low. The green reading meant he was clear.

"Good," said Ophelia, replacing the styletometer. "Let's talk about how you are doing."

They spent about 15 minutes talking about his comings and goings. Her aim was to help him relax and to gain a little rapport before getting on with the "instructions." This was one of Ophelia's skills—getting clients to relax in her presence—and she enjoyed being in control of her interaction style. All the while, she was watching him, looking for any cues that something might be wrong, that he might be trying to hide something.

Then she asked about his job, testing out how well he was doing with his supervisor. His answer was hesitant, and she realized this was an area to probe further.

With a bit of relief, he told her that his boss at the supermarket where he worked was giving him a hard time about his conviction. He wanted to quit. They talked about it for awhile, and she convinced him to stick it out for awhile longer. Mentally, she made a note to report the problem, knowing that a community relations specialist would follow up with the supervisor to try to head off any trouble. Wilson's job was a good one, and if he quit he would have trouble finding something in its place. Better to get the supervisor to stop the harassment.

After they had talked about the job for awhile, and Wilson seemed a bit more settled about it, Ophelia changed the subject.

"How's Angela? Could I talk to her?"

Wilson said he would have to wake her up, and when Ophelia said "Thanks," he realized that she intended to talk to his daughter anyway. So he went to get her.

A few minutes later, Angela walked out yawning and wearing her nightgown. She was a cutie—a redhead with big freckles.

Ophelia broke into a big smile and reached out, taking Angela's little hands into her own.

"Angela, how are you?" she asked sweetly. She and Angela had talked several times before, and she sensed that Angela liked her. By holding her hand, Ophelia would be able to talk to Angela for awhile and, without being obvious, check her arms for marks.

They talked about Angela's schoolwork and the play she was going to be in this term. Satisfied that there was no evidence of physical abuse, Ophelia gave Angela a hug and sent her back to bed.

It was routine to check for any evidence of violence for all child sex offenders who lived with children. Ophelia was very good at it—children seldom realized what she was doing. This was just another of the many ways that Ophelia had talents that justified being a specialist.

Being a specialist was very important, of course. Regular CCWs had a hard job. They got routine cases with mediocre profiles of risk and problems—and they got lots of them. It was not unusual for them to have as many as 300 cases to keep track of, and the compuwork, videophoning, and coordinations were a huge headache. And all they ever seemed to do was monitor payments of fines and performance of community service. No wonder turnover was so high for these jobs.

The specialists got better pay and better benefits and had much more interesting work organized into more reasonable workloads. There were three child-sex offender specialists in Middlesex County, and they co-shared a total of about seventy cases. Ophelia loved her work—and she was known to be good at it.

After Angela left the room, Ophelia complimented Wilson on how lovely a child she was. Then she asked to talk with Myra. Alone.

Her conversations with Myra were always a little strained, for Myra had never gotten over her partner's arrest and conviction. But her willingness to stand behind him— that and the lack of evidence that sexual misconduct had occurred with Angela —persuaded the judge to put Wilson on Special Probation rather than sentence him to three years in prison. He would be on probation for a full decade, according to his profile. Myra would have plenty of time to get used to supervision, which would grow gradually less frequent as Wilson continued to show no new misconduct and continued to respond well to therapy.

The most discomfort between Ophelia and Myra came when she asked about Wilson's sexuality with her. Even though Ophelia was very good at handling this sensitive area, Myra was embarrassed to discuss it. But according to his profile, his heterosexual adjustment was a key indicator of his overall adjustment.

An hour after arriving, Ophelia left Wilson's apartment. She was satisfied that all was well there, and she felt good about it. Wilson, she thought, had a great chance to make it.

Back in the company car, she entered the data about her visit. It took just a minute or two because the accountability system was designed to record what were called "key indicators" very efficiently. While Ophelia was free to add anything she wished, her experience was that the system usually asked everything that was important. Profiles again!

Once done with the Wilson report, she again asked for "instructions." The computer routed her to her next case, one Florence Trueblood.

But halfway to the Trueblood house, the computer voice abruptly chimes out the words, "Override. Override. Override." Ophelia took manual control of the car and pulled over. The computer screen gave her information that one of her cases—a Vernon Granger—was being questioned by police about his daughter's accusation that he had beaten her up. The instruction was to go immediately to Granger's house to investigate and—according to office policies—consider making an arrest. She put on her siren and sped away to Granger's.

The override was itself office policy. Specialists took pride in making their own arrests: the saying was, "The specialists clean up after themselves." By making their own arrests, specialists reinforced the importance of their work and kept their credibility high with courts and the police. It was a matter of pride.

When Ophelia arrived at Granger's, the police were about to handcuff him. She recognized one of the officers and went to him to learn what had happened. She learned that the daughter had been reported missing by Mrs. Granger, and that an hour or so ago the girl had been found hiding in some bushes near the edge of the city's main park. She told the police she had run away because she was afraid of her dad. There were ugly bruises on her head and arms. Granger denied everything, but they decided to make an arrest anyway.

Ophelia asked permission to take over on the arrest, and the police agreed to let her. They had learned that the specialists handled these situations very well, and they could save a lot of police time by letting CCWs do the dirty work. She went over to Granger, read him his rights, handcuffed him, and put him in the back of her car.

The whole arrest process—taking him to the precinct, booking him, and filing the appropriate information with headquarters—took nearly two hours. By the time she was done, she was tired, hungry—and a bit angry. After talking to Granger's daughter, Ophelia had decided to ask for a semen exam. The results weren't in, but she was pretty sure they would be positive. If so, Granger was looking at a long sentence: He was already on parole for assaulting a daughter from a prior marriage. The shame of it was that the whole family—Granger, his wife, and the three daughters—had been watched closely and in continual therapy ever since the wedding—as a condition of parole. How did people get themselves into these problems?

Back in her car, she asked again for "instructions." The computer said mutely, "Well done, Ms. Edison." Ophelia answered back absently. "Kiss my butt" and requested her lunch break. It was approved.

Lunch improved her mood a little, and the next three hours went fairly smoothly. She made four routine home visits—unusually, all without a hitch. By 3 P.M., it was time for "group."

One of the job satisfactions for specialists was participation in treatment. It was an area where she was able to use her skills and knowledge regarding sex offenders to best effect. It was also one of the few areas left where the accountability system allowed her free rein. By office policy, she was left completely on her own during the hour and a half of group. She wasn't even interrupted for an arrest.

Her co-therapist was Dana Richardson, a clinical social worker who was experienced with sex offenders. They conducted a weekly group therapy program for eight probationers or parolees convicted of child sex offenses. During group, they discussed a wide range of feelings and reactions the offenders had, and they confronted the offenders about the rationalization they used to excuse their behavior.

The groups were one of the main reasons Ophelia liked the job. Much of her work involved monitoring offenders, and sometimes this work could get oppressive and heavy-handed. The group was a way to humanize her work, dealing with the lives of her clients and helping them work through their adjustment problems. It was also a great way for her to grow professionally. In addition to her contact with Dana, a man with whom she shared mutual respect, she had monthly meetings with a psychologist who consulted with Dana and her about the group's progress.

Today's particular group session was exhilarating. One of the members had made a new friendship with a divorcee who had a young son. The group spent a lot of time focusing on the issues surrounding disclosure of his past to the woman. By the time group was over at 4:30, Ophelia had overcome her anger about the Granger episode and accepted it as a part of the job.

Learning to live with failure—not internalizing it when it happened—was probably the most difficult aspect of the job for Ophelia. When her sex offenders failed, it was almost always a tragedy that damaged a child's life. That made it hard to get over the feeling that "she could have done something to prevent it," a common feeling among her peers.

That was why she felt compassion without sympathy when she arrested someone for violating the rules. On the regular probation caseloads, people were almost never revoked from probation for mere rules violations. There had to be a new arrest to force the system to take action. But for the specialists, the stakes were too high. The first indication that a person was sliding into misconduct was always met with swift and stern action. There could be no other way.

Sometimes, though, after she arrested one of her clients for a new offense, she was tempted to leave the job. After all, there were plenty of correctional businesses out there she could work for: electronic monitoring, drug-control systems, work camps, and so on. In the last twenty years there had been a proliferation of nonprison programs for criminals, and they were all grouped together and called "intermediate sanctions." More than 40 percent of offenders were sent to one or another of these private programs. Only a handful were put on probation or parole and thereby assigned to community control.

By the end of her group session, she was pretty drained, which was typical. She and Dana talked for awhile about the clients in the group, after which she spent twenty minutes recording information about the session into the accountability system. It was important to record everything, because at the end of the year she would be evaluated. Her performance—arrests, groups, client progress, policy adherence, and so forth, all added together in a master formula—would be computed. Based on her score, and based on how the score compared to everyone else, she would receive a raise and a bonus. Ophelia was proud that she scored in the top 20 percent of staff every year on the job.

Her day had lasted nearly twelve hours, and she felt it was high time she left the office. On her way out the door, she inserted her index finger into the bioreader machine that stood at the end of the office hallway. The bioreader was a combined drug-testing device and physical checkup machine. It took her blood pressure, tested for illegal substances, and checked for developing infections. The machine, which helped prevent employee stress and work-related maladies, was another accomplishment of the work of the union.

The light burned green—"no problem"—and she unconsciously nodded a "thanks" to the inert device and headed out the door. Machines seemed to get better treatment than people these days.

She would make a stop at the health club; regular visits there reduced her health insurance costs and resulted in another work bonus. Then she would get a bite to eat on her way home. By now, the office car was in use by another CCW, so she would have to walk home from the health club. It was only a few blocks, and she didn't mind the stroll. The spring air smelled unusually clean, and she felt good about herself. She broke into a whistle.

EXPLANATION

Only people stupid enough to bet on the Baltimore Colts to defeat the New York Jets in the 1968 Super Bowl would try to predict the nature of community corrections in 2010. I did the former, and so I did the latter.

But the reader should be advised that it not only is hazardous to one's intellectual health to believe that one can foresee the future, but also a proven idiocy. In 1967, when the presidential commission ushered in an era called "reintegration," everyone foresaw the coming of a decade of community corrections. The prison was seen as an outdated and proven failure. Treatment methods in the community were seen as the only truly effective methods for dealing with crime as well as the certain wave of the future. Experts geared up for a generation of prison reform and community programming.

What then happened? During the 1970s and 1980s, America's prison population experienced a growth unprecedented in American history. The number of citizens locked up in prisons quadrupled, from fewer than 200,000 in 1967 to more than three-quarters of a million in 1990. The imprisonment rate per 100,000 citizens tripled from 97 in 1967 to 293 in 1990. Every failure should be successful.

The point is that, however confident one might feel that the future is clearly laid out before one's eyes, the future that eventually occurs is bound to disappoint. Bearing this in mind, I offer the above speculative leap to the year 2010. It was based on a few ideas about some things that I think are likely to happen over the next twenty years.

Before getting into the predictions, I need to clarify a couple of terms used throughout. Sometimes, I will use the term *traditional* probation or parole supervision. By this, I mean the regular agencies' practices, which have remained fairly stable over the last century. In the case of probation, this means offenders who are assigned to the oversight of an officer in lieu of a prison sentence. For parole, "traditional" programs are those where an offender is released by a parole board and is placed under the supervision of a parole officer. My use of the term "traditional" means that there are "nontraditional" versions of these programs: Intensive probation, electronically monitored supervision, and special early release programs are illustrations.

This distinction is important because, as my predictions make clear, community supervision is increasingly splitting into two, sometimes quite different versions. The traditional versions remain funded and respected about as much as they always have: not very well. The "new" versions are high-profile, ambitious attempts to be responsive to the main complaints people have lodged about traditional methods.

There is also one dominant force that will shape every aspect of the next two decades in corrections. The capacity of the prison system is finite. The rest of the criminal justice system can produce as many offenders as it can—and the capacity of law enforcement and the courts to produce them has accelerated—but prisons can absorb only so many offenders. The rest have to go to other correctional assignments.

Because of this, there will always be a powerful need for nonprison correctional alternatives. It is not merely a matter of justice—although for many, perhaps most, offenders a prison sentence is not just a punishment—it's a matter of economics.

With these points in mind, let us proceed to the predictions.

TEN PREDICTIONS

1. *Specialized nontraditional supervision services will predominate in field services.* In the 1980s, research and programming have both documented the complexity of criminality, from the general idea of criminal careers to the specific examples of drug-using offenders, sex offenders, and violent criminals. There is no way that a single person, carrying a heterogeneous caseload comprising all types of felons, can be a fully capable "expert" in how to deal with all of them. Specializing caseloads into subgroups of more homogeneous types of problems is an idea that simply makes sense.

2. *Intermediate sanctions options will grow in number and size.* Intermediate sanctions are types of punishment that fall in severity between traditional probation and traditional parole. Since the mid-1980s, there has been a proliferation of correctional programs that are not as lenient as probation but not as severe as prison. Besides being politically popular, these programs are a public-relations godsend to community corrections. They advertise themselves as "tough," they

cost far less than prison, and many have been shown to have very low recidivism. With a good "rep," a real demand, and a history of delivery on its promises, it is hard to see how intermediate sanctions are not the correctional growth industry of the future.

3. *Traditional probation and parole supervision will handle a decreasing share of the offender population.* It follows from the first two predictions that the future of the traditional supervision methods is not a bright one. This does not mean that community-based sanctions will be unimportant by 2010. Frankly, there is no way that corrections can survive without a strong, healthy nonprison component. Yet there is also no way that full funding of nonprison alternatives is feasible.

    The likely scenario is that traditional types of community supervision—which have not enjoyed strong support in criminal justice since the 1960s—will languish. Instead, growing emphasis will be given to correctional approaches that are not as expensive as prison, but which do not align themselves with traditional techniques.

4. *Private-sector involvement in community corrections will have grown to become a powerful factor in policy and program development.* We already have seen a growth of privatization in community corrections. The profits have apparently been enough that new businesses are starting in many areas of the country. The conditions for new businesses are ideal. Correctional crowding guarantees a large pool of potential "customers." Disquiet about traditional methods guarantees a business environment sympathetic to new ideas and new businesses.

5. *A probation officer will lose a civil liability suit for $5 million.* The liability of probation and parole officers has grown dramatically in recent years. Some agencies now calculate liability settlements into their annual budgetary projections.

    Civil liability occurs when a probation or parole officer fails to supervise a client according to established policies and procedures, enabling the client to commit a new crime. Already, there have been suits that resulted in awards to victims of more than $1 million. The only thing that will stop an eye-popping, multimillion-dollar award against a probation agency is a legislative cap on the size of allowable civil damages.

6. *Accountability-oriented systems will dominate new technologies.* In the last decade, the story about community corrections has been its growing reliance on systems of accountability. The most obvious example is the National Institute of Correction's Model Case Management System. This approach sets specific standards for supervision contracts and bases the distribution of cases among officers on time-study data about prior performance. There has also been an emphasis placed on managerial supervision of the work of line officers, especially as it relates to conformity with policy and procedure.

    Two forces have spawned this wave of accountability measures: (1) the powerful threat of agency liability and (2) the fact that funding is increasingly dependent on showing that programs are effective. These forces will continue to grow in importance over the next twenty years, and so agencies will be even more inclined to remedy them by developing techniques of improved accountability.

7. *The amount of "formal" discretion exercised by line workers in community corrections will diminish.* Accountability systems, when they work well, have one

main result: They reduce the range of decisions officers can make regarding their clients. They do so by reducing the amount of discretion that officers have concerning how to manage their cases.

The loss of discretion is an important change in the nature of the job for the officer. For many officers, what makes the job interesting and challenging is the chance to "work with people." The phrase, as they use it, connotes the ability to be creative in case management, to respond to cases with gut feelings and seat-of-the-pants decisions. It makes the officer feel like something of an artist—or maybe more like a cowboy or a "Lone Ranger"—in control of his or her own caseload as though it were a domain.

8. *Treatment programs will make a comeback in the field, especially those based on a "partnership" between corrections and a treatment provider.* Evidence is growing that treatment is one of the best ways to control clients' criminal behavior. It is a surprising circumstance, after all the criticism that has been applied to the concept, to find that in the mid-1990s, treatment programs appear to be more important than ever as a part of the correctional arsenal.

The nature of the treatments have changed, of course. They are no longer the general "counseling" approaches designed to generate "insight" into the causes of criminal behavior. They are much more structured interventions—treatment systems—that combine behavior monitoring and control with cognitive counseling. They presume a depth of knowledge about particular patterns of criminal behavior, so they are often done collaboratively with "experts."

9. *The importance of information technologies will overwhelm traditional practices in virtually every way.* It would be remarkable if the computer age, which has transformed the world of work, did not also change the nature of probation and parole work. The only real question is, "How will the work change?"

The description of the need for accountability systems has already shown how important information will be for parole and probation agencies. Critical to accountability is the ability to demonstrate what has been done about cases, and this requires recording information about actions. Moreover, it is information about offenders that provides treatment profiles, classification scores, and instructions for supervision from case-management systems. It is impossible to think of the future of community supervision without also thinking about information.

10. *Labor-management relations in probation and parole will be increasingly vitriolic.* If earlier predictions are correct, then the job will change a great deal in the coming years. Officers' discretion will be essentially eradicated, at least formally. All actions will be sifted through the "opinion" of a computerized prepackaged set of policies and procedures. Liability for failures to follow the procedures will be higher than ever.

In the face of these pressures, local professional organizations will be more and more inclined to focus on bread-and-butter labor issues instead of problems of the profession. Salaries, wages, benefits, and working conditions will be the area of contention between government and workers. Probation and parole organizations will become increasingly antagonistic about these issues.

FIVE MORE TENTATIVE PREDICTIONS

1. *Caseloads will not be the only way in which probation and parole caseloads are organized.* The caseload is an administrative convenience; it allows the "boss" to decide how to hand cases out and how to hold officers accountable. When there are new accountability systems available, the caseload will be valuable only to the degree that it manages cases well.

2. *Revocation of community supervision status will become dual track: Regular cases will be revoked only for new arrests, and specialized cases will be revoked for rules violations.* Already it is difficult to get a case revoked from traditional community supervision without evidence of a new crime. This has not been the case for the special programs, however: These normally have very high "technical" failure rates. There is no obvious reason why this trend would stop.

3. *A completely private community corrections system will be tried somewhere on an experimental basis.* Depending on how the privatization experiments turn out, this is a likely scenario. After all, private vendors provide medical services to government on a contractual basis. Why not extend this to community corrections? The promise will be pretty tempting: better service at less cost. Some jurisdiction somewhere is bound to try it. The only thing that would interfere would be a resounding failure of correctional privatization in other spheres. This seems unlikely.

4. *Fines and community service will replace traditional probation for nonserious, low-risk offenders.* These are cheap, effective, and popular sanctions.

5. *Supervision role conflict will be considered unimportant.* Evidence is mounting that far too much has been made of the "conflict" between law enforcement and social work in community supervision. Increasingly, it will be recognized that the role is not a duality of two ideas, but an integration of two themes: control and change.

FIVE DEFINITE PREDICTIONS (PROBABLY)

1. *Risk prediction will not be more accurate.* There are a few ways to improve profiling systems to increase prediction accuracy. But in the long run, prediction will not become more refined until people become more predictable. This is a problem of evolution and is not going to be resolved in two decades.

2. *Every state will experience a "Willie Horton" case—a situation in which a serious offender who is released into the community commits a heinous crime.* Failure—and its effects on the system—will continue to be uniform experience in community corrections. Nothing will eradicate it—the only solution is to prepare for it.

3. *The probation or parole officer's task uncertainty will not diminish.* All of the above means that the work of the probation officer will still contain a great deal of subtlety. Seeing how offenders act, making interpretations of their behavior, managing the interaction of supervision—this will be the main content of the job. No amount of performance structuring can eliminate it.

4. *The use of "electronic monitoring" will have topped out.* Such use is limited to only certain kinds of cases—those whose effective management is augmented by making sure they are home at certain times. The number of cases fitting this profile will be finite and will not feed an ever-expanding industry.

5. *One or more of my predictions will not pan out.* No comment.

QUESTIONS FOR THOUGHT AND DISCUSSION

Chapter 28: "Life on the Inside: The Jailers," by Andrew Metz

1. How would you characterize the author's view of contemporary correctional officers?
2. What are some immediate threats that a correctional officer must confront?
3. What are the essential skills required of a correctional officer?

Chapter 29: "The Imprisonment of Women in America," by Pauline Katherine Brennan

1. What are the current social demographics of women in prison?
2. How do they differ from their male counterparts?
3. Are prisons currently able to meet the special needs of female prisoners?
4. What is the role of aftercare programs for female prisoners?

Chapter 30: "The Needs of Elderly Offenders," by Delores E. Craig-Moreland

1. What does research tell us about the number of elderly offenders in prison?
2. Why has this number increased in recent years?
3. What are some of the medical problems of elderly offenders that must be addressed by prison administrators?
4. What about safety and security issues?

Chapter 31: "Behind Bars: Substance Abuse in America's Prison Population," National Center on Addiction and Substance Abuse, Columbia University

1. Of the total number of adults currently incarcerated, how many have a substance abuse problem?
2. What are some external factors accounting for an increased number of substance-involved offenders?
3. Discuss treatment effectiveness in correctional facilities.
4. What role have America's prisons played in the "war on drugs"?

Chapter 32: "Rethinking the Assumptions About Boot Camps," by Dale Colledge and Jurg Gerber

1. What are the advantages of using a multiple goal typology when evaluating boot camps?
2. Are all boot camps created equally? Explain.

Chapter 33: "A Decade of Experimenting With Intermediate Sanctions: What Have We Learned?" by Joan Petersilia

1. What was the impetus for intermediate sanctions programs?
2. Have intermediate sanctions programs worked?
3. What is the ultimate goal of intermediate sanctions programs?

Chapter 34: "The Evolving Role of Parole in the Criminal Justice System," by Paul Cromwell

1. What is the difference between probation, parole, and pardon?
2. Discuss parole guidelines. How does this method of parole decision-making differ from the traditional methods?

3. What brought about the change in criminal justice philosophy in the mid-1970s? What were the consequences to the system?
4. Should parole be used as a safety valve for prison populations? Why or why not?

Chapter 35: "This Man Has Expired: Witness to an Execution," by Robert Johnson

1. Has the rate of executions been going up or down over the past fifteen years?
2. Explain what the death watch team is and the goals of the team.

Chapter 36: "Maxxing Out: Imprisonment in an Era of Crime Control," by Melissa E. Fenwick

1. What are super maximum-security facilities?
2. What is the prison industrial complex? How has it altered the correctional community?
3. Are super maximum-security facilities an outcome of political rhetoric? Explain.

Chapter 37: "Ophelia the CCW: May 11, 2010," by Todd R. Clear

1. How may new technology affect the delivery of probation and parole services in the future?
2. Out of all the predictions made by the author, which two do you think will have the greatest impact on crime control in the future?

INDEX